THE A-Z OF
WOLVES

Express & Star

THE A-Z OF
WOLVES

Compiled by Tony Matthews
with John Hendley and Les Smith

**The Breedon Books
Publishing Company
Derby**

First published in Great Britain by
The Breedon Books Publishing Company Limited
Breedon House, 44 Friar Gate, Derby, DE1 1DA.
1999

ISBN 1 85983 157 5

Printed and bound by Butler & Tanner Ltd., Selwood Printing Works,
Caxton Road, Frome, Somerset.

Colour separations and jacket printing by Green Shires Group Ltd,
Leicester.

Introduction

I have attempted to make this A-Z of Wolverhampton Wanderers Football Club as comprehensive as possible, utilising all the statistical information available which I have obtained from various sources.

I started compiling this book some 12 years ago but in the interim period I was fortunate to have one or two elaborated publications on the Molineux club published, along with a series of paper backs covering the star players who have donned the famous gold and black colours over the years. Now all the information from those previous books has been pasted together and used as one to bring you an extensive record of a club which has won the Football League championship three times, the FA Cup on four occasions, the League Cup twice and played against many of Europe's finest sides.

A pen-picture biography of each and every player who has appeared for Wolves at first team level is featured in this book. Wolves' playing record against every club they have met at competitive level is there for all to see. There is an international section covering all the players who have represented their country whilst serving with Wolves.

There are attendance facts, records of sendings-off, details of all those men who have managed Wolves down the years, the story of Molineux and much much more.

I have, hopefully, covered everything there is to know on Wolverhampton Wanderers Football Club but with so much to write about I will admit that somewhere down the line I will have missed the odd statistic, a relevant fact, one or two important milestones, player's feats, a manager's decision etc. etc. But I have done my best – with the help of some ardent and dedicated Wolves supporters.

Wolverhampton Wanderers is a big club – it has been for so many years. Unfortunately its team has yet to play in the Premiership – in fact Wolves were last in the top flight of English football fifteen years ago (in 1984) and since then they have played in and won the old Third and Fourth Divisions but sadly, for their supporters, they have now been based in the Nationwide League Division One for a decade, having twice missed out in the play-off semi-finals and more recently finished an agonising seventh in the First Division.

Wolves will be back. The Molineux Stadium, with its splendid internal facilities, is one of the finest grounds in the country. The support is certainly there – the average attendance will be 25,000 at least if the team is doing well.

The Molineux club is a sleeping lion, a phoenix ready to rise from the flames – and as we approach the Millennium one feels that pretty soon Wolves will be playing Premiership soccer.

Thousands of people certainly hope so…

Acknowledgements

First and foremost I would like to say a big thank you to the *Express & Star* for the tremendous assistance given to me regarding the publication of this book.

Also I would like to acknowledge the support afforded by Anton Rippon and his staff at Breedon Books of Derby.

There have also been contributors who have helped me compile this Wolves A-Z, none more so than Les Smith, John Hendley and Scott Pritchard, who between them have worked overtime, especially the latter two, with the task of proof-reading. Thank you sincerely.

And I cannot forget Graham Hughes who once again has allowed me to use several of his Wolves photographs.

I am also indebted to quite a few fellow football statisticians up and down the country whose work – perhaps unknowing to them – I have referred to to clarify certain facts and figures, and of course there is Ray Spiller and several members of the Association of Football Statisticians who have helped in many departments.

I have referred to scores of soccer books to obtain and confirm information and these include excellent publications by Dr Percy M. Young and Mike Slater.

I would also like to say thank you to my wife Margaret who once again has assisted me no end throughout the compilation of this book.

Thank you one and all.

ABANDONED/POSTPONED MATCHES

Over 18,000 fans were in attendance at the Wolves against West Bromwich Albion First Division game at Molineux on Boxing Day 1962 when heavy snow caused it to be abandoned at half-time with Wolves winning 2-0. The re-arranged fixture, played almost three months later, on 16 March 1963, attracted a crowd of 22,618 and this time Wolves ran out convincing winners by 7-0.

Other abandoned matches involving Wolves include (all in the League) against Everton (home) on 18 November 1893 (snow intervened with the visitors 2-0 up at half-time); against Liverpool (home) on 14 March 1903 (halted after 50 minutes due to heavy rain with the Merseysiders again 2-0 in front); against Leeds United (away) on 12 December 1936 (called off in the 83rd minute due to a fierce blizzard with Wolves ahead at the time, but playing without goalkeeper Alex Scott (sent-off) and Stan Cullis (injured) and at Blackpool on 14 January 1961, when fog caused the referee to call off the proceedings after only nine minutes with the score sheet blank.

Due to the arctic weather conditions that gripped Britain during the winter of 1947, Wolves played only one League game (away to Leeds United) between 19 January and 28 February.

Similarly, during the bitterly cold winter of 1962-63, mainly due to heavy snow and ice, Wolves managed to fulfil only three League games and one FA Cup-tie between 16 December and 8 March. Their third-round Cup clash at Nottingham Forest, due to be played on 5 January, finally took place 24 days later after ten postponements.

ABERDEEN

Wolves met Aberdeen three times, finally beating them 6-5 on penalties to win the Los Angeles Soccer League in 1967 (see under *Los Angeles Wolves*).

Five years later, in May 1972, Wolves again took on the 'Dons', playing them in four friendly matches in Canada and the USA. Each side won twice, Wolves 3-0 in Vancouver and 4-0 in Los Angeles, Aberdeen 3-1 in San Francisco and 3-0 in Seattle.

The first time the teams met was in a friendly at Pittodrie Park in January 1954 when the Dons beat Wolves 5-3.

In May 1972 Wolves and Aberdeen faced each other again when they toured North America/Canada. This time they played four exhibition matches – Wolves lost 3-1 and 3-0 in San Francisco and Seattle respectively but won 3-0 and 4-0 in Vancouver and Los Angeles to balance the books.

Goalkeeper John Burridge, defenders Steve Wright and Frank Munro and forwards Jack Beattie and Mixu Paatelainen all represented both clubs, while Mark McGhee was a striker with the Dons (1979-84) and later managed Wolves (1995-98).

ACADEMICA DEL COIMBRA

Wolves' playing record against Academica is:
UEFA Cup

Venue	P	W	D	L	F	A
Home	1	1	0	0	3	0
Away	1	1	0	0	4	1
Total	2	2	0	0	7	1

Wolves started their march towards the 1972 UEFA Cup Final with a comfortable 7-1 aggregate win over the Portuguese side Academica Del Coimbra in the opening round which was played over two legs in September 1971. A crowd of 23,349 saw the Molineux clash which ended in an easy win for Wolves, who then went to Portugal and ran up another convincing scoreline in a game which was attended by just over 11,000 fans. Derek Dougan hit a hat-trick in the latter victory and Wolves defender John McAlle had the honour of scoring in both legs. Danny Hegan became the first Wolves player to receive marching orders in a European competition when he was sent-off in the second leg in Portugal.

ACCRINGTON

Wolves' record against Accrington is:
Football League

Venue	P	W	D	L	F	A
Home	5	5	0	0	19	4
Away	5	1	1	3	11	18
Totals	10	6	1	3	30	22

FA Cup

Venue	P	W	D	L	F	A
Away	1	1	0	0	3	2

Wolves first met Accrington in an away League game on 6 October 1888 and a crowd of 5,000 witnessed a thrilling 4-4 draw.

The return fixture that season, played in front of 3,000 fans at Dudley Road two months later, resulted in a 4-0 win for Wolves.

The following season (New Year's Day) the Lancashire side gained sweet revenge by inflicting a 6-3 defeat on Wolves, Prendergast scoring a hat-trick for Accrington.

Wolves then whipped Accrington 5-0 at Molineux on 14 September 1891, when Joseph Heath became the first player ever to score from the penalty spot in a League game. Wolves scored four goals in the space of 10 minutes during the second half of this fixture, one of them coming while the visitors' defender Arthur Elliott was off the pitch changing his 'knickers' so reported the *Accrington Observer*.

The last season Wolves and Accrington met at League level was in 1892-93. The Wanderers won 5-3 at Molineux with Joe Butcher netting all five goals, but then amazingly lost the away fixture by 4-0, fielding practically the same side.

The only FA Cup-tie between the clubs was played in 1890-91 when Wolves squeezed into the third round 3-2 after extra-time.

Player with both clubs: Sammy Thomson.

ACCRINGTON STANLEY

Wolves' playing record against Stanley is:
Football League

Venue	P	W	D	L	F	A
Home	1	1	0	0	5	1
Away	1	0	0	1	0	1
Totals	2	1	0	1	5	2

FA Cup

Venue	P	W	D	L	F	A
Home	1	1	0	0	2	0

The two League matches were played in the Third Division North in September 1923. Just over 5,200 fans saw Stanley win 1-0 at Peel Park, and there were almost 14,500 fans present at Molineux a week later to see Wolves romp to a convincing 5-1 victory with Stan Fazackerley scoring a hat-trick.

Wolves' FA Cup triumph over Stanley was achieved in 1910-11 when a crowd of 13,500 saw them win a first round tie 2-0 with George Hedley scoring twice.

Players with both clubs include: Stan Fazackerley, Walter Gummery, Henry Howell, Fred Keetley, Fred Marsden, Alf Tootill, 'Pongo' Waring and Walter Weaver.

Associated with both clubs: Ted Ivill (later reserve-team coach), John Aspin, Tom Allen, Tony Bond, Walter Cressy, Albert Latham, Ron Morgan, Chris Pearce and Doug Roberts (Wolves Reserves – Morgan also Wolves wartime guest), Billy Wrigglesworth (Stanley trainer 1950s) and Gary Pierce (Stanley manager).

ADDENBROOKE, John Henry

Jack Addenbrooke was Wolves' manager from August 1885 to June 1922 and for a short while during that time he was also landlord of the Molineux Hotel. Born in Wolverhampton in 1865, he played football for St Luke's School, Blakenhall (1875-77) and was appointed secretary of the team at the age of 10. Four years later he attended Saltley College (Birmingham) and after his educational studies were over he returned to Wolverhampton to pursue a teaching career, commencing with a two-year spell at Bushbury School. During his time here he became associated with Wolves, playing regularly for the second team. In August 1885 he was appointed the first paid secretary of the club, a position which later took in the managerial duties (as we know them today). He held office for a club record 37 years – until the summer of 1922 – and during his time at the club Wolves moved into their Molineux home, became founder members of the Football League, won the FA Cup twice (in 1893 and 1908) and were beaten in the Final three times (1889, 1896 and 1921). He was also involved in the recruitment of several

Wolves' 1893 FA Cup winning side. Jack Addenbrooke is standing extreme right behind the stair rail.

quality players including Billy Malpass, George Fleming, England goalkeeper Tom Baddeley, Bill Wooldridge, George Edmonds, Jackery Jones, Billy Harrison, Noel George and Revd Kenneth Hunt, the famous amateur international. He was unfortunately taken ill in June 1922 and was declared unfit for work by Doctor Wolverson. He was allowed six months leave, but sadly, on 7 September of that year he died.

Addenbrooke was presented with the long-service medal by the Football League in 1908-09 and his record as Wolves manager was 1,124 games, 454 wins, 220 draws and 450 defeats.

ADMISSION PRICES

Before the commencement of League football in 1888-89, the general charge for admission to a Wolves home game varied from 1d (½p) and 6d (3p). The 6d charge remained as a minimum entrance fee until after World War One (1919) when it was increased to one shilling (5p). For the next 23 years that shilling admission price remained in force, but for the 1942-43 wartime season it went up to 1s 3d (7p). From then on increases on the minimum entrance fee and the highest admittance charge, have both been gradual. Here is a guide to the dearest adult admission prices to Molineux since 1955:

Season	Terraces	Seats
1955-56	2s (10p)	4s 6d (23p)
1960-61	2s 6d (13p)	5s (25p)
1963-64	3s (15p)	6s (30p)
1964-65	3s 6d (18p)	7s 6d (38p)
1965-66	4s (20p)	8s 6d (43p)
1967-68	5s (25p)	10s (50p)
1970-71	9s (45p)	15s (75p)
1972-73	50p	88p
1974-75	60p	£1.00
1978-79	£1.00	£1.50
1979-80	£1.30	£2.30
1980-81	£1.50	£2.50
1981-82	£2.00	£3.00
1984-85	£2.50	£5.00
1985-86	£3.00	£5.00
1987-88	£3.00	£6.00
1989-90	£4.00	£7.00
1990-91	£4.50	£7.50
1992-93	£6.00	£9.00
1993-94	-	£12.00
1994-95	-	£14.00
1995-96	-	£15.00
1996-97	-	£15.00
1997-98	-	£17.00
1998-99	-	£16.00

A Family Ticket was introduced during the mid-1990s.

Season Tickets

An 1880s ground season ticket to watch Wolves cost the supporter 3s (15p) – in those days a club used to play between 15 and 20 home matches per season.

When League football arrived in 1888-89, the average price for a season ticket was 5s (25p).

At the turn of the century (1900-01) the price had risen to 10s (50p) and in the first season after World War One (1919-20) a season ticket at Molineux was priced at 15s (75p).

Over the next 20 years or so the overall price rose slowly – in 1930 supporters paid 30s a time (£1.50); in 1934 it had risen to £2 per season ticket and just before League football was suspended in 1939 the cost had climbed to three guineas (£3.15p)

Immediately after World War Two, the admission charge had reached £4 a time; it was £5 ten years later (in 1956) and in 1960 the average price of a season ticket was £8.

Between 1961 and 1974 season ticket prices went up slowly – from £9 to £10 to £12 to £15 to £18 and for the 1974-75 campaign fans at Molineux were paying up £20, plus an extra £6 for five cup matches and £17 (plus £5) in the main stand.

In 1979-80, the price of a Wolves season ticket for an adult (in the main stand) was around the £60 mark (this was the norm up and down the country for the majority of First Division clubs). And since then the general cost of a season ticket has risen steadily, from £50 (terraces) and £100 (seats) in 1984-85, from £60/£120 in 1987-88, from £84/£147 in 1989-90, from £126/£198 in 1992-93, from £147/£200 in 1994-95 to a highest of £273 for the 1996-97 campaign. Obviously prices fluctuated, depending on where the supporter to chose to watch his football. For season 1998-99 the dearest season ticket at Molineux was £339 and the cheapest £234 and in 1999-2000 the same tickets were priced at £355 and £249 respectively.

Complimentary Tickets
For Football League matches, the visiting club can normally claim a total of 37 complimentary tickets – 25 for use by the players, manager and coach – and 12 for the directors. There is no set limit on how many complimentary tickets the home club can issue.

All-Ticket Games
Nowadays, all-ticket matches at Molineux have a crowd limit in the region of 28,500 put on them by the local police in conjunction with the club itself (for safety reasons).

Fifty years ago, certainly up until the late 1940s, there had been no all-ticket matches involving Wolves at Molineux (only for scheduled FA Cup semi-finals). The first game made all-ticket is believed to have been made all-ticket at Molineux was the Wolves v West Bromwich Albion sixth-round FA Cup-tie on 26 February 1949 when the attendance was set at 55,700 (in fact, 55,648 fans actually attended the game).

Since then several matches (in various competitions) have had the 'all-ticket' tag placed on them, and in recent years, there have been 'all-ticket' arrangements made for visiting supporters to Molineux.

AGE
Oldest
The oldest player to appear in a competitive first team game for Wolves has been Archie Goodall (born in Belfast on 19 June 1864) who made the last of his seven appearances for Wolves on 2 December 1906 against Everton at home (League Division One) at the age of 41 years, five months and two days.

David Stokes, who was a shade over 40 years of age when he lined up at outside-right against Sheffield Wednesday at Hillsborough on 11 April 1921 – also the last of seven League outings for the club.

Defender Lawrie Madden was aged 37 years, 222 days when he played his last game for Wolves against Derby County on 8 May 1993.

Youngest
The youngest player ever to appear in a first team match for Wolves has been the Scotsman Cameron Buchanan who was just 14 years, 57 days old when he starred in a wartime Football League North game against West Bromwich Albion at Molineux on 26 September 1942.

Billy Wright was only 15 years, seven months and 17 days old when he played in his first senior game for Wolves against West Bromwich Albion in a wartime Midland Regional League game on 23 September 1939.

Winger Jimmy Mullen was 16 years, 43 days old when he made his Wolves debut in a First Division League game against Leeds United on 18 February 1939. Then a fortnight later Mullen became the youngest player to appear in an FA Cup-tie for Wolves when he starred in their sixth-round win over Everton on 4 March. He was reserve for the Final that year (v Portsmouth).

Mullen scored for Wolves against Coventry City in a wartime game on his 17th birthday – just four hours after signing professional forms for the club.

Dave Wintersgill was just 22 days short of his 17th birthday when he made his Wolves League debut against Blackburn Rovers on 28 August 1982.

Wolves fielded two 16-year-old wingers – Mullen and Alan Steen – in their home League game against Manchester United in March 1939 (won 3-1).

On 27 September 1941 against Leicester City (away) Wolves fielded their youngest-ever team – average age 17 years. Ashton was the oldest member of the side, aged 18 years, six months.

The average age of the Wolves team against Birmingham in a Regional wartime game on 16 March 1940 was 19 years, seven months.

Ryan Green became the youngest-ever player to appear in a full international match for Wales when he lined up for his country against Malta in June 1998, at the age of 17 years and 226 days.

Matthew Murray – aged 16 years, 277 days – was Wolves' substitute goalkeeper for the FA Cup replay with Charlton Athletic in 1997-98, He was also on the bench for both Cup clashes with Wimbledon, but failed to get on in any of the three matches.

AINSCOW, Alan
A hard-working Lancastrian midfielder, born in Bolton on 15 July 1953, Alan Ainscow played initially for Blackpool (1969-78) and then, in turn, for Birmingham City (1978-81), Everton (1981), Barnsley (on loan in 1982), Eastern FC in Hong Kong (in 1983), Wolves (from July 1984 to December 1985), Blackburn Rovers (1985-89), Rochdale (1989), Horwich RMI (August 1990), Flint Town United (July 1991) and finally Ellesmere Port (as coach 1992). Capped by England at youth team level, Ainscow helped Birmingham win promotion from Division Two in 1980 and starred in well over 500 senior games as a professional at club level. *Wolves record: 62+3 apps. 6 goals.*

ALDERSHOT
Wolves' playing record against the Shots is:
Football League

Venue	P	W	D	L	F	A
Home	2	2	0	0	4	0
Away	2	2	0	0	4	2
Totals	4	4	0	0	8	2

Play-Offs

Home	1	0	0	1	0	1
Away	1	0	0	2	0	2
Totals	2	0	0	2	0	3

Wolves first did battle with Aldershot in their 1986-87 Fourth Division campaign. A crowd of under 3,000 saw the Wanderers win 2-1 at the Recreation Ground and there were 3,357 fans present at Molineux to witness the return fixture which Wolves won 3-0, Andy Mutch scoring twice.

At the end of the season Wolves and the Shots met in the Play-offs. Sadly for Wolves they missed out on promotion, Aldershot winning 3-0 on aggregate – 2-0 on home soil and 1-0 at Molineux, where the winning goal came in the 83rd minute.

For the 1988-89 season Aldershot were joined in the Third Division by Wolves and the two meetings this term went in favour of the Wanderers, who won 1-0 at Molineux, Steve Bull the scorer, and 2-1 away when 'Bully' again hit the target.

Players with both clubs include: David Barnes, George Berry, Chic Brodie, Steve Claridge, Bobby Gould (assistant manager of the Shots), Andy King, Tony Lange, Tommy Langley, Bertie Lutterloch, Jimmy Melia (player-manager of the Shots), David Miller and Alan Steen.

Also associated: Andy Beattie (Wolves manager), Billy Crook, Stan Cullis, Tom Galley, Jimmy Jinks, Frank Taylor and Horace Wright (Wolves players) – all wartime guests with Aldershot.

Nicky Clarke (left) puts in a challenge during the 1987 Play-off game against Aldershot.

ALDERTON, James

A wing-half from Wingate, County Durham (born 6 December 1924) Jimmy Alderton joined Wolves in December 1941 and made 111 appearances for the Wanderers during the hostilities (plus a handful afterwards) and was a guest player with Chester before transferring to Coventry City in October 1947 for a small fee. He starred in 60 first-team matches for City up to May 1952, when he withdrew from competitive soccer through injury. Alderton died in May 1998.

Wolves record: 15 apps.

ALLEN, Harry

Born in Walsall on 19 January 1866, Allen was a formidable defender, 'rather rash at times' but nevertheless a great competitor for Wolves, whom he joined in 1886 after spending three years with Walsall Town Swifts. Capped by England on five occasions, he appeared in two FA Cup Finals for Wolves – 1889 and 1893 – skippering the side in the second when he collected a winners' medal after he scored the only goal against Everton at Fallowfield (Manchester). After retiring through injury in October 1894 he became a publican in Wolverhampton. Allen died suddenly in Walsall on 23 February 1895, aged 29.

Wolves record: 152 apps. 13 goals.

ALLEN, Ronald

Allen was Wolves' manager from September 1965 to November 1968 and during that time he guided the team back into the First Division (1967). Born in Fenton, Stoke-on-Trent on 15 January 1929, Allen played junior football for a number of teams in the Potteries and in 1944 signed for Port Vale as an outside-right. He made steady progress with the Valiants and after World War Two he established himself in the first team. In March 1950 he was transferred to West Bromwich Albion for a fee of £20,000 and in the next 11 years at The Hawthorns he scored well over 230 goals in more than 600 senior appearances, helped the Baggies win the FA Cup (1954) and collected five full England caps as well as representing the country's 'B' team, the FA XI and the Football League. He left Albion in May 1961 to join Crystal Palace, later taking over as player-coach at Selhurst Park. He retired in March 1965, and six months later, after a brief coaching spell at Molineux, a short period as acting-manager, Allen finally took over as Wolves' boss from Andy Beattie. He did reasonably well with the club for the first two-and-a-half years or so, and four of his finest signings were Derek Dougan, snapped up for a bargain £50,000 fee in March 1967, defender Frank Munro (bought from Aberdeen), wing-half Mike Bailey (lured from Charlton) and full-back Derek Parkin (secured from Huddersfield). Among others, he also introduced goalkeeper Phil Parkes, defender John McAlle, strikers John Richards (signed by Allen as an apprentice in 1967, he made his debut in 1970) and inside-forward Alun Evans to League soccer, selling teenager Evans to Liverpool for £100,000. Allen's days at Molineux were numbered following a crushing 6-0 home defeat at the hands of Liverpool in late September 1968 and five weeks later he left the club, to be replaced by Bill McGarry. Thereafter Allen remained in football as follows: Athletic Bilbao (manager, 1969-71), Sporting Lisbon (manager, 1972-73), Walsall (manager, 1973), West Bromwich Albion (scouting adviser, January 1977, then team manager, June to December 1977), football adviser to Saudi Arabian FA (1978), Panathinaikos, Greece (manager, 1980), WBA (manager for a second time from July 1981 to May 1982, then general manager to 1983). He remained in association with the Baggies as a shareholder (just failing to get onto the board of of directors) and later acted as assistant coach, a position he held until ill-health set him back in 1996. Indeed, Allen played in an end-of-season friendly for Albion against Cheltenham Town in 1995, aged 66. He has been ill (in a Sutton Coldfield nursing home) for the last 18 months (1998-99).

Ronnie Allen, the former Albion and England star who managed Wolves.

Allen scored goals at first team level for 22 years: 1944-65 inclusive, and he held the Albion record for most League goals (208) from 1961-78 until it was bettered by current holder Tony Brown. West Bromwich Albion entertained Aston Villa in a testimonial match for Allen at The Hawthorns on 3 August 1997. In all he netted 234 goals in 458 senior games for Albion.

Allen's record as Wolves manager was 150 games played, 66 won, 35 drawn and 49 lost.

ALTRINCHAM

Wolves began their 1965-66 FA Cup campaign with an emphatic 5-0 third round victory over non-League Altrincham at Molineux on 22 January. Almost 30,500 fans were in attendance to see Ernie Hunt (2), Hugh McIlmoyle, Bobby Woodruff and Dewar (own goal) score the goals.

Players with both clubs include: Paul Edwards and Matt Carrick (Wolves Reserves).

Also associated: Tommy Docherty was manager of both clubs and Nicky Boland (Wolves Reserves).

AMALGAMATION

The amalgamation of St Luke's School (Blakenhall) and the Wanderers Cricket Club in 1879 led to the formation of Wolverhampton Wanderers Football Club.

AMATEURS

The Revd Kenneth Hunt is perhaps the best known amateur footballer ever to play for Wolves. A Corinthian wing-half, he helped the team win the 1908 FA Cup Final and won 20 caps for England as an amateur (1907-21), represented Great Britain in the Olympic Games of 1908 (winning a soccer gold medal) and also gained two full caps (both in 1911).

Percy Corbett was a first-team player with Wolves (1906-08) who represented England seven times in Amateur internationals.

Outside-right Dick Topham, who starred for Wolves in the 1890s, won two England Amateur caps, while centre-half Bill Slater, who skippered Wolves to victory in the 1960 FA Cup Final, played six times for the England Amateur side (1952-54) as well as collecting 12 caps for his country at senior level. Slater was, in fact, registered as a semi-professional at Molineux and indeed was the last amateur footballer to appear in an FA Cup Final (1960).

Wolves star of the-mid 1920s, Evan Edwards, was capped several times by Wales as an amateur.

Prior to professionalism being introduced to British football in 1885, among the early Wolves stars, who were regarded at the time as amateurs worthy of international recognition, were goalkeeper Ike Griffiths, full-backs Tommy Cliff and Charlie Mason, half-backs Alf Davidson, Jack Baynton, Arthur Lowder and Tom Blackham and forwards Arthur Lowder, Jack Brodie and Ted Hadley.

Lester Finch, a distinguished amateur footballer with Leytonstone in the 1930s/40s was a wartime guest for Wolves.

ANDERSON, Edward Walton

Ted Anderson was born in Newcastle on 17 July 1911 and played his early football in the North East with Jarrow. In July 1930 he was recruited by Wolves from Worksop Town but played only three League games, all in the left-half position in place of Dai Richards, before leaving for Torquay United in December 1931.He later assisted West Ham United (1933-35), Chester (1935-37) and Tranmere Rovers (1937-48) as well as Everton, New Brighton and Wrexham as a wartime guest. On retiring in the summer of 1948 Anderson returned to Newcastle. Anderson (who died in Birkenhead on 23 March 1979) enjoyed tennis and swimming. *Wolves record: 3 apps.*

ANDERSON, Nicholas

Played for Wolves in the first season of the Football League competition in 1888-89. A stocky centre-forward, born locally *c.*1865, Anderson failed to make an impact at Molineux and left the club in May 1889. *Wolves record: 2 apps.*

ANGLO-ITALIAN CUP

Wolves have played in this competition on four occasions, the results of which are:

1969-70

v Fiorentina	(home)	2-1	Att. 14,262
v Lazio	(home)	1-0	Att. 11,953
v Fiorentina	(away)	3-1	Att. 13,120
v Lazio	(away)	0-2	Att. 43,973

1992-93

v Tranmere Rovers	(away)	1-2	Att. 3,361
v Peterborough United.	(home)	2-0	Att. 3,091

1993-94

v Stoke City	(home)	3-3	Att. 9,092
v Birmingham City	(away)	2-2	Att. 2,710

1993-94

v Lecce	(away)	1-0	Att. 1,795
v Ascoli	(home)	0-1	Att. 9,599
v Venezia	(away)	1-2	Att. 750
v Atalanta	(home)	1-1	Att. 7,265

That attendance of 750 for the game in Italy against Venezia on 5 October 1994 is believed to have been the lowest ever audience to witness a Wolves competitive game at home or away.

Summary:

P	W	D	L	F	A
12	5	3	4	17	15

ANNIS, Walter

Born in Wolverhampton in 1874, Annis was a hard-tackling defender who, as part of a fine half-back line at Molineux with initially Ted Pheasant and George Fleming, and later with Jack Whitehouse, Pheasant and for a time, George Walker, gave Wolves splendid service for seven seasons. He joined the club from Stafford Road FC in August 1898, having earlier assisted Wolverhampton St Luke's, and he left Molineux for Cradley Heath in April 1905. Annis died in Wolverhampton in 1944.

Wolves record: 147 apps. 1 goal.

APPEARANCES

Football League

Full-back Derek Parkin holds the record for most League appearances for Wolves – 501 – made between 1967 and 1982. Billy Wright amassed 490, Steve Bull 472, Ron Flowers 467, Kenny Hibbitt 466, Peter Broadbent 452, Jimmy Mullen 445, Geoff Palmer 416, John McAlle 406, John Richards 385, Bert Williams 381, Mike Stowell 365, Mike Bailey 361 and Albert Bishop 357 – these being the only players to have made more than 350 appearances in the said competition.

FA Cup

England internationals Harry Wood and Billy Wright, each with 48, share the club record for most FA Cup appearances for Wolves. Kenny Hibbitt played in 47 FA Cup games, Derek Parkin in 46, John McAlle and John Richards 44 each and Dicky Baugh (senior) 42.

League Cup

Kenny Hibbitt, with 36 appearances, is Wolves' record-holder in the League Cup competition. Derek Parkin starred in 35 matches, Steve Bull, Geoff Palmer and John Richards played in 33, Mike Bailey 29 and John McAlle 27.

UEFA Cup

Derek Dougan and John McAlle each played in 18 UEFA Cup matches for Wolves; both Kenny Hibbitt and Frank Munro turned out in 17; goalkeeper Phil Parkes appeared in 16, Derek Parkin in 15 and three players – Jim McCalliog, John Richards and Dave Wagstaffe – all starred in 14.

European Cup

Wolves represented England in this competition in 1958-59 and 1959-60, fulfilling a total of eight matches. Five players appeared in each of those eight fixtures – Peter Broadbent, Norman Deeley, Ron Flowers, Gerry Harris and Bobby Mason.

European Cup-winners' Cup

Wolves played four games in this competition in season 1960-61 and only two players – Norman Deeley and Eddie Stuart – appeared in each one.

Senior Competitions

Taking into consideration all senior competitions Wolves have participated in, the players who have appeared in most first-team games for the club are: Derek Parkin 609, Kenny Hibbitt 574, Steve Bull 559, Billy Wright 541, Ron Flowers 512, John McAlle 508, Peter Broadbent 497, Geoff Palmer 496, Jimmy Mullen 486, John Richards 485, Mike Bailey 436, Mike Stowell 424, Bert Williams 420 and Dave Wagstaffe 404.

Goalkeeper Tom Baddeley was the first player to appear in more than 300 games for Wolves and 'keeper Mike Stowell beat Bert

Williams' record of 420 senior appearances for Wolves when he took the field against West Bromwich Albion at Molineux in April 1999.

Consecutive appearances

Goalkeeper Phil Parkes made a club record 127 consecutive League appearances for Wolves over a period of three years – between September 1970 and September 1973. All told he lined up in 171 first team games during that same period.

Parkes beat the previous record of 126 successive League outings which had been set by another goalkeeper, Noel George, between 1922 and 1926.

Two other players, both full-backs, Cecil Shaw (1930s) and Bobby Thomson (1960s) had unbroken League sequences of 120 and 121 respectively in the Football League competition for Wolves with Shaw making 163 all told (including Cup games).

Ever-presents

Full-back Jackery Jones holds the record for being an ever-present most times for Wolves in a complete League season – total five – between 1901 and 1907. Three players who had ever-presents records on four occasions, are Albert Bishop (between 1906-15), Derek Parkin (between 1968-79) and Mike Stowell (1990s) while George Fleming (1897-1900) and Noel George (1921-25) were ever-presents three times each.

The greatest number of players who were ever-presents in a single League season for Wolves is four – in 1902-03, 1903-04 and 1976-77.

In Wolves' first-ever League campaign of 1888-89, only two players – Harry Allen and Dicky Baugh – appeared in all 22 games.

Central League

Right-half Bill Baxter (starting in 1945) made a record 213 Central League appearances for Wolves before transferring to Aston Villa in 1954. Full-back Gerry Taylor made 209 appearances (1966-75).

500 Club

Derek Parkin made his 500th League appearance for Wolves against Middlesbrough (away) on 6 March 1982. He is the only Wolves player to amass 500 appearances in this competition (Billy Wright made 490).

ARKWRIGHT, Ian

Arkwright, an England schoolboy international, had only a handful of outings for Wolves, all in 1978-79, when he wore the No.10 shirt. Born in Shafton near Barnsley on 18 September 1959, he represented Yorkshire Boys before joining the club as an apprentice in 1975, turning professional in September 1977. He left Molineux for Wrexham in March 1970 and later had loan spells with Scunthorpe United (November-December 1981) and Torquay United (March/April 1984) before quitting League football at the end of the 1983-84 season. *Wolves record: 4 apps.*

ARROWSMITH, Arthur

Inside-forward Arthur Arrowsmith played once for Wolves, lining up against Birmingham in October 1908 in place of Walter Radford. Born at Finchfield, Wolver-

hampton in 1880, he started out with Compton FC and joined Coventry City in July 1904. Two years later he gained a Junior International cap when he represented the Birmingham Association against Scotland Juniors. In August 1906 he left Highfield Road for Stoke and made almost 40 appearances for the Potters before signing for Wolves in July 1908. He left Molineux for Willenhall Swifts in April 1909 and died in 1954, aged 74. *Wolves record: 1 app.*

ARSENAL

Wolves' playing record against the Gunners is:

Football League

Venue	P	W	D	L	F	A
Home	45	18	11	16	81	67
Away	45	8	13	24	65	108
Totals	90	26	24	40	146	175

FA Cup

Venue	P	W	D	L	F	A
Home	5	2	1	2	7	5
Away	5	0	0	3	3	6
Neutral	2	0	0	2	0	3
Totals	10	2	1	7	10	14

Wartime

Venue	P	W	D	L	F	A
Home	1	0	1	0	1	1
Away	1	0	0	1	2	3
Void	1	0	1	0	2	2
Totals	3	0	2	1	5	6

Colchester Cup Final

Venue	P	W	D	L	F	A
Neutral	1	1	0	0	1	0

The first-ever League meeting between Wolves and Arsenal took place on 24 September 1904, when 20,000 fans saw the Gunners win a Second Division game 2-0 in London. The return fixture at Molineux on

Action from the FA Cup tie between Wolves and Arsenal in January 1926.

21 January 1905 ended in a 4-1 win for Wolves in front of 8,500 spectators

Wolves' best League win over the Gunners is 6-1 – achieved on two occasions, both at Molineux. The first triumph came on the opening Saturday (31 August) of the 1946-47 season when over 50,000 fans saw Jesse Pye scored a hat-trick on his League debut for Wolves. Then 12-and-a-half years later, on 7 March 1959, two goals apiece from the England duo of Peter Broadbent and Norman Deeley, set Wolves up for another resounding 6-1 victory.

Arsenal's best over Wolves is 7-0 in a First Division game at Highbury in December 1934 when Ted Drake netted a four-timer.

Arsenal also ran up a 7-1 scoreline at Molineux, on 5 November 1932 when a 43,570 crowd saw the fireworks produced by the Gunners' trio of David Jack (3 goals), Cliff Bastin (2) and Jack Lambert (2).

There have been only two gates of over 60,000 at Molineux – the second best is that of 61,267 for the fourth-round FA Cup-tie against Arsenal on 22 January 1938. The Gunners won 2-1.

A white ball was used for the first time at Molineux during Wolves' home League game with Arsenal in March 1950, when over 53,000 saw Johnny Walker score twice in the 3-0 defeat of the Gunners.

After being a goal down at the break, Wolves scored five times in the space of 20 minutes during the second-half of their snow-riddled First Division game against the reigning champions Arsenal at Molineux in November 1971 to win the contest 5-1. The best 'goal' of the five was Dave Wagstaffe's effort which won him 'Goal of the Month' award.

In season 1960-61 Wolves doubled-up over Arsenal in some style, winning 5-3 at Molineux and 5-1 at Highbury. Ted Farmer scored a hat-trick in the home win.

The previous season, the two First Division encounters had produced 14 goals from two draws: 3-3 on Wolves' soil and 4-4 in London when eight different names figured on the scoresheet.

The last time Wolves and Arsenal met in the League was in season 1983-84 when the Gunners took all six points, winning 2-1 at Molineux and 4-1 at Highbury.

Arsenal beat Wolves 2-0 in the FA Cup semi-final at Villa Park in March 1980 and repeated that victory with a 1-0 scoreline on the same ground in the 1997 FA Cup semi-final when Hans Segers' miscued clearance set up the game's only goal.

It was 2-1 to Arsenal when the teams met in a fourth-round FA Cup-tie at Molineux in January 1998, Dennis Bergkamp's double-deflection giving the Gunners a narrow victory in front of a 27,500 plus crowd which realised record attendance receipts for a game at Molineux of £319,141. 50p

The Colchester Cup Final was played in 1938 between Wolves and Arsenal at Layer Road in front of 18,000 fans and Wolves' winning goal came from Harry Thompson.

Players with both clubs include: Vince Bartram, Eddie Clamp, Don Cock, Bobby Gould, Val Gregory, Adam Haywood, John Heath, Jackie Henderson, Bryn Jones, Bob McNab, Jon Purdie, Alan Sunderland and Arthur Worrall.

Also associated: Don Howe (Wolves amateur trialist, Arsenal player, coach, assistant manager and manager), Bob Wilson (Wolves amateur, Arsenal goalkeeper), John Barnwell (Arsenal player, Wolves manager), Tommy Docherty (Arsenal player, Wolves manager), George Jobey (Arsenal player, Wolves manager), Chris Evans (Arsenal player, Wolves coach), Nigel Sims (Arsenal guest), Billy Wright (Wolves player, Arsenal manager), Ray Hankin (Arsenal trialist), Laurie Scott (Arsenal player, Wolves wartime guest), Eric Jones and Billy Wrigglesworth (Wolves players, Arsenal wartime guests) and Tommy Rudkin (Wolves Reserves).

ASCOLI

Wolves were beaten 1-0 at Molineux by the Italian Serie 'B' side Ascoli in a preliminary round of the Anglo-Italian Cup in September 1994. The Italians had Benetti sent-off and their all-important goal was a 'rocket' scored by Marcato in the 57th minute. The attendance was a creditable 9,599.

ASHALL, George Henry

Stocky left-winger Ashall had two fine seasons with Wolves: 1936-38. He joined the club from Frickley Colliery in February 1936 and made a goalscoring debut in the gold and black against Grimsby Town the following month. On leaving Molineux in July 1938, he signed for Coventry City and remained at Highfield Road until the summer of 1948 when he drifted into non-League football before finally hanging up his boots in 1952. Ashall, who was born in Killamarsh, Derbyshire, on 29 September 1911, represented the Football League against the Scottish League in 1937 and guested for Northampton Town during the war. He died in May 1998.
Wolves record: 94 apps. 19 goals.

ASHINGTON

Wolves' playing record against Ashington is:
Football League

Venue	P	W	D	L	F	A
Home	1	1	0	0	1	0
Away	1	1	0	0	7	1
Totals	2	2	0	0	8	1

Both these games were played in the Third Division North in season 1923-24. Just Under-17,000 fans saw Harry Lees give

Wolves victory at Molineux in late December, while there were 3,000 spectators present for the trip to Ashington on 5 January when Tom Phillipson netted a hat-trick in Wolves' emphatic victory.

Players with both clubs include: Edward Carter, Frank Green and Ray King (Wolves amateur).

ASHLEY, Kevin

A quick-recovering full-back who loved to overlap, Ashley was born in Kings Heath, Birmingham on 31 December 1968 and played junior football for Wheelers Lane School before joining Birmingham City on YTS forms in June 1984. He turned professional in December 1986 and after 67 outings for Blues was transferred to Wolves for £500,000 in September 1990. He had a useful first season at Molineux, but after that struggled with his form and finally left the club in August 1994 to join Peterborough United on a free transfer. He later played for Doncaster Rovers, Telford United in the Vauxhall Conference (1996-97) and then for Bromsgrove Rovers (under the managership of ex-Wolves star Steve Daley) before teaming up with Shifnal Town in 1998-99. Ashley is now a postman and lives in Halesowen.
Wolves record: 97+2 apps. 1 goal.

ASHTON, Derek O.

Solid full-back or centre-half, born in Worksop, Notts on 4 July 1922, Ashton represented Worksop schools and joined Wolves in 1941. He played throughout the hostilities, accumulating 151 games for the Wanderers in wartime and FA Cup football. But with so many quality defenders at Molineux around that time, Ashton was allowed to leave Wolves for Aston Villa in May 1946. He played in eight games for Villa before moving into non-League soccer with Wellington Town in 1951.
Wolves record: 4 apps.

ASTILL, Leonard Victor

Len Astill was a reserve outside-left for Wolves in the mid-1930s, breaking into the first team in April 1935 after playing initially as an amateur in the 'A' side. Born in Wolverhampton on 30 December 1916, he was educated at Hordern Road and Old Hall Schools and played for Wolverhampton Boys in the English Schools Shield Final against Islington at Highbury in 1931 in front of 13,531 fans. It was his form in this game that led to Major Frank Buckley recruiting him to Wolves. Astill progressed through the 'A' and reserve teams and made his debut for Wolves in a 2-1 win over Stoke. In May 1935, a month after representing the Birmingham County FA against the Scottish Junior FA at The Hawthorns and the Irish Free State, he was surprisingly transferred to Blackburn

Rovers and later assisted Ipswich Town, linking up with Gilbert Alsop, one of the greatest goalscorers of his time, and Colchester United (from March 1938). Astill retired from the game during the early part of the war and started a business as market trader in Walsall, later becoming a newsagent in Telford. A fine club cricketer, he died on 6 January 1988.

Wolves record: 2 apps.

ASTON, Harry

Aston was a speedy, wholehearted utility forward, born in Bloxwich in October 1855 who attended Spon Lane School, West Bromwich and played for the George Salter Works team before becoming a key member of West Bromwich Albion's first senior squad in 1879-80. He left the Throstles for Wolves in July 1885 and the following summer switched to Burslem Port Vale for whom he made over 40 appearances. He later assisted Preston North End (briefly) and Oldbury Town and retired in 1891. Aston died in West Bromwich c.1914.

Wolves record: 5 apps. 4 goals

NB. Aston scored Albion's first recorded goal against Black Lake Victoria in a friendly in December 1879.

ASTON, Jack

Centre-half Jack Aston (no relation to Harry, above) was one of the first dominant defenders to pull on a Wolves shirt. Born in Wednesbury in 1863, he spent a couple of seasons at the club, from July 1884 to May 1886, having been recruited from local junior football. After leaving Wolves he served with several minor teams including Willenhall Pickwick, Stafford Road and Oldbury Saints.

Wolves record: 5 apps. 3 goals.

ASTON SHAKESPEARE

Wolves have met the Birmingham-based club once – in a second-round FA Cup-tie at Dudley Road on 5 November 1887. A crowd of 2,500 saw Wolves win 3-0 with goals from Hunter, Shaw and Griffiths.

ASTON VILLA

Wolves' playing record against the Villa is:

Football League

Venue	P	W	D	L	F	A
Home	48	21	12	15	86	68
Away	48	12	10	26	64	109
Totals	96	33	22	41	150	177

FA Cup

Home	5	1	3	1	8	8
Away	5	0	1	4	5	10
Neutral	2	2	0	0	4	1
Totals	12	3	4	5	17	19

League Cup

Home	2	0	1	1	2	3
Away	3	0	0	3	3	6
Totals	5	0	1	4	5	9

Norman Deeley's winning goal against Aston Villa in the 1960 FA Cup semi-final.

Wartime

Home	9	1	1	7	10	24
Away	10	2	2	6	17	26
Totals	19	3	3	13	27	50

As founder members of the Football League, Wolves met Villa on the opening day of the competition – 8 September 1888 – at Molineux. A moderate crowd of 2,500 witnessed the 1-1 draw with full-back Gershom Cox scoring an own-goal to earn Wolves a share of the points.

Wolves' best League victory over Villa is 6-3 (away) on 18 April 1892 (Division One). Harry Wood scored a hat-trick for Wolves that day in front of 8,000 fans. Villa had lost 3-0 in the FA Cup Final to West Brom shortly before this game.

When Villa were defeated 5-2 at Molineux in a First Division match in September 1934, Billy Hartill was the Wolves star man, netting all his side's goals in front of 29,047 fans.

The previous December, Wolves had beaten Villa 4-3 at Molineux with ten men following the sending-off of Charlie Phillips, later to play for Villa. While just 24 hours before (Christmas Day 1933) Villa had roasted Wolves 6-2 at Villa Park before a 57,000 crowd to record their joint second biggest League win over the Wanderers.

Villa also won 6-2 at home on the last day of the 1890-91 League season (14 March).

Villa's best win over Wolves is 6-0, achieved at home in November 1905 (Division One) when the turnout was 20,000. The reverse fixture that season ended Wolves 4 Villa 1 at Molineux.

Wolves also lost 5-0 on Villa soil in League games in April 1893 and April 1897, and went down 5-1 at Villa Park in the First Division in December 1949 when 69,492 spectators packed into the ground – a record for a League game at Villa Park. Only 48 hours earlier Wolves had whipped Villa 4-0 at Molineux when the attendance was almost 40,000.

In December 1947, a record crowd of 68,099 had witnessed the Villa-Wolves League encounter at Villa Park. This stood for exactly two years.

Villa won 4-0 on Wolves' territory in December 1894 and again in November 1978.

During the Wolves against Villa League game at Molineux in August 1961, there was a bottle-throwing incident; Wanderers' full-back John Harris broke his leg and Ted Farmer (Wolves) and Derek Dougan (Villa) both scored twice in the 2-2 draw before a 31,703 crowd.

In the League game at Molineux in February 1981, Wolves' Peter Daniel broke a leg as Villa gained a crucial victory (1-0) on their way to the championship.

The last League meeting between the clubs was at Villa Park on 25 February 1984 when Villa won 4-0 in front of 18,257 fans.

Wolves have completed seven League doubles over Villa, who in turn have achieved nine over Wolves, the last in 1980-81.

The teams first met in the FA Cup in season 1886-87, Villa going through at the fourth attempt by 2-0 after scores of 2-2, 1-1 and 3-3, on their way to winning the trophy.

Villa again ousted Wolves from the competition, winning 3-1 at Molineux en route to the 1892 Final.

A 32nd minute goal by winger Norman Deeley at the Birmingham Road end gave

Wolves a 1-0 win over Aston Villa in the FA Cup semi-final showdown at The Hawthorns in March 1960 which was witnessed by almost 55,600 fans. And Wolves again beat Villa on Albion soil in a fifth round second replay in March 1965 when Hugh McIlmoyle scored a hat-trick on a snowbound pitch in front of a 37,534 crowd.

Villa knocked Wolves out of the League Cup over two legs in seasons 1981-82 (5-3 on aggregate) and 1989-90 (3-2). The fifth clash at Villa Park in season 1995-96 attracted a 39,277 crowd who saw Villa win 1-0.

Wolves beat Villa 2-1 and 5-0 in a soccer tournament in the USA in 1969. Derek Dougan scored in each game against his old club.

A crowd of 39,333 witnessed the home wartime fixture against Aston Villa on 31 March 1945 which ended in a 1-0 win for Wolves.

Players with both clubs include: Derek Ashton, Bill Baxter, Tom Bennett, Paul Birch, Andy Blair, Mark Blake, Peter Broadbent, Mark Burke, John Burridge, Gordon Clayton, Gordon Cowans, Tony Daley, Will Devey, Dicky Dorsett, Derek Dougan, Alun Evans, Steve Froggatt, Andy Gray, George Harper, George Harris, Bob Iverson, Mick Kenning, George Kinsey, Dariuz Kubicki, Bobby McDonald, Peter McParland, Derek Mountfield, Dennis Parsons, Charlie Phillips, Roy Pritchard, Cyrille Regis, Phil Robinson, Geoff Sidebottom, Nigel Sims, Fred Smart, Gordon Smith, Les Smith, Cyril Spiers, Barry Stobart, Bobby Thomson, Mark Walters, Tom 'Pongo' Waring, Guy Whittingham, Evan Williams and Peter Withe.

Also associated: Stan Collymore, Arthur Conway, Geoff Crudgington (Wolves Reserves), George Harper, George Harris, Frank Moss (he made 283 appearances for Villa after leaving Molineux where he had been a reserve), Bert Smart, Jim Travers and Gareth Williams (all Wolves Reserves), Matt Forman, Matt Hellin, Arnold Henshall, Darren Middleton, Dennis Pearce, David Stokes (all Villa Reserves), Billy Kellock (Villa junior), Ian Ross (Wolves reserve and also caretaker-manager), Arthur Thomas (trialist); Mark Jones (Villa schoolboy), Alex Scott (Villa wartime guest), Frank Broome, Colin Gibson, Freddie Haycock, Jock Mulraney, Frank O'Donnell and Tom Wood (Villa players, Wolves wartime guests).

Major Frank Buckley was a player at Villa Park, who later managed Wolves. Tommy Docherty, Brian Little, Graham Taylor and Graham Turner all managed both clubs, with Little also playing for Villa. Jim Barron kept goal for Wolves and later became assistant manager at Villa Park.

John Ward was assistant manager to Taylor at Villa Park and in 1998-99 became assistant boss to Colin Lee at Molineux. Ron Atkinson

was a junior with Wolves and a reserve at Villa Park before later managing Villa. Bill Shorthouse was a player at Wolves and later coach at Villa Park and Steve Harrison was a Wolves coach and Villa's assistant manager.

Doug Ellis (current Villa chairman) has been a director of both clubs.

ATALANTA
A Molineux crowd of 7,265 saw Wolves held to a 1-1 draw by Italy's Serie 'B' side Atalanta in an Anglo-Italian Cup preliminary round clash in November 1994. Lee Mills scored for Wolves in the first half.

ATKINS, Mark Nigel
The versatile Mark Atkins has occupied a number of positions in his League career which began in 1986 with Scunthorpe United whom he joined two years earlier as a teenager. Born in Doncaster on 14 August 1968, and a winner of England Schoolboy honours, Atkins played in 66 games for the Iron before transferring to Blackburn Rovers for £45,000 in June 1988. In the next seven years, he amassed more than 300 appearances for Rovers, helping them win the Premiership in 1994-95. He was sold to Wolves for £1 million in September 1995 and over the next two campaigns gave Wolves excellent service, mainly as a central defender although occasionally filling in at right-back and in midfield. Atkins was released by Wolves in May 1999.
Wolves record: 140+11 apps. 11 goals.

ATKINSON, Hugh A.
Hardworking Irish midfielder, who could also play at left-back, Atkinson was born in Dublin on 8 November 1960. His early football was with Cabinteely Youth Club and Dundrum Boys before he joined Wolves as an apprentice in 1976, turning professional in November 1978. He spent five years as a professional at Molineux, up to November 1983, when he was sold to Exeter City, later assisting York City (July 1984) and Darlington (on loan, March/April 1985).
Wolves record: 52 apps. 3 goals.

ATTENDANCES
Highest
The record attendance at Molineux (before it became an all-seater stadium) was 61,315 for the FA Cup-tie with Liverpool on 11 February 1939.

Since Molineux became an all-seater stadium, Wolves' best home crowd has been that of 28,544 against Leicester City, FA Cup, fifth round, in February 1995.

The biggest League Cup audience at the ground is 28,369 – for the Coca-Cola clash with Nottingham Forest (lost 3-2) in October 1994.

A 'best' League crowd of 28,298 attended

the game with. Stoke City (Division One) on 14 January 1995.

The current capacity of Molineux (at 1999) is 28,550.

Only one other 60,000 plus crowd has assembled at the ground – 61,267 against Arsenal, also in the FA Cup, on 22 January 1938.

The biggest League attendance at Molineux has been that of 56,661 against West Bromwich Albion (Division One) on 15 October 1949.

The top League Cup audience is 41,031 for the semi-final second leg clash against Swindon Town on 12 February 1980.

In European football, Wolves' best home crowd has been the 55,747 turnout against ASK Vorwaerts in the European Cup on 7 October 1959.

In wartime football, the highest crowd at Molineux for a Wolves game was that of 43,038 against Sunderland for the Football League North Cup Final on 30 May 1942.

The best 'League' attendance at Molineux during World War Two was that of 42,684 against Birmingham on 20 April 1946.

In non-competitive football, the top attendance at Molineux is 55,480 for the Wolves v Moscow Dynamo friendly on 9 November 1955.

The biggest attendance for any game involving Wolves was that of 99,370 for the 1939 FA Cup Final v Portsmouth at Wembley.

A crowd of 98,776 witnessed the 1960 FA Cup Final between Wolves and Blackburn Rovers; around 80,000 saw the European Cup clash involving Barcelona and Wolves at the Nou Camp Stadium in Spain in February 1960 and crowds of over 70,000 were present to see Wolves take on Moscow Spartak and Moscow Dynamo in friendly matches in the Russian capital in August 1955.

A then record crowd, for the competition, of 80,841 attended the 1988 Sherpa Van Trophy Final between Wolves and Burnley at Wembley – around 40,000 of them supporting Wolves.

The best crowd for a League game involving Wolves is that of 75,043, which assembled at Stamford Bridge for a vital First Division clash v Chelsea in April 1955.

During World War Two the average attendance at Molineux for Wolves' home games was 11,745 – the average in 1944-45 was 13,409 and in 1945-46 it was 25,079.

The biggest League crowd ever to assemble at Villa Park is 69,492 for the visit of Wolves on 27 December 1949.

Lowest
The two lowest crowds ever recorded for competitive games at Molineux are believed to be those of just 900 – for the First Division fixture with Notts County on 17 October

1891 and for the encounter with Blackburn Rovers, in the same Division, on 28 November 1891.

On 18 March 1986, a crowd of 2,205 saw the Bury game at Molineux – Wolves' lowest home attendance in the Football League since 19 December 1892, when an estimated 2,000 fans witnessed the encounter with Accrington.

The lowest crowd for a cup-tie at Molineux (involving Wolves) has been 1,618 for the Freight Rover Trophy match with Torquay United on 22 January 1986.

In the FA Cup, Wolves' smallest home crowd has been 2,000 for their Dudley Road ground ties against Long Eaton Rangers on 27 October 1883 (Wanderers' first-ever game in this competition); v Derby St Luke's on 31 October 1885 and v Crosswell's Brewery on 13 November 1886.

The lowest FA Cup attendance at Molineux is 3,000 for the Wolves v Small Heath game on 1 February 1890.

The lowest League Cup turnout at Molineux has been 3,256 for the Wolves v Lincoln City clash on 26 August 1986.

Molineux's smallest European crowd is 14,530 v Lokomotiv Leipzig in the UEFA Cup on 7 November 1973.

Just 1,198 fans saw Wolves' home Regional wartime game with Birmingham on 19 December 1942.

Perhaps the lowest crowd ever to watch a competitive game involving Wolves has been that of just 750 for the Anglo-Italian Cup-tie against Venezia (away) on 5 October 1994.

The friendly between Wolves and Pavi Kavatski Gradjanski Sportski Klub in November 1936 attracted a crowd of just 646 to Molineux.

Points of Interest

Wolves' best average home League attendance for a season is 45,346 in 1949-50.

The lowest seasonal average for a full League programme at Molineux is 3,710 in 1985-86.

For the first season at Molineux (1889-90) Wolves averaged 5,436 at their 11 home League matches and in the first season of League football (in 1888-89) Wolves' home average at their Dudley Road ground was 4,600.

The biggest League crowd ever recorded at The Hawthorns – 60,945 – saw the Albion-Wolves First Division derby on 4 March 1950.

A record crowd of 51,455 at Highfield Road saw the vital Second Division promotion battle between Coventry City and Wolves in April 1967.

Fratton Park's biggest League crowd – 50,248 – attended the Portsmouth v Wolves First Division game on 1 October 1949.

Luton Town's biggest League turnout – 27,911 – packed into Kenilworth Road for the visit of Wolves in November 1955.

The record attendance at Old Trafford – 76,962 – did not feature Manchester United. It was for the Grimsby Town v Wolves FA Cup semi-final clash in March 1939.

The top attendance at Blundell Park is 31,653 – for the Grimsby Town v Wolves FA Cup-tie in February 1937.

Liverpool's best-ever attendance – 61,905 – saw the FA Cup clash with Wolves in February 1952.

Blackpool's record home attendance of 38,098 was set against Wolves (Division One) on 17 September 1955.

An reported unofficial record crowd of 25,052 packed into Sincil Bank to see Wolves beat Lincoln City 1-0 in a third-round FA Cup-tie in January 1958, though the Imps official record attendance was set against Derby County nine years later.

Reports state that almost 49,000 fans (a record) saw the Leicester City v Wolves sixth-round FA Cup-tie at Filbert Street in March 1960.

A crowd of 8,679 saw the Wolves v Stoke game at Molineux in December 1983 – the first time the attendance figure had fallen below 10,000 for a League match at Molineux since March 1937 when just 6,113 fans saw the clash with Portsmouth.

In March 1934, a crowd of 5,489 witnessed the Sheffield Wednesday v Wolves First Division fixture, one of the lowest on record at Hillsborough for a competitive game.

Over a six-year period – 1979-80 (when they won the League Cup) to 1985-86 – Wolves' lost 22,074 fans as their average home League attendance dropped from 25,784 to an all-time low of 3,710.

For the first League season after World War Two (1946-47) Wolves' average home crowd was 43,307 – a rise of over 14,000 from the last pre-war campaign in 1938-39 when their average was 29,335

In 1967-68, following promotion to the First Division, Wolves' average home League crowd rose by more than 8,500 to 33,264.

Record Attendances

This is how the attendance record was subsequently broken at each of Wolves' main grounds:

At Dudley Road

2,000	v Long Eaton Rangers	FA Cup	27 Oct 1883
3,000	v Derby St Luke's	FA Cup	8 Nov 1884
3,000	v Preston North End	FA Cup	21 Nov 1885
6,000	v Preston North End	Friendly	17 Apr 1886
7,000	v Aston Villa	FA Cup	15 Jan 1887
8,600	v West Bromwich A	League	15 Dec 1888
		Equalled previous attendance	

At Molineux

4,000	v Walsall Town	Walsall Cup	20 Mar 1886
4,000	v Aston Villa	Friendly	2 Sep 1889
4,000*	v Notts County	League	7 Sep 1889
8,000	v Aston Villa	League	21 Dec 1889
19,000	v West Bromwich A	League	26 Dec 1889

20,000	v Sunderland	League	26 Dec 1891
21,945	v Aston Villa	FA Cup	13 Feb 1892
22,200	v Aston Villa	League	26 Dec 1895
27,489	v Aston Villa	League	26 Dec 1896
29,981	v Southampton	FA Cup	18 Feb 1905
33,028	v Chelsea	FA Cup	25 Feb 1911
36,800	v Blackburn Rovers	FA Cup	15 Jan 1920
39,658	v Derby County	FA Cup	3 Feb 1921
40,079	v Liverpool	FA Cup	3 Feb 1923
40,283	v West Bromwich A	FA Cup	27 Feb 1924
42,083	v Arsenal	FA Cup	9 Jan 1926
48,949	v Hull City	FA Cup	19 Feb 1927
52,112	v Aston Villa	League	27 Dec 1932
53,097	v Arsenal	League	19 Sep 1936
56,799	v Grimsby Town	FA Cup	24 Feb 1937
57,751	v Sunderland	FA Cup	6 Mar 1937
61,267	v Arsenal	FA Cup	22 Jan 1938
61,315	v Liverpool	FA Cup	11 Feb 1939

Biggest crowds at Molineux

61,315	v Liverpool	FA Cup	11 Feb 1939
61,267	v Arsenal	FA Cup	22 Jan 1938
57,751	v Sunderland	FA Cup	6 Mar 1937
56,799	v Grimsby Town	FA Cup	24 Feb 1937
56,661	v West Bromwich A	League	15 Oct 1949
56,590	v West Bromwich A	League	14 Nov 1953
56,283	v Tottenham Hotspur	League	23 Apr 1960
55,998	v Arsenal	League	18 Oct 1947
55,778	v Darlington	FA Cup	15 Feb 1958
55,648	v West Bromwich A	FA Cup	26 Feb 1949
55,648	v Arsenal	League	4 Nov 1950

Top 20 away crowds (all games)

99,370	v Portsmouth	FA Cup Final	29 Apr 1939
98,920	v Leicester City	FA Cup Final	30 Apr 1949
98,776	v Blackburn Rovers	FA Cup Final	7 May 1960
97,886	v Manchester City	L.Cup Final	2 Mar 1974
96,527	v Nottingham Forest	L. Cup Final	15 Mar 1980
80,841	v Burnley	Sherpa Van T.	29 May 1988
80,000	v Barcelona	European Cup	10 Feb 1960
80,000	v Moscow Spartak	Friendly	27 Aug 1955
79,229	v Glasgow Rangers	ECWC	29 Mar 1961
76,962	v Grimsby Town	FA Cup semi-f	25 Mar 1939
75,322	v Everton	League	27 Dec 1954
75,043	v Chelsea	League	9 Apr 1955
75,000	v Moscow Dynamo	Friendly	12 Aug 1955
74,967	v Newcastle United	FA Cup Final	25 Apr 1908
72,805	v Tottenham Hotspur	FA Cup Final	23 Apr 1921
72,631	v Manchester United	FA Cup semi-f	2 Apr 1949
72,569	v Everton	FA Cup	31 Jan 1948
69,492	v Aston Villa	League	27 Dec 1949
68,099	v Aston Villa	League	26 Dec 1947
67,782	v Manchester City	League	23 Aug 1947

Top 10 Away League attendances

75,322	v Everton		27 Dec 1954
75,043	v Chelsea		9 Apr 1955
69,492	v Aston Villa		27 Dec 1949
68,099	v Aston Villa		26 Dec 1947
67,782	v Manchester City		23 Aug 1947
67,311	v Arsenal		4 Sep 1937
66,967	v Manchester United		5 Apr 1947
66,796	v Tottenham Hotspur		20 Jan 1951
63,781	v Chelsea		27 Sep 1952
63,572	v Aston Villa		27 Dec 1948

AUSTRIA (FK)

Wolves' playing record against the Austrians is:

European Cup-winners' Cup

Venue	P	W	D	L	F	A
Home	1	1	0	0	5	0
Away	1	0	0	1	0	2
Totals	2	1	0	1	5	2

Wolves have featured in the European Cup-winners' Cup competition once – in 1960-61 – and their first 'tie' was the two-legged encounter against FK Austria. After losing their away game in front of 25,000 fans in mid-October, Wolves stormed back and went nap in the second leg at Molineux on 30 November in front of 31,699 fans, thus winning the tie 5-2 on aggregate. Peter Broadbent and Johnny Kirkham both scored twice and Bobby Mason once in that crushing 5-0 victory.

BADDELEY, Thomas

Baddeley was an excellent goalkeeper, as 'safe as houses' and despite his 5ft 9ins. and 11 stone frame, he feared no-one and often dived bravely at opponents' feet. The fourth member of the Baddeley clan, he was born in Bycars, Stoke, on 2 November 1874 and commenced his career with Burslem Swifts in 1890. In September 1893 he signed for Burslem Port Vale and after more than 70 outings for the Valiants he moved to Wolves for £50 in October 1896 after being suspended for signing a second professional form for

Tom Baddeley played 315 times for Wolves.

an another club. He spent the next 11 seasons at Molineux (up to 1907) when he switched to Yorkshire to sign for Bradford Park Avenue (being a founder member of that club – playing in the first League game v Hull City in September 1908). During March and April 1910 he played eight games for Stoke and finally called it a day in 1911 after briefly assisting Whitfield Colliery FC. Winner of five England caps (1903-04), Baddeley could throw a ball out up to 50 yards (an unusual feature for a 'keeper of his era) and in a fine career accumulated almost 400 appearances at club level, being the first Wolves player to star in 300 matches. He died in Hartshill, Stoke-on-Trent on 24 September 1946.
Wolves record: 315 apps.

BAILEY, Herbert

Herbert Bailey was a reserve utility forward, born locally c.1870, who played for Wolves in season 1891-92. He was recruited as cover for Messrs Devey, Heath and Topham, and when released from Molineux he signed for Willenhall Pickwick.
Wolves record: 1 app.

BAILEY, Michael Alfred

Mike Bailey gave Wolves splendid service, contributing greatly to the club's long-awaited revival in the 1970s as a wing-half, who oozed confidence. Capped twice by England (v USA in 1964 and Wales in 1965), Bailey also won five Under-23 caps, was voted Midland Footballer of the Year in 1967 and in 1974 skippered Wolves to victory in the League Cup Final against Manchester City. Born in Wisbech on 27 February 1942, Bailey was a pupil at Edward Worlidge and Alderman Leech Schools (Gorleston). He was a junior with Precasters FC and after a short spell with Gorleston signed amateur forms for Charlton Athletic (May 1957), turning professional in March 1959. Prior to him joining Wolves, he broke a leg against Middlesbrough, but made a full recovery and arrived at Molineux for £40,000 in March 1966. Then, over the next 11 years, Bailey became a big favourite with the club's fans. His contract with Wolves was cancelled in January 1977 and five months later he signed for Minnesota Kicks (NASL) for £15,000. After 17 months as player-manager of Hereford United (from June 1978 to October 1979) he became chief coach at his old club Charlton (from October 1979, taking over as manager in March 1980 and holding office until June 1981). He then managed Brighton and Hove Albion (from June 1981 to December 1982); coached briefly in Cyprus (1983-84); was player-manager of Bexley FC (1985-86); acted as co-manager of New Valley FC, while at the same time penning a column in a Sunday Newspaper; managed non-League Fisher Athletic (from December

1989 to January 1991) and then held a coaching position coupled with that of reserve team manager/coach at Portsmouth in season 1992-93 before becoming general manager of Leatherhead (ICIS League). Bailey who was granted a testimonial (Wolves v WBA) in 1976, later scouted for Blackburn Rovers, Newcastle, Everton and Derby County
Wolves record: 436 apps. 25 goals.

BAILLIE, Joseph M.

Joe Baillie was a powerfully built full-back, born in Dumfries, Scotland on 26 February 1929, who, for 18 months at Molineux, was first reserve to the likes of Bill Shorthouse and Eddie Stuart. After 177 appearances for Celtic and having represented Scotland 'B' and the Scottish League, as well as having won a Scottish Cup winners medal in 1951 as a half-back, he was recruited by Wolves' manager Stan Cullis in December 1954, and left Molineux for Bristol City in June 1956. Twelve months later he went to Leicester City and played in 80 League and Cup games for the Filbert Street club before rounding off his senior career with a spell at Bradford Park Avenue (1960-61). Baillie was tragically killed in a car crash in Glasgow in March 1966.
Wolves record: 1 app.

BAKER, Charles

Inside-forward Charlie Baker, described as a 'neat dribbler', was born in Stafford in February 1870. He played for Stafford Rangers, Stoke (from April 1889 to May 1891), Wolves (from August 1891 to February 1893), Stoke, for a second time (from January 1893 to June 1894) and Southampton St Mary's (from August 1894 to April 1896) when he retired from competitive football. He later returned to his home town of Stafford and again assisted Stafford Rangers before finally hanging up his boots in 1900 to pursue a shoemaking trade. Baker, who was presented with a gold watch on his departure from The Dell, died c.1940.
Wolves record: 41 apps. 10 goals.

BAKER, James Edward

Strong, forceful wing-half, 6ft tall and weighing over 12st, Jack Baker deputised for Frank Higham during his time at Molineux. Born in the Rhonda Valley at Trethomas on 27 March 1904, he played for Lovell's Athletic before joining Wolves in May 1926. From Molineux he went to Coventry City (May 1929) and after a second spell with Lovell's (1932) he returned to Highfield Road in February 1933. He later assisted Bristol City (from June 1935) and Colchester United (1937-41) before retiring during the war. Baker died in Coventry on 27 March 1979.
Wolves record: 17 apps.

BANSFORD, George

An amateur inside-forward, recruited by Wolves soon after World War One, George Bansford was born in Wednesfield in 1894 and played for Dudley Road Methodists, St Matthews's Church, West Park Juniors and Bushbury Rovers prior to moving to Molineux in August 1919. He had one season with Wolves, leaving to join Lanesfield Rovers in May 1920. His only League game in the gold and black was the 1-0 away win at Grimsby in September 1919. There is no record of him playing beyond 1922.

Wolves record: 1 app.

BARCELONA

Wolves' playing record against the Spanish club is:

European Cup

Venue	P	W	D	L	F	A
Home	1	0	0	1	2	5
Away	1	0	0	1	0	4
Totals	2	0	0	2	2	9

Spanish giants Barcelona knocked Wolves out of the European Cup in the second round of the 1959-60 competition with a crushing aggregate victory. A crowd of around 80,000 packed the Nou Camp Stadium and saw Barcelona win the first leg in style on 10 February. Then, despite Wolves having a mountain to climb, a massive crowd of 55,535 attended Molineux for the return fixture on 2 March, which the star-studded visitors also won comfortably, Sandor Koscis scoring four of his side's five goals.

In July 1998, Barcelona played a pre-season friendly against Wolves at Molineux where a crowd of more than 18,000 saw the Spanish club win a hard fought contest by 3-2.

Player with both clubs: Ronnie Ekelund (Wolves trialist).

BARKER, George

Full-back George Barker partnered George Walker in Wolves' defence during the first season of the 20th century. Born in Blakenhall in February 1875, he played local football in the Wolverhampton League before going north to Merseyside to join Everton in 1896. From there he went to Bristol City (1898) and then returned to the Black Country to sign for Wolves. His brief spell at Molineux lasted from December 1900 to September 1901, when he was forced to retire through injury.

Wolves record: 13 apps.

BARKER, Richard

Richie Barker, born in Burton upon Trent on 23 November 1939, did not play League football until joining Derby County at the age of 28 in October 1967, having previously assisted Morris Sports FC, Burton Albion (two spells), Loughborough, Matlock Town (1963), and the Canadian side, Primo

Hamilton (on loan). He helped the Rams win the Second Division in 1969 and later assisted Notts County, gaining a Fourth Division championship medal with them in 1971. After breaking a leg playing for Peterborough, whom he served from September 1971, he moved into management, first as assistant to Alan Durban at Shrewsbury, and when Durban left for Stoke in February 1978, Barker took the manager's chair at Gay Meadow. Ten months later he moved to Wolves (as assistant to John Barnwell). In June 1981 he became manager of Stoke, staying there until December 1983 before returning to Meadow Lane as boss in November 1984 (to April 1985). He then coached Ethnikos (Greece) and Zamalek (Egypt) prior to becoming Ron Atkinson's assistant at Sheffield Wednesday in February 1989 to May 1995. Barker is now chief scout at West Bromwich Albion.

BARLOW, Herbert

Bert Barlow spent less than eight months at Molineux and amazingly ten weeks after leaving the club he won a FA Cup winners medal with Portsmouth who ironically defeated Wolves 4-1 in the 1939 Final at Wembley when he scored one of the goals. An inside-right, Barlow was born in Kilnhurst, Yorkshire on 22 July 1916 and played for Silverwood Colliery and Barnsley (July 1935) before teaming up with Wolves (on the 'never never') in June 1938. He switched to Fratton Park in February 1939 and played for Pompey for the next 10 years, transferring to Leicester City in December 1949. He ended his playing career with Colchester United (July 1952-May 1954). Barlow, who guested for Barnsley, Brighton, Chelsea and Rotherham United during the war, appeared in well over 300 games at club level and helped Portsmouth win the First Division championship in 1949, netting eight goals.

Wolves record: 3 apps. 1 goal.

BARNES, David

Strong, athletic full-back or midfielder, Barnes was born in Paddington, London on 16 November 1961. On leaving school he joined Coventry City as an apprentice (June 1977) and turned professional at Highfield Road in May 1979. Three years later he was transferred to Ipswich Town and in October 1982 was recruited by Wolves, manager Graham Hawkins paying £30,000 for his signature. He did very well at Molineux during his three year stay before switching to Aldershot in August 1987. From there he went to Sheffield United for £50,000 (July 1989) and helped the Blades win promotion to the First Division in 1990. He made over 100 appearances for United before transferring to Watford for £50,000 in January 1994. Unfortunately he was troubled by an Achilles tendon injury during his time at Vicarage

Road and was given a 'free' in the summer of 1996 when he moved to Colchester United, helping them reach the Auto Windscreen Shield Final at Wembley. His contract was cancelled at Layer Road in March 1997 by mutual consent.

Wolves record: 107 apps. 4 goals.

BARNET

Wolves' record against Barnet:

League Cup

Venue	P	W	D	L	F	A
Home	1	1	0	0	5	0
Away	1	0	0	1	1	2
Totals	2	1	0	1	6	2

After losing the away leg of a first round Worthington League Cup-tie at Underhill in mid August 1998, Wolves bounced back to win the return leg 5-0 at Molineux a week later in front of a 15,000 plus crowd. Steve Bull grabbed a hat-trick in the second leg clash. Wolves have yet to play Barnet in a League match.

Played for both clubs: Dougie Freedman.

Associated with both clubs: Bob McNab (as a player), Bobby Gould (Wolves player) and Don Howe (Wolves trialist, Barnet coach), Jimmy Jinks (wartime guest), Dave Barnett and Robert Sawyers (Wolves apprentices).

BARNSLEY

Wolves' playing record against Barnsley is:

Football League

Venue	P	W	D	L	F	A
Home	32	17	8	7	69	33
Away	31	5	9	17	36	66
Neutral*	1	0	0	1	2	4
Totals	64	22	17	25	107	103

FA Cup

Away	1	1	0	0	3	1

The League game on a neutral ground was, in fact, a Wolves 'home' League fixture, played in November 1919 on a snow-covered at The Hawthorns after Molineux had been 'closed' for two home matches. Wolves ended up with nine men, goalkeeper Teddy Peers and winger Billy Harrison both going off injured.

The first League meeting between Wolves and Barnsley was played at Oakwell in December 1906 where a goal by George Hedley gave the visitors a 1-0 Second Division victory in front of 4,000 spectators. Wolves completed the double over the Tykes when they won the return fixture 5-1 at Molineux in the April.

Wolves' biggest League win over Barnsley is 9-1 – achieved in a Second Division fixture at Molineux on 5 November 1926. The gold and black fireworks that day were in celebration of the hat-tricks scored by Wilf Chadwick and Tom Phillipson.

Seven months earlier (in April 1926) Wolves had beaten the Tykes 7-1 on the same pitch when Phillipson this time netted a four-timer.

Wolves also won 5-0 at home in March 1912 when Billy Halligan claimed a hat-trick.

Barnsley's biggest League win over Wolves is 7-1 – in a Second Division match at Oakwell in October 1909. The Tykes also ran up a 5-0 scoreline at the same venue in November 1907 and 84 years later (in March 1991) repeated that victory with a 5-0 drubbing of Wolves at Molineux, all the goals being scored by different players.

Wolves conceded three goals in four minutes during their Second Division League game at Oakwell in September 1984. They eventually lost 5-1.

In season 1996-97, as they were making their way towards the Premiership, the Tykes held Wolves to a 3-3 draw at Molineux only to lose 3-1 at Oakwell in the return fixture.

Barnsley pipped Wolves for the second automatic promotion place in the First Division in 1996-97 despite dropping five points to the Wanderers by losing 3-1 at Oakwell and drawing 3-3 at Molineux (Wolves were 3-1 up in the latter game).

Dean Richards scored for both teams at Oakwell in March 1999. He gave Barnsley the lead early on and after Wolves had fought back from being 2-0 down, Richards grabbed a dramatic late winner for the Wanderers injury-time to keep them in a Play-off position in Division One.

Wolves' FA Cup victory over Barnsley came in the fifth round in 1930-31 before a 33,385 Oakwell crowd.

Players with both clubs include: Alan Ainscow, Herbert Barlow, Alan Birch, Andy Blair, John Chadburn, Don Goodman, Francis Green, George Lax, Gary Pierce, Jimmy Seal, Peter Shirtliff (Barnsley player-coach), Jack Short, Robin Van der Laan, Paul Walker, Harry Walters, Tom 'Pongo' Waring, Gareth Williams.

Also associated: Arthur Hetherington and Tom Smalley (Barnsley trialists), John Jarman (Wolves reserve, later coach and Barnsley player), Bobby Downes (Barnsley player, Wolves coach), Herbert Barlow, Stan Burton and John Taylor (Wolves players, Barnsley wartime guests), John Myers (Barnsley reserve), John Hartson, Tom Ellis, John Thomas and Jim Travers (Wolves Reserves), John Stainsby and Barry (Wolves amateurs), and Chris Pearce (Wolves junior).

BARNWELL, John

Barnwell was manager of Wolves for three years – from November 1978 to November 1981 – and in 1980 proudly led his team to victory in the League Cup Final at Wembley, having previously seen his side lose to Arsenal in the 1979 FA Cup semi-final. A Geordie, born in the North-East at Newcastle-on-Tyne on 24 December 1938, Barnwell was an amateur inside-left with Bishop Auckland before turning profession-

al with Arsenal in November 1956. He spent over seven years at Highbury, making more than 160 senior appearances and scoring 24 goals. In March 1964 he switched to Nottingham Forest and after netting 22 times in 182 League games during his for six years at the City Ground, he joined Sheffield United.

He retired as a player in 1971 after amassing a League record of 329 appearances and 47 goals as well as gaining youth and Under-23 caps for England. In July 1977, Barnwell stepped into management with Peterborough United from where he joined Wolves. He made some excellent signings (and sales) during his time at Molineux, although he did admit that it was hard making the transfer from the Third to the First Division in one swift move. Indeed, it was Barnwell who arranged the transfer to Wolves of striker Andy Gray for £1.15 million and the sale of midfielder Steve Daley to Manchester City for roughly the same amount early in the 1979-80 season, as well as the recruitment of 'Crazy Horse' himself Emlyn Hughes from Liverpool, all this after a serious car crash in March 1979 had left him with a fractured skull. Thankfully he recovered from that horrific accident (which had threatened his career in football) and he duly continued in the game. (Brian Garvey had taken over the reins at Molineux during Barnwell's enforced absence). Soon after this mishap Barnwell was voted Midland Sports Personality of the year (1979-80) by the Variety Club. After a disappointing run of results soon after the start of the 1981-82 season Barnwell came under intense pressure and it was no surprise when he left the club with Wolves situated at the bottom end of the First Division table. He had, in fact, received legal advice before terminating his contract. For Barnwell there followed a period out of the game before a brief sojourn in Saudi Arabia got him back into the routine.

He became manager-coach of AEK Athens and was then banned from working in Greece (January 1984) before moving back to England to eventually take over at Notts County (June 1987). He led the Magpies into the Third Division Play-offs at the end of his first season at Meadow Lane. His next move was to struggling Walsall in mid-January 1989, but sadly he couldn't save the Saddlers from losing their Second Division status as they were passed on the way by Wolves. Barnwell was sacked by Walsall in March 1990 and for a time came out of football, although still contributing to a soccer magazine as well as summarising at certain matches. In 1992-93 he acted as a scout for several clubs before joining Third Division strugglers Northampton Town as a consultant to player-manager and ex Wolves star Phil Chard. In July 1996 Barnwell was given the

job as chairman of the League Managers' Association.

BARRACLOUGH, William

Outside-left Bill Barraclough was born in Hull on 3 January 1909. He served Wolves from June 1928 until October 1934 when he was transferred to Chelsea for £1,500. After more than 80 games for the Londoners, he switched to Colchester United and before retiring in the war, he assisted Doncaster Rovers. His career began with Bridlington Town from where he joined Hull City, whom he served prior to his move to Molineux. Barraclough, who won a Second Division championship medal with Wolves in 1932, later worked as a clerk in the Humberside docks and was also a fruit merchant. A keen golfer and respected tennis player, he died in his native Hull on 6 August 1969.
Wolves record: 183 apps. 19 goals.

BARRETT, Scott

Goalkeeper Barrett was given his League debut by Wolves boss Tommy Docherty in 1984. Born at Ilkeston, Derbyshire on 2 April 1963, he played for his local club, Ilkeston Town and was a junior with Notts County before signing for Wolves in September 1984. He moved from Molineux to Stoke City for £10,000 in July 1987 and had 60 first-team outings for the Potters, to August 1992, when he signed for Colchester United, this after loan spells at Layer Road (January 1990) and Stockport County (March 1990). He left Colchester for Gillingham in August 1992 and three years later signed for Cambridge United (August 1995). In 1998 passed the milestone of 150 appearances for the Abbey Stadium club. A loan spell with non-League Kingstonian (August 1998) preceded Barrett's move to Leyton Orient. In 1992 Barrett appeared on BBC's *Question of Sport*.
Wolves record: 35 apps.

BARRON, James

Goalkeeper Jim Barron had a fine career, accumulating 416 League appearances between 1963 and 1981. The son of a former Blackburn Rovers and Darlington 'keeper, Barron was born on 19 October 1943 in Tantobie in the North East of England. He joined Wolves as an amateur in 1960 from Newcastle West End Boys Club, having previously starred for Raby Street School and Byker and Newcastle Boys, as a goalkeeper and inside-right. It was as a goalkeeper, though, that Barron was to star. He signed professional at Molineux in November 1961 and after winning an FA Youth Cup medal in 1962, he made his League bow against Everton the following year. Unfortunately with Fred Davies holding the fort, Barron's chances of regular first-team football were limited and in April 1965 he was sold to

Chelsea. He failed to establish himself at Stamford Bridge and in March 1966 went to Oxford United. At the Manor Ground he did well, making over 150 senior appearances for the Us before trying his luck with Nottingham Forest (July 1970 – August 1974). He made a further 155 League appearances for Forest and then added 79 to his tally with Swindon Town (to August 1977) before ending his career with 21 League games for Peterborough, retiring in May 1981. Barron then became assistant manager at Mansfield and returned to Molineux as coach/assistant manager (1981-83), later having a third spell with Wolves as coach prior to becoming boss at Cheltenham in November 1989, at the same time running a goalkeeping school in the Gloucestershire area. He lost his job at Cheltenham in October 1990, but was then given the position of goalkeeping coach by Howard Kendall at Everton. He was later appointed assistant manager to Ron Atkinson at Villa Park (1992-93) and then, after serving a short prison sentence following a car crash which killed his wife, he became assistant-boss at Sheffield United (under Steve Thompson) and had a big hand in team tactics as the Blades' chased promotion and reached the FA Cup semi-final in 1997-98. In November 1998 Barron left Bramall Lane to become a coach with Birmingham City. Barron's son played in goal for Cheltenham Town when he was manager of the Vauxhall Conference club.
Wolves record: 8 apps.

BARROW

Wolves playing record against Barrow is:
Football League

Venue	P	W	D	L	F	A
Home	1	1	0	0	3	0
Away	1	0	1	0	2	2
Totals	2	1	1	0	5	2

FA Cup

Away	1	1	0	0	4	2

The two League meetings took place in 1923-24 when Wolves won the Third Division North title. En route they collected three vital points off Barrow over the Easter weekend, with Jimmy Harrington scoring twice in the 3-0 win at Molineux.

Wolves' FA Cup triumph over Barrow was achieved at Holker Street in a third round tie in January 1959, when winger Norman Deeley netted twice in front of a full-house crowd of 18,900.

Players with both clubs include: Brian Birch, Joe Blackett, Jack Gardiner, Andy Mutch and Peter Withe.

Also associated: Shane Westley (Wolves player, assistant manager of Barrow), Jimmy Baker and Gordon Brown (Wolves Reserves), Andy Beattie (Wolves manager, Barrow secretary-manager), Jack Harris (Wolves Reserves) and Joe Harvey (Wolves reserve and Barrow manager).

BARTLEY, John Patrick

A well-built, proportionate player, Jack Bartley spent less than two seasons as a reserve at Molineux, occupying the inside-right berth. Born in New Washington, County Durham in February 1908, Bartley played for Spennymoor United from May 1926 before joining Wolves in December 1928. He left Molineux for Walsall in June 1930 and after a brief spell with Usworth Colliery FC, he rounded off his career by having a brief spell with Stockport County (1932-33) with no first-team outings.
Wolves record: 2 apps.

BARTRAM, Vincent

Goalkeeper Vince Bartram was born in Birmingham on 7 August 1968 and was a West Brom fan up until he joined Wolves from Oldswinford FC in May 1985. A pupil at the Hagley RC School, Bartram represented Halesowen and Stourbridge District Boys and was recruited to Molineux when Wolves had a goalkeeping crisis. He never got a good run in the first team and when Graham Turner arrived Mark Kendall became first choice. Loan spells with Blackpool in 1989-90 and West Brom in 1990-91 plus a stint with Cheltenham Town (under Jim Barron) preceded his transfer to Bournemouth for £165,000 in August 1991. He matured at Dean Court and made 162 appearances for the Cherries before moving to Arsenal for £400,000 in August 1994, as reserve to John Lukic and David Seaman. In February 1997 Bartram returned to Molineux on loan for a month as cover for Stowell and he also had a spell at Huddersfield (October 1997). In March 1998 he moved to Gillingham and helped them reach the Second Division One999 Play-off Final at Wembley, where they lost on penalties to Manchester City after leading 2-0 in the dying moments of normal time.
Wolves record: 10 apps.

BATE, Walter William

Wolves acquired the services of utility forward Billy Bate from Darlaston in the summer of 1919. Born in West Bromwich c.1895, he stayed at Molineux for a season, signing for West Smethwick in August 1920.
Wolves record: 11 apps. 5 goals.

BAUGH, Richard

Full-back Dickie Baugh was born in Wolverhampton on 14 February 1864. He attended St Luke's School (Blakenhall) and played for Rose Villa, Wolverhampton Rangers and Stafford Road before joining Wolves in May 1886. Capped twice by England (in 1886 and 1890) he appeared in three FA Cup Finals during his ten years with Wolves, gaining a winners' medal in 1893. He left Molineux for Walsall in September 1896, and retired a year later through injury. Baugh died in Wolverhampton on 14 August 1929.
Wolves record: 227 apps. 1 goal.

BAUGH, Richard Horace

Son of Dickie senior, Baugh junior was born in Wolverhampton on 6 March 1902, a week after Wolves had qualified for the FA Cup semi-final. He, too, was a fine full-back, a grafter, keen and resilient who also played for Stafford Road before joining Wolves in August 1918, turning professional a year later. After missing the 1921 FA Cup Final through injury, Baugh was induced by an agent to join Cardiff City (April 1921). However, a joint FA and Welsh FA Commission, investigated the issue and subsequently cancelled the deal, fining Cardiff £50 and Baugh £20, while also severely censuring him. After another three seasons at Molineux, Baugh was transferred to West Bromwich Albion in June 1924. He made 65 appearances for the Baggies before moving to Exeter City in May 1929, later assisting Kidderminster Harriers, from May 1932 to April 1936 when he retired. Dickie Baugh died in 1972.
Wolves record: 120 apps. 4 goals.

BAXTER, Thomas William

Born in Mansfield on 1 February 1903, Tom Baxter was a fast, energetic outside-left who spent two seasons at Molineux from August 1927. He joined Wolves from Mansfield Town and left the club for Port Vale in August 1929. He helped the Valiants win the Third Division North title in 1930 and made almost 60 appearances for the Potteries club before returning to Mansfield in May 1931. Thereafter he had two spells with Margate Town (1932 and 1933), served briefly with Carlisle United and rounded off his career in Ireland with Distillery. Earlier Baxter had played for Warsop Church Lads, Welbeck Colliery, Newark Town and Worksop Town before signing for Mansfield in 1927. He died in Cannock on 21 August 1987.
Wolves record: 53 apps. 15 goals.

BAXTER, William

Wing-half Bill Baxter was a patient man who served in the Royal Navy and had to wait seven years before making his League debut for Wolves against Everton in December 1948. Born in Methill, Fife, on 21 September 1924, he joined the groundstaff at Molineux on leaving The Vale of Leven School in August 1939 and turned professional in September 1945, having guested Leicester City, Mansfield Town and Notts County during the war. After battling on, mainly in the second team, Baxter, who made a record 224 reserve team appear-

ances for Wolves (213 in the Central League) finally left Molineux for Aston Villa in November 1953. He added more than 100 senior outings to his career tally during the next four years at Villa Park before retiring in June 1957 to become Villa's third-team coach. He was the club's assistant manager in the early 1960s and was reserve-team trainer for two years: 1965-67. He later managed the Scottish club East Fife (1968-70).
Wolves record: 47 apps. 1 goal.

BAYLY, Martin J.
Republic of Ireland Youth international midfielder Bayly was given his senior debut with Wolves by manager Graham Hawkins in 1983 as a teenager. Born in Dublin on 14 September 1966, Bayly played schoolboy football in his home city and after a brief spell with Little Bray FC joined Wolves as an apprentice in 1982, turning professional in July 1984. Although voted the club's 'Young Player of the Year' in 1984, he was perhaps too fragile to make a real impact in competitive League football and on leaving Molineux in July 1985 had a brief association with Coventry City before drifting into non-League soccer.
Wolves record: 11 apps.

BAYNHAM, Albert
Outside-right Albert Baynham was born in the Black Country c.1880 and joined Wolves from Halesowen at the start of the 1903-04 season. He replaced Fellows on the wing and did a fine job in the first team for well over two seasons before suffering a serious knee injury in December 1905. He left Molineux in the summer of 1906, but played very little football after that, retiring during World War One.
Wolves record: 77 apps. 4 goals.

BAYNTON, John M.
One of the original founder members of the club in 1877, Jack Baynton served Wolves for 12 years (to 1889) before retiring through injury. A pupil-teacher at St Luke's School, he lined up initially for Blakenhall St Luke's, as a centre-half, appearing in his first-match on 15 March 1877. He then officially joined Wolves, acting as secretary and treasurer in the early days, and seven years later helped them win their first trophy, the Wrekin Cup (1884). He also starred in the club's first FA Cup-tie v Long Eaton Rangers (October 1883). Not the tallest of defenders at 5ft 9 ins, he then surprisingly changed positions to become a goalkeeper, taking over between the posts in the club's first League campaign of 1888-89 when he conceded 32 goals in 18 appearances. He also helped Wolves reach that season's FA Cup Final when they lost 3-0 to Preston North End (his last game for the club). A wholehearted outfield player and team captain, Baynton was also a very capable goalkeeper. On retiring from football he became a teacher at All Saints School, Hockley, Birmingham. He also took up refereeing (like his pal Jack Brodie) and officiated in several first-class matches. Born at Rushock Wood, Wolverhampton in March 1859, Baynton died at Alfreton, Derbyshire in May 1939, aged 80.

As a 'keeper, Baynton once scored a goal from almost 100 yards, fly-kicking the ball downfield and between the posts when playing in a game at Dudley Road.
Wolves record: 28 apps.

BEASANT, David John
Goalkeeper Dave Beasant was secured on loan by Wolves in January 1993, following an injury to Mike Stowell. One of the tallest 'keepers in the country at 6ft 3ins, Beasant was born in Willesden on 20 March 1959 and played his early football with Edgware Town before turning professional with Wimbledon in June 1979. He became a very popular figure at Plough Lane and in 1988 became the first keeper to captain an FA Cup winning side, leading the Dons to a 1-0 victory over Liverpool after he himself had also become the first man to save a penalty in such a Final. He made over 400 appearances for Wimbledon, whom he helped rise from the Third to the old First Division. A month after his Wembley glory, he left Plough Lane for Newcastle United for £800,000 but seven months later he was back in London, having left St James' Park for Chelsea in a £725,000 deal. Capped by England 'B' on seven occasions and twice at senior level, he helped Chelsea win the ZDSC at Wembley, and all told played in more than 150 games for the Stamford Bridge club. He left Chelsea for Southampton in a £300,000 deal in November 1993, following his short spell with Wolves and also a period on loan with Grimsby Town (October 1992). Beasant passed the personal milestone of 100 outings for Saints in 1996-97 and during the early part of the 1997-98 campaign he was loaned out to Nottingham Forest, the club he joined on a permanent basis in November 1997, helping them regain their Premiership status in 1998. But Forest returned to the Nationwide League after only one season in the top flight.
Wolves record: 5 apps.

BEATS, William Edwin
An opportunist goalscorer, totally reliable, determined and clever, Billy Beats arrived at Molineux in June 1895 for just £80 (plus a benefit match guaranteed to raise a further £50) after serving with Porthill Victoria, Port Vale Rovers (1899) and Burslem Port Vale (from 1891 – he scored a hat-trick in Vale's 4-1 Staffordshire Cup win over Wolves in March 1894). Beats spent the next eight seasons with Wolves, amassing a fine record at club level, while twice representing England, as well as being in the national team on the day of the Ibrox Park disaster (5 April 1902). Born at Wolstanton, Staffs, on 13 November 1871, Beats was a regular in the Wolves side until 1901 and played in the 1896 FA Cup Final against Sheffield Wednesday. He left Molineux in May 1903 for Bristol Rovers and two years later skippered Rovers to the Southern League championship. In August 1906 he returned to the Potteries, teaming up again with Port Vale. In May 1907, when Vale were faced with a financial crisis and after he had taken his appearance tally with the Valiants up to 130 (47 goals), he joined Reading. In the summer of 1911, he was appointed trainer at Bristol Rovers and switched back to Elm Park in the same capacity in 1914. On quitting football, in 1917, Beats became a publican, taking over the Truro Inn in Castle Street, Reading – a position he held until 1936. He died in Reading on 6 April 1939.
Wolves record: 199 apps. 73 goals.

BEATTIE, Andrew
Beattie was manager at Molineux for a year: September 1964 to September 1965. The former Scottish international took over from Stan Cullis, but after a disastrous season which saw Wolves relegated to the Second Division for the first time since 1932, he was replaced by Ronnie Allen just a few weeks into the 1965-66 campaign. Born at Kintore, Aberdeenshire on 11 August 1913, Beattie was a junior footballer with Inverurie Loco and then Kilmarnock prior to joining Preston North End for £135 in 1935. He spent 12 years at Deepdale, making over 130 senior appearances before the hostilities and many more during the war, when he also guested for Aldershot, Bradford City, Clapton Orient, Derby County, Leicester City, Manchester City, Northampton Town and Notts County. He played in two FA Cup Finals, picking up a losers' medal in 1937 and a winners' prize 12 months later, and gained seven full caps for Scotland, as well as starring in five wartime and Victory internationals. A superb defender, who was capable of outwitting the trickiest opponent, Beattie retired from 'match play' in March 1947 to become secretary-manager of Barrow. He then held a similar position with Stockport County (March 1949 to April 1952) before being appointed manager of Huddersfield Town, holding office at Leeds Road until November 1956. Whilst at Huddersfield he also took charge of the Scottish national team for four months: February-June 1954. After a short period out of football, Beattie was given the manager's job at Carlisle United (May 1958-March 1960) and during

his time in office at Brunton Park, he again looked after the Scottish national team: March 1959 to October 1960. In September 1960 he had become manager of Nottingham Forest, taking over from Billy Walker. He remained at the City Ground until July 1963 and prior to his appointment at Wolves, Beattie was caretaker-manager of Plymouth Argyle (October 1963 to March 1964). On leaving Wolves, Beattie remained in the game, joining Peter Doherty at Notts County as professional advisor (December 1965) later taking the position of General Manager at Meadow Lane. Two years later he became assistant manager to ex-Wolves player John Harris at Sheffield United (October 1967) and at various times after this he coached and scouted for a number of clubs including Brentford, Liverpool, Notts County, Walsall and Wolves. Beattie died at Rushcliffe on 20 September 1983, aged 70.

BEATTIE, John Murdoch

Beattie was a quality inside-forward, possessing a fierce right-foot shot, who played all his senior football with top-Division clubs. Born in Newhills, Scotland on 28 May 1912, and after playing for Hall Russells FC he began his professional career with Aberdeen in August 1931. In September 1933 he was transferred to Wolves for £1,500 and was first choice at Molineux until leaving for Blackburn Rovers in December 1934 for £5,000. In January 1937, a player-exchange deal plus £2,000 took him to Birmingham and 12 months later he was sold to Huddersfield Town for £2,500. And from February 1938 to May 1946, Beattie was registered with Grimsby Town, who had paid £2,500 for his services. He retired in 1950 after guesting for Walsall. Beattie died in Wolverhampton on 15 January 1992.
Wolves record: 46 apps. 13 goals.

BELENENSES (OS)

Wolves' playing record against the Portuguese side is:
UEFA Cup

Venue	P	W	D	L	F	A
Home	1	1	0	0	2	1
Away	1	1	0	0	2	0
Totals	2	2	0	0	4	1

The Portuguese club was Wolves' opponents in a first round UEFA cup-tie early in the 1973-74 season. On 26 September Wolves travelled to Portugal and took control of the tie with a well-merited victory in front of almost 9,000 fans. It was a harder challenge at Molineux a week later in front of a 16,000 plus crowd, but Wolves did enough to win 4-1 on aggregate and so progress through to the next round.

Former Wolves player Jimmy Melia was manager of Belenenses for over two years, from October 1983 to November 1985.

BELL, John

Centre-half Jackie Bell was recruited to the Molineux playing staff in the summer of 1894 from Bacup. Mainly a reserve, he was not retained for the following season and left Wolves for Grimsby Town in July 1895. Born in Dundee in June 1877, he played initially for Dundee Wanderers and then Renton before joining Bacup. After 77 League games for Grimsby he assisted Chesterfield Town (from June 1899 – making 54 League appearances), Millwall Athletic (August 1900 – over 50 outings) and Leicester Fosse (May 1903 to May 1904). An engine fitter by trade, there is no doubt that Bell played his best football with Grimsby where he had steady influence on the team and specialised in feeding the attack.
Wolves record: 6 apps. 2 goals.

BELL, Norman

An inside or centre-forward, Bell spent a little over ten years at Molineux, initially joining Wolves as an apprentice in July 1971 and turning professional in November 1973. Often referred to as 'Super Sub' he was born in Sunderland on 16 November 1955 and played local junior football prior to signing for Wolves. He unfortunately broke a leg during Wolves' FA Cup-tie with Crystal Palace in 1978-79. He left Molineux in November 1981 for Blackburn Rovers, but was then forced to give up League soccer in 1983 through injury, although he did make a comeback in non-League football in 1984-86. He is now in business in Blackburn.
Wolves record: 100 apps. 24 goals.

BELLAMY, Gary

Prior to joining Wolves for £17,000 in September 1987, full-back or central defender Gary Bellamy appeared in over 200 games for Chesterfield, helping the Spireites win the Fourth Division championship in 1985. Recruited by manager Graham Turner to bolster up the defence, Bellamy went on to give Wolves tremendous service over the next five years, being a key member of the side which gained promotion from the Fourth to the Second Division in successive seasons as well as winning the Sherpa Van Trophy at Wembley. He also skippered the side before a niggling injury began to interrupt his performances. After a loan spell with Cardiff City (March-May 1992) with whom he won a Welsh Cup winners medal, Bellamy signed for Leyton Orient for £30,000 in September 1992. He went on to play in more than 150 games for the London club before pulling out of League football in June 1996 when he joined Chelmsford City as player-coach and commercial manager. Born in Worksop on 4 July 1962, Bellamy first signed for Chesterfield in July 1978, turning professional two years later.
Wolves record: 165 apps. 9 goals.

BELLIS, George Alfred

George Bellis was described as being 'a big, powerful fellow' who scarcely knew his own strength. Few could get by him.' Born the son of a company sergeant major in the Royal Engineers at Kirkee in India on 8 June 1904, Bellis attended St John's School in Seaforth, Lancashire and started playing football with Waterloo FC in 1921. He then assisted LMS Railway United (in Formby) and also Seaforth Fellowship FC before signing amateur forms for Southport in August 1923. A year later – after serving his apprenticeship as an electrician – he became a professional and in May 1927 was transferred to Wrexham for £150. From there he joined Wolves for £600 in June 1929, replacing Tom Pritchard. After making a successful debut against West Bromwich Albion on the opening day of the 1929-30 Second Division campaign, Bellis went on to appear in roughly half of Wolves' games that season. But following the arrival at Molineux of Jack Nelson in November 1932, his first-team outings became limited and the following month he was sold to Burnley. In June 1935 he moved to Bournemouth, served with Wellington Town from June 1937 to May 1939 and during the war he guested for Tranmere Rovers. An electrician by trade, Bellis died in Seaforth on 6 January 1969, aged 64.
Wolves record: 43 apps.

BENEFITS/TESTIMONIAL MATCHES

Over the years several Wolves players have been granted testimonials and/or benefits by the club, including (since 1946-47): Mike Bailey, Peter Broadbent, Steve Bull, Ray Chatham, Robbie Dennison, Derek Dougan, Ted Farmer, Ron Flowers, Kenny Hibbitt, John McAlle, Jimmy Mullen, Geoff Palmer, Phil Parkes, Derek Parkin, John Richards

Ally Robertson shakes hands with Emlyn Hughes before his first testimonial, as an Albion player, in 1980.

(two), Alistair Robertson, Andy Thompson, Dave Wagstaffe, Dave Woodfield and Billy Wright.

Mullen and Wright's testimonial match was a joint affair in 1959.

Ally Robertson's testimonial was against his former club West Bromwich Albion, as was Mike Bailey's.

Albert Fletcher (in October 1891, Wolves 3 All Star XI 0) was the first Wolves player to receive a benefit. He was followed four years later by Billy Beats and in 1899 by Jack Tonks.

Jack Whitehouse and Billy Wooldridge had a joint benefit match (Wolves v Derby County) in 1905-06. Ted Watson was granted a benefit by Wolves in 1928.

BENNETT, Michael

Born in Bolton on 24 December 1962, full-back Mick Bennett was an apprentice at Burnden Park for almost two years before turning professional in January 1980. A compact player, he moved to Wolves in June 1983, but stayed less than a season at Molineux before transferring to Cambridge United in March 1984. From there he went to Bradford City (August 1986) and then had a good spell with Preston North End (September 1986-September 1992), helping them to runners-up spot in Division Four in 1986-87. Bennett was a non-contract player with Bradford City before joining Carlisle United in July 1990. He dropped out of League soccer to sign for Northwich Victoria two years later.
Wolves record: 8 apps.

BENNETT, Thomas McNeill

Born in Falkirk on 12 December 1969, Scotsman Tom Bennett signed for Wolves on a free transfer from Aston Villa in July 1988 having failed to make the breakthrough at Villa Park. A versatile defender, he spent five years at Molineux before leaving for Stockport County for £75,000 in June 1995 and two years later starred for the Edgeley Park club as they won promotion to Division One for the first time in the club's history. He broke his leg in a game at Birmingham in January 1998, but thankfully made a full recovery.
Wolves record: 133 apps. 2 goals.

BENTON, John

Burly wing-half, born in Wolverhampton in 1865, Jack Benton played for Wolves during their first season of League football (1888-89). Previously with St Phillip's FC, Stafford Royal and Willenhall White Star, he later assisted Blakenhall and Wightwick. He died in Wolverhampton c.1932.
Wolves record: 1 app.

BERRY, George Frederick

Central defender George Berry became a firm favourite with the fans wherever he played. Berry was born in the town of Rostrop, West Germany on 19 November 1957. His father was a Jamaican, his mother Welsh (she came from Mountain Ash, Glamorgan) and he had a Scottish grandfather. Berry, who was educated at Holy Trinity and St Thomas of Canterbury schools (both in Blackpool), joined Wolves as a youngster in 1973 after playing junior football for Bipsham FC (Blackpool) and in Handsworth as well as having trials with Ipswich Town. He turned professional in November 1975 (aged 18) and went on to give Wolves sterling service, helping them win the Football League Cup in 1980. He left Molineux for Stoke City in the summer of 1982 and went on to star in 260 competitive matches for the Potters, scoring 30 goals, a third of them from the penalty spot. He had a loan spell with Doncaster Rovers in 1984 and rounded off his senior career with brief spells at Peterborough United, Preston North End and Aldershot. In 1992 he teamed up with Stafford Rangers, later becoming their commercial manager. Four years later Berry left Stafford to take a full-time job with the PFA, working alongside Chief Executive Gordon Taylor and Brendan Batson. And in 1998 he took a position with PFA Enterprizes Ltd. (Manchester branch). Berry won five full caps for Wales – his first against West Germany. Berry was granted a testimonial while with Stoke and while he was at the Victoria Ground he also had his own local radio programme on BBC Radio Stoke.
Wolves record: 160 apps. 6 goals.

BEST, Robert

Bobby Best was born in the village of Mickley on 12 September 1891 and was an enterprising outside-right, who was signed from Sunderland in June 1922. He spent less than a season at Molineux before leaving for Durham City in May 1923, later assisting Hartlepools United (1924-27). Prior to joining Sunderland in August 1911, Best had been with Mickley Colliery FC. His record for the Wearsiders was 25 goals in 94 outings.
Wolves record: 23 apps.

BETTELEY, Richard Harold

Dick Betteley had five excellent years at Molineux and afterwards he spent a further six seasons with West Bromwich Albion, whom he helped win the Second Division championship in 1911. A wonderfully consistent performer Betteley was born in Bradley, Bilston on 14 July 1880. He played for Bilston Schools, Bradley Athletic, Priestfield Albion, Bilston St Leonard's and Bilston United before signing for Wolves in August 1901. A fee of £100 took him to The Hawthorns in May 1906 and after his service with the Baggies he rounded off his career with a second spell at Bilston United, retiring through injury in May 1914. Betteley later ran the Town Hall Stores in Bilston. He died in Wolverhampton on 20 August 1942.
Wolves record: 123 apps. 1 goal

BEVAN, Frederick Walter

Tricky inside-forward with good shot, Fred Bevan spent three seasons with Wolves, mainly as a reserve. Born in Walsall c.1880, he played initially for Walsall Dynamos and then Darlaston before moving to Molineux in August 1903. He left Wolves in May 1906 for Stourbridge and later assisted Bilston (from May 1907) and Bloxwich Strollers (1909). Bevan died in Wednesbury c.1940.
Wolves record: 38 apps. nine goals
Some reference books spell his name as Bevin.

BICKNELL, Roy

Centre-half Roy Bicknell graduated through the junior ranks at Molineux, but his career with Wolves shortlived and he left the club for Charlton Athletic in May 1947. Born in Doncaster on 19 February 1926, he came south in 1942 and turned professional with Wolves three years later, having guested for Notts County and Swindon Town in the war. From The Valley he went to Bristol City (June 1949-June 1952) and rounded off his League career with Colchester United, retiring in May 1955. He then ran a cafe and later managed Clacton Town (from April 1958-60). Bicknell became a bookmaker in 1963.
Wolves record: 1 app.

BIGGINS, Steven James

A good player in the lower Leagues, centre-forward Steve Biggins was born in Walsall on 26 June 1954, and served with Hednesford Town before breaking into League football with Shrewsbury Town in December 1977, following his £6,000 move from Cross Keys. In July 1982 he switched to Oxford United for £8,000 and then a £20,000 transfer took him to Third Division Derby County in October 1984. He was still at the Baseball Ground when he served with Wolves, on loan, during March/April 1985. He later assisted Port Vale, also on loan, in March 1986 and after a brief spell in Sweden with FC Trelleborg, he signed as a non-contract player with Exeter City (October 1986), later assisting for Telford United (gaining a runners-up medal in the 1988 FA Trophy Final) and Worcester City.
Wolves record: 4 apps.

BIRCH, Alan

Brother of Paul Birch (see below), Alan was a goalscoring midfielder. Born in West Bromwich on 12 August 1956 he had three trial games with West Bromwich Albion in 1971, before joining Walsall as an apprentice

in 1972, turning professional at Fellows Park in August 1973. From the Saddlers he went to Chesterfield for £40,000 in July 1979 and two years later Wolves secured his services for the healthy sum of £180,000. Unfortunately Birch never fitted in at Molineux and after barely seven months at the club he moved to Barnsley in February 1982, returning to Chesterfield (August 1983) and thereafter having spells with Rotherham United (March 1984), Scunthorpe United (June 1986) and Stockport County (December 1987 to April 1988). All told Birch scored more than 100 goals in well over 500 appearances in senior football. He helped Chesterfield beat Glasgow Rangers to win the Anglo-Scottish Cup in 1980-81.
Wolves record: 18 apps.

BIRCH, Brian

A brainy inside-forward with good ball control who gained England youth caps as a teenager before going on to score over 60 goals in more than 200 appearances in his 12 years at senior club level. Born in Salford near Manchester, on 18 November 1931, Birch represented Salford Boys and England and Great Britain Schools before joining Manchester United as a junior in 1946, turning professional in May 1949. He moved from Old Trafford to Molineux in March 1952, but spent only nine months with Wolves before transferring to Lincoln City in December of that year. Afterwards his career took him everywhere: to Boston United (1955), Barrow (June 1956), Exeter City (for £3,000 in September 1958), Oldham Athletic (January 1960), Rochdale (£750 in March 1961), coach in the Phillipines (June 1962), Mossley FC (1963), coach to Sydney FC in Australia (February 1964), Ellesmere Port as a player (August 1966 to January 1967) and finally as junior coach with Blackburn Rovers (from November 1967 to May 1968). He was very popular with the press.
Wolves record: 3 apps. 1 goal.

BIRCH, Paul

Born in Birmingham on 20 November 1962, Paul Birch, a right-sided midfield player, with flair and stamina, began his career as an apprentice with Aston Villa. He turned professional in July 1980 and went on to score 29 goals in 219 appearances in the next 11 years for the Birmingham club with whom he won a European Super Cup medal in 1982, also helping them clinch promotion from Division Two in 1988, as well as gaining an FA Youth Cup winners medal in 1980. In February 1991 he was transferred to Wolves for £400,000 and gave the Molineux club excellent service until 1996 when, after a brief loan spell with Preston North End (March 1996), he moved to Doncaster Rovers (July 1996), before joining Exeter City in March

Bert Williams comes under pressure against Birmingham City in September 1949.

1997. Birch was granted a testimonial match in August 1991 (Villa v Wolves). In July 1998 Birch made his debut for non-League side Halesowen Town.
Wolves record: 149+17 apps. 19 goals.

BIRD, Horace

Outside-right Horace Bird was a reserve team player with Wolves during the first two seasons after World War One (1919-21). Born in Smethwick c.1895, he played for Handsworth Victoria and Walsall Reserves before moving to and after leaving Molineux he also assisted Bloxwich Strollers.
Wolves record: 3 apps.

BIRMINGHAM CHARITY CUP (LORD MAYOR'S)

This competition started in 1881 and ran through until 1965 when it was renamed the Birmingham Senior Amateur Cup. Wolves appeared in eight Finals, the details being:

1889 Aston Villa 3	Wolves 0	(at Edgbaston)
1890 Aston Villa 2	Wolves 1	(at Perry Barr)
1891 Aston Villa 3	Wolves 0	(at Stoney Lane)
1892 Wolves 2	Small Heath 1	(at Aston Lower Grounds)
1894 Aston Villa 3	Wolves 1	(at Aston Lower Grounds)
1903 Wolves 3	WBA 2	(at Aston Lower Grounds)
1930 Aston Villa 5	Wolves 1	(at Villa Park)
1932 Aston Villa 2	Wolves 1	(at Villa Park)

In 1887 Aston Villa and Wolves reached the Final, but Villa withdrew and the cup was awarded to Wolves by default.

BIRMINGHAM CITY

Wolves' playing record against the Blues is:

Football League

Venue	P	W	D	L	F	A
Home	52	35	6	11	102	53
Away	52	17	16	19	73	74
Total	104	52	22	30	175	127

FA Cup

	P	W	D	L	F	A
Home	3	2	0	1	5	4
Away	1	0	1	0	1	1
Total	4	2	1	1	6	5

League Cup

	P	W	D	L	F	A
Home	1	1	0	0	3	2
Away	2	1	0	1	2	1
Total	3	2	0	1	5	3

Anglo-Italian Cup

	P	W	D	L	F	A
Away	1	0	1	0	2	2

Wartime

	P	W	D	L	F	A
Home	9	5	2	2	19	14
Away	8	2	1	5	7	11
Total	17	7	3	7	26	25

The first League meeting between the two clubs took place in October 1894 when Wolves won 2-1 at Molineux, Joe Butcher and Harry Wood the Wolves scorers. Three weeks later Blues gained sweet revenge with a terrific 4-3 victory at Muntz Street, In fact, at half-time Wolves led 3-0, but inspired by Frank Mobley, who scored twice, the home side stormed back to register a memorable win.

In season 1895-96 Wolves achieved their biggest League win over Blues, beating them 7-2 at Molineux, Billy Beats and Harry Wood both scoring twice for the Wanderers in front of 4,000 fans.

In May 1950 Wolves sent Blues back into the Second Division when they won 6-1 at Molineux with Jesse Pye and Jimmy Mullen each scoring twice.

In season 1957-58 Wolves completed the League 'double' over Blues, winning both First Division games by 5-1. Jimmy Murray scored a hat-trick in the Molineux encounter. Three seasons later Ted Farmer grabbed four goals when Wolves again crushed Blues 5-1.

Another 5-1 victory for Wolves arrived in March 1964, at Molineux, when winger Terry Wharton scored twice.

It was Birmingham City 3 Wolves 6 in the First Division clash at St Andrew's in October 1961, Bobby Mason scoring twice for the Wanderers in front of a 29,000 crowd. And the following season (March 1963) a seven-goal thriller on Blues' soil again went in Wolves' favour, this time by 4-3.

Wolves' whipped Blues 4-0 at St Andrew's in a live television game in September 1992 when Darren Roberts scored a hat-trick.

Blues' best League victory over Wolves is 4-1 – achieved three times: in February 1905, January 1914 and November 1920.

In August 1948, the biggest crowd for a Wolves v Birmingham League game at Molineux – 54,361 – witnessed the 2-2 draw.

Two Wanderers' defenders – George Showell and David Woodfield – scored for both teams in derby matches between 1958 and 1966.

When Wolves were beaten 1-0 in a Nationwide League game at St Andrew's in October 1997, the winning goal was scored by former Molineux midfielder Chris Marsden, who was making his debut for Blues, while Paul Simpson (on loan from Derby County) and Lee Naylor were playing their first games for Wolves.

Blues caused a major upset when, as a Second Division side, they knocked out League champions elect Wolves in the third round of the FA Cup in season 1953-54, winning 2-1 at Molineux in front of 36,784 crowd.

The last occasion the teams met in the FA Cup was in season 1995-96 when Wolves edged through to the fourth round with a 2-1 home win in front of 28,000 fans after a 1-1 draw at St Andrew's.

Blues beat Wolves on the away goal rule to win a first round League Cup-tie on aggregate in season 1988-89 (Wolves tri-umphed 3-2 at Molineux, but lost 1-0 at St Andrew's).

One of Birmingham's lowest home attendances this century – just 2,710 – witnessed the Anglo-Italian Cup-tie v Wolves in 1993-94 which ended all square at 2-2.

Dennis Westcott scored a hat-trick when Wolves defeated Blues 6-2 in a Midland Regional League game in December 1939.

On 14 April 1945 Wolves defeated Birmingham 1-0 at Molineux in a second round, second leg Regional League Cup-tie. Bill Morris struck the winning goal in the 63rd minute of extra-time. After 120 minutes of normal and extra-time, the referee told the players that he would call a halt to the proceedings when a goal was scored. Morris netted at approximately 5.45pm, the game having kick-off at 3pm.

Wolves defeated Blues 8-2 in a Birmingham Senior Cup-tie in 1896-97,

In October 1896 Wolves were beaten 2-0 by Blues in a friendly match at Crystal Palace – a game arranged to help boost the funds of the London club.

Players with both clubs include: Alan Ainscow, Kevin Ashley, Jack Beattie, Colin Brazier, Jackie Brown, Walter Bunch, Brian Caswell (also coach), Steve Claridge, Wayne Clarke, Will Devey, Keith Downing, Tony Evans, Joe Gallagher (later Blues Community officer), George Getgood, Ian Handysides, Roger Hansbury, Bob Hatton, Harry Haynes, Harry Hooper, Alex McIntosh, Chris Marsden, Dick Neal, Jack Needham, Mike O'Grady, John Paskin, Charlie Phillips, Brian Roberts, Phil Robinson, Ken Rowley, Vinny Samways, John Smith, Bobby A. Thomson, Bobby G. Thomson and Peter Withe.

Also associated: Major Frank Buckley (Blues player 1909-11, Wolves manager), Billy Ellis (Wolves junior reserve, then later had 35 games for Blues: 1927-29); Bill Booth (reserve with Blues and Wolves), Stan Cullis (player and manager of Wolves, manager of Birmingham City); Garry Pendrey (Birmingham player and manager, Wolves assistant manager); Bill Shorthouse (Wolves player, Blues coach); Jim Barron, Fred Davies and Derek Jefferson (Wolves players, Blues coaches); Jack Acquaroff (Blues and Wolves) and Sammy Brooks (Blues) wartime guests, Bob Iverson, Albert Kay and Jack Shelton (Blues wartime guests); Jock Mulraney (Blues player, Wolves wartime guest), Dave Barnett and Stuart Storer (Wolves apprentices), Bob Coy (Blues junior trialist); Tony Godden (Wolves trialist), George Waddell (Wolves reserve, Blues trialist), Steve Mardenborough (Blues Reserves); Dave Latchford (Wolves Reserves), goalkeeper Billy Rose; Ian Ross (Wolves reserve and caretaker-manager, Blues coach), Tom Trevellyan Jones, Jim Travers and George Waddell (Wolves Reserves), James Dailey,

Tom Jones and Barry Squires (Wolves amateurs) and Fred Davies (Wolves player, Blues coach). Mel Bird worked in the ticket office at Molineux for many years before 'transferring' to St Andrew's where he did a similar job.

BIRMINGHAM COMBINATION

Wolves won the championship of the Birmingham Combination in season 1934-35, fielding a mixture of reserve and junior players.

BIRMINGHAM AND DISTRICT LEAGUE

Wolves won the Birmingham and District League on four occasions – in 1892-93 (when they registered 15 wins from 18 games); in 1897-98 (when they accumulated 21 victories from their 30 matches); in 1898-99 (when they retained the trophy with 29 wins from 34 starts) and in 1900-01 (when again they recorded 29 victories).

The team finished runners-up in 1896-97, 1899-1900 and 1905-06 and they also occupied third place on four occasions: in 1893-94, 1895-96, 1908-09 and 1909-10

Their lowest placing in this League was 17th in 1907-08.

Wolves' best win in the Birmingham and District League is 14-0 v Shrewsbury Town in November 1895 when David Black scored four goals and Jack Miller and Tommy Green three apiece.

Wolves' heaviest defeat in this competition is 10-1, away to Willenhall in April 1920.

They also lost 9-0 at Hereford in March 1920.

Wolves went a record 30 games without defeat during 1900-02. In comparison they failed to win any of 15 League games during 1907-08.

Dan Nurse, with a total of 158, made most Birmingham and District League appearances for Wolves (1894-1901); goalkeeper Jim Stringer made 147 (1898-1905), Albert Brookes 133 (1910-15), Walter Tuft 132 (1895-1900) and Ted Juggins 122 (1902-07). Walter Swift made a record 84 consecutive League appearances between January 1895 and December 1899) while both Winston Crump (1893-95) and Jimmy Stringer (1900-02) each had runs of 56.

Tommy Green scored most goals – 61 – between 1894 and 1896; Joe Jones netted 53 (1898-1903), Frank Pope hit 48 (1900-06) and Dick Richards claimed 43 (1912-22).

Green also holds the record for scoring most goals in a Birmingham and District League game for Wolves – six against Smethwick Works on 19 January 1895 – and he shares the record with George Harper, Billy Wooldridge, Harry Parsonage, Ernie Francis and Jack Sambrook, for scoring in six consecutive League games

Wolves' full record in the Birmingham and District League:

P	W	D	L	F	A	Pts
806	442	124	240	1911	1228	1008

In 1921 they moved into the newly-formed Central League.

BIRMINGHAM SENIOR CUP

This competition has been in existence since 1875. Wolves first entered in season 1877-78 and up until 1905 fielded, in the main, their first team as did all the other major teams in the Midlands area.

Here are details of Wolves' exploits in the Final of this annual competition:

1889	Aston Villa 2	Wolves 0
1892	Wolves 5	WBA 2
1893	Wolves 3	Aston Villa 1
1894	Wolves 3	WBA 3

(each team held trophy for six months)

1897	Walsall 2	Wolves 1
1898	Walsall 3	Wolves 0
1900	Wolves 2	Burslem Port Vale 1

(game abandoned after 80 minutes – score allowed to stand)

1902	Wolves 1	Aston Villa 0
1904	Aston Villa 3	Wolves 1
1907	Birmingham 5	Wolves 3
1909	Aston Villa 2	Wolves 1
1913	Burslem Port Vale 1	Wolves 0
1924	Wolves 2	Aston Villa 1
1987	Burton Albion 2	Wolves 2
Replay	Wolves 2	Burton Albion 1
1999	Birmingham City 4	Wolves 1

In the replay of the latter Final v Burton, Wolves, fielding practically a reserve side, scored through Jon Purdie and Matt Forman and the attendance at Molineux was 1,125. This game was actually played at the start of the 1987-88 season.

Venues for Wolves' 14 Finals – 1889 County Ground, Edgbaston; 1892, 1894 and 1897 – Perry Barr; 1893 – Aston Lower grounds; 1898, 1900 and 1909 – Villa Park; 1902 and 1904 – The Hawthorns; 1907 – St Andrew's; 1913 – Victoria Ground, Stoke; 1924 – Molineux; 1987 Burton (first leg) and Molineux (second leg), 1999 – St Andrew's (800 crowd).

BISHOP, Alfred John

Born in the heart of the Black Country, in Stourbridge, on 8 April 1886, Alf Bishop began his Football League career as a centre-half with Wolves in December 1906 after signing from Halesowen. He switched to wing-half the following season, and went on to give the Molineux club supreme service until 1920, some of that time as skipper. Bishop won a FA Cup winners medal in 1908 when he lined up in the middle line with Billy Wooldridge and the Revd Kenneth Hunt. An ever-present in Wolves' ranks on four occasions, he guested for Merthyr Town in 1917 and returned to play in six Victory

League games for Wolves in 1919. On leaving Molineux in July 1920, Bishop signed for Wrexham, but spent only a short time with the Welsh club before retiring in 1923. He died in 1938, at the age of 52.
Wolves record: 357 apps. 6 goals.

BISHOP AUCKLAND

Wolves took on, and defeated, the northern amateur side 3-0 in County Durham in the first round of the FA Cup on 13 January 1906. An enthusiastic crowd of 7,122 attended the game.

Associated with both clubs: John Barnwell (Bishop's player, Wolves manager) and Mick Gooding (Bishop's amateur, Wolves player).

BISSET, George

George Bisset was a useful winger or inside-forward who joined Wolves from Old Trafford in November 1921 and left Molineux for Pontypridd in February 1924. In his time with the club he worked very well alongside Sammy Brooks and centre-forward George Edmunds. Born in Cowdenbeath, Scotland on 25 January 1897, he started off with Glencraig Thistle, played next for Third Lanark (1914-15), and during World War One served in the Army. In November 1919, he teamed up with Manchester United, making 42 appearances for the Reds, some in place of the great Billy Meredith. After his spell with Pontypridd (January 1924), Bisset spent two years with Southend United, retiring in May 1926.
Wolves record: 44 apps. 10 goals.

BLACK, David Gibson

When David Black joined Wolves in July 1893, he was already a Scottish international, having gained what was to be his only cap four years earlier against Ireland. Able to play at inside or outside-left, he was born in Hurlford, Ayrshire on 22 January 1870, Black played his early football for his home town club, Hurlford and in 1889 was transferred to Grimsby Town. Two years later he switched to Middlesbrough and moved south to Molineux in 1893. Ten months after scoring for Wolves in the 1896 FA Cup Final defeat by Sheffield Wednesday, Black left the club for Burnley. He then had a useful spell with Tottenham Hotspur in the Southern League before retiring in 1901. He died in Wolverhampton on 14 December 1951, in his 80s, David Black's great grandson, Malcolm, is now an avid Wolves supporter, living at Bishop's Castle, near Wolverhampton.
Wolves record: 83 apps. 17 goals.

BLACK, John

A Scotsman from Helensburgh (born on 10 November 1957) left-winger John Black played for Wolves' second and third teams for three seasons before breaking into the senior

side during the 1977-78 campaign. Having turned professional at Molineux in December 1975, he failed to make an impression and left the club for Bradford City in January 1980, later spending the 1983-84 season with Hereford United before dropping into non-League football where he stayed until 1988.
Wolves record: 6 apps.

BLACKBURN ROVERS

Wolves' playing record against Rovers is:

Football League

Venue	P	W	D	L	F	A
Home	38	23	7	8	102	58
Away	38	8	8	22	44	83
Total	76	31	15	30	146	141

FA Cup

Venue	P	W	D	L	F	A
Home	1	1	0	0	1	0
Away	6	1	2	3	9	11
Neutral	3	2	0	1	5	2
Total	10	4	2	4	15	13

As founder members of the Football League, Wolves first met Rovers in season 1888-89 and on 29 September four goals were shared at Dudley Road. The return fixture at Ewood Park, three weeks later, also ended in a 2-2 draw. During this same season Wolves met Blackburn in the semi-final of the FA Cup and after a 1-1 draw, Wolves progressed into the Final with a 3-1 replay win.

Wolves' best League victory over Rovers is 8-1 in a First Division match at Molineux in November 1935. Wolves also won 6-1 at home in November 1891 when Dick Topham scored a hat-trick. Rovers were defeated 5-0 at Molineux in January 1959 and there were two 5-1 victories for Wolves, both at home, in 1893-94 and 1947-48,

All five forwards scoring in the latter game. Wolves recorded two successive 5-3 home wins over Rovers – first in December 1932 – when Billy Hartill netted a hat-trick and then in March 1934.

That latter victory was sweet revenge for Wolves, who earlier in the season had been thrashed 7-1 by Rovers at Ewood Park when Thompson claimed a hat-trick.

In season 1962-63, the two League games between Wolves and Rovers produced another 12 goals. Wolves won 4-2 at Molineux in September (2 goals for Alan Hinton) and then Rovers, on 13 May, raced to a 5-1 victory at Ewood Park, Fred Pickering scoring a hat-trick.

There was fighting between rival supporters on the pitch at Molineux before Wolves' 4-0 home League win over Blackburn Rovers in September 1966 and when the teams met in the return fixture at Ewood Park in the January Wolves' Dave Wagstaffe was sent-off in the 0-0 draw.

In successive seasons (1989-90 and 1990-91) Wolves beat Blackburn 3-2 away but then lost by the same scoreline at home.

Blackburn's Mick McGrath puts through his own goal in the 1960 FA Cup Final against Wolves.

Wolves have so far met Rovers in three FA Cup semi-finals and in one FA Cup Final. The semi-final showdowns took place in 1888-89 when the Wanderers won 3-1 (after a 1-1 draw); in 1889-90 when they lost 1-0 and in 1892-93 when they clinched a Final place with a 2-1 victory. The FA Cup Final was in 1960, when, in front of 98,954 fans (receipts £49,816) goals by Norman Deeley (2) and Mick McGrath (own-goal) gave Wolves a 3-0 victory against 10-man Rovers, who sadly lost full-back Dave Whelan with a broken leg.

Blackburn Rovers visited Molineux just prior to the start of the 1998-99 season to play Wolves in Robbie Dennison's testimonial match.

Players with both clubs include: Alan Ainscow, Len Astill, Mark Atkins, Jack Beattie, Norman Bell, Paul Bradshaw, Gordon Cowans, Chris Crowe, Derek Dougan, Tim Flowers, Freddie Goodwin, Graham Hawkins, Ken Knighton, Robbie Slater, Dave Wagstaffe and Dennis Westcott.

Also associated: Bobby Downes and ex-Wolves player Robert Kelly were on the coaching staff at both Molineux and Ewood Park; Brian Birch played for Wolves (1952) and later became a junior coach with Rovers (1967-68). Alan Boswell was a reserve with Rovers; Tom Finn was secretary at Molineux and Ewood Park; Sammy Chung (Wolves manager and Rovers' chief scout); Ian Miller (Rovers player, Wolves coach), Tom Bond, Ernie Brooks, Laurie Calloway, Gerald Farrell and Billy McCall (Wolves Reserves) and Chris Pearce (Wolves junior, Rovers player).

BLACKETT, Joseph

Left-back Joe Blackett was recruited by Wolves for the 1896-97 season following the departure of George Fleming, Tommy Dunn and Harry Wood. He fitted in well alongside Jack Eccles. Born in Newcastle-upon-Tyne in June 1875, he played first for Newcastle United and after a spell with Gateshead, joined Loughborough Town in June 1896. From there he switched to Wolves (May 1896) and was an ever-present in his initial campaign at Molineux and missed only one game in 1898-99 and one the following season. To everyone's surprise he was then snatched away from Wolves by Derby County in April 1900. But while at the

Baseball Ground, Blackett suffered ill-health, and likewise when serving with Sunderland (April 1901) and Middlesbrough (1901 to May 1905). He later assisted Luton Town (to June 1906) and Leicester Fosse (to May 1909 – signed for £115). A three-year stint as player-manager of Rochdale followed (to May 1912) and he next served with Barrow (June 1912-July 1913) before rounding off his footballing life as Reading's trainer (August 1913-May 1915). Blackett represented the England XI in the Annual Players' Union international at Ibrox Park in March 1900 and was selected for the Football League against the Irish League in Belfast in October 1904. He helped Middlesbrough win promotion in 1902 and guided Rochdale to the championship of the Lancashire Combination. On leaving Reading he spent four years in the Army during World War One. He made over 300 appearances at club level. It is believed that Blackett died c.1940.
Wolves record: 103 apps. 12 goals.

BLACKHAM, Arthur Thomas

Born in Blakenhall, Wolverhampton in July 1859, Blackham attended and played for St

Luke's School, and after serving with Stafford Royal, joined Wolves in August 1883. He managed only a season with the club when he was forced into early retirement in May 1884 after breaking a leg playing wing-half in a Birmingham Cup-tie against Aston Cross the previous December. After this set-back he became Wolves' official linesman (1885) and also worked on the club's Committee, looking after travel arrangements. Later on he was appointed steward of the Blakenhall Conservative Club, holding office for over four years before taking over as licensee at The British Crown (on Dudley Road). He was steward of the Bilston-based Conservative Club after that and in the meantime also ran a successful general stores in Colway Road, Wolverhampton. A fine cricketer-footballer, Blackham died at Bushbury, Wolverhampton in June 1945, aged 85.

Wolves record: 15 apps. 7 goals.

BLACKPOOL

Wolves' playing record against Blackpool is:

Football League

Venue	P	W	D	L	F	A
Home	45	26	9	10	86	55
Away	45	16	7	22	60	80
Total	90	42	16	32	146	135

FA Cup

Venue	P	W	D	L	F	A
Home	1	0	1	0	0	0
Away	1	0	0	1	0	1
Total	2	0	1	1	0	1

League Cup

Venue	P	W	D	L	F	A
Home	1	0	1	0	1	1
Away	2	1	0	1	2	2
Total	3	1	1	1	3	3

Wartime

Venue	P	W	D	L	F	A
Home	1	1	0	0	1	0
Away	1	0	0	1	1	6
Void	1	0	0	1	1	2
Total	3	1	0	2	3	8

Wolves and Blackpool first met each other at League level in 1906-07 (Division Two). The game at Molineux finished all square at 1-1, while Wolves won 2-1 at Bloomfield Road.

Wolves have recorded two 4-0 home League wins over the Seasiders – in March 1913 when Billy Halligan scored twice in front of just 2,500 fans and in March 1921 when Henry Hargreaves netted on two occasions.

When Wolves won 3-2 at Blackpool in October 1926, they came back from 2-0 down and Tom Phillipson even missed a penalty.

Wolves also won 4-1 at Molineux in March 1927 (two goals for Tom Phillipson), in February 1954 (helped by a Roy Swinbourne hat-trick on their way to the First Division championship) and in December 1956 (when Dennis Wilshaw notched a treble).

Blackpool hammered Wolves 7-2 at

Bloomfield Road in January 1962, Ray Charnley scoring four of the Seasiders' goals.

On 17 September 1955, a record Bloomfield Road crowd of 38,098 saw Blackpool beat Wolves 2-1 in a First Division game.

The 2-2 League draw between the Seasiders and the Wanderers at Bloomfield Road in October 1976 was marred by a crowd disturbance caused a hold-up in play after a missile was thrown on to the pitch.

The two FA Cup meetings took place in season 1949 50 and it was Blackpool, who eventually entered the semi-finals after a replay.

Thanks to a Derek Dougan goal, Wolves beat Blackpool 1-0 at Bloomfield Road to win a fifth-round League Cup replay in November 1972 – sweet revenge for a 2-1 elimination from the same competition by the Seasiders in 1968-69.

When Blackpool defeated Wolves 6-1 in a wartime Football League Cup-tie in January 1942, Stan Matthews, Stan Mortensen and Ronnie Dix were among the scorers.

Players with both clubs include: Alan Ainscow, Vince Bartram, John Burridge, Danny Crainie, Mark Crook, Jack Curnow, Tony Evans, John Farley, George Farrow, Bob Hatton, Adam Haywood, Des Horne, Emlyn Hughes, Freddie Kemp, Eric Nixon, Gary Pierce, Billy Rafferty, Bill Slater, Paul Stewart, John Teasdale, Dave Wagstaffe.

Also associated: Major Frank Buckley (manager of both clubs), Lionel Hayward and Frank O'Donnell (Blackpool players, Wolves wartime guests), Jock Mulraney (Blackpool trialist, Wolves guest), Cecil Shaw and Ernie Stevenson (Blackpool guests), Martin James, Keith Pritchett and Henry Turley (Wolves Reserves), Graham Newton (Wolves junior, Blackpool reserve) and Bobby Downes (Wolves coach, Blackpool player-coach).

BLACKWELL, Steven G.

Born in Wolverhampton on 8 June 1967, Steve Blackwell was a member of the successful Wolverhampton Town Boys side before joining Wolves as a YTS, turning professional in November 1984. He failed to make the grade as a midfielder and was released by the club the following year. In 1998-99 Blackwell was playing for Wednesfield. A Wolves supporter as a lad, Blackwell was later arrested after being involved in a criminal offence.

Wolves record: 1 app.

BLADES, Paul Andrew

Defender Blades began his playing career as a junior with Derby County, turning professional at the Baseball Ground in December 1982. An England Youth international, he appeared in 200 games for the Rams and gained a Second Division championship

medal in 1987 before transferring to Norwich City for £700,000 three years later. From Carrow Road he joined Wolves, manager Graham Turner paying £325,000 for his services in August 1992. He did very well at Molineux, performing in both full-back berths as well as a central defender. Blades left Molineux for Rotherham United for £10,000 in July 1995, and the following year helped the Millers win the Auto Windscreen Shield at Wembley. In June 1997 he moved to non-League Hednesford Town, teaming up with his former Molineux colleague Robbie Dennison. Blades became player-manager of Gresley Rovers in 1999.

Wolves record: 127 apps. 3 goals.

BLAIR, Andrew

Scotsman Blair is one of the few players to score a hat-trick of penalties in a major competition doing so for Sheffield Wednesday against Luton Town in a Milk Cup-tie in November 1984. A stylish midfielder, Blair was born in Kirkcaldy on 18 December 1959 and attended Nicholas Chamberlain School at Bedworth. He played for Bedworth Juniors and Warwickshire County Boys before joining Coventry City as an apprentice in July 1975, turning professional in October 1977. A shade under four years later he was transferred to Aston Villa for £300,000 and it was from there that he came to Wolves for a three-month loan spell (October-December 1983). In August 1984 he left Villa Park for Sheffield Wednesday for £60,000, but in March 1986 he returned to the Villa for a fee of £100,000. Loan spells with Barnsley (March/April 1988) and Northampton Town (March/April 1989) preceded his move to Kidderminster Harriers in August 1989 and afterwards Blair assisted Nuneaton Town prior to taking a coaching job with Racing Club of Warwick in 1991-92. Capped five times by Scotland at Under-21 level, Blair made his Villa debut at Wembley in the 1981 Charity Shield draw with Spurs; he was on the bench when Villa won the European Cup in 1982 and helped them lift the European Super Cup in season 1982-83. He made over 200 League appearances all told.

Wolves record: 10 apps.

BLAKE, Mark Anthony

Midfielder Mark Blake was born in Nottingham on 16 December 1970 and signed professional forms for Aston Villa in July 1989 after two years as an apprentice. Following a loan spell with Darlington (October 1990 when he played alongside ex-Wolves star Steve Mardenborough) Wolves also acquired him on loan in January 1991, and in May 1993 he was transferred by Villa to Portsmouth for £400,000. The following March, Blake became Leicester City's record buy when he moved from Fratton Park to

Filbert Street for £360,000. In May 1996, he was released by Leicester and three months later signed for Walsall. Capped by England at Schoolboy and Youth team levels, he went on to play in nine Under-21 internationals for his country.

Wolves record: 2 apps.

BLAKENALL ST LUKE'S SCHOOL

Most of the founder members of Wolverhampton Wanderers were or had been associated with St Luke's School, which was officially opened on Monday 11 November 1861. The in-house pupils used to play their sport on a strip of land off Goldthorn Hill, near to the home of Sir Alfred Hickman who later became president of the Wolves club and did so much to further the development of football in the area. Mr W Harry Barcroft, who was appointed headmaster of the said school in the summer of 1873, aged 21, was perhaps mainly responsible for starting a football team at the School when he presented two of his pupils, Jack Baynton and Jack Brodie, with a case-ball. They, in turn, persuaded Thomas Blackham, James Hill and George Worrell to join them for kick-abouts. Blakenhall St Luke's School side was boosted by further players, and friendly matches were arranged on a regular basis. In November 1876, the St Luke's players and former pupils called for a general meeting at the School, where it was proposed that the new name for their team should be St Luke's FC. In 1879 St Luke's merged with the Wanderers Cricket Club to form Wolverhampton Wanderers FC.

BLUNT, William

Hard-shooting inside-forward Billy Blunt was signed by Wolves from Stafford Rangers in August 1908 as cover for Jack Shelton, George Hedley and Walter Radford. He played mainly in the Reserves during his first season at Molineux, but then burst into life the following campaign when he top-scored with 27 goals, including four-timers against Leicester Fosse (League) and Reading (FA Cup). He was then transferred to Bristol Rovers in the summer of 1912, following the emergence of the two Needhams. Blunt, who was born in Bilston in 1886 and educated in Stafford, later assisted Bath City and Taunton Town. He retired in 1916 and died in 1962, aged 76.

Wolves record: 61 apps. 42 goals

Billy Blunt's younger brother, Sidney, (born in April 1902) was also associated with Wolves, as well as playing for Worcester City, Bilston United, Lichfield City, Port Vale, Shrewsbury Town and Hednesford Town.

BOLTON WANDERERS

Wolves' playing record against the Wanderers is:

Keith Curle in action at the Reebok Stadium against Bolton's Scott Sellers in 1998-99.

Football League

Venue	P	W	D	L	F	A
Home	53	33	10	10	129	55
Away	53	14	10	29	68	104
Totals	106	47	20	39	197	159

Play-Offs

Home	1	1	0	0	2	1
Away	1	0	0	1	0	2
Totals	2	1	0	1	2	3

FA Cup

Home	5	1	1	3	3	7
Away	4	2	1	1	5	4
Totals	9	3	2	4	8	11

FA Charity Shield

Away	1	0	0	1	1	4

Wartime

Home	1	0	1	0	2	2
Away	1	0	0	1	1	2
Totals	2	0	1	1	3	4

As founder members of the Football League, Wolves and Bolton first met in this competition in season 1888-89. Wolves won their home game 3-2, while Bolton took theirs at 2-1.

In March 1890, Wolves beat Bolton 5-1 at Molineux, thanks mainly to a hat-trick from David Wykes.

Another big Wolves win followed in April 1896 when Bolton were beaten 5-0 at Molineux and this scoreline was repeated in December 1946 when hot-shot Dennis Westcott rattled in four goals.

Wolves then repeated this scoreline at Burnden Park in August 1948 when wingers Jimmy Mullen and Johnny Hancocks both scored twice in front of a near 34,000 crowd.

Wolves' best win over the Trotters at League level is 7-1 – achieved at home in September 1950. Roy Swinbourne (3) and Johnny Hancocks (2) led the goal chase that day in front of a 46,764 crowd.

In August 1957, in their first home League game of the season, Wolves whipped Bolton 6-1 with Norman Deeley and Jimmy Murray both scoring twice.

Bolton's best win over Wolves is 6-0 – achieved at Burnden Park in December 1890 (John McNee netted a hat-trick) and the Trotters followed that up with a convincing 6-1 victory on the same ground in December 1894, when this time Charlie Henderson scored three goals.

A crowd of 37,400 saw Wolves crushed 6-1 at Bolton in February 1955 (Ray Parry claimed a treble in this game) and another big win for came at Burnden Park in February 1995 when they whipped Wolves 5-1.

When Wolves won 1-0 at Burnden Park on the last day of the 1976-77 Second Division League season it meant that Nottingham Forest were promoted instead of Bolton Wanderers.

On their way to FA Cup glory in 1893, Wolves beat Bolton in the third round, winning 2-1 at Molineux after a 1-1 draw.

In 1957-58 Bolton went all the way to the FA Cup Final where they beat Manchester United, and en route they knocked out Wolves 2-1 in the fourth round in front of 55,621 spectators at Burnden Park.

The first FA Cup-tie to take place at the Reebok Stadium was between Bolton and Wolves on 2 January 1999. It ended in a 2-1 win for the visitors, Robbie Keane scoring both goals.

Bolton came back from a goal behind to prevent Wolves from making the 1994-95 First Division Wembley Play-off Final. Two goals from John McGinlay in the second leg at Burnden Park in front of 20,041 fans gave the Trotters a 2-0 home win (3-2 on aggregate) and left Graham Taylor's men – and supporters – totally distraught. In the first leg at Molineux which attracted an audience of 26,153, Wolves completely dictated the play, especially in the second-half and the corner count was 19-1 in their favour.

Bolton beat Wolves in the annual FA Charity Shield game at Burnden Park in October 1958 in front of 36,029 fans. The South African Cliff Durandt scored for Wolves.

In November 1986, Wolves were defeated 3-0 by non-League Chorley at Bolton's Burnden Park ground in a first round, second replay of the FA Cup. The first game had also been played at Bolton and ended all square at 1-1.

Bolton beat Wolves 4-3 on aggregate in the semi-final of the League Cup (North) in May 1945.

Players for both clubs include: Mick Bennett, Alan Boswell, Simon Coleman, Bill Crew, Hugh Curran, George Eccles, Tony Evans, Jack Griffiths, Roger Hansbury, Bob Hatton, Charlie Henderson, Billy Hughes, Joe Keetley, Mixu Paatelainen, Jack Stanley, David Stokes, Terry Wharton and Billy Wrigglesworth.

Also associated: Ian Greaves (Bolton player and manager, also Wolves manager); Fred Scotchbrook and Ted Vizard (Bolton players, Wolves managers); David Felgate and Albert Picken (Wolves Reserves), Jermaine Wright (Bolton trial before Wolves); John Griffiths (Wolves wartime guest); Horace Wright (Bolton wartime guest), Stan Cullis (Bolton trialist), Ted Ivill (Bolton amateur) and Geoff Lomax (Wolves player, football in the community officer at Bolton in the 1990s).

BONSON, Joseph

One-time Schoolboy sprint champion in Yorkshire, Bonson was a hefty six-footer who played as an inside or centre-forward. He progressed through the junior ranks at Molineux (with Wath Wanderers) and signed professional forms in July 1953. In season 1953-54 he netted 48 goals for Wolves 'A' team in the Birmingham League, claimed 14 in the FA Youth Cup and four in the Central League. His first-team outings, however, were limited owing to the presence of some fine forwards, and in November 1957 Bonson was sold to Cardiff City for £5,000. In June 1960 he went to Scunthorpe United (in an exchange deal involving Peter Donnelly) and thereafter served with Doncaster Rovers (February 1962), Newport County (June 1962), Brentford (June 1964) and Lincoln City (January-May 1967). In a fine career he hit 132 goals in 313 League games. Bonson, who was born in Barnsley on 19 June 1936, sadly died in 1991 aged 55.
Wolves record: 12 apps. 5 goals.

BOON, Reginald

Reg Boon was an orthodox centre-forward who signed for Wolves in May 1905. From Stafford Rangers. A local man, born c.1880, he served with a number of Midland-based non-League teams including Tettenhall and Featherstone Rangers after leaving Molineux.
Wolves record: 3 apps. 1 goal

BOOTH, Charles

Charlie Booth was born in Gainsborough in 1869 and joined Wolves at the age of 20 from his home town club, Gainsborough Trinity in August 1889. He spent three seasons at Molineux, occupying in the main the outside-left position. In May 1892 he left Wolves for Royal Arsenal and later assisted Loughborough Town (1894-95). Booth died in Wolverhampton on 17 September 1898 after a short illness.
Wolves record: 73 apps. 10 goals.

BOOTH, Colin

Colin Booth was a fine marksman who netted over 150 goals in almost 350 senior appearances at club level. Born at Middleton, near Manchester, on 30 December 1934, he attended and played for Newton Heath Secondary School and starred for Manchester Boys v Swansea in the English Schools Final of 1950. An England Schoolboy international trialist, he also skippered the Lancashire Boys County FA Representative side before joining Wolves as a junior in June 1950, turning professional in January 1952. Booth battled hard to earn a place in Wolves' first team and when he did play he always gave a good account of himself. He helped the Wanderers win the League title in successive seasons: 1957-59, and also gained an England Under-23 cap. He left Molineux for Nottingham Forest in October 1959 for £20,000; in August 1962 he transferred to Doncaster Rovers and signed for Oxford United for a then record fee of £7,500 in July 1964 before retiring through injury in May 1967.
Wolves record: 82 apps. 27 goals.

BOSWELL, Alan Henry

Boswell was an eccentric goalkeeper, yet still had an excellent career between the posts. Born in Wednesbury on 8 August 1943, he was educated in Walsall and represented south east Staffs Schools as a teenager before signing for Walsall as a junior in 1958, turning professional at Fellows Park in August 1960. He made his League debut for the Saddlers in November 1961 and played over 60 games for the club before moving to Shrewsbury Town in August 1963. Whilst at Gay Meadow, he amassed 222 League appearances, up to September 1968, when he was recruited to Molineux by Wolves boss Ronnie Allen, who signed him as cover for

Phil Parkes. Unfortunately, after only a handful of first-team outings and reluctant to play in the Reserves, he left Molineux to join Bolton Wanderers in October 1969. In July 1972 he returned to the Midlands to sign for Port Vale, playing in almost 100 games for the Valiants up to May 1974. He then had a brief spell with Blackburn Rovers before teaming up with Oswestry Town (1975-80). After that he chose to play in charity matches up to 1985. In his senior career Boswell made almost 500 appearances, 435 at League level. As a Vale player, he was sent-off for fighting against Swansea City in April 1973.
Wolves record: 10 apps.

BOSWELL, William

Billy Boswell began his career as a wing-half, but developed into a direct inside-forward, who had a long time in the game. Born in Cradley Heath on 5 August 1902, he played for Tansey Green Rovers, Coombe Wood Colliery and Walsall (from December 1924) before joining Wolves in May 1925. He spent a little over two seasons at Molineux (mostly in the Reserves) before transferring to Gillingham in November 1927. From there he moved to Worcester City (July 1928) and afterwards assisted Burton Town (December 1930), Oldham Athletic (signed for £275 in January 1932), Burton Town again (April 1932) and finally Kidderminster Harriers (June 1934-May 1936). He won two Birmingham League championship medals with Worcester (1928-29 and 1929-30) when he scored 90 goals (44 and 46 respectively). Boswell died in Kidderminster on 14 June 1977.
Wolves record: 9 apps. 5 goals.

BOTTO, Anthony Lewis

Goalkeeper Lew Botto was born in Jarrow on 12 July 1898, and after 'learning the game' with Hebburn Colliery, Durham City (August 1923-June 1926), Stockton and then Shildon, he moved to Molineux in May 1927 where he contested the No.1 position with Noel George, Jack Hampton and Alf Canavon. Botto spent less than two years with Wolves before transferring to Norwich City in February 1929 – and when making his debut for the Canaries, his name on the team-sheet was down as G. O. Alie – and quite regularly afterwards he was referred to as A. L. Blotto. In September 1929, he moved from Norwich to Nelson and two months later was back in the North East with Jarrow FC. He retired in May 1932 and died in Jarrow on 4 June 1953.
Wolves record: 16 apps.

BOTTRILL, Walter Gibson

Yorkshireman Walter Bottrill was an inside-forward – a clever schemer, over elaborate at times – who served with seven different

League clubs over a period of 15 years: 1922 to 1936 inclusive. Born in Elston, Yorkshire on 8 January 1903, he started his career with South Bank FC, then assisted Middlesbrough (1922-24), Nelson (1924-28), Rotherham United (1928-29), York City (1929-30), Wolves (from 20 July 1930 to 16 June 1933), Huddersfield Town (for £2,000 – 1934-35) and finally Chesterfield. He retired through injury in 1936 after scoring well 105 goals in 314 League appearances at club level. He later became a publican in Yorkshire where he died *c*.1975.

Wolves record: 109 apps. 44 goals.

BOULD, George

Inside-forward George Bould was a Wolves player for just one season: 1907-08. Born in Tettenhall in 1885, he played for Goldthorn Alexandra, St Saviour's FC and Penkridge before moving to Molineux. On leaving Wolves Bould assisted Darlaston and then Bilston Town, retiring during World War One. He died in Wolverhampton *c*.1951.

Wolves record: 6 apps. 1 goal

BOURNEMOUTH (AFC)

Wolves' playing record against the Cherries is:

Football League

Venue	P	W	D	L	F	A
Home	2	1	0	1	3	4
Away	2	0	1	1	3	4
Totals	4	1	1	2	6	8

FA Cup

Home	1	0	0	1	0	1
Away	1	1	0	0	2	1
Totals	2	1	0	1	2	2

Freight Rover Trophy

Home	1	1	0	0	4	3

Wolves and Bournemouth first met in the Football League in season 1985-86 – and it was the Cherries who came out best, winning both games by a 3-0 scoreline.

Wolves' only League win over the Cherries was by 3-1 at Molineux in December 1990 when 15,400 fans were present.

Wolves defeated Bournemouth 2-1 at Dean Court in a third-round FA Cup-tie in January 1948. Almost 24,000 fans saw Jimmy Mullen score twice that afternoon.

A goal by former West Bromwich Albion left-winger Reg Cutler gave Third Division (South) underdogs Bournemouth a tremendous 1-0 FA Cup win at Molineux in a fourth round tie in January 1957. During the course of the game, which was witnessed by over 42,000 fans, Cutler also ran into an upright at the South Bank End of the ground, causing it to snap at the base.

A crowd of just 1,923 saw Wolves beat Bournemouth 4-3 at Molineux in a Freight Rover Trophy game in December 1986 when both Steve Bull and Paul Dougherty netted twice.

Running repairs to a goalpost during Wolves FA Cup tie against Bournemouth in 1957.

Players with both clubs (at first team level): Vince Bartram, George Bellis, John Bradford, Steve Claridge, Bill Colley, Fred Davies, George Farrow, Billy Gold, John Kirkham (also wartime guest), John McDonald, Fred Marsden, Neil Masters, George Marshall, Fred Pincott, Billy Rafferty and Ernie Whittam.

Also associated: Cameron Buchanan (Wolves wartime player) and Gareth Williams, Fred Davies; Bill McGarry (manager of both clubs) and Wolves Reserves Graham Newton, Tom Paton, Micky Reid, John Rowley, John Rutter and Arnold Stephens plus Bob Iverson (Bournemouth wartime guest).

Over a ten-year period between 1930 and 1939 inclusive an astonishing total of 38 former or future Wolves players (at various levels) were registered with Bournemouth. They were: Len Adkins, Walter Akers, George Bellis, Kenny Bird, John Bradford, Ted Buckley, Wilf Bucknall, Meynell Burgin, Roy Burns, Bill Colley, Billy Elliott, George Farrow, Jack Flaherty, Billy Gold, Joe Harvey, Arthur Keeley, Reg Kirkham, Billy Langley, George Lax, James Lovery, John McDonald, Fred Marsden, Ronnie Morgan (also a Wolves wartime guest), Tom Gracie Paton, Fred Pincott, Robert Redfern, Jack Rowley (loan), Billy Sellars, Len Smart, George Smith, Billy Smith, Ernie Tagg, Eden Taylor, John Turner, Richard Twiss, Ernie Whittam, Fred Wilson and Laurie Woodward.

BOWDLER, John Charles Henry

Born in Shrewsbury on 24 April 1869, Jack Bowdler was an inside or outside-left who won five caps for Wales between 1890 and 1894. After skippering the Shrewsbury School team, he helped found Shrewsbury Town Football Club (in 1886) and spent four excellent years at The Old Racecourse Ground, Copthorne, being regarded as the Shrews best player in 1889-90. So much so that in August 1890 – after he had won three Welsh Cup winners medals in successive seasons from 1887 – Bowdler became the first Shrewsbury Town player to join a Football League club when he moved to Molineux for a fee of £50. He stayed two years with Wolves and after a season with Blackburn Rovers (1892-93) he returned to Shrewsbury where he stayed until May 1897. In 1895, Bowdler qualified as a solicitor and later served Shrewsbury Town as secretary and then chairman. In 1901 he came to the Shrewsbury's financial rescue by putting in money from his personal savings to keep the club afloat. Bowdler was a member of the Shropshire FA and served on the town's council from 1901. During World War One he was a corporal in the Shropshire Regiment and for some years also acted as an agent for the local MP. He died in Shrewsbury on 18 July 1927.

Wolves record: 25 apps. 3 goals.

BOWEN, George

A hard-shooting inside or centre-forward, Bowen moved to Molineux from the Staffordshire League side Bridgetown Amateurs in July 1899, as cover for Billy Beats. Born in Walsall *c*.1875, he was a first-team regular during the 1900-01 campaign, but then left the club to sign for Liverpool (with George Fleming) in May 1901. After struggling to get into the Liverpool side, making only two appearances, he returned to Molineux for a second spell in November 1901 and left for

Burslem Port Vale in June 1904. Bowen retired from League soccer in April 1906 and went to work in a factory in Bilston, but continued to play local football for various non-League clubs. Bowen died c.1950.
Wolves record: 56 apps. 16 goals.

BOWEN, Thomas George

Tommy Bowen was a forceful inside-right, forever involved in the action, who was recruited by Wolves from Walsall in March 1924 (with Ben Timmins) in a combined deal worth just £130. Standing only 5ft 5ins. tall he spent five seasons at Molineux, up to June 1928, when he was transferred to Coventry City. He quit League football when he left Highfield Road and moved to Kidderminster Harriers in August 1930. Bowen was born in West Bromwich on 16 January 1900 and played for Bush Rangers before having a brief spell as an amateur with Birmingham (1920), signing for Walsall in July 1921. As a Coventry player he gained representative honours when appearing for the Birmingham and District side against the FA XI in September 1925. He scored 17 goals in 81 games for Walsall. He died c.1972.
Wolves' career: 94 apps. 24 goals.
NB. Bowen's son, Tom junior, played for Walsall and Newport County.

BOXLEY, Frank

Goalkeeper Frank Boxley was a Black Country man, born in Cradley Heath in August 1887. He joined Wolves from Cradley St Luke's in April 1909, immediately after winning a Junior international cap against Scotland. Brought to Molineux initially as cover for Tommy Lunn, he was a first-team regular from September 1910 and February 1912 and was perhaps unlucky to lose his place in the side to Teddy Peers. Strong and physical, he left Molineux in April 1912, when he transferred to Shrewsbury Town, later having a brief spell with Wellington Town. During World War One, he badly injured his back, forcing him into an early retirement at the age of 30.
Wolves record: 74 apps.

BRADBURY, Shaun D.

Shaun Bradbury made his senior debut for Wolves in October 1991, wearing the No. 9 shirt against Shrewsbury Town in a League Cup-tie at Gay Meadow. His Football League baptism followed more than six months later when he scored two cracking goals in a 3-1 win over Millwall. Unfortunately he failed to maintain this form and in May 1994 he joined Hereford United, later assisting Shifnal Town. Bradbury, who was born in Birmingham on 11 February 1974, joined Wolves as an apprentice in June 1990 and turned professional in June 1992.
Wolves record: 3 apps. 2 goals.

BRADFORD CITY

Wolves' playing record against the Bantams is:
Football League

Venue	P	W	D	L	F	A
Home	13	7	4	2	30	12
Away	13	3	4	6	19	29
Totals	26	10	8	8	49	41

FA Cup

Venue	P	W	D	L	F	A
Home	2	2	0	0	5	2
Away	4	0	2	2	2	8
Totals	6	2	2	2	7	10

Wolves and City first met in the Football League in season 1906-07. The game at Molineux ended in a 1-1 draw while Wolves were victorious in Yorkshire by 3-2.

Wolves beat City 4-1 in February 1923, 7-2 on Christmas Day 1926 and 6-0 in January 1930 – all at Molineux. Francis Burrill scored a hat-trick in that win in 1923; Tom Phillipson grabbed five goals to celebrate Christmas in 1926 and both Jimmy Deacon and Billy Hartill scored two goals apiece in that triumph in 1930.

Bradford won 6-2 at Valley Parade in February 1908 to register their best ever League victory over the Wanderers.

Two years earlier Bradford City had whipped Wolves 5-0 in a second-round FA Cup-tie at Valley Parade (February 1906) before a 17,000 crowd.

Wolves beat City 1-0 in a first-round replay on the way to winning the FA Cup in 1908, and then, in 1931, after a 0-0 draw in Yorkshire, they progressed into the fifth round of the competition with a 4-2 replay win at Molineux when Walter Bottrill netted twice.

On 18 February 1998, Steve Bull scored his 300th competitive goal for Wolves against Bradford City in a midweek League game at Molineux.

A year later – in May 1999 – City won 3-2 at Molineux to clinch their place in the Premiership. Former 'Wolf' Lee Mills scored one of City's goals in front of Molineux's best crowd of the season – 27,589.

Players with both clubs include: Michael Bennett, John Black, Billy Bryant, Arthur Buttery, Gordon Cowans, Don Goodman, Irvine Harwood, Micky Holmes, Martin Johnson, Stuart McMillan, Lee Mills, Eric Nixon, John Oldfield, John Preece, John Price, Dean Richards, Tim Steele, Reg Weaver and Steve Wright.

Also associated: Major Frank Buckley (City player, manager of Wolves), Tom Barkas, Joe Black, John Crudgington, John Hartson, Joe Harvey, Martin Jones, James Lovery, Phil Nicholls, George Smith and George Waddell (all Wolves Reserves), Andy Beattie (City wartime guest, Wolves manager), Stan Burton (City wartime guest), Jim Mulvaney and Laurie Scott (City players, Wolves wartime guests), Malcolm White (Wolves junior), Edward Wilby (Wolves amateur), and Albert Flatley (Wolves trialist, City guest).

BRADFORD, John

Jack Bradford was a left-half who was always involved in the action. He was born in Pilsley, Derbyshire on 9 April 1895 and played for Hucknall Byron FC and Grimsby Town (from May 1920) before joining Wolves in March 1924. He was an ever-present in the Wanderers side in his first season, lining up across the middle with Mitton and Caddick. He left Molineux for Bournemouth in October 1927 and later assisted Letchworth Town (as player-coach from May 1931). Bradford, whose cousin John William, played for Birmingham and Walsall, died at Hitchin, Herts in August 1969.
Wolves record: 80 apps.

BRADFORD (PARK AVENUE)

Wolves' playing record against Park Avenue is:
Football League

Venue	P	W	D	L	F	A
Home	12	5	6	1	24	10
Away	12	3	3	6	11	20
Totals	24	8	9	7	35	30

FA Cup

Venue	P	W	D	L	F	A
Home	1	1	0	0	3	1
Away	1	0	0	1	0	3
Totals	2	1	0	1	3	4

Wolves and Park Avenue first met at League level in season 1908-09 (Division Two). The teams drew 1-1 at Molineux, but Park Avenue were comfortable 4-1 victors in Yorkshire.

Wolves also lost 5-1 at Park Avenue in April 1913 and they went down again by a 4-1 scoreline on the same ground in November 1928.

Wolves' best win of the eight recorded over Bradford in the League is 6-0 at Molineux on 28 March 1932 – on their way to winning the Second Division championship. Walter Bottrill and Jimmy Deacon both scored twice that day.

Twenty four hours later, Wolves, fielding the same team, met Bradford for the last time in the Football League – and they went down 2-1 in the return fixture at Park Avenue.

Dennis Westcott scored twice when Wolves beat Park Avenue 3-1 at Molineux in a third-round FA Cup-tie in January 1939. This was the start of a superb run which took the Wanderers all the way through to the Final.

Players with both clubs include: Tom Baddeley, Joe Baillie, Joe Davies, Vic Fox, Irvine Harwood (amateur and professional), George Henson, Kenny Hibbitt, Martin Johnson, Norman Lewis, Harry Scott, John Taylor, Paul Walker (amateur at Park Avenue).

Also associated with both clubs: Jack Rowley (Wolves reserve and guest, Bradford manager), George Jobey (Park Avenue player in 1914, manager of Wolves), Glen Andrews, Stuart Darfield, Joe Harvey, and John E. Taylor (all Wolves Reserves) and Albert Flateley (Wolves trialist, Bradford guest).

BRADLEY, Claude

Claude Bradley was a lithe wing-half, who spent the 1891-92 season at Molineux. Born in Walsall in 1868, he played for Birchills FC before signing for Wolves and afterwards assisted Dudley Town. He died in Birmingham c.1938.
Wolves record: 6 apps.

BRADLEY, Patrick J.

Pat Bradley was a reserve outside-left, who spent three seasons at Molineux – from July 1924 to May 1927. Born locally in 1901, he left the Wolves for Gillingham and later returned to the Midlands to play for Walsall Wood, later assisting Brownhills Albion.
Wolves record: 5 apps.

BRADSHAW, Paul William

Goalkeeper Paul Bradshaw was Wolves' record signing when he joined the club from Blackburn Rovers for £150,000 in September 1977. Commanding his area well, he was a fine shot-stopper, handled crosses with confidence and remained at Molineux until August 1984, when he signed for Vancouver Whitecaps, managed by Johnny Giles. Born in Altrincham on 28 April 1956, Bradshaw represented Altrincham and Cheshire Boys and had trials with Manchester United in 1971 before becoming an apprentice with Blackburn in January 1972, turning professional at Ewood Park in July 1973. He played for England Youth and made over 80 appearances for Rovers prior to his move to Wolves. He quickly gained a place in the first team at Molineux and remained there until May 1982, when replaced by John Burridge. After his spell in the NASL Bradshaw joined West Bromwich Albion (February 1985) being one of Giles' first recruits after he'd taken over as manager at The Hawthorns for a second time. He stayed at Albion until June 1986 and after a coaching spell with Walsall, signed for Bristol Rovers on a non-contract basis, later assisting Newport County (1987-88) before undertaking a second term at The Hawthorns. In May 1990 Bradshaw left Albion for Peterborough United, teaming up with former colleague George Berry. On retiring from the game in 1992 he returned to live and work in Wolverhampton. Twice voted Wolves Player of the Year in 1981 and 1982, Bradshaw won four England Under-23 caps with Blackburn and in 1980 helped Wolves win the League Cup at Wembley.
Wolves record: 243 apps.

BRAZIER, Colin J.

Colin Brazier could occupy a variety of positions, mainly in defence and was generally a steady player, giving nothing away. Born in Solihull on 6 June 1957, he played for Northfield Town before joining to Wolves as an apprentice in June 1973, turning professional at Molineux in August 1975. He spent the next six seasons vying for a first-team place with several quality players and in June 1981 was transferred to the NASL club, Jacksonville Teamen. He returned to England to sign for Birmingham City in October 1982, but fell out with manager Ron Saunders at St Andrew's and in March 1983 signed for AP Leamington, quickly re-entering the Football League with Lincoln City the following month. From Sincil Bank he switched to Walsall (August 1983) and then had an excellent spell with Kidderminster Harriers (October 1986 to June 1990). A League Cup winner with Wolves in 1980 (as sub), Brazier twice represented the England semi-professional team in 1987.
Wolves record: 91 apps. 2 goals.

BRAZIER, Gilbert

A forceful inside-left, Gil Brazier was a regular in the Wolves' side during the 1884-85 season, but then found it difficult to get first-team football following the arrival of Harry Wood. Born in Beckbury, near Shifnal in August 1860, he played for Shifnal before joining Wolves in April 1884. He left the club in August 1886 to join Lyttleton Rangers. Brazier died in Wolverhampton.
Wolves record: 2 apps. 1 goal.

BREAKWELL, Arthur James

The versatile Archie Breakwell was a strong player with an eye for goal who joined Wolves as a centre-forward from Sedgley in September 1904. He did very well in the second team before establishing himself in the senior side the following year, where he played superbly well alongside Corfield and Wooldridge. Unfortunately an injury ruined his career at Molineux and in 1907 he was transferred to Brierley Hill, later assisting Bilston. Born in Gornal in 1879, Breakwell died in Tipton c.1960.
Wolves record: 24 apps. 3 goals.

BRENTFORD

Wolves' playing record against the Bees is:

Football League

Venue	P	W	D	L	F	A
Home	8	5	0	3	19	13
Away	8	2	1	5	10	18
Totals	16	7	1	8	29	31

Sherpa Van Trophy

Home	1	1	0	0	4	0

Wartime

Home	1	1	0	0	1	0
Away	1	0	1	0	0	0
Cup Final	1	0	1	0	1	1
Totals	3	1	2	0	2	1

A crowd of over 28,400 saw Wolves win their first Football League game with Brentford on 28 September 1935 by 3-2 at Molineux. However, the tide turned when the return fixture took place at Griffin Park in February as the Bees raced to an emphatic 5-0 victory.

Wolves, though, quickly gained revenge and beat Brentford 4-0 at home in February 1937 and they then ran up a convincing 5-2 victory, again at Molineux, in January 1939 when Dennis Westcott (3) and Dickie Dorsett (2) were the marksmen.

In a First Division fixture at Griffin Park in January 1947, Brentford recorded an excellent 4-1 win over Wolves and they repeated that scoreline at Molineux in a Third Division game in January 1986.

A hat-trick by Steve Bull helped Wolves defeat Brentford 4-0 at home in a Sherpa Van Trophy game in January 1988.

On 6 June 1942, Wolves drew 1-1 with Brentford at Stamford Bridge in a challenge match between the winners of the League Cup North (Wolves) and the London Cup.

Jimmy Mullen gave Wolves a 50th minute lead but Ernie Collett equalised a quarter-of-an-hour from time. The attendance was 20,174.

Players with both clubs include: Joe Bonson, Peter Broadbent, Chic Brodie, Joe Hodnett, Eric Jones, Mark Lazarus, Gerry McAloon, Jon Purdie, Harry Rowbotham, David Richards, Bill Slater, Alf Walker and Shane Westley.

Also associated: George Poyser (Wolves reserve, scout and coach, Brentford player and assistant trainer); Dickie Dorsett, Eric Jones, Dennis Westcott and Bill Wrigglesworth (all Brentford wartime guests), Frank Broome (wartime guest for both clubs), Arthur Beattie (Wolves manager, Brentford coach), Colin Lee (Brentford player, Wolves manager), Don Cock (Brentford reserve), Keith Pritchett, and Dave Silman (Wolves Reserves) and Kenneth Horne (Wolves amateur).

BREWSTER, George

Scotsman George 'Dod' Brewster was precisely the right height and build for a centre-half, six feet tall and 13 stones in weight. He was born in the Aberdonian village of Culsalmond on 7 October 1893 and scored nine goals in 112 appearances for Aberdeen over a period of eight years from August 1912, having earlier gained winners' medals in both League and Cup competitions with the junior club, Aberdeen Mugiemoss. He guested for Ayr United and Falkirk during the war and in January 1920, left Pittodrie for Everton for £1,200. In November 1922, after almost 70 outings for the Merseysiders, he was transferred to Wolves as manager George Robey sought to bolster up his defence. Sadly Brewster never settled down at Molineux and

after spending barely six months in the Midlands he moved to Lovells Athletic (May 1921), quickly switching his loyalties to Wallasey United. From March to August 1924 he coached the Brooklands Wanderers in New York and on his return to Scotland became player-manager of Inverness. A much-liked and well-respected gentleman, both on and off the field, Brewster was a great sheet-anchor at the heart of the defence, never letting his side down. He is believed to have died in Scotland *c*.1963, aged 70.
Wolves record: 13 apps.

BRICE, Gordon Henry Joseph

When skipper Stan Cullis retired as a player in April 1947, Wolves manager Ted Vizard went out and secured the services (on Cullis' recommendation) of the Luton Town centre-half Gordon Brice, bringing him to Molineux for £10,000. Brice, nicknamed 'Whiz', played in the first quarter of the 1947-48 season but then lost his place in the side to Bill Shorthouse (following a 5-1 defeat at Charlton). He appeared in only one more senior game for the club before being sold to Reading in March 1948. Born in Bedford on 4 May 1924, and educated at Bedford Secondary Modern School, Brice played for Bedford St Clement's before joining Luton Town as an amateur in June 1939. Owing to World War Two, he had very little time for football, but when peace was restored, he rejoined the Hatters and appeared in over 50 games for the Kenilworth Road club before switching to Wolves. From Reading, for whom he played in more than 200 games, he went to Fulham (December 1952) and remained at Craven Cottage until May 1956, when he signed for Ayr United. He remained in Scotland where he ran a successful hotel. A useful Northamptonshire and Bedfordshire cricketer, Brice scored 412 runs in the County Championship at an average of 13.73. He also took 72 wickets (ave. 33.69) with a best return of 8-124 and claimed 14 catches. He returned to his native Bedford in the 1970s and still lives there today.
Wolves record: 12 apps.

BRIGHTON AND HOVE ALBION

Wolves' playing record against Albion is:
Football League

Venue	P	W	D	L	F	A
Home	7	1	0	6	7	14
Away	7	0	3	4	6	17
Totals	14	1	3	10	13	31

FA Cup

Away	1	1	0	0	3	2

League Cup

Away	1	1	0	0	3	2

The first nine League games between Brighton and Wolves all ended in victories for the Seagulls. The tenth and 11th encoun-

ters both finished all square at 1-1, Brighton won the 12th game (3-2) while the 13 battle resulted in a 3-3 draw. Wolves finally recorded their first win over Albion in December 1992, at the 14th attempt, gaining a 2-0 triumph at Molineux.

When Brighton beat Wolves 3-1 at Molineux in December 1979, Peter Ward scored a hat-trick for the visitors.

On 4 May 1985 Brighton hammered Wolves 5-1 at The Goldstone Ground – a defeat which condemned the Wanderers to relegation. After the game Wolves' boss Tommy Docherty said: "An official asked for two of my players to take a dope test. I offered him the referee instead."

Wolves knocked Albion out of the FA Cup 3-2 in the third round in January 1979 after a tense affair at The Goldstone Ground, which attracted a 25,217 crowd.

Wolves' League Cup win over Albion arrived in season 1969-70 when Hugh Curran netted twice in that 3-2 scoreline in front of 33,859 fans at Hove.

Players with both clubs include: Ken Davies, John Humphrey, Alan Jackson, Albert Lumberg, Bertie Lutton, Archie Needham, Jack Nightingale, Geoff Sidebottom, Mike Small, Tony Towner, Ken Whitfield, Jack Williams and Eric Young.

Also associated: Ron Bennett, Bill Booth, Reg Hipkin, Charlie Livesey, Robert Redfearn, Billy Richards, Doug Roberts and George Willis (all Wolves Reserves); Mike Bailey (Wolves player, Brighton manager); Jimmy Melia (Wolves player, Brighton coach and manager); Major Frank Buckley (Brighton player, Wolves manager); Paul Emblen (Wolves trialist), George Holley (Brighton player, Wolves trainer); Bill McGarry (Wolves manager, Brighton scout); Herbert Barlow, Jackie Brown and Arthur Rowley (all Brighton wartime guests), Jim Mulvaney and George Paterson (Brighton players, Wolves wartime guests), Chris Evans (Brighton player, Wolves coach) and Ray Crawford (Wolves player, Brighton coach).

BRINDLEY, Christopher

Chris Brindley was a reserve central defender at Molineux from November 1986 to June 1988. He left Wolves to join the Vauxhall Conference side Telford United where he teamed up with another ex-Wanderers player, Paul Grainger. He moved to Kidderminster Harriers for a then record fee for the Aggborough club of £20,000 in August 1992 and helped them win the GM Vauxhall Conference three years later. Born in Cannock on 5 July 1969, Brindley played for Hednesford Town before embarking on his career with Wolves and in March 1999 he returned to Keys Park for a second spell.
Wolves record: 9 apps.

BRISTOL CITY

Wolves' playing record against City is:
Football League

Venue	P	W	D	L	F	A
Home	25	14	9	2	47	20
Away	25	11	3	11	37	32
Totals	50	25	12	13	84	52

FA Cup

Home	1	1	0	0	1	0

Sherpa Van Trophy

Home	2	2	0	0	6	1

Wartime

Home	1	0	0	1	1	2
Away	1	0	0	1	2	4
Totals	2	0	0	2	3	6

Wolves won their first two League games with City in season 1911-12. They triumphed 3-1 at Molineux and 3-2 at Ashton Gate. Jack Needham and Tommy Yule scored in both games for the Wanderers.

The Wolves-City League game in September 1920 ended in a 0-0 draw, but George Edmonds had a 'goal' ruled out despite the ball passing clean through the City net.

When Wolves beat City 5-2 at home in a Second Division game in March 1928, Reg Weaver netted a hat-trick – and Billy Hartill weighed in with a treble in Wolves' 4-2 home win in November 1931. Five months later Wolves completed the double over City with a 4-0 victory at Ashton Gate.

Four penalties were awarded during the Bristol City v Wolves League game at Ashton Gate on the opening day of the 1977-78 season. City scored two, but Wolves (in the case of Willie Carr) netted one and missed one. City won the match 3-2.

When City were beaten 4-0 by Wolves at Molineux in October 1990, Steve Bull was a hat-trick hero and four years later it was Irish international David Kelly who took the limelight with a superb second-half hat-trick in Wolves' 5-1 League win at Ashton Gate (November 1994).

Just 48 hours after Mark McGhee had lost his job as manager at Molineux (on 7 November 1998) Wolves, under the guidance of caretaker-boss Colin Lee, beat Bristol City 6-1 at Ashton Gate in a First Division League game with Irish international David Connolly scoring four times. This was Wolves' best away win since they beat Hereford United at Edgar Street by the same score in October 1976.

Wolves' hard-earned 1-0 FA Cup win over City was achieved in season 1972-73, John Richards' goal seeing them through to the fifth round in front of a 30,849 crowd.

In Wolves' Sherpa Van Trophy clash with City in November 1987, Steve Bull netted twice in his side's 3-1 win, and it was Bully's hat-trick which helped see off City by a convincing 3-0 scoreline (at home) in the same competition in January 1989.

Players with both clubs include: Joe Baillie, James E. Baker, George Barker, Roy Bicknall, Tommy Burden, Davey Burnside, Chris Crowe, Keith Curle, Dicky Davies, Bobby Gould (also City manager), Jack Hamilton (also City manager at both first and reserve team levels), Sid Homer, Ernie Hunt, Scott McGarvey, Hugh McIlmoyle, Paul McLoughlin (amateur/professional), John Pender, Jason Roberts, George Showell, Walter Tuft, Clive Whitehead and Les Wilson.

Also associated: Mark McGhee (City apprentice, Wolves manager), Colin Lee (City player, Wolves manager), John Ward (City manager, assistant manager at Molineux); George Hedley (Wolves player, City manager); Jack Hamilton, Martin James, John Jones, Joey Jones, Jimmy Rogers, Tommy Rudkin, George Smith, Reg Smith, John T. Turner and Ken Wimshurst (all Wolves Reserves), Billy Hartill (City reserve), Bill Coley and Fred Pincott (City wartime guests).

Wolves signed teenager Jimmy Morgan from Bristol City in the summer of 1920, but before he had played at any level for the Wanderers, Morgan was killed when he fell from a train while travelling to Wolverhampton from his home in the West Country on 2 September of that year.

BRISTOL ROVERS

Wolves' playing record against the Pirates is:
Football League

Venue	P	W	D	L	F	A
Home	6	2	1	3	12	10
Away	6	1	5	0	9	5
Totals	12	3	6	3	21	15

League Cup

Home	1	1	0	0	4	0

Watney Cup

Away	1	0	0	1	0	2

Wolves first met Rovers at League level in season 1976-77 (Division Two). Wolves won 5-1 at Eastville in December and then doubled up with a 1-0 home victory in April.

Rovers won a seven-goal thriller at Molineux by 4-3 in September 1985 when Andy King scored twice for Wolves watched by just 3,241 hardy supporters.

Wolves' emphatic 4-0 home win over Rovers in the League Cup thrilled a 20,553 crowd at Molineux in October 1972 when Jim McCalliog netted twice.

Wolves lost to Rovers 2-0 in the 1972 Watney Cup Final at Eastville before a sun-bathed, sleeveless shirt crowd of 12,489.

Players with both clubs include: Billy Beats (also Rovers trainer), Billy Blunt, Paul Bradshaw, Arthur Buttery, Keith Curle, Jack Ellis, Bobby Gould (also Rovers manager), Hillary Griffiths, Billy Hartill, Irvine Harwood, Kenny Hibbitt (also assistant manager at Rovers), Sid Homer, Gwyn Jones, George Kinsey, Tansey Lea, James Mason, Jack Preece, John Price, Jason Roberts, Jack Smith, Joe Smith, John Timmins, David Walker, Arthur Weare, Tom Wildsmith and Maurice Woodward.

Also associated with both clubs: John Ward (manager of Rovers, assistant-boss of Wolves); Ted Buckley, Fred Chadwick, Herby Hayle, James Mason, Matthew O'Mahoney, Bill Prendergast, Billy Richards, Jack Smith, Len Smith, Ernie Whatmore and Francis Wragge (all Wolves Reserves), Paul McLoughlin (City trial), John Angus (Wolves reserve, Rovers wartime guest), Andy Gurney (Rovers player, Wolves trialist) and Garry Pendrey (Wolves coach, Rovers player).

BROADBENT, Peter Frank

Peter Broadbent was a brilliant inside-forward who spent 14 years with Wolves. Born in Elvington, near Dover, Kent on 15 May 1933, he played for Dover prior to joining Brentford in May 1950 and from Griffin Park he was transferred to Molineux for £10,000 in February 1951. Playing under manager Stan Cullis, Broadbent was the workhorse in the middle of the field. He helped Wolves win three League championships and the FA Cup as well as gaining seven full England caps, plus more at 'B' and Under-23 levels. He also represented the Football League XI and was the scorer of Wolves' first-ever goal in a European competition (v the German outfit Schalke '04) in November 1958. He left Wolves in January 1965 for Shrewsbury Town and later served with Aston Villa, Stockport County and Bromsgrove Rovers. On retiring he opened a baby-wear shop in Halesowen.
Wolves record: 497 apps. 145 goals.

BROCKSTOPP, Albert Arthur

Arthur Brockstopp played only one season of first-team football for Wolves – in 1894-95 – during which time he lined up on the left-wing in three League games. He was born locally c.1870 and was signed from Ironbridge. All told he spent three years at Molineux, up to 1896 when he moved to Willenhall.
Wolves record: 3 apps.

BRODIE, Charles Thomas

Scotsman 'Chic' Brodie spent seven months with Wolves – from February to September 1961 – during which time he played in one League game, at home against Manchester United on 11 February when he replaced goalkeeper Malcolm Finlayson in a 2-1 win in front of 38,526 fans. In fact, during the year of 1961 Brodie played in three different divisions of the Football League (Fourth, First and Third) in consecutive League games – for Aldershot on 4 February, then for Wolves and finally for Northampton Town. Born in Duntocher on 22 February 1937,

Brodie began his career in Scotland with Partick Avondale in 1952, gaining Schoolboy international honours at the age of 15. In March 1954 he signed as a professional for Manchester City, but failed to break into the first team at Maine Road and left the club for Gillingham in July 1957. Twelve months later he was transferred to Aldershot and after his spell at Molineux, he played in 87 League games for Northampton Town (up to November 1963) and a further 201 for Brentford (to May 1971). In a fine career, Brodie amassed a grand total of 466 senior appearances between the posts (403 in the Football League) and, in fact, his League days were brought to an abrupt end by a dog, which ran into him on the field at Griffin Park, causing him injury. On leaving Brentford Brodie assisted Margate and in 1971 was on the receiving end of Ted MacDougall's record-breaking nine-goal bombardment when Bournemouth won a FA Cup-tie against the non-League side by 11-0. Later on Brodie became a London taxi driver and was involved in a road accident in Westminster – the driver of the other vehicle being no other than Geoff Hurst.
Wolves record: 1 app.

BRODIE, John Brant

Born in the village of Wightwick near Wolverhampton on 30 August 1862, Jack Brodie was a splendidly gifted footballer would could, and would, play in any position on the field, having good pace, excellent ball control, a keen eye and powerful shot. Educated at St Luke's School, Blakenhall and later a pupil-teacher at Saltley College, Birmingham, Brodie helped form Wolverhampton Wanderers FC in 1877 and he continued to serve the club as a player until retiring in the summer of 1891. He then took up refereeing which he did outside his teaching duties as assistant headmaster at St Peter's School, Wolverhampton. In 1913, some 36 years after he had initially signed for Wolves, Brodie was opted onto the board of of directors at Molineux where he was always a very popular person, frequently livening up the proceedings with his witty remarks. Capped three times by England as an inside-forward between 1889 and 1891, he netted in his first international against Ireland, helping England win 6-1.

He also claimed Wolves' first competitive goal – scoring against Long Eaton Rangers in the club's initial FA Cup-tie in October 1883. He was Wolves' top-scorer during the five year period to 1888 when League football was introduced and at the end of that season was a bitterly disappointed man as Wolves' skipper when Preston North End beat the Wanderers 3-0 to win the 1889 FA Cup Final. Brodie guested for neighbours West Bromwich Albion v Aston Villa in July 1886.

He died in Wolverhampton on 16 February 1925.
Wolves record: 65 apps. 44 goals.

BROOKES, Albert Arthur

Signed as cover for full-back Ted Collins, Arthur Brookes (some reference books give his name as Brooks) was a powerfully built player. A Brummie, born in Small Heath in 1888, he played for Bordesley Rangers and Small Heath Taverners prior to joining Wolves in May 1910. He remained at Molineux until May 1915 when he moved to Newport County. He made 133 Birmingham League appearances for Wolves in those five seasons. Brooks did not play competitive football after World War One.
Wolves record: 14 apps.

BROOKS, Albert Walter

After a brief spell with Rotherham County, rugged right-back or centre-half Albert Brooks (whose name sometimes appears with an 'e') spent three seasons at Molineux – July 1913 to May 1915. Playing mostly in the Central League side, he deputised in the first team for Albert Bishop, Bob Young, Albert Groves and Alf Riley during that time. He played briefly for Newport County after the war, retiring in 1922. Brooks was born in Sheffield in 1888 and died c.1940.
Wolves record: 18 apps.

BROOKS, Samuel Ernest

Goalscoring left-winger Sammy Brooks, at 5ft 2ins tall and barely eight stone in weight is one of the smallest and lightest players ever to appear in a first team game for Wolves, doing so between August 1910 and July 1922. Born in Brierley Hill on 28 March 1890 and educated at Bent Street School, he joined Wolves after service with local teams Brierley Hill Corinthians, Brierley Hill Alliance, Bilston United (September 1906) and Cradley Heath. Known as the 'Little Giant' he spent 12 seasons at Molineux and after guesting for Birmingham during the war, he moved to London to sign for Tottenham Hotspur. He played only 16 times for Spurs who transferred him to Southend United in December 1923. From there he joined Kidderminster Harriers (June 1925) and finished his career with spells at Cradley Heath and Stourbridge, retiring in 1927. Capped by England against Wales in the 1919 Victory international, Brookes also represented the Football League against the Irish League in October 1914 and was a member of the Wolves side beaten 1-0 by Spurs in the 1921 FA Cup Final. He died in Wolverhampton on 13 January 1960.

Sammy's brother Ernie played for Blackburn Rovers, Wolves (Reserves) and Brierley Hill Alliance.
Wolves record: 246 apps. 53 goals.

BROWN, Henry Stamford

Harry Brown was born Workington on 23 May 1918 and joined Wolves from his home town club, Workington, in 1938. Basically a reserve outside-left at Molineux, he played in two away League games for Wolves right at the end of that last pre-war season when Stan Burton moved to Portsmouth. He was still on the books at Molineux when the war broke out, but after the hostilities made his way to Hull City for whom he appeared in 22 League games in 1946-47 before going back to Cumbria.
Wolves record: 2 apps.

BROWN, John

Outside-right Jackie Brown was born in Belfast on 8 November 1914. He worked and played for William Ewart and Son before joining Belfast Celtic in 1933. From there he joined Wolves (December 1934) and spent two years at Molineux, up to October 1936 when he signed for Coventry City, transferring to Birmingham in September 1938. He remained at St Andrew's throughout the war when he guested for Brighton, Crystal Palace and Watford. He finally left Blues to sign for Barry Town in January 1948, spending only five months with the Welsh club. From May 1948 to June 1951 he played for Ipswich Town and then announced his retirement through injury. Brown – 5ft 8in tall and weighing 11st – sprang to fame as a teenager in Ireland whilst serving his apprenticeship in the linen trade. He never really settled at Molineux although he did gain the first three of his ten full caps with Wolves, later adding two Republic of Ireland caps to his collection with Coventry. He had a direct approach to football and was a good crosser of the ball.
Wolves record: 31 apps. 7 goals.

BROWN, William

Scotsman Bill Brown was a tall, confident-looking right-half whose cleverness was manifest to everybody. He served Wolves for one season (1928-29) before losing his place to George Lax. Born in Burnbank, Hamilton on 17 November 1902, he played for Belshill Athletic and Coventry City (from June 1925 to May 1928). On leaving Molineux he moved to Norwich City (May 1929) and spent two years with the Canaries before returning to the Midlands to play (as an amateur) for Boulton and Paul Works FC (May 1931 to April 1932). He later retired to Norfolk where he died (in Norwich) on 16 November 1985.
Wolves record: 34 apps.

BRYAN, John Thomas

A well built, orthodox winger Jack Bryan came in for ten games during the 1899-1900 season, playing mainly on the right. A native of Wolverhampton (born c.1877) he spent

three years at Molineux (from July 1898) predominantly as a reserve before leaving to join Blakenhall in the summer of 1901. He later played for Willenhall.
Wolves record: 10 apps. 2 goals.

BRYANT, William

Right-winger Bill Bryant was born in Shildon on 26 November 1913. A pupil at Timothy Huckworth School in County Durham, he represented Durham Boys and played for Bishop Auckland Training Centre Juniors and Cockfield FC before joining Wolves in September 1931. He spent two seasons at Molineux, acting as reserve to Mark Crook and Charlie Phillips, leaving Wolves for Wrexham in October 1933. He later served with Manchester United (October 1934), Chester (as a guest in 1941-42), Bradford City (November 1945), Luton Town (1946), Altrincham (1946-47) and Stalybridge Celtic, retiring c.1950. He won a Darlington Junior League Championship medal with Bishop Auckland TCJ, gained a Second Division championship medal with Manchester United in 1935-36 and played in both legs of the wartime League Cup Final of 1945. Bryant died in County Durham in November 1975.
Wolves record: 5 apps.

BRYCE, Frederick

A solidly built Welshman, born in 1905, goalkeeper Fred Brice conceded 12 goals in his two League outings for Wolves, letting in five at Preston and seven at Fulham in January 1928. His career collapsed after that and he left Wolves during the following summer to join Nuneaton Borough, later serving with Bedworth and Rugby Town. He joined Wolves from Flint Town early in 1928.
Wolves record: 2 apps.

BUCHANAN, Cameron

Scottish inside-forward Cameron Buchan was born on 31 July 1928 in Airdrie, and in September 1942 created a footballing record when, at the age of 14 years, 57 days, he made his senior debut for Wolves in a wartime Football League North game against West Bromwich Albion at Molineux in front of 8,382 spectators. Buchanan went on to play in 18 wartime games for Wolves, scoring six goals, including a hat-trick against Southampton in 1945. He left Molineux for Bournemouth in August 1949 without ever playing in a major League or FA Cup game for the Wanderers. And after serving the Cherries for over seven years, during which time he scored 19 goals in 83 Third Division (South) matches, he was transferred to Norwich City (October 1956), eventually drifting into non-League football the following year. In later life Buchanan moved to Devon where he became associated with Tiverton Town.

BUCKLAND, Mark C.

Mark Buckland was a hardworking midfielder, born in Cheltenham on 18 August 1961, who played for AP Leamington for three years before joining Wolves in February 1984. A scaffold worker by trade, he did well during his time at Molineux and after leaving Wolves (in 1985) moved to Kidderminster Harriers, later assisting Cheltenham Town and Gloucester City (1992-94). He won medals with both the Harriers and Cheltenham.

Wolves record: 56 apps. 5 goals.

BUCKLEY, Major Franklin Charles

Major Frank Buckley was associated with the game of football for 53 years. One of five brothers, he was born in Urmston, Manchester on 9 November 1882 (three years later his brother Charles who became Aston Villa's chairman, was born on the same day) and after school he enlisted in the Army (1898). He served in the Boer War and in the summer of 1903, at the age of 22, joined Aston Villa as an attacking defender. Unfortunately he failed to make the grade at Villa Park and in July 1905 was transferred to Brighton and Hove Albion. In August 1907 he switched to Manchester United and thereafter had spells with Manchester City (to July 1909), Birmingham (to August 1911), Derby County (to July 1914) and Bradford City. He retired as a player towards the end of World War One after serving with the 17th Middlesex Regiment (known as the Footballers' Battalion) when he became a Commanding officer, attaining the rank of Major in 1918.

Whilst with Derby, Buckley gained his only England cap (v Ireland in 1914) having helped County win promotion to the First Division two years earlier. In March 1919, he was appointed manager of Norwich City, a position he held until May 1920, when he left football briefly to become a commercial traveller in London. In July 1923 he returned to the game as Blackpool's manager and after spending four years at Bloomfield Road, he switched to Molineux, taking over the manager's hot seat in June 1927 from Fred Scotchbrook. The next 17 years saw Buckley make Wolves into a solid and capable First Division side. They won the Second Division championship in 1932, reach the FA Cup Final in 1939 And win the wartime League Cup in 1942. He introduced several quality players to the club, some young, some old, a few already established professionals and a handful of inexperienced ones. Included among his 'finds' were Stan Cullis, Tom Galley, Joe Gardiner, Billy Hartill, Bryn Jones, Wilf Lowton, Jimmy Mullen, Charlie Phillips, Cecil Shaw, Dennis Westcott and Billy Wright. When in charge at Molineux,

various headlines in the local and national press referred to Buckley as the 'baby snatcher' and the 'kidnapper' and even the club was called the 'football factory.' Buckley left Wolves in March 1944, handing over the reins to Ted Vizard. From May 1946 to May 1948 he was in charge of Hull City and then spent five seasons (to the summer of 1953) as team manager of Leeds United, bringing the great John Charles into the football arena. After leaving Elland Road, Buckley managed Walsall until retiring in June 1955. When he moved into the Molineux hot seat, he introduced himself to the players and staff without too much superfluous ceremony. Indeed, he immediately instructed the players as to routine, issued each one with a printed rule book and clearly emphasised that these were to be strictly observed at all times, demanding punctuality as well. He brought in several old items of equipment for the gym including a rowing machine. Known as the 'Iron Major' Buckley was unequivocal, progressive, ambitious and voluble. His ideas were freely communicated to the local and national press. He publicly stated that he was totally against the use of the white football (Cowdenbeath had experimented with one in Scotland) and he also revealed that it was he who had initially advocated the numbering of players' jerseys for the benefit of supporters. Football was like war to him – the team simply had to win matches to succeed. Buckley designed a brand new strip – black and gold vertical striped shirts, black shorts – and his first match in charge saw Wolves draw 2-2 at home with Manchester City. In his first four seasons in charge Wolves had mixed fortunes in Division Two, before winning promotion in 1932. In 1936-37 Buckley transferred a complete team from Molineux for less than £20,000. In 1938 he sold inside-forward Bryn Jones to Arsenal for a record fee of £14,000 – and immediately bought himself a Welsh terrier and called it 'Bryn Jones.' It was common knowledge that Major Frank Buckley, who died on 22 December 1964, was a ruthless disciplinarian and that youngsters at Molineux were genuinely afraid of him. But he was a terrific manager, one of the very best, certainly in the Wolves camp.

BUCKLEY, Patrick McCabe

Scottish outside-left Pat Buckley amassed a splendid record in Wolves' reserve team, scoring 55 goals in three complete seasons: 1964-65 to 1966-67, including a haul of 33 in the latter campaign. Born in Leith on 12 August 1946, he was signed from Third Lanark in February 1964, but his first-team outings were restricted owing to the presence of Dick Le Flem and Dave Wagstaffe, and in January 1968 he was transferred to Sheffield United. He later assisted Rotherham United

(from June 1972) and quit first-class soccer the following May (1973).

Wolves record: 29 apps. 8 goals.

BULL, Stephen George

Now regarded as the greatest goalscorer in Wolves' history, Steve Bull was born in Tipton on 28 March 1965. On leaving school he worked in a bed-making factory and at weekends played for Tipton Town. In 1984 he joined West Bromwich Albion and played in their intermediate side before being offered a full professional contract at The Hawthorns in 1985. After just nine first-team appearances for the Baggies (three goals scored) he was transferred to Wolves by manager Ron Saunders in a deal which also involved Andy Thompson, Bull being valued at £65,000, the transaction going through on 21 November 1986. He made his Wolves debut the following day (against Wrexham) and scored the first of more than 300 goals for the club against Cardiff City in a Freight Rover Cup-tie at Ninian Park on 2 December. (His 300th came in February 1998 v Bradford City in a League game). He ended his first 'half season' at Molineux with 19 goals and in 1987-88 netted a staggering 52, collecting a Sherpa Van Trophy winners' medal at Wembley and helping Wolves win the Fourth Division title in the process. A Third Division championship medal was also won the following year. By now a cult hero at Molineux, Bull, forceful and with a powerful right foot shot couldn't stop scoring. Having earlier represented England at 'B' and Under-21 levels, he won the first of his 13 full caps in May 1989 v Scotland, scoring to mark the occasion. 'Bully', as he became affectionately known, was also taken by England boss Graham Taylor to the World Cup Finals. He knows he failed to hit the dizzy heights on the international scene (remember Gary Lineker was around at the same time) but the goals still flowed thick and fast at club level – 64 in the League in three seasons (1991-94) and in 1997-98 he reached two personal milestones: his 300th senior goal of his career (for Albion, Wolves and England) and his 300th competitive goal for Wolves, the winner (2-1) over Bradford City at Molineux in February 1998. Granted a testimonial in 1996-97 (Wolves v Santos), Bull agreed to stay at Molineux until the end of his career – despite Wolves twice missing out on the Play-offs which may well have brought Premiership football for 'Bully' and of course, for Wolves. And in August 1998 to show he was still goal-hungry he whipped in his 18th hat-trick for the club in a 5-0 League Cup win over Barnet at Molineux. Injuries severely disrupted the 1998-99 season – and how Wolves' missed him.

Senior football apart, Bully also scored five goals in a friendly for Wolves v FC Smedly

Steve Bull, a great Wolves hero of recent times.

apprentice in June 1985 and turned professional in February 1987. He won England schoolboy honours at the age of 15, playing twice at Wembley and scoring a hat-trick against Holland. After becoming a professional he then added youth caps to his collection, but failed to establish himself at Villa Park, transferring to Middlesbrough for £50,000 in December 1987. A loan spell with Darlington (October 1990) preceded his move to Wolves for £25,000 in March 1991. He had some good runs in the first team at Molineux, but after another loan period, this time with Luton Town (March 1994) and a trial with Tottenham Hotspur, he moved to Port Vale (August 1994) where he remained until May 1995 when he signed for Fortuna Sittard on a free transfer. He had trials with Sporting Lisbon in May-June 1994.
Wolves record: 77 apps. 14 goals.

BURLEIGH, James

Utility forward Jim Burleigh spent two seasons at Molineux (from July 1890 to May 1892) where he played most of his football in the Reserves. Born locally *c.*1869, he remained an amateur throughout his career and after leaving Wolves assisted several non-League teams in and around the Wolverhampton and Willenhall areas.
Wolves record: 2 apps.

BURNLEY

Wolves' playing record against the Clarets is:

Football League

Venue	P	W	D	L	F	A
Home	50	32	9	9	117	47
Away	50	17	13	20	79	85
Totals	100	49	22	29	196	132

FA Cup

	P	W	D	L	F	A
Away	1	0	0	1	0	3

League Cup

	P	W	D	L	F	A
Home	1	1	0	0	2	0
Away	1	0	1	0	1	1
Totals	2	1	1	0	3	1

Sherpa Van Trophy

	P	W	D	L	F	A
Neutral	1	1	0	0	2	0

FA Charity Shield

	P	W	D	L	F	A
Away	1	0	1	0	2	2

Wolves and Burnley were founder members of the Football League, and they first met in this competition on 22 September 1888 when Wolves won 4-1 to record their first-ever League victory. Wolves also won the return fixture at Turf Moor that season by 4-0, Harry Wood scoring twice.

In the third meeting between the clubs – in December 1889 – Wolves raced to an explosive 9-1 home victory with Harry Allen, Jack Brodie, Harry Wood and David Wykes scoring two goals apiece.

Burnley's first win over Wolves arrived in November 1890 – at the sixth attempt. They achieved a 4-2 scoreline at Turf Moor in front of 3,500 fans.

(Sweden) in July 1994 and whilst recovering from injury he rattled in another five against Peterborough United in a third team game. West Brom boss Ron Saunders allowed Bull to leave The Hawthorns because he thought his first touch wasn't good enough. A year or so after buying him, Wolves manager Graham Turner said: "Okay his first touch still isn't good, but he usually scores with his second." July 1999 Bull announced his retirement because of injury.
Wolves record: 542+17 apps. 306 goals.

BUNCH, Walter Wilbert S.

Walter Bunch was a reserve defender, capable of occupying several positions, but preferring the full-back berth. Born in Weston-Super-Mare in 1872, he played for Compton Colts, Willenhall Institute and Blakenhall prior to spending four seasons at Molineux (August 1895 to May 1899). He left Wolves for Walsall and after 72 games for the Saddlers, had a spell with Birmingham (from September 1901 to April 1902, appearing in three games). He retired through illness and injury in May 1902, although he did turn out occasionally in later years for Stourbridge Swifts and Lye Commadores, playing his last game in 1905. Bunch then became licensee of the Golden Lion in Chell Street, Dudley before moving to the West Country. He died in Somerset.
Wolves record: 7 apps.

BURKE, Mark Stephen

Born in Solihull on 12 February 1969, midfielder Mark Burke joined Aston Villa as an

Wolves began the 1895-96 League season with a thumping 5-1 home win over Burnley. And they ran up a useful 4-0 home victory in April 1899 when Billy Beats scored twice.

Another 5-1 Wolves victory followed in March 1908 (two goals here for both George Hedley and Wally Radford) and in November 1908 Radford scored a hat-trick in Wolves' 5-3 win at Turf Moor.

Burnley doubled up over Wolves in season 1930-31 with two 4-2 victories, but Wolves quickly retaliated with two 3-1 wins the following season on their way to the Second Division title.

The crowd of 16,737 for the Wolves-Burnley League game in April 1952 was the first below 20,000 at Molineux for 13 years – since April 1939. Burnley won 2-1.

Two seasons later Burnley were the only team to complete the double over Wolves when Wanderers became League champions for the first time in 1953-54.

The following season Wolves swept to an impressive 5-0 home win with Ron Flowers and Roy Swinbourne both scoring twice.

In between times, Wolves played their 1,000th away League game – losing 2-0 at Turf Moor in November 1952.

In season 1959-60 Wolves won 6-1 at home (two goals for Gerry Mannion), but lost 4-1 at Burnley, and in the First Division game at Turf Moor in November 1960, Wolves were 3-1 up at one stage but eventually lost 5-3.

In mid-April 1963 Wolves slammed Burnley 7-2 at Molineux in front of 21,562 fans. Peter Broadbent and Alan Hinton both scored twice.

Derek Dougan came off the subs' bench and scored with his first touch in Wolves' 3-2 win over Burnley at Turf Moor in September 1970.

Wolves completed another double over Burnley in 1974-75 (winning 4-2 at home and 2-1 away) and ace marksman John Richards scored the fastest-ever Wolves goal from the start of a game when he netted after only 12 seconds of the First Division game with Burnley at Turf Moor in November 1975. Wolves eventually won 5-1.

The 100th League game between the two clubs took place at Molineux in season 1994-95 and ended in a 2-0 victory for Wolves.

In January 1970, Wolves were knocked out of the FA Cup in the third round by Burnley, but then the Wanderers gained some revenge by beating the Clarets 3-1 on aggregate in a second round League Cup-tie in 1979-80 when Geoff Palmer scored in each game.

The Sherpa Van Trophy triumph over Burnley was achieved at Wembley in the Final of that competition in May 1988 when almost 81,000 fans saw Robbie Dennison and Andy Mutch score the goals.

The Charity Shield game at Turf Moor in August 1960 ended all square at 2-2. The crowd of 19,873 saw Jimmy Murray and Norman Deeley net for FA Cup holders Wolves against the League champions Burnley.

Players with both clubs include: George Bellis, David Black, Gordon Clayton, Paul Cook, Gordon Cowans, Steve Daley, Peter Daniel, Tommy Dunn, Roger Eli, Joe Gallagher, Ray Hankin, Roger Hansbury, Henry Hargreaves, Micky Holmes, Mark Kendall, Reg Kirkham, Steve Kindon, Geoff Palmer, John Pender, Barry Powell (also Wolves coach), Alex Scott, Paul Stewart, Dave Thomas, Walter Weaver and Peter Zelem.

Also associated: Mick Docherty (Burnley player, Wolves coach); Chris Pearce (Wolves junior, Burnley player); George Paterson (Burnley player, Wolves wartime guest), Bill Shorthouse (Burnley wartime guest), Tom Mayson (reserve), Jack Mitton (Wolves player, Burnley amateur); John Ward (assistant manager at both clubs).

BURNS, William

Irishman Billy Burns had two spells with Wolves – the first from December 1925 to January 1926 and the second during season 1928-29. A capable centre-half, born at Newtonards, Belfast in 1904, he played his early football with Nortonville FC (Belfast) and after unsuccessful trials with Stoke (August-September 1923) he signed for Glentoran. He was transferred to Wolves after gaining County Antrim Shield and Irish League championship medals. After his first spell at Molineux, Burns spent a short time in America before returning to Ireland to assist Dublin Shelbourne and when he left Wolves second time round he signed for Ards. In June 1929, Burns was recruited by Workington, but he never settled in Cumbria and went back to the Emerald Isle in May 1930 where he rounded off his career by assisting a handful of minor clubs including Belfast St Peter's. Once rated the best centre-half in Ireland, Burns was a strong defender, a powerful header of the ball and fearless on the ground. He represented the Irish League v The Football League in October 1924 and coached briefly in Washington (USA) in the early 1930s.
Wolves record: 4 apps.

BURNSIDE, David Gort

Davey Burnside was a ball-playing inside-forward who appeared in more than 450 competitive games in a 20-year career. Born in Kingswood, Bristol on 10 December 1939, he attended and played for Kingswood Secondary Modern School and represented Bristol and District Boys before signing for Bristol City as an amateur. In December 1955 he joined the groundstaff at West Bromwich Albion and turned professional at The Hawthorns in February 1957. Over the next five years or so he made 135 appearances for the Baggies, gained England Youth and Under-23 honours and in 1960 entered the European footballers 'Heading' competition which saw him finish runner-up with 495 headers to the Austrian George Kaul's amazing tally of 3,025. From Albion Burnside moved to Southampton for £17,000 in September 1962. He played for Crystal Palace from December 1964 to September 1966 when he joined Wolves, linking up again with manager Ronnie Allen, whom he had been with at West Brom and Palace. After a good spell at Molineux during which time he helped Wolves regain their First Division status (1967) he left the club in March 1968 and switched south to Plymouth Argyle, later assisting Bristol City (December 1971), Colchester United (March 1972), Bath City (as player-manager April 1972 to March 1973), Walsall (as assistant manager, August-December 1973), Cadbury Heath (as a player, August 1974 to May 1975), Bridgwater Town (player-manager August 1975 to May 1979) and finally Taunton Town (September 1979 to June 1980). He then retired to take up coaching, and between July 1983 and December 1996 was associated with the FA, mainly looking after the England Youth side and helping bring through some exceptionally fine players. Over the last two years or so he has been director of Youth Football at Bristol City.
Wolves record: 43 apps. 5 goals.

BURRIDGE, John

A fitness fanatic all his life, consistent goalkeeper John 'Budgie' Burridge had a superb career between the posts, and when he quit top-class football in 1996-97, he had accumulated an appearance record bettered by only one other keeper in the history of the game – Peter Shilton. Burridge played in 917 competitive matches at senior club level (it was over 1,000 if you include friendly matches etc.). He started out with Workington, whom he joined as an apprentice in 1968, turning professional in January 1970. He left the Cumbrian club for Blackpool in a £100,000 deal in April 1971 and over the next 27 years his career went as follows: Aston Villa (£100,000, September 1975), Southend United (loan, January 1978), Crystal Palace (£65,000, March 1978), Queen's Park Rangers (£200,000, December 1980), Wolverhampton Wanderers (£75,000, August 1982), Derby County (loan, September 1984), Sheffield United (£10,000, October 1984), Southampton ((£30,000, August 1987 – to replace Shilton.), Newcastle United (£25,000, October 1989), Hibernian (July 1991), Newcastle United (free transfer, August 1993), Scarborough (free, October 1993), Lincoln City (free, December 1993),

Enfield (February 1994), Aberdeen (free, March 1994), Barrow (September 1994), Dumbarton (free, October 1994), Falkirk (November 1994), Manchester City (free, December 1994), Notts County (free, August 1995), Witton Albion (October 1995), Darlington (free, November 1995), Grimsby Town (free, December 1995), Gateshead (January 1996), Northampton Town (January 1996), Queen of the South (March 1996), player-manager of Blyth Spartans (July 1996), Scarborough (on loan, December 1996). He was 45 years of age when he played his last competitive game for Scarborough in the Auto Windscreen Shield game v Notts County in December 1996, being the oldest player ever to appear for that club. And he also became the oldest ever Darlington player when he kept goal for the Quakers in December 1995, aged 44. He was part time goalkeeping coach at both Newcastle United and Leeds United while playing for Blyth Spartans. Burridge won an Anglo-Italian Cup winners medal with Blackpool in 1970, a League Cup winners medal with Villa in 1977, a Second Division championship medal with Crystal Palace in 1979 and a Scottish Premier League Cup winners medal with Hibernian 1991. 'Budgie' helped Wolves win promotion from Division two in 1983 and the following season was voted the club's Player of the Year. He set the record for being Lincoln City's oldest-ever footballer, aged 42 years, 57 days v Rochdale in 1994 and in April 1995 he created another record of being the oldest player to star in the Premiership – keeping goal for Manchester City v Newcastle United at the age of 43 years, four months and 26 days. Burridge, who was born in Workington on 13 December 1951, was at loggerheads with Wolves during 1984-85 and at one stage refused to play in goal.

Wolves record: 81 apps.

BURRILL, Frederick

Fred Burrill could play equally well at left-half or as an inside-forward. A skilful dribbler, born at Manor Park, East London in 1894, he was recruited by Wolves from Southend United in May 1920, having earlier assisted East London Schools and West Ham United (1911-14). He appeared in the 1921 FA Cup Final against Tottenham Hotspur, but two years later he left Molineux to join Charlton Athletic (July 1923). He later assisted Walsall (May 1924 to May 1925) before drifting into non-League soccer (to 1930). Burrill died at Whitechapel, London on 31 July 1962.

Wolves record: 69 apps. 17 goals.

BURTON, Stanley

Yorkshireman Stan 'Dizzy' Burton was born at Thurnscoe on 3 December 1912 and died

in Sheffield on 10 February 1977. An out-and-out attacker down the right-wing, he represented Yorkshire Schools at the age of 14 and started his career, in earnest, with Wombwell FC, later joining Thurnscoe Victoria (1931) from where he switched to Doncaster Rovers (February 1933). Five and a half years later (in September 1938) he was transferred to Wolves for £4,000 – and quickly established himself in the first team. He left Molineux for West Ham United on 29 April 1939 in a record £6,000 transfer, just five days after having played in the FA Cup Final against Portsmouth. He then turned out for the Londoners v Manchester City in the final League game of that season, thus becoming the only footballer in history to appear in the FA Cup Final, and then afterwards in a League match for a different team in the same season. During the war Burton guested for several clubs in Yorkshire including Barnsley, Bradford City, Doncaster Rovers, Leeds United and Sheffield Wednesday.

Wolves record: 32 apps. 4 goals.

BURTON UNITED

Wolves' playing record against United is:

Football League

Venue	P	W	D	L	F	A
Home	1	1	0	0	3	0
Away	1	0	0	1	1	4
Totals	2	1	0	1	4	4

The two League games between Wolves and Burton were played in the Second Division season of 1906-07. Former Bloxwich Strollers star Arthur Hawkins scored twice in Wolves' 3-0 win at Molineux.

Players associated with both clubs (various levels): Billy Boswell, Will Devey, George Harper, Arthur Hawkins, Adam Haywood and Jack Stanley.

BURY

Wolves' playing record against the Shakers is:

Football League

Venue	P	W	D	L	F	A
Home	25	15	8	2	54	16
Away	25	4	1	20	20	50
Totals	50	19	9	22	74	66

FA Cup

Home	1	1	0	0	2	0
Away	1	0	0	1	0	1
Totals	2	1	0	1	2	1

Wolves first met Bury in the Football League in season 1895-96. They won 1-0 at Molineux, but lost 3-0 to the Shakers at Gigg Lane.

In April 1903, Bury ran up their biggest League win over Wolves, beating them 4-0 at home.

Wolves' best League wins over Bury have been those of 7-0 in November 1930 when Billy Hartill netted a hat-trick; 6-0 in December 1931 (when Jimmy Deacon and

Charlie Phillips both scored twice) and 4-0 in March 1989 (when Steve Bull grabbed a hat-trick).

Wolves doubled up over the Shakers in season 1997-98, winning 4-2 at Molineux and 3-1 at Gigg Lane. Robbie Keane and Steve Bull both scored twice in the first match.

A crowd of just 2,205 witnessed the Wolves v Bury League encounter at Molineux in March 1986 – the lowest in this competition since 1892. It ended all square at 1-1.

Wolves played both their 2,000th away League game and their 4,000th in all at Gigg Lane on 2 March 1999, when they drew 0-0 with lowly Bury.

Walter Radford scored both goals in Wolves' 2-0 FA Cup win over Bury in season 1907-08 as they moved towards that Final victory over Newcastle

Players with both clubs include: Paul Edwards, Roger Eli, John Farley, Chris Greene, Alan Jackson, Jack Mitton and John Paskin.

Also associated: David Felgate (Wolves Reserves), Jack Acquaroff (Bury player, Wolves wartime guest), Albert Flatley (Wolves trialist), Albert Groves (Bury guest), Ian Miller (Bury player, Wolves coach).

BUTCHER, Joseph Henry

Joe Butcher's claim to fame was to score all five goals for Wolves in a 5-3 League victory over Accrington in November 1892. He was also the youngest player on the pitch (at 18) when Wolves defeated Everton 1-0 in the 1893 FA Cup Final. An out-and-out centre-forward, with a powerful right-foot shot, Butcher was born in Willenhall in February 1875, and joined Wolves from Wolverhampton East End in June 1892. He spent just over three seasons at Molineux before transferring to West Bromwich Albion for £25 in September 1895. Unfortunately before he could make his senior debut for the Throstles he suffered a crippling knee injury which forced him into an early retirement at the age of 21. He chose to go into business in Wolverhampton and certainly had a good life, living until he was 83. He died in Derby on 29 March 1958.

Wolves record: 76 apps. 31 goals.

BUTLER, Paul J.

Paul Butler was an eager-beaver wing-forward, who was never really a first-team regular at Molineux. Born in Stockton-on-Tees on 9 June 1964, he joined Wolves as a junior at the age of 16 and turned professional in June 1982. He was on the bench more often than not during the 1982-83 and 1983-84 seasons before becoming surplus to requirements. At this juncture (January 1984) he went on loan to Hereford United and after Tommy Docherty had taken over as manager, Butler joined the Edgar Street club on a permanent basis in February 1985. He made almost 120 appearances for the Bulls who then sold him to Hartlepool United in July 1987. He failed to continue his good form at the Victoria Ground and in May 1988 Butler given a free transfer to enter non-League soccer in County Durham.

Wolves record: 21+14 apps. 2 goals.

BUTTERY, Arthur J.

Regarded as a good schemer, Arthur Buttery was basically a reserve inside-forward during his time at Molineux. Born in Hednesford on 20 December 1908, he played for Hednesford Town for four years, while also having unsuccessful trials with Motherwell and Swansea Town, before joining Wolves in November 1929. He spent three years at the club, up to June 1932 when he was transferred to Bury, later assisting Bradford City (January 1937), Walsall (June 1938) and Bristol Rovers (July 1939). He guested for Walsall and Wolves during the World War Two.

Wolves record: 10 apps. 6 goals.

CADDICK, William

Centre-half Bill Caddick – whose grandfather William senior had been a reserve team goalkeeper with Wolves between 1880-83 – had seven excellent seasons at Molineux, being a regular in the side in five of those campaigns. Born at Wolverhampton on 14 March 1898, he attended St Luke's School until he was 15. He then played for All Saints FC (Wolverhampton) and for the Third Battalion Grenadier Guards between 1916-19. In 1919-20 he became a professional footballer with Wellington Town (Birmingham and District League). Both Aston Villa and Wolves then sought his signature and it was the latter who secured his services in December 1920, Wolves signing him as cover for Maurice Woodward and Joe Hodnett. Caddick who stood 6ft 1in tall and weighed 12 stones, had to wait until 10 March 1921 before making his senior debut (at Stoke) and by the following October had established himself as a regular member of the first team, holding his position until Sammy Charnley replaced him in 1925. Caddick, who helped Wolves win the Third Division North championship in 1923-24, returned to Wellington Town in June 1927. After spending three years with Stafford Rangers (1928-31), helping them twice with the Keys Cup (1928 and 1929) he retired and later became licensee of the Hop Pole pub on Oxley Moor Road, Wolverhampton. Caddick junior died on 13 June 1981 at Maldon, Essex. He was 84.

Wolves record: 154 apps. 2 goals

NB: William Caddick senior was born in Wolverhampton on 20 July 1859 and died in Wolverhampton on 17 February 1898, aged 40. An ironmonger's clerk, he was a commit-tee member, auditor and also kept goal for Wolves' teams.

CALLANAN, William W.

Bill Callanan was a solid centre-half, who played mainly reserve team football during his two years with Wolves – June 1907 to May 1909. Born in Featherstone, Staffs in June 1885, he started his career with Oxley St Mark's and joined Wolves from Willenhall Pickwick. He left Molineux to sign for Bilston Town and died c.1951 in Wolverhampton.

Wolves record: 3 apps.

CAMBRIDGE UNITED

Wolves' playing record against United is:

Football League

Venue	P	W	D	L	F	A
Home	5	2	1	2	8	6
Away	5	0	3	2	4	6
Totals	10	2	4	4	12	12

FA Cup

	P	W	D	L	F	A
Home	1	0	0	1	0	1

League Cup

	P	W	D	L	F	A
Home	1	0	0	1	0	1
Away	1	0	0	1	1	3
Totals	2	0	0	2	1	4

A crowd of 4,571 saw the Cambridge United-Wolves game at the Abbey Stadium in November 1982 – then the lowest League attendance a Wolves team had played in front of since 1927. This was also the first League meeting between the two clubs and United won 2-1.

Wolves beat United 3-0 at Molineux in October 1987 to record their best victory so far.

United ousted Wolves from the League Cup in 1980-81, winning comfortably over two legs. And ten years later United did it again, upsetting Wolves by beating them 1-0 at Molineux in the third round of the FA Cup in January 1991.

Players with both clubs include: Scott Barrett, Michael Bennett, Steve Claridge, Roger Eli, Roger Hansbury, Micky Holmes, Keith Lockhart, Steve Mardenborough, Jon Purdie, Floyd Streete, Tony Towner and Shane Westley.

CANAVON, Alfred

Goalkeeper Alf Canavon joined Wolves from Stafford Rangers in May 1925. At six feet tall and weighing 12 stones, he certainly looked the part, but found it difficult to get first-team football during his three seasons at Molineux owing to the form Noel George. He was, in fact, a regular in the Reserves throughout 1925-26 before breaking into League football the following year. Born in Coventry in 1904, Canavon left Wolves for Shrewsbury Town in July 1928 and later assisted Newtown Albion and Wellington White Star, retiring during World War Two.

Wolves record: 15 apps.

CANNON, Alfred A.

Alf Cannon was a reliable wing-half, who deputised for both Arthur Fletcher and Arthur Lowder during his two seasons with the club. Born in Cannock c.1865, he played for Cannock Royal and Easington White Rose before joining Wolves in August 1887. He left Molineux for Springhill Athletic in May 1889.

Wolves record: 7 apps.

CAPTAINS

Over the years Wolves have had many fine captains, including Stan Cullis and Billy Wright, who both led the team out at Wembley on FA Cup Final day (1939 and 1949 respectively). Bill Slater was also a FA Cup Final skipper (1960) while Mike Bailey and Emlyn Hughes both lifted the Football League Cup (in 1974 and 1980) and Ally Robertson held aloft the Sherpa Van Trophy in 1988.

Prior to that, Jack Brodie had skippered Wolves in the 1889 FA Cup Final; Harry Allen led the team in the 1893 Final; Billy Malpass was captain in the 1896 Final; Bill Wooldridge lifted the trophy in 1908 and Val Gregory was in charge of the team in the 1921 Final.

Prior to the mid-1930s, when Cullis took over the mantle, Wolves had been skippered in the Football League by Allen, Dicky Baugh, Dick Betteley, Albert Bishop, Brodie, Bill Caddick, Gregory, Hillary Griffiths (1890s), Billy Harrison, Reg Hollingworth, the Revd Kenneth Hunt, Jackery Jones, Wilf Lowton, Malpass, Harry Wood (1895-96) and Wooldridge among others. And since World War Two, in addition to those mentioned earlier, Gary Bellamy, Steve Bull, Keith Curle, Ian Atkins, Dean Richards, Ally Robertson and John De Wolf have all skippered Wolves at sometime or another.

Larry Kelly was just 17 years of age when he skippered Wolves in season 1942-43 – possibly the youngest ever captain at the club.

Stan Cullis (Wolves) who was born in 1915, became England's youngest-ever captain at the age of 22 when he led his country during the 1937-38 season.

Besides Cullis, Billy Wright (England) and Derek Dougan (Northern Ireland) both skippered their countries.

Wright skippered his country in a record 90 internationals and when he led England for the fiftieth time, in April 1955, Scotland were hammered 7-2 at Wembley (Dennis Wilshaw scoring four goals on his debut).

CARDIFF CITY

Wolves' playing record against the Bluebirds is:

Football League

Venue	P	W	D	L	F	A
Home	18	11	3	4	42	21
Away	18	7	7	4	34	22
Totals	36	18	10	8	76	43

FA Cup

	P	W	D	L	F	A
Home	1	0	0	1	1	2
Away	1	0	1	0	0	0
Neutral	1	1	0	0	3	1
Totals	3	1	1	1	4	3

Freight Rover Trophy

	P	W	D	L	F	A
Away	1	1	0	0	1	0

Wartime

	P	W	D	L	F	A
Home	2	1	0	1	3	3
Away	2	0	0	2	1	4
Totals	4	1	0	3	4	7

Wolves and Cardiff first met in the Football League in season 1920-21 and it was the Welsh side who took the honours, winning both matches: 2-0 in Cardiff and 3-1 at Molineux.

In April 1930, Dicky Rhodes, playing at inside-right, scored twice in Wolves' 4-0 home win over Cardiff in front of just 5,108 fans.

The following season (November) Wolves won 4-1 at Molineux.

Around 10,000 Cardiff fans made the trip to Molineux for the opening League game of the 1952-53 season but they had nothing to celebrate at the end of the day as Wolves won 1-0 with a goal by Jimmy Mullen.

The following year three late goals by Wolves beat Cardiff City 3-1 in the First Division game at Molineux.

Wolves' greatest away win in the Football League came at Ninian Park in September 1955 when they hammered luckless Cardiff 9-1 before more than 40,000 fans. Johnny Hancocks and Roy Swinbourne both scored hat-tricks that day with one of Swinbourne's goals a cheeky back-heeler.

A rare Friday night League game at Cardiff in February 1962 (re-arranged as not to clash with a rugby international at the nearby Arms Park) saw Wolves win 3-2, Terry Wharton scoring twice.

In September 1965 the first post-war Second Division meeting between the clubs resulted in a competent 4-1 away win for Wolves with Hugh McIlmoyle netting twice. Wolves doubled up this season, winning 2-1 at Molineux.

The following season (September 1966) Terry Wharton hit a hat-trick as Wolves whipped Cardiff 7-1 at Molineux. Cardiff had been beaten 3-0 at Molineux three weeks earlier.

On their way to winning promotion in 1976-77 Wolves beat Cardiff City 4-1 at Molineux in late April to all but clinch their First Division place.

A Fourth Division game at Molineux in February 1988 ended Wolves 1 Cardiff 4 – the Welsh club's best-ever League victory over the Wanderers.

Wolves beat Cardiff City 3-1 in a replay to reach the 1921 FA Cup Final against Tottenham. The teams had fought out a goal-less draw in the first game at Anfield where the attendance was almost 42,000, but in the replay at Old Trafford Wolves came good and won in style with goals from Dick Richards, George Edmonds and Sammy Brooks. The attendance here was 44,863.

A goal by Steve Bull – his first in a Wolves shirt – earned his side a 1-0 win at Cardiff in a Freight Rover Trophy game in December 1986. It was a pity that only 1,201 fans were there to witness this famous goal.

Cardiff, with ex-Wolves man Jason Roberts in their side, won promotion from the Third Division in 1998-99 with another former 'Wolf' Kenny Hibbitt, the club's director of football.

Players with both clubs include: Gary Bellamy, Joe Bonson, Glenn Crowe, Fred Davies, Keith Downing, Tony Evans, John Farrington, Roger Hansbury, Bob Hatton, Billy Kellock, Paul McLoughlin, Steve

Roy Swinbourne on target in the 9-1 drubbing of Cardiff City in 1955.

Mardenborough, James Myers, Ernie Stevenson, Ronnie Stockin, Nigel Vaughan, Bobby Woodruff,

Also associated: Bill Booth, Ernie Carless, David Felgate, Ron Hewitt and Billy Moore (all Wolves Reserves), Terry Harkin (Wolves junior), Dicky Baugh (subject of transfer row), Ray Goddard, Bryn Jones, Jack Smith and Billy Wrigglesworth (City wartime guests), Colin Gibson (City player, Wolves wartime guest), Kenny Hibbitt (Wolves player, Cardiff manager) and Cyril Spiers (Wolves player, Cardiff manager).

CARL ZEISS Jena

Wolves' playing record against Jena is:
UEFA Cup

Venue	P	W	D	L	F	A
Home	1	1	0	0	3	0
Away	1	1	0	0	1	0
Totals	2	2	0	0	4	0

En route to the 1972 UEFA Cup Final, Wolves overcame the East German side Carl Zeiss Jena 4-0 on aggregate in the third round.

The first leg was played on a snowbound pitch in Jena on 24 November 1971 in front of 9,764 fans when John Richards scored the game's only goal. The return leg was played a fortnight later and this time Wolves won well with Derek Dougan netting twice before a crowd of 24,135.

CARLISLE UNITED

Wolves playing record against Carlisle is:
Football League

Venue	P	W	D	L	F	A
Home	7	5	1	1	15	5
Away	7	4	0	3	9	6
Totals	14	9	1	4	24	11

FA Cup

Venue	P	W	D	L	F	A
Home	1	1	0	0	3	1
Away	1	1	0	0	2	0
Totals	2	2	0	0	5	1

The first time Wolves met United was in season 1965-66 (Division Two). The game at Molineux went Wolves' way by 3-0 but United won their home game at Brunton Park by 2-1.

Alan Sunderland netted a hat-trick in Wolves' 4-0 home win over Carlisle in October 1976. And Gary Bellamy hit a rare goal when Wolves beat United 3-1 in a Fourth Division fixture at Molineux in March 1988.

Wolves ended a run of 19 League games without a win by recording a 1-0 victory at Carlisle in April 1985 (a goal by Tony Evans in the 62nd minute did the trick).

The first of the two FA Cup clashes took place at Carlisle in the third round in January 1927 before 15,000 fans and the second was played at Molineux, also in the third round, in January 1962 when Terry Wharton netted twice for Wolves.

Players with both clubs include: Tom Baxter, Michael Bennett, Derek Clarke, Mick Coady, Ted Elliott, Willie Forbes, Bob Hatton, Leslie Heelbeck, Micky Holmes, Geoff Lomax, Scott McGarvey, Hugh McIlmoyle, Derek Mountfield, Eric Nixon, Billy Rafferty, Peter Shirtliff, Alan Steen, Ernie Tagg and Bob White.

Also associated: Andy Beattie managed both clubs, David Oliphant and John Sanderson (Wolves Reserves).

CARR, William McIanny

Willie Carr was a slightly built but highly effective midfielder who worked tirelessly, feeding his strikers and grafting hard throughout his career. Born in Glasgow on 6 January 1950, Carr moved south as a youngster and after attending Cambridge Schools, signed as an apprentice for Coventry City (July 1965), turning professional at Highfield Road two years later. In March 1975 after more than 250 appearances for the Sky Blues he was transferred to Wolves for £80,000 and in the next seven years gave the Molineux faithful some vintage moments. Carr played six times at full international level for Scotland and also won four U/23 caps as well as helping Wolves win the Second Division championship in 1977 and the League Cup in 1980. On leaving Wolves in August 1982, he teamed up with Millwall and from The Den he joined Worcester City (August 1983) and later assisted Willenhall Town and Stourbridge before retiring in 1988.
Wolves record: 289 apps. 26 goals

It was Carr, accompanied by Ernie Hunt (a former Wolves player) who instituted the famous donkey-kick (as seen on TV in November 1970). When Coventry were awarded a free-kick on the edge of the penalty area, Carr stood over the ball and then casually flicked it up and backwards for Hunt to volley into the net.

CARTER, Edward Thomas

An efficient, well built centre or left-half, Ted Carter stood in for Alf Riley and Albert Kay during his two-year stay at Molineux. Born at Harrington, Cumberland, in April 1895, he played for Ashington from August 1919 to June 1921 when he joined Wolves. On leaving Molineux in August 1923 he went back north to sign for Durham Town. Carter died *c.*1959.
Wolves record: 17 apps.

CARTWRIGHT, Archibald

Reserve inside-forward for Wolves over a two-year period: August 1907 to June 1909. Born in Wolverhampton in 1885, Archie Cartwright played for Bankside Wanderers and Willenhall Pickwick before joining Wolves and on his departure from Molineux he signed for Bilston Town. He died in Wolverhampton.
Wolves record: 2 apps.

CARTWRIGHT, Ian J.

A useful player on his day but one who never really produced consistent form at League level. Cartwright was born at Brierley Hill on 13 November 1964 and joined Wolves as a youngster on leaving school in the summer of 1980, turning professional in September 1982. He was released by the club in May 1986 when he moved into local non-League football.
Wolves record: 61 apps, 2 goals.

CASTLECROFT GROUND

On 29 September 1956, Wolves' new training ground, situated at Castlecroft, with its own stand and excellent floodlights, was officially opened by Sir Stanley Rous, secretary of the Football Association.

CASUALTIES
Deaths

These players (associated with Wolves) suffered an early death, either during their respective careers or soon after they had quit football: Harry Allen, Noel George, Ian Handysides, Jimmy Morgan, Ted Pheasant, Jimmy Utterson and David Wykes, while Joe Rooney and Billy Parker were two Wolves players who lost their lives during World War Two.

- Allen died suddenly in Walsall in 1895, aged 29.
- Goalkeeper George died in Lichfield in 1929, aged 31.
- Handysides died of a brain tumour in Solihull in 1990, aged 27.
- Morgan (aged 19) had been signed from Bristol City in 1920, but was killed when he fell from a train travelling from the West Country to the Midlands before he had played for Wolves.
- Pheasant died of peritonitis in 1910, aged 33.
- Utterson was only 21 when he died of brain damage.
- Wykes died of typhoid fever and pneumonia in 1895, aged 28.
- Two ex-Wolves players – full-back Joe Baillie and centre-half Reg Hollingworth – both died in cars, the former in a crash in Glasgow in 1966, the latter of a heart attack in Birmingham in 1969.

Injuries

Goalkeeper William George Walker had the misfortune to break his leg shortly before half-time when making his Football League debut for Wolves in the local derby away at West Bromwich Albion on 28 December 1929. The Baggies were 3-1 up at the time of Walker's misfortune and Wolves eventually lost the game 7-3. This was Walker's only appearance for the club.

Striker Don Goodman suffered a fractured skull when playing for Wolves against

Huddersfield Town at Molineux on 27 April 1996. At first the injury threatened to end his career, but after long periods of intensive treatment, the Yorkshireman regained full fitness and returned to first-team action in 1997.

John McAlle came on as a substitute for Wolves against Watford in a fifth-round FA Cup-tie at Molineux in February 1980 and broke his leg almost immediately. He was out of League action for over a year.

Centre-forward Roy Swinbourne was forced to retire with a knee injury in 1957, three months before his 28th birthday.

Ted Farmer, another striker, quit football through injury in 1964 at the age of 24.

James Hill was forced to retire through injury in 1884 at the age of 22.

CASWELL, Brian

Caswell had an excellent professional career as a defender or midfielder. He spent 14 years with Walsall – his first club – signing as a junior in June 1971, turning professional in September 1973 and remaining there until August 1985. He played in 458 League and Cup games and scored 19 goals. Born in Wednesbury on 14 February 1956, he attended and played for Wood Green School prior to linking up with the Saddlers and on leaving Fellows Park he joined Doncaster Rovers. He stayed only three months at Belle Vue before transferring to Leeds United. His brief association with Wolves came in January 1987 when he had a month's loan at Molineux. He retired in May 1987 and later coached at both Birmingham City (1990) and Stoke City. Caswell still plays in Charity matches and in 1992 helped the ex-players of West Bromwich Albion win the over 35s Cup at Wembley.

Wolves record: 1 app.

CELTIC (GLASGOW)

Wolves met the famous Scottish club four times in friendly matches, three in the 1950s. The first encounter took place on 17 April 1894 when Wolves lost 4-2 in Glasgow, Lowder and Worrall their scorers.

On 14 October 1953 The Buoys visited Molineux for the second meeting and were beaten 2-0 by Wolves under floodlights just two weeks after a South African XI had come over to play a game to 'officially' switch on the lights.

On 20 September 1954, Wolves were then invited north of the border 60 years after their first visit to play Celtic at Parkhead in a game arranged to officially turn out the Glasgow club's new floodlights.

This time the game ended all square at 3-3 after a terrific all-action contest.

Five years later, on 12 October 1959, Wolves again played Celtic at Parkhead and on this occasion they won 2-0.

Associated with both clubs: John Baillie, Danny Crainie, Tommy Docherty (Celtic player, Wolves manager), Gerry McAloon, Mark McGhee (Celtic player, Wolves manager), Jim Melrose, Frank Munro and Evan Williams. Jock Mulraney and Frank O'Donnell were wartime guests with Wolves who also assisted Celtic

CENTRAL (PONTINS) LEAGUE

Wolves first put out a reserve team at competitive level in 1891-92 when they entered the Shropshire District League. (They had earlier played friendly matches and entered the Birmingham Junior Cup in 1884-85).

They played in the Shropshire League for just one season before transferring to the Birmingham and District League in 1892-93 where they remained until 1921 when, with seven other clubs – Birmingham, Derby County, Leeds United, Sheffield United, Stoke and West Bromwich Albion – they entered the Central League (known now as the Pontins League since 1990-91). The seven sides that left the League all joined the newly-formed Third Division North. From 1921 the Central League consisted entirely of reserve teams from Football League clubs and Wolves remained in the League until 1986 when they resigned. They re-entered the competition after an absence of three years.

The Central League was formed in 1911 and Lincoln City were the first champions.

Wolves have so far won the Central League championship six times, starting in season 1931-32 when they collected a then best points tally of 61 while also scoring 126 goals. When they won the title in 1958-59 (for the sixth time) they equalled the record for most championships.

They then gained a hat-trick of triumphs, commencing in 1950-51, duly retaining the trophy in 1951-52 and adding a third success in 1952-53. A total of 126 games were played over these three campaigns and Wolves' second team ran up 80 victories, scored 288 goals (including two centuries of 110 and 101 in the first two seasons) and they amassed 181 points out of a possible 252.

Wolves' last two Central League championship wins came back-to-back, in seasons 1957-58 and 1958-59, when they scored 112 and 131 goals respectively. The latter total is their-best ever goal-haul at reserve team level in a single campaign.

Wolves have finished runners-up in the competition on three occasions: 1946-47, 1949-50 and 1962-63, and they have taken third place no fewer than ten times.

Wolves played five seasons in the Pontins League Division Two between 1983-84 and 1991-92 and were runners up in the latter campaign, having earlier gained promotion in 1989-90 when finishing in fourth place.

9-0 is Wolves' best Central/Pontins League win – achieved on two occasions v Sheffield United (h) in January 1959 (Jimmy Murray scored a hat-trick) and v Chesterfield (h) in December 1960 when Murray netted a double hat-trick (six goals) which is a club record.

Wolves' heaviest defeat has been 10-3 away at Newcastle in November 1934. They also lost 9-2 at Blackburn in November 1927 and 8-1 at Sheffield Wednesday in September 1929 as well as suffering three 7-0 reverses at Leeds in 1928, at Notts County in 1985 and away to Derby County in 1994.

In 1998-99 Wolves registered one of their best-ever reserve team wins over their arch rivals West Bromwich Albion when they beat the Baggies 5-0 at The Hawthorns.

Barry Stobart scored a record 110 Central League goals for Wolves between 1955 and 1964. Les Smith netted 74, Tudor Martin 72, Ken Whitfield 70 and Ted Farmer 68.

Tudor Martin scored 49 goals for Wolves' Reserves (League and Cup) in 1931-32 (a club record). He netted a total of 74 at reserve team level for Wolves in two seasons (1930-32) and netted in a record eight consecutive games during August and September 1931 – a feat he repeated in February and March 1932.

The fewest goals Wolves Reserves have netted in one single Central League campaign is 19, back in season 1982-83.

Wolves Reserves conceded a record 129 goals in 1927-28.

Wolves obtained a record 70 points in 1958-59 (two points for a win) and 68 in 1991-92 (three points). The fewest points gained has been 13 in season 1982-83.

A record 32 wins were registered in 1958-59 but only three were gained in 1982-83.

Wolves lost nine successive Central League games in seasons 1907-08 and 1981-82

Wolves drew 18 Central League matches in 1971-72 and suffered a record 23 defeats in 1927-28.

Wing-half Bill Baxter appeared in a club record 213 Central League matches for Wolves between 1945 and 1954. Gerry Taylor made 207 (1966-75), Les Smith 206 (1945-56), Barry Stobart 197 (1955-64) and George Showell 195 (1951-63).

Goalkeeper Jack Hampson made a club record 95 consecutive Central League appearances for Wolves (January 1923 to February 1925).

Wolves second team met the Rest of the Central League side five times during the 1950s. The results were:

29 September 1951 Wolves 3 (Deeley, Walker, Whittaker) Central League 1

27 September 1951 Wolves 2 (Whittaker 2) Central League 0

3 October 1953 Wolves 3 (Smith pen. J. Taylor, D. Taylor) Central League 2

15 November 1958 Wolves 1 (Durandt) Central League 2

24 October 1959 Wolves 6 (Read 2, Mason 2, Farmer, Stobart) Central League 0

All games were played at Molineux.

Wolves' overall record in the Central/Pontins League (1921-99)

P	W	D	L	F	A
2,746	1,289	573	894	5,177	4,051

CHADBURN, John

The moustachioed John Chadburn could play as a right-back or right-winger. A plucky footballer, he had good pace and always gave a battling performance. Born in Mansfield in February 1873, he represented Mansfield and District schools as a teenager before joining Lincoln City in 1892. Two years later he moved to Notts County from where he signed for Wolves in October 1897. He remained at Molineux for a little over two years before transferring to West Bromwich Albion in January 1900. He went on to play in almost 50 first-team games for Albion, helping them win the Second Division title in 1902. In May 1903 Chadburn switched to Liverpool, and thereafter had relatively short spells with Barnsley, Mansfield Town (1905), Reading (1906), Plymouth Argyle (1907) and Swindon Town, retiring from competitive football in 1909. He died in Mansfield in December 1923 after a short illness.

Wolves record: 12 apps. 1 goal

CHADWICK, Wilfred

Inside-forward Chadwick was a soccer 'nomad' and during a lengthy career served with eight different clubs at various levels: Bury juniors (1917), Nelson (November 1920), Rossendale United (August 1921, for whom he hit 35 goals in 23 games), Everton (from February 1922), Leeds United (signed in November 1925), Wolverhampton Wanderers (from August 1926), Stoke City (£250 in May 1929 – signed for £250) and Halifax Town (from October 1930 to May 1932). He was top-scorer at Goodison Park in 1923-24 with 30 goals and in all netted 55 times in his 109 appearances for the Merseysiders. In League action alone, Chadwick claimed 104 goals in 251 outings. A clever and at times very creative player, he was born in Bury on 7 September 1900 and died in the same Lancashire town on 14 February 1973.

Wolves record: 101 apps. 44 goals.

CHAPMAN, Campbell

Born in Sutton-in-Ashfield on 28 June 1963, midfielder Campbell, son of the former Wolves manager Sammy Chapman and brother of Cavan, began his career with Peterborough United whom he joined as an apprentice in 1978, turning professional in July 1981. He failed to make the grade at London Road and in 1982 joined non-League Bilston Town from where he switched to Wolves in December 1984. He did reasonably well at Molineux before signing as a non-contract player for Crewe Alexandra in November 1986. He remained at Gresty Road until May 1987 and later took over as player-manager of Willenhall Town (1992-93).

Wolves record: 58 apps. 4 goals.

CHAPMAN, Cavan

Younger brother of Campbell, Cavan Chapman was also a midfield player born at Emsworth on 11 September 1967 who came to Wolves on the YTS in June 1983, turning professional in September 1984. He failed to produce the goods and was released by the club two years later in May 1986. He later had a month's trial with West Bromwich Albion.

Wolves record: 1 app.

His only appearance for Wolves was in the No.9 shirt alongside his brother at Cardiff in a Second Division match in February 1985.

CHAPMAN, Samuel E.C.

Chapman had two separate spells in charge of Wolves – the first from August to September 1985 and his second from November 1985 to August 1986. Former England star Mike Channon was tipped to become the first player-manager in Wolves' history following Tommy Docherty's departure from Molineux in the summer of 1985, but surprisingly Chapman, the club's chief scout at the time, was given the job as care-taker-manager instead. He was under considerable pressure from the word go. He took the job as a temporary measure until Bill McGarry returned to the club. McGarry arrived but then left after only 61 days in office, and Wolves gave Chapman the opportunity of a second spell in the hot seat. Born in Belfast on 16 February 1938, did all he could at Molineux but things never worked out for the Irishman. He gave debuts to 18 players among them Andy Mutch, signed from non-League Southport. But results were a disaster and Wolves slithered into the Fourth Division at the end of the 1985-86 campaign. Chapman struggled on through the summer before handing over the duties to Brian Little. A year after leaving Wolves, Chapman was appointed chief scout of Leicester City and had 14 men working for him up and down the country. As a player himself, Chapman occupied the wing-half berth and served, in turn, with Shamrock Rovers, Mansfield Town (October 1956), Portsmouth (February 1958) and Mansfield again, from December 1961 to May 1964, when he retired. He won one 'B' cap for Northern Ireland and appeared in 216 Football League games, scoring 51 goals.

CHARD, Philip J.

During his career Phil Chard occupied a number of positions in defence and midfield. Born in Corby, Northamptonshire, on 16 October 1960, he joined Nottingham Forest as an amateur (1975) but failed to make the breakthrough and left to sign for his home team Corby Town (1976) from where he switched to Peterborough United in January 1979. He played well over 170 games for Posh before transferring to Northampton Town in August 1985. After 115 outings for the Cobblers he was signed by Wolves boss Graham Turner in March 1988 and in the next 18 months helped the Wanderers win promotion from the Fourth to the Second Division in successive seasons. Chard left Molineux in October 1989 to rejoin Northampton Town. He later took over as player-manager (April 1992) and held office until the summer of 1993 when he was replaced by former Wolves boss John Barnwell.

Wolves record: 38 apps. 5 goals.

CHARITY SHIELD (FA)

Wolves have played for the FA Charity Shield on five occasions, the details being:

19 Dec 1949 v Portsmouth (at Highbury)	1-1
29 Sep 1954 v West Bromwich Albion (home)	4-4
6 Dec 1958 v Bolton Wanderers (away)	1-4
15 Aug 1959 v Nottingham Forest (home)	3-1
13 Aug 1960 v Burnley (away)	2-2

Over 35,000 attended Highbury to witness the 1-1 draw with First Division champions Portsmouth in 1949.

Future Wolves manager Ronnie Allen scored a hat-trick for West Bromwich Albion in the 4-4 draw at Molineux in 1954 when over 45,000 packed into for the evening kick-off.

More than 36,000 fans attended the clash at Burnden Park in 1958 between the two Wanderers of the Football League in 1958.

There were 32,329 spectators present at Molineux to see FA Cup holders Nottingham Forest beaten by three goals to one.

And just under 20,000 supporters were present at Turf Moor to witness the 2-2 draw between FA Cup holders Wolves and League champions Burnley in 1960.

Summary of results:

P	W	D	L	F	A
5	1	3	1	11	12

CHARLTON ATHLETIC

Wolves' playing record against Athletic is:

Football League

Venue	P	W	D	L	F	A
Home	30	20	7	3	68	27
Away	30	12	6	12	47	46
Totals	60	32	13	15	115	73

FA Cup

	P	W	D	L	F	A
Home	5	4	1	0	11	3
Away	2	0	1	1	2	5
Totals	7	4	2	1	13	8

League Cup

	P	W	D	L	F	A
Home	1	0	1	0	0	0
Away	1	1	0	0	2	1
Totals	2	1	1	0	2	1

Wartime

Home	1	0	0	1	1	2
Away	1	0	1	0	1	1
Totals	2	0	1	1	2	3

Wolves and Charlton first met at League level on Boxing Day 1929 (Division Two). The game at Molineux ended in a 4-0 win for Athletic whose former Wolves player Tom Pritchard broke his left leg in the 50th minute with his parents and sisters watching from the stand.

The return fixture took place on New Year's Day when Charlton won again 2-0 in very heavy conditions.

In 1936-37, Wolves beat Charlton 6-1 at home but lost 4-1 at The Valley. Wolves scored five goals in a 20-minute spell during the second-half of that encounter at Molineux.

In 1938-39, Wolves doubled up over the Addicks, winning 3-1 at home and 4-0 in London. Dicky Dorsett scored twice in each game.

Dennis Westcott netted his 100th League goal for Wolves in the 2-0 win over Charlton in March 1947.

When Wolves crashed to a 5-1 defeat at Charlton in October 1947, Sammy Smyth took over between the posts for the injured Bert Williams.

Wolves collected two championship-winning points when they easily defeated Charlton 5-0 at Molineux in April 1954. Johnny Hancocks even missed a penalty against Charlton's legendary goalkeeper Sam Bartram who was making his 500h League appearance.

Wolves recorded their best League win over Charlton in February 1957 when they beat them 7-3 at Molineux. Wolves led 3-0 after 23 minutes. At this juncture Charlton were going through a bad patch – they conceded 36 goals in just seven matches.

In September 1982 a crowd of just over 13,000 saw Wolves beat Charlton 5-0 at Molineux. Charlton finished the game with 10 men – and five different players scored for Wolves.

The return fixture at The Valley in May 1983 saw Wolves clinch promotion to the First Division with a 3-3 draw (after being 3-0 up). Charlton's three goals came in the space of 12 second-half minutes.

Steve Bull scored his 200th League goal for Wolves in a 3-2 defeat at Charlton in April 1995.

In 1945-46 Charlton beat Wolves 6-3 on aggregate in a fourth-round FA Cup-tie. After a losing 5-2 at The Valley from being 2-1 up, Wolves could only scramble a 1-1 draw at Molineux and went out of the competition to the eventual Finalists.

On a snow-covered Molineux pitch in February 1955, Wolves produced a superb display of football to beat Charlton 4-1 in a fifth-round FA Cup-tie with Dennis Wilshaw scoring a first-half hat-trick in front of more than 49,000 spectators.

On their way to winning the FA Cup in 1960, Wolves accounted for Charlton by 2-1 at home in the fourth round.

And in the fourth round of the 1996-97 season Wolves drew at The Valley 1-1 before knocking the Addicks out 3-0 at Molineux.

The League Cup encounters took place in 1995-96 when Wolves fought hard and long in the away leg to win through to the fourth round

Players with both clubs include: Mike Bailey (also Charlton coach), Roy Bicknell, Francis Burrill, Ray Crawford, Cliff Durandt, Noel Dwyer, John Humphrey, Ted Ivill, Mick Kearns, Mick Kenning, Tony Lange, Lawrie Madden, Jim Melrose, John Pender, Tom Pritchard, Peter Shirtliff, Mike Small, Tony Towner and Shane Westley.

Also associated: James E. Baker, Bill Barron, Jock Basford, Andy De Bont (trialist), Reg Hipkin and Cyril Pearce (all Wolves Reserves) and Bobby Gould (Wolves player, Charlton coach), Albert 'Sailor' Brown and Bill Johnson (Wolves wartime guests), Jock Mulraney (Wolves and Charlton wartime guest) and Paul Emblen (Wolves trialist).

CHARNLEY, Samuel

Rather small for a centre-half at 5ft 10in tall and 11st 9lbs in weight, Scotsman Sammy Charnley was, nevertheless, a sturdy defender, who performed exceedingly well in the Wolves middle line between Jack Mitton and Albert Kay during the mid-1920s. Born in Craigneuk, near Motherwell in 1902, Charnley moved to Molineux from Burnbank Athletic in January 1925, initially as cover for Billy Caddick. He remained with Wolves until August 1928 when, following the emergence of Tom Pritchard, he was transferred by Major Buckley to York City, later assisting Dartford and then Kettering Town (September 1929 to May 1931) before moving back to Scotland to round off his career.

Wolves record: 55 apps. 1 goal.

CHATHAM, Raymond Harold

Ray Chatham was a real character, the dressing room comedian, who played as a semi-professional throughout his career, being a representative for an engineering firm based in the Midlands. Born in Wolverhampton on 20 July 1924, Chatham spent much of his childhood in Coventry and as a 16-year-old represented Coventry schoolboys before joining Wolves the following year from Oxley FC. Initially a centre-forward, Chatham was converted into a centre-half. During the transitional wartime season of 1945-46 he scored 16 goals for Wolves, but with Dennis Westcott and Jesse Pye the main attackers, he decided to change positions – for the best. After receiving a benefit in 1950, Chatham was transferred to Notts County (January 1954), but when the Magpies were relegated in 1958, he left Meadow Lane (after more than 130 appearances) and drifted into non-League soccer, ending his career in Kent with Margate. He retired in 1962 to concentrate on his job as a rep working in London. Chatham died in May 1999.

Wolves record: 86 apps. 2 goals.

CHELSEA

Wolves' playing record against Chelsea is:

Football League

Venue	P	W	D	L	F	A
Home	46	21	12	13	95	61
Away	46	15	14	17	73	87
Totals	92	36	26	30	168	148

A goal for Sammy Smyth against Charlton in November 1948.

Bert Williams dives at the feet of Chelsea's McNichol in April 1955.

FA Cup

Home	2	1	0	1	2	3
Away	1	0	0	1	0	1
Totals	3	1	0	2	2	4

Wartime

Home	1	0	1	0	1	1
Away	1	1	0	0	1	0
Totals	2	1	1	0	2	1

The first time Wolves met Chelsea at League level was in season 1906-07 (Division Two) and it was the Londoners who came out on top, winning both games: 2-1 at Molineux and 4-0 at Stamford Bridge.

In 1911-12 Chelsea beat Wolves 4-0 at Stamford Bridge while Wolves won 3-1 at Molineux.

Harry Scott scored twice for Wolves in a 3-3 draw with Chelsea at Stamford Bridge in March 1926.

In September 1933, Wolves crashed 5-2 at Molineux to Chelsea – their worst home defeat at the hands of the Londoners.

Thirteen goals were scored in the two League games between Wolves and Chelsea in 1934-35. A crowd of 48,000 saw Chelsea win 4-2 at Stamford Bridge while 32,700 witnessed the return game at Molineux when Wolves triumphed 6-1, all seven goals coming from different players.

Unruly fans got onto the pitch and uprooted a goalpost during Wolves' home League game with Chelsea in November 1936. The visitors won 2-1.

The first Wolves v Chelsea League game at Molineux after World War Two resulted in a 6-4 home win for the Wanderers with three players – Willie Forbes, Johnny Hancocks and Dennis Westcott – each scoring twice.

In September 1951 an eight-goal thriller at Molineux went Wolves' way by 5-3, Jesse Pye scoring twice for the Wanderers. In fact, during the last six minutes of this game four goals were scored, Wolves going from 4-0 up to win 5-3.

The Wolves v Chelsea First Division game at Molineux in February 1953 attracted just 13,957 spectators – the lowest League attendance at the ground since May 1937. It ended all square at 2-2.

When Wolves won the First Division title in 1953-54, they whipped Chelsea 8-1 at Molineux in late September – their best win over the Blues. Over 36,000 fans saw Johnny Hancocks score a hat-trick that day.

Peter Sillett's match-winning penalty for Chelsea towards the end of the First Division game at Stamford Bridge in April 1955, virtually clinched the League title for the Londoners in front of 75,043 fans. Billy Wright conceded the spot-kick by handling Seamus O'Connell's shot.

Jimmy Greaves scored five of Chelsea's goals in their 6-2 League victory over Wolves at Stamford Bridge in August 1958.

Wolves beat Chelsea 5-1 at at Stamford Bridge in a League game on 30 April 1960 just a week before they travelled back to London to defeat Blackburn Rovers in the FA Cup Final.

After a 3-3 draw with Chelsea in London early in the 1960-61 season, the return fixture at Molineux went all one way, Wolves winning in style by 6-1 with Jimmy Murray netting a hat-trick.

The following season a nine-goal thriller at Stamford Bridge ended in Wolves' favour by 5-4, Chris Crowe scoring twice.

It was goals all the way in season 1963-64 with Wolves winning 4-1 at home and 3-2 away – Terry Wharton scored twice at Molineux and Ray Crawford likewise at Stamford Bridge.

Hugh Curran scored four times for Wolves against Chelsea in 1969-70 – netting both his sides goals in the 2-2 away draw and then adding two more when Chelsea were beaten 3-0 at Molineux.

When Wolves beat Chelsea 7-1 at home in March 1975, six different Wanderers' players

figured on the scoresheet, John Richards netting twice.

Chelsea drew their penultimate League game 1-1 in front of a near 33,465 crowd at Molineux in May 1977 to clinch promotion back to the First Division, going up with Wolves.

Chelsea have so far completed eight League doubles over Wolves, who in turn have recorded seven over Chelsea, the last in 1974-75.

Wolves lost 1-0 to Tottenham Hotspur in the 1921 FA Cup Final at Stamford Bridge.

Chelsea knocked Wolves out of the FA Cup at the quarter-final stage in season 1993-94, winning a tight contest 1-0 at Stamford Bridge in front of a near capacity 29,340 crowd.

The 1958 FA Youth Cup Final between Wolves and Chelsea was a classic encounter. After losing the first leg 5-1 at Stamford Bridge when Chelsea were inspired by Jimmy Greaves, Wolves' youngsters stormed back and took the return fixture 6-1 at Molineux to record a stunning 7-6 aggregate victory. Ted Farmer netted four of Wolves' goals in that return leg.

Wolves played Chelsea five times on their Caribbean tour in 1964. They won two, 3-1 and 4-2, but lost the other three by 3-2, 3-0 and 2-0.

Players with both clubs include: Billy Barraclough, Jim Barron, Dave Beasant, Richard Deacon, Michael Gilkes, Ray Goddard, Tommy Langley, Jim McCalliog, Stuart McMillan, Jack Smith and Reg Weaver.

Also associated: Tommy Docherty (managed both clubs); Colin Lee (Chelsea player, Wolves manager), Frank Upton (Chelsea player and assistant manager, Wolves coach), Bobby Gould (Wolves player, Chelsea assistant manager); John Harris (Wolves Scottish wartime international, Chelsea defender), Don Howe and Charles Livesey, (Wolves amateur, Chelsea coach); Keith Downing (Chelsea trial), Billy Gold and James Lee, Herbert Barlow, Billy Crook, Eric Jones, Bert Williams and Billy Wrigglesworth (all Chelsea wartime guests) and Frank Munro (Chelsea trialist).

CHELTENHAM TOWN

Wolves knocked non-League Cheltenham Town out of the FA Cup in the first round of the 1987-88 competition, beating them 5-1 at Molineux in front of 10,541 fans. Steve Bull scored a hat-trick.

Players with both clubs include: Vince Bartram, Chris Brindley, Mark Buckland, Mel Eves, Andy Gray, Tony Lange, Steve Mardenborough, Barry Powell, Jon Purdie and Darren Wright.

Also associated: Jim Barron and Ally Robertson (Wolves players, Cheltenham managers). In May 1940 Dennis Westcott

(Wolves) was paid £4 to play for Cheltenham against Worcester City – the maximum wage at the time was £1.50.

CHESTER CITY

Wolves' playing record against Chester is:

Football League

Venue	P	W	D	L	F	A
Home	1	1	0	0	3	1
Away	1	0	1	0	1	1
Total	2	1	1	0	4	2

FA Cup

Venue	P	W	D	L	F	A
Home	1	1	0	0	1	0

Wartime

Venue	P	W	D	L	F	A
Home	4	3	0	1	11	7
Away	4	4	0	0	11	2
Total	8	7	0	1	22	9

The two League games took place in season 1988-89 and Andy Mutch scored in both games for Wolves. The clash at Chester attracted 8,236 fans.

A goal by Kenny Hibbitt gave Wolves their 1-0 FA Cup victory over Chester in the fifth round of the FA Cup in 1976-77.

Guest player Jimmy Jinks scored a hat-trick for Wolves when they beat Chester 6-1 in a Football League North game at Molineux in January 1945.

Players with both clubs include: George Ashall, Ted Anderson, Bob Coy, Ted Elliott, Gerry Mannion, Cyrille Regis, Mike Stowell, Guy Wharton, Ernie Whittam, Dave Wintersgill and Peter Zelem.

Also associated: Graham Turner (Chester player, Wolves manager); Chris Evans (Chester player, Wolves coach); Jock Basford, Tommy Burden, John Evans, David Felgate, Ron Hewitt, Dennis Isherwood, Arthur Keeley, Bill Prendergast, David Read, John T. Turner, Trevor Walters and Arthur Wilson (all Wolves Reserves), Ray King (amateur) and Jimmy Alderton, Bill Bryant, Bill Coley, Johnny Hancocks, Fred Pincott and Guy Wharton (all Chester wartime guests).

CHESTERFIELD

Wolves' playing record against the Spireites is:

Football League

Venue	P	W	D	L	F	A
Home	7	6	1	0	15	2
Away	7	2	2	3	8	10
Total	14	8	3	3	23	12

FA Cup

Venue	P	W	D	L	F	A
Home	1	1	0	0	6	0

League Cup

Venue	P	W	D	L	F	A
Home	1	0	1	0	1	1
Away	1	1	0	0	3	1
Total	2	1	1	0	4	2

The first two League games took place in season 1906-07, Wolves winning 2-1 at Molineux but losing 3-2 at Chesterfield.

George Hedley scored twice for Wolves in their 3-0 home win over Chesterfield in January 1909 and Walter Bottrill and Charlie Phillips both netted twice in Wolves' 6-0 victory over Chesterfield in September 1931.

The last time the teams met in the League was in January 1989, when Wolves were triumphant by a goal to nil at Molineux, Nigel Vaughan the scorer.

That emphatic 6-0 FA Cup victory by Wolves came in the third round of the 1948-49 competition at Molineux when over 40,000 fans saw Jesse Pye and Sammy Smyth each score twice.

The two League Cup games were played in 1994-95, Wolves winning a second round tie 4-2 on aggregate. There were almost 15,000 fans present to see the clash at Molineux.

Players with both clubs include: John Bell, Gary Bellamy, Alan Birch, Walter Bottrill, Nicky Clarke, Bob Coy, Mick Gooding, Joe Hodnett, Mark Kendall, Lawrie Madden, Cyril Ordish, Fred Price, Darren Roberts, Phil Robinson, David Thompson, Dennis Westcott, Billy Wrigglesworth, Jermaine Wright and Harry Wright.

Also associated: George Swift (Wolves player, Chesterfield secretary), Joe Miller and Bill Tudsley (Wolves Reserves) and Meynell Burgin (Chesterfield wartime guest).

CHORLEY

Wolves' playing record against Chorley is:

FA Cup

Venue	P	W	D	L	F	A
Home	1	0	1	0	1	1
Neutral	2	0	1	1	1	4
Total	3	0	1	2	2	5

After three attempts and 300 minutes of action, non-League Chorley sensationally knocked Fourth Division Wolves out of the FA Cup in the first round in November 1986. The initial encounter took place at Burnden Park, Bolton where a crowd of 4,887 witnessed a 1-1 draw. The Molineux replay, three days later, also ended in a 1-1 draw after extra-time in front of 4,790 fans and then in the second replay, again at Bolton, 5,421 witnessed a Chorley victory by 3-0.

Wolves boss Graham Turner said after this ignominious defeat: "Ally Robertson pulled a thigh muscle after only ten minutes play and was still our best player. That says a lot."

This was the first time Wolves had been knocked out of the competition by a non-League side since losing to Mansfield Town of the Midland League in January 1929.

Played for both clubs: Jack Nelson.

Associated with both clubs: Tony Bond, Chris Pearce, Richard Twiss and George Waddell (all Wolves Reserves).

CHRISTMAS DAY

Wolves have played 27 League games on Christmas Day (most of them having an 11am or 12 noon kick-off).

The first was in 1901 when they travelled to Derby County only to lose 3-1.

The first one at Molineux was in 1906 when Stockport County held Wolves to a 1-1 draw, and Wolves' first Christmas Day victory arrived the following year when Billy Harrison's goal saw off Gainsborough Trinity.

In 1909 it was Harrison again who took the limelight, scoring the only goal of the away game at West Bromwich Albion and amazingly the same player made it a hat-trick of Christmas Day goals when he netted Wolves' effort in the 1-1 draw with Leicester Fosse in 1911.

On 25 December 1914 Wolves crashed 5-1 at Hull and in 1922 they were well and truly walloped at Coventry City, losing 7-1 in front of 16,000 crowd at Highfield Road.

Two goals by Tom Phillipson earned Wolves victory at Oldham (2-1) in 1925 and the same player scooped a five-timer 12 months later when Bradford City were trounced 7-2 at Molineux.

A trip to London over Christmas 1929 ended in a 4-0 defeat at Charlton and the following season Wolves went down 2-0 at Oldham.

In 1931 a crowd of over 33,000 saw Wolves beaten 3-2 at home by Manchester United and there were 50,000 at Villa Park in 1932 when Wolves won 3-1, aided by two goals from Jimmy Deacon.

However, it was a completely different story in 1933 when Villa gained revenge by slamming Wolves 6-2 on Christmas Day in front of 57,000 fans.

Bob Iverson, Tom Smalley and Billy Wrigglesworth scored in Wolves' 3-0 win at Bolton on Christ's birthday 1935 and the following year Huddersfield were defeated 3-1 at Molineux with Tom Galley among the scorers.

The first post-war Christmas Day League match was in 1946 when a Johnny Hancocks goal gave Wolves a 1-0 at Sunderland, and Jesse Pye and Sammy Smyth both netted twice in Wolves' 4-0 home win over Aston Villa in 1948 when the crowd was almost 40,000.

Three years later in December 1951, Wolves shared six goals at Villa Park in front of an audience of 49,525 and then in December 1956 Wolves played their last ever Christmas Day match, travelling south to London, where they lost 2-1 to Charlton Athletic in front of a near 16,000 crowd. And Colin Booth had the pleasure of scoring Wolves' last goal.

CHUNG, Cyril

Sammy Chung – as he was unversally known – managed Wolves for five months – from June to November 1976, serving between the reigns of Bill McGarry and John Barnwell. Known affectionately as Sammy, Chung was born in Abingdon, Oxford on 16 July 1932 to a Chinese father and English mother, and was a part-time professional with Headington United (now Oxford United) before moving into the Football League as a wing-half with Reading in August 1949. After completing his Army service in November 1951 he signed professional forms at Elm Park and remained there until January 1955 when he switched to Norwich City for £6,000. A year-and-a-half later he moved to Watford where he stayed for eight years, amassing almost 250 League and Cup appearances for the Hornets, scoring 25 goals. During his time at Vicarage Road, Chung gained his FA coaching badge and graduated to player-coach with Watford. In July 1963 he came in contact with Bill McGarry for the first time when the former England international became manager of the Hornets. McGarry gave Chung three months to prove his worth as a coach. He did just that and when McGarry left to become boss of Ipswich Town in 1964, he took Chung with him, and in double-quick time, between them they guided the Portman Road club to the top of the Second Division. In 1967 Chung became manager of the Swedish side, IFK Vastera before returning to England as McGarry's assistant at Wolves, taking over the mantle himself as team manager at Molineux in 1976. He left Wolves for the United Arab Emirates, but when Mick Mills was appointed boss of Stoke City in May 1985, he asked Chung to be his No.2 (the pair having worked together at Ipswich). Chung remained at the Victoria Ground for two years, leaving the Potteries to take over as manager of the Beazer Homes League side Tamworth where he stayed until January 1993. After a brief association as scout with Blackburn Rovers, he was named manager of Doncaster Rovers in July 1994, a position he held until 1997. In January 1999, at the age of 66, Chung was appointed director of football in Barbados.

CHURCH (THE)

In 1912-13 Wolves had two Reverends on their books – Kenneth Hunt and Billy Jordan. This was the first time two parsons had ever been registered with the same club in a Football League season.

CLAMP, Harold Edwin

Eddie Clamp was a wing-half, who was dubbed 'Chopper' by the fans at Molineux. Born in Coalville (Leicestershire) on 14 September 1934, he was a pupil at the village state school and actually joined Wolverhampton Wanderers halfway through his paper round. This was in 1949. Wolves' boss Stan Cullis immediately placed him the club's nursery team, Wath Wanderers, where his game developed rapidly. Clamp turned professional in April 1952 and made his

senior debut in the gold and black; strip in March 1954 against Manchester United at Old Trafford in front of almost 39,000 fans. This was the start of a superb career for Chopper, who won two First Division championship medals (1958 and 1959) and an FA Cup winners medal in 1960. He also received four England caps (1958) when he starred alongside his team-mates Billy Wright and Bill Slater to form an all-Wolves half-back line. Clamp left Molineux in November 1961 to sign for Arsenal for £12,000, but he never settled in London and left Highbury after only 10 months, switching to Stoke City in September 1962 to be re-united with his former Wolves colleague Eddie Stuart. He helped the Potters regain their First Division status in 1963 and played in 62 games (two goals scored) during his time at the Victoria Ground before leaving for Peterborough United in October 1964. After a season at London Road (when he took his career tally up to 335 League games) Clamp then had brief spells with Worcester City and Lower Gornal, and finally called it a day in 1970, although he still figured in the occasional charity match for the Wolves Old Stars. Thereafter he ran his own business and was a regular visitor to both the Victoria Ground and Molineux right up until his death on 10 November 1995. Clamp's mother was the laundry lady at Molineux during the 1950s.
Wolves record: 241 apps. 25 goals.

CLARIDGE, Stephen

Since making his League debut for Bournemouth in 1984, striker Steve Claridge has made and scored goals wherever he's played. A real workhorse, no matter what the circumstances, he often had his socks rolled down near his ankles as he grafted tirelessly away. Born in Portsmouth on 4 October 1966, he began his career at Fratton Park in 1982, but he failed to make the breakthrough and in November 1984 moved to nearby Bournemouth. After Dean Court he was on the books of Crystal Palace and Weymouth before signing for Aldershot in October 1988. From the Recreation Ground, Claridge went to Cambridge United for £75,000 in February 1990; he joined Luton Town for £160,000 in July 1992, only to return to the Abbey Stadium four months later, this time for £195,000. In January 1995, Birmingham City boss Barry Fry took Claridge to St Andrew's for a fee of £325,000 and in March 1996, almost four times that amount changed hands when a record £1.2 million deal was struck with Leicester City. Some of that money was quickly paid back as Claridge netted the Wembley Play-off winner, which shot the Foxes into the Premiership. Then he helped Leicester win the Coca-Cola Cup and get into Europe. His next move on the football merry-go-round took Claridge from

Filbert Street to Wolves in March 1998 for £350,000, but he never really settled in at Molineux and was transferred to Portsmouth for £200,000 in August 1998. Then when Wolves played Pompey in a League game soon after his move, he was involved in a penalty incident which saw Keith Curle sent-off. In season 1998-99 Claridge reached the milestone of 500 appearances at club level – and he's scored almost 140 goals
Wolves record: 5+1 apps.

CLARKE, Derek

A member of the famous footballing family, Derek Clarke, like his brothers Allan and Wayne, was also a fine goalscorer. Born in Willenhall on 19 February 1950, he left school in 1965 and immediately joined Walsall, turning professional at Fellows Park in December 1967. From there he moved to Molineux (May 1968) but owing to the number of established goalscorers in the camp, he was allowed to leave Wolves for Oxford United for £11,500 in October 1970. He did well at the Manor Ground, scoring 40 goals in less than 200 League and Cup games before switching to Leyton Orient in August 1976. He played for the Londoners in their 1978 FA Cup semi-final defeat by Arsenal and the following year, after a loan spell with Carlisle United (October 1978) Clarke dropped into non-League soccer in the south east.
Wolves record: 3 apps.

CLARKE, Nicholas J.

Defender Nicky Clarke was born in Willenhall on 20 August 1967 and joined the Molineux apprentice staff on leaving school in June 1983, turning professional in February 1985. He took time to establish himself in the first team, but then a terrible knee injury sidelined him for two seasons before he left Molineux for Mansfield Town in December 1991 for a fee of £25,000. The following season Clarke helped the Stags win promotion from Division Four. He later had a loan spells with Chesterfield (March/April 1993), Doncaster Rovers (December 1993) and Preston (March 1994) before moving into non-League football with Bromsgrove Rovers, switching to Bilston Town in August 1997.
Wolves record: 88+9 apps. 1 goal

CLARKE, Wayne

A former England schoolboy and youth international and West Midlands representative player, Clarke had two spells with Wolves. The first lasted eight years from June 1976 and the second time was on loan in September 1991. Born in Willenhall on 28 February 1961, Clarke, a natural goal-poacher, like his two senior brothers Allan, Derek and Frank) was signed initially by Wolves as

an apprentice at the age of 15 and turned professional in March 1978. He was transferred from Molineux to Birmingham City for £80,000 in August 1984 and then after scoring 43 goals in 105 games for Blues he left St Andrew's in March 1987 to join Everton for £500,000. Whilst at Goodison Park he quickly gained a League Championship medal, but the arrival on Merseyside of Tony Cottee prompted his departure to Leicester City in July 1989 for £500,000. In January 1990 Clarke moved to Manchester City and after loan spells with Shrewsbury Town, Stoke City and Wolves, he quit Maine Road to team up with his old Wolves colleague Kenny Hibbitt at Walsall (August 1992). He gave the Saddlers excellent service before returning to Shrewsbury Town for two seasons from July 1993. He then quit senior soccer and entered non-League football with Telford United as player-manager in August 1995, resigning his position in November 1996. In all Clarke netted over 130 goals in more than 500 League appearances during a fine career. In 1999 Clarke surprisingly became a postman.
Wolves record: 171 apps. 33 goals

When Wolves were relegated at the end of the 1981-82 season it completed an unhappy sequence for the Clarke family. The Wolves striker became the fifth brother to suffer a similar fate with a different club. Allan was with Fulham when they went down in 1967-68, and Leicester City in 1968-69; Frank with Carlisle in 1974-75, Derek with Oxford in 1975-76 and Kevin with Walsall in 1978-79. Allan, as manager of Leeds United in 1981-82, also suffered a similar experience.

CLAYTON, James Gordon George

Former policeman Clayton was a tall, strapping centre-forward with a fine scoring record. Born in Sunderland in July 1910, he joined Wolves from Shotton Colliery in October 1932 and spent five years at Molineux before transferring to Aston Villa in October 1937. Clayton helped Villa win the Second Division title that season, but in October 1938 he was sold to Burnley. He retired in 1945 after guesting for Swansea Town during World War Two
Wolves record: 55 apps. 39 goals.

CLEWS, Malcolm Derek
Born in Tipton on 12 March 1931, inside-forward Malcolm Clews was at Molineux at a time when there was ample strength in all front-line positions – consequently his first-team outings were limited to just one. He signed for Wolves on leaving school in 1946 and turned professional under manager Stan Cullis in February 1948. Amazingly he stayed with the club for the next six years, playing happily in the Reserves before deciding to leave Molineux for Lincoln

City in February 1954. He played just seven games for the Imps who released him in May 1955 when he entered non-League football back in the West Midlands. Clews also played a lot of club cricket.
Wolves record: 1 app.

CLIFF, Thomas
A hard-nut defender, born in Wolverhampton in December 1860, Cliff joined the club from St Luke's in August 1883, but spent only two years with Wolves before moving to Excelsior in 1885.
Wolves record: 4 FA Cup apps.

COACHING/TRAINING STAFF
Here is a list of Wolves' first-team trainers: 1890 to date, remembering that from the mid-1960s the trainer became commonly known as the club's physiotherapist:

1880s	Beaumont Shaw
1890-97	Jack Lewis
1891-1920	Albert Fletcher
1905-08	Edward Judson
1915-20	Jackery Jones
1918-45	Jack Davies
1920-23	Elijah (Eli) Morse
1922-32	George Holley
1931-35	Jack Bradford
1945-48	Jack Smith
1943-69	Jack Dowen
1944-64	Joe Gardiner
1946-69	George Palmer
1957-64	Bill Shorthouse
1971-78	Toby Anderson
1978-80	Kevin Walters
1980-82	John Maylam
1983-85	Denis Conyard LCSP (Phys)
1985-86	Eddie Edwards
1986-94	Paul Darby
1994-99	Barry Holmes
1995-99	Dave Hancock
1998-99	Kevin O'Leary

John Jackson was assistant trainer at Molineux in the early 1900s. He played for Singers FC (Coventry), managed Loughborough, was trainer at West Bromwich Albion (early 1890s), did a similar job at Liverpool (1895-96), managed Brighton United from 1898 to 1900, Brighton and Hove Albion from 1901 to 1905 and Blackpool in 1907-08.

Harry Dillard was Wolves' reserve-team trainer for 27 years from 1892 to 1919. He earlier played for Walsall Town Swifts and was also the Swifts' official umpire in first-team matches.

John Henry (Jack) Davies was born in Wrexham and during his time as trainer at Molineux, Wolves won both the Second and Third Division North championships, the wartime League Cup and lost in the Final of the FA Cup (1939).

Up until the 1960s trainers invariably acted also as coaches.

Wolves Coaches
Over the years, certainly since just after World War One, Wolves had a senior coach working for the team manager, as well as other coaches working with the Reserves and youth teams. Here is a list of some of the coaches who have been employed at Molineux:

1920/30s	Jack Bradford, Valentine Gregory
1940s	Jack Gardiner, Jack Davies, Jack Nelson
1950s	Jack Screen, Alf Crook, Cyril Sidlow
1965-66	Ronnie Allen
1966-68	Ron Bradley
1967-69	Gerry Summers
1967-70	Gordon Eddlestone,
1967-72	Sammy Chung*
1970-74	John Jarman
1976-79	Brian Owen
1978-79	Brian Garvey
1979-80	Richie Barker*
1979-82	Ian Ross
1981-84	Jim Barron
1982-84	Ron Bradley
1983-85	Frank Upton
1984-85	Mick Docherty
1985-87	Greg Fellows
1986-87	Garry Pendrey*
1988-91	Barry Powell
1989-90	Jim Barron
1989-94	Garry Pendrey*
1991-95	Chris Evans
1994-96	Steve Harrison/Stuart Gray/Robert Kelly
1995-96	Bobby Downes*/Ian Miller Chris Turner/Mike Hickman John Ward*
1999	Keith Downing

(*also acted as assistant manager)
George Palmer (masseur/physiotherapist) served in the Navy for 26 years attaining the rank of warrant officer.

Mick Docherty was at Molineux when his father Tommy was manager of Wolves.

Former Wolves 1930s winger Eric Jones was on the coaching staff at Lilleshall (late 1950s). He also acted as trainer-coach with Port Vale in 1962.

Wolves 1950s trialist Don Howe became a prominent member of the FA coaching staff during the 1970s, a position he holds today. He also coached with Arsenal, Galatasary (Turkey), Leeds United, England 'B', in Saudi Arabia, Bristol Rovers, Wimbledon and Barnet.

Chris Evans later became Wolves' youth development officer.

Tony Lacey (ex-Stoke City and Port Vale) became Wolves' youth recruitment officer in 1998.

COADY, Michael Liam
Mike Coady was brought back to England from the Australian club Sidney Olympic in

January 1985 by Wolves manager Tommy Docherty. A steady full-back, he unfortunately failed to impress at Molineux and after spending two-and-a-half years with the club, he was transferred to Lincoln City. Born in Dipton, County Durham on 1 October 1958, Coady had played for Sunderland (apprentice June 1975, professional from July 1976) and then Carlisle United (from July 1980 to 1982) before trying his luck 'down under'. He made over 50 League appearances during his time at Brunton Park.

Wolves record: 14+1 apps. 1 goal

COCK, Donald James

Strong, bustling utility forward with a fierce shot, who was a regular goalscorer as well as being a fine distributor of the ball throughout his career. Born at Hayle, Cornwall on 8 July 1896, and brother of the former Chelsea, Everton and England star Jack Cock, and Herbert, once of Brentford, Don played Army football in 1917-18 and was a reserve with Brentford before joining Fulham in June 1919. He then had a two-and-a-half year association with Notts County (October 1922 to March 1925, signed for £1,750) prior to teaming up with Arsenal for £4,000. He stayed at Highbury only a few months, moving across London to Clapton Orient for £1,500 in October 1925. From there he joined Wolves for £1,000 in July 1927, but spent barely six weeks at Molineux before going to Newport County in a £750,000 deal in September of that same year. Cock, who broke a leg whilst at Highbury, died at Bradmore, Wolverhampton on 31 August 1974.

Wolves record: 3 apps. 1 goal.

COCKER, Leslie James

As a teenager Cocker won 11 England youth caps as a wing-half, skippered Wolves' Staffordshire League side to the championship in 1957-58 and was also a member of the club's successful FA Youth Cup winning side that same season. He spent five years in the Reserves at Molineux, playing in the shadows of Messrs Clamp, Slater and Flowers among others. Born in Wolverhampton on 18 September 1939, and educated in the town, Cocker joined Wolves as a junior in 1956, turned professional in June 1958 and was released in 1960. He later became senior trainer with Leeds United (under Don Revie) and spent several memorable years at Elland Road, also acting as trainer to various England teams over the same period (1960s-early 1970s).

Wolves record: 1 app.

COLCHESTER CHALLENGE CUP

The Final of the 1938 Colchester Challenge Cup was between Wolves and Arsenal at Layer Road and attracted a bumper crowd of 17,584. Both teams fielded mixed sides consisting of first and second team players, and Wolves ran out 1-0 winners, Harry Thompson scoring.

COLCHESTER UNITED

Wolves' playing record against United is:

Football League

Venue	P	W	D	L	F	A
Home	2	2	0	0	4	0
Away	2	0	1	1	1	3
Totals	4	2	1	1	5	3

Play-Offs

	P	W	D	L	F	A
Home	1	0	1	0	0	0
Away	1	0	1	0	2	2
Totals	2	0	2	0	2	2

Wolves' four League meetings with Colchester were over two successive seasons of Fourth Division football (1986-88). United's only victory was a 3-0 success at Layer Road on 31 October 1986 while Wolves' recorded two 2-0 scorelines, both at Molineux, in March 1987 and April 1988.

The two Play-off games were the home and away legs of the 1986-87 Fourth Division semi-final, which Wolves won on the away goal rule after a disappointing performance at Molineux. The 4,829 attendance at Layer Road was United's best of the season.

Players with both clubs include: James Baker, Billy Barraclough, Scott Barrett, Herbert Barlow, David Barnes, Roy Bicknell, Davey Burnside, Ray Crawford, Roger Hansbury and Brian Owen.

Also associated: Brian Garvey (United player, Wolves coach), Bert Barlow (United guest), Bill Prendergast (Wolves Reserves).

COLEMAN, Simon

Experienced central defender, signed on a month's loan from Bolton Wanderers in September 1997 when injuries disrupted Wolves' back four plans. Simon Coleman was born in Worksop on 19 October 1966 and began his professional career with Mansfield Town in July 1985. He played almost 120 games for the Stags before a £400,000 transfer took him to Middlesbrough in September 1989. From Ayresome Park he moved to Derby County for £300,000 in August 1991 and in January 1994 Sheffield Wednesday boss Trevor Francis engaged him at Hillsborough for £325,000 after he had made almost a century of appearances for the Rams. Coleman's next move – in October 1994 – saw him join Bolton Wanderers for £350,00, and he did well with the Lancashire club, helping them win a place in the Premiership in 1997. After returning to the Reebok Stadium, from his loan spell at Molineux Coleman moved to Southend United in February 1998.

Wolves record: 3+1 apps.

COLEY, William Ernest

Bill Coley was a well built, hard-tackling left-half who spent six years at Molineux during which time he played mainly in the reserve and intermediate teams. Born in Wolverhampton on 17 September 1916, he played for Dudley Road School. He represented Wolverhampton Town Boys (playing alongside Len Astill) and served with Belle Vue Rovers before joining with Wolves as an amateur in May 1931, turning professional in September 1933. Four years later, in May 1937 he was transferred to Bournemouth. In July 1938 he switched to Torquay United (for £500) and in August 1947 Coley signed for Northampton Town, having guested for the Cobblers as well as Chester, Bristol City and Tranmere Rovers during the war. He later served with Exeter City (from July 1951) before retiring in May 1953. At that juncture he returned to Northampton as reserve-team coach, a position he retained until May 1955. He scored seven goals in 112 games for Northampton and was, in fact, the first Cobblers player to be sent-off after the war. He was fined £2 for this misdemeanour. In later years he became a hotelier on the south coast, playing club cricket until well past his sixtieth birthday.

Coley's father, Albert, played for Wolves' second team in 1906.

Wolves record: 2 apps.

COLLEY, A. J. Robert

Bob Colley played two seasons with Wolves – 1899-1901 – and during that time acted as reserve outside-right. He was later with Newtown and Shrewsbury Town (1907-08), Wellington Town, Stafford Rangers (1911-12) and Darlaston. He was a local man, born c.1875 whose father ran an ironmonger's shop in Wolverhampton.

Wolves record: 8 apps. 2 goals.

COLLINS, Edward

Full-back Ted Collins was a rock-hard performer, born in Wolverhampton on 16 June 1884, who started his career with Bilston United and played next for Verity Athletic (Birmingham Works Association) and Brownhills Albion before joining Wolves in August 1907, quickly making his senior debut for the club against rivals West Bromwich Albion. He formed a fine partnership with Jack Jones and remained at Molineux until 1915 when he moved to Sunbeam Motors, later assisting Newport County (from 1917), Notts County (albeit briefly in 1919-20) and Hednesford Town. During the hostilities Collins guested for Port Vale and Walsall, and once scored five goals for the Saddlers as an emergency centre-forward. He helped Wolves win the FA Cup in 1908. It is believed he died in the 1960s.

Wolves record: 307 apps.

COLOURS

The first colours donned by Wolves players back in the 1870s were blue and white striped jerseys. In 1881 the blue stripes were changed to red ones, possibly because of a certain team down the road. And one of the earliest colour photographs seen of Wolves depicts the players clad in red and white striped jerseys and black shorts.

Come 1891 the decision was taken to change the kit to gold and black diagonal halves (black shorts), thus representing the town's motto of 'Out of darkness cometh light.' This, in fact, was the strip worn by the club which won the FA Cup in 1893.

The following year a gold and black striped shirt was introduced and in 1896 the stripes became much broader and were worn on and off until after World War Two when a slimmer stripe was brought in.

In 1923 the colour of Wolves jerseys changed again – this time to being basically all gold with a black collar and 'V' which was on the front and back of each shirt.

This design was short-lived and in 1926 the gold and black striped shirt returned, although shortly after the club chose to have a brief flirtation with gold shirts graced with two black hoops just below the collar accompanied with the traditional black shorts.

Come the end of the 'roaring twenties' the Molineux directors decided on another kit change – one which was to last for over 25 years – this being an old gold shirt, with button-up black collar and cuffs and black shorts. And when Wolves played in the 1939 FA Cup Final, a badge was sewn on to the front of each player's jersey – this was believed to be the first time that the town's coat of arms, or indeed, any badge/insignia had ever been seen on a Wolves football shirt.

At the start of the 1954-55 season the colour of the shirts changed from old gold to gold and the button-up collar was replaced with a 'V' neck design. This kit was kept for over a decade, until relegation was suffered from the top flight in 1965 and during Wolves' time in the Second Division, numbered gold shorts matched the gold shirts.

But once First Division football was back at Molineux manager Billy McGarry reverted back to black shorts – this also being a popular choice with the fans.

Since then, the world famous gold shirt and black shorts have remained in place, to a certain extent, although occasionally slightly different designs have been utilised with black pencil-stripes coming into view at one time, along with several new logos including the 'WW' badge, among others. And there have also been many sponsors' names which have taken up a prominent position on the front of each shirt since the early 1980s.

Over the years Wolves' change strip has changed considerably and there have been instances whereby the players have worn all white, all light blue, black and white, occasionally red and white, even green and black and yellow. In the early days it is said that from time to time hooped shirts were worn as well as quartered jerseys.

COMMERCIAL MANAGERS (1978-1999)

Wolves first appointed a commercial manager in 1978. He was the former World Cup Final referee, Jack Taylor. Since then five other men have held the position: Joe Witherington (two spells), Nick Mannering, Mark Witherington, Keith Butler and the man in office now (1999) Gary Lever, who first watched Wolves as an eight-year-old in 1968.

Eric Woodward, former player Derek Dougan and Gordon Dimbleby (1985-86) have all held the post of chief executive at Molineux, and in 1992 David Clayton (formerly with Goodyear) was appointed director of marketing and public affairs at Molineux, holding office until 1997.

CONNOLLY, David James

Connolly, a Republic of Ireland international forward, was signed by Wolves boss Mark McGhee on a year's loan from the Dutch club Feyenoord in August 1998 – the deal finally going through after four months of negotiations. Born in London of Irish parents on 8 August 1977, Connolly signed professional forms for Watford – his first club – in November 1994, and he scored eight goals in his first 13 League games for the Hornets, six of which were as a substitute. He went to Holland in the summer of 1997 but never really succeeded over there and was always looking to come back to England. In November 1998 he became a big hero with the Wolves fans by scoring four goals in an emphatic 6-1 League win at Bristol City.
Wolves record: 20+15 apps. 6 goals.

CONWAY, Arthur Albert J.

A former Halesowen player (1905-07), right-half Conway signed for Wolves in the summer of 1908 after failing to make the grade with Aston Villa. He took time to establish himself at Molineux and, indeed, it wasn't until the following season that he finally gained a permanent position in the side. Surprisingly, in July 1910 after being replaced by Albert Groves, he left Wolves and joined his old club Halesowen, later assisting Cradley Heath and Netherton. Conway was born in Stourbridge in 1886 and died in the Black Country *c.*1951.
Wolves record: 30 apps.

COOK, Paul Anthony

Midfielder Cook was born in Liverpool on 22 February 1967 and began his career with Marine before becoming a professional with Wigan Athletic in July 1984. In May 1988, after 100 appearances for Wigan, he was transferred to Norwich City for £73,000 and in November 1989 Cook arrived at Wolves for £250,000 (a record sale for the Canaries). With an excellent left foot, he did well at Molineux initially, being the club's penalty-taker in 1991-92, but thereafter his form deteriorated and in August 1994 he was sold to Coventry City for £600,000, switching north to sign for Tranmere Rovers in February 1996 for a further £250,000. In October 1997 Cook moved again, this time from Prenton Park to Stockport County, also for £250,000, replacing former Wolves player Chris Marsden at Edgeley Park, who was sold to Birmingham City. During 1997-98 Cook passed the milestone of 400 League appearances at club level but after losing his place in the Hatters' side the following campaign he was eventually loaned out to Burnley (May 1999), signing full-time the following month.
Wolves record: 209+5 apps. 21 goals.

COOPER, Jeremiah

Strong-running inside-forward, always thirsty for the ball, Cooper was a member of Wolves' first-ever Football League side which met Aston Villa on 8 September 1888. Unfortunately a serious ankle injury forced him out of the side and in May 1891, he left Molineux for Stourbridge Standard. Born in Heathtown, Wolverhampton in 1865, he played for Milton FC and Amblecote Nomads before signing for Wolves in August 1888. It is believed Cooper died in Bradford in the 1940s.
Wolves record: 26 apps. 6 goals.

CORBETT, Percy Baxter

Percy Corbett remained an amateur all his life. He occupied the inside-left berth in the main, and appeared in the Wolves side which started on the road to winning the FA Cup in 1908. Born in Penn, Wolverhampton in February 1885, Corbett played most of his football with the Wulfrunians club and was recruited by Wolves for a six-year period, starting in August 1905 although he was a first-team player for only two seasons: August 1907 to April 1909. An England amateur international, capped seven times between 1905 and 1910, he also represented the Birmingham County Youth team and the Birmingham County Amateur side. He died in Merry Hill, Wolverhampton in August 1940. Percy is not related to Walter Samuel Corbett, who won an Olympic soccer gold medal in 1908.
Wolves record: 8 apps. 3 goals.

CORFIELD, Sidney

Corfield was a stylish centre-half whose career was disrupted by his parents. A Black

Country man, born at Princes End, Tipton in June 1883, he attended St Martin's School, Tipton and played for Toll End Wesley (1900) before joining West Bromwich Albion as a professional in November 1902. He made just eight first-team appearances for the Baggies before his mother and father pulled him out of the game and asked him to go into engineering. Corfield was out of football for at least 15 months, up to August 1905 when he was enticed back into the game by Wolves who signed him to help bolster up a rather leaky defence. Sadly Corfield never really commanded a first-team place at Molineux although he did remain at the club for four years, his best season coming in 1905-06 when he played in 29 senior games. In 1909 he left Wolves for Wrexham with whom he won two Welsh Cup winners medals (1910 and 1911) before returning to the Midlands to sign for Tipton Victoria, retiring in 1915. A useful cricketer with West Bromwich Dartmouth in 1913 and 1914, Corfield died in West Bromwich in 1941.
Wolves record: 47 apps. 3 goals.

CORICA, Stephen Christopher

Skilful, industrious right-sided midfielder, born in Cairns, Australia on 24 March 1973, Steve Corica joined Wolves for £1.1 million from Leicester City in mid February 1996. He had been a big success in Australian soccer with Marconi FC of Sydney before moving to England to join Leicester in August 1995 for £325,000 (the fee decided by a FIFA tribunal). He played under Mark McGhee at Filbert Street and had no hesitation in following his boss to Molineux. He did well in his first season with Wolves despite a few injury problems and in 1997 was called into the Australian World Cup squad, coached by former England boss Terry Venables.
Wolves record: 74+16 apps. 4 goals.

CORONATION CUP

To celebrate the Coronation of Queen Elizabeth II, Wolves met neighbours West Bromwich Albion in a friendly match at The Hawthorns on 4 May 1953. A crowd of 5,802 saw Wolves win 3-1 with goals from Ron Flowers, Roy Swinbourne and Johnny Hancocks. George Lee netted for the Baggies.

The Wolves team was: Sims; Short, Pritchard; Baxter, Shorthouse, Flowers, Hancocks, Broadbent, Swinbourne, Wilshaw, Clews.

COUNDON, Cuthbert

A competent utility forward, Coundon – nicknamed 'Kid' – was signed from Southampton in July 1928. Unfortunately he had been struck down by diphtheria in December 1927 and never really recovered his full health, and as a consequence was transferred to Southend United in May 1929. Born in

Sunderland on 3 April 1905, Coundon represented Sunderland and District Schools, played for Mercantile Dock XI and Jarrow (1923) before moving 400 miles to The Dell in April 1925. From Southend he switched to Guildford City (July 1930) and in September 1935 was appointed trainer-coach of Sutton United. Coundon died in Sutton, Surrey on 18 December 1978.
Wolves record: 13 apps. 1 goal

COVENTRY CITY

Wolves' playing record against City is:
Football League

Venue	P	W	D	L	F	A
Home	22	8	6	8	22	20
Away	22	5	3	14	19	42
Totals	44	13	9	22	41	62

FA Cup

Venue	P	W	D	L	F	A
Home	2	1	1	0	3	1
Away	2	0	1	1	1	4
Totals	4	1	2	1	4	5

League Cup

Venue	P	W	D	L	F	A
Home	1	1	0	0	2	1

Wartime

Venue	P	W	D	L	F	A
Home	8	4	3	1	12	7
Away	8	2	2	4	11	13
Totals	16	6	5	5	23	20

The clubs first met in the Football League in 1919-20 (Division Two) when Wolves won 2-0 at Molineux and City 1-0 at Highfield Road.

Wolves' best wins at League level (goals scored) have been 4-2 at Coventry in November 1924 (Division Two) and 3-0 at home in April 1973 (Division One). In contrast the Sky Blues have inflicted several big wins over Wolves including those of 7-1 at home on Christmas Day 1922; 4-0 at Highfield Road in February 1921 and March 1978, and two 3-0 scorelines in May and November 1979.

A record crowd at Highfield Road of 51,455 (6,000 supporting Wolves) witnessed the vital Second Division promotion clash on 29 April 1967 which Coventry won 3-1 on their way to the championship. Wolves were also promoted that season, as runners-up, finishing a point behind the Sky Blues.

Mick Ferguson of Coventry City became the first opposition player to score at hat-trick against Wolves at Molineux for 16 years when he helped the Sky Blues to a 3-1 win in October 1977.

Wolves met the Sky Blues three times in the 1983-84 FA Cup competition. After two 1-1 draws it was the Sky Blues who finally progressed into the fourth round with a solid 3-0 win in the second replay at Highfield Road.

Wolves' League Cup win was at home in the fourth round in season 1995-96 when a crowd of 24,628 attended Molineux.

Wolves beat Coventry City 3-0 in Cork and 6-3 in Belfast on their Irish tour in 1963.

In April 1999, a Pontins League match at Highfield Road ended: Coventry City Reserves 7 Wolves Reserves 0 – and Wolves fielded 12 players during the course of the game with first team experience.

Players with both clubs include: Jimmy Alderton, Arthur Arrowsmith, George Ashall, James Baker, David Barnes, Martin Bayly, Andy Blair, Tommy Bowen, Bill Brown, Jackie Brown, Willie Carr, Paul Cook, Charlie Cross, Tom Davison, Paul Edwards, Steve Froggatt, Jack Gardiner, Bobby Gould (also City manager), Kenny Hibbitt, Frank Higham, Ernie Hunt, Eleander Juggins, Bobby McDonald, Alex McIntosh, Steve Mardenborough, Andrew Marr, Chris Marsden, Jim Melrose, Barry Powell (later coach at both clubs and Community officer at Coventry), Billy Rafferty, Cyrille Regis, Brian Roberts (also coach at Coventry), Graham Rodger, Robert Rosario, Ken Rowley, Steve Sedgley, John Smith, Terry Springthorpe and Ted Watson.

Also associated: Emilio Aldecoa (Wolves Reserves), Don Howe (Wolves trialist, Coventry City manager); Graham Newton (Wolves junior); Robert Allen, Tom Allen, Bill Brown, Dave Clements, Micky Cook, Ernie Hackett, Ron Hewitt, Tom Langley, David Meeson, Billy Morgan (he made 150 appearances for City after leaving Molineux), James Rogers and Joe Stone (all Wolves Reserves); Garry Pendrey (Wolves coach and assistant manager, Coventry coach).

COWANS, Gordon Sidney

Midfielder 'Sid' Cowans was born in Cornworth on 27 October 1958. His career began in earnest when he joined Aston Villa as an apprentice in 1974, turning professional in September 1976. In the next nine years he helped Villa win the League Cup (1977), the First Division title (1981), the European Cup (1982) and the European Super Cup (also in 1982). He was capped by England, later taking his tally of full caps to 10, as well as representing his country in two 'B' and five U/21 internationals, having earlier played at youth team level. From Villa Park he went to the Italian club Bari for £500,000 in July 1985, but returned to Villa for half that amount in July 1988, having had three good years in Serie 'A', making almost 100 appearances. In November 1991, a fee of £2000,000 took Cowans to Blackburn Rovers, but surprisingly in July 1993, he returned for a third spell with Aston Villa. His next move was to Derby County for £80,000 in February 1994 and his association with Wolves commenced in December 1994 when the Rams accepted £20,000 for his departure. Almost a year later – in December 1995 – Cowans was on the road again, this time to Sheffield United on a free transfer. He switched clubs once more early in the 1996-97 season when he went to

Bradford City, and before the campaign had ended he signed for Stockport County, helping the Edgeley Park side win promotion to the First Division. The much-travelled Cowans, who was replaced in the Stockport midfield by former Wolves man Chris Marsden, was then linked with the vacant manager's job at Hereford United following the departure from Edgar Street of former Wolves boss Graham Turner. Cowans passed the personal milestone of 800 appearances at club level during the 1997-98 season (75 goals scored). In August 1997 he joined Burnley as player-coach under his former England colleague Chris Waddle, moving up to reserve-team manager at Turf Moor in 1998 when Waddle left.
Wolves record: 40+6 apps. 1 goal

COY, Robert A.

Coy had a number of central defensive partners during his time at Molineux including Joe Gallagher, George Berry, John Pender and Alan Dodd. Born in Birmingham on 30 November 1961, he joined Wolves as an apprentice in 1977 and turned professional on his 18th birthday two year later. He made his senior debut for Wolves against Tottenham in September 1981 and in 1982-83 helped Wolves win promotion from the Second Division. As the team were slithering back down, Coy was transferred to Chester City (with colleague Dave Wintersgill) in March 1984, and in later years he served with Northampton Town (from August 1986 to May 1987), Aylesbury United (to July 1989) and Moor Green (August 1989 to March 1993), skippering the latter club for three seasons to 1992. Earlier in his career Coy was a promising goalkeeper and played in an England Schoolboys Under-15s trial match as well as having a brief spell as a junior with Birmingham City (1976).
Wolves record: 44+3 apps.

CRABTREE, Jack

Son of the Aston Villa and England player Jimmy Crabtree, Jack's career in League was cut short after he had been wounded during World War One. Born in Bournbrook, Birmingham in September 1887, Crabtree played for Bourneville FC before joining Wolves in July 1912. He spent two years as a left-half at Molineux and left for Kings Heath prior to serving his country at War (from April 1915). He retired on returning home (1919) and although he turned out in various charity matches, he never really took up football again and became secretary of a local team in the Birmingham area. Crabtree died in King's Heath, Birmingham c.1950.
Wolves record: 11 apps.

CRAINIE, Daniel

Danny Crainie was a fast raiding, slightly

built forward, who became the 'forgotten' man of English football when he was discarded by Wolves in 1985 and then abandoned in the Australian outback. But the likeable Scot bounced back with Airdrieonians and during the next few years often caught the headlines of the Scottish newspapers. Born in Kilsyth on 24 May 1962, Crainie joined Celtic in 1978 and won a League championship medal at the age of 19. But when manager Billy McNeill left Parkhead to join Manchester City, David Hay took over and Crainie's days at Celtic were numbered. In December 1983 he was transferred to Molineux, but in truth he never really settled down in the Midlands despite scoring a couple of marvellous goals, one a real beauty at West Brom. After a loan spell with Blackpool (March/April 1985) he left Wolves for Dundee but quickly opted for a change of scenery in Australia, signing for the South Melbourne club, Hellas, whose fans were mostly Greek immigrants. From there he switched to Wollongong City – and that's where things really went wrong for Crainie. Playing alongside Paul Mariner, Trevor Francis and Alan Brazil one week, he suddenly found himself stranded after the club's millionaire-owner walked out. He returned to Britain shortly afterwards to play briefly for Airdrieonians (1990-91) and then entered non-League football.
Wolves record: 71+2 apps. 4 goals.

CRAWFORD, Raymond

Crawford remained a prolific goalscorer throughout his career and when he retired in May 1971 he had netted well over 300 times in more than 600 appearances as a professional, including a League record of 290 goals in 476 outings. Born in Portsmouth on 13 July 1936, his career saw him serve, in turn, Portsmouth (as a professional in December 1954), Ipswich Town (September 1958), Wolves (signed in September 1963), West Bromwich Albion (from February 1965), Ipswich Town again (for three years from March 1966), Charlton Athletic (March 1969), Kettering Town (on loan) and finally Colchester United (for one season, commencing June 1970). He was capped twice by England and also played for the Football League. He helped Ipswich win the League championship in 1962 and the Second Division title in 1961. After leaving Layer Road he had a brief spell with Durban City (South Africa), coached at Brighton, Portsmouth and in New Zealand and then returned to Fratton Park as youth-team manager, later taking charge of Fareham Town and Winchester City. Crawford also played for Malaysia while on National Service over there, and he is still Ipswich Town's champion marksman of all-time with 227 League and Cup goals, which included a

five-timer in a European cup clash with the Maltese side FC Floriana in September 1962.
Wolves record: 61 apps. 41 goals.

CREW, E. William

Billy Crew was a gritty performer who loved to battle it out in the middle of the park. Born at Little Lever, Bolton in 1898, he played for the Great Lever club before joining Bolton Wanderers in July 1922. From Burnden Park he switched to Wolves (May 1923) but spent only a season at Molineux before moving to Tranmere Rovers (May 1924). After that he served with Pontypridd (August 1925), Merthyr Town (October 1925), Southend United (May 1929), Wigan Borough (September 1930), Burton Town (1933) and Mossley (June 1936), retiring in May 1938, aged 40. He helped Wolves win the Third Division North title when deputising for skipper George Getgood at right-half. Crew died in Manchester in 1961.
Wolves record: 8 apps.

CREWE ALEXANDRA

Wolves' playing record against the Alex is:

Football League

Venue	P	W	D	L	F	A
Home	5	3	1	1	9	5
Away	5	2	3	0	5	1
Total	10	5	4	1	14	6

FA Cup

Venue	P	W	D	L	F	A
Home	1	0	1	0	2	2
Away	1	1	0	0	3	1
Total	2	1	1	0	5	3

Wartime

Venue	P	W	D	L	F	A
Home	4	3	0	1	14	8
Away	5	3	0	2	10	15
Total	9	6	0	3	24	23

Wolves took three points off Crewe when winning the Third Division North title in 1923-24. They won 1-0 at Molineux and drew 0-0 at Gresty Road.

A hat-trick by Peter Bodak helped Crewe to a 3-2 win over Wolves at Molineux in January 1987.

Wolves beat the Alex (away) in January 1988 (Division Four) when Andy Mutch scored twice.

In another Fourth Division match on Wolves soil in January 1986, Crewe were 3-2 victors in front of just 3,759 fans.

When the teams met in the League again – in season 1997-98 – Wolves won both matches, 2-0 at Gresty Road and 1-0 at Molineux.

The two FA Cup games were played in 1891-92 when Wolves won a first-round replay 3-1 after Crewe had battled out a 2-2 draw at Molineux. David Wykes scored in both games for Wolves.

Crewe inflicted upon Wolves an 8-1 defeat in a wartime Football League (North) game at Gresty Road in April 1943.

Players with both clubs include: Francis Burns, Campbell Chapman, Bill Coley, Paul

Edwards, Roger Eli, Walter Featherby, Francis Greene, Frank Green, Billy Harrison, Harry Hughes, Eric Jones, Tony Lange, Angus McLean, Jimmy Melia (Alex player-manager), John O'Connor, John Oldfield, Trevor Owen, Albert Picken, Val Rouse, Alex Scott, Jack Stanley, George Swift, Geoff Thomas, Stuart Watkiss and Jermaine Wright.

Also associated: Arthur Allman, Jock Basford, Joe Clarke, Maurice Doyle, David Felgate, George Gilchrist, Cecil Hardstaffe, Terry Harkin, Dennis Isherwood, Michael Kelly, Alf Lythgoe, Phil Nicholls, Bill Prendergast, Les Redfearn, Alan Stephens and George Willis (all Wolves Reserves), Johnny Hancocks, Bill Parker, Ernie Tagg and Tom Waring (Crewe wartime guests), Frank Broome (Crewe player, Wolves wartime guest) and Greg Fellows (Alexandra player, Wolves coach).

CRICKETER FOOTBALLERS

One of the finest all-round sportsman to play for Wolves was Henry Howell, who besides being a talented footballer also starred in county cricket for Warwickshire and played in Test matches for England as well as representing the MCC. Howell played 15 seasons for Warwickshire and in five Test Matches for England v Australia in the 1920s. He scored over 1,650 runs and took 975 wickets in a splendid career.

Wolves' defender Walter Victor Fox scored over 6,650 runs for Worcestershire between 1923 and 1932 and also played cricket for Abertillery CC in Wales.

Wolves' 1940s centre-half Gordon Brice played first-class cricket for both Northamptonshire and Bedfordshire and his fellow centre-half Sid Corfield was a regular in West Bromwich Dartmouth's Birmingham League side in seasons 1913 and 1914.

Wolves' 1930s full-back Jack Dowen was a very useful all-rounder in local club cricket, while brothers Alf and Billy Crook also played local club and works league cricket in the Wolverhampton area during the 1940s and 1950s.

Ron Howells was a cricketer on Warwickshire's Club and Ground; Wolves' 1920s defender Tommy Davison was an excellent all-round cricketer in the Derbyshire District League; Irvine Harwood spent many years playing in the Bradford League and Tom Galley, too, was a regular on the cricket square.

Welsh international John Matthias played cricket for Brougham CC in the 1890s; defender Jack Nelson played Lancashire League cricket; 1930s full-back Cecil Shaw was a very good minor cricketer in the Mansfield, Wolverhampton and Handsworth (Birmingham) areas and 1950s/60s winger Terry Wharton played for Brewood Cricket Club for 13 years.

Other Wolves players who were good cricketers included Len Astill, Bill Coley, Charlie Phillips, Billy Richards, Tom Smalley and Cyril Spiers.

Former Wolves' secretary Keith Pearson was a fine club cricketer who played for Milford Hall Cricket Club for a number of years and so too were commercial managers Keith Butler and Gordon Dimbleby.

CROOK, Alfred R.

Alf Crook was a reserve full-back at Molineux. Born at Brewood on 13 August 1923, he joined Wolves from Boulton and Paul's FC for the 1942-43 wartime season and after a handful of outings in the various Regional Leagues, he finally made his senior debut in the FA Cup semi-final replay against Manchester United in April 1949, when he replaced the injured Lawrie Kelly. Crook was allowed to leave Wolves at the end of the 1948-49 season and is now an avid member of the ex-players' association.
Wolves record: 2 apps.

CROOK, Mark Stanley

A diminutive outside-right or outside-left, Crook was born in Morby, Yorkshire on 29 June 1903. He developed his football with Wombwell before breaking into senior competition with Blackpool, making a much bigger impact with Swindon Town prior to joining Wolves on 4 October 1929. Terrier-like in his persistency, Crook was only 5ft 5ins. tall and weighed 10st. 8lbs, but always gave a good account of himself against the much stronger full-backs. He made his debut for Wolves v Bristol City just 24 hours after joining the club and his last outing was at Sunderland in January 1935. His best season came in 1932-33 when he made 25 appearances, helping Wolves win the Second Division championship. He left Molineux for Luton Town in May 1935 and retired during the early part of the war when he took up scouting, recommending several players to both Wolves and Walsall. It was Crook who formed Wolves' nursery side, Wath Wanderers, when he took over the facilities of the Brampton Welfare Football Club in the late 1940s. Crook died in Wath-on-Deane, Lancashire on 1 December 1977.
Wolves record: 81 apps. 16 goals.

CROOK, William Charles

Left-back or wing-half Billy Crook was a key member of the Wolves side during the early post-war years, winning a FA Cup winners' medal in 1949. Born in Wolverhampton on 7 June 1926, and educated at Wolverhampton Grammar School, he joined the club as a 14-year-old from Boulton and Paul's FC on schoolboy forms in August 1940, became an amateur in July 1941 and turned part-time professional in August 1943. After establish-

ing himself in the side during the hostilities, when he also guested for Aldershot and Chelsea, Crook found himself a regular in the Wolves side in 1946 after more than 120 wartime appearances. In October 1954, having by now lost his place in the first team, he was transferred to Walsall, where he stayed until 1956, retiring four years later after a period in non-League soccer. During his playing days Crook trained as a structural draughtsman and later took up employment in this field with Rubery Owen and Co. (Darlaston). He was also a fan of Dixieland jazz. Like his brother he is also a member of the ex-Wolves' players' association.
Wolves record: 221 apps. 3 goals.

CROSS, Charles Alon

Charlie Cross was a sturdy full-back, signed from Crystal Palace in August 1928. Born in Coventry on 15 May 1900, he played initially for Sideley Deasy FC and then made 11 League appearances for Coventry City before joining Palace in 1922. He played over 220 League games for the London club but never really settled in the Midlands and he spent just a season with Wolves, acting as reserve to Harry Shaw before leaving for Merthyr Town in June 1029. He later returned to Coventry.
Wolves record: 3 apps.

CROSSWELL'S BREWERY

Wolves recorded their best ever FA Cup win over Crosswell's Brewery, beating them 14-0 in a second round tie at their Dudley Road ground on 13 November 1886. That afternoon a crowd of around 2,000 saw Tom Hunter (4), Tommy Knight (3), Jack Brodie (3), Bernie Griffiths (3) and Harry Allen score for the rampant Wanderers. The last quarter-of-an-hour of this tie was played in semi-darkness (owing to Crosswell's late arrival at the ground).

CROWE, Christopher

Born in Newcastle-on-Tyne on 11 June 1939 and educated at St John's school (Edinburgh) Chris Crowe played for Edinburgh Boys and gained England schoolboy and youth honours as a teenager before adding four Under-23 caps and one senior cap to his tally, After trials with Hearts he joined Leeds United, signing as a junior at Elland Road in July 1954 and turning professional in June 1956. Tutored briefly by the great John Charles, Crowe made over 100 appearances for the Yorkshire club who then sold him to Blackburn in March 1960. He had 51 League outings for Rovers before transferring to Wolves in February 1962. He remained at Molineux for two-and-a-half years, up to August 1964, when he moved to Nottingham Forest. A blond inside-forward, he made 74 appearances for Forest, later adding a further 67 to his collection with Bristol City (between January 1967 and September 1969) and 13 with his last English club, Walsall, whom he served for a season (1969-70) after a spell in New Zealand with Auburn. Crowe ended his career with Bath City (February-May 1971).

Wolves record: 85 apps. 24 goals.

CROWE, Glenn Michael

A determined left-footed striker, born in Dublin on Christmas Day 1977, Glen Crowe joined Wolves as a trainee on leaving school in 1994 and turned professional in July 1996 after completing his YTS course. Capped by the Republic of Ireland at both Youth and Under-21 levels, he went on loan to Exeter City in February and March 1997 before returning to appear in the Play-offs for Wolves at the end of that season. He was booked on his debut v Reading in April 1996 and scored in his second game v Charlton Athletic. In October/November 1997 Crowe was again loaned out, this time to Cardiff City and after returning to Molineux he was later transferred to Plymouth Argyle (January 1999 after a month's trial at Home Park). *Wolves' record 6+4 apps. 1 goal.*

CRUMP, Winston Howard

Left-half, born in Smethwick in 1870, Winston Crump played for Smethwick Centaur, West Smethwick and Wednesfield before joining Wolves in September 1894. He stayed nine months at Molineux before leaving to join Bloxwich in May 1895. Crump died in Coventry c.1943.

Wolves record: 1 app.

CRYSTAL PALACE

Wolves' playing record against Palace is:

Football League

Venue	P	W	D	L	F	A
Home	17	9	5	3	19	13
Away	17	4	6	7	21	29
Totals	34	13	11	10	40	42

Play-Offs

	P	W	D	L	F	A
Home	1	1	0	0	2	1
Away	1	0	0	1	1	3
Totals	2	1	0	1	3	4

FA Cup

	P	W	D	L	F	A
Home	3	1	1	1	4	6
Away	3	1	1	1	4	5
Totals	6	2	2	2	8	11

League Cup

	P	W	D	L	F	A
Away	1	1	0	0	2	1

Wolves and Palace first met each other at League level in season 1921-22 (Division Two), and it was the Londoners who had the better of the exchanges, drawing 1-1 at home and winning 1-0 at Molineux.

The following season Palace whipped Wolves 5-0 at The Nest with George Whitworth scoring a hat-trick.

After Wolves had beaten Palace 3-1 at Molineux in April 1925, the teams didn't

Steve Bull in action against Crystal Palace.

meet again in the Football League until season 1965-66 when Wolves doubled up by winning both matches 1-0.

Almost 27,000 fans at Selhurst Park saw Palace inflict upon Wolves their heaviest defeat during their promotion-winning season of 1966-67, winning 4-1 on the last day of the campaign.

The first time Wolves met Palace in the top flight was in November 1969 when the Eagles won 2-1 at Selhurst Park.

A seven-goal thriller at Palace ended in a 4-3 win for Wolves in November 1982, Mick Matthews scoring twice.

In the mid 1990s Palace came to Molineux and won 2-0 and 3-0, while Wolves travelled to London and came away with a 3-2 victory and a 3-2 defeat. Australian midfielder Steve Corica netted two classy goals in that win at Selhurst Park in November 1996.

Wolves lost to Palace 4-3 on aggregate in the First Division Play-off semi-final of 1996-97 and so missed out on a trip to Wembley for the second time in three seasons. Palace won 3-1 at Selhurst Park in front of a 21,000 plus crowd but lost 2-1 at Molineux before 26,403 spectators – and they went on to beat Sheffield United 1-0 in the Final to gain a place in the Premiership.

The first of the six FA Cup games took place in season 1908-09, but Wolves, the holders of the trophy, went out in the first round beaten by Southern League Palace 4-2 after extra-time in London following a 2-2 draw at Molineux.

In March 1995, Palace again beat Wolves in the FA Cup, this time in the quarter-final replay. After a 1-1 draw at Selhurst Park, Palace raced to a convincing 4-1 victory at Molineux.

Players with both clubs include: Davey Burnside, John Burridge, Steve Claridge, Charlie Cross, Neil Emblen, Tony Evans, Dougie Freedman, Adam Haywood (Palace player-coach), John Holsgrove, John Humphrey, Revd Kenneth Hunt, David Jordan, Tommy Langley, Mark Lazarus, Frank Manders, Kevin Muscat, Archie Needham, Simon Osborn, Tom Raybould, Jamie Smith, Paul Stewart, Alf Somerfield, Geoff Thomas, Albert Thorpe, Alf Tootill, George Walker (founder-player of Palace, 1904), Terry Wharton, Bobby Woodruff and Eric Young.

Also associated: Jackie Brown, Eric Jones and Arthur Rowley (all Palace wartime guests), Ronnie Allen (Palace player-coach, Wolves manager and coach); Cyril Spiers (Wolves player, Palace manager), Ron Bennett, Stan Collymore, Fred Hanson, Joe Millbank, Tommy Reece and Alf Somerfield (all Wolves Reserves). Reece and Laurie Scott also Wolves wartime guests.

CULLIS, Stanley

Stan Cullis was one of a rare breed, a footballer who achieved outstanding success as a player and as a manager. Furthermore, he achieved both with the same club, Wolverhampton Wanderers. Born in

Stan Cullis, a great Wolves player and manager.

Ellesmere Port, Cheshire on 25 October 1915, Cullis, who had trials with Bolton Wanderers at the age of 16, joined Wolves in February 1934 from his local Wednesday club, thus beginning a career which saw him make his mark as a fine centre-half. He made his Football League debut, at home to Huddersfield Town 12 months after arriving at Molineux, and was appointed skipper of the first team before he was 20. Indeed, he was a natural leader and went on to captain England, initially at the age of 22, the youngest ever at that time (in 1937-38). He went on to gain 12 full caps, plus a further 20 in wartime when he was part of a quite brilliant international half-back line comprising Joe Mercer, himself and Cliff Britton. Cullis captained the Wolves side in the last pre-war FA Cup Final, which the Molineux club lost to Portsmouth, and altogether he made over 170 senior appearances for the club, up to his retirement in May 1947. And but for seven seasons lost to the war (when he guested for Aldershot, Fulham and Liverpool) he would probably have doubled that appearance tally, although he did turn out in 24 Regional League and Cup matches during the hostilities when on leave from the South Staffs Territorials, with whom he became a CSMI, serving in Italy. Prior to his last League game for Wolves against Liverpool at Molineux on 31 May 1947 when over 50,000 fans turned out, Cullis had coached in Norway (1946) and on retiring he became assistant to manager Ted Vizard, eventually taking over from Vizard in the summer of 1948 to begin an even more successful career in charge of the team. He led Wolves to victory in two FA Cup Finals (first as the youngest manager at the age of 33 years, 187 days in 1949 v Leicester City and secondly in 1960 v Blackburn Rovers). He also guided the Wanderers to three League Championships (in 1953-54, 1957-58 and 1958-59) as well as to runners-up in the top flight. He also led the team in the European Champions Cup and was in charge when a series of famous foreign teams came over to play Wolves under the Molineux floodlights in the 1950s. He later managed Birmingham City (1964-68), steering Blues to both the League Cup and FA Cup semi-finals. Cullis, on retiring from football, had a successful period when he penned an interesting column in the local *Express and Star* sports paper. He now lives in retirement with his wife in Malvern.
Wolves record: 171 apps.

CUP FINALS

Wolves have played in eight FA Cup Finals to date, those of:
1889 v Preston North End (lost 3-0)
1893 v Everton (won 1-0)
1896 v Sheffield Wednesday (lost 2-1)
1908 v Newcastle United (won 3-1)
1921 v Tottenham Hotspur (lost 1-0)
1939 v Portsmouth (lost 4-1)
1949 v Leicester City (won 3-1)
1960 v Blackburn Rovers (won 3-0).

Wolves have also appeared in two League Cup Finals, winning them both:
2-1 v Manchester City in 1974
1-0 v Nottingham Forest in 1980.

The 1972 UEFA Cup Final featured Wolves against Tottenham Hotspur when victory went to the Londoners 3-2 on aggregate.

Wolves defeated Burnley 2-0 at Wembley to win the 1988 Sherpa Van Trophy Final.

In 1971 Wolves defeated the Scottish club Heart of Midlothian in the Final of the Texaco Cup, winning 3-2 on aggregate.

In the 1941-42 wartime Football League Cup, Wolves defeated Sunderland 6-3 on aggregate in the two-legged Final.

Wolves' teenagers have played in five FA Youth Cup Finals – 1953 v Manchester United (lost 9-3 on aggregate); 1954 v Manchester United (lost 5-4 on aggregate); 1958 v Chelsea (won 8-7 on aggregate); 1962 v Newcastle United (lost 2-1 on aggregate) and 1976 v West Bromwich Albion (lost 5-0 on aggregate).

Wolves won the Lord Mayor of Birmingham Charity Cup in 1892 and 1903; won the Birmingham Senior Cup in 1892, 1893, 1894 (shared), 1900, 1902, 1924 and 1987; were successful in the Wrekin Cup Final of 1884 (the club's first trophy win) and lifted the Staffordshire Cup in 1888, 1897, 1901, 1904 (shared), 1922, 1935, 1936, 1937, 1938, 1950, 1952 and 1967.

Wolves also played in the Final of the US Tournament in 1967 when they beat Aberdeen 6-5 after extra-time to win the trophy and in 1938 they beat Arsenal 1-0 at Layer Road in the Final of the Colchester Challenge Cup.

CURLE, Keith

Central defender Curle skippered Manchester City for five years before transferring to Wolves for £650,000 in August 1996. He began his career with Bristol Rovers as an apprentice in 1979, turning professional at Eastville in November 1981. In November 1983 he was sold to Torquay United for £5,000 and in March of the following year returned to Bristol to sign for City for £10,000. After gaining an Associated Members Cup winners medal and playing in almost 150 games for the Ashton Gate club, Curle was transferred to Reading for £150,000 in October 1987. From Elm Park, where he helped the Royals win the Full Members Cup, he switched to Wimbledon for £500,000 in October 1988, and in his three years with the Dons, appeared in 112 senior matches. He left Wimbledon for Maine Road in a £2.5 million deal in August 1991 and during his time with City won three England caps to go with four 'B' caps gained earlier. He made 204 appearances for Manchester City and, ironically, prior to the start of the 1995-96 campaign, he fractured his ankle playing in a friendly against Wolves. A fine penalty taker, Curle who was born in Bristol on 14 November 1963, was kept out of the Wolves side for almost six months through injury from the time he joined the club, finally making his full debut in January 1997. In December 1998 he was appointed player-coach at Molineux.
Wolves record: 120+1 sub.apps 8 goals.

CURNOW, John Lester

Jack Curnow, at almost 6ft 3ins and 13st 6lbs,

was one of the tallest and heaviest goalkeepers in the country during the 1930s. A Yorkshireman, born at Lingdale, Saltburn on 31 January 1910 and joined Wolves as a professional from non-League football in 1934 and made his First Division debut at Chelsea four days before Christmas 1935 when he deputised for the injured Jack Weare. Curnow, a fine judge of crosses, failed to hold down a regular first-team place at Molineux and was transferred to Blackpool in December 1936. From Bloomfield Road he switched to Tranmere Rovers (May 1937) and during the war assisted Hull City (1939-45). He retired in 1946 with well over 100 senior appearances under his belt.
Wolves record: 8 apps.

CURRAN, Hugh Patrick

Hugh Curran enjoyed a fine goalscoring record in the Football League with 163 goals in 404 games in a career which began with Millwall in 1964 and ended at Oxford United in 1979. For Wolves he scored 47 goals in 98 appearances. Curran was born in Glasgow on 25 September 1943 and was an apprentice with Manchester United before being released and joining Shamrock Rovers in the League of Ireland. Then followed a spell with Third Lanark before he was given a trial by Millwall. They allowed him to drift into the Southern League with Corby Town before he finally joined the Lions for £3,000 in March 1964. After 27 goals in 57 League games for Millwall, Curran moved to Norwich City for £10,000 in January 1966 and for the Carrow Road club he netted a further 46 goals in 112 League games. That induced Wolves to pay £60,000 for his signature in January 1969 and by the time he left for Oxford in September 1972, for £50,000, he had played five times for Scotland. The only other major honour he won was as a member of Wolves' team which finished runners-up in the 1972 UEFA Cup Final. Bolton signed him for £40,000, but Curran returned to the Manor Ground in July 1977 and retired through injury in March 1979.
Wolves record: 91+7 apps. 47 goals.

CURTIS, Frank

Born in Llanelli in 1890, inside or centre-forward Frank Curtis served Wolves before, during and after World War One. He moved to Molineux from his home town club, Llanelli in June 1914 and after scoring more than a goal every two games, surprisingly left Wolves for Reading in May 1920. Curtis later had useful spells with both Bilston United and Kidderminster Harriers, before returning to South Wales to work in engineering.
Wolves record: 42 apps. 25 goals.

CUTLER, Eric R.

Amateur inside-forward Eric Cutler cap-

tained the England Schools team in 1914-15 and was one of the many players recruited by Wolves immediately after World War One. He stayed at Molineux for just two seasons (1919-21) before drifting back into non-League soccer. A local man, born c.1898, he later became a licensee in Wolverhampton.
Wolves record: 18 apps. 4 goals.

DALEY, Anthony Mark

Due to injury, fast raiding winger Daley made his full debut for Wolves a year after he had intended, but after only one outing as a substitute under his former manager Graham Taylor he broke down again and then missed all of the 1996-97 campaign. Born in Birmingham on 18 October 1967, Daley attended and played for The Holte Comprehensive School, Lozells, represented Birmingham Boys and joined Aston Villa as an apprentice in the summer of 1983, turning professional on 31 May 1985. After playing for his country at youth team level, he bided his time at Villa Park before gaining a regular place in the first team. Once in, he stayed and did extremely well, going on to win one 'B' and seven full England caps as well as helping Villa win the League Cup in 1994. After scoring 38 goals in 290 appearances for the Villains, Daley was sold to Wolves for a club record £1.25 million in June 1994 but with injury plaguing him continuously, he managed just 24 outings in his first three seasons at Molineux. Daley was given a free transfer from Wolves in May 1998 and two months later he teamed up with his former boss at Villa Park, Graham Taylor, at Watford and helped the Hornets reach the 1999 First Division Play-off Final and promotion.
Wolves record: 20+7 apps. 4 goals.

DALEY, Stephen J.

A Yorkshireman, born in Barnsley on 15 April 1963, Steve Daley was rated highly as a youngster and in the mid-1970s he was a key figure in Wolves midfield, driving forward, looking for openings and always keen to have a shot at goal himself. He helped Wolves reach the UEFA Cup Final in 1972 and win the Football League Cup Final in 1974. Three years later he was an ever-present when Wolves lifted the Second Division championship. After almost 250 appearances for Wolves, Manchester City boss Malcolm Allison paid a then British transfer record fee of £1,437,500 for Daley's signature on 5 September 1979. Three days later that money was reinvested when Wolves almost broke that record by signing Andy Gray from Aston Villa for £1.15 million. Whilst at Molineux, Daley had also won England Youth honours and played six times for the England 'B' team. At Maine Road he appeared in only 53 full games and scored four goals before joining

Burnley in November 1983. He later played for Walsall, Lye Town, Kettering Town and the Old Wulfrunians whilst in the early 1980s Daley had two spells in the NASL with Seattle Sounders (1982) and San Diego Sockers (1984). After a short period working for a brewery in the West Midlands, Daley returned to football as manager of Vauxhall Conference side Telford United in June 1997. In the summer of 1998 Daley switched clubs, leaving Telford to take charge of Bromsgrove Rovers, replacing Brian Kenning.
Steve's father, Alan Daley, was associated with Mansfield Town (two spells), Hull City, Doncaster Rovers, Scunthorpe United, Stockport County, Crewe Alexandra and Coventry City between 1946 and 1961.
Wolves record: 218+26 apps. 43 goals.

DALY, Maurice

Attacking left-back or orthodox left-winger Daly spent five seasons at Molineux (July 1973 to May 1978) during which time he struggled to gain a regular place in the side, his best campaign being his last in 1977-78 when he had 28 senior outings under manager Sammy Chung. Born in Dublin on 28 November 1955, he graduated via the well respected Home Farm club in the Irish Republic before moving to Wolves. He left Molineux for Sweden after gaining two full caps for his country.
Wolves record: 31+5 apps. 1 goal.

DANIEL, Peter William

Peter Daniel, who was born in Hull on 12 December 1955, was the driving force in Wolves' midfield for six years (1978-84), making a total of 194 senior appearances for the club and scoring 16 goals. He joined Wolves from Hull City for £82,000 in May 1978 and helped the Molineux club to League Cup glory in 1980 and to promotion to the First Division in 1983. He was capped three times by England Under-21s and also played three times for the Under-23s. Daniel broke his right leg in a match against Aston Villa in February 1981 but made a quick recovery. He had a spell in the NASL with Minnesota Kicks before leaving Wolves for Sunderland in May 1984 and he later played for Lincoln City and Burnley, totalling almost 400 League appearances in his career which ended when he retired in May 1988.
Wolves record: 194 apps. 16 goals.

DANKS, Richard

Born in Bilston in March 1865, centre-forward Dicky Danks, a former pupil at Saltley College, joined Wolves as a 22-year-old in the summer of 1887 after scoring over 20 goals for Stafford Road the previous season. He guested for Burslem Port Vale late on in 1887, and joined the Potteries' club on a permanent basis in the summer of 1888. He was

appointed secretary of the Vale in October 1889 (whilst still a registered player) but in November 1893 was released and became associated with Wednesbury Town, later assisting Wednesbury Old Athletic. Danks died on 19 November 1929.
Wolves record: 3 apps.

DARLINGTON

Wolves' playing record against the Quakers is:

Football League

Venue	P	W	D	L	F	A
Home	5	5	0	0	12	5
Away	5	1	2	2	9	11
Total	10	6	2	2	21	16

FA Cup

Venue	P	W	D	L	F	A
Home	2	2	0	0	9	2
Away	1	1	0	0	4	0
Total	3	3	0	0	13	2

Wolves first met the Quakers in the Third Division North in 1923-24, winning 2-0 at Molineux and drawing 1-1 at the Feethams. Two seasons later, following promotion for both clubs a year apart, Wolves doubled up over Darlington, winning 4-3 away in late April after having won by a goal to nil at Molineux early in March. The last two League meetings took place in 1986-87 when Wolves won 5-3 at home (a hat-trick for Steve Bull) following a 2-2 draw at Darlington when Andy Mutch netted twice.

Wolves' three FA Cup wins over the Quakers came in January 1924 by 3-1 in round three; in February 1958 by 6-1 in the fifth round when a crowd of 55,778 saw Jimmy Murray net a hat-trick, this being one of the biggest audiences a Darlington side has ever played in front of; and in January 1998 when Wolves won another third round tie, this time by 4-0 at the Feethams, scoring three of their goals late on.

Players with both clubs include: Hugh Atkinson, Mark Blake, Jimmy Deacon, Richard Deacon, Evan Edwards, Charlie Henderson, Harry Lees, Lawrie Madden, Steve Mardenborough, Darren Roberts, Jimmy Seal, Guy Wharton and Dave Wintersgill.

Also associated: Richard Deacon (Darlington junior), Evan Edwards, Charlie Henderson (trialists), Mick Connaboy, Jack Harris, Ian McDonald, Ron Hewitt, Mike Spelman, Jeff Wealands (Wolves Reserves) and Jack Dowen, Jimmy Mullen, Cyril Sidlow, Frank Taylor and Guy Wharton (all Darlington wartime guests).

Brian Little managed both clubs; Chris Evans was a player at Feethams and a coach at Wolves and Ray Hankin played for Wolves and managed Darlington.

DARWEN

Wolves' playing record against Darwen is:

Football League

Venue	P	W	D	L	F	A
Home	2	1	1	0	4	3
Away	2	1	0	1	5	4
Total	4	2	1	1	9	7

FA Cup

Venue	P	W	D	L	F	A
Home	2	2	0	0	7	0
Away	1	0	1	0	0	0
Total	3	2	1	0	7	0

Wolves scored in all four League games against Darwen, their best win coming away from home in March 1892 by 4-1. Darwin's only victory over the Wanderers was a 3-1 scoreline at home (Division One) in March 1894 when the crowd was given as just 2,000.

Wolves beat Darwen 5-0 in a third-round FA Cup-tie at Molineux in February 1893. Dick Topham scored twice that day in front of 12,000 fans.

DAVIDSON, Alfred R.

Alf Davidson was a short, stocky right-half, fresh-faced, with black wavy hair, who had good footwork and was always totally committed. Born in Wolverhampton *c.*1861, he helped Wolves win their first-ever trophy – the Wrekin Cup – in 1884 having joined the club from Blakenhall in April 1883. He left Wolves to play for Wednesfield St Luke's in 1886. Davidson died in Birmingham in 1923.
Wolves record: 5 apps.

DAVIES, Frederick

Fred Davies, who was born in Liverpool on 22 August 1939, was spotted by Wolves when he kept goal for Borough United in the Welsh League. He joined the Molineux staff in April 1957 but had to wait almost five years before making his senior debut, when he played in an FA Cup-tie against arch rivals West Brom before a 46,000 crowd at Molineux. The following week he made his League debut, against Spurs, in front of another near-46,000 Molineux attendance. It was the first of 369 League appearances for Davies playing for Wolves, Cardiff City and Bournemouth. In 1966-67 he helped Wolves to win promotion from the Second Division and he had made over 170 senior appearances by the time he signed for Cardiff in January 1968. Davies was then transferred to Bournemouth in July 1970 and served the Cherries until May 1974, starring in their Fourth Division promotion run of 1970-71. After retiring he became trainer-coach at Norwich City (under John Bond) and later worked for Blackpool, Swansea City and Birmingham City. He had a brief spell as manager of Merthyr Tydfil, then became assistant to Bond at Shrewsbury Town before taking over as manager at Gay Meadow in May 1993. One of his first signings was the former Wolves player, Wayne Clarke, and he duly led the Shrews to the Third Division championship in 1994. Davies was sacked as

manager of Shrewsbury (after relegation to the Third Division) in May 1997 and became boss of Weymouth (December 1997). A little over four months later (April 1998) he sadly died at the age of 58.
Wolves record: 173 apps.

DAVIES, Harry Joseph

Robust right full-back Harry Davies feared no-one. He was a real hefty player who joined Wolves from Bamford Athletic in March 1898 and remained at Molineux until May 1901, following the emergence of George Walker and the arrival of Jackery Jones. Born in Wednesbury *c.*1873, he deputised initially for George Eccles and then partnered Joe Blackett and later John Matthias and George Fleming before being transferred to Shrewsbury Town. From August 1902 to July 1904 he assisted Gainsborough Trinity; he was with Doncaster Rovers until March 1905 and ended his League career with Hull City, leaving the Tigers in May 1907. Davies's son, Harry junior, played for Stoke City. Davies himself died on 23 September 1963.
Wolves record: 72 apps.

DAVIES, Josiah Joseph

Joe Davies was a stylish footballer who could occupy a number of positions, playing mainly in defence as a right-half. A Welshman, born in Cefn Mawr near Ruabon in July 1865, he played for Druids (1882-86), Newton Heath (1886-90) and West Bromwich Albion (briefly in August 1890) before joining Wolves in September 1890. He was replaced in the Wanderers side by Hill Griffiths and after two-and-a-half years at Molineux he left the club to sign for Kidderminster Olympic (May 1893), returning to Druids for a second spell in May 1894. One of five brothers, four of whom were capped by Wales: Lloyd, Thomas, Robert and himself (seven caps won between 1887 and 1894) Davies, was a solid player, very reliable, and was very disappointed not to make Wolves' 1893 FA Cup Final team. On retiring from football he became a farmer in Wales and in later years ran a butcher's shop in Cefn. Davies died in his native Cefn Mawr on 7 October 1943.
Wolves record: 39 apps.

DAVIES, Kenneth

Davies was a nippy winger, born in Doncaster on 20 September 1923, who joined Wolves in 1943. He did well during the last three wartime seasons, but even then found it difficult to hold down a first-team place with Johnny Hancocks the regular outside-right. Davies was subsequently transferred to Walsall in June 1946. After two seasons at Fellows Park he moved south to Brighton and Hove Albion (May 1948). He

remained at Hove until 1950, returning to the Midlands to live and work – and play non-League soccer. He retired as a player in 1957 and sadly died in 1995.
Wolves record: 2 apps. 2 goals.

DAVIES, Richard

Inside-forward Dicky Davies played first-team football for Wolves for only one season: 1898-99, when he partnered right-winger John Tonks and centre-forward Billy Beats. An aggressive footballer, born in Quarrington Hill, Durham in August 1876, he played initially for Admaston FC before joining Manchester City in 1894. From there he moved to Hanley and after two seasons with Leicester Fosse (1895-97) he switched to Glossop North End, then Bristol St George before signing for Wolves in May 1898. He never quite reached the level required to become an established League player and after leaving Molineux in June 1901 he assisted Reading, later serving with Bristol City, Shrewsbury Town (June 1902) and Wellington St George (1903). He died in Shrewsbury in 1939.
Wolves record: 11 apps. 2 goals.

DAVIES, Royston

An outside-right, Roy Davies spent five months with Wolves during which time he deputised for Mark Crook at the start of the League programme, getting himself sent-off against Hull City in his seventh outing. A useful footballer, with good pace, he was born in South Wales *c.*1905 and joined the Wanderers from Ebbw Vale in June 1929. On leaving Molineux he joined West Ham United and later played for Reading, staying three seasons at Elm Park before returning to the Midlands to sign for Walsall Wood, later assisting Lichfield. He died *c.*1970.
Wolves record: 9 apps.

DAVISON, Thomas Reay

Tommy Davison played two seasons with Wolves in the mid-1920s when he stood in for centre-half Bill Caddick, acting as the team's sheet anchor in both constructional and defensive terms. He was recruited from Durham City in June 1923 after making more than 60 appearances for the northern club. Described in the press as being 'durable, as smart with his head as his feet' Davison was born in County Durham on 3 October 1901 and played initially for Tanfield Lea Juniors before joining his home town club in 1920. In July 1925, after failing to oust Caddick from the pivotal role, he left Molineux for Derby County and had 85 games for the Rams before switching to Sheffield Wednesday in February 1931. From Hillsborough he moved to Coventry City (July 1932) and after exactly 100 appearances for the Sky Blues he signed for Rhyl Athletic

(July 1935) where he became player-coach, retiring out of football in 1939 after a brief spell with Bath City. An ex-pit worker, Davison was keen on greyhounds as well as being an accomplished crown green bowler and excellent all-round cricketer. He died in Derby on 1 January 1971.
Wolves record: 10 apps. 1 goal.

DE WOLF, Johannes

Injuries ruined De Wolf's career at Molineux. The tall, long-haired Dutchman, who won eight caps for his country before joining Wolves for £620,000 from Feyenoord on 6 December 1994, made less than a dozen appearances during the second half of the 1994-95 season and was restricted to only a fraction over that amount the following

Dutchman Johannes De Wolf, nearly an inspired signing.

campaign when rumours suggested that he could well be in line for the player-manager's job at Molineux. This never materialised and after 18 months with Wolves, De Wolf returned to Holland, re-signing for Feyenoord, whom he later coached before moving in the same capacity to Sparta Rotterdam. Born in Schniedam on 10 December 1962, and standing 6ft 2ins. tall and weighing 14 st. 6lbs, he had a varied career in Holland before settling down with Feyenoord for whom he made over 50 senior appearances. His goal tally for Wolves included a hat-trick in a 4-2 win at Port Vale in February 1995 – becoming the first Wolves defender to achieve this feat for 92 years, since Ted Pheasant netted a treble in a 3-0 victory over Newcastle in March 1902. De Wolf, unable to settle in the Black Country, left Molineux in the summer of 1996.
Wolves record: 32+1 apps. 5 goals.

DEACON, James

Born to Irish parents in Glasgow on 4 January 1906 and brought up with his younger brother Richard (see below) in Darlington, Jimmy Deacon was a big

favourite with the Wolves fans during the early 1930s. At 5ft 7ins. tall and weighing barely 11 stones, he was not the tallest or heaviest of strikers, but he always gave a good account of himself against the some of the toughest defenders in the game. He had excellent ball skills and was often applauded for his artistry by players and supporters alike. Deacon never attempted anything flashy and averaged a goal every three games for Wolves whom he joined in the summer of 1929 from Darlington. After gaining a Second Division championship medal in 1933, he left Molineux in October 1934 for Southend United and retired from competitive football in 1939 after a short association with Hartlepools United.
Wolves record: 158 apps. 55 goals.

DEACON, Richard

Also born in Glasgow on 26 June 1911, inside-forward Dicky Deacon, brother of Jimmy (above) was brought up in Darlington and was an apprentice fitter at a locomotive works before turning to football. He played for Alliance Juniors, Albert Hill United and Darlington Juniors before having unsuccessful trials with Wolves in September 1928. He then assisted Cockfield FC and returned to Molineux as a professional in January 1930 after a brief trial period with Fulham. His first-team outings for Wolves were restricted and each time he did get a game he replaced his brother in attack. On leaving Wolves in June 1931, Deacon signed for West Ham United. Three years later he transferred across London to Chelsea (June 1934); played for Glenavon before the turn of the year and in October 1935 joined Northampton Town. Deacon junior was with Lincoln City (August 1936 to October 1939) and guested for Northampton during the war. After the hostilities he retired to go and live in the North-East. He died in May 1986, aged 74.
Wolves record: 3 apps. 1 goal.

DEAKIN, Enoch

Enoch Deakin, born in Wolverhampton *c.*1888, was a 1910-11 reserve inside-forward with Wolves, who made only a handful of senior appearances, replacing the Needham brothers on four occasions and George Hedley once. A pupil at Coven Council School, he joined the club from Bilbrook FC in April 1910 and left Molineux for Willenhall Pickwick in October 1911. Standing only 5ft 4ins tall, he died in Wolverhampton in 1947.
Wolves record: 5 apps. 1 goal

DEAN, John

Jack Dean was an outside-right or left, born in Wolverhampton *c.*1880, who played first-team football for Wolves during the early part of the 20th century when he acted, in the main, as understudy to Jack Miller. He played initially for Willenhall White Star and signed for Wolves in August 1901. On his release from Molineux in the summer of 1903 he joined Darlaston.

Wolves record: 4 apps.

DEANS, Harold

Right-winger Harry Deans was a valuable member of Wolves' first-team squad in the mid-1880s and, indeed, was a regular in the side in 1884-85. Born in Wolverhampton *c.*1865, he played for Wednesbury Town and Bilston after leaving Wolves.

Wolves record: 2 apps.

DEBT

Wolverhampton Wanderers Football Club was £2 million in debt in 1981. This prompted chairman Harry Marshall to eventually resign. The receiver was called in (July 1982) and at that time it was a strong possibility that the club would go out of business.

DEBUTS

Eleven players made their senior debuts for Wolves as well as appearing in their first-ever FA (English) Cup-tie when they lined up against Long Eaton Rangers on 27 October 1883. They were: Ike Griffiths, Tommy Cliff, Charlie Mason, Alf Davidson, Jack Baynton, Tom Blackham, James Hill, Arthur Lowder, Jack Brodie, Ted Hadley and John Griffiths.

The 11 Wolves players who made their Football League debuts on the opening day of the then newly-formed competition v Aston Villa on 8 September 1888 were: Jack Baynton, Charlie Mason, Dickie Baugh, Albert Fletcher, Harry Allen, Arthur Lowder, Tommy Hunter, Jerry Cooper, Nicholas Anderson, Walter White and Alf Cannon.

A total of 19 players were given League debuts by Wolves in that initial League campaign of 1888-89; 17 players got their League baptisms for the Wanderers during the course of the 1919-20 season and 16 played their first League games for the club in season 1946-47.

The team which lined up for Wolves in the club's first-ever competitive European match v Schalke '04 in the European Champions Cup on 12 November 1958, was: Geoff Sidebottom, Eddie Stuart, Gerry Harris, Bill Slater, Billy Wright, Ron Flowers, Micky Lill, Bobby Mason, Peter Broadbent, Colin Booth and Norman Deeley.

The first time Wolves participated in a League Cup-tie was against Mansfield Town at Molineux on 13 September 1966 and the players on duty that night were: Fred Davies, Joe Wilson, Bobby Thomson, Mike Bailey, David Woodfield, John Holsgrove, Terry Wharton, Ernie Hunt, Hugh McIlmoyle, Bob Hatton and Dave Wagstaffe.

Wolves made their debut in the 'old' Second Division on Saturday 1 September 1906 when they drew 1-1 with Hull City at Molineux in temperatures touching 90 degrees Fahrenheit. The team that day was: Tom Baddeley, Eleander Juggins, Jack Jones, Alf Bishop, Sid Corfield, Amos Lloyd, Jack Hopkins, George Hedley, Billy Wooldridge, Jimmy Gorman and Jack Pedley.

Wolves' first-ever encounter in the Third Division North was against Chesterfield (away) on 25 August 1923 and the players on duty that afternoon were: Noel George, Ted Watson, Harry Shaw, George Getgood, Billy Caddick, Albert Kay, Jack Harrington, Stan Fazackerly, Albert Legge, Harry Lees and Evan Edwards.

DEELEY, Norman Victor

The late 1950s were a great time for Wolves' versatile winger Norman Deeley, for the Wednesbury-born star gained two League championship medals, was capped twice for England, against Brazil and Peru, and then in 1960 scored two goals as Blackburn Rovers were beaten in the FA Cup Final at Wembley. Deeley, who was born in the Staffordshire town on 30 November 1933, was allegedly the smallest lad ever to play for England Schoolboys when in 1948 he stood only 4ft 4in, but his size did not daunt Wolves, who signed him as an amateur before he turned professional in December 1950. He grew a foot in the meantime and made his League debut at right-half in August of the following year, yet it was not until 1955-56, after a few games at inside-forward, that he switched to the wing. National Service cost him many appearances but in 1957-58, when Wolves lifted the League title, Deeley missed only one game. And when they retained it the following season he was absent only four times. Deeley eventually left Molineux in February 1962, when he joined up again with his former Wolves colleague Bobby Mason at Leyton Orient for whom he netted nine goals in 73 outings before going into non-League soccer with Worcester City (July 1964), Bromsgrove Rovers (August 1967) and Darlaston (September 1971), retiring in 1974. Living in his native Wednesbury, he became manager of the Caldmore Community Agency in Walsall and also took the post of steward for Walsall FC's VIP lounge.

Wolves record: 237 apps. 73 goals.

DEN HAAG

Wolves' playing record against the Dutch side is:

UEFA Cup

Venue	P	W	D	L	F	A
Home	1	1	0	0	4	0
Away	1	1	0	0	3	1
Total	2	2	0	0	7	1

Wolves met and easily beat the Dutch First Division side Den Haag on aggregate in the second round of the UEFA Cup in 1971-72. The away leg took place on 22 October and in front of almost 16,500 fans Wolves cantered to a comfortable win. The return leg at Molineux three week later attracted a crowd of 20,299 and this time Wolves eased home even more convincingly, three of their goals coming from Dutch defenders Weiner, Mansfield and Van Der Burgh, who diverted shots from Kenny Hibbitt, Derek Dougan and Jim McCalliog past their own frustrated goalkeeper.

DENNISON, Robert

Wolves signed Dennison from neighbours West Brom in March 1987 and some two years later the winger had gained Fourth and Third Division championship medals, a Sherpa Van Trophy winners' medal and been capped at full international level by Northern Ireland. Born at Banbridge on 30 April 1963, Dennison joined Albion for £40,000 from Irish League club Glenavon in September 1985. Unable to hold down a place in Albion's first team, he switched to Molineux shortly after Bull and Thompson had made similar journeys. He cost Graham Turner only £20,000 but established himself as a key performer, playing wide on the left as Wolves went from the Fourth to the Second Division. Dennison, who won 18 full caps for Ireland (with West Brom and Wolves) as well representing his country at both youth and 'B' team levels, finally left Molineux in June 1997 after 11 years service, joining the Vauxhall Conference side Hednesford Town where he teamed up with another ex-Wolves star, Paul Blades. Dennison was rewarded with a testimonial by Wolves in 1997-98, having a match at Molineux against Premier League side Blackburn Rovers. In December 1998 Dennison left the Pitmen to sign for Hereford United where he teamed up again with his former manager Graham Turner and playing colleague Keith Downing.

Wolves record: 316+37 apps. 49 goals.

DERBY COUNTY

Wolves' playing record against the Rams is:

Football League

Venue	P	W	D	L	F	A
Home	61	27	15	19	119	79
Away	61	16	10	35	91	144
Total	122	43	25	54	210	223

FA Cup

Home	4	1	1	2	6	9
Away	5	0	2	3	5	10
Neutral	2	1	0	1	2	2
Total	11	2	3	6	13	21

Wartime

Home	4	2	1	1	11	5
Away	5	0	2	3	6	14
Total	9	2	3	4	17	19

Like Wolves, Derby County were founder members of the Football League and the teams first met at this level on 3 November 1888, when a Harry Wood hat-trick gave Wolves a 4-1 home win in front of 6,000 spectators at Dudley Road.

The return fixture that season resulted in a 3-0 win for the Rams.

The two League games in 1890-91 produced 15 goals. Wolves won 5-1 at Molineux when Jack Brodie scored twice but a rampant Derby raced to a record 9-0 victory at The Baseball ground, Scotsman Johnny McMillan grabbing a five-timer.

Derby doubled up over Wolves in 1893-94 – winning 4-2 at Molineux and 4-1 at home. Johnny Allan (2), Steve Bloomer and McMillan found the net for the Rams in both matches.

Bloomer was a hat-trick hero when Derby beat Wolves 5-2 at home in October 1895 and he scored all four goals when Wolves were pipped 4-3 at the Baseball Ground in September 1896. The Cradley Heath centre-forward, however, wasn't so lethal when Wolves crashed 6-2 to the Rams in February 1899 – Bloomer only netted once.

A nine-goal thriller at Derby in September 1900, ended in a 5-4 win for Wolves (Billy Beats scoring twice) and another Billy – Wooldridge – scored a hat-trick when Wolves whipped the Rams 7-0 at Molineux on the last day of the 1905-06 season (this was also the chosen benefit match for Wooldridge and Jack Whitehouse).

Wolves lost 5-0 at Derby in September 1909, won 4-0 at Molineux in September 1924 and were held 4-4 at home by Wolves in a real cracking encounter in December 1932 when Billy Hartill (Wolves) claimed a hat-trick.

On Christmas Day 1934 Charlie Phillips (3) and Tudor Martin (2) helped Wolves to a comfortable 5-1 home win over the Rams, while that scoreline was reversed at Derby in September 1936 when Dally Duncan scored twice.

The first two League meetings after World War Two took place in the space of 24 hours in April 1947, Derby winning 2-1 at the Baseball Ground and Wolves 7-2 at Molineux when future 'Ram' Jesse Pye scored a hat-trick.

Pye scored twice more when Wolves beat Derby 4-1 at home in February 1950.

With County going down in 1953, they didn't meet Wolves again until season September 1965 (Division Two) and it was Peter Knowles who stole the show, rapping in a fine hat-trick in Wolves' 4-0 home win.

The following season Wolves won 5-3 at Molineux and 3-0 at the Baseball Ground over the Christmas period, Bob Hatton and Terry Wharton scoring in both matches, and John McGovern netted twice when Derby won 4-2 at Molineux in August 1970.

Jim McCalliog scores from the spot against champions-elect Derby in 1971-72 after Dougan had been brought down.

Wolves ran up two more 4-0 home wins in April 1974 (Steve Kindon scored twice) and April 1979, while the Rams secured a 4-1 home win in November 1978 and a 4-2 success, also at home, in August 1985, as well as winning 4-0 at Molineux in four months later.

Steve Bull was Wolves' top man with a treble in his side's healthy 4-0 win at Derby in November 1993.

In April 1995, a six-goal thriller between the Rams and the Wolves at the Baseball ground ended all square at 3-3. Paul Simpson (later to join Wolves) scored twice for the Rams, while Dean Richards grabbed a brace for the Wanderers.

Wolves reached the FA Cup Final of 1896 by beating Derby 2-1 in the semi-final at Perry Barr. And on their way to the Cup Final in 1921 Wolves again conquered the Rams, beating them 1-0 in a second replay at Molineux following a 1-1 draw at the Baseball Ground.

The last FA Cup meeting between the teams was in 1970-71 when the Rams won a fourth round encounter 2-1 at home in front of 40,576 fans.

Wolves suffered one of their heaviest home defeats in FA Cup football when they crashed 6-3 at Molineux against Derby County in a third round tie in January 1933, Jack Bowers scoring a hat-trick for the Rams in front of 31,000 fans.

Jack Rowley, guesting for Wolves from Manchester United, scored all eight goals in an 8-1 Football League North victory over Derby at Molineux in November 1942.

Players with both clubs include: Steve Biggins, Joe Blackett, Paul Blades, John Burridge, Simon Coleman, Gordon Cowans, Tom Davison, Jimmy Dunn, Stan Fazackerley, Billy Halligan, John Hamilton, Jack Hampton, Rob Hindmarch, Alan Hinton, George Kinsey, Billy Livingstone, John McAlle, Alex McDougall, Stuart McMillan, David Miller, Lee Mills, Les Mynard, Albert Picken, Barry Powell, Jesse Pye, John Richards, Paul Simpson, Floyd Streete and Robin Van der Laan.

Also associated: George Bakewell and John Griffiths (Wolves guests); Major Frank Buckley (County player, Wolves manager), Tommy Docherty (manager of both clubs), George Jobey (manager of both clubs), Keith Pearson (secretary and director of Wolves, secretary of County), Gerry Summers (coach at Wolves, Derby chief scout), Andy Beattie (County wartime guest, Wolves manager), John Griffiths and Bert Williams (also County wartime guests), Richie Barker (Derby player, Wolves assistant manager/coach) and Frank Upton (Derby player, Wolves coach); Justin Bray (Wolves reserve, Derby schoolboy).

DERBY ST LUKE'S

Wolves' playing record against St Luke's:

FA Cup

Venue	P	W	D	L	F	A
Home	2	1	1	0	7	0
Away	1	0	0	1	2	4
Total	3	1	1	1	9	4

Wolves had mixed results again Derby St Luke's. In 1884-85, after a first round tie at Dudley Road had ended goalless before 3,000 fans, Wolves travelled to Derby for the replay and lost 4-2 in front of barely 1,000 spectators.

The following season Wolves gained sweet revenge by winning another first round tie, this time by 7-0 at home when five different players figured on the scoresheet.

DERRY CITY

Wolves' playing record against Derry is:
Texaco Cup

Venue	P	W	D	L	F	A
Home	1	1	0	0	4	0
Away	1	1	0	0	1	0
Total	2	2	0	0	5	0

Wolves defeated the Northern Irish League club Derry City in the semi-final of the 1970-

71 Texaco Cup competition, winning 1-0 away and 4-0 at home. Over 10,000 saw the victory in Ireland on 1 December when Bobby Gould found the net, and there were almost 15,800 present at Molineux on 23 March to see Wolves clinch a place in the Final with a resounding victory, Gould again on target along with Hugh Curran, Mike O'Grady and Derek Parkin.

Associated with both clubs: Alan Sunderland (senior player with Wolves and Derry) and Terry Harkin (a reserve with Wolves (1960) who later assisted Derry and then became a director of the Irish club).

DEVELOPMENT ASSOCIATION

The Wolverhampton Wanderers Football Club Development Association was formed in 1962 and has been a thriving concern ever since.

DEVEY, William

Will Devey – from the famous Midlands' footballing family – could play in a variety of positions, including those of wing-half and inside-forward. Born in Birmingham on 12 April 1865, his career took him to Wellington Road FC, Aston Unity (1882), Small Heath Alliance, now Birmingham City (from August 1885), Wolves (from August 1891 to December 1892), Aston Villa (January 1893), Walsall Town Swifts (May 1894), Burton Wanderers (1895), Notts County (1896-98), Walsall again (early 1898) and Small Heath again (from July 1898). Retiring in 1900, he was a player with skill rather than strength, who did well with every club he served. He died in Birmingham on 10 June 1935.
Wolves record: 42 apps. 18 goals.

DIAZ, Isidro

Born in Valencia, Spain on 15 May 1972, right-winger 'Izzy' Diaz joined Wolves 'on trial' in September 1997 from Wigan Athletic. He failed to impress and soon went back to Springfield Park after appearing in only one senior game, coming on as a substitute in the League at Oxford. Diaz was signed by Wigan from Balaguer (Spain) in July 1995.
Wolves record: 0+1 app.

DILLARD, Henry James

In the summer of 1892 Wolves' committee appointed Harry Dillard as the club's reserve team manager, a position he held until shortly after World War One. Earlier, Dillard had put in a lot of hard work in helping to build up the Wolves first team. Born in Tewkesbury, Gloucestershire, c.1858, Dillard was taken to Sheffield with his family at the age of two. On returning to the Midlands, he attended Wesley School, Pelsall and later became a founder-member of Walsall Swifts

(1874-75). He played for that team for a time until a knee injury halted his progress. He then became the Swifts' official match umpire (a key position in the game at that time). From 1918 to 1940 Dillard represented Wolverhampton Wanderers on the Birmingham County FA and was presented with more than 30 different medals by various clubs and associations for his dedicated service to the game. A much respected figure and an avid Wolves supporter all his life, Dillard died c.1950.

DIRECTORS

Wolves became a Limited Liability Company in the summer of 1892 and immediately the club formulated a board of of directors.
Since then scores of local businessmen have been members of the Wolves' board of of directors as well as many ex-players, including internationals John Brant Brodie, Derek Dougan, John Richards and the late Billy Wright.

DOCHERTY, Thomas Henderson

Tommy Docherty was manager of Wolves for 13 months – from June 1984 to July 1985. Born in Pershore, Glasgow on 24 April 1928 and raised in the Gorbals district of the city, he started kicking a ball around the back streets at the age of eight and in 1942 went to work in a bakery. He then started playing junior football for St Paul's Guild FC and after assisting Shettlestone Juniors and the Highland Light Infantry while in the forces in Palestine, he signed for Glasgow Celtic in July 1948. In November 1949 Docherty was transferred to Preston North End and made over 350 appearances for the Deepdale club, gaining runners-up medals in the First Division in 1953 and FA Cup Final the following year as well as helping the Deepdale club win the Second Division title in 1951. In August 1958 he moved to Arsenal for £28,000, and had the misfortune to break an ankle playing against his former club Preston in October 1959. He recovered full fitness and in September 1961 switched to Chelsea as player-coach. He decided to retire as a player in January 1962 with more than 450 senior games under his belt, which included 25 full international appearances for Scotland. He was immediately appointed team manager at Stamford Bridge and quickly guided Chelsea back into the First Division as well as seeing them lift the League Cup in 1965. In May 1967 he took the London club to Wembley where they lost the FA Cup Final to Spurs and in October of that year he resigned as manager after being banned by the FA following incidents during Chelsea's trip to Bermuda. For a year from November 1967, the 'Doc' managed Rotherham United and then had 28 days in charge at QPR

(November-December 1968). He quit Loftus Road after being refused permission to spend £35,000 on new players. Twelve days after leaving Rangers he was appointed manager of Aston Villa but with Third Division football threatening Villa Park, he was sacked (January 1970). Within a matter of weeks the 'Doc' became boss of the Portuguese side, FC Porto, a position he held until April 1971. His next job was with Hull City, as assistant to manager Terry Neill, also a former Arsenal player, and in September 1971 he took over as caretaker-manager of the Scottish national team, moving up to manager two months later. He retained that post until December 1972 when he left to take over at Manchester United. Under his control United won the Second Division championship in 1975 and twice reached the FA Cup Final, but soon after winning the trophy in 1977, Docherty was sacked after admitting to having an affair with Mary Brown, wife of the club's physiotherapist (he later married her). Down but not out, the 'Doc' returned to football as Derby County boss in September 1977 and he remained at the Baseball Ground for two years before resigning. He then went back to QPR for a second spell in charge, but within a short period of time was sacked by chairman Jim Gregory, who then re-instated him nine days later. The axe finally fell on Docherty again in October 1980 and two months later he decided to try his luck down under when he was appointed manager of the semi-professional club Sydney Olympic in Australia. In June 1981 he returned to England as manager of his former club Preston North End, but that job lasted for only six months. He returned to Australia to link up as coach with South Melbourne who promptly sacked him after eight months in office. This brought him to Wolves, but following relegation to the Second Division at the end of his first season in charge, the 'Doc' was ousted yet again and after being out of football for awhile he was given the manager's job at Vauxhall Conference side Altrincham. One of the soccer's most controversial characters, Tommy Docherty who had over 40 years in the game and was associated with 15 clubs in a paid capacity, now earns his money as a popular after dinner speaker.

DODD, Alan

Born in Stoke-on-Trent on 20 September 1953, 'Doddy' joined the junior ranks of Stoke City on leaving school in 1969 and turned professional in October 1970. He made his first-team debut in November 1972 and after establishing in the side, became a class player, with a lot of skill, both in the air and on the ground. But despite his excellent club form (he scored four goals in 416 games for the Potters in two spells) he never gained

full England honours, collecting just six Under-23 caps for his efforts. Nevertheless, as a club man, Dodd was quite superb and he was eventually sold to Wolverhampton Wanderers for £40,000 in November 1982 after more than 12 years at Stoke. He helped Wolves win promotion back to the First Division, but then returned to Stoke under manager Bill Asprey in January 1985, initially on a monthly contract. He stayed with the club until the end of the season when he went over to Sweden to assist Elfsborg. He then played for GAIS Gothenburg and Elfsborg (again) before having two League games for Port Vale in 1986. Dodd later turned out for Cork City, Landskrona Bols as well as non-League Rocester and Goldenhill Wanderers before returning to Rocester as player-coach (1992-93). He later assisted Ball Haye Green Young Men's Club.
Wolves record: 99 apps. 6 goals.

DONCASTER ROVERS
Wolves' playing record against Rovers is:
Football League

Venue	P	W	D	L	F	A
Home	2	1	0	1	2	2
Away	2	2	0	0	3	0
Total	4	3	0	1	5	2

Wolves completed the double over Rovers when claiming the Third Division North title in 1923-24. They were 1-0 victors at Molineux and 2-0 winners at Belle Vue. Rovers' only triumph over Wolves was a 2-1 scoreline at Molineux in a Third Division match in October 1985 in front of just 4,324 fans.

Players with both clubs include: Billy Barraclough, George Berry, Paul Birch, Joe Bonson, Colin Booth, Stan Burton, Brian Caswell, Harry Davies, Billy Gold, Ernie Hunt, Fred Keetley, David Miller, Mark Rankine, Darren Roberts, Colin Taylor, Andy Turner, Billy Walker, Tom Wildsmith and Jermaine Wright.

Also associated: Ron Morgan (Wolves reserve and wartime guest), Stan Burton and George Laking (Doncaster wartime guests), Ron Flowers (Rovers amateur), Sammy Chung (manager of both clubs) and Ian Miller (Rovers player, Wolves coach).

DORSETT, Richard
Dicky Dorsett spent 18 years in top-class soccer, serving in the main with just two clubs – Wolves and Aston Villa. Born in Brownhills, Staffs. on 3 December 1919, he represented Walsall and District Boys and the Birmingham County FA before joining Wolves as a junior in April 1935, turning professional on his 17th birthday the following year. He was still a teenager, learning the game, when he scored Wolves' goal in their 4-1 FA Cup Final defeat by Portsmouth in 1939, and prior to that event he had netted two four-timers in League games for the Wanderers – against Leicester City in 1938 and Everton a year later, both in the First Division. Nicknamed the 'Brownhills Bomber' Dorsett was a hard-shooting player whose career at Molineux was severely disrupted by the war. Indeed, although serving in the RAF he played for the Wolves in every season during

the hostilities (except 1940-41) scoring 42 goals in 61 appearances. He also guested for Brentford, Grimsby Town, Liverpool, QPR and Southampton during the hostilities when on leave from the RAF. He surprisingly left Molineux for Villa Park in September 1946 and over the next seven years, during which time he was successfully converted into a rugged, no-nonsense defender, Dorsett gave the Claret and Blue faithful plenty to cheer about, scoring 36 goals in 271 appearances. In January 1950, however, his playing days nearly came to an abrupt end when he was involved in a serious car accident, but he recovered to play another three years with Villa. After retiring Dorsett was given a coaching job at Villa Park and in July 1957 was appointed assistant trainer at Liverpool. He returned to the Midlands in 1962 to take over the running of a local junior side near Lichfield and still resides in Brownhills today. Dorsett is the nephew of the former Manchester City and West Bromwich Albion brothers Joe and George Dorsett.
Wolves record: 52 apps. 35 goals.

DOUGAN, Alexander Derek
Centre-forward Derek Dougan was one of the most colourful footballers of his day, once shaving his head completely bald. Always a big favourite with the fans, he played for Distillery, Portsmouth, Blackburn Rovers, Aston Villa, Peterborough United, Leicester City and Wolves, won 43 caps for Northern Ireland (some as captain) and by the time his playing career was over he had

Derek Dougan lies in the net celebrating his goal against Den Haag in the 1971-72 UEFA Cup.

scored 262 goals in 692 senior appearances. Born in Belfast on 20 January 1938, Dougan had a brief spell in the Irish League before joining Portsmouth in August 1957, by which time he had been capped at Schoolboy, Youth and Amateur level as a wing-half and central defender. Pompey switched him to centre-forward and after he had scored nine goals in 33 League games (his first against Wolves in November 1957 in a 1-1 draw), Blackburn signed him in March 1959. The Doog, as he became known, scored 25 goals in 59 First Division games for the Ewood club and appeared against Wolves in the 1960 FA Cup Final. In August 1961, Joe Mercer signed him for Villa for £15,000 to replace Gerry Hitchins, who had gone to Inter-Milan, and at Villa Park, Dougan continued to score goals with 26 in 60 League and Cup games. Then he moved to Peterborough in June 1963, for £21,000 and scored 38 goals in 77 League games for the Posh before yet another move, this time to Leicester for £25,000 in May 1965. With the Filbert Street club he netted 35 goals in 68 League games before what he describes his 'best move' to Wolves for £50,000 in March 1967. Dougan came just in time to help Wolves back to Division One and it was certainly a successful time for both player and club: Dougan gained a League Cup winners' award in 1974 and a UEFA Cup runners-up medal in 1972. He made a quick impression, scoring a hat-trick on his home debut, against Hull, and altogether hit five trebles for the club. He was also Wolves' top scorer in 1967-68, 1968-69 and 1971-72. Altogether for Wolves he scored over 120 goals in more than 320 senior games. A former PFA chairman, who also managed Kettering Town for a spell, Dougan returned to Molineux in August 1982, as chairman and chief executive, a post he held until the arrival of the Bhatti brothers. He moved to Codsall, near Wolverhampton, and became involved in raising money for the Duncan Edwards Medical Centre.

Dougan suffered a heart attack in 1997, but thankfully recovered after treatment.

Dougan's brother was married on the same day as Queen Elizabeth and Prince Philip, and another brother was born on the same day as Prince Charles, while 'Doog' himself became a father of a boy on the day after the Queen had given birth to her fourth child.

In 1998 it was revealed that Dougan might be considering a takeover bid for Stoke City football club – but nothing materialised.

Dougan scored more goals in League football than any other Irishman – 219. And he is one of the few players to score a hat-trick in the Football League, FA Cup, League Cup and in a European competition.
Wolves record: 307+16 apps. 123 goals.

DOUGHERTY, Paul

Nicknamed 'Pee-Wee' midfielder Dougherty, at 5ft 2ins, became one of the smallest players ever to star in a Football League match for Wolves when he made his debut against neighbours West Bromwich Albion at Molineux in April 1984. A terrier-type performer, he became a big hit with the fans. Born in Leamington Spa on 12 May 1984, he joined Wolves as an apprentice in June 1982 and turned professional in May 1984. In February/March 1985 he went on loan to Torquay United before being released by Wolves in May 1987, following relegation to the Fourth Division. At this point he chose to go and play his football in the US Major Indoor League with San Diego, but returned to England within two years. In September 1992, having played for several non-League sides round the Midlands, Dougherty was given a two-week trial by West Bromwich Albion, playing in two reserve matches without impressing The Hawthorns management team.
Wolves record: 47 apps. 5 goals.

DOWE, Jens

German midfielder Jens Dowe joined Wolves for £200,000 from the Bundesliga club HSV Hamburg in October 1996, but remained at Molineux for barely seven months before leaving to sign for Sturm Graz for £100,000. Born in Rostock, Germany on 1 June 1968, Dowe never settled in England and he turned out to be a rather expensive player as far as Wolves were concerned.
Wolves record: 5+3 apps.

DOWEN, John Stewart

As a youngster Jack Dowen represented Walsall Boys and played for England v Scotland and Wales in Schoolboy internationals in 1929. And later on, in 1934, he starred for the Birmingham County FA v Scotland. A stocky, but quite robust full-back, Dowen, who never acknowledged defeat, was born in Wolverhampton in November 1914 and joined Wolves from Courtaulds FC as an amateur in March 1931, turning professional in August 1932. Acting as reserve to Wilf Lowton, Reg Hollingworth, Bill Morris and George Laking, his outings in the first team were limited and in October 1935 he was transferred to West Ham United, only to return to Molineux in October 1936. This time he stayed for two years before moving to Hull City (June 1938). During the war he guested for Wolves as well as Hull City, Darlington and Leeds United and later returned to the club as first-team trainer, a position he held until the early 1970s. After this he occasionally did some coaching and scouting, was kitman and the all-purpose odd-job man and had been associated with Wolves for some 50 years when he eventual-

ly left the club in 1982. Dowen, who played a lot of club cricket, died in September 1994.
Wolves record: 12 apps.

DOWNING, Keith Gordon

Nicknamed 'psycho', Keith Downing was a hard-working midfielder, often in trouble with referees for his over-robust style of play, but always totally committed to playing football. Born in Oldbury, West Midlands on 23 July 1965, he had an unsuccessful spell with Chelsea as a teenager and after serving with Mile Oak Rovers (Tamworth) he joined Notts County in May 1985. From Meadow Lane he switched to Wolves on a free transfer in August 1987 and had a fine career at Molineux, helping the team win both the Third and Fourth Division championships (in successive seasons) as well as the Sherpa Van Trophy. He left Wolves for Birmingham City in July 1993 and 12 months later switched to Stoke City for whom he made 24 appearances before joining Cardiff City in August 1995, quickly switching to Hereford United after only a month at Ninian Park. Under his former manager Graham Turner, he helped the Bulls reach the Third Division Play-offs in 1996. Downing retired in 1997 and became a representative for a Dudley publishing company, later returning to assist Hereford after they had been relegated to the Vauxhall Conference. He was appointed player-coach (still under Turner) at Edgar Street in 1998 but in March 1999 he made it full circle by going back to Molineux as youth-team coach in place of Chris Turner.
Wolves record: 200+28 apps. 11 goals.

DUDLEY, Robert

Bob Dudley was a left-half and his only first-team appearance for the club came in the last game of the inaugural League season v Notts County at Molineux on 23 February 1889, when he replaced Arthur Lowder, who was 'rested' before a vital third-round FA Cup-tie v Sheffield Wednesday. Born in Audley in 1864, Dudley joined Wolves from Audley Welfare in early February 1889 and left for Warwick County seven months later. He then assisted Bradley Primitives (1890), Wallbrook FC and Bilston Royal before retiring in 1900. Dudley died in Albrighton in 1932.
Wolves record: 1 app.

DUNDEE

Wolves' playing record against Dundee is:
Texaco Cup

Venue	P	W	D	L	F	A
Home	1	0	1	0	0	0
Away	1	1	0	0	2	1
Total	2	1	1	0	2	1

Dundee were Wolves' first opponents in the 1970-71 Texaco Cup competition. The two-legged tie was played in September. Wolves won narrowly on Tayside and then drew 0-0 at Molineux to go through on aggregate. The respective gates were 9,892 at Dens Park and 13,042 at Molineux.

Associated with both clubs: Dave MacLaren (goalkeeper), Frank Upton (coach) and Trevor Walters (Wolves Reserves).

Dundee's near neighbours United have yet to play Wolves at competitive level, but five players have been associated with both clubs: Andy Gray, Frank Munro, John Paskin, Mixu Paatelianen and Dave Richards.

DUNN, Edwin
Ed Dunn played for Wolves during the last season prior to World War One. Born in Coventry c.1891, he was a short, stocky footballer, occupying the inside-right berth. He joined the Molineux staff from Nuneaton Town in July 1914 and after the hostilities had ended, signed for Rugby Town at the start of the 1919-20 campaign. He died in Rugby in 1967.
Wolves record: 16 apps. 3 goals.

DUNN, James
Son of the former Everton and Scotland inside-forward and 'Wembley Wizard' of the same name, Jimmy Dunn was born in Edinburgh on 25 November 1923 and was playing for a junior side called St Theresa's in the Merseyside and District League when Wolves signed him as an amateur in 1941. He became a professional in November the following year, but after some success in wartime football (he played in some 100 games when free from his duties as a railway fireman) Dunn found himself in the Reserves at Molineux when the Football League resumed in 1946. A former railway fireman, Dunn played only three times when Wolves went all the way to the wire in that season's League championship race. But the following season he gained a more regular place and in 1949 he collected a FA Cup winners' medal after an outstanding season as partner to outside-left Jimmy Mullen. The following season he was troubled with a serious back injury, but fought back and was a valuable asset until the 1952-53 season, when he played in the first game, but then lost his place and in November was transferred to struggling Derby County. The Rams hoped that Dunn might help them retain their First Division status but after only six weeks he suffered a cartilage injury which necessitated an operation. Derby were looking at their first-ever season in the Third Division North when they released Dunn to Southern League club Worcester City in the summer of 1955. It had not been a successful time, but Dunn had still managed 21 goals in 58 games for Derby. From June 1957 to May 1959 he played for Runcorn and then after managing

the Roebuck licensed house, Penn, he became a coach at West Bromwich Albion (initially under Jimmy Hagan) and twice went to Wembley with the Baggies. He later worked as a physiotherapist at the Edgbaston Clinic (to 1984) and was then arepresenta-tivein Dudley while running his own gymnasium in the jewellery quarter in Birmingham. He retired in 1988 and chose to live in Halesowen and when possible still plays tennis at the Quinton Tennis Club.

DUNN, Richard R.
Dicky Dunn was given just one League outing by Wolves, as a replacement for the injured Bob Young in the away Second Division game at Bradford Park Avenue in April 1913 and it was a game he quickly wanted to forget as Wolves lost 5-1. Born in Lichfield c.1890, Dunn played for Cannock before joining Wolves in July 1912. He left Molineux in May 1915 to go to war and on his return signed for Hednesford Thistle with whom he stayed for three years, retiring in May 1922. Dunn died in 1946.
Wolves record: 1 app.

DUNN, Thomas
Tommy Dunn was a moustachioed full-back, rather on the small side, both in height and weight, but a player who always gave a good account of himself against a variety of opponents. A Scotsman, born in 1869, he played for East Stirlingshire prior to teaming up with Wolves in August 1891. He spent six years at Molineux, during which time he appeared in the 1896 FA Cup Final defeat by Sheffield Wednesday. After being replaced in the first team by Harry Wood (who switched from inside-left), Dunn had a disagreement with the Wolves committee and left the club for Burnley in November 1896, later assisting the Kent club, Chatham (from November 1897) before returning to Scotland where he ended his career.
Wolves record: 102 apps.

DURANDT, Clifford Michael
A South African left-winger, born in Johannesburg on 16 April 1940, Cliff Durandt attended KES School in his home town and played for Marist Brothers before joining Wolves as a professional in June 1957. Over the next six years he was in and out of the Wolves first team and in March 1963, manager Stan Cullis transferred him to Charlton Athletic for a fee of £15,000. Two years later Durandt returned to South Africa to play for Germiston Callies. 'Capped' by his country at the age of 16 (v Wolves in a friendly – hence his move to Molineux.) Durandt also represented Transvaal Province at both rugby and swimming. He now lives in his native Johannesburg.
Wolves record: 49 apps. 10 goals.

DURHAM CITY
Wolves' playing record against Durham is:
Football League

Venue	P	W	D	L	F	A
Home	1	1	0	0	2	1
Away	1	1	0	0	3	2
Total	2	2	0	0	5	3

Wolves defeated Durham at home and away when winning the Third Division North championship in 1923-24. Harry Lees scored twice in both matches which were played on Christmas Day and New Year's Day respectively.

Associated with both clubs: Bobby Best, Edward Carter, Tom Davison and Martin Johnson.

DWYER, Noel M.
Irishman Noel Dwyer played Gaelic football and hurling as a teenager. Born in Dublin on 30 October 1934, he was one of several promising goalkeepers developed at Molineux during the 1950s. He arrived at the club from Ormeau FC in August 1953, signing professional forms two months later. He spent the next five years at Molineux, acting as understudy to the likes of Bert Williams, Malcolm Finlayson, Fred Davies and Geoff Sidebottom. He finally made his League debut (in place of Sidebottom) in 1957, but in December of the following year was transferred to West Ham United. In August 1960, Dwyer moved to Swansea Town and after more than 150 appearances for the Vetch Field club, with whom he won a Welsh Cup winners medal in 1961 (v Bangor), he switched to Plymouth Argyle in January 1965. There he took over between the sticks from Dave MacLaren, who ironically moved to Wolves. Dwyer rounded off his League career with Charlton Athletic (December 1965 to May 1966), finishing with 213 League games under his belt. Capped 14 times by the Republic of Ireland between 1960-65, he also represented his country's 'B' team and on retiring (sadly through cartilage trouble) he became licensee of the Trafalgar public house in Wimblebury, later moving to Claregate, Tettenhall. One of Dwyer's three daughters (a former model) married former England striker Frank Worthington. Dwyer died in December 1992 aged 58.
Wolves record: 5 apps.

EASTOE, Peter R.
Although he was never really given a chance at Molineux, Peter Eastoe was a fine marksman, who amassed an excellent scoring record in League football of 95 goals in 330 appearances. Born at Dorden, Tamworth on 2 August 1953, he attended Dorden Junior and Polesworth High Schools, represented Nuneaton and District Boys, and played junior football for Glascote Highfield and Warton Hatters before signing as an appren-

tice for Wolves in June 1970, turning professional 12 months later. Capped by England Youth eight times, Eastoe found it difficult to break into the Wolves first team and in November 1973 he signed on a temporary transfer for Swindon Town, making the move permanent for £88,000 in March 1974. He finished as top scorer for the Robins in 1973-74 and 1974-75 but then became a soccer nomad, playing in turn for Queen's Park Rangers (£80,000, March 1976), Everton (player-exchange involving Mike Walsh, March 1979), West Bromwich Albion (£250,000 plus future Wolves player Andy King, July 1982), Leicester City (on loan, October 1983), Walsall (on loan, August-September 1984), Huddersfield Town (on loan, March-April 1984), Wolves (on loan, February 1985, during which time he made over half his Wolves appearances), Sporting Farense, Portugal (transfer July 1985), Atherstone Town (August 1988) Bridgnorth Town (1989), Atherstone Town again (1990), Alvechurch (manager, August 1991 to April 1992) and Nuneaton Borough (assistant manager 1992-93). He top-scored for QPR in season 1977-78 and played in two FA Cup semi-finals (for QPR and Everton). His best spell was at Goodison Park where he scored 33 goals in 115 games for the Merseysiders.
Wolves record: 14+3 apps. 1 goal.

EARLY YEARS

During the 11 years prior to the introduction of League football, Wolverhampton Wanderers Football Club developed rapidly and was, at the time, one of the strongest clubs in the Midlands. After playing their first match, in March 1877 (under the name of Blakenhall St Luke's) right up until their very first League game against Aston Villa on 8 September 1888, they had some outstanding contests up and down the country and most of the time proved worthy and difficult opponents.

The club was blessed with some excellent footballers, some of whom became established internationals, while others did far better for the club off the field than on it. There were quite a few people who became household names, either on the administration side, as committee members, as out and out players (at various levels), as respective trainers of the various teams, as club directors and/or as coaches.

Wolves won their first trophy – the Wrekin Cup – in 1883-84, the same season they first entered the FA (English) Cup when they lost in the second round to rivals Wednesbury Old Athletic.

Local derbies against Black Country neighbours West Bromwich Albion commenced in 1882 and in 1889 the team reached the FA Cup Final, losing 3-0 to double winners Preston North End.

Of the more famous players who donned the club's colours in the late 1870s were Jack Brant Brodie, a pupil teacher at St Luke's school, Jack Baynton, Charlie Mason, Thomas Blackham, James Hill and George Worrall. Mason, in fact, was Wolves' first England international.

Once into the 1880s, the likes of Ike Griffiths, Arthur Lowder, Alex Pearson, Ted Hadley, Alf Davidson, Tommy Cliff and Arnold Smith were on the scene, and when League football got underway Wolves' first team comprised: Baynton, Dickie Baugh, Mason; Albert Fletcher, Harry Allen and Lowder; Tommy Hunter, Jerry Cooper, Nicholas Anderson, Walter White and Alf Cannon.

As that initial League campaign progressed, into the side came Tommy Knight, William Crispin Rose, Harry Wood and David Wykes, Rose and Wood winning international honours for England.

ECCLES, George Samuel

Full-back George Eccles was described as being a 'grand tackler and untiring worker' who played the game 'professionally, never committing a bad foul.' Born in Newcastle-under-Lyme, Staffs. in 1874, Eccles started out with Wolstanton Brotherhood FC and then played, in turn, for Stoke St Peter's, Titbury Town, Middleport and Burslem Port Vale (June 1893), He broke his collarbone with Vale, but made a full recovery and was transferred to Wolves in May 1896. He took over from Dickie Baugh at right-back and proved a fine replacement, although he surprisingly he left Molineux after only two seasons, transferring to Everton in April 1898. Four years later he signed for West Ham United (May 1902) and rounded off his career with short spells at Preston North End (from 1904) and Bolton Wanderers. His only goal for Wolves was a cracking 30-yard drive against Nottingham Forest in April 1897 which earned a 2-1 victory. Eccles made over 50 appearances for Vale, 60 for Everton and 64 for West Ham. Eccles died in Bolton on 18 December 1945.
Wolves record: 37 apps. 1 goal.

EDGE, Robert

Outside-left Bob Edge, brother of Alf Edge, who played for Walsall, had a useful time with Wolves whom he served for almost four years from August 1893 to May 1897. He was born in Wolverhampton c.1871 and played for St Phillip's Church team before joining Wolves. On leaving Molineux he played for Loughborough and later returned to the Wolverhampton area to play for Excelsior FC (local league).
Wolves record: 25 apps. 8 goals.

EDMONDS, George William Neville

George Edmonds, a centre-forward, who was born in Holborn on 4 April 1893, played his early football with St Stephen's FC, Andrew's, with whom he gained a Drinking Trades Cup winners' medal, and St Albans City. He joined his local side Watford as a professional in 1912 and helped them win the Southern League championship in 1915. He played for England in a Victory International before moving to Wolves in the 1920 close season. Edmonds made his Football League debut against the club he was later to join, Fulham, in August of that year, and by the time he left Molineux in September 1923, he had been leading scorer in each of his three seasons as a Wanderers player, and played in the 1921 FA Cup Final against Tottenham Hotspur at Stamford Bridge. He formed a fine strike force with Stan Fazackerley, but became unsettled when Wolves dropped into the Third Division North, so the club allowed him to move to Fulham. Alas, he never broke into the Cottagers' League side and eventually returned to Watford in 1926. The following year he entered non-League football before retiring in May 1929. Into his 90s he was living in a rest home in Ryde on the Isle of Wight, where he died on 10 December 1989, aged 96.
Wolves record: 126 apps. 42 goals.

EDWARDS, Dean S.

Born in Wolverhampton on 25 February 1962, striker Dean Edwards joined Shrewsbury Town on leaving school and turned professional at Gay Meadow in February 1980. A spell abroad with Pallosuera (Finland) preceded a move to Telford United in 1983 and from Buck's Head he transferred to Wolves in October 1985. Unfortunately Edwards failed to find favour at Molineux, but his game developed considerably after leaving Wolves for Exeter City in March 1987. From St James' Park he switched to neighbouring Torquay United (July 1988) and in the summer of 1992 entered non-League soccer with Yeovil Town, signing for Stafford Rangers in 1993 before going back to South Devon to become manager of Bideford Town. He made over 120 appearances for Torquay, whom he helped reach the Final of the Sherpa Van Trophy at Wembley in 1989 as well as the Fourth Division promotion Play-offs. He quit Bideford in July 1998 to take over Striker's pub near to his old hunting ground at Plainmoor.
Wolves record: 30+4 apps. 10 goals.

EDWARDS, Evan Jenkin

Welsh amateur international winger who could also play as an inside-forward or left-half, Edwards was a fine footballer with great vision and telling shot. Born in Merthyr on 14 December 1898, he served his home town club, Merthyr Town from August 1920 before joining Wolves for £750 in May 1923. After

two years at Molineux he returned to Wales to sign for Mid Rhondda in July 1925, later assisting Swansea Town (October 1925), Northampton Town (July 1926), Halifax Town (September 1927), Ebbw Vale (early 1928), Darlington (August 1928) and Clapton Orient (September 1929 to May 1930). He helped Wolves win the Third Division North championship in 1924 when he linked up superbly well down the left with Shaw, Kay and Lees. It is understood that Edwards died in Merthyr c.1958.
Wolves record: 70 apps. 13 goals.

EDWARDS, Neil Anthony

Versatile forward Neil Edwards was born in Rowley Regis on 14 March 1966 and played for Oldswinford before becoming a professional with Wolves in August 1985. He spent three years at Molineux – breaking his leg in a 5-2 win at Burnley in February 1987 before pulling out of League football in May 1988 after a recurring knee injury, initially suffered with Wolves. He signed for Kettering Town at this juncture and remained there for two years.
Wolves record: 32+4 apps. 7 goals.

EDWARDS, Paul Ronald

Ginger-haired full-back Paul Edwards was a solid performer, who joined Wolves from Coventry City in August 1992 for £100,000. Always giving a good account of himself, he began his career with Altrincham before entering League football with Crewe Alexandra in January 1988. He made over 100 appearances for the Alex who then sold him to Coventry for £350,000 in March 1990. He was in and out of the side at Highfield Road and jumped at the chance of moving to Wolves. Unfortunately in his two years at Molineux he struggled from time with injury and in January 1994 was transferred to West Bromwich Albion for £80,000. At The Hawthorns Edwards again suffered with a back injury as well as undergoing a hernia operation and after 57 games for the Baggies he was loaned out to Bury (February 1996). He signed for the Gigg Lane club on a permanent basis a month later, before joining Hednesford Town in September of that same year. In season 1998-99, after two years recuperating from a serious stomach injury at his Coventry home, Edwards was appointed assistant manager of Paget Rangers.
Wolves record: 48+3 apps.

ELI, Roger

Tall, well built utility player, equally at home in defence or midfield, Roger Eli spent just over 18 months at Molineux, from January 1986 to August 1987. Born in Bradford on 11 September 1965 he joined Leeds United as an apprentice on leaving school and turned professional at Elland Road in September 1983.

Wolves recruited him from the Yorkshire club at a time when things were going badly on the pitch at Molineux. Unfortunately Eli's presence had little effect on the team's overall performances and on leaving the club he signed for Cambridge United on a non-contract basis. A month after moving to The Abbey Stadium, Eli went to Crewe Alexandra and after that served with Northwich Victoria, York City (November 1988), Bury (non-contract, January 1989), in Hong Kong, Burnley (July 1989), Scunthorpe United (1994) and finally Partick Thistle, with whom he was briefly in spring 1995 before retiring.
Wolves record: 18+3 apps.

ELLIOTT, Edward

Goalkeeper Ted Elliott played second fiddle to Bert Williams during his two-and-a-half years with Wolves. Born in Carlisle on 24 May 1919, he was registered with his home town club, Carlisle United, for ten years (from 1936) making less than 30 senior appearances for the Cumbrians. In March 1946 he joined Wolves and remained at Molineux until October 1948 when he was transferred to Chester. He played in a further 59 League games while at Sealand Road before rounding off his career with Halifax Town (November 1950 to May 1952). Strong-armed with good positional sense, Elliott kicked long, could throw a ball out some 50 yards and was a clean puncher, although at times he was suspect under pressure.
Wolves record: 7 apps.

ELLIS, John

When Wolves won the Second Division championship in 1932-33 goalkeeper Jack Ellis played in half of his side's 42 matches, doing well in most of them. Born at Tyldesley, Lancashire on 25 January 1908, Ellis joined Wolves three months into the 1930-31 season having played four years in his native county and briefly as an amateur with West Bromwich Albion (May-October 1930). From Molineux, Ellis switched to Bristol Rovers (July 1934) and following the arrival of Joe Nicholls from Spurs he moved to Hull City (August 1938), rounding off an interesting career with Clapton Orient (July 1939-45). A fine figure of a man, standing almost six feet tall and weighing around 12 stones, Ellis could deal expertly with high crosses and kicked well out of his hands. Unfortunately he was on the wrong end of Bristol Rovers' 12-0 drubbing by Luton Town in a Third Division (South) match in 1936 when Joe Payne scored 10 goals.
Wolves record: 26 apps.

EMBLEN, Neil Robert

Born in Bromley, Kent on 19 June 1971, the versatile Neil Emblen played for

Sittingbourne before becoming a professional with Millwall in November 1993, the Lions paying £175,000 for his signature. After only 13 games for the London club, Wolves stepped in with a £600,000 bid and brought Emblen to Molineux where he did well until suffering a torn hamstring on a summer tour in 1996. The injury lingered on, yet after regaining full fitness he established himself in the side once more, occupying a number of positions, including those of right-back, centre-half and sweeper, although his best berth was that of an attacking midfielder. However, Emblen was hurt again in March 1997 (at Bradford) and in the August manager Mark McGhee transferred him to Premiership newcomers Crystal Palace for £2 million, only for him to return to Molineux for a second spell in March 1998 for £900,000.
Wolves record: 131+18 apps. 12 goals.

EUROPEAN FOOTBALL

Wolves have played 32 games in seven seasons of European Football.

As English First Division champions, they entered the European Champions Cup in 1958-59 and 1959-60 and their prize for beating Blackburn Rovers in the 1959-60 FA Cup Final was a place in the European Cup-winners' Cup the following season. They have also had four campaigns in the UEFA Cup: 1971-72, 1973-74, 1974-75 and 1980-81, qualifying for the latter two competitions following League Cup success at Wembley. This is Wolves' full European record:

P	W	D	L	F	A
32	16	6	10	59	44

Wolves played their first European Cup game against the German side, Schalke '04, at Molineux on 12 November 1958 before a crowd of 47,767. They were held to a 2-2 draw with Peter Broadbent scoring both Wolves goals. The Germans won the away leg 2-1.

In the same competition the following season Wolves succumbed to the Spanish giants Barcelona in the second round, losing 9-2 on aggregate, after they had ousted ASK Vorwaerts and Red Star.

Wolves' first taste of European Cup-winners' Cup action saw them overcome F.K. Austria 5-2 on aggregate, but then they slipped up in the semi-finals against Glasgow Rangers, going out 3-1 over two legs.

Entering the UEFA Cup for the first time in 1971-72, Wolves went all the way to the Final by knocking out Academica Del Coimbra (Portugal), FC Den Haag (Holland), Carl Zeiss Jena (East Germany), Juventus (Italy) and Ferencvaros (Hungary). They met Tottenham Hotspur in the two-legged Final and after losing 2-1 at Molineux could only draw 1-1 at White Hart Lane and so lost the trophy 3-2 on aggregate.

In season 1973-74, Wolves went out of the UEFA Cup to Locomotiv Leipzig on the away goal rule (4-4 on aggregate); the following season they fell at the first hurdle, beaten 5-4 over two legs by FC Porto and in 1980-81 PSV Eindhoven conquered Wolves' conquerors, winning 3-2 on aggregate in the first round.

European Facts and Figures
Derek Dougan and John McAlle, with 18 appearances apiece, have played in most European Cup games for Wolves. Kenny Hibbitt and Frank Munro made 17.

Dougan with 12 goals (all in the UEFA Cup, including a hat-trick in a win over Academica Del Coimbra in 1971) was Wolves' top European scorer. Peter Broadbent netted seven times, including Wolves' first-ever strike in a European competition (v Schalke '04).

A crowd of 80,000 saw the Barcelona-Wolves European Cup clash in the Nou Camp Stadium in February 1960 – the biggest attendance for a Wolves game in Europe. Just over 79,000 fans witnessed Wolves' Cup-winners' Cup clash with Rangers at Ibrox Park in 1961.

A top Molineux crowd of 55,747 saw the Wolves v ASK Vorwaerts European Cup encounter in October 1959.

Wolves were one of only ten founder members of the Cup-winners' Cup competition in 1960-61. They played in two rounds – the quarter and semi-finals.

Johnny Kirkham scored Wolves' first Cup-winners' Cup goal, in a 5-0 win over FK Austria at Molineux in November 1960.

Danny Hegan was the first Wolves player to be sent-off in Europe – dismissed against the Portuguese University side, Academica Del Coimbra (away) in September 1971.

Three visiting defenders conceded own-goals when Wolves beat the Dutch side, FC Den Haag 4-0 in a second round, second leg clash at Molineux in November 1971.

A vital penalty save by goalkeeper Phil Parkes earned Wolves a 2-2 draw with Ferencvaros in the semi-final, first leg clash in the impressive Nep Stadium of the 1971-72 UEFA Cup. Defender Frank Munro headed a vital late equaliser in this game.

'Lofty' Parkes again saved a penalty (from the same player, Szoke) in the return leg against the Hungarians, and Munro once more netted a vital goal as Wolves went through to meet Spurs in the Final.

The 1971-72 UEFA Cup Final was the first major European Final involving two British (English) clubs – Wolves and Tottenham Hotspur.

EVANS, Alun William

Born in Stourport-on-Severn on 30 September 1949, the son of the former West Bromwich Albion and Wales wartime international by the same name, striker Alun Evans became Britain's costliest teenager when he was transferred from Wolves to Liverpool for £100,000 in September 1968. Earlier in his career, after winning England caps at Schoolboy, Youth and Under-23 levels, he was regarded as a star of the future but sadly he never reached the heights expected of him. A pupil at Bewdley State School, he represented mid-Worcester Boys and Birmingham Schools, and after a trial with Aston Villa he signed as an apprentice with Wolves (July 1965), turning professional in October 1966. A blond striker, quick off the mark with an eye for goal, Evans did quite well at Molineux, hence his big-money move to Anfield, and for the Merseysiders he scored 21 goals in 79 League games, appearing in the 1971 FA Cup Final. His stay at Anfield was marred by a much publicised night club incident which resulted in Evans receiving a badly gashed face leaving him scarred him for life, and he also underwent a cartilage operation. He moved to Aston Villa for £72,000 in June 1972, and three years later gained a League Cup winners' medal. Nine months after that Wembley clash with Norwich City – and a haul of 17 goals in 72 outings – he was transferred to Walsall for £30,000. While at Fellows Park he played more in midfield than as a striker and amassed 101 appearances (8 goals) up to July 1978 when, after a trial, he joined the Australian club, South Melbourne. From there he went to Hellas FC and returned to Melbourne for £10,000 in August 1979, retiring two years later. Evans chose to stay in Australia and now resides with his wife and family in Cheltenham, Victoria.
Wolves record: 20+2 apps. 4 goals.

EVANS, Anthony

Born in Liverpool on 11 January 1954, striker Tony Evans was an electrician working in Lancashire and playing for Formby FC. From there he became a professional with Blackpool (June 1973) and two years later moved to Cardiff City. At Ninian Park he established himself as a very useful striker and from then until the end of his career scored some excellent goals. From Cardiff he switched to Birmingham City (July 1979) and in August 1983 (after 33 goals in 76 games for Blues) he signed for Crystal Palace (August 1983). In April 1984 he found his way to Molineux, but found it difficult to fit into a struggling side and after loan spells in 1985 with Bolton Wanderers (February) and Exeter City (March-April) he teamed up with Swindon Town in readiness for the start of the 1985-86 campaign. After more than a year with the Robins Evans moved back to the Midlands to sign for Walsall on a non-contract basis in September 1986 and later that year he was recruited by Stafford Rangers, later returning to Molineux as 'football in the community officer' in 1991. In his senior career Evans scored well over 100 goals in 300 appearances (87 in 254 League games). He netted a four-timer for Cardiff against Bristol Rovers in a League Cup-tie in August 1976.
Wolves record: 24+3 apps. 6 goals.

EVANS, Jasper

Rock-solid left-half, Jasper Evans played for Wolves in the mid-1880s, but his career was cut short by a persistent knee injury. Born in Wednesbury c.1861, he played for Wednesbury White Rose, King's Hill FC and Wednesbury Town before joining Wolves in August 1885. He left the Wanderers for West Bromwich Standard in May 1887 and retired a year later. He died in Darlaston in 1938.
Wolves record: 3 apps.

EVERTON

Wolves' playing record against the Merseysiders is:

Football League

Venue	P	W	D	L	F	A
Home	57	29	9	19	112	77
Away	57	11	11	35	51	118
Total	114	40	20	54	163	195

FA Cup

	P	W	D	L	F	A
Home	3	1	2	0	4	2
Away	3	1	0	2	4	6
Neutral	1	1	0	0	1	0
Total	7	3	2	2	9	8

League Cup

	P	W	D	L	F	A
Away	1	0	0	1	1	4

Wartime

	P	W	D	L	F	A
Home	1	1	0	0	11	1
Away	1	0	0	1	1	2
Total	2	1	0	1	12	3

As founder members of the Football League, Wolves first met Everton in 1888-89 and were victorious in both encounters, winning 5-0 at Molineux and 2-1 on Merseyside.

Wolves had to wait almost 50 years before bettering that five-goal scoreline and they did in style, thrashing Everton 7-2 at Molineux in a First Division match in February 1937 when Gordon Clayton scored four times in front of a 36,551 crowd. Two years later, in February 1939, League-champions elect Everton, were hammered 7-0 by a rampant Wolves side at Molineux. On this occasion Dicky Dorsett was the star-performer with four goals watched by almost 40,000 fans.

In May 1933, Wolves saved themselves from relegation to the Second Division by defeating Everton (the FA Cup holders) 4-2 at Molineux on the final day of the season. A crowd of almost 35,500 saw Jack Hetherington score twice and have a hand in another of Wolves' goals that afternoon.

Over 31,000 spectators saw Wolves beat

A goal for Dennis Wilshaw against Everton in January 1950.

Everton 4-0 in a League game at Molineux in November 1950 and a similar crowd witnessed a 4-1 win for Wolves on the same ground in January 1961 when Jimmy Murray netted twice.

Everton quickly avenged that first season slaughter by beating Wolves 5-0 at home in September 1890 and at the turn of the century they ran up successive home wins over the Wanderers of 5-1 (in September 1900) and 6-1 (in September 1902).

Everton also ran up three excellent home wins of 4-0 in November 1930, 5-1 in December 1932 and 5-2 in February 1935.

In post-war League football, Everton's best wins over Wolves have been 4-0 at Goodison Park in March 1962 and January 1969, when the crowd topped 48,000, 4-2 at Molineux in April 1965 and by the same score at home in September 1967, when almost 51,500 fans were present.

Wolves' striker Derek Dougan was sent-off in the home League game against Everton in October 1969. Wolves lost 3-2, there was crowd trouble with 100 fans injured and many more arrested. Dougan was banned for six weeks.

John Richards' hat-trick in Wolves' 4-2 win over Everton in April 1973 culminated with a superb left-foot volley.

Wolves were officially relegated to the Second Division after losing 2-0 to Everton at Goodison Park in April 1984. And to run salt into the wounds, ex-Wolf Andy Gray scored one of the Merseysiders' goals that day. This, in fact, was the last time Wolves and Everton met at League level.

The first FA Cup meeting between Wolves and Everton was in the Final of 1893 at Fallowfield, Manchester – and in front of a then record crowd of over 45,000 (receipts £2,559) Wolves took the trophy 1-0 thanks to a long range goal by skipper Harry Allen, whose speculative effort hit into the sun sailed over the Everton 'keeper's head and into the unguarded net.

Everton were then defeated in 1920-21 (by 1-0) and 1938-39 (by 2-0) as Wolves again made their way to the Final again where they lost on both occasions.

The usually reliable Johnny Hancocks missed a penalty in a fourth-round FA Cup-tie with Everton at Molineux in January 1947. The game ended 1-1 and Everton won the replay 3-2.

Everton knocked Wolves out of the competition after a replay in 1966-67, winning 3-1 at Goodison Park after a 1-1 draw at Molineux.

In front of a 19,065 crowd at Goodison

Park and despite a fine goal by Steve Bull, Wolves lost their only League Cup-tie with Everton by 4-1 in October 1991, Peter Beagrie scoring twice for the home side.

Everton beat Wolves 3-2 on penalties (after a 1-1 draw) in the Mercantile Credit League Centenary Festival at Wembley in April 1988. Robbie Dennison scored for Wolves in normal time in front of a 21,446 crowd.

Two guest players – Jack Rowley (5 goals) and Frank Broome (3) scored eight times between them when Wolves defeated Everton 11-1 at Molineux in a wartime Football League Cup-tie in March 1942.

Archie Goodall became the oldest player ever to appear in a competitive game for Wolves when, at the age of 41 years, five months and two days, he played his last game in a gold and black shirt against Everton at Molineux in the First Division on 2 December 1905. A crowd of 4,000 saw Everton win 5-2.

Players with both clubs include: Alan Ainscow, George Barker, George Brewster, Wilf Chadwick, Wayne Clarke, Peter Eastoe, George Eccles, Stan Fazackerley, Dick Forshaw, Andy Gray, Billy Hartill, Ernie Hunt, Revd Billy Jordan, Andy King, Micky Lill, Tom Mayson, Johnny Morrissey, Derek Mountfield, Darren Oldroyd, Billy Owen,

Vinny Samways, Mike Stowell, Dave Thomas, Sammy Thomson, Walter Weaver, Frank Wignall and Bob Young.

Also associated: Edward Anderson (Everton wartime guest); Andy Mutch (Everton apprentice); Dave Clements and Les Smith (Wolves Reserves), Dick Richards (Everton trial), Bobby Downes (Wolves coach, Everton scout) and Jim Barron (Wolves player, Everton coach) and Harry Potts (coach).

EVES, Melvyn John

Born at Wednesbury on 10 September 1956, striker Mel Eves scored 53 goals in 214 senior games during his 11 years on the Molineux staff, helping Wolves to the Second Division championship in 1977 and the League Cup in 1980. He joined the club as an apprentice in July 1973 and became a full-time professional in July 1975. Eves, who was Wolves' leading scorer with 19 goals in 1982-83, also won three England 'B' caps, against Singapore (twice) and New Zealand. During the early 1980s, there was a feeling that Eves had not been treated fairly and after suffering a series of injuries he left Wolves for Sheffield United in December 1984, after a loan spell with Huddersfield Town. In August 1986, the Blades let him go to Gillingham and he later spent short loan spells with Mansfield Town, Manchester City and West Bromwich Albion. He retired in the 1989 close season after an impressive record of 67 League goals in 243 appearances with his seven League clubs. Eves later played for Telford United and Cheltenham Town in the GM Vauxhall Conference League, for Old Wulfrunians and took part in charity matches.
Wolves record: 202+12 apps. 53 goals.

EXETER CITY

Wolves' playing record against the Grecians is:

Football League

Venue	P	W	D	L	F	A
Home	2	1	1	0	5	2
Away	2	2	0	0	7	3
Total	4	3	1	0	12	5
FA Cup						
Home	1	1	0	0	3	1
Away	1	0	1	0	2	2
Total	2	1	1	0	5	3
League Cup						
Home	1	1	0	0	5	1
Freight Rover Trophy						
Away	1	0	1	0	1	1

Wolves conceded two penalties and had defender Ally Robertson sent-off, but still beat Exeter 3-1 at St James' Park in a Fourth Division game in May 1987.

After an excellent 2-2 draw at home to Wolves in a third-round FA Cup-tie in January 1978, Exeter eventually bowed out of the competition when they lost the replay 3-1 at Molineux.

Wolves easily accounted for Exeter City in the only League Cup meeting between the clubs, winning a fourth-round tie at Molineux on a Tuesday afternoon in November 1973 by 5-1 with John Richards and Kenny Hibbitt both scoring twice in front of just 7,623 fans.

A meagre crowd of 1,278 turned out to witness Wolves' 1-1 Freight Rover Trophy draw at Exeter in January 1986.

Players with both clubs include: Hugh Atkinson, Richard Baugh jnr, Steve Biggins, Brian Birch, Paul Birch, Bill Coley, Glenn Crowe, Dean Edwards, Tony Evans, Vic Fox, Ray Goddard, Francis Hemingway, Sammy Holt, John Kirkham, Tommy Langley, Wilf Lowton, Jack Mitton, Tim Steele, Clive Whitehead and Horace Wright.

Also associated: Jock Basford (Wolves reserve, Exeter manager); Eric Jones (Wolves player, City wartime guest); Cyril Spiers (Wolves player, City manager) and Jack Angus (he made 265 appearances for Exeter: 1934-48 after leaving Molineux), Mick Connaboy, Jimmy Gill, Herby Hoyle, Steve Pugh, John Rutter, Bernie Singleton, George Willis (all Wolves Reserves) and James Dailey (Wolves amateur).

FAIR PLAY LEAGUE

In season 1977-78 Wolves won a prize in the Daily Mail/Vernons Pools Fair Play League. They had only one player sent-off (Bob Hazell against Arsenal in the FA Cup), conceded five penalties, received 16 bookings (the lowest by a First Division club) and gave away the least number of free-kicks.

FAMILY LINKS

Brothers to play for Wolves at first team level include full-backs Richard (senior) and Richard (junior) Baugh; midfielders Campbell and Cavan Chapman; strikers Derek and Wayne Clarke; defenders Alf and Sammy Crook; Jackery and Joseph Jones from Wellington; the Welshmen Dai and Billy Richards; inside-forwards Jimmy and Richard Deacon; Ike and John Griffiths (1880/90s) and Reg and Walter Weaver, Joe and Ted White and utility players Archie and Jack Needham.

The brothers Arthur and Jack Rowley were together at Molineux during the 1939-45 wartime period.

Wolves reserve Ernie Brooks and first-team regular Sammy Brooks were brothers (either side of World War One).

Jack Shelton, an inside-forward with Wolves in the 1930s and later a full-back with Walsall, was both son and stepson of ex-Wolves star Jack Shelton who won a FA Cup medal in 1908. And when he died his widow married Wolves player Jack Needham.

Chris and Matthew Clarke became the first set of twins to join Wolves when they signed YTS forms in June 1997.

Chapman, father of Campbell and Cavan, was Manager of Wolves in the 1980s.

Graham Turner had his son, Mark, at Molineux with him when he was Wolves' manager.

Billy Blunt and his brother Sidney were both associated with Wolves between the two world wars.

The Moss brothers, Craig and Paul, were at Molineux together during the 1970s, Craig made the first team, Paul didn't.

Tom Galley was the uncle of John Galley.

1990s striker Jason Roberts is the nephew of another ex-Wolves goalscorer Cyrille Regis.

William Caddick senior was a reserve goalkeeper with Wolves from 1880-83 and between 1920 and 1927 his grandson, William Caddick junior, was a defender – and captain – of Wolves, helping them win the Third Division North championship in 1924.

The Bhatti brothers were associated with Wolves in the 1980s.

The Haywards, Sir Jack, the club's millionaire businessman owner and his son, Jonathan, have been associated with Wolves since the early 1990s.

FARLEY, John R.

Versatile winger John Farley served with six different League clubs in 12 years between 1969 and 1981. Born in Middlesbrough on 21 September 1951, he played initially for Stockton (1967) and after that assisted Watford (July 1969), Halifax Town (on loan September 1971), Wolves (May 1974), Blackpool (on loan October 1976), Hull City (May 1978) and Bury (August 1980 to May 1981). He appeared in more than 250 senior games as a professional and netted over 20 goals, laying on plenty more for his colleagues. He helped Watford establish themselves in the Second Division during his five-year stay at Vicarage Road.
Wolves record: 38+5 apps.

FARMER, James Edward

Although centre-forward Ted Farmer played only four seasons of League football for Wolves before his career came to a cruel and premature end at the age of 24, he made his mark with a splendid scoring record of 44 goals in only 62 games. And even in his fleeting international career, he wrote his name large with two Under-23 caps, against Israel and Holland in 1961 and a hat-trick against the Dutch. In the 1960-61 season he scored 28 goals in only 27 League games, including four goals against Birmingham City at

Molineux in March. He was born in Rowley Regis on 21 January 1940 and played for Wednesbury High School, Rowley Regis Boys and Dudley and District Schools. Outside school he turned out on Saturday afternoons for Wednesbury Commercial and Wednesbury Youth Club, and in November 1955 he scored 21 goals in one day, with 13 in the morning and eight in the afternoon. Those sort of goalscoring exploits soon came to the attention of local League clubs and Wolves won the race to sign him in the 1956 close season. In his first season with Wolves juniors, Farmer netted a remarkable total of 86 goals. Wolves made him a full-time professional in August 1960 and on his League debut, at Old Trafford of all places, he scored twice in a 3-1 victory over Manchester United. Between his debut day and 21 January 1961 he scored 21 goals in only 17 League games and had a hat-trick against Arsenal to his name. There followed those four goals against Birmingham City and another four against Manchester City as Wolves won 8-2 on the opening day of the 1962-63 season. He seemed set to become the goalscoring sensation of the day when injury struck and he played only six games in 1963-64 before retiring. He was plagued by injuries, suffering a damaged bladder, broken leg against Fulham in December 1961 (which wasn't diagnosed until five weeks later), numerous dislocations, twists, cracks and concussion. Farmer later published a book about his career and he was also the licensee of the Lamp Tavern in Dudley.
Wolves record: 62 apps. 44 goals.

FARRINGTON, John

John Farrington was an out-and-out winger, rather on the slim side, but fast and clever nonetheless. Born at Lynemouth on 19 June 1947, he joined Wolves as a junior in 1963 and turned professional in June 1965. In the next four years he drifted in and out of the first team before leaving Molineux for Leicester City in October 1969. He did very well at Filbert Street and after scoring 18 goals in 118 League appearances he moved to Cardiff City (November 1973). From Ninian Park he switched to Northampton Town (October 1974) and hit over 30 goals in more than 250 outings for the Cobblers up to 1981 when he dropped into non-League soccer, serving first with AP Leamington and later managing Barlestone of the Influence Combination (1991-92).
Wolves record: 35+3 apps. 5 goals.

FARROW, George Henry

One of the few players who served Blackpool before and after World War Two, George Farrow was born in Whitburn on 4 October 1913 and played for Whitburn Boys before becoming a professional with Stockport County in October 1930. In January 1932 he left Edgeley Park for Molineux, signed by Major Buckley as cover for right-half Dicky Rhodes. A reliable performer, he played in a quarter of Wolves' games on their return to the First Division, but was then sold to Bournemouth in July 1933, later playing for Blackpool (June 1936). After the hostilities he signed for Sheffield United (January 1948) and retired in May 1950.
Wolves record: 12 apps.

FAZACKERLEY, Stanley Nicholas

Stan Fazackerley was another forward who spent only a short time with Wolves, barely three seasons, yet he too became a big favourite with the fans, helping the club to the Third Division North championship in 1923-24. Born in Preston on 3 October 1891, Fazackerley, a tall and skilful inside-forward, played with local club Lands End United and had an unsuccessful trial with Preston North End before going over to North America where he spent a season with Charleston in the Boston League in 1910, helping them win the title. He returned to England to sign for Accrington Stanley, then in the Lancashire Combination, before Hull City recruited him in April 1912. Sheffield United were impressed enough to pay £1,000 for his signature in March 1913 and Fazackerley scored one of the Blades' goals in their 3-0 win over Chelsea in the 1915 FA Cup Final, called the 'Khaki Final' because so many soldiers home on leave from the Western Front were present in the crowd. Everton paid a then British record fee of £4,000 for him in November 1920 and he arrived at Molineux, with Everton's George Brewster, in November 1922. Fazackerley was in George Jobey's team that won the Northern Section title and it was Jobey, then manager of Derby, who signed Fazackerley for the Rams in March 1925, after the player had been loaned out to Kidderminster Harriers whilst on Wolves' transfer list. Derby had a centre-forward problem and Fazackerley was one of three men tried in the first six games of 1925-26. For Fazackerley it was the end of the road anyway and he retired on medical advice in April 1926. As a Sheffield United player he toured South Africa with the FA in 1920 and once scored 11 goals for Hull City in a 16-1 friendly match win over a Trondheim and District XI in Norway in May 1912. He died in Sheffield on 20 June 1946.
Wolves record: 77 apps. 32 goals.

FEATHERBY, Walter Leonard

One of soccer's globetrotters, inside-forward Len Featherby had a wide and varied career which spanned almost 20 years. Born in King's Lynn on 28 July 1905, he began his playing days with Whitefriars FC in 1921 and then went on to assist Lynn Town, Norfolk County, Glasgow Rangers (as a trialist in January 1924), Norwich City (signing as an amateur in May 1924 and turning professional June 1924), Northfleet (early October 1927), Millwall (late October 1927), Peterborough and Fletton United (March 1928), Merthyr Town (August 1928), Wolves (signed in January 1929), Reading (June 1930), Queen's Park Rangers (from May 1931 – no first-team games), Mansfield Town (December 1931), Crewe Alexandra (July 1932), Merthyr Town again (for one season from July 1933), Plymouth Argyle (March 1934), Notts County (June 1935) and finally King's Lynn (August 1938 to October 1939). An avid pigeon fancier, Featherby retired during the war and later became a cricket groundsman in Norfolk. He represented Norfolk County and gained a Senior Cup winners medal with King's Lynn in April 1939 and during his time in football turned down lucrative jobs with senior clubs in the north of England and in Switzerland. Featherby died in King's Lynn on 22 February 1972.
Wolves record: 21 apps. 6 goals.

FELLOWS, Arthur

Wolves signed inside or centre-forward Archie Fellows in the summer of 1901 from Willenhall Pickwick. He stayed at Molineux for two seasons before injuries forced him to drop out of League football. He was given a free transfer in May 1903 and signed for Darlaston, later assisting Halesowen and Netherton. He was born in Wednesfield c.1880.
Wolves record: 55 apps. 8 goals.

FERENCVAROS

The Hungarian club Ferencvaros were victims of Wolves in the 1971-72 UEFA Cup semi-final. The first leg, played on 5 April in Hungary, ended 2-2 before a near 45,000 crowd. The second leg at Molineux two weeks later attracted over 28,000 fans and resulted in a narrow 2-1 victory for Wolves, who went through 4-3 on aggregate. Frank Munro was one of the Wolves' heroes against the Hungarians, scoring in both games.

FERGUSON, Darren

Son of the Manchester United manager Alex Ferguson, midfielder Darren Ferguson joined Wolves from Old Trafford for £250,000 in January 1994 after appearing in 30 games for United. Born in Glasgow on 9 February 1972, he joined the Reds as a junior in 1988 and turned professional in July 1990. After representing Scotland at youth team level, Ferguson went on to gain five Under-21 caps as a tidy, hard-working midfielder, very competitive who occasionally let his enthusiasm boil over – he was sent-off playing for

Wolves against against Bolton in October 1996. In November 1998 Ferguson had a trial with the Italian Serie 'B' side Cosenza, but quickly returned to Britain after a near riot broke out at the club's training ground following the sacking of boss Juliano Sonzongni. In January 1999, Ferguson was on his travels again, this time to the Dutch side Sparta Rotterdam, on a month's loan.
Wolves record: 122+27 apps. 10 goals.

FERGUSON, John James

Outside-right Jack Ferguson joined Wolves in August 1928 from Spen Black and White FC. He spent just over a season at Molineux before transferring to Watford in October 1929. Born in Rowland's Gill in 1904, and played for Grimsby Town in season 1926-27 (3 League games).
Wolves record: 20 apps. 4 goals.

FERRES, Walter F. Joseph

Goalkeeper Walter Ferres was born in Bloxwich in 1886 and joined Wolves from Willenhall Swifts in August 1907. Reserve to Tommy Lunn and Jim Stringer, he conceded five goals on his League debut at Barnsley and stayed at Molineux until May 1907 when he moved to Wednesfield, later assisting Darlaston, Greets Green Primitives and Cradley Town. He died *c*.1950.
Wolves record: 2 apps.

FINLAYSON, Malcolm

Although he had played in 229 League games for Millwall, goalkeeper Malcolm Finlayson was a relatively unknown Third Division South player when Wolves paid £4,000 for him in August 1956 to eventually replace the great Bert Williams, who was nearing he end of his illustrious career. Finlayson appeared only 13 times in his first season at Molineux but in the summer of 1957, Williams retired and Finlayson went on to make over 200 appearances for Wolves, winning two League championship medals and an FA Cup winners' medal during his time at Molineux. He was virtually an ever-present for a number of seasons before Fred Davies took over in January 1962. Finlayson's last appearance at Anfield in September 1963, when he suffered a broken finger. He retired at the end of that season. Finlayson became a very successful businessmen with a number of foundries, and in June 1982 he was appointed vice chairman of Wolves, although the appointment was short-lived when a new regime took over. He was born in Dumbarton on 14 June 1930 and played for Renfrew Juniors before Millwall signed him during the 1947-48 season. In November 1948, Finlayson was injured in the 20th minute of a League game at Walsall and was taken to hospital. When he returned the second half was 18 minutes old and Millwall were losing 3-1, so Finlayson

scaled a wall, resumed his place in goal and inspired the Lions to a 6-5 victory.
Wolves record: 203 apps.

FIORENTINA

Italy's Serie 'A' side Fiorentina were beaten by Wolves twice in the qualifying group in the 1970 Anglo-Italian Competition. The first clash at Molineux (watched by 14,262 fans) ended in a 2-1 Wolves victory, and the second in Florence (in front of a 13,120 crowd) saw the Wanderers triumph 3-1. Derek Dougan scored in both games.

FIVE-A-SIDE

Wolves won the National Five-a-Side soccer competition in successive seasons, in 1975-76 and 1976-77. They beat Spurs in the first Final and then defeated Stoke City in the Final 12 months later to retain the trophy.

FLEMING, George

Hard-tackling left-half George Fleming was born at Bannockburn, Stirlingshire, on 20 May 1869 and joined Wolves from East Stirlingshire in July 1894 to become one of six Scottish players on the Molineux club's books. Fleming enjoyed his time with Wolves, making 187 senior appearances and scoring seven goals. He did not appear in the 1896 FA Cup Final defeat by Sheffield Wednesday, but played 30 times when Wolves finished third in Division One in 1897-98. In May 1901, with the emergence of Jack Whitehouse, Fleming was transferred to Liverpool, thus leaving Wolves without any Scots on their books. He was a firm favourite at Anfield, making 83 appearances for the Merseysiders and gaining a Second Division championship medal in 1905 before retiring to become assistant trainer at the club. He died in August 1922.
Wolves record: 187 apps. 7 goals.

FLETCHER, Albert Thomas

Wing-half Albert Fletcher, who was born in Wolverhampton on 4 June 1867, was a man who was huge in both body and spirit, a real 'man mountain' who nevertheless possessed a great deal of skill. He joined Wolves in 1886, when secretary Jack Addenbrooke paid a golden sovereign for his signature from Willenhall Pickwick, and went on to make 120 senior appearances for the club, 58 of them in the Football League. Fletcher played in the 1889 FA Cup Final against Preston North End and gained two England caps, both against Wales, in 1889 and 1890. His career came to a sad end when he suffered a broken leg during a game against Aston Villa at Perry Barr and in July 1891 he finally gave up his plans for a comeback. His Molineux days were really just beginning, though, for he spent the next 29 years with Wolves, first as assistant trainer from 1891 to 1896 and

then as successor to chief trainer Jack Lewis. Albert Fletcher left Wolves in August 1920, aged 53, and he died in the town on 16 August 1938.
Wolves record: 76 apps. 2 goals.

FLO, Haavard

The first Norwegian to sign for Wolves, Flo was a £750,000 buy from the German Bundesliga side Werder Bremen in January 1999. A forceful striker, who can also play in midfield, Flo had already won 15 full caps for Norway when he moved to Molineux. A member of his country's France '98 World Cup squad, he was born in 1970 and had been with Bremen for three seasons, having earlier assisted FC Aarhus. He made his debut for Wolves in the home League game with Watford four days after signing and admitted: "English football is quicker than what it is in Germany, much quicker."
Wolves record: 19+1 apps. 6 goals.

FLOODLIGHTS

In the summer of 1953, the first set of floodlights, comprising 60 lamps, similar to those at the famous Yankee Stadium in New York, were erected at Molineux. They were officially switched on later that year when a South Africa National team came over to play an under-strength Wolves side in a friendly on 30 September and were defeated 3-1.

The first League game to be staged under the Molineux lights was Wolves against Tottenham Hotspur in April 1956 when the Wanderers ran out convincing 5-1 winners, Bill Slater netting with two penalty kicks.

Four years later, in 1957, a new set of lights were installed with the old ones being sold to Blackpool. Set on four pylons and rising 146 feet above the pitch, they were some of the best in the country at that time.

As the years rolled by and televised soccer became more and more positive, so clubs changed to better floodlighting, and in 1969 Wolves acquired another brand new set of lights, this time at a cost of £20,000.

During the 1970s and 1980s, with European football and colour TV firmly taking hold, high quality lamps had to be used and Wolves kept up with the Jones's all down the line. And when the Molineux stadium was redeveloped with Sir Jack Hayward's millions, yet another high quality set of floodlights were assembled, this time at a cost of almost £100,000.

Rays of Light

Wolves met neighbours West Bromwich Albion at Cross Keys in 24 March 1953 in a friendly arranged to officially 'switch on' the Hednesford Town floodlights. The Baggies were beaten 4-2.

Celtic invited Wolves to Parkhead for a friendly in October 1954 to officially switch

Ron Flowers (extreme left) joins his teammates and manager Stan Cullis to admire the Football League championship trophy in 1954.

on their new floodlighting system. This game ended 3-3.

On 28 November 1983, Wolves beat Cardiff City 5-3 in a friendly to officially turn on the new floodlighting system at Ninian Park.

Wolves have visited several other venues to 'officially' switch on the floodlights of that club, among them: Bristol City (Ashton Gate) in February 1951; Hull City (Boothferry Park), March 1953; Bilston Town (Queen Street) also in March 1953; Bury (Gigg Lane) in October 1953; Hendon in September 1962; Greenock Morton (Cappielow Park) in October 1962; Eastwood Town (Notts.) in February 1981; Forest Green Rovers in October 1981 (won 6-1); Dudley Town in November 1981 (won 6-1); Bridgnorth Town in October 1982; Willenhall Town in August 1982; Halesowen Town in February 1984 and Rushall Olympic in November 1984.

FLOWERS, Ronald

In the 1950s, Wolves were famed for their half-back line and Ron Flowers, of the striking blond hair, immense stamina and powerful shot was one of its stars. Born in Edlington, near Doncaster, on 28 July 1934,

Flowers starred with his local grammar school team, Doncaster Rovers juniors and the Doncaster and Yorkshire Boys side before he joined the Wolves nursery side, Wath Wanderers, in July 1950, turning professional in 1952. Flowers made his League debut at home to Blackpool in September that year and celebrated with a headed goal before a crowd of 49,000. He gained three League championship medals with Wolves and an FA Cup winners' medal as well as winning 49 full England caps, two for the Under-23s and playing for the Football League. He spent 15 years as a professional at Molineux, appearing in more than 500 senior games (467 in the League alone) and scoring almost 40 goals. His international career began in 1955 and he was still in contention 11 years later as a member of England's original pool of 40 for the 1966 World Cup finals. He helped Wolves regain their First Division place before, in September 1967, moving to Northampton Town. He later became player-coach of the Cobblers before becoming player-manager of Wellington Town. They were renamed Telford United by the time he guided them to the FA Trophy Final at Wembley and in 1971 he resigned to concentrate on running his Wolverhampton sports outfitters

shop. His father and brother both played for Doncaster Rovers.

Wolves record: 512 apps. 37 goals.

FLOWERS, Timothy

Tim Flowers, born at Kenilworth on 3 February 1967, replaced John Burridge in Wolves' goal at the start of the 1984-85 season after joining the staff at Molineux as an apprentice in June 1983 and turning professional in August 1984. Wolves' manager Tommy Docherty gave him his League debut at home to Sheffield United on the opening day of the season and he made 38 appearances that season and 72 in all before he signed for Southampton after a loan period at The Dell. The Saints wanted to groom Flowers to take over from Peter Shilton and paid Wolves £70,000 for him in June 1986. Eventually, after two loan spells at Swindon Town, Flowers replaced Shilton who had gone to Derby County. He gained his first full England cap against Brazil in the summer of 1993, during the USA Cup competition, to go with the Youth and Under-21 honours he had won whilst with Wolves, and in November 1993 – after 242 appearances for Saints – he joined Blackburn Rovers for £2.4 million. It was a world record fee for a goalkeeper and Liverpool had been prepared to pay it but Flowers wanted to join Blackburn and refused to speak with the Anfield management. He helped Rovers into European football for the first time, as Premiership champions and in 1998 he became the first goalkeeper to appear in 200 Premiership matches, although soon afterwards he asked for a transfer from Ewood Park. In February 1995 Flowers was sent-off after only 72 seconds play when keeping goal for Blackburn against Leeds United – another Premiership record.

Wolves record: 72 apps.

FOLEY, Dominic

Striker Dominic Foley was born in Cork on 7 July 1976 and was educated at The Christian Brothers School in Charleville. He played Gaelic football before taking up soccer and in due course signed for Wolves direct from the St James' Gate club in the Irish Republic for £35,000 in August 1995. But with Steve Bull, Don Goodman and Iwan Roberts ahead of him, his first-team appearances were limited. An Irish Under-21 international, he had only 26 senior outings for Wolves before having loan spells with Watford (February-April 1998), Notts County (December 1998), Lincoln City (January 1999) and the Greek club, Ethnikos (February-May 1999). He scored a hat-trick on his debut for Ethnikos whose manager was Howard Kendall. In July 1999 Foley joined Watford.

Wolves record: 4+22 apps. 3 goals.

FA CUP

Wolves first entered the FA (English) Cup in season 1883-84 and to date (to May 1998) they have played 324 games in the annual competition.

Their full record (1883-1999) is:

P	W	D	L	F	A
335	157	76	102	613	430

Wolves have appeared in eight FA Cup Finals, winning four and losing four.

In 1893 they beat Everton 1-0 at Fallowfield (Manchester) when Harry Allen scored the vital goal ten minutes into the second-half in front of 45,000 spectators (receipts £2,559). A speculative high ball from Allen was lost in the sun by the Everton 'keeper Billy Scott and it dropped behind him into the unguarded net. This was the first time the Final had been decided outside London.

Their second victory was 3-1 over a strong Newcastle United side at the Crystal Palace in 1908 when 74,967 fans (paying £5,998 in receipts) saw four players whose surnames all began with the letter 'H' score the goals – George Hedley, Billy Harrison and the Revd Kenneth Hunt for Wolves and Howie for Newcastle.

A delighted Harrison became the father of triplets on the same day Wolves won the Cup in 1908 (25 April).

When lifting the Cup in 1908, Wolves were in the Second Division and finished as low as ninth that season – the lowest position occupied by a League team winning the coveted trophy.

Wolves' third success was achieved in 1949 when they overcame fellow Midlanders Leicester City 3-1 at Wembley before a 98,920 crowd (receipts £39,300). On target that afternoon were Jesse Pye (2) and Sammy Smyth, the latter's goal being described as the best seen in any Cup Final up to that time.

The last occasion Wolves lifted the coveted trophy was in 1960 when they beat the ten men of Blackburn Rovers 3-0 with right-winger Norman Deeley netting twice and Mick McGrath conceding an own-goal. The attendance at Wembley was 98,776 (with receipts of £49,816), and Dave Whelan was the unlucky Rovers' player, carried off with a broken leg.

Wolves' four Final defeats were suffered in the space of 50 years between 1889 and 1939.

Preston North End beat Wolves 3-0 at Kennington Oval in the 1889 Final before a 22,250 crowd. The Deepdale club went on to clinch the double that season.

Sheffield Wednesday then ruined Wolves' hopes of success in the 1896 Final, winning 2-1 at the Crystal Palace in front 48,836 fans (receipts £1,824). Scotsman David Black scored for the Wanderers.

A crowd of 72,805 (receipts £13,414) saw Tottenham Hotspur's Jimmy Dimmock score the only goal of the rain-swept 1921 Final which was staged at Stamford Bridge. And underdogs Portsmouth, with two former Molineux players in their side, Herbert Barlow and Guy Wharton, lifted the Cup in 1939 with a convincing 4-1 win at Wembley.

Wolves' 1939 FA Cup winning players. Back row (left to right): Morris, Galley, Scott, Taylor, Gardiner. Front: Mullen, Burton, McIntosh, Cullis, Westcott, Dorsett, Maguire.

Dicky Dorsett netted Wolves' consolation goal in front of 99,370 fans (receipts £29.116).

Dicky Baugh (senior) and Harry Wood both appeared in three FA Cup Finals for Wolves.

Wolves' record in the FA Cup Final:

P	W	D	L	F	A
8	4	0	4	12	12

Wolves have also been beaten in six semi-finals – losing to Blackburn Rovers in 1890, Newcastle United in 1951 (after a replay), Leeds United in 1973, Arsenal in 1979, Tottenham Hotspur in 1981 (again after a replay) and Arsenal in 1998.

Winger Jimmy Mullen was only 16 years of age when he played for Wolves in the 1939 FA Cup semi-final victory over Grimsby Town at Old Trafford.

FA Cup Facts and Figures

Wolves' best FA Cup win to date has been that of 14-0 over Crosswell's Brewery in a second round tie at Dudley Road on 2 November 1886. That afternoon a crowd of 2,000 saw Tom Hunter (4), Jack Brodie (3), Tom Knight (3), Bernie Griffiths (2), Harry Allen and Joe Law (own goal) score the goals.

Wolves defeated Watford 10-0 at Molineux in a first-round replay on 24 January 1912. On a chilly midweek afternoon, a crowd of 8,751 saw Irishman Billy Halligan lead the goal-rush with a fine hat-trick.

Wolves' third biggest FA Cup victory was a 9-1 victory over Wrexham at home in a third round tie on 10 January 1931. Over 28,000 attended this encounter when Billy Hartill (4) and Charlie Phillips (3) were in terrific goalscoring form.

Wolves defeated Stoke 4-0 at home in the third round of the 1889-90 competition, but the visitors lodged a strong protest over the state of the Molineux pitch. The FA upheld their protest and ordered the tie to be replayed. Wolves were again in convincing form and won easily by 8-0 with Jack Brodie scoring five times.

Non-League Lovells Athletic were thrashed 8-1 by Wolves in a third round second leg game at Molineux in January 1946. Tom Galley scored a hat-trick and Wolves went through 12-3 on aggregate.

Wolves' biggest away win in the competition is 5-0, achieved twice – in a first round tie at Reading in January 1910, when Billy Blunt scored four goals and in the 1939 semi-final against Grimsby Town at Old Trafford when a record crowd for the ground of 76,962 saw Dennis Westcott also net a four-timer.

Wolves also beat Grimsby 5-2 at Blundell Park in January 1955 when over 26,000 spectators saw Dennis Wilshaw score twice.

The heaviest defeat suffered by Wolves in the FA Cup competition is 6-0, away at Rotherham in a first round tie in November 1985.

Wolves also lost 6-3 at Molineux against Derby County in January 1933 and were swept aside 5-1 also at Molineux by West Ham United (from the Southern League) in February 1910. Another heavy home defeat was 5-3 at the hands of Manchester United in a quarter-final clash in March 1965 when the crowd was 53,581.

Wolves were undefeated in their first 19 home FA Cup games. They lost their 20th encounter 3-1 to Aston Villa in the third round in February 1892.

Wolves' first FA Cup-tie was their home clash with Long Eaton Rangers on 27 October 1883. A crowd of 2,000 saw them register a 4-1 victory with Jack Brodie (2) and John Griffiths (2) their scorers.

Wolves' first defeat in the competition came soon after when they lost 4-2 to Wednesbury Old Athletic (away) on 1 December 1883.

The first FA Cup-tie to be staged at Molineux was the Wolves v Old Carthusians match on 2 February 1889. A crowd of 6,000 saw Wolves win 4-3 with Tom Knight scoring twice.

Since League football was introduced in 1888, Wolves have been beaten by clubs from a lower Division in the FA Cup 11 times – Queen's Park Rangers (Southern League) 1899-1900, Southampton (Southern League) 1904-05, Crystal Palace (Southern League) 1908-09, West Ham United (Southern League) 1909-10, Cardiff City (Southern League) 1919-20, Mansfield Town (Midland League) 1928-29, Birmingham City (Division Two) 1953-54, Bournemouth (Division Three South) 1956-57, Huddersfield Town (Division Two) 1960-61, Watford (Division Two) 1979-80 and Chorley (Multi-Part League) 1986-87.

The team Wolves have met most times in the FA Cup is Aston Villa (12). They have had 11 encounters against both Derby County and Sheffield United and have opposed Blackburn Rovers, Sheffield Wednesday and West Bromwich Albion on 10 occasions.

Over 40 of Wolves' draws in the FA Cup have been by the scoreline of 1-1 while their highest-scoring draw has so far been 3-3.

Wolves suffered their 100th defeat in the FA Cup when they lost 2-1 at home to Portsmouth in a third round tie at Molineux in January 1997.

Full-back Bobby Thomson made his senior debut for Wolves in the third-round FA Cup-tie with West Bromwich Albion at Molineux in January 1962. Almost 46,500 fans saw Albion win 2-1.

Jack Brodie, Tom Knight and Dennis Westcott have each scored two hat-tricks in FA Cup competition for Wolves. The last player to claim a hat-trick in the tournament was Steve Bull, doing so against non-League side Cheltenham Town (now a Football League club) at Molineux in November 1987.

Harry Wood and Billy Wright share the record of appearing in most FA Cup matches for Wolves – 48. Kenny Hibbitt played in 47 and Derek Parkin 46.

John Richards scored a record 24 FA Cup goals for Wolves; Jack Brodie claimed 22 and Dennis Westcott 19.

Since the formation of the Football League in 1888, Wolves have met the following non-League clubs in the FA Cup – Altrincham, Carlisle United*, Cheltenham Town, Chorley, Crystal Palace*, Lincoln City*, Lovells Athletic, Mansfield Town*, Walsall and West Ham United*.

*Wolves met these clubs in their pre-League days.

FA YOUTH CUP

Wolves entered the FA Youth Cup at the outset of the competition in 1952-53. Their first match saw them defeat Wellington Town 5-0 away. They progressed through to the Final that season, losing to Manchester United 9-3 on aggregate after going down 7-1 before 20,934 fans at Old Trafford and then drawing the return leg at Molineux 2-2 in front of a 14,208 crowd. Included in the Wolves team were Eddie Clamp, Les Smith and Colin Booth, all of whom entered League football with the Wanderers.

Wolves were beaten Finalists the following season (1953-54) when once more Manchester United took the trophy, winning 5-4 on aggregate after a terrific contest. The teams drew 4-4 at Molineux when the attendance was 18,246 before United edged a 1-0 victory at Old Trafford, cheered on by a crowd of 28,651.

In the Wolves line-up for this Final were the likes of Geoff Sidebottom, Garry Harris, Bobby Mason and Jimmy Murray.

In 1957-58 Wolves won the FA Youth Cup at the sixth time of asking, beating Chelsea 7-6 in a superb Final. Wolves knocked out neighbours West Bromwich Albion, Aston Villa, Stoke City, Leicester City and Bolton Wanderers en route to the Final and after losing the first leg 5-1 in front of 19,621 fans at Stamford Bridge, no-one gave them any hope of turning round that four-goal deficit. But turn it round they did and after playing some terrific football witnessed by a crowd of 17,074, Wolves ran out 6-1 winners at Molineux to take the Cup 7-6 on aggregate Ted Farmer netted four goals in the second leg.

Stan Cullis' Wanderers were beaten in the 1961-62 Final by Newcastle United 2-1 on aggregate (it was 1-1 at Molineux in front of a 13,916 crowd and 1-0 to United at St James' Park when the turnout was 20,588). Earlier Wolves had accounted for Birmingham City,

Smith (centre) opens the scoring for Wolves against Manchester United in the second leg of the 1952-53 FA Youth Cup Final.

Notts County, Stoke City, Aston Villa and Chelsea. In 1962-63 and 1970-71 they lost in the semis to West Ham United and Arsenal respectively, but reached their fourth Final in 1975-76, when this time, after knocking out Birmingham City, Fulham, Tottenham Hotspur and Newcastle United, they succumbed to rivals West Bromwich Albion 5-0 on aggregate, losing both legs. They went down 2-0 at home in front of 11,875 spectators and then crashed 3-0 at The Hawthorns when the crowd was 15,558. Bob Hazell and George Berry were in defence for Wolves while Martin Patching was in midfield.

A further semi-final appearance arrived in season 1981-82 when the Wolves youngsters were beaten by Graham Taylor's Watford, but since then the FA Youth Cup has not been a good competition for the Wanderers.

In 13 years from 1952 Wolves' youngsters were unbeaten in 35 FA Youth Cup matches at Molineux, recording 28 victories.

Wolves' record win in the competition is 11-1 at home against Spalding in 1953-54. Joe Bonson scored four times and Wolves led 8-1 at half-time.

When Wolves defeated Walsall 10-0 at Molineux in 1954-55 centre-forward Harry Middleton scored five goals.

Other big wins have seen Wolves beat both Peterborough United and Leicester City by 9-0 scorelines in 1955-56 and 1957-58 respectively.

Wolves' best away win in the Youth Cup is 8-0 at Shrewsbury in 1968-69. Wolves also won 8-1 at Corby Town in 1960-61 and 7-1 at Walsall the previous season. In 1994-95 Wolves' youth team beat Cambridge United 6-2 away in a first-round replay.

Wolves' heaviest Youth Cup defeat is 7-1, suffered twice, at Old Trafford against Manchester United in the semi-final, first leg of 1952-53 and at Highfield Road against

Coventry City in 1985-86. They also lost 6-1 at Bolton in 1972-73.

In season 1995-96 Wolves were beaten 6-5 at Molineux in a first round tie by Birmingham City.

Joe Bonson and Les Cooper share the record for scoring most FA Youth Cup goals for Wolves – total 15. Bonson's tally includes a five and a four in season 1953-54. Winger Les Smith netted 13 (including two hat-tricks) and Peter Eastoe claimed 11.

The most appearances made by a Wolves player in FA Youth Cup football is 20 by Frank Bolton and Les Cooper; Peter Knowles made 19.

This is Wolves' complete record in the FA Youth Cup: 1952 to 1999

P	W	D	L	F	A
173	87	34	52	429	258

See *Youth Football*

FOOTBALL LEAGUE

Along with 11 other clubs – Accrington, Aston Villa, Blackburn Rovers, Bolton Wanderers, Burnley, Derby County, Everton, Notts County, Preston North End, Stoke and West Bromwich Albion – Wolves were founder members of the Football League in 1888.

Their first match was against Aston Villa on 8 September of that year and it ended in a 1-1 draw at Dudley Road. Villa's full-back Gersom Cox scored an own-goal for Wolves.

Wolves' first League win was achieved at home against Burnley on 22 September 1888 when they triumphed by 4-1 in front of 4,000 spectators.

The team had suffered its first League defeat at the hands of Preston North End at Deepdale a week earlier, losing 4-0.

Wolves ended their first League season in third position with 28 points, winning 12

and drawing four of their 22 fixtures. Their goal-average was 51 for and 37 against.

Wolves have won the Football League (First Division) championship three times: 1953-54, 1957-58 and 1958-59. They have taken the Second Division title twice: 1931-32 and 1976-77; carried off the Third Division prize once, in 1988-89, collected the Third Division North crown in 1923-24 and lifted the Fourth Division trophy in 1987-88. Wolves finished runners-up in the 'old' First Division in 1937-38, 1938-39, 1949-50, 1954-55 and 1959-60.

When Wolves won the League title in season 1953-54 they became the first club ever to achieve top spot in the First, Second and Third Division North Divisions – and when they became Fourth Division champions in 1987-88, they were the first team ever to achieve the titles of four different divisions.

The longest season of League football played by Wolves was that of 1946-47 which began on 31 August and finished nine months later on 31 May.

Wolves' record in the Football League: 1888-1999

Division One

P	W	D	L	F	A
2270	911	506	853	3876	3671

Division One/Two

1516	607	359	550	2340	2104

Division Three

134	61	39	34	229	174

Division Four

92	51	16	25	151	93

All Divisions

4012	1630	920	1462	6596	6042

League Play-offs

P	W	D	L	F	A
8	3	1	4	7	10

Wolves made their worst-ever start to a League season in 1983-84 (Division One) when they recorded only one win (3-1 at West Bromwich Albion) in their opening 19 matches under Graham Hawkins' management, going 15 games before that victory at The Hawthorns.

Wolves won only four games out of 24 from the start of the 1985-86 season up to the turn of the year.

In 1964-65 Wolves won only one of their opening 15 First Division games and in 1968-69 they triumphed only four times in the first 17 League games under managers Ronnie Allen and Bill McGarry.

Wolves' 1,000th home League game was v Manchester City on 8 November 1952 (won 7-3). Their 1,000th away game was at Burnley on 29 November 1952 (lost 2-0) and their 2,000th game overall was v Preston at Molineux on 22 November 1952 (lost 2-0). Their 2,000th home League fixture was v Huddersfield Town on 27 February 1999

Wolves first-team squad 1991-92, the season they finished 11th in the old Division Two before it became Division One with the advent of the Premiership.

(drew 1-1) and both their 2,000th away League and game and their 4,000th in all was at Gigg Lane v Bury on 2 March 1999 (drew 0-0).

FOOTBALL LEAGUE CUP

The Football League Cup was first played for in season 1960-61.

It wasn't compulsory at the outset for every club to enter the competition, and Wolves, along with a number of other top-line teams did not compete until the mid-1960s, Wolves entering for the first time in 1966-67.

Now they have played 100 games in the said competition which, since 1982, has carried sponsorship: Milk Cup, Littlewoods Cup, Rumbelows Cup, the Coca-Cola Cup and the Worthington Cup.

Wolves' League Cup record (to the end of the 1998-99 season) is:

P	W	D	L	F	A
100	43	19	38	147	124

Wolves' have won the Football League Cup twice – in 1974 and 1980 – both times at Wembley.

Manchester City were their victims in the 1974 Final, when a crowd of 97,886 (receipts £161,500) saw Kenny Hibbitt and John Richards score the goals which saw off City.

Then six years later, a tap-in goal by Andy Gray, after a mix-up between Peter Shilton and Dave Needham in the penalty area, was enough for Wolves to beat Nottingham Forest 1-0 in front of 96,527 spectators (receipts £625,000).

Four Wolves players – Geoff Palmer, Derek Parkin, Kenny Hibbitt and John Richards – appeared in both of those winning Finals.

Wolves have appeared in three League Cup semi-finals, beating Norwich City over two legs in 1973-74 and Swindon Town on aggregate in 1979-80, but they were defeated by Tottenham Hotspur, 4-3 on aggregate, in 1972-73.

A crowd of 41,031 paid then record Molineux gate receipts of £80,839 to see that midweek semi-final second leg with Swindon in 1980.

Wolves' biggest League Cup win has been that of 6-1 at home to Shrewsbury Town in a second round, first leg encounter in September 1991. Paul Birch and Steve Bull both scored two goals apiece that night in front of 12,229 fans.

Wolves also accounted for Millwall 5-1 at Molineux in September 1968; beat Bristol Rovers 4-0 at home in October 1972; whipped Exeter City, also at Molineux, in November 1973 when only 7,623 fans

attended on a cold Wednesday afternoon during the electricity-ban and beat Fulham 5-1 at Craven Cottage in the second round in season 1995-96.

Wolves' heaviest League Cup defeat is 5-0, suffered twice, at Fulham in the third round in October 1966 (their first defeat in the competition) and then at Sunderland in a second round, second leg clash in October 1982.

Wolves' biggest home defeat in the League Cup has been 3-1, by Fulham in September 1974 and by Luton Town in August 1977.

One of the closest League Cup encounters involving Wolves was their tie at Manchester City in September 1971 which ended in a 4-3 defeat in front of 29,156 fans.

Wolves' first-ever League Cup-tie was at home to Mansfield Town on 13 September 1966 when they won 2-1 before 12,098 spectators. Bobby Thomson and Mike Bailey were the Wanderers' goalscorers that night.

Kenny Hibbitt, with 36, has appeared in most League Cup games for Wolves; Derek Parkin starred in 35, Geoff Palmer and John Richards in 33 and Mike Bailey 29.

John Richards and Steve Bull each netted a record 18 League Cup goals; Kenny Hibbitt scored 12.

Of Wolves' eight home draws in the

Wolves skipper Mike Bailey holds aloft the Football League Cup at Wembley in 1974.

League Cup, six have been by a scoreline of 1-1.

The team Wolves have met most times in the League Cup competition has been Swindon Town – eight.

Some of Wolves' embarrassing defeats in the competition have been those at Mansfield Town (1-0 in 1975); at Reading (1-0 in 1978); against Cambridge United (3-1 away and 1-0 at home in 1980); against Walsall (1-0 at home in 1985), against Lincoln City (2-1 at Molineux, in 1986) and at home to AFC Bournemouth (2-1 in September 1998).

FOOTBALL LEAGUE JUBILEE TRUST FUND

Wolves entertained Staffordshire neighbours Stoke City in two League Jubilee Fund games in successive seasons leading up to the outbreak of World War Two.

In August 1938 Wolves won 4-3 at Molineux and the following August Wolves were again triumphant, this time by 4-2 with Dicky Dorsett netting a hat-trick.

FOOTBALLER OF THE YEAR

Two great Wolves stars, Billy Wright (in 1952) and Bill Slater (in 1960) received the accolade of Footballer of the Year – and both players skippered FA Cup winning teams.

Wright was also runner-up in the prestigious European Footballer of the Year poll in 1957.

In 1972-73 Wolves' striker John Richards collected two awards – those of Midland Footballer of the Year and the national Young Player of the Year.

FORBES, William

Signed by manager Ted Vizard from Dunfermline Athletic in September 1946, ever-reliable wing-half or inside-forward Willie Forbes had great stamina. Born in Glasgow on 25 May 1922, he played for Glasgow United prior to joining Dunfermline, and after leaving Wolves, in December 1949, he joined Preston North End, whom he helped win the Second Division title in 1951, finish runners-up in the First Division in 1953 and reach the FA Cup Final the following year. All told, Forbes

played in well over 200 games for the Deepdale club before signing for Carlisle United in July 1956. When he retired in May 1958 he had well over 250 senior appearances in his locker.

Wolves record: 75 apps. 23 goals.

FORD, Clive

A promising youngster, who supported West Bromwich Albion during his school days, utility forward Clive Ford failed to reach the heights expected of him at Molineux and he was mainly a reserve during his time with Wolves. Born in West Bromwich on 10 April 1945, he represented West Bromwich Town and joined Wolves as a junior in 1960, turning professional in October 1962. He left Molineux for Walsall in December 1964 and after 14 League outings for the Saddlers he switched to Lincoln City, making over 50 first-team appearances for the Imps before ending his senior career.

Wolves record: 2 apps.

FORMAN, Matthew Charles

Born in Evesham on 8 September 1967, cen-

tral midfielder Matt Forman was an apprentice at Villa Park for two years before turning professional in September 1985. He failed to make the grade with the First Division club and in August 1986 was transferred to Wolves. After leaving Molineux in September 1988 Forman played for Burton Albion, Oldbury United, Evesham United and Transatlantic FC (in America) before returning to Evesham for the 1992-93 season.
Wolves record: 28+1 apps. 5 goals.

FORMATION OF CLUB

Wolverhampton Wanderers Football Club was officially formed in 1877 and it was all down to the youthful enthusiasm of three men named John. Two were pupil-teachers from St Luke's School Blakenhall, namely John Baynton and John (Jack) Brodie, while the third was John Addenbrooke, who was at the time in the preliminary stages of his scholastic profession. All three were registered players with the St Luke's junior football team and they were backed all the way by Sir Alfred Hickman, later president of Wolves, whose home overlooked a piece of land off Goldthorn Hill where games were played.

At an historic first meeting on 10 November 1876, held at St Luke's school, those attending were asked if they were interested in playing football? The response was excellent and things developed quickly after that. The record books show that the first game played by the newly-formed Wolves was a 12-a-side fixture against Stafford Road FC on 13 January 1877 on Windmill Field in Goldthorn Hill. Some 600 spectators witnessed an emphatic 8-0 defeat for the young Wolves team, who lined up with Harry Barcroft in goal; Frank Hampson, David Hedges, James Adams, Oscar Rowbotham, George Worrall and Walter Kendrick in defence and John Baynton, Ernest Newman Richard Myatt, Billy Jacks and Jack Foster as forwards. John Ward was the team's official umpire.

Two months later, in March 1877, John Addenbrooke (who later became secretary-manager of Wolves), John Baynton, John Brodie, Arthur Lowder, Ike Griffiths and Richard Baugh all agreed to put pen to paper and become the first official signed-up players of Wolverhampton Wanderers Football Club. And the rest is history.

FORSHAW, Richard

Dick Forshaw could play at inside-right or centre-forward. Born in Preston on 20 August 1895, he attended school in Gateshead and played local football in the north-east with St George's Church Lads' Brigade (Gateshead) and Gateshead St Vincent's before entering the Army in 1914. He guested for both Middlesbrough and Nottingham Forest during the hostilities and after being demobbed he signed for Liverpool in June 1919. He became a star player at Anfield and scored 117 goals 266 appearances for the Merseysiders, helping them twice win the First Division championship in 1922 and 1923. In March 1927 he surprisingly moved across Stanley Park to sign for Everton, transferring to Molineux in August 1929 after helping the Toffeemen win the League title in 1928. He never really settled in with Wolves, although he was now aged 35, and after only a handful of outings he moved to Hednesford Town in August 1930, later assisting Rhyl Athletic from October 1930 to May 1931 when he retired.
Wolves record: 6 apps. 4 goals.

FOWNES, Walter Jeremiah

Wally Fownes spent five seasons a reserve full-back with Wolves. Born in Coseley c.1885, he played for Wednesbury St Paul's and Wood Green Rovers before joining the staff at Molineux in August 1906. He left the club to join Willenhall in 1911.
Wolves record: 12 apps.

FOX, William Victor

Vic Fox was a hefty defender, who loved a challenge. He was a reserve for biggest part of his time at Molineux, appearing in less than 50 first-team matches in a six-year spell, his best season coming in 1927-28 when he had 24 outings, mainly as partner to full-back Ted Watson. Born in Middlesbrough on 8 January 1898, Fox attended Council School in Middlesbrough, represented Teesside Juniors and South Bank Schools before joining South Bank East End from where he was transferred to Bradford Park Avenue, moving to Middlesbrough in 1918 and turning professional in May 1919. In October 1924 he was signed by Wolves and in August 1930 left Molineux for Newport County, later playing for Exeter City (September 1931), Manchester Central (November 1931), Bradford Park Avenue again (March 1932) and Nantwich Town (August 1932-34). Fox, who made well over 100 appearances for Middlesbrough, was also a very useful cricketer with Worcestershire (1923-32). A middle order right-hand batsman and occasional bowler he scored 6,654 runs in 281 innings spread over 163 county matches for an average of 26.61. His highest score was 198. He also took 87 catches and managed two wickets for 137 runs. He topped the 1,000 run mark in season three times with a best aggregate total of 1,457 (average of over 31) in 1929. Fox also played for Abertillery CC. His father, Billy Fox, was a Middlesbrough player in the 1880s and a Northern-based cricket professional who was instrumental in seeing his son make the grade with both the small and large balls. Fox junior died in Withington, Manchester on 17 February 1949.
Wolves record: 49 apps.

FRANCIS, Ernest

Wolves recruited centre-forward Ernest Francis from local junior football in July 1912. Born c.1891, he stayed at Molineux until football was abandoned owing to World War One, playing mostly in the Reserves. He did not re-sign for Wolves after the hostilities.
Wolves record: 10 apps. 3 goals.

FREEDMAN, Douglas Alan

Born in Glasgow on 21 January 1974, striker Dougie Freedman made a terrific start to his Wolves career by scoring on his debut against Swindon Town at Molineux on 18 October 1997, two days after joining the club from Crystal Palace on a month's loan (later signing permanently in a deal which took Jamie Smith to Palace). A trainee with Queen's Park Rangers, Freedman signed professional forms at Loftus Road in May 1992 but never got a first team outing and moved to Barnet on a free transfer in July 1994. He scored 32 goals in 57 appearances for the Underhill club, four coming in one game against Rochdale in September 1995. After that salvo he switched to Palace for £800,000, and did very well at Selhurst Park, netting 34 times in 103 games for the Eagles. A hat-trick hero for the Eagles against Wolves in the 1995-96 League game at Selhurst Park, he scored another two goals past Wolves in the 1997 Play-off semi-final, first leg clash in London which ultimately led to Palace going on to win a place in the Premiership after they had beaten Sheffield United in the Final at Wembley. Capped by Scotland as a schoolboy, Freedman went on to represent his country eight times at Under-21 level and he also gained a 'B' cap. He was sold by Wolves to Premiership newcomers Nottingham Forest for £850,000 in August 1998.
Wolves record: 30+5 apps. 12 goals.

FREIGHT ROVER TROPHY

Wolves played in this sponsored competition in seasons 1985-86 and 1986-87 before it became the Sherpa Van Trophy. Their first opponents were Exeter City (away) on 14 January 1986, the game ending all square at 1-1 in front of 1,278 fans. Eight days later Wolves met another Devon side, Torquay United, at Molineux and again were held to a 1-1 draw in front of 1,616 hardy supporters. These two results meant that Wolves were eliminated from the competition.

However, the following season they did make progress from the Preliminary stages by beating Cardiff City 1-0 at Ninian Park on 2 December 1986, courtesy of Steve Bull's first goal in a gold shirt in front of 1,201 spectators, and defeating Bournemouth 4-3 at Molineux when Bull (2) and Paul Dougherty (2) scored the goals watched by only 1,923 onlookers. But then, on 26 January 1987, a visit from Hereford United saw Wolves go out of the tournament, beaten by a goal to nil before a 2,892 crowd. Summary:

P	W	D	L	F	A
5	2	2	1	7	6

FRIENDLY MATCHES

In their early years Wolves, like all other clubs, played scores of friendly matches, concentrating initially with fixtures against local sides in the Midlands region. As time went by so the team travelled further afield, but when League football was introduced (1888) the number of friendlies (per season) was reduced and this was the case thereafter. Between 1877 and 1939 it is believed that Wolves played around 1,000 friendly matches (perhaps more) and one of their first overseas tours of any note took them to France in the summer of 1933 where they played four games against the Racing Club de Paris, Marseilles, Nice and Nimes. Their match in Nice developed into a fiery affair, and ended in such civil disturbance that Major Frank Buckley escorted his players off the field before the final whistle. Perhaps surprisingly Nice were invited back to Molineux for a return game the following year and so began a contact with foreign clubs which subsequently grew much more intimate as the years ticked by.

The first foreign side to visit Molineux after World War Two was Norkopping (Sweden) who forced a 1-1 draw in November 1946.

Wolves beat a South African XI 3-1 at home on 30 September 1953, in a friendly game that officially saw the switching-on of the first set of Molineux floodlights, installed for £25,000.

Over a period of ten years – between 1953 and 1962 inclusive – Wolves staged 17 friendly matches under the Molineux lights. They won 13 and drew four and there were many outstanding encounters, including classic matches against Moscow Spartak in November 1954 (won 4-0), against Honved (Hungary) in December 1954 (won 3-2), against mighty Real Madrid (in October 1957) won 3-2 and against Tiflis Dynamo (in November 1960) drew 5-5.

As well as the many friendly matches, Wolves have also played several testimonial and benefit matches (all classed as friendlies) for star players at Molineux (and elsewhere) and among those staged at Molineux have been the following:

1962	Wolves 4 International XI 4
	(Wright and Mullen Benefit)
1965	Wolves 5 International XI 8
	(Broadbent Benefit)

1970	Wolves 8 England XI 4
	(Flowers testimonial)
1974	Wolves 2 International XI 5
	(Woodfield testimonial)
1975	Wolves 1 International XI 2
	(Wagstaffe testimonial)
1975	Wolves 0 Don Revie XI 0
	(Dougan testimonial)
1976	Wolves 3 West Bromwich Albion 0
	(Bailey testimonial)
1978	Wolves 0 Midland All Stars XI 5
	(Parkes testimonial)
1978	Wolves 2 Tottenham Hotspur 1
	(McAlle testimonial)
1979	Wolves 1 Midland Select XI 4
	(Parkin testimonial)
1981	Wolves 2 Derby County 1
	(Hibbitt testimonial)
1982	Wolves 2 Moscow Dynamo 4
	(Richards testimonial)
1983	Wolves 4 Leicester City 1
	(Palmer testimonial)
1985	Wolves 4 Selected XI 1
	(Richards testimonial)
1997	Wolves 1 Santos, Brazil 1
	(Bull testimonial)

As a Wolves player, former West Bromwich Albion defender Ally Robertson had a testimonial match: Wolves against the Baggies, on his old stamping ground in 1988.

Foreign tours have been a key feature of Wolves' pre and end-of-season activities since 1948 and among the many trips abroad made by the club over the last 50 years have been the following: to the Netherlands 1948; South Africa 1951 and 1957; Russia 1955; USA and Canada 1963; Caribbean 1964; Switzerland 1966; USA again in 1967 (for a tournament which they won) and 1972; New Zealand 1972; Norway 1975; Sweden 1976, 1978 and 1983; Spain 1980 and Malta 1985, plus Irish and Scottish tours as well.

Wolves' record friendly win is that of 19-1 v Manchester East End (away) in November 1888 when Jack Brodie scored seven times Harry Wood six.

Wolves' biggest home friendly win is 15-0 v Stourbridge in 1882-83 when Brodie scored six goals this time and Arthur Lowder four.

The first foreign club side to beat Wolves in a friendly at Molineux was the German side, Hanover '96 who won 2-1 in August 1971.

The lowest attendance ever for a first team game at Molineux – just 646 – saw the friendly with the Pavi Kavatski Gradjabnski Sportski Klub in November 1936.

FROGGATT, Stephen Junior

Steve Froggatt completed his transition from outside-left to wing-back during the 1996-97 season when he regained his form and fitness after serious injury and illness problems following his transfer to Molineux from Aston Villa for £1 million in July 1994. Froggatt was capped twice by England at Under-21 level during his time at Villa Park, which lasted from June 1989 when he became a junior, turning professional in January 1991. In all he made 44 appearances for Villa and scored three goals. Fast and clever, he enjoyed taking on his opponent when playing as an out-and-out winger with Villa, but then, under Mark McGhee at Wolves, his style changed and he developed into a fine attacking wing-back, winning selection to the PFA's First Division side in 1997. In September 1998, Froggatt was – perhaps surprisingly in supporters' minds – transferred from Molineux to Coventry City for a club record fee of £1.9 million. In the Premiership he did very well, playing as a wide midfielder under Gordon Strachan's managership.

Wolves record: 112+8 apps. 11 goals.

FULHAM

Wolves' playing record against the Cottagers is:

Football League

Venue	P	W	D	L	F	A
Home	30	16	9	5	60	33
Away	30	10	7	13	36	48
Total	60	26	16	18	96	81

FA Cup

Away	1	1	0	0	1	0

League Cup

Home	3	2	0	1	4	3
Away	3	2	0	1	7	6
Total	6	4	0	2	11	9

Wartime

Home	1	1	0	0	2	0
Away	1	0	0	1	1	3
Total	2	1	0	1	3	3

Wolves and Fulham first met at League level in season 1907-08 (Division Two) when each team won its home game with scores of 2-0 at Molineux and 2-1 in London.

In November 1910, a crowd of 9,000 saw Wolves beat Fulham 5-1 at Molineux, which was to remain their best victory over the Cottagers for 49 years.

In between times Wolves lost 4-2 at home in February 1913, went down 4-1 in London in December 1926 and crashed to a 7-0 defeat at Craven Cottage in February 1928 (when Sid Elliott scored a hat-trick).

In September 1959, Wolves hammered luckless Fulham 9-0 in a First Division encounter at Molineux in front of 41,692 fans who saw in-form Norman Deeley score four goals and lay on two more for his colleagues.

Amazingly, later on in the season Fulham gained sweet revenge with a 3-1 win at the Cottage, following up in April 1961 with a competent 4-2 win on Wolves' soil.

In December 1962 a smart hat-trick from left-winger Alan Hinton helped Wolves to a convincing 5-0 away win over Fulham and in April 1964 two goals from Jimmy Melia helped Wolves again whip the Londoners, this time by 4-0 at Molineux.

On their way to promotion in 1976-77, Wolves beat Fulham 5-1 at Molineux in the February when Steve Daley and Kenny Hibbitt both scored twice and drew 0-0 in London.

Fulham virtually condemned Wolves to relegation from the Second Division when they won 4-0 at Craven Cottage in April 1985.

Season 1988-89 saw Wolves win 5-2 at home and draw 2-2 at Fulham, Steve Bull scoring a hat-trick in the victory at Molineux.

The one FA Cup-tie between the teams took place at Craven Cottage in season 1920-21 and it was Wolves who came out best, winners by a goal to nil on the way to the Final against Spurs.

Wolves' first-ever League Cup defeat was a 5-0 drubbing at the hands of Fulham at Craven Cottage in October 1966 when Allan Clarke scored twice And as holders of the trophy, the Wanderers were knocked out of the competition by Fulham who won 3-1 at Molineux in September 1974.

Wolves ran up one of the best away performances in the League Cup when they beat Fulham 5-1 at Craven Cottage in October 1995 to go through into the next round 7-1 on aggregate.

And when Wolves visited Craven Cottage for a second round first leg League Cup encounter in September 1997, debutant Sanjuan Jesus Garcia (from Real Zaragoza) scored to give them a 1-0 advantage. The return game at Molineux finished with the same scoreline (1-0 in Wolves' favour).

Players with both clubs include: Gordon Brice, Don Cock, George Edmonds, Jackie Henderson, Tony Lange, John McDonald, Stacey North, Billy Richards, Harry Rowbotham, Jamie Smith and Alf Tootill.

Also associated: Richard Deacon (Fulham trialist), Stan Cullis and Eric Jones (Wolves players, Fulham wartime guests), Charlie Mitten (Fulham player, Wolves wartime guest), John Griffiths (Fulham and Wolves guest), and Arthur Rowley (Wolves wartime player, Fulham star).

GAINSBOROUGH TRINITY

Wolves' playing record against Trinity is:
Football League

Venue	P	W	D	L	F	A
Home	6	4	2	0	8	1
Away	6	3	0	3	6	4
Total	12	7	2	3	14	5

All 12 League games between Wolves and Trinity were in Division Two and took place over a period of six years: 1906-12. Wolves' best win of the seven recorded over Trinity is 4-0 at Molineux in October 1908, when Walter Radford scored twice in front of 7,000

fans. Wolves also won 3-1 away in December 1910, Billy Harrington netting twice this time. Trinity's three victories were all by the same score of 1-0.

Players with both clubs include: Charlie Booth, Harry Davies, Jack Hamilton and Billy Walker.

Also associated: Charlie Brawn (Wolves Reserves).

GALLAGHER, John Christopher

A totally committed midfielder or emergency striker, Jackie Gallagher was born in Wisbech on 6 April 1958 and played for March Town before turning professional with Lincoln City in February 1976. Over the next decade he served, in turn, with Kings Lynn, Peterborough United (two spells: from April 1980 and August 1985), Torquay United (August 1982) and Wisbech Town (1983-84) before joining Wolves in June 1987. He spent two years at Molineux, gaining a Sherpa Van Trophy winners medal as sub as well as helping Wolves win both the Fourth and Third Division championships in successive seasons. Gallagher left Molineux for non-League Kettering Town in May 1989.
Wolves record: 13+23 apps. 5 goals.

GALLAGHER, Joseph Anthony

Joe Gallagher began his career as a right-back, but the lack of manoeuvrability resulted in him converting to the centre-half position where he became a commanding figure, especially in the air although at times looked a little awkward on the ground. Born in Liverpool on 11 January 1955, he represented Lancashire and Merseyside Schools and in 1970 joined Birmingham City as a junior, turning professional at St Andrew's on his 17th birthday.

He established himself in the first team and went on to score 23 goals in 335 appearances for Blues, gaining an England 'B' cap in 1980. The following August (1981) he was perhaps surprisingly sold to Wolves for £350,000, but his stay at Molineux was a relatively short one, lasting until December 1982, when he switched to West Ham United following a newspaper article in which he admitted that he couldn't give full effort out on the field of play as he was in dispute with the club. In August 1983 he moved north to Burnley; he played for Padiham (on loan) in 1984 and then five years later became manager of Coleshill Town. He returned to St Andrew's as Blues' Community Liaison officer in November 1990, staying in office for a year when he took over as boss of Atherstone United.
Wolves record: 34 apps. 1 goal.

GALLEY, John Edward

John Galley was a useful centre-forward, who

started his League career with Wolves and ended it with Hereford United. Born in Clowne on 7 May 1944, he joined the Molineux groundstaff as a junior in 1959 and turned professional in May 1961. With so many good strikers at the club, Galley found it hard to get first-team football and consequently, in December 1964, he was transferred to Rotherham United. Three years later (after scoring 48 goals in 112 League appearances for the Millers) he switched to Bristol City where he averaged a goal every two games for the Robins (netting 84 in 172 League outings). In December 1972 he moved to Nottingham Forest and after a loan spell with Peterborough United (October 1974) he rounded off an eventful career by scoring ten goals in 80 League matches for Hereford United (December 1974 to May 1977). All told at League level, Galley, the nephew of Tom who also played for Wolves (see below), netted 151 goals in 413 matches – a fine return.
Wolves record: 6 apps. 2 goals.

GALLEY, Thomas

Tom Galley was one of those great club men, a loyal servant, who was on Wolves' books for well over 13 years, playing in almost 280 senior matches (including 75 in wartime) and appearing without complaint in whatever position suited his manager best. Galley was born in Hednesford on 4 August 1915

Tom Galley, 49 goals in 204 appearances for Wolves.

and played as an amateur for Notts County and Cannock Town before signing as a part-time professional for Cannock in August 1933. Wolves secured him on full professional forms in April 1934 and with them he played in seven different positions. He scored 11 goals in the 1938-39 season when he was an ever-present, appeared in the FA Cup Final, skippered the 1942 wartime League (North) Cup winning team which beat Sunderland, won two England caps (against Sweden and Norway in 1937) and also played for the Football League. During the war he served in France and Germany with the Royal Artillery and guested for Aldershot, Clapton Orient, Leeds United and Watford. After scoring over 40 goals in more than 200 senior games, he left Molineux in November 1947 and moved to Grimsby Town, who were also in the First Division albeit in relegation trouble. He skippered the Mariners but after only 33 League games (two goals scored), he was forced to retire from League soccer because of injury. Galley – who played club cricket for 30 years – returned to the Midlands to sign for Kidderminster Harriers in August 1949, and in May 1950 was appointed player-coach of Clacton Town before retiring in June 1960. He is the uncle of John Galley, who played for Wolves in the early 1960s. Tom Galley died in June 1999.
Wolves record: 204 apps. 49 goals.

GALVIN, David

Born in Denaby on 5 October 1946, defender Dave Galvin joined Wolves as a junior and turned professional at Molineux in May 1965. He understudied Dave Woodfield for a number of years but only managed a handful of senior appearances before transferring to Gillingham in October 1969, ending his League career with Wimbledon (August 1977 to May 1979). He scored 17 goals in 245 League games for the Gills, helping them win promotion from the Fourth Division in 1973. He also assisted Wimbledon in their rise from the Fourth Division.
Wolves record: 5 apps.

GAMES (MOST IN A SEASON)

Wolves played a record 61 competitive games in 1987-88 – the most in a season.

They fulfilled 46 in the League (Division Three); three in the FA Cup; four in the League Cup and eight in the Sherpa Van Trophy.

Two players – goalkeeper Mark Kendall and striker Andy Mutch – appeared in every match, while Steve Bull missed just two League games.

GARDINER, Donald C.

A reserve midfielder to Kenny Hibbitt and Willie Carr, Don Gardiner was released by Wolves in May 1975 having been at Molineux

since July 1972 when he joined the club as an apprentice, turning professional in August 1973. Born in Jamaica on 30 August 1955, he had an unsuccessful trial with Coventry City immediately prior to him joining Wolves.
Wolves record: 1+2 apps.

GARDINER, John G.

A knee injury, suffered during the opening months of his Wolves career, ended left-half Jack Gardiner's stay at Molineux. Born in Hamilton, Scotland in July 1904, he attended and played Blantyre Victoria and Motherwell before joining Coventry City in May 1926. Two years later he signed for Wolves, but injury resulted in him leaving Molineux for Norwich City in November 1928. He later assisted Kettering Town (from July 1929), Walsall (June 1930), Workington Town (1931), Barrow (August-September 1932) and Lancaster Town (October 1932-May 1933).
Wolves record: 3 apps.

GARDINER, Joseph B.

Born at Bearpark, County Durham on 23 August 1916, Joe Gardiner was one of Major Buckley's 'Babes', a player who came through the ranks after joining Wolves as an amateur in December 1932. Buckley signed Gardiner on professional forms as soon as the player was 17 and he went on to make almost 140 League and Cup appearances for Wolves after developing into an effective defender after Buckley had chosen to switch him following an unsuccessful start as a centre-forward. Born in the same Durham mining village as the great Derby and England winger Sammy Crooks, Gardiner played for Durham County Boys, and the Wolves scouting net quickly picked him up. He soon gained representative honours with Wolves, representing the Football League against the Scottish League at Molineux when he was 22. The following year he made a Wembley appearance as a member of the Wolves' team beaten by Portsmouth in the 1939 FA Cup Final. He first became a regular in the Wolves' first team during the 1936-37 season and continued to play during the war (49 outings) until retiring in 1944. He stayed on at Molineux on the training staff, then went to Birmingham City, where he remained until 1964. He later returned to his beloved Wolves where he did some scouting for club (up to the early 1980s) and, in fact, Gardiner was associated with the Molineux side for some 50 years (as player, trainer and scout). Gardiner, who retired to live at Sedgley, near Dudley, was also trainer to the full England team on two occasions. He died in Wolverhampton in 1997, aged 81.
Wolves record: 139 apps. 2 goals.

GARRATLY, George

George Garratly, born at Walsall in October 1888, began his career with Walsall

Constitutionals in 1904 and then played for Bloxwich Strollers, where Walsall spotted him in February 1908. A solid defender, Garratly appeared in the Birmingham League for the Saddlers and in the summer of 1909, Wolves signed him. He remained at Molineux until 1920, making over 230 senior appearances for Wolves. He played alongside Ted Collins from 1910-11 to 1914-15 and their full-back pairing was considered to be the best outside the First Division. Although his career was interrupted by World War One, Garratly was still playing for Wolves in 1919-20 before handing over to George Marshall. He ended his career with Hednesford Town, retiring to take over as manager at Cross Keys. In 1923 he recommended Jack Harrington to Wolves. Garratly died c.1952.
Wolves record: 232 apps. 6 goals.

GATE RECEIPTS

Here are the details of how the Molineux gate receipts record has been broken over the last ten years:

£91,137 v Torquay United, Sherpa Van Trophy Area Final, 18 April 1989

£109,655 v Aston Villa, League Cup, second round second leg, 4 October 1989

£110,623 v Sheffield Wednesday, FA Cup third round, 6 January 1990

£114,574 v Bolton Wanderers, FA Cup fourth round 24 January 1993

£129,300 v Bristol City, League Division One, 14 August 1993

£135,410 v Middlesbrough, League Division One, 28 August 1993

£150,045 v Oxford United, League Division One, 28 December 1993

£191,105 v Crystal Palace, FA Cup third round, 8 January 1994

£209,979 v Ipswich Town, FA Cup fifth round, 19 February 1994

£236,972 v Leicester City, FA Cup fifth round, 18 February 1995

£273,004 v Birmingham City, FA Cup third-round replay, 17 January 1996

£276,168 v Tottenham Hotspur, FA Cup fourth round, 7 February 1996

£319,141 v Arsenal, FA Cup fourth round, 24 January 1999.

GATESHEAD

Wolves never played a competitive game against the North East club when they were called Gateshead. However, prior to that Wolves did come face to face with South Shields, Gateshead's previous name. (See *South Shields*).

GEORGE, Noel

Noel George was serving with the RASC in Salonika during World War One when he discovered his talent for goalkeeping during

Wolves goalkeeper Noel George, seen here practising, was a great influence in the 1920s.

recreational periods, and in April 1919 he won praise for his performance for a Salonika XI against an Italian XI at Aldershot. He was born at Lichfield on 26 December 1897 and had played in Hednesford Town's forward line before the war. Wolves signed him in the summer of 1919 and he made his League debut in February 1921 at Nottingham Forest. His first senior appearances had come two days earlier, in a Thursday afternoon FA Cup replay victory over Derby County at Molineux and he appeared in that season's Final when Wolves lost 1-0 to Spurs at neutral Stamford Bridge. George went on to play in almost 250 senior games for Wolves (222 in the Football League), his last appearance being a 4-0 defeat at Ashton Gate in November 1927. By then he was in the early stages of a terminal illness. He battled bravely against it before dying peacefully in his sleep at Lichfield on 16 October 1929. Wolves had originally signed him as an eventual successor to Welsh international Teddy Peers, and he replaced Peers permanently at the start of the 1921-22 season. Altogether, George missed only 18 out of the next 190 League games and was an ever-present in 1921-22, 1923-24 and 1924-25. In 1925-26 and 1926-27 he missed many games through injury before his final illness. When Wolves won the Third Division championship in 1923-24, George conceded only 31 goals in 42 games.
Wolves record: 242 apps.

GETGOOD, George
Known affectionately as 'Goodman', Scotsman George Getgood was born in Coylton, Ayrshire on 15 November 1892. He played for Ayr United, Reading (July 1914 to August 1921), Birmingham (to March 1922) and Southampton before transferring to Wolves in January 1923. He skippered Wolves and made almost 60 appearances for the first team before leaving for Kidderminster Harriers in March 1925. He later assisted Aberdare Athletic (from July 1926), Shrewsbury Town (November 1926), Bathgate, Bo'ness and Nuneaton Town (February-May 1929). He helped Wolves win the Third Division North championship. Getgood died in Kidderminster on 22 July 1970.
Wolves record: 59 apps. 1 goal.

GIBBONS, Leonard
Len Gibbons was an efficient junior footballer but after turning professional he never quite reached the heights to make his mark in the Football League. Born in Wirral on 22 November 1930, he signed for Wolves as an amateur in 1946, joined the full-time staff in February 1948, but with so many good class full-backs at the club, he was then released in the summer of 1953 and entered non-League soccer.
Wolves record: 29 apps.

GILKES, Michael Earl
Left-sided midfielder Michael Gilkes joined Wolves from Reading in March 1997 for a fee reported to be £155,000 – signed by his former manager Mark McGhee. A Londoner, born near Hackney Marshes on 20 July 1965, he played for Waltham Borough Boys (London) before joining Leicester City as a junior. He failed to make an impression at Filbert Street, quickly moving south to join Reading as a professional in July 1984. He made his senior debut for the Royals soon after arriving at Elm Park, and went on to accumulate 486 appearances, scoring 52 goals before moving to Wolves, having earlier had loan spells with both Chelsea (January/February 1992) and Southampton (March 1992). He helped Reading win the Third Division title in 1986, the Full Members' Cup Final of 1988 and the Second Division championship in 1994. He was awarded a testimonial at Elm Park in 1996-97. Unfortunately he was injured shortly after joining Wolves and took time to regain full fitness.
Wolves record: 34+6 apps. 1 goal.

GILL, G. Arthur
Archie Gill played for Wolves' first team during the 1921-22 season when he replaced the injured Dick Richards on the left-wing. Born locally *c.*1901, he assisted St Barnard's and Victoria Swifts before joining Wolves and on leaving Molineux he signed for Stourbridge.
Wolves record: 7 apps.

GILLINGHAM
Wolves' playing record against Gillingham is:
Football League

Venue	P	W	D	L	F	A
Home	2	1	0	1	7	4
Away	2	1	0	1	3	3
Totals	4	2	0	2	10	7

Wolves first met the Gills when they slipped into the Third Division in 1985-86. The two fixtures that season both went against Wolves, Gillingham winning 3-1 at Molineux in front of 3,543 fans and 2-0 at The Priestfield Stadium.

The teams met again in 1988-89 (also in Division Three) and this time Wolves doubled up over the Gills, winning 3-1 away and 6-1 at Molineux when the attendance was almost 12,600. Andy Mutch scored twice in the latter game.

Players with both clubs include: Scott Barrett, Bill Boswell, Chic Brodie, Mel Eves, David Galvin, Adam Haywood, Joe Hodnett, Jack Hopkins, John Humphrey, Mike Kent, Stuart McMillan, James McVeigh, Neil Masters, John O'Connor, Albert Picken, Harry Rowbotham, Sid Tyler, George Walker, Jack Williams and Nigel Williams.

Also associated: Pat Bradley, Cyril Poole, Jim Travers and Les Williams (all Wolves Reserves), goalkeeper Andy Poole (reserve with both clubs); Albert Hoskins (manager of both clubs) and Gerry Summers (Gills manager, Wolves coach).

GLOSSOP NORTH END
Wolves' playing record against Glossop is:

Football League

Venue	P	W	D	L	F	A
Home	10	8	2	0	27	3
Away	10	5	1	4	16	17
Totals	20	13	3	4	43	20

Wolves ran up three successive home wins over North End – 4-0 in September 1899, 4-0 in January 1907 and 5-0 in January 1908. A crowd of 6,000 saw the latter victory when Jack Shelton and Percy Corbett both scored twice. Glossop's best win over Wolves is 5-1 at home in February 1911. The last time the teams met was in season 1914-15 when Wolves completed the double, winning 4-0 at home and 2-0 at Glossop.

Players with both clubs include: Dicky Davies, Archie Goodall, Archie Needham, Harry Rowbotham and Frank Whitehouse.

GOALS AND GOALSCORERS

Players who have scored over 100 goals for Wolves (wartime not included). Steve Bull 306, John Richards 194, Billy Hartill 170, Johnny Hancocks 168, Jimmy Murray 166, Peter Broadbent 145, Harry Wood 127, Dennis Westcott 124, Derek Dougan 123, Kenny Hibbitt 114, Roy Swinbourne 114, Jimmy Mullen 112, Dennis Wilshaw 112, Tom Phillipson 111 and Andy Mutch 106.

Players with more than 100 League goals for Wolves: Bull 249, Hartill 162, Hancocks 158, Murray 155, Richards 144, Broadbent 127, Wood 110, Swinbourne 107, Westcott 105, Wilshaw 105 and Phillipson 104.

The first player to score a League goal for Wolves was the Aston Villa defender Gersom Cox (an own-goal) in the 1-1 draw at Dudley Road on 8 September 1888.

The first Wolves player to score a League goal was Walter White against Burnley (home) on 22 September 1888.

Wolves' first Second Division goal was netted by full-back Jackery Jones against Hull City (at home) on 1 September 1906.

Wolves' first Third Division North goal came from Harry Lees in the home game against Rotherham on 27 August 1923.

Wolves entered the old Third Division in season 1985-86 and the scorer of their first goal in this section was Neil Edwards in the away game with Brentford on 17 August 1985.

A year later and Wolves were in the Fourth Division for the first time – and the player who netted the first goal in this department was Peter Zelem from the penalty spot against Cambridge United at Molineux on 23 August 1986.

Wolves' first FA Cup goal was scored by Jack Brodie against Long Eaton Rangers on 27 October 1883.

Wolves entered the Football League Cup for the first time in 1966-67 and the player who claimed the club's first goal in this com-

John Richards, one of the most prolific goalscorers in Wolves' history.

petition was Bob Hatton against Mansfield Town at Molineux on 13 September 1966.

Wolves' first European goal was scored by Peter Broadbent against FC '04 Schalke (Germany) at Molineux on 12 November 1958.

Dennis Westcott reached his century of League goals for Wolves in only his 109th match (against Charlton in March 1947). Steve Bull reached the 100 mark in his 126th outing; Billy Hartill in his 130th and Tom Phillipson in his 135th.

The first player to score 100 goals for Wolves was Harry Wood, reaching that milestone in September 1897 against Preston (his 215th match in the competition). His first was scored against Accrington nine years earlier, in October 1888.

Wood was also the first player to score on both his FA Cup and Football League debuts for Wolves: doing so against Derby St Luke's in 1885 and Accrington in 1888.

Bob Hatton scored on his League Cup debut for Wolves (v Mansfield Town in 1966) and in his first League game (same year against Portsmouth).

Dennis Westcott's strike-rate for Wolves was exceptional – a goal every 0.8611 of a game.

John Richards scored a hat-trick for Wolves in the FA Cup-tie against Charlton in 1976 after coming on as a substitute.

Tom Phillipson scored in 13 consecutive League games for Wolves, commencing 6 November 1926 and ending on 9 February 1927.

Wolves scored 100 and more League goals four seasons running from 1957 to 1960. In a total of 128 First Division matches they netted 422 times – and indeed, they scored 516 goals in the space of five season: 1956-60 inclusive.

In contrast, they went 535 minutes without scoring a goal in season 1981-82.

Wolves netted five times in 15 minutes either side of half-time when they defeated Manchester City 8-1 in a First Division match at Molineux in August 1962.

Wolves secured five goals in 20 minutes of their First Division League with Arsenal at Molineux in November 1971 – coming back from 1-0 down to win 5-1.

Four goals were scored in the last six minutes of the Wolves against Chelsea First Division game at Molineux on 22 September 1951. The score jumped from 4-0 to Wolves to 5-3.

John Richards scored after only 12 seconds for Wolves at Burnley in a First Division game in November 1975 – the quickest goal from the start of a game by a Wolves player.

Billy Wright found the net after only 19 seconds of his side's League Division One game against the reigning champions Everton at Goodison Park in October 1946.

Bob Hatton scored after only 29 seconds of his Wolves League debut against Portsmouth in a 3-1 win in October 1966.

Wolves goalkeeper Andy De Bont was beaten by a long-range shot from Phil Mason after only five seconds of a friendly game against Worcester City in 1995.

Barry Stobart netted a club record 110 Central League goals for Wolves between 1955 and 1964.

Derek Dougan's 200th League goals of his career arrived when he was a Wolves player – against West Ham United (home) in August 1972. His first arrived 15 years earlier for Portsmouth against Wolves in November 1957.

Wolves' centre-forward Dennis Westcott topped the First Division scoring charts in season 1946-47 with a total of 38 goals.

Steve Bull scored 102 goals in two seasons for Wolves – 52 in 1987-88 and 50 in 1988-89. He became the first player to top the 50-goal mark for 27 years when achieving that feat in 1988 and thus became the first player since Middlesbrough's George Camsell in 1926-28 to net a century of goals in the space of two seasons.

Bull was also the first player to score 50 or more goals in a season twice and the first to register to half centuries in successive campaigns.

Wolves' Roy Swinbourne scored 17 goals in the opening 14 games of the 1955-56 League season.

Wolves did not score a goal between 17 November 1984 and the 13 April 1985 – a total of 1,002 minutes – covering the part of two games and the whole of another ten. They failed to find the net in 12 home fixtures that season, compared with only six blank sheets away from Molineux.

In season 1950-51 Wolves lost 19 First Division matches by the odd goal and finished fourth in the table.

GODDARD, George

Centre-forward George Goddard was 30 years old when Major Frank Buckley signed him as cover for Billy Hartill in December 1933. Although he appeared in less than 20 games for Wolves, he more than earned his wages with a dozen goals in that brief spell, all of them coming in the 1933-34 season. In October 1934 he was on his way again, to Sunderland where he scored six goals in 14 games. From Roker Park he moved to Southend United in mid-March 1936 and after his playing days were over he took over a butcher's shop in London and later ran a cafe. Goddard, who was born at Gomshall, Surrey, on 20 December 1903, first played for Redhill FC and represented Surrey as an amateur before QPR signed him as a professional in 1926, taking him from his job in a local bus garage. He Rangers' leading scorer in each of his six full seasons with them, netting 36 goals in 1928-29, 37 in 1929-30 and a club record 189 overall in League and FA Cup matches. In December 1933, Rangers let him go to Brentford, but he did not appear in their first team prior to joining Wolves. Goddard died in Kingston-on-Thames on 24 March 1987.

Wolves record: 18 apps. 12 goals.

GODDARD, Raymond

Left-half Ray Goddard was born in Ecclesfield, Sheffield on 17 October 1920 and joined Wolves in September 1928 from Red Rovers FC. World War Two seriously disrupted his career at Molineux and after his military service, which took him to Burma and Ceylon with the Army soccer team, and a few games as a guest for Cardiff City, he left the club to sign for Chelsea in September 1946. In July 1948 he moved from Stamford Bridge to Plymouth Argyle, played over 150 League and Cup games for Exeter City between December 1949 and May 1954 and rounded off his footballing career as player-manager of Bideford Town (June 1954 to April 1956). He returned to the West Midlands and lived in Dudley until his death, in Gornal, on 1 February 1974.

Wolves record: 4 apps.

GOLD, James William

Goalkeeper Billy Gold deputised for Alex Scott during the 1936-37 season. Secured by Wolves from Bournemouth in December 1936, Gold was a tall, well built 'keeper whose appearances were restricted owing to the form of Scott and he left Molineux for Chelsea in May 1937 where he became reserve to Vic Woodley. Born in the village of Birkenshaw, Strathclyde in 1914, Gold played initially for Ballieston Juniors, moving to Bournemouth in January 1931. He failed to make Chelsea's first team and in February 1938, left Stamford Bridge to sign for Doncaster Rovers, retiring in 1946 after guesting for Rotherham United during the war.

Wolves record: 16 apps.

GOMEZ, Fernando

Spanish-born midfielder, who his senior debut for Wolves in a 5-0 Worthington League Cup win over Barnet in August 1998, scoring his first goal in English football soon afterwards in a 2-0 away win over Watford. He was 33 when he joined Wolves from Valencia where he had been since 1985 during which time he had scored 117 goals in 457 Spanish League games and 17 goals in 117 Cup matches. Capped eight times by his country at senior level, he also played in five Under-21 internationals and in 24 Under-18 games for Spain. A fine passer of the ball, Gomez quickly added confidence and composure to the Wolves midfield and his presence on the field was significant as Wolves made an exceptional start to the 1998-99 season.

Wolves record: 21+2 apps. 2 goals.

GOODALL, Archibald Lee

Inside-right-cum-centre-half Archie Goodall was well past his 41st birthday when he joined Wolves in October 1905. And when he played his last game for the club (against Everton on 2 December 1905) he was aged 41 years, five months and two days – the oldest player ever to don a Wolves shirt. An Irishman, born in Belfast on 19 June 1864, he was raised in Scotland and moved down to England as a teenager. After playing for Liverpool Stanley, he signed for Preston North End in 1887, served briefly with Aston Villa (from October 1888), then scored 52 goals in 423 games for Derby County between May 1889 and May 1903, helping the Rams twice reach the FA Cup Final and finish runners-up in the League championship. One of the great characters ever to play for Derby, he caused some alarm when, in 1898, he tried to unload his Cup Final tickets on which he had speculated. He also refused to play in extra-time in a United Counties League Cup Final (against West Bromwich Albion) because he said his contract ended after 90 minutes. On leaving the Baseball Ground, Goodall, who was capped eight times by Northern Ireland between 1898 and 1902, played for Plymouth Argyle from where he switched to Glossop North End (in January 1904), finally linking up with Wolves in October 1905 and staying until January 1906, when he retired. After this Goodall toured Europe and America with a strongman act, walking around with a massive metal hoop. He was a keen sportsman and followed his country avidly at football, cricket and tennis. In later life he worked and lived in North London and died in the capital on 29 November 1929, aged 75. His brother John also played for Preston North End, Glossop and Derby County.

Wolves record: / apps.

GOODING, Michael Charles

As a younger player Mick Gooding was a studious, hardworking midfielder, preferring the left-hand side of the field. Later on in his career he developed into an efficient player-manager, always putting unlimited effort and enthusiasm into his game. Born in Newcastle on 12 April 1959, he played for Bishop Auckland before entering the Football League with Rotherham United in July 1979. After three years at Millmoor during which time United won the Third Division crown, he switched to Chesterfield (December 1982) and in September 1983 returned to Rotherham for a second spell, which lasted until August 1987 when he signed for Peterborough United. From London Road he was transferred to Wolves for £85,000 in September 1988 but stayed just 15 months at Molineux before moving to Reading for £65,000 in December 1989, having assisted the Wanderers in winning the Third Division title. At Elm Park he teamed up with Jimmy Quinn and between them they helped Reading win the Second Division championship in 1994 and in 1995-96 Gooding himself was elected the Royals Player of the Year for the third time in five seasons. He was released by Reading in the summer of 1997 along with his co-manager Quinn. In July 1998 Gooding was appointed assistant manager of Southend United.

Wolves record: 52+2 apps. 5 goals.

GOODMAN, Donald Ralph

Striker Don Goodman's playing career almost came to an abrupt end when he suffered a depressed fracture of the skull in Wolves' penultimate League game of the 1995-96 season against Huddersfield Town. Thankfully after some nervous moments and several hours of medical care and attention, he recovered full fitness and went on to serve the club until May 1998 when he was given a free transfer to join the Japanese J-League club, Sanfrecce Hiroshima (July 1998). In December 1998 Goodman returned to England to play on loan for Nationwide League club Barnsley, and in March 1999 he moved to Scotland to sign for Motherwell. Born in Leeds on 9 May 1966, he played

junior football for Collingham before signing professional forms for Bradford City in July 1984. He went on to score 22 goals in 86 outings for the Yorkshire club and was with the Bantams at the time of the Bradford fire disaster. In March 1987, Goodman was sold to West Bromwich Albion for £50,000 and he did supremely well at The Hawthorns, amassing a fine record of 63 goals in 181 senior appearances. Then, in December 1991, Sunderland came in with a £900,000 bid and took Goodman away from West Brom – much to the annoyance of the Baggies' fans. At Roker Park he continued to find the net and claimed 44 more goals in 132 outings for the Wearsiders before his £1.1 million transfer to Wolves in December 1994. Teaming up with Steve Bull and David Kelly, who subsequently moved to Sunderland, Goodman was also asked to play wide as well as behind the front two, and he had some excellent games, his pace and determination proving decisive. During 1999 he reached the milestone of 600 appearances and 175 goals at senior level.
Wolves record: 142+12 apps. 39 goals.

GOODWIN, Frederick James

Born in Stockport on 4 January 1944, Freddie Goodwin was a useful midfielder, who represented Stockport and Cheshire schools before joining Wolves as a junior in June 1959, turning professional in January 1961. He had a lot of excellent players challenging him for a position in the first team at Molineux, but he battled on and made almost 50 appearances for the club before transferring to his native Stockport County in January 1966. He later served with Blackburn Rovers (March 1970), Southport (October 1971), Port Vale (July 1972), Macclesfield Town (1973-74), Stockport County again (August 1974), New Mills FC, Stalybridge Celtic and Ashton United, before taking up a coaching position in New Zealand with FC Stopout. He then became assistant-coach to the New Zealand national side and thereafter coached Papatoetoe FC and Hutt Valley United.
Wolves record: 46+1 apps.

GORMAN, James

Jim Gorman had a fine goalscoring record as an inside-forward in non-League football, but failed to make the grade in a higher level. Born in Stourbridge *c.*1883, he played (and scored well) for Woodside Albion and Halesowen before joining Wolves in April 1906. From Molineux he moved to Stoke (April 1907) and from July 1909 to May 1910 assisted Croydon Common. He then returned to the Black Country to round off his career with Dudley Town (August 1910) and Stourbridge (1912), retiring in 1914. Gorman, who also served in the Police Force

(based in Halesowen) died in Dudley *c.*1950.
Wolves record: 9 apps. 4 goals.

GOULD, Robert Alfred

Centre-forward Bobby Gould was another much-travelled footballer, serving eight clubs between 1964 and 1980, scoring 160 goals in 439 League games. Born in Coventry on 12 June 1946, he became an apprentice at Highfield Road in July 1962 and signed full-time professional forms in June 1964. His playing career went as follows: Coventry City (40 goals in 78 games); Arsenal (from February 1968, 16 goals in 65 games); Wolves (June 1970-September 1971 and December 1975-October 1977); West Bromwich Albion (from September 1971, 18 goals in 52 games); Bristol City (from December 1972, 15 in 35); West Ham United (from November 1973, 15 in 51); Bristol Rovers (from October 1977, 12 in 36) and Hereford United (from September 1978-May 1980, 13 in 45). He was also a non-contract player with Aldershot and Wimbledon. After ending his playing days, Gould worked as a coach or assistant manager at Aldershot, Chelsea, Charlton, and QPR, and managed Bristol Rovers (twice), Wimbledon (who he took to FA Cup glory in 1987), West Brom and Coventry (twice) and in 1996 was named team manager of Wales, a position he resigned in June 1999. In his first spell as a Wolves player Gould helped them finish fourth in Division One in 1970-71 and although he couldn't prevent them from being relegated during his second spell at Molineux, he was in the Second Division championship-winning side in 1976-77.
Wolves record: 81+12 apps. 39 goals.

GRAY, Andrew Mullen

Striker Andy Gray became the second most expensive footballer in Britain (behind Steve Daley) when Wolves paid Aston Villa the princely sum of £1,150,000 in September 1979. Gray, who was born in Glasgow on 30 November 1955, had always been a colourful figure wherever he played and it was appropriate that the transfer forms should be signed on the pitch in front of 24,580 fans, before the home game against Crystal Palace. Gray scored over 40 goals for Wolves, the most vital being the winner against Nottingham Forest in the 1980 League Cup Final at Wembley. A centre-forward, who was never afraid to go in where it hurt, Gray first played for Clydebank Strollers before joining Dundee United in 1970. He became a full-time professional in May 1973 and made over 75 appearances for the Tayside club, including the 1974 Scottish Cup Final when he gained a runners-up medal. Villa signed him for £110,000 in September 1975 and in 114 senior appearances for them he scored 69 goals. In 1977 he played in the two drawn

Andy Gray became the second most expensive footballer in Britain when Wolves paid Aston Villa £1.15 million in September 1979.

games of the League Cup Final and was voted Player of the Year and Young Player of the Year by the PFA. In July 1985, Gray left Wolves for Everton in a £250,000 deal and in only two seasons at Goodison he collected winners' medals in the FA Cup, League championship and European Cup-winners' Cup. Against Watford in the 1985 FA Cup Final he scored a somewhat controversial goal, apparently heading the ball out of Steve Sherwood's hands. Villa signed Gray for a second time in July 1985, for £150,000, and then followed a loan spell with Notts County before his old Villa boss Ron Saunders signed him for West Bromwich Albion for £25,000. Still his career was not over and early in 1988-89, Gray was signed by Glasgow Rangers, a club he helped win the Skol Cup almost immediately, followed by the Scottish Premier League title. At the end of the season, his job done, he was released and went to play for Cheltenham Town before rejoining Villa in the summer of 1991, this time as assistant manager to Ron Atkinson. Gray was capped 20 times by Scotland as well as winning Under-23, Youth and Schools caps, and his overall career tally shows well over 200 goals in more than 600 senior club matches. He left Villa to pursue a career in television and became a familiar face as an analyst with BSkyB. In June 1997 he was linked with the vacant manger's job at his former club Everton, but declined the offer, choosing to stay with Sky instead.
Wolves record: 159+3 apps. 45 goals.

GREATWICH, Frank Edwin

A reserve outside-right Frank Greatwich played in Wolves' League side in season 1897-98. Born locally *c.*1874, he spent just two seasons at Molineux, leaving for Stourbridge in May 1899.

Wolves record: 2 apps.

GREAVES, Ian D.

Ian Greaves was manager at Molineux for barely six months – from February to August 1982. In that time Wolves won only five League games and they suffered relegation to the Second Division. A Lancastrian, born in Oldham on 26 May 1932, Greaves started his career in non-League football with Buxton United and went on to become a sturdy full-back with Manchester United whom he served from May 1953 until December 1960 when he joined Lincoln City. He made 75 senior appearances whilst at Old Trafford, playing in the 1958 FA Cup Final defeat by Bolton Wanderers – the team he supported as a lad. He also gained a League championship medal in 1955-56. From Sincil Bank he moved to Oldham Athletic (May 1961), announcing his retirement in May 1963. Five years later he stepped into management with Huddersfield Town where he remained until 1974. He then took charge of Bolton Wanderers with whom he stayed for six seasons. At the start of the 1980-81 campaign Greaves was appointed assistant manager of Hereford United (under Frank Lord) and later on he took over from Ron Barry as team boss of Oxford United, a position he held until moving to Molineux for his six month reign. In January 1983, after an enforced 'long holiday' Greaves returned to football management with Mansfield Town. He held his job at Field Mill until 1989 when he was sacked. As a manager Greaves guided both Huddersfield (1970) and Bolton (1978) to the Second Division championship; in 1985 he lifted Mansfield into the Third Division and two years led the Stags to victory in the Freight Rover Trophy Final at Wembley. On four occasions Greaves was voted Manager of the Month – once at Huddersfield and three times with Bolton.

GREEN, Alfred Thomas

Reserve centre-forward Tommy Green appeared in Wolves' League side during the 1895-96 season when he replaced Billy Beats. Born in Wolverhampton *c.*1873, he was signed from Willenhall in August 1894, and on leaving Molineux in the summer of 1896, he teamed up with Tettenhall Sentinels, later assisting Bushbury. He scored 61 goals in two seasons of Birmingham and District League soccer for Wolves: 1894-96.

Wolves record: 2 apps.

GREEN, Francis

Frank Green was a big, burly inside-forward, six foot two inches tall, 13 stones in weight, who had a good spell at Molineux, finishing second top-scorer in 1928-29 with 16 goals. Born in Ashington, County Durham in 1905, Green played for his home town club Ashington before joining Wolves from Frickley Colliery in November 1927, as cover for Messrs Cock, Phillipson and Chadwick. He left the club in October 1929 for Crewe Alexandra, later playing for Peterborough and Fletton United, Crewe again (January 1931), Barnsley (June 1931), Racing Club De Paris (1933-34), Northwich Victoria (June 1935), Rhyl Athletic and briefly with Nantwich Town before retiring in 1939. He netted ten goals in 45 games for the Alex.

Wolves record: 38 apps. 17 goals.

GREEN, John Asher

Sprightly, well proportioned reserve inside-forward, born in St Helens in September 1894, Jack Green joined Wolves from Prescot Cables in August 1919 and left Molineux for Formby the following year. He later assisted Liverpool R.M. Services FC and died on Merseyside *c.*1966.

Wolves record: 6 apps. 1 goal.

GREEN, Ryan

Ryan Green became the youngest-ever player to appear in a full international match for Wales when he lined up for his country against Malta in June 1998, aged 17 years, 226 days. A right full-back, born in Cardiff in 1970, he joined Wolves as a trainee on leaving school and, in fact, had not made a senior first-team appearance before receiving his first full cap. Before he had actually signed professional forms for Wolves Green turned down offers from four other clubs: Blackburn Rovers, Norwich City, Swansea City and his home town club Cardiff City. In April 1999 Green agreed a new contract with Wolves which will keep him at Molineux until the year 2002.

Wolves record: 1 app.

GREENE, Christopher

Irish inside-forward or wing-half Chris Greene never really settled at Molineux. Born in Dublin in 1908, he played in Leinster League football as a youngster and developed his skills with Brideville FC and then Shelbourne (from 1926) before joining Southport in August 1933. Wolves paid £500 for his services in November 1933, with another £500 available if he made his mark at Molineux. Unfortunately he didn't, and in May 1936 he was sold to Swansea Town. He later assisted Bury (from December 1937) and retired during the war. Greene died in Ireland *c.*1978.

Wolves record: 7 apps. 2 goals.

GREENOCK MORTON

Wolves' playing record against Morton is:

Texaco Cup

Venue	P	W	D	L	F	A
Home	1	0	0	1	1	2
Away	1	1	0	0	3	0

Wolves played the Scottish club Morton at home and away in the second round of the Texaco Cup competition of 1970-71. Over 10,000 fans saw Wolves comfortably win the first leg at Cappielow Park in October, but then a fortnight later, just under 14,000 attended Molineux to see the Wanderers lose 2-1.

Associated with both clubs: Hugh McIlmoyle (striker with Wolves and Morton) and Mark McGhee (Wolves manager, Morton player).

GREGORY, John Theodore

Reserve outside-right Jack Gregory spent most almost a year in Wolves' second team before making his senior debut late in the 1908-09 campaign against Leeds City at Molineux. Born in Wolverhampton *c.*1887, he joined Wolves from Victoria Road Swifts and left Molineux (in 1910) for Dudley Town, later playing for St Phillip's FC

Wolves record: 1 app.

GREGORY, Valentine Francis

Val Gregory was born at Hendon, Middlesex on 14 February 1888, St Valentine's Day, hence his first name. A wing-half, he played for Reading, Watford (1910) and Arsenal (from September 1914, although he played only wartime games for the Gunners) before joining Wolves for £3,500 in May 1920. Gregory had three excellent seasons at Molineux, making over 100 senior appearances and gaining a FA Cup runners-up medal in 1921 when he skippered the side against Tottenham Hotspur. After retiring in May 1925 he became coach and then trainer at Molineux before leaving the club through ill health in 1938. Gregory died at Heathtown, Wolverhampton on 10 March 1940.

Wolves record: 106 apps. 2 goals.

GRIFFIN, Alfred

Outside-left Alf Griffin joined Wolves in August 1892 at the age of 21 from Walsall, having previously assisted Brierley Hill Alliance. Born in Walsall on 3 June 1871 and educated in his native town, he became a firm favourite with the Molineux fans and was on the wing when Wolves won the FA Cup in 1893. He was transferred back to Walsall in the summer of 1896 and retired five years later following a serious ankle injury. He hit 34 goals in 88 games for the Saddlers in his two spells at the club. Griffin died *c.*1945.

Wolves record: 76 apps. 14 goals.

GRIFFITHS, Bernard

Outside-left Bernie Griffiths was one of the early stars in Wolves' pre-League days, being a regular in the first team for two years. Born in Pendeford in 1868, he played for Wolverhampton Rangers before joining Wolves in the summer of 1886. He scored seven FA Cup goals in season 1886-87, and when Crosswell's were beaten 14-0, he claimed two of those goals and helped set up eight more for his colleagues. He left Wolves in August 1888 to sign for Lanesfield, later assisting Sedgeley. He did c.1925.

Wolves record: 8 apps. 8 goals.

GRIFFITHS, Hillary

Wing-half Hill Griffiths gave Wolves splendid service for 12 years during which time he made over 200 first-team appearances and skippered the side for three seasons. Born in Wednesfield in August 1871, he joined Wolves from Wednesfield Rovers in April 1899 and left Molineux for Burton Swifts in 1901. He later played for Reading, Nottingham Forest, Bristol Rovers (May 1904), Millwall (October 1905) and Kidderminster Harriers (from December 1905), retiring in 1907. He starred for Wolves in the 1896 FA Cup Final and was unlucky not to have gained international honours, injuries ruining his chances. Two of Griffiths's elder brothers, John and Jabez, were also useful footballers. Hillary Griffiths died in Worcester in 1940.

Wolves record: 201 apps. 1 goal.

GRIFFITHS, Isaac

Goalkeeper Ike Griffiths was first choice for Wolves for four seasons: 1883 to 1887. Indeed, he was the first recognised 'keeper at the club. Born in Willenhall in 1862, he played in all of Wolves' first 14 FA Cup-ties and made his League debut against Burnley at Molineux in October 1890 – seven years after joining the club from Wolverhampton Rangers, having earlier played for Wednesbury St Peter's. Griffiths was a confident 'keeper who loved to 'fly-kick' the ball to safety rather than collect it with his hands. A knee injury restricted his performances from 1888 onwards and in 1891 he retired to go into business in Wolverhampton. He died in 1938.

Wolves record: 15 apps.

GRIFFITHS, Jabez

Signed from Wednesfield Rovers in 1882, Jabez Griffiths played regularly for Wolves in the 1883-84 season. An outside-left – born locally c.1860 – he netted in the Final of the Wrekin Cup which Wolves won 11-0 – their first trophy success.

Wolves record: 2 apps. 2 goals.

GRIFFITHS, John

Jack Griffiths was a full-back who acted as reserve to first Harry Shaw and then Cecil Shaw during his time at Molineux. Born in Fenton, Staffs, on 15 September 1909, he worked as a potter and played football for the local Boys Brigade team and for Shirebrook FC, before joining Wolves in May 1929. After three years at Molineux he was transferred to Bolton Wanderers (June 1932), moving to Manchester United in March 1934, before becoming player-coach with non-League Hyde United in May 1939. He played in more than 175 games whilst at Old Trafford, helping United win promotion from the Second Division in 1938, the same year he figured in an England international trial match. During the war, Griffiths guested for Derby County, Notts County, Port Vale, Stoke City and West Bromwich Albion, returning to Hyde in 1945. He also qualified as a masseur during the hostilities.

Wolves record: 6 apps.

GRIFFITHS, Joseph B.

Born in New Tredegar in 1910, and no relation to any of the other players of the same name, Joe Griffiths made one appearance for Wolves in February 1931 (at Reading) when he replaced Billy Hartill. He left Molineux in May 1931 and spent the next two years with Stockport County (scoring 33 goals in 48 League appearances). He was forced to quit top line soccer through injury.

Wolves record: 1 app.

GRIFFITHS, John Charles Ruskin

John Griffiths was a useful centre-forward, who served Wolves during the last two League seasons prior to World War One (1913-15). Born in Wednesfield in 1888, he played his early football with Bushbury White Star and Goldthorn Park before joining Willenhall from where he switched to Molineux in July 1913. He did not figure after the war.

Wolves record: 13 apps. 2 goals.

GRIMSBY TOWN

Wolves' playing record against the Mariners is:

Football League

Venue	P	W	D	L	F	A
Home	30	19	5	6	82	28
Away	30	9	5	16	29	45
Total	60	28	10	24	111	73

FA Cup

	P	W	D	L	F	A
Home	1	1	0	0	6	2
Away	3	1	1	1	6	4
Neutral	1	1	0	0	5	0
Totals	5	3	1	1	17	6

League Cup

	P	W	D	L	F	A
Home	1	0	1	0	1	1
Away	1	0	1	0	0	0
Neutral	1	1	0	0	2	0
Totals	3	1	2	0	3	1

ZDSC						
Away	1	0	0	1	0	1

Wartime

	P	W	D	L	F	A
Away (void)	1	0	1	0	0	0

Wolves and Grimsby first met at League level in season 1901-02 and each team won their respective home game: Wolves 2-0, Town 3-0.

Billy Wooldridge scored twice in a competent 5-0 Wolves' victory at Molineux in March 1907 and nine months later (December) Jack Shelton netted a hat-trick in Wolves' 5-1 home win.

It was goal galore in December 1909 when Wolves ran up their joint best League win over Grimsby, beating them 8-1 at Molineux in a second Division match in front of 5,000 fans. Four players – Blunt, Hedley, Radford and Pedley each scored twice.

Wolves ran up two 4-1 wins over Grimsby in the last two seasons prior to World War One, at Molineux in January 1914 and at Blundell Park in January 1915.

Starting their home League programme after World War One, Wolves hammered Grimsby 6-1 at Molineux in September 1919 before a 10,000 crowd. And when they won the Third Division North title in 1923-24 Wolves whipped the Mariners 4-1 at home with Stan Fazackerley and Tudor Martin both netting twice.

Grimsby achieved their best League success over Wolves in May 1927, when they won 6-0 at home with Joe Robson scoring four times, one a net-busting penalty.

When Wolves won 5-2 at Molineux in April 1937, Gordon Clayton reaped a hat-trick following his double-strike in an FA Cup victory two months earlier.

During the last season before World War Two, Wolves scored a total of 14 goals against the Mariners in three meetings (two in the League and one in the FA Cup semi-final).

In the League encounters, after winning 4-2 at Cleethorpes, they doubled up by winning 5-0 at home with a hat-trick for Dennis Westcott.

Wolves equalled their best League win over Grimsby in their first home game of the 1947-48 season (27 August). Jesse Pye (3), Sammy Smyth (2) and Dennis Westcott (2) led the goal-rush in that 8-1 romp in front of 43,289 spectators.

A week later Wolves won 4-0 at Blundell Park with Willie Forbes netting twice on this occasion.

It was then another 35 years before Wolves and Town met again in the League. This time a Second Division match at Molineux in November 1982 ended in a 3-0 win for Wolves in front of 12,701 fans. Wayne Clarke scored twice.

Wolves crashed to a crushing 5-1 defeat at Grimsby in November 1984 when David Barnes conceded a silly own-goal.

In September 1995 it was Wolves 4

Grimsby 1 at Molineux and when Wolves won 3-1 on Mariners' soil in August 1996, all their goals came from ace striker Steve Bull.

Wolves beat the Mariners 6-2 in a fifth-round replay at Molineux in February 1937, with Gordon Clayton and George Ashall both netting twice in front of a midweek crowd of almost 57,800.

Two years later, in the FA Cup semi-final at Old Trafford, a record attendance of 76,962 saw Wolves thrash luckless Grimsby Town 5-0 with Dennis Westcott netting four of the goals (two in the last three minutes). It was unfortunate for the Mariners who had their goalkeeper George Moulson taken off injured after only 21 minutes play.

Sixteen years on – in January 1955 – Wolves and Grimsby met again in the FA Cup and once more the Wanderers came out on top, winning a third round tie at Blundell Park by 5-2 with Dennis Wilshaw netting twice in front of 26,114 fans. The Mariners were 2-0 up in this tie (through Albert Stokes and Ray Harrison) and an hour had gone before Wolves began to play. Then the floodgates opened and the goals rained in thick and fast from the reigning League champions.

After a 0-0 draw at Blundell Park and a 1-1 showdown at Molineux, Wolves finally eclipsed Grimsby from the League Cup in 1979-80, winning 2-0 at neutral Derby.

Under 1,600 fans saw the Mariners knock Wolves out of the Zenith Data Systems Cup in 1991-92.

Players with both clubs include: Dave Beasant, Jack Beattie, John Bell, David Black, John Bradford, Jack Ferguson, Tom Galley, George Harper, George Harris, Charlie Henderson, Scott McGarvey, Tom Mayson, Tom Raybould, Graham Rodger, Ronnie Stockin, Phil Stoutt and Billy Tennant (later Grimsby's reserve team manager).

Also associated: David Felgate and Jack Ferguson (Wolves Reserves), Dickie Dorsett, John Harris and Frank Wildman (all Grimsby wartime guests) and John Ward (player with Grimsby, Wolves assistant manager).

GROSVENOR, Sidney Victor

Full-back Sid Grosvenor was signed as cover for Jack Jones and Dick Betteley – but with these two fine players holding their form he failed to establish himself in the first team and left after three years at Molineux. Born in Wolverhampton c.1882, Grosvenor played for Willenhall Swifts prior to joining Wolves in August 1903 and on leaving Molineux in 1906 had a brief spell with Walsall before signing for Stafford Royal.
Wolves record: 2 apps.

GROUNDS

Wolves' first major ground was Windmill Field, situated in Goldthorn Hill which they utilised for two years: 1877-79.

The capacity was approximately 2,000 but very rarely did they get crowds above the 1,000 mark.

For the next two years the club played their home games on John Harper's Field which lay directly opposite Stroud's Niphon Works in Lower Villiers Street. Again attendances weren't all that large and an audience of 2,000 was regarded as a good turnout.

From 1881 Dudley Road was Wolves' home. This was situated on one of the many main roads leading out of Wolverhampton and had the Fighting Cocks public house directly across the road.

Wolves played their first ever FA Cup-tie here against against Long Eaton Rangers on 27 October 1883, which they won 4-1 in front of 2,000 spectators.

Wolves' first Football League game also took place at Dudley Road when they were held to a 1-1 draw by Aston Villa on 8 September 1888 before a crowd of 2,500.

The best crowd for a Wolves home game at Dudley Road is believed to have been that of 10,000 for a third-round FA Cup-tie against Sheffield Wednesday on 2 March 1889.

Wolves stayed at Dudley Road for eight years, until the summer of 1889, when Molineux was declared ready for use – although during this period (1881-89) it is believed that certain matches were played on the Blakenhall Wanderers Cricket Ground which stood behind the Fighting Cocks pub.

Molineux, therefore, has been home to Wolverhampton Wanderers for 109 years and is now rated one of the best stadiums outside the Premiership with an all-seated capacity of 28,500. (See Molineux).

Neutral Grounds
Molineux was closed down for a short period of time by the Football League during the first season after World War One.

Following crowd disturbances towards the end of a home League game with Bury on 18 October, Wolves were forced to play two scheduled home games on a neutral ground, and they chose The Hawthorns, where they were beaten 4-2 by Barnsley on 29 November 1919 and drew 2-2 with Stockport County on 6 December.

Here are other instances of neutral grounds where Wolves have played major competitive matches:

16 Mar 1889 v Blackburn Rovers, FA Cup semi-final, Gresty Road, Crewe
23 Mar 1889 v Blackburn Rovers, FA Cup semi-final replay, Gresty Rd, Crewe
30 Mar 1889 v Preston North End, FA Cup Final, The Oval
8 Mar 1890 v Blackburn Rovers, FA Cup semi-final, Baseball Ground, Derby
4 Mar 1893 v Blackburn Rovers, FA Cup semi-final, Town Ground, Nottingham
25 Mar 1893 v Everton, FA Cup Final, Fallowfield, Manchester
21 Mar 1896 v Derby County, FA Cup semi-final, Perry Barr, Birmingham
18 Apr 1896 v Sheffield Wednesday, FA Cup Final, Crystal Palace
29 Feb 1904 v Derby County, FA Cup second round, second replay, Villa Park
28 Mar 1908 v Southampton, FA Cup semi-final, Stamford Bridge
25 Apr 1908 v Newcastle United, FA Cup Final, Crystal Palace
19 Mar 1921 v Cardiff City, FA Cup semi-final, Anfield, Liverpool
23 Mar 1921 v Cardiff City, FA Cup semi-final replay, Old Trafford
23 Apr 1921 v Tottenham Hotspur, FA Cup Final, Stamford Bridge
15 Mar 1937 v Sunderland, FA Cup sixth round second replay, Hillsborough
25 Mar 1939 v Grimsby Town, FA semi-final, Old Trafford
29 Apr 1939 v Portsmouth, FA Cup Final, Wembley
26 Mar 1949 v Manchester United, FA Cup semi-final, Hillsborough
2 Apr 1949 v Manchester United, FA Cup semi-final replay, Goodison Park
30 Apr 1949 v Leicester City, FA Cup Final, Wembley
19 Dec 1949 v Portsmouth, FA Charity Shield, Highbury
10 Mar 1951 v Newcastle United, FA Cup semi-final, Hillsborough
14 Mar 1951 v Newcastle United, FA Cup semi-final replay, Leeds Road
26 Mar 1960 v Aston Villa, FA Cup semi-final, The Hawthorns
7 May 1960 v Blackburn Rovers, FA Cup Final, Wembley
1 Mar 1965 v Aston Villa, FA Cup fifth round, second replay, The Hawthorns
2 Nov 1968 v Nottingham Forest, League Division One, Meadow Lane, Nottingham
21 Aug 1971 v Leeds United, League Division One, Leeds Road, Huddersfield
7 Apr 1973 v Leeds United, FA Cup semi-final, Maine Road, Manchester
2 Mar 1974 v Manchester City, League Cup Final, Wembley
31 Mar 1979 v Arsenal, FA Cup semi-final, Villa Park
18 Dec 1979 v Grimsby Town, League Cup fifth round, second replay, Baseball Ground, Derby
15 Mar 1980 v Nottingham Forest, League Cup Final, Wembley
11 Apr 1981 v Tottenham Hotspur, FA Cup semi-final, Hillsborough
15 Apr 1981 v Tottenham Hotspur, FA Cup semi-final replay, Highbury

15 Nov 1986 v Chorley, FA Cup first round,
  Burnden Park, Bolton

24 Nov 1986 v Chorley, FA Cup first round,
  second replay, Burnden Park,
  Bolton

16 Apr 1988 v Everton, Mercantile Credit
  League Festival, Wembley

29 May 1988 v Burnley, Sherpa Van Trophy
  Final, Wembley

5 Apr 1998 v Arsenal, FA Cup semi-final,
  Villa Park

When entering the Birmingham Senior and Staffordshire Senior Cup competitions, Wolves occasionally played Finals on neutral grounds, the details of which appear under those separate headings. Wolves also played the 1938 Colchester Challenge Cup Final and the 1942 Wartime Challenge Cup Final on neatral grounds.

GROVES, Albert

Albert Groves, born in Newport, Monmouthshire in January 1886, was one of the smallest centre-halves ever to play for Wolves at 5ft 7in, although in those days, of course, the position was more a true midfield link than defensive stopper. Groves joined Wolves from Aberdare Athletic in August 1909 and remained at Molineux until May 1920 when he was appointed player-manager of Birmingham League side Walsall. By then he had scored 20 goals in more than 200 League and Cup games for the Wanderers. Groves made his debut at home to Manchester City on the last day of the 1909-10 season and he appeared in several positions thereafter, including inside-right in 1912-13, when he hit ten goals in Division Two. During World War One he served in the Army and guested for Port Vale, Bury and Sunbeam Motors (Coventry). In 1919 he re-signed for Wolves, but soon afterwards, with other players coming through the ranks, he decided to try his luck in management, taking over at Walsall for one season before handing over to Jack Burchell when the Saddlers became founder-members of the Third Division North. Continuing as secretary at Fellows Park until 1924, he still played competitively, however, scoring eight goals in 36 appearances during Walsall's first season back in the Football League. In all he made 79 Football League appearances for the Saddlers, netting 15 goals. He also played in 12 FA Cup-ties for Walsall and in 33 other senior games. Later he turned out for Willenhall before becoming licensee of the Hope and Anchor pub, Bloxwich Road, Willenhall. Groves died c.1960.
Wolves record: 217 apps. 20 goals.

GUELLIAM, Richmond Cedric

An amateur trialist at Molineux, inside-left Rich Guelliam celebrated his debut for Wolves by scoring at Anfield. Born in Wolverhampton c.1880, he played for Wolverhampton White Star and Birch Coppice before linking up with Wolves in September 1901. Three months later he left the club to sign for Wrens Nest FC and later assisted Dudley. Guelliam died in Dudley c.1935.
Wolves record: 2 apps. 1 goal.

GUEST PLAYERS

During World War Two, Wolves recruited the services of 42 guest players to assist them in Regional League and Cup football and they were: Jack Acquaroff (24 apps. 18 goals), Arthur Bailey, George Billingsley, Harry Bowden, Frank Broome, Albert R. Brown, Jack Dowen, Len D. Emanuel, Mick Fenton, Lester Finch, Neil Franklin, Colin Gibson, Freddie Haycock, Wilf Heathcote, Jim Hooks, Dick Houghton, Harry Iddon, Jimmy Jinks, Bill Johnson, David Johnstone, Davey Jones, Reg Kirkham, Joe McCormick, Johnny McDonald, Dick Marsh, Irving Methley, Charlie Mitten, Jack Morby, Jock Mulraney, Ron Morgan, Frank O'Donnell, George Paterson, Tommy Reece, Arthur Rowley, Jack Rowley (scorer of 17 goals in only seven games), Laurie Scott, Jack Shelton, Tom Smalley, Jack Smith, Bernard Streten, Guy Wharton and Tom Wood.

During their respective careers, Broome (Aston Villa), Franklin (Stoke City), Jack Rowley (Manchester United), Scott (Arsenal), Smalley (Norwich City) and Streten (Luton Town) were all capped by England, O'Donnell (Preston North End, Blackpool, Aston Villa and Nottingham Forest) represented Scotland, Smith (Wolves, Chelsea) won Welsh caps in wartime games while Finch (Barnet) was an England amateur international. And the following all had excellent careers – Acquaroff (with Norwich City), 'Sailor' Brown (Charlton, Nottingham Forest and Aston Villa), Fenton (Middlesbrough), Gibson (Newcastle and Aston Villa), Haycock (Aston Villa), Jinks (Millwall), McCormick (Bolton Wanderers and Rochdale), McDonald (Liverpool and Tranmere Rovers), Methley (Walsall), Mitten (Manchester United), Mulraney (Birmingham City, Aston Villa and Shrewsbury Town), Arthur Rowley became the champion League goalscorer of all-time serving with West Bromwich Albion, Fulham, Leicester City and Shrewsbury Town), Shelton (Walsall – whose father played for Wolves: 1907-10), Wharton (Wolves and Portsmouth) and Wood (Aston Villa).

Like Wharton, Dowen, Kirkham, Smalley and Smith also played for Wolves before the war, while Arthur Rowley was an amateur at Molineux before joining West Bromwich Albion.

GUMMERY, Walter Harry

Walter Gummery was a smart outside-left, who played for Wolves during the mid 1920s, having his best season in 1924-25. Born in Worcester on 1 March 1900, he played for St Thomas's Boys' Club, Hammerford Lads' and Worcester City before moving to Molineux in August 1923. He left Wolves for Accrington Stanley in May 1926. Gummery died in Sutton on 19 October 1974.
Wolves record: 10 apps. 1 goal.

GUTTRIDGE, William Henry

Nicknamed 'Chopper', full-back Bill Guttridge was a fine defender. Born in Darlaston on 4 March 1931, he worked and played for Metroshaft Works before joining Wolves as an amateur in 1947, turning professional in March 1948. He spent the next six years at Molineux playing mainly in the Reserves, but in November 1954 he left for Walsall where he immediately gained a first-team place. He went on to appear in well over 200 games for the Saddlers, helping them win promotion from the Fourth to the Second Division. He retired in May 1962 and later coached the youngsters at Fellows Park.
Wolves record: 7 apps.

HADLEY, Edmund

A relatively unknown inside-forward, born in Tettenhall c.1865, Edmund Hadley played for Wolves from September 1883 to May 1885. He joined the club from Wednesfield Rovers, having earlier played for Stafford Road, and left for Bilston Saints. He died in December 1929.
Wolves record: 3 apps.

HALES, Frederick F.

Utility forward Fred Hales was perhaps too lightweight to make his mark in senior football. Born in Oldbury in 1898 and a pupil at Matthew Boulton School, he joined Wolves from the Hardy Spicer Works FC in June 1920 and left Molineux for Darlaston in 1922, later assisting Bloxwich Strollers. He died in Walsall in 1957.
Wolves record: 2 apps. 1 goal.

HALIFAX TOWN

Wolves' playing record against Halifax is:
Football League

Venue	P	W	D	L	F	A
Home	3	1	0	2	5	3
Away	3	1	1	1	7	7
Totals	6	2	1	3	12	10

League Cup

Away	1	1	0	0	3	0

Wolves inflicted a 4-0 defeat on Halifax at Molineux in their Third Division North championship-winning season of 1923-24. Over 14,700 saw Stuart McMillan score twice. Over 60 years later, in March 1987, Wolves won a terrific Fourth Division match at The

Shay by 4-3 when Andy Mutch scored twice in front of just 2,079 fans. Halifax's two wins over Wolves came in the 1980s and were both by 2-1. Over 8,000 Fans saw Wolves easily beat the Shaymen in a second round League Cup-tie in October 1973 – en route to the Final.

Players with both clubs include: Wilf Chadwick, Evan Edwards, Ted Elliott, John Farley, Joe Gallagher, Billy Kellock, Fred Kemp, Teddy Maguire and Mick Matthews.

Also associated: Jim McCalliog (Wolves player, Halifax manager), Jim Mulvaney (Halifax player, Wolves wartime guest), Albert Flatley (Wolves trialist), Larry Kelly (Halifax wartime guest), Cyril Hannaby and Malcolm White (Wolves juniors), and Martin James, James Lee and Willie Morgan (Wolves Reserves).

HALLIGAN, William

Irish international forward Billy Halligan, born at Athlone in August 1890, had a career that spanned 20 years and took in nine Football League clubs (and 14 in total). He first played for Belfast Distillery, Belfast Celtic and Cliftonville in the Irish League before joining Leeds City in 1909. Derby County signed him in February 1910 and he became a Wolverhampton Wanderers player in June 1911, for £450. In his career netted over 100 goals in more than 220 senior appearances. His two seasons with Wolves were spent in the Second Division before he was transferred to Hull City in May 1913, for what was then City's record fee of £600. For the Tigers he scored 28 goals in 64 games, then played for Manchester United and Rochdale as a guest in World War One before joining Preston North End in July 1919. Oldham Athletic signed him in January 1920, then he went to Nelson (July 1921) and ended his career in non-League football with Boston Town and Wisbech Town, finally retiring in 1924 at the age of 39. Although on the small side, he could play in any of the three central forward positions and proved a more than useful marksman. He was capped twice at senior level against Wales in January 1911 and against England in February 1912. He also played for an All-Ireland XI v England in Dublin in 1912, in two Victory Internationals against Scotland in 1919-20 and for the Irish League against the Scottish League in 1909. Halligan died c.1950.
Wolves record: 73 apps. 41 goals.

HAMILTON, A. John

Wing-half Jack Hamilton was born in Ayrshire in 1872 and played for Glasgow United (1890) and Ayr United (1891) before moving to the Midlands to sign for Wolves in June 1894. Unfortunately he failed to make his mark at Molineux and was quickly released, moving to Derby County in November of that same year. He then switched to Ilkeston Town before having useful spells with Gainsborough Trinity, Loughborough Town, Bristol City (making 142 appearances for the Robins between 1897-1900), Leicester Fosse (September 1900), Watford (April 1901), Wellingborough (July 1902), Fulham (as a player in August 1903, then as assistant manager at Craven Cottage: 1904-08 and head trainer: 1908-10). He returned to Ashton Gate as reserve team manager and then managed City's League side during World War One (May 1915 to August 1919) and actually came out of retirement to play in two matches when City were short of players before returning north of the border to assist Heart of Midlothian and then Airdrieonians in a coaching capacity. He died in Scotland c.1944.
Wolves record: 4 apps.

HAMPTON, John William

Goalkeeper Jack Hampton was a member of the first-team squad at Molineux for five years from 1922, although for most of the time he had to play second fiddle to Noel George. Born in Wolverhampton in 1899, he played for Wellington Town (seasons 1917-19) and joined Wolves from Oakengates Town in May 1920. He left Molineux for Derby County in June 1927 (teaming up with manager George Jobey) and after gaining a First Division runners-up medal with the Rams he was transferred to Preston North End in May 1930, later assisting Dundalk (from June 1931 to May 1933).
Wolves record: 51 apps.

HANCOCKS, John

Tiny outside-right Johnny Hancocks, who was only 5ft 4in tall and wore size-two boots, had a magnificent record with the great Wolves team of the post-war period. In played in well over 350 senior games and scored more than 160 goals, 158 of which came in 343 League outings, all of them in the old First Division. Born at Oakengates, Salop, on 30 April 1919, he played for Oakengates Town before Walsall signed him on professional forms. He scored on his League debut for the Saddlers in a 2-2 draw at Fellows Park in the Third Division (South) in October 1938, and by the end of the season had netted ten goals in 37 competitive matches. He scored 32 times in 94 wartime games for Walsall, guested for Chester, Crewe Alexandra and Wrexham and represented the Army and Western Command after joining up as a PT instructor. Wolves signed him on 11 May 1946, for a bargain fee of £4,000, and the hard-shooting winger went on to collect an FA Cup winners' medal in 1949 and a League championship medal in 1954. He won three full England caps, scoring twice on his debut in a 6-0 win against Switzerland at

Johnny Hancocks, the tiny winger who made such a huge impact on Wolves after World War Two.

Highbury, and also represented the Football League. Even after Harry Hooper had replaced him on Wolves' right wing in 1956-57, Hancocks, who actually refused to re-sign for Wolves in 1950-51 after failing to agree terms, continued to delight the Molineux crowd in the Central League team. He eventually moved to Wellington Town (later Telford United) and after a spell as their player-manager he ended his career with Cambridge United (then in the Southern League), Oswestry and GKN Sankey. He later worked at Maddock and Sons, ironfounders, in his hometown of Oakengates before retiring in 1979, on his 60th birthday. Alas, he later suffered a stroke but still followed the fortunes of his former clubs through newspapers and TV. One of Wolves' greatest players died on 19 February 1994.
Wolves record: 378 apps. 168 goals.

HANDYSIDES, Ian Robert

As a youngster Ian Handysides was hailed as the new Trevor Francis when he began his professional career at St Andrew's, but the high expectations proved to be a millstone round his neck and despite him winning England Youth team honours, he never really hit the heights with Birmingham City. Born in Jarrow on 14 December 1962, Handysides represented Durham Boys before joining Blues as an apprentice in June 1978, turning professional in January 1980. Four years later he was transferred to Walsall for £17,000 and after rejoining Blues in March 1986, he had a loan spell at Molineux during September/October 1986. He was then forced to retire through ill-health in October 1988 after developing a brain tumour. He underwent surgery and seemed to be on the road to recovery, but further tumours appeared on his spinal chord and sadly he died in Solihull on 17 August 1990, aged 27. *Wolves record: 11 apps. 2 goals.*

HANKIN, Raymond

Striker Ray Hankin had a useful career during the 1970s and 1980s although his goals were less frequent in the latter part of his time in League football. Born in Wallsend on 2 February 1956, he started his professional days with Burnley in February 1973 having been at Turf Moor for almost two years as an apprentice. In September 1976 he transferred to Leeds United for £180,000. In March 1980 he switched to Vancouver Whitecaps, had a trial with Arsenal in January 1982, played for Shamrock Rovers after that and returned to England with Middlesbrough in September 1982 for a fee of £80,000. He served Peterborough United from September 1983 and was sacked after being sent off five times. He arrived at Molineux in March 1985 at a time when Wolves were on the slide. Capped by England at both youth and Under-23 levels, Hankin scored almost 100 goals in close on 300 appearances in League and Cup football before dropping into non-League football with Whitby Town in March 1986. He later assisted Blue Star FC, Guisborough Town (July 1987), Northallerton (as manager 1989) and then managed Darlington from March to July 1992. *Wolves record: 9+1 apps. 1 goal.*

HANN, Charles William

Charlie Hann was a reserve outside left who spent three years at Molineux. Determined, with a good shot, he was born in Wolverhampton c.1903, and played for several local clubs including Bilston White Star and Wesley Methodists before joining Wolves in August 1924. He left Molineux in May 1927 and signed for Darlaston, later assisting Penkridge. *Wolves record: 14 apps. 2 goals.*

HANSBURY, Roger

Goalkeeper Roger Hansbury had a long career in the game. Born in Barnsley on 26 January 1955, he represented Yorkshire Youths before joining Norwich City as an amateur in 1971, turning professional on his 18th birthday. Loan spells with Bolton Wanderers (March 1977), Cambridge United (November 1977) and Leyton Orient (December 1978) preceded his transfer to Eastern Athletic in Hong Kong in December 1981. He then returned to England to sign for Burnley in August 1983 and afterwards assisted Cambridge United for a second time (July 1985), Birmingham City (March 1986),

had loan spells with Sheffield United (October-November 1987), Wolves (March-April 1989), Colchester United (August 1989) and Cardiff City (October 1989), signing permanently for the Welsh club for £20,000 in December 1989. He retired from Football League action the following year and entered the non-League scene. Hansbury's career was disrupted early on by a broken leg (at Norwich) but he recovered full fitness and did well generally with every club he served, making over 300 senior appearances in total. *Wolves record: 6 apps.*

HARDWARE, James

Jimmy Hardware was a handy player to have in reserve. He acted as understudy for half-backs Bishop and Hunt during his two-year stay at Molineux. Born in Finchfield, Wolverhampton in September 1886, he played for Tettenhall Institute and Hurst Lane Social before joining Wolves in August 1907. In May 1910 he was allowed to leave for Bilston United and later assisted Willenhall Pickwick and Whitwick White Star. Hardware died in Wolverhampton c.1957. *Wolves record: 9 apps.*

HARGREAVES, Henry Harold

Inside-left Harold Hargreaves was sent-off for the only time in his career playing for Wolves against Leeds United in December 1922. He was suspended for a month (January 1923) and left Molineux at the end of that season. A thrustful inside-forward with deadly shot, he was born at Higham, Lancashire on 3 February 1899 and played for Great Harwood and Nelson before joining Wolves in November 1921. He spent almost two years at Molineux, leaving for Pontypridd in June 1923, and later assisting Tottenham Hotspur (December 1923), Burnley (March 1926), Rotherham (May 1928), Mansfield Town (May 1930), Rossendale United (October 1930) and Barnoldswick Town (March 1931 to April 1932). He scored 13 goals in 39 games for Spurs. Hargreaves died in Nelson on 18 September 1975. *Wolves record: 55 apps. 8 goals.*

HARPER, George

Inside-forward George Harper spent four seasons with Wolves, his best two coming in 1899-1900 and 1900-01 when he was a regular in the first team, top scoring in the former campaign with 10 goals. Smart on the ball, fast with a strong shot, he was born in Birmingham in May 1877 and worked and played for the Saltley Gas Company before joining Burton United. From there he went to Aston Villa, then to Hereford Thistle, linking up with Wolves in August 1897. In May 1901 he was transferred to Grimsby Town

and from November 1902 to 1904 he assisted Sunderland. Harper died on 14 July 1914. *Wolves record: 66 apps. 21 goals.*

HARRINGTON, Jack A.

There were few more exciting wingers in the 1920s than Jack Harrington, who made his Football League debut for Wolves on the opening day of the 1923-24 season, at Chesterfield. It was also Wolves first-ever game in the Third Division North and they drew 0-0. Halligan held his place in the side for five seasons, injuries permitting, and in all he made 117 senior appearances, scoring ten goals and laying on many more for his colleagues. He helped Wolves win the Northern Section title in his first season and then helped them re-establish themselves in the higher division. Although an outside-right with Wolves he had previously played on either flank for Hednesford Town and was a big favourite at the Cross Keys. He had been recommended to Wolves by a former player at Molineux, George Garratly. Harrington, who was born at Bloxwich in 1901, had earlier made his name as a fine local sprinter who could reportedly break the 11-second barrier for the 100 yards. After leaving Molineux in June 1928 he was on Northampton Town's books until June 1929, making six League appearances before going back to non-League football with Brierley Hill Alliance and retiring in 1933. At the time of writing he is in his 98th year and probably the oldest surviving former Wolves player. *Wolves record: 117 apps. 10 goals.*

HARRIS, George

Goalkeeper George Harris played for Wolves during the late 1890s. Reserve to first Billy Tennant and then Tom Baddeley, he was a steady performer who conceded a total of ten goals in his seven senior outings. Born in Redditch in 1875, he played for Headless Cross FC, Redditch Excelsiors and briefly for Aston Villa (1895 as reserve to Tom Wilkes) before joining Wolves in July 1896. In May 1900 he left Molineux for Grimsby Town and later assisted Portsmouth (from November 1901), Redditch and Kidderminster Harriers. Harper died in Alcester on 27 June 1910. *Wolves record: 7 apps*

HARRIS, Gerald W.

Left-back Gerry Harris made more than 260 senior appearances for Wolverhampton Wanderers, yet he might have been a West Bromwich Albion player had he accepted the offer of a trial with the Baggies, albeit as an outside-left. Harris was born at Claverley, near Bridgnorth, on 8 October 1935 and was playing for Bobbington FC in the Wolverhampton Amateur League when Wolves scout George Norris took him to Molineux during the 1953-54 season. Harris signed professional forms in January 1954 and after gaining a first-team place in 1956-57 he won League championship medals in consecutive seasons, 1957-58-59, and a FA Cup winners' medal in 1960. A hard-tackling defender, he also came to the notice of the England selectors and gained four Under-23 caps. Harris remained at Molineux until April 1966 when he was transferred to neighbours Walsall. He played in only 15 League games for the Saddlers, two of them as a substitute, before retiring in May 1967 through injury, although he still managed to turn out in charity matches for a while. A keen bowls player, he captained the Bridgnorth club, Bylet, and today he lives in a converted farm house in Claverley.

Wolves record: 270 apps. 2 goals.

HARRIS, John

John Harris was the first Wolves player to play for Scotland, doing so in a wartime international in 1944-45. Born in Glasgow on 30 June 1917, he was an amateur with Swindon Town before joining Swansea Town as a professional in August 1934 at the age of 17. From the County Ground he went to Tottenham Hotspur (February 1935) and signed for Wolves in May 1939. Unfortunately the hostilities in Europe completely ruined his playing career for six years and, in fact, when peace arrived he surprisingly left Molineux for Chelsea in August 1945 for a fee of £8,000, having guested for Grimsby Town and Southampton. He remained at Stamford Bridge for 13 years, up to July 1956 when he became player-manager of Chester, holding office there until July 1959, when he was appointed manager of Sheffield United. He was at Bramall Lane until July 1963 when he was moved upstairs to the position of general manager for the season 1968-69. He was then given a second stint as United boss from August 1969 to December 1973 and after that was made chief scout at Bramall Lane before coaching United's arch rivals Sheffield Wednesday (1972-75). As a full-back Harris won a two Regional League wartime runners-up medals; with Wolves (in 1944 and 1945) and a First Division championship medal with Chelsea in 1955 at the age of 37. And as a manager he gained two League Division Two runners-up medals in 1961 and 1971 with Sheffield United. Harris died on 24 July 1988, aged 71.

HARRIS, David John

Full-back Harris graduated through the ranks at Molineux and for seven years (injuries apart) he was understudy to the likes of his namesake Gerry, Eddie Stuart, George Showell and Bobby Thomson, among others, before leaving Wolves for neighbouring Walsall. Born at Upper Gornal, on 3 April 1939, he joined Wolves as a junior

Wolves, 1908 FA Cup winners. Back row (left to right): A. Fletcher (trainer), Revd K. R. G. Hunt, J. Jones, W. Wooldridge, T. Lunn, E. Collins, A. Bishop. Front row: W. Harrison, J. Shelton, G. Hedley, W. Radford, J. Pedley.

in June 1955 and turned professional in May 1958. His transfer to Fellows Park was finalised in January 1965 and after four years as a player with the Saddlers, he had a spell as reserve team manager-coach at Fellows Park before ending his career with Rushall Olympic (May 1970 to June 1974). Unfortunately Harris broke his leg in only his second game for Wolves against Aston Villa early in the 1961-62 season, and after recovering full fitness he then broke his other leg in 1963-64. As Walsall's skipper he did an excellent job as partner to Frank Gregg, making over 80 appearances. Harris was injured during the pre-match warm-up before the kick-off in a game at Northampton in March 1968 and was replaced by Nick Atthey.

Wolves' career: 3 apps.

HARRIS, John W.

Reserve centre-forward Jack Harris played for Wolves during the mid-1920s. Born locally on 18 March 1896, he served with Bilston Commodores and Bilston Central before moving to Molineux in August 1924. On leaving Wolves in May 1926 he signed for Watford, and later assisted Darlington, Hartlepools United, Wolves (again as a reserve in 1928), Barrow and Spennymoor United, retiring in 1931.

Wolves record: 6 apps. 2 goals.

HARRIS, Walter T.

Wally Harris had one season of first-team football with Wolves, that of 1908-09 when he acted, in the main, as reserve to George Hedley and Jack Shelton. He was born in Wolverhampton in 1887 and played locally for Queen's Park Athletic and Willenhall before joining Wolves from Redditch. When he left the club in April 1909 he signed for Dudley Town and later served with Blakenhall.

Wolves record: 5 apps. 1 goal

HARRISON, William Ewart

Dashing winger Billy Harrison joined Wolves from Crewe Alexandra in the 1907 close season for a transfer fee of just £400, and by the end of his first season with the Molineux club he had gained an FA Cup winners' medal after scoring a brilliant individual goal in the Final against Newcastle United. Harrison soon found himself a favourite with the Wolves supporters. He was described as a 'master of the game' and he could either use great pace to get past a full-back, or tease the same defender with some mazy dribbling skills. Harrison was small, standing only 5ft 4in tall, but he was never afraid to go in with the burliest defenders and he took plenty of knocks in a Wolves career that saw him make almost 350 senior appearances and score close on 50 goals before being transferred to Manchester United in October 1920. He scored five times in 46 games for United before his next move, to Port Vale in September 1922. He joined Wrexham in June 1923 and retired in May the following year. Harrison was almost 37 when he left big-time football but he carried on playing in charity games until he was well past his 40th birthday. He was another former Wolves player who excelled on the bowling green and he was also landlord of the Rose and Crown public house in Tettenhall for many years. Billy Harrison was born at Wypunbury on 27 December 1886 and played his early football with Hough United, Crewe South End and Willaston White Star. He died in Wolverhampton in August 1948.

Wolves record: 345 apps. 49 goals.

HARTILL, William John

They called him 'Artillery Billy' and it was certainly an appropriate name for a striker who amassed a terrific goalscoring record with Wolves. He was their leading marksman

in seasons: 1929-30, 1930-31, 1931-32, 1932-33 and 1934-35. and finished second to Tom Phillipson in 1933-34. Hartill was born in Wolverhampton on 18 July 1905, in the same street as his best pal and later Wolves colleague Dicky Rhodes. Indeed, Hartill followed Rhodes into the same Wolverhampton school's side. Leaving his educational studies behind him, Hartill joined the Royal Horse Artillery and served as a bombardier. He scored over 70 goals in two seasons for the R.H.A. XI and the Army team before obtaining his demob to join Wolves in August 1928. After starting in the Central League team, he made his League debut in November 1928, at Bradford, and scored his first two League goals at Stamford Bridge the following March. His style pleased the fans with its sweeping passes to the wings before he got into position for the return crosses which brought him many of his goals, and he was good with his head and possessed a powerful kick in either foot, specialising in the hook shot. With Hartill in their side, Wolves regained their First Division status in 1931-32 (when he scored four of his 16 hat-tricks) but three years later – after representing the Football League (Midland) XI – he was transferred to Everton. He made only five appearances for Everton, scoring one goal, and his last appearance for them was a 4-0 drubbing at Molineux. The same year moved across Stanley Park to Liverpool, where he made another five appearances, this time without managing a goal. He ended his career at Bristol Rovers (1935-38 – scoring 19 goals in 36 League games). Billy Hartill died in Walsall on 12 August 1980.
Wolves record: 234 apps. 170 goals.

HARTLAND, Frederick

Goalkeeper Fred Hartland made his only first-team appearance for Wolves at Blackpool in a Second Division League game in April 1921 when he replaced Teddy Peers in a 3-0 defeat. Born in West Bromwich in 1902, he was an amateur with West Bromwich Albion for a season before joining Wolves in 1920 and he left Molineux for Smethwick Highfield in 1922.
Wolves record: 1 app.

HARTLEPOOL UNITED

Wolves' playing record against the Pool is:
Football League

Venue	P	W	D	L	F	A
Home	3	3	0	0	8	2
Away	3	2	1	0	2	0
Totals	6	5	1	0	10	2

Wolves first met the Pool in season 1923-24 when they doubled up, winning 2-1 at Molineux and 1-0 at the Victoria Ground, on their way to taking the Third Division North title. Wolves' best win of the five gained so far is 4-1, at home in the Fourth Division on 9

May 1987, when Steve Bull rounded off the season with a hat-trick in front of 8,610 fans.

Players with both clubs include: Bobby Best, Paul Butler, Jimmy Deacon, Keith Lockhart, Tom Mulholland, Mark Venus and Chris Westwood (Hartlepool trialist).

Also associated: Fred Mitcheson (Wolves trialist); Andy De Bont, Jack Harris and Michael Spelman (Wolves Reserves), Angus McLean (Wolves player, United manager), Albert Flatley (Wolves trialist), Teddy Maguire (Hartlepools wartime guest) and Mick Docherty and Chris Turner (both Hartlepool managers and Wolves coaches).

HARWOOD, Irvine

Inside-forward Irvine Harwood was basically a reserve during his one season at Molineux. Born in Bradford on 5 December 1905, he played for Manningham Mills FC, Bradford Park Avenue (May 1929) and Bradford City (May 1931) before joining Wolves in June 1933. On leaving Molineux he signed for Bristol Rovers (May 1934) and later assisted Walsall (from May 1936) before retiring in 1940. Harwood was an exceptionally fine cricketer who played in the strong Bradford League for 15 seasons. He died in Walsall in June 1973.
Wolves record: 6 apps.

HASSALL, Josuah

Joe Hassall, a very competent goalkeeper, became first choice between the posts for Wolves in season 1894-95 after Billy Rose had left for Loughborough Town. Hassall, who had been reserve at Molineux for two years prior to that, stood six feet tall and weighed over 12 stones. He was born in Wednesfield in November 1871 and played his early football with St George's FC, Stafford Rangers (1888-91) and Heath Moor. He made his debut early in the 1892-93 season (replacing Rose briefly) but in 1894-95 he was an ever-present. Then, out of the blue, he was taken ill, leaving Rose free to return to Molineux and claim back his place. In the meantime Hassall was admitted to hospital where he sadly died 12 months later of pneumonia at the age of 24.
Wolves record: 52 apps.

HATFIELD, Ernest

Full-back Ernie Hatfield failed to make an impact at Molineux and after only four first-team appearances was sold to Southend United in May 1931. Born in Mansfield on 16 January 1905, he played his early football with Frickley Colliery and Wombwell Athletic before joining Sheffield Wednesday in November 1927. Three years later (having made only one appearances for the Owls) he was transferred to Wolves (April 1930), but spent only a season at Molineux. After two years at Southend he went to Dartford

(August 1933).
Wolves record: 4 apps.

HAT-TRICKS

Dennis Westcott claimed a total of 19 hat-tricks for Wolves – seven in the Football League, two in the FA Cup and ten during World War Two.

Steve Bull has notched 18 trebles and Billy Hartill netted 16 (15 in the League, including four in 1931-32). Roy Swinbourne and Tom Phillipson each netted seven (all in the League).

Dutchman John De Wolf's goal tally for Wolves included a hat-trick in a 4-2 win at Port Vale in February 1995 – making him the first Wolves defender to achieve this feat for almost 93 years, since Ted Pheasant netted a treble in a 3-0 victory over Newcastle in March 1902.

John Richards scored a hat-trick for Wolves against Charlton Athletic in an FA Cup-tie in 1976 after coming on as a substitute.

Wolves' first League hat-trick was also the first in that competition at Molineux – scored by Harry Wood (3 goals) against Derby County at home in November 1889. Wood also grabbed Wolves' first hat-trick in an away League game – at Aston Villa in April 1892.

Wolves' first hat-trick scorer at Molineux was Jack Brodie, who achieved the feat in an 8-0 FA Cup replay victory over Stoke in February 1890.

Three weeks later David Wykes netted Wolves' first League treble at Molineux – doing so against Bolton Wanderers.

Steve Bull scored a record six hat-tricks for Wolves in season 1988-89 including two four-timers.

Wolves players between them have scored eight hat-tricks against Leicester Fosse/City – a record.

Three defenders from the Portuguese side FC Den Haag contributed greatly by scoring a 'hat-trick' of own-goals in Wolves' 4-0 home UEFA Cup win in November 1971.

Wolves inflicted three big defeats upon Manchester City in the space of seven years and each time a player scored a four-timer – Roy Swinbourne in a 7-2 triumph in August 1955, Jimmy Murray in a 5-1 victory in August 1956 and Ted Farmer in an 8-1 thrashing in August 1962.

Dennis Westcott and Dicky Dorsett scored four goals apiece in Wolves' 10-1 home League win over Leicester City in April 1938.

Roy Swinbourne scored a hat-trick against both Manchester clubs – City and United – in successive months during the 1952-53 season.

Swinbourne also netted three hat-tricks in four games in 1955-56 – against Manchester City, Cardiff City (away) and Huddersfield Town.

Joe Butcher bagged all five Wolves goals in their League win over Accrington in November 1892 – his first and only hat-trick for Wolves.

In December 1946, Dennis Westcott scored a four-timer on successive Saturdays for Wolves against Liverpool at Anfield and Bolton at Molineux.

Tom Hunter (4 goals) claimed Wolves' first FA Cup hat-trick – against Crosswell's Brewery (home) in a record 14-0 win in November 1886. Jack Brodie and Tommy Knight also scored three goals in this tie, but Hunter grabbed his third goal first. And in fact this is the only occasion whereby three hat-tricks have been scored by Wolves players in the same game.

Derek Dougan scored Wolves' first hat-trick in a major European game – against the Portuguese side Academica Coimbra (away) in the UEFA Cup in September 1971.

Steve Bull registered a hat-trick of hat-tricks for Wolves in the Sherpa Van Trophy competition – against Brentford in January 1988 and v Port Vale and Bristol City the following season.

Jesse Pye (against Arsenal in August 1946) and Dennis Wilshaw (against Newcastle United in March 1949) scored hat-tricks on their League debuts for Wolves.

Ken Whitfield scored only three League goals for Wolves – a hat-trick against Blackpool in December 1952.

Bobby Woodruff headed three goals for Wolves in the home League game with Sunderland at Easter 1965 – the only player to achieve this feat.

Guesting for Wolves from Manchester United, Jack Rowley scored all eight goals against Derby County in a wartime game in November 1942.

Former Wolves' amateur footballer Billy Holmes, scored a hat-trick on his Wedding Day for Southport against Carlisle United in October 1954.

Jimmy Millar scored a hat-trick for Sunderland in three separate League games against Wolves between 1891 and 1900.

HATTON, Robert John

Bob Hatton was a fine marksman who netted 217 goals in 620 League games during a 20-year career. Born in Hull on 10 April 1947, Hatton played for Wath Wanderers from June 1962 before joining Wolves' apprentice staff in June 1963, turning professional in November 1964. In March 1967 he was transferred to Bolton Wanderers after failing to establish himself in the first team at Molineux. From Burnden Park he moved to Northampton Town (October 1968) and after a spell with Carlisle United (from July 1969 to October 1971) he signed for Birmingham City where he linked up with Bob Latchford and Trevor Francis. After hit-

ting 73 goals in 218 outings for Blues, Hatton switched to Blackpool (July 1976); two years later he signed for Luton Town and in July 1980 became a Sheffield United player. After helping the Blades win the Fourth Division title he left Bramall Lane and served with Cardiff City from December 1982, helping the Bluebirds rise from the Third to the Second Division, before quitting League soccer the in May 1983. He later played for Lodge Cotterill FC (Birmingham Sunday League side) and also worked on local radio, while employed by a Birmingham-based Insurance Company.
Wolves record: 13 apps. 8 goals.

HAWKINS, Arthur

Bustling centre-forward Archie Hawkins had one excellent season with Wolves, that of 1906-07 when he averaged almost a goal every two games. Powerful, with pace and excellent right-foot shot, he was sadly plagued by injuries, suffering a broken arm, dislocated shoulder, cracked ankle and damaged knee all within the space of 12 months. Born in Wolverhampton c.1884 he joined Wolves in August 1905 from Heath Town Conservatives and with his career in doubt after those injury problems, he was released by the club in April 1907 and signed for Kidderminster Harriers.
Wolves record: 20 apps. 9 goals.

HAWKINS, George

Durable full-back who had a useful kick, George Hawkins was born in West Bromwich c.1862 and played for West Bromwich Standard and Wednesbury Old Athletic before joining Wolves in the summer of 1885. He left the club to sign for Walsall Victoria in August 1886 after failing to hold down a regular first-team place.
Wolves record: 3 apps.

HAWKINS, Graham Norman

Born in Darlaston on 5 March 1946, Graham Hawkins was a central defender who joined Wolves as an apprentice in June 1961 and turned professional two years later. He made his League debut in the local derby against West Bromwich Albion in October 1964, but failed to hold down a regular position in the first team. In December 1967 he was transferred to Preston North End and after a spell with Blackburn Rovers (August 1974 to January 1978) he became Port Vale's player-youth coach for £6,000. In May 1978 he was upgraded to first-team coach at Vale Park and became assistant manager there seven months later. Unfortunately he was dismissed by the Valiants in September 1979 and immediately took out an unfair dismissal claim, but this was dropped when he received an acceptable compensation offer in April 1980. After a spell as assistant manager

at Shrewsbury Town, Hawkins returned to Molineux as Wolves boss on 1 August 1982 stepping into the job vacated by Ian Greaves. He guided Wolves back into the First Division in his first season, but was then sacked after Wolves had attained their worst seasonal record in living memory, winning only six League games and suffering 25 defeats as relegation was suffered once more. Hawkins, who was replaced by Tommy Docherty, became disillusioned with English football and chose to go and coach in Saudi Arabia.

Hawkins' record as Wolves manager was played 88, won 26, drawn 27, lost 35 (exactly 100 goals scored).
Wolves record: 29+6 apps.

HAYES, JACK Walter

Welsh international goalkeeper Teddy Peers missed two games in the 1913-14 season, and in his place stood Walter Hayes. A native of Oldbury (born in 1894) he joined the staff at Molineux from Hednesford Town in November 1912, having earlier assisted Brownhills Albion. He actually played as an emergency left-half for Wolves Reserves against Birmingham Trams in a Birmingham Cup-tie at Molineux a month after joining the club. Efficient enough, the chance of regular first-team football with Wolves was limited and in July 1914 he was allowed to leave the club to sign for Preston North End. He later returned to the Black Country to play for Cradley Heath and Lye Town. Hayes died in 1965.
Wolves record: 2 apps.

HAYNES, Harold

Wolves recruited centre-half Harry Haynes from non-League soccer. Basically a reserve, he had one splendid season at Molineux, that of 1894-95, when he played at the heart of the defence between Hill Griffiths and Billy Malpass. Born on 21 April 1873 in Walsall. Haynes played briefly for his home town club before joining Walsall Unity in 1891. He found his way to Molineux in February 1893 and spent two-and-a-half years with Wolves before transferring to Birmingham in July 1895. A year later he moved to Southampton St Mary's, but was forced to retire through injury in 1900 after helping Saints win the Southern League championship three seasons running: 1896-99 and reach the 1898 FA Cup semi-final. He later became landlord of the Turk's Head and Edinburgh Castle pubs in Southampton. Haynes died suddenly in Southampton on 29 March 1902.
Wolves record: 24 apps. 2 goals.

HAYWARD, Sir Jack

Multi-millionaire businessman Sir Jack Hayward, an avid supporter since he was a young lad, bought Wolverhampton

Wanderers Football Club in May 1990 and immediately placed his son, Jonathan, and former player Billy Wright, on the board. Straightaway he set about redeveloping the Molineux Stadium and in the next seven years put £19 million into the club as Wolves strived to get into the Premiership.

Born at Dunstall (near the racecourse) on 14 June 1923 and a pupil at Stowe Public School, he used to crawl under the turnstiles as a youngster to get inside Molineux to watch his favourites in action. In 1941, at the age of 18, he entered the RAF, obtaining his wings after training in Canada and the USA. Posted to India. Hayward volunteered as a glider pilot for war service against the Japanese on the India/Burma border. Demobbed in 1946, after attaining the rank of flight lieutenant, he then worked in South Africa for many years and took charge of his father's business in the USA The business was moved to the Bahamas and over the last 40 years or so, the island has been developed into a thriving economy, with a fine airport, a seaport, a major tanker terminal and established electrical and water companies – all owned by Sir Jack who also purchased Lundy Island off the Devon coast (for the National Trust in 1969). He brought the first iron ship, Brunel's *SS Great Britain*, back from the Falkland Islands so that it could be restored in this country; he paid £1 million for a hospital in Port Stanley, after the Falklands War, and made a healthy donation towards the building of MCC's Indoor Cricket School. For his wonderful achievements Jack Hayward was knighted by the Queen in 1986.

Married in 1948, Sir Jack Hayward has a daughter and two sons, Jonathan and Rick.

In March 1994 he was the man who sacked Wolves boss Graham Turner and employed Graham Taylor in his place. In November 1995 he dismissed Taylor 'after lack of success' (Taylor spent £7.5 million on players) and replaced him with Mark McGhee.

In May 1997 Sir Jack vowed he would not continue to bail out the club. Four month later, in September 1997, he took over as chairman at Molineux, moved his son to vice-chairman and appointed ex-player John Richards, as marketing director.

Just four weeks after assuming the chair Sir Jack paid off an £8 million bank overdraft, this taking his total investment into the club to more than £40 million, and immediately said: "I want to make a fresh start – this is now a new era."

In March 1998, he underwent a triple heart by-pass in Los Angeles and recovered sufficiently well to attend Wolves' FA Cup semi-final with Arsenal at Villa Park.

Four months into another new season – in November 1998 – he sacked manager Mark McGhee, and within a matter of days

appointed Colin Lee as caretaker-boss, soon afterwards giving him the job full-time until the end of the season.

HAYWARD, Jonathan

Jonathan Hayward, Sir Jack's son, was born in Nassau, Bahamas on 10 June 1957. After being educated at Durlston Court School in Hampshire, he followed in his father's foot-steps and moved to Stowe School. There he became a useful sportsman, captaining the rugby, hockey and crickets teams. He played rugby for Buckinghamshire County and represented Sussex Under-19s at cricket. For two years after leaving school he played regularly for Sussex's second team prior to going to the Royal Agricultural College in Cirencester. Married in 1979 (to Fiona) the Haywards have a daughter (Laura, born in 1982) and since 1984 they have resided on a 1,200 acre farm in Northumberland, where their son Rory was born in 1986. Four years later Jonathan was appointed vice-chairman at Molineux, taking over as chairman in 1992, a position he held until September 1997 when his father took over the post. A Football League director from 1992 to 1994, Jonathan was also a governor at Wolverhampton Grammar School before leaving Molineux.

HAYWOOD, Adam S.

Utility forward Adam Haywood was a veritable trojan for work, quick and decisive, who joined Wolves from New Brompton (later Gillingham) in 1901. Born at Horninglow, Burton upon Trent on 17 May 1875, he stood only 5ft 5in tall and weighed 10st and had appeared in a North v South England trial before taking over from George Harper in the Wolves side. In May 1905 Haywood left Molineux for West Bromwich Albion; he was transferred from The Hawthorns to Blackpool in December 1907 and for season 1910-11 was player-coach at Crystal Palace. Before joining Southern League club New Brompton he played for Burton Ivanhoe, Burton Wanderers, Swadlincote, Woolwich Arsenal and Queen's Park Rangers. Haywood died in May 1932.
Wolves record: 113 apps. 28 goals.

HAZELL, Robert Joseph

Born in Kingston, Jamaica on 14 June 1959, tough-tackling centre-back Bob Hazell signed as an apprentice for Wolves June 1975 and turned professional in May 1977. He was the first black player to represent the Molineux club in a senior game, he made his League debut at Newcastle United in December 1977. And was also the first black player to score for Wolves (against Manchester City in March 1978). He won England youth, Under-21 and 'B' caps for England during his first spell at Molineux,

which lasted until September 1979 when he joined Queen's Park Rangers. Four years later, after 106 League outings for the London club, he moved to Leicester City and in September 1985 played one more game on loan with Wolves before joining Luton Town in August 1986. A spell with Reading preceded his transfer to Port Vale in December 1986. Unfortunately a back injury ruined his career and in June 1989 he was released by the Valiants after appearing in exactly 100 senior games for the Potteries club. Hazell is now resident in Walsall and working for the Birmingham Social Services (1999).
Wolves record: 36+1 apps. 1 goal.

HEART OF MIDLOTHIAN

Wolves' playing record against Hearts is:
Texaco Cup

Venue	P	W	D	L	F	A
Home	1	0	0	1	0	1
Away	1	1	0	0	3	1
Totals	2	1	0	1	3	2

Wolves won the 1971 Texaco Cup Final by defeating the Scottish First Division side Hearts 3-2 on aggregate. Over 26,000 attended Tynecastle to see Wolves gain a two-goal advantage from the first leg, but with almost 28,500 present at Molineux, Hearts made a game of it by winning the second leg 1-0.

Associated with both clubs: Chris Crowe (Hearts trialist, Wolves player) and Jimmy Hamilton (Wolves player, Hearts coach).

HEATH, John Frederick Joseph

Joseph Heath had the distinction of scoring the first ever penalty goal in the Football League – for Wolves against Accrington on 14 September 1891. Born in Bristol *c*.1869, he moved to the Black Country as a young lad and played for Bushbury Principals and Lye Cross before joining Walsall Town Swifts. He joined Wolves in August 1891 from Wednesbury Old Athletic. A centre-forward or half-back, slimly built, Heath spent two

years at Molineux (the second of which saw him on the club's injured list) before joining Arsenal in June 1893. He served the Gunners for two years during which time he scored seven times in 12 senior games and also acted as reserve-team coach in 1894-95. In September 1895 he moved to Gravesend United before rejoining Arsenal (as a reserve) in September 1896, returning to the Midlands to play for Pendeford between 1899 and 1901. Whilst with Arsenal second time round he won a Kent League championship medal and then added a Sevenoaks Charity Cup medal to his collection with Gravesend in 1897-98. Heath also had the pleasure of netting Arsenal's first ever League hat-trick – in a 4-0 win over his former club Walsall Town Swifts in September 1893. He died in Willenhall c.1935.
Wolves record: 12 apps. 4 goals.

HEDLEY, George Albert
Born at Southbank, Northumberland on 3 May 1876, centre-forward George Hedley scored a goal every three games for Wolves after joining them from Southampton in May 1906. He began his career as an amateur in the Northern League before turning professional with Sheffield United in May 1898. In 1899 he gained his first FA Cup winners' medal when the Blades beat Derby County in the Final, and in 1902 he scored the first goal when United beat Southampton in another Final. In 1901 he had won his only England cap and also collected a FA Cup runners-up medal. Torn heart muscles threatened his career, but he defied medical advice to sign for Southampton in May 1903. Hedley soon became a star at The Dell, scoring 30 goals in 70 games and helping the Saints win the Southern League title before moving to Wolves where he collected his third FA Cup winners' medal, scoring a priceless goal in the 1908 victory over Newcastle United. After seven fine years at Molineux he became manager of Bristol City from April 1913 until April 1915. They were a Second Division club at the time and he guided them to eighth and 13th place. He became a publican in Bristol, from 1918 to 1941 and then returned to Wolverhampton to run a boarding house, but died in the town on 16 August 1942. For his three League clubs he scored 125 goals in 385 League games. Besides his England cap, which came against Ireland, he also played once for the Football League.
It is said that Hedley wore the same pair of boots for ten years and when he played in the 1908 FA Cup Final there were no fewer than 17 patches on them.
Wolves record: 214 apps. 74 goals.

HEDNESFORD TOWN
Wolves have played the Pitmen several times over the years, in benefit matches, testimoni-al games, friendlies, various challenge matches and in minor non-League and intermediate Cup competitions.
Shortly before and for a number of years after the Football League was formed, the Pitmen and Wolves met each other quite often, mainly in friendlies, and there were some entertaining encounters.
On 17 February 1894, a benefit match at Hednesford's old Anglesey Ground saw Wolves win 2-0 in front of 3,000 fans and the following year, on a snow-covered pitch, the Wanderers were again victorious by 4-2 with 2,000 spectators present this time. Wolves fielded a strong team in this second game which included goalkeeper Swallow, full-back Haynes, wing-half Reynolds and forwards Roberts, Crump, Bell and Edge. Bell, in fact, scored a hat-trick.
In March 1953, Wolves and West Bromwich Albion played each other in a friendly match to officially switch on Hednesford Town's newly-erected floodlights. Wolves won 4-2.
Players with both clubs include: Steve Biggins, Paul Blades, Joe Bonson, Chris Brindley, Arthur Buttery, Robbie Dennison, Dick Forshaw, George Garratly, Noel George, 'Tosh' Griffiths, John Griffiths, Jack Harrington, Derek Jefferson, Jimmy Kelly, Arthur Lloyd, Harry Lloyd, Alex McIntosh, John Miller, Teddy Peers, Tom Picken, Jack Robinson, Jack Rostance, Dale Rudge, Harry Shaw and Arthur Tatem.
Also associated: Wolves Reserves Johnny Cullen, Sid Nicholls and Granville Palin; John Griffiths (war guest); Graham Newton (Wolves junior, Town player).

HEELBECK, Leslie Walter
Les Heelbeck was a tremendously hardworking reserve half-back, who always gave a sound performance when called into action. A Yorkshireman, born in Scarborough in July 1909, he played for Thorne Amateurs, Newark Town and Carlisle United (from July 1931) prior to joining Wolves in March 1932. He left Molineux for Rotherham United in June 1934, skippering the Millerman in his first season, and after a spell with his home town club, Scarborough (from June 1937) he retired in 1941. Heelbeck died in Scarborough on 25 March 1998.
Wolves record: 8 apps.

HEGAN, Daniel
Danny Hegan had loads of ability, a midfielder with style, great vision and an excellent passing skills, he unfortunately allowed his social life to ruin his football career. Born of Irish parentage in Coatbridge, Scotland on 14 June 1943, he attended Coatbridge and Ballieston Schools, represented Glasgow Boys and Rutherglen Youths and had trials with Sunderland (August 1958) prior to joining Albion Rovers in August 1959. In September 1961 Sunderland paid £6,000 for his signature and he spent two years at Roker Park before moving south to Ipswich Town for £20,000 in July 1963. Six years later Hegan was transferred to West Bromwich Albion in a player-exchange deal involving Ian Collard, and from The Hawthorns he switched to Molineux for £50,000 in May 1970. After more than three years with Wolves, Hegan was sacked for 'persistent infringement of club rules' and duly returned to Sunderland (November 1973) and after that he went to South Africa to play for Highlands Park FC and Johannesburg Spurs before having trials with Partick Thistle (April 1975). He returned to Highlands Park for four months to August 1975 and his last club was Coleshill (Warwickshire). He retired in 1978 to become soccer coach at Butlin's Holiday Camp, Clacton. Capped by Northern Ireland on seven occasions, Hegan helped Ipswich win the Second Division title in 1968, played for Wolves in the 1972 UEFA Cup Final and in his career amassed a total 280 League appearances, scoring 42 goals. In January 1982 Hegan was sued for libel by Billy Bremner of Leeds United; Bremner won the case and was awarded £100,000 in damages. Hegan also blotted his copybook by becoming the first Wolves player to be sent-off in a European competition v Academica Coimbra in the UEFA Cup in September 1971.
Wolves record: 65+5 apps. 8 goals.

HEIGHT
Tallest
Perhaps the tallest outfield player ever to represent Wolves was the versatile Tom Galley, who was almost 6ft 4ins in height.
Goalkeepers Jimmy Utterson and Alec Scott were both 6ft 4ins tall, and Cyril Spiers, Nigel Sims, Malcolm Finlayson, Fred Davies, Paul Bradshaw, Tim Flowers, Phil Parkes and Mike Stowell all stood 6ft 3ins.
Shortest
Wolves' 1980s midfielder Paul Dougherty, known as 'Pee-Wee' and left-winger Sammy Brookes (1910-22) were only 5ft 2ins. tall when they played for the club. John Smith (1904 era) was 5ft 3ins.while Enoch Deakin, from the 1880s, and 1950's wingers Norman Deeley and Johnny Hancocks were all 5ft 4ins tall. Midfielder Nigel Vaughan (from the 1980s) is another on the list of short players.

HELLIN, Matthew Karl
Matt Hellin never never settled in English League football and during his time at Molineux he played in just one first team game – lining up at left-half against Cambridge United at home on the opening Saturday of Wolves' first-ever Fourth Division campaign on 23 August 1986. A Welshman, born in Merthyr on 12

September 1966, Hellin was a junior and then professional with Aston Villa before transferring to Molineux in August 1986. On leaving Wolves in the summer of 1987 he returned to South Wales.

Wolves record: 1 app.

HEMINGWAY, Cyril Francis

Cyril Hemingway was a creative inside-forward whose career was spent mainly in the Devon area. A Yorkshireman, born in Rotherham in February 1904, and educated in that town, he represented the County Schools and played for Rotherham United from January 1926, top scoring for the Yorkshire club in 1926-27. He moved to Torquay United (June 1928) and on to Exeter City in June 1929. He was the Grecians leading marksman in his only season at St James' Park before joining Wolves in May 1930. On leaving Molineux in September 1931, he returned to Torquay and later assisted Dartmouth United (July 1932). On his retirement in 1934, he became a publican in the famous harbour town of Dartmouth, where he died c.1979.

Wolves record: 4 apps.

HENDERSON, Charles J.

Inside-forward Charlie Henderson had a fine career which spanned 16 years. Born in Durham in April 1870, he played for South Bank (1885), Darlington as a trialist (1886), Grimsby Town (April 1902 to February 1933), Leith Athletic (March 1893), Bolton Wanderers (August 1893), Wolves (signed for £20 in April 1895), Sheffield United (season 1896-97), Dundee Harp (1898) and Edinburgh Thistle (1899-1901). He was in the Wolves side for the 1896 FA Cup Final against Sheffield Wednesday and top-scored for Bolton in his first season at Burnden Park. He died in Scotland c.1944.

Wolves record: 36 apps. 11 goals.

HENDERSON, John Gillespie

Jackie Henderson was an energetic, pacey Scottish international forward who could play on the wing or through the middle. Born in Montrose on 17 January 1932, he joined Portsmouth as a teenager and turned professional at Fratton Park on his 17th birthday, four months before Pompey won the First Division championship, which they retained the following season. Henderson went on to score 70 goals in 217 League games for Portsmouth before transferring to Wolves in March 1958. Unfortunately he failed to settle in the Midlands and after only five months moved to London to join Arsenal (October 1958). He notched 29 goals in just over 100 First Division games for the Gunners prior to rounding off his career with Fulham (January 1962 to May 1964). He won seven

full caps for his country and also starred in two 'B' internationals.

Wolves record: 9 apps. 3 goals.

HENSHALL, Albert V.

Albert Henshall replaced Harry Hampton in the Wellington Town attack when the great centre-forward joined Aston Villa in 1904. A resolute performer with good pace, he did well in non-League soccer but failed to make the grade with Wolves. Born in Wellington in 1882, he joined Wellington Town in 1900 and after a spell with Whitchurch (August 1905) he moved to Molineux as a trialist in September 1905, returning for a further spell with Wellington in 1907. Henshall died in Whitchurch in 1944.

Wolves record: 2 apps.

HENSON, George Horace

Centre-forward George Henson spent just two seasons at Molineux, making all his first-team appearances in 1935-36. Signed from Northampton Town in August 1935, Henson was born in Stoney Stratford, Buckinghamshire on 25 December 1911 and played his early football with Stoney Stratford and Wolverton before signing for the Cobblers as an amateur in 1932, turning professional a year later. He scored 18 goals in 52 games before leaving to join Mexborough, signing for Wolves in 1934. He left Molineux in May 1936 for Swansea Town and then played for Bradford Park Avenue in 1937-38, finishing up as top scorer in the Second Division that season with 27 goals. Henson moved to Sheffield United six months before the outbreak of World War Two and didn't figure again in League football after the hostilities.

Wolves record: 6 apps. 1 goal

HERBERT, Ricki L.

Ricki Herbert played for Wolves during two very poor seasons: from October 1984 to May 1986. A hard-tackling defender, who preferred the left-hand side, he could also occupy the full-back position but he was always under pressure with the rest of his colleagues during his time at Molineux.
Born on 10 April 1961 in New Zealand, he joined Wolves from Sydney Olympic (Australia) and won his first full cap for New Zealand against Australia in 1985-86. He returned to Australian football when leaving Wolves.

Wolves record: 47+2 apps.

HEREFORD UNITED

Wolves' playing record against United is:
Football League

Venue	P	W	D	L	F	A
Home	3	3	0	0	5	1
Away	3	2	0	1	8	4
Totals	6	5	0	1	13	5

Freight Rover Trophy

Home	1	0	0	1	0	1

Sherpa Van Trophy

Away	2	1	1	0	4	2

The first time Wolves met Hereford in a League game was at Edgar Street in October 1976. A crowd of 13,891 packed into the ground to see Sammy Chung's team win handsomely by 6-1 with Bobby Gould (2), Steve Kindon, Alan Sunderland, Willie Carr and Steve Daley finding the net. This stayed as Wolves' best away win for 22 years until they equalled it at Bristol City in 1998.

The Bulls defeated Wolves in a Freight Rover Trophy game at Molineux in January 1987 in front of a meagre 2,892 crowd.

Less than two years later, in November 1988, Wolves drew 2-2 with United at Edgar Street in a Sherpa Van Trophy group match and then, in the same competition, after both clubs had made progress, they met again on Hereford soil in the Area semi-final – and this time Wolves won 2-0.

Players with both clubs include: Mike Bailey (player-manager of Hereford), John Black, Sid Blunt, Shaun Bradbury, Paul Butler, Robbie Dennison, Keith Downing (as player and coach), John Galley, Bobby Gould, Frank Higham, Derek Jefferson, Fred Kemp, Richard Leadbetter, Paul McLoughlin, Steve Mardenborough, Gerry O'Hara, Dennis Parsons, Brian Roberts, Darren Roberts, Billy Rotton, Peter Russell, Cecil Shaw, Tim Steele, John Teasdale, Albert Thorpe, Mark Turner, Nigel Vaughan, Stuart Watkiss.

Also associated: Graham Turner (managed both clubs and later chairman and director of football at Edgar Street); Colin Lee (Wolves manager), Ian Greaves (Wolves manager, Hereford assistant manager), John Barnwell (Wolves manager, Hereford assistant manager), Steve Crompton, Andy DeBont, Steve Devine, Kevin Charlton, Ron Hewitt, Gavin Mahon and Quinton Townsend (all Wolves Reserves) and Ian Ross (Wolves coach, caretaker-manager, Hereford non-contract player).

HETHERINGTON, John Arthur

Yorkshireman Jack Hetherington was a useful inside or outside-left. Born in Rotherham on 7 August 1908, he played initially for Dalton United before joining Wolves in the summer of 1928 as cover for Tom Baxter. When Baxter was transferred Hetherington became first choice on the left wing and did very well for three seasons before losing his place to Billy Barraclough. He eventually left Molineux for Preston North End in January 1935 after almost 100 appearances for the Wolves. He moved from Deepdale to Swindon Town in 1936 and then spent two seasons with Watford before the war ruined his career. Hetherington died in April 1977.

Wolves record: 95 apps. 24 goals.

HEYWOOD, David Ian

As a youth team player David Heywood looked set for a bright future in the game, but he never developed into a League footballer and consequently drifted out of the spotlight in the mid-1980s. Born in Wolverhampton on 25 July 1967, full-back Heywood joined the Molineux camp on a YTS in 1983. He turned professional in November 1984, but was released into non-League soccer two years later when he joined Burton Albion, later assisting Kettering Town, Halesowen Town and Worcester City (August 1991) and Halesowen again (from February 1993).
Wolves record: 8 apps.

HIBBITT, Kenneth

Yorkshireman Kenny Hibbitt was born in Bradford on 3 January 1951, and for 16 years starred in Wolves midfield, making more than 570 first-team appearances and thus the £5,000 that Wolves boss Ronnie Allen paid Bradford Park Avenue for his services look the bargain of the decade. Ironically, Allen left his job within 48 hours of completing Hibbitt's signing, but the youngster stayed and prospered. Hibbitt joined Wolves in November 1968, after making only 15 League appearances for Bradford, and remained at Molineux until August 1984. He was an industrious, creative midfielder who also found time to score over 100 goals for Wolves, including a precious effort in the 1974 League Cup Final victory over Manchester City at Wembley and a club record nine penalties the following season.

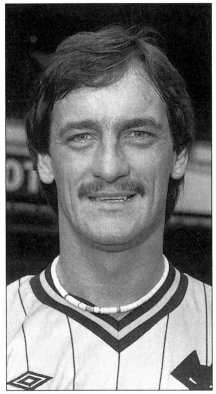

Kenny Hibbit made 544 appearances and scored 114 goals for Wolves.

Six years later he collected a second League Cup winners' trophy when Wolves beat Nottingham Forest in the Final. Two years after receiving a testimonial in 1981-82, Hibbitt was allowed to move to Coventry City and in August 1986 the Sky Blues transferred him to Bristol Rovers. When he returned to Molineux in 1989, as Rovers coach, the South Bank saluted him in recognition of the magnificent service he had given their club. Alas, his illustrious playing career had finally come to an end when he suffered a broken leg playing for Rovers against Sunderland in February 1988. As assistant to Gerry Francis he helped steer Bristol Rovers to the Third Division title and the Leyland DAF Trophy Final in 1989. In May 1990 he was appointed team manager of Walsall and three years later led the Saddlers into the Third Division Play-offs, signing a new two-year contract at the Bescot Stadium soon afterwards. But in 1995 he quit to become manager of Cardiff City, later assuming the role of director of football and coaching at Ninian Park (initially under manager Russell Osman). Hibbitt won one major international honour, an England Under-23 cap as a substitute against Wales in 1970-71. His brother Terry, also a midfield player, assisted Leeds United, Newcastle and Birmingham City.
Wolves record: 522+22 apps. 114 goals.

HIGGS, Harold

Born in Stourbridge in 1900, goalkeeper Harry Higgs joined Wolves from Halesowen in time for the kick-off at the start of the first season after World War One (1919). He was reserve to Teddy Peers and therefore got very little opportunity to try his luck in the League side. He eventually left the club for Darlaston in July 1920.
Wolves record: 3 apps.

HIGHAM, Frank

Hefty wing-half, 6ft 1in inch tall and 12st 6lbs in weight, Frank Higham spent three years at Molineux during which time he acted as reserve to Mitton, Kay and Bradford. Born in Daventry in September 1905, he played for Walsall (March 1925) before joining Wolves in May 1925. In June 1928 he was transferred to Coventry City and two years later signed for Lincoln City. Higham then entered non-League soccer and played in turn for Worcester City, Nuneaton, Evesham Town and Hereford United before retiring in 1939.
Wolves record: 42 apps. 2 goals.

HILL, James

Utility forward Jimmy Hill was born in Wolverhampton in April 1862 and joined Wolves in 1877-78 as a founder member from Spittal Strollers. He broke into the first

team within six months and remained at the club until 1884 before his career was cut short with a serious knee injury at the age of only 22. He was heart broken at the time and although he tried to make a comeback at a lower level, he was a cripple before he had tuned 40. He later worked in a factory in Surrey. In 1953 Hill was a guest at the Charlton v Wolves game at The Valley. He died in London two years later, aged 93.
Wolves record: 1 app.

HILL, J. Albert

Albert Hill was Wolves' reserve centre-forward for two seasons: 1928-30. He was never a serious threat to the likes of regular forwards Deacon, Hartill and Marshall but nevertheless he was a dedicated footballer who never accepted defeat. Born in Rotherham *c.*1907 he played for several clubs locally before joining Wolves in July 1928. He left Molineux in May 1930 and signed for Wrexham.
Wolves record: 2 apps.

HILL, James Thomas W.

Goalkeeper Jimmy Hill spent two seasons as a reserve with Wolves. Born in Aldridge in 1888, he left Blakenhall for Molineux in July 1909 and moved to Darlaston in May 1911 after only a handful of senior appearances for the Wanderers replacing first Billy Lunn and then Frank Boxley. Hill was unfortunate to suffer with arm and back injuries during the early part of his career. He died in 1950.
Wolves record: 3 apps.

HINDMARCH, Robert

Hard-tackling defender Rob Hindmarch was born in Stannington near Morpeth on 27 April 1961. He joined Sunderland as a youngster and turned professional at Roker Park in April 1978 after representing England at youth team level. He went on to make well over 100 League appearances for the Wearsiders and after a loan spell with Portsmouth (in December 1983) he moved to Derby County in July 1984. He spent the next six years at the Baseball Ground, amassing almost 200 outings for the Rams and helping them win the Second Division title in 1987 before he joined Wolves in June 1990 for £325,000. He stayed at Molineux until May 1993 when he was given a free transfer, moving quickly into non-League football with Telford United.
Wolves record: 43+1 apps. 2 goals.

HINTON, Alan

Winger Alan Hinton's real career highlights came at Derby County, after Brian Clough had rescued him from relative obscurity as he drifted along with Nottingham Forest. But it was with Wolves that Hinton, who was born in Wednesbury on 6 October 1942,

began his career and where he won the first of his first three full England caps. An out-side-left who could cross the ball with remarkable accuracy, Hinton also possessed a tremendous shot in his left foot, whether cutting in for goal or from dead-ball situations. He played for South-East Staffordshire and Birmingham County Schools before turning professional with Wolves in October 1959. Hinton's League debut came in January 1961 and altogether he made almost 80 first-team appearances for Wolves and besides his full cap, he appeared for England's Youth and Under-/23 teams. Hinton moved to Nottingham Forest in January 1964 where he won another two full caps and hit 24 goals in 123 first-team appearances before Clough signed him for Derby in September 1967 for £30,000. On his transfer, a Forest committee member reportedly said that the Rams would soon want their money back, but he reckoned without Clough's and Peter Taylor's motivational skills. Hinton appeared in well over 300 senior games for Derby, scoring 83 goals. He helped the Rams win the Second Division title and was a key member in two League championship winning sides. Unfortunately he played little in 1975-76, following the tragic death of his young son, Matthew, and eventually went to work in the North American Soccer League with Dallas Tornado (March 1977), switching to Vancouver Whitecaps (October 1977), Tulsa Roughnecks (October 1978), Seattle Sounders (November 1979-January 1983) and Tacoma Stars (1986). With Vancouver in 1978 he set a new record for 'assists', his 30 beating the old record set jointly by Pele and George Best. In 1980 Hinton was voted the NASL Coach of the Year, but when the NASL eventually folded, he moved to the Major Indoor Soccer League with Tacoma. Hinton later quit soccer altogether and now helps his wife run a real estate business in the United States.
Wolves record: 78 apps. 29 goals.

HODNETT, Joseph Edward

Centre-half Joe Hodnett played for Wolves during the first four seasons after World War One. Born in Wolverhampton on 18 July 1896, he began his career with Willenhall in 1914 and moved to Molineux in August 1919 when the team was being rebuilt after the war. At first he found himself in reserve – at one stage he appears to have been Wolves' fourth-choice pivot – but he managed a few games each season and appeared in the 1921 FA Cup Final against Spurs at Stamford Bridge. That was his best season with 34 League and Cup appearances and he was one of the stars of the Cup run, but in 1923 Wolves, with several options at centre-half, transferred him to Pontypridd. He later played for Chesterfield (June 1924), Merthyr

Town (May 1925), Brentford (August 1926) and Gillingham (June 1927) before returning to the Midlands to join Stafford Rangers in August 1928. Before he retired in 1935-36 he had also played for Stourbridge, Halesowen, Dudley Town and Brierley Hill Alliance. He died at Willenhall on 12 November 1943.
Wolves record: 85 apps. 5 goals.

HOLLIFIELD, Michael

A player who showed a lot of ability as a teenager, full-back Mike Hollifield was never a first choice player at Molineux. Born in Middlesbrough on 2 May 1961, he had trials at Ayresome Park before joining Wolves as an apprentice in June 1977, turned professional in April 1979 and left the club for Hull City in August 1983. He made 45 League appearances for the Tigers before moving to Tranmere Rovers in July 1985, remaining at Prenton Park until May 1986.
Wolves record: 25 apps.

HOLLINGWORTH, Reginald

Centre-half Reg Hollingworth was one of the more unfortunate footballers to have played for Wolverhampton Wanderers. True, he made 180 senior appearances for Wolves, but just before he was due to play in an England international trial at Huddersfield, he was injured playing for Wolves at Barnsley in March 1932, just when a cap was considered a near-certainty. Then in 1936, another injury forced him to retire. Hollingworth, who was born at Rainworth, near Mansfield, on 17 October 1909, was a fine centre-half, tall and strong and with attacking instincts. He first played for Nuffield Colliery and as an amateur for Mansfield Town before Wolves signed him from Sutton Junction FC in November 1928. Apparently Mansfield wanted to sign him as a professional but couldn't afford another paid player. Hollingworth helped Wolves to the Second Division title in 1931-32, when he was a regular until the injury at Oakwell, which kept him out for the rest of that season and half the next. After leaving Molineux he joined the Staffordshire police force. He then worked at Goodyears before being employed as a manager by Batchelor Robinson and Company in Balsall Heath for 22 years. Hollingworth's death was tragic – he died after suffering a heart attack whilst driving a car along Sandy Lane, Sparkbrook, on 8 July 1969.
Wolves 180 apps. 8 goals.

HOLMES, Michael Anthony

Micky Holmes, who was born in Blackpool on 9 September 1965, was a hard-working midfielder who served Wolves from November 1985 to July 1988 and did well in difficult circumstances, making over 100 senior appearances and winning a Fourth Division championship medal and a Sherpa

Van Trophy winners medal in 1988. A former Bradford and West Yorkshire Schools player, Holmes joined Bradford City from Yeadon Colliery in July 1983, but after only five sub-stitute appearances they released him to Hamileff FC and he was on Burnley's book as a non-contract player (without making a senior appearance) before Wolves signed him. After leaving Molineux, he played for Huddersfield Town, Cambridge United, Rochdale and Torquay United prior to a £15,000 transfer to Carlisle United in February 1992. During 1993-94 he passed the 250 mark in career appearances. In 1991 Holmes helped Torquay to victory in the Fourth Division Play-off Final against Blackpool at Wembley.
Wolves record: 89+15 apps. 13 goals.

HOLSGROVE, John William

Powerful defender John Holsgrove cost Wolves £18,000 when they signed him from Crystal Palace in May 1965. He was recom-mended to Wolves by Palace player-coach Ronnie Allen, who later became his manager at Molineux. Holsgrove, who was born at Southwark on 27 September 1945 and had been on the books of both Arsenal and Spurs as an amateur, spent only one season in Palace's first team, making 22 appearances after joining them as a junior on their groundstaff. But the former England Youth international was at Molineux considerably longer, making 202 senior appearances before he was transferred to Sheffield Wednesday in June 1971. He enjoyed a fine understanding with Dave Woodfield at Wolves, and later with Frank Munro, and although he missed some of the season through injury, he was a key player in the 1966-67 promotion to Division One. After returning to the team in January 1967 he made 97 consecutive appearances until February 1969. He lost his place after John McAlle was introduced to the team by Bill McGarry. In four seasons at Hillsborough, Holsgrove made 104 appearances before ending his career with Stockport County, where he spent half a season before retiring through injury in 1976. His son, Paul, played for Aldershot and Luton and had loan spells with Wimbledon, West Bromwich Albion and Stoke City among others.
Wolves record: 200+2 apps. 7 goals.

HOLT, Sidney Oscar

Inside-forward Sid Holt looked very promis-ing early on in his Wolves career, but the pressures of League football got to him and he failed to make an impact at senior level. Born in the village of Cornworthy, South Devon in 1885, Holt played for Buckfastleigh before joining Wolves in August 1907. He remained at Molineux for a season, leaving for Torquay United in May 1908, and later

assisting Exeter City and Newton Abbot. Holt died in Totnes in 1958.
Wolves record: 8 apps.

HOLYHEAD, Joseph J.

Born in Wolverhampton in August 1880, Joe Holyhead played for Willenhall Swifts and Wednesbury Old Athletic before joining Wolves in August 1902. He spent a season at Molineux, leaving for Port Vale in September 1903 (initially on trial) and later serving with Swindon Town (May 1907), Wellington Town (July 1908) and Walsall White Star (August 1910). Holyhead, who made over 140 first-team appearances for the Vale, retired towards the end of World War One, and died in Walsall *c*.1951.
Wolves record: 6 apps.

HOMER, Sidney

Outside-right Sid Homer – born in Bloxwich on 14 January 1903 – was highly rated when playing on the wing for Bloxwich Strollers and in the summer of 1925 he was taken on as a full-time professional at Molineux. He had an excellent first season with Wolves, appearing in 18 League games in place of Billy Harrington. The following campaign wasn't so good and in May 1927 he was transferred to Bristol Rovers. He spent three years at Eastville (making 38 appearances) before switching to neighbouring Bristol City in November 1929. At Ashton Gate he became a real star and over the next five-and-a-half years scored 18 goals in 179 appearances for the Robins before quitting League soccer to play for Worcester City, retiring through injury at the age of 31.
Wolves record: 29 apps. 2 goals.

HONOURS

Defenders Billy Wright, Emlyn Hughes and Bill Slater along with ex-World Cup referee Jack Taylor, who became Wolves' commercial manager, all received the OBE for services to football. Slater also received the CBE.

Wolves' owner and chairman Jack Hayward is now Sir Jack, having been knighted in 1986. Wolves' deputy chairman in 1999 was Derek Harrington, CBE

And prior to that Wolves' president during the early part of the 20th century was Sir Alfred Hickman Bart.

Rachael Heyhoe-Flint (a member of the Wolves board of of the directors) was awarded with the CBE for services to cricket in 1972.

HONVED

Wolves met and defeated the great Hungarian side 3-2 in a prestigious floodlit friendly at Molineux in December 1954. The BBC TV cameras were present along with some 55,000 and they saw Honved, fielding several star players who had twice helped Hungary beat England 6-3 at Wembley and

7-1 in Budapest, take a 2-0 lead inside the first quarter-of-an-hour. But Wolves, urged on by their supporters, stormed back and after a Johnny Hancocks penalty had gone in just before the break, the home side took control during the second period. Roy Swinbourne headed in the equaliser from Dennis Wilshaw's astute lob in the 74th minute and within two minutes Swinbourne cracked in the winner after some fine build-up play involving Les Smith and Wilshaw.

HOOPER, Harold

Harry Hooper enjoyed a fine career that spanned 13 years, took in over 320 senior appearances and saw him play for four League clubs. Born at Pittington, County Durham, on 14 June 1933, Hooper is the son of a former Nelson, Sheffield United (he skippered their 1936 FA Cup Final side) and Hartlepools United footballer also called Harry. Hooper junior joined West Ham United as a full-time professional in December 1950, after the Upton Park club had appointed his father to their training staff. Earlier, young Harry had played for Hylton Colliery and as an amateur with Sunderland. A former Durham youth sprint champion he scored 44 goals in 119 Second Division games for the Hammers, winning six England 'B' caps and two at Under-23 level as well as playing for the Football League. When Wolves paid £25,000 for him to succeed Johnny Hancocks it was the most any club had paid for a winger at that time. Hooper, happiest on the right flank, scored 19 goals in 39 League games, all in 1956-57 when he was top scorer. In December 1957, with Norman Deeley now established on the right wing at Molineux, Hooper moved to Birmingham City, thus taking no part in Wolves' championship season. The Blues paid £19,500 for him and he scored 42 goals in 105 games for them, appearing in the 1960 Fairs Cup Final against Barcelona. In September 1960 he was transferred to Sunderland, a local boy going home, and made 65 League appearances for the Wearsiders before joining Kettering Town in May 1963. He left football in 1967 and went into business in Kettering.
Wolves record: 41 apps. 19 goals.

HOPKINS, John

Wolves signed winger Jack Hopkins from Liverpool's reserve team in March 1904. And over the next two seasons he gave some excellent performances on the left flank when called in to deputise for Jack Miller. Unfortunately he could never hold down a regular first-team place and in 1906 was transferred to New Brighton. Born on Merseyside *c*.1882, Hopkins later worked near the Mersey shipyard.
Wolves record: 47 apps. 14 goals.

HORNE, Desmond

Several players from South Africa found their way to Britain in the 1950s, amongst them outside-left Des Horne, who was born in Johannesburg on 12 December 1939 and signed for Wolves in December 1956. Horne was an out-and-out winger, fast and direct, but Jimmy Mullen was in possession of the number-11 shirt at Molineux and Horne had to wait until the first day of the 1958-59 season to make his debut, at home to Nottingham Forest. He made only eight appearances that season as Wolves regained the League championship, but began to establish himself the following season and gained an FA Cup winners' medal in 1960, when Wolves beat Blackburn in the Final. Altogether he made 52 appearances for Wolves, scoring 18 goals, before being transferred to Blackpool in March 1961. For the Seasiders, Horne made 188 League appearances, also scoring 18 goals. His time at Bloomfield Road saw Blackpool struggling in Division One, but he helped them to a League Cup semi-final in 1962. In 1966 he returned to South Africa where he now runs his own air-conditioning business, although his daughter works in Wolverhampton. Horne incidentally was the second South-African born winger to play in a FA Cup Final, following Blackpool's Bill Perry in 1953.
Wolves record: 52 apps. 18 goals.

HORTON, Thomas Ezekial Bruce

Teak-tough inside-forward, very unorthodox in his play, Tom Horton was born in Birmingham in 1863 and played for Crosswell's Brewery before joining Wolves in August 1885. He spent a season with the club and in August 1886 signed for West Bromwich Standard, later assisting Stafford Rangers. He died in Stafford *c*.1928.
Wolves record: 2 apps. 1 goal.

HOSKINS, Albert Herbert

Bert Hoskins was born in Southampton in 1885 and played for St Mary's Guild and Freemantle FC (Hampshire) before joining Southampton in 1904. A useful forward with good pace, he scored three goals in 21 games for Saints before transferring to Shrewsbury Town. In May 1908 he was recruited by Wolves but failed to make the grade at Molineux and left after a short while to sign for Dudley Town, later assisting St Peters FC, Darlaston and Wellington Town where he became club secretary. In August 1919 he returned to Molineux as assistant to then manager/secretary Jack Addenbrooke. He progressed well and became Wolves secretary himself in 1922. Two years later, in June 1924, he was handed the manager's job at Wolves – and was indeed, a proud man. Hoskins looked after team affairs at Wolves for two years, seeing the team finish sixth in the Second Division in 1924-25, but his appointment was short-lived and in March 1926 he left Wolves to take over a similar position at Gillingham, holding office there for four years. Thereafter he remained in the game as a trainer, coach and scout, working for several non-League clubs until 1940. Hoskins died on 19 February 1968.

Hoskins' record as Wolves manager was played 78, won 34, drawn 13, lost 31.

Wolves record: 14 apps. 2 goals.

HOWELL, Henry

Henry Howell was born in Smethwick on 28 June 1895 and besides being a useful centre or inside-forward, he also played Test cricket for England and County cricket for Warwickshire. As a footballer he starred for St Michael's Youth Club and Burslem Swifts before joining Wolves in July 1913. During the war he guested for Stoke and Port Vale and soon after re-signing for Wolves (August 1919) he had a trial with Southampton (1920) and later assisted Northfleet FC (1921), Accrington Stanley (October 1922-23) and Mansfield Town. As a cricketer, Howell spent 15 years with Warwickshire (1913-28), appearing in 198 first-class matches. He twice toured Australia with the MCC (in 1920-21 and 1924-25), playing in five Tests against the Aussies. In his career as an all-rounder, Howell played in 227 competitive matches and scored 1,679 runs in 326 innings (111 not-outs) for an average of 7.80. His bowling figures were much better – 20,700 runs conceded, 975 wickets taken for an average of 21.23. His best return was 10-51 against Yorkshire at Edgbaston in 1923 when he became the first Warwickshire bowler to take all ten wickets in an innings. He claimed five wickets in an innings 75 times and 10 in a match on 18 separate occasions. He took over 100 wickets in a season six times with a best tally of 161 in 1920 (average 17.91). Howell died in Selly Oak on 9 July 1932.

His brother, A. L. Howell, also represented Warwickshire CCC.

Wolves record: 41 apps. 8 goals.

HOWELL, William Thomas R.

Signed as full-back cover by secretary-manager Jack Addenbrook from Wellington Town in August 1900, Bill Howells (sometimes his name was seen without the 's') stayed at Molineux for one season before transferring to Willenhall Pickwick in August 1901. He was born in Shrewsbury *c.*1878.

Wolves record: 1 app.

HOWELLS, Ronald

Tall, slim wing-half, Ron Howells, besides being an efficient footballer, was also a very accomplished cricketer, playing for the Warwickshire Club and Ground. Born the son of a Rugby Union international in the Rhondda Valley on 3 August 1935, he was educated in Coventry and represented the County Schools before joining Nuneaton Borough. From there he switched to Molineux, becoming a professional in July 1953. He stayed with Wolves for six years before transferring to Portsmouth in March 1959, later assisting Scunthorpe United (June 1961) and Walsall (July 1963 to May 1964). He amassed well over 150 senior appearances at club level.

Wolves record: 9 apps.

HOWLEY, John T.

Jack Howley arrived at Molineux as a junior office boy in 1923 and stayed with Wolves for the rest of his working life, until the arrival of manager Bill McGarry. He was club secretary for 20 years (June 1948 to June 1968), the last five being combined with the duties of general manager. A dedicated Wolves man, Howley sadly died on 23 March 1971. His daughter, Christine, who lives in Wombourne, has been a regular supporter at Molineux to this day.

HUDDERSFIELD TOWN

Wolves' playing record against Town is:

Football League

Venue	P	W	D	L	F	A
Home	32	19	8	5	89	45
Away	32	10	4	18	34	51
Totals	64	29	12	23	123	96

FA Cup

Home	3	1	2	0	4	2
Away	2	0	0	2	2	5
Totals	5	1	2	2	6	7

League Cup

Away	1	0	0	1	0	1

Wolves and Huddersfield first met in the Football League in season 1910-11 (Division Two) and it was the Yorkshire side who took the honours, winning 3-0 at Molineux and 3-1 at Leeds Road.

Wolves' first victory over Town was a 2-1 home success in September 1912 and in February 1915 they ran up their second victory with a 4-1 win at Molineux in front of just 3,000 spectators.

There was an absence of League action between the clubs for some 12-and-a-half years (from April 1920 to September 1932) before Wolves lost 3-2 at Huddersfield only to gain sweet revenge with a thrilling 6-4 victory at Molineux in February 1933 when over 22,000 fans saw Wolves' ace Billy Hartill score four goals.

The following season (September 1933) Wolves raced to a solid 5-2 home win over Town with Jack Hetherington a hat-trick hero on this occasion.

An amazing coincidence occurred during two successive Wolves v Huddersfield Town League games at Molineux in the late 1930s.

In the 86th minute of the First Division encounter on Christmas Day 1936, Wolves defender Stan Cullis handled inside the penalty area and Hayes scored from the spot in his side's 3-1 defeat. Some 14 months later, on 16 February 1938, in the next Wolves-Huddersfield match, Cullis again conceded a penalty in the 86th minute by using his hands, and again Hayes stepped up to score from the spot, but this time Town won 4-1. Alex Scott was the Wolves goalkeeper in both games.

In between times, Wolves had 'keeper Scott sent-off when they lost 4-0 at Huddersfield on 28 December 1936.

The first post-war League encounter, staged at Molineux in October 1946, resulted in a 6-1 win for Wolves (Jesse Pye scoring twice) and in October 1948 Wolves went one better, thrashing the Yorkshire club 7-1 with Pye grabbing a hat-trick this time round.

Amazingly, in September 1949, Wolves hammered Huddersfield at home once more, again to the tune of 7-1 and again it was that man Jesse Pye who was the thorn in the Town' side with another treble in front of a 45,559 crowd.

Coincidence or not – Wolves registered their third 7-1 League win over Huddersfield at Leeds Road in a First Division game in September 1951, Jimmy Dunn weighing in with three goals on this occasion. And towards the end of Wolves' 1953-54 championship-winning campaign they rattled third-placed Huddersfield 4-0 at Molineux only to lose the return fixture by 2-1 at Leeds Road 24 hours later.

A ten-goal thriller on Wolves' soil in February 1955 was witnessed by a crowd of 30,666, and those present saw the Wanderers triumph 6-4 with a hat-trick from Johnny Hancock, who gave former Wanderers' full-back Larry Kelly a roasting.

Wolves doubled up over Town in 1955-56, winning 4-0 at home (with a Roy Swinbourne hat-trick) and 3-1 away – and it was then ten years before the teams met again in the League.

On their way to winning the Third Division title in season 1988-89 Wolves whipped Huddersfield 4-1 at Molineux with goal from Steve Bull (2), Andy Mutch and Floyd Streete.

On 27 February 1999 Wolves played their 2,000th home game in the Football League against Huddersfield Town (drew 1-1).

Wolves' first FA Cup-tie against Huddersfield also saw them record their only victory in the competition over the Yorkshire club. It was a 2-0 triumph at Molineux in the fifth round in February 1951 when 52,708 fans saw Jimmy Dunn score twice.

Wolves' 1-0 League Cup defeat was suffered at Leeds Road in September 1967.

Players with both clubs include: Vince Bartram, Jack Beattie, Walter Bottrill, Peter Eastoe, Mel Eves, Micky Holmes, Lawrie Kelly, Steve Kindon, Bob McNab, Chris Marsden, Mike O'Grady, John Oldfield, Derek Parkin, Gary Pierce, Iwan Roberts, Phil Robinson, Phil Stoutt, Andy Turner, Paul Walker, Bob White, Peter Withe (Town player-coach) and Ernie Whittam.

Also associated: Andy Beattie and Ian Greaves (managed both clubs); Bill McGarry (Huddersfield player, Wolves manager), Alf Lythgoe (a Wolves reserve who scored 46 goals in 79 games for Town after leaving Molineux in mid 1930s) and Ian Ross (Wolves coach, caretaker-manager, Town manager).

HUGHES, Emyln Walter, OBE

Emlyn Hughes was a vastly experienced defender with 657 League, Cup and European appearances with Liverpool to his name when John Barnwell signed him for Wolves in August 1979. In addition to his rich haul of honours gained with the Merseysiders – he captained them when they first won the European Cup – Hughes also won 59 full England caps and Barnwell saw him as the man to help solve the problem of a leaky defence which had just conceded 150 goals in two seasons – and it worked.

With Hughes at the centre of their rearguard, Wolves opened the season with two clean sheets and by the end of it Hughes was lifting the League Cup after victory over Nottingham Forest at Wembley. Wolves also climbed from 18th to sixth in Division One. Hughes also added three more England caps to his collection as a Wolves player, but his was only ever going to be a short-term signing, and in September 1981 he became player-manager of Rotherham United, after appearing in 76 first-team games for Wolves, who were relegated at the end of the season. Hughes ended his career with Hull, Swansea City and Mansfield, although he never appeared for the Stags. Footballer of the Year in 1977, with Liverpool he won four League championship medals, two European Cup winners' medals and two UEFA Cup winners' medals, a FA Cup winners' medal and appeared in several other Finals. He was born in Barrow on 28 August 1947, the son of a Great Britain Rugby League international, and first played for Roose FC and Blackpool (from September 1964) before Liverpool signed him in March 1967 for £65,000. He was on the board at Hull City for a season and worked in television, most notably as one of the captains in *A Question of Sport* on BBC. He was awarded the OBE for his services to football.
Wolves record: 75+2 apps. 2 goals.

HUGHES, Harold

Born in Cheshire in 1881, Harry Hughes was reserve to Jack Whitehouse and Ernie Jones during his time at Molineux. He joined Wolves from Crewe Alexandra in July 1905 and left for Leamington Town in May 1906. He later played for Stafford Rangers (1907-08) and then Hanley Swifts (1909) before retiring in 1910. Hughes died in Warwick c.1939.
Wolves record: 9 apps.

HUGHES, William H.

Billy Hughes was a forceful centre-forward, who scored 51 goals in 102 games for Bolton Wanderers before moving to Molineux in September 1913. Born in Stourbridge in 1890, Hughes played for Norton Hall FC, Stourbridge Standard and Connah's Quay before moving into the professional ranks at Burnden Park in April 1908. Unfortunately his association with Wolves was cut short through a knee injury, forcing him to retire in May 1914. After helping Bolton win promotion to the First Division in 1911, the Trotters were fined £28 by the Football League for misleading Hughes into assuming he would receive £200 in lieu of a benefit match if he left Burnden Park.
Wolves record: 24 apps. 10 goals.

HULL CITY

Wolves' playing record against the Tigers is:

Football League

Venue	P	W	D	L	F	A
Home	23	11	5	7	49	29
Away	23	6	3	14	21	55
Totals	46	17	8	21	70	84

FA Cup

	P	W	D	L	F	A
Home	2	1	0	1	1	1
Away	2	1	1	0	4	2
Totals	4	2	1	1	5	3

League Cup

	P	W	D	L	F	A
Home	1	0	1	0	1	1
Away	1	0	1	0	0	0
Totals	2	0	2	0	1	1

The first time Wolves met Hull City in a League game was at Molineux (Division Two) in September 1906 when a crowd of 6,000 witnessed a 1-1 draw played in a 90 degree temperature- the hottest weather ever to greet Wolves in a League game.

The return fixture this season ended in a convincing 5-1 win for the Tigers for whom Joe Smith and John Manning each scored twice.

Wolves thrashed Hull 8-0 in a Second Division game at Molineux in November 1911 when two players – Billy Halligan and Jack Needham – both scored hat-tricks.

Hull gained revenge for that hiding in December 1913 when they crushed Wolves 7-1 on Humberside in another Second Division fixture which attracted 8,000 fans, who saw ex-Wolf Halligan score four times against his former team-mates.

Another big Hull win came on Christmas Day 1914 when Wolves were beaten 5-1 at Anlaby Road, but there was an even heavier thrashing for the Molineux men who were walloped 10-3 by the Tigers in December 1919 in front of 8,000 spectators. Billy Mercer (4) and Sammy Stevens (3) led the goal-chase for the rampant Tigers who a week earlier had lost 4-2 at Molineux. (Nineteen goals in two games that season).

Wolves' first League game of 1927 saw Wolves beat Hull 5-2 at Molineux, Tom Phillipson and Wilf Chadwick scoring two each.

Wolves lost 4-2 and then won 4-2 in successive home League games against Hull in September 1928 and September 1929, but there followed a break of almost 38 years before the teams meet again. This was in March 1967 when a Derek Dougan hat-trick on his home debut, gave Wolves a 4-0 win in a vital Second Division match.

Wolves' best FA Cup win over Hull is 3-1 at Boothferry Park in a third round tie in January 1969. Derek Dougan again scored twice that day in front of more than 27,500 fans.

The two League Cup games were played in season 1990-91, and it was the Tigers who went through on the away goal rule after the side's had drawn 0-0 at Boothferry Park.

Players with both clubs include: Billy Barraclough, Harry Brown, Jack Curnow, Peter Daniel, Harry Davies, Jack Dowen (also wartime guest), Jack Ellis, John Farley, Stan Fazackerley, Billy Halligan, Mick Hollifield, Emlyn Hughes, David Jordan, Ken Knighton, Mick Matthews, Jack Needham, Bill Parker, Harry Scott, Jack Taylor and Kim Wassall.

Also associated: Major Frank Buckley (manager of both clubs), Brian Garvey (Hull player, Wolves coach), Jack Acquaroff and Neil Franklin (City players, Wolves wartime guests), Henry Brown, Cyril Hannaby, James Lee, Billy Lucas, Paul Moss, Cliff Sherwood, Trevor Walters, Jeff Wealands and Gareth Williams (all Wolves Reserves), Paul Todd (Wolves trialist).

HUMPHREY, John

Cockney right-back John Humphrey was born at Paddington on 31 January 1961. Educated at Aylestone High School Kensal Rise, he played for Bourne Hall Youth Club in Bushey, Herts, where he was spotted by Wolves manager Sammy Chung, who quickly signed him as an apprentice in 1977. After being upgraded to the professional ranks in January 1979, Humphrey established himself in the senior side in 1981-82, but found himself in a side fighting an unsuccessful battle against relegation to Division Two. The next season, though, they bounced straight back as runners-up and Humphrey was an ever-present. Of course, those were

topsy-turvy days at Molineux and 12 months on, Humphrey found himself back in the Second Division with Wolves. Another year later and he was facing Third Division football as Wolves hurtled straight down the League. In July 1985, before he could sample the questionable delights of Third Division football Humphrey was rescued by Charlton Athletic. He spent five years with the London club, appearing in 231 games, helping the Addicks back to the First Division in his first season at Selhurst Park (to where Charlton had just moved) and to the 1987 Full Members' Cup Final in 1987, when they lost to Blackburn. In July 1990 he was transferred to Crystal Palace for £400,000 and helped Palace win the Zenith Data Systems Cup in 1991. In December 1993 he joined Reading on loan as Palace went on to win the First Division title and so regain their Premiership status. In July 1995 Humphrey had a second spell with Charlton and in August 1996 he joined Gillingham, moving to struggling Brighton and Hove Albion in January 1997. In November 1997 Humphrey signed for non-League Chesham United having made 681 first-class appearances.
Wolves record: 164 apps. 3 goals.

HUNT, Revd Kenneth Reginald Gurney

A top-class footballer in the mould of Revd Kenneth Hunt could not exist today, of course. But back in the early 1900s there was still room for the gifted amateur to make his mark alongside full-time professionals. Hunt, who was born at Oxford on 24 February 1884, but who attended Wolverhampton Grammar School, remained an amateur throughout his playing days as a creative wing-half. His career began at Trent College in Derbyshire before he gained a soccer Blue at Oxford University three years in succession. Naturally, he played for the great amateur side, Corinthians, and he also assisted several other clubs including Leyton, Crystal Palace, Wolves and Oxford City. He gained 20 England Amateur caps but also played twice for the full international side, both in 1911, against Scotland and Wales, when he was officially listed as a Leyton player but was also helping Wolves. Indeed, he appeared for Wolves from 1906 to 1920, as and when his studies and other work allowed, and altogether played in 61 senior games for the club and scored two goals, one of them coming in the 1908 FA Cup Final when Newcastle United were beaten 3-1 at

the Crystal Palace. That was his best season for Wolves with 21 League appearances and seven in the Cup and ended with a winners' medal. The same year he also won an Olympic gold medal with the Great Britain soccer team. In 1913 he played for Oxford City in the FA Amateur Cup Final and after World War One turned out for Eccleshall Comrades and Stafford Rangers. Hunt was ordained in 1909 and as a house-master at Highgate School, North London, between 1909 and 1945 he did much for public schools soccer. Hunt was an FA Council member for many years before retiring through ill health in 1949. He died on 28 April that year, at Heathfield in Sussex.
Wolves record: 61 apps. 2 goals.

HUNT, Roger ('Ernie')

Midfielder 'Ernie' Hunt had a memorable start to his Wolves career. He was signed from Swindon Town by manager Andy Beattie on the morning of 17 September 1965, with every expectation of making his debut at Southampton the following day. But four hours after the signing was completed, Beattie resigned. Hunt, not surprisingly, decided that he wasn't quite ready, and the following day sat in the stand at The Dell and

Wolves in 1987. Back row (left to right): Mutch, Barnes, Robinson, Bull, Edwards, Purdie, Dennison, Stoutt. Middle: Paul Darby (physiotherapist), Clarke, Streete, Kendall, Bartram, Bellamy, Brindley, Graham Turner (manager). Front: Thompson, Jones, Forman, Robertson, Downing, Holmes, Smith.

watched his new club go down 9-3. Things got better for both player and club, however, and Hunt soon settled down in the Wolves midfield and in 1966-67 helped them win promotion back to the First Division. He had an excellent striking record for a midfielder with 35 goals in only 82 appearances for Wolves before he was transferred to Everton for £80,000 in September 1967. Six months later Coventry bought him for £70,000 and at Highfield Road he teamed up with future Wolves men Willie Carr and Bobby Gould. It was Hunt and Carr who perfected the infamous 'donkey-kick' which resulted in a spectacular goal on BBC's *Match of the Day* before the innovative kick was outlawed. After a loan spell with Doncaster Rovers, Hunt ended his career with Bristol City before he retired in May 1974 with an overall tally of 165 goals to his name in 467 League appearances. He became landlord of the Full Pitcher public house in Ledbury and later worked as a window cleaner. Hunt, who was born in Swindon on 17 March 1943, played for Wiltshire Boys but was working for British Rail when Bert Head signed him for Swindon as an amateur in 1957. He became a full-time professional in March 1960 and with Swindon he won three England Under-23 caps and appeared in 214 League games for the Wiltshire club, scoring 82 goals.

Wolves record: 82 apps. 35 goals.

HUNTER, Thomas

Wolves signed utility forward Tommy Hunter from Walsall in the summer of 1886. He had failed to establish himself with the Saddlers, but made a fine start to his career with the Wanderers, scoring plenty of goals in the various friendly matches played by the club. He also claimed five goals in the FA Cup in his first season, including a four-timer in a 14-0 win against Crosswell's Brewery on 13 November. When League football arrived in September 1888, Hunter was in Wolves' line-up for their opening game against Aston Villa (1-1) and in fact, he was also in the side which registered their first-ever League win, 4-1 over Burnley, when he scored a fine goal. He was subsequently released by Wolves in the summer of 1889 after picking up a knee injury. He joined Stourbridge and later played for Pelsall before retiring in 1892. Hunter was born in Walsall in 1864 and died in Wolverhampton in 1935.

Wolves record: 35 apps. 13 goals.

INTERNATIONAL WOLVES

Here are details of international/representative honours won by players whilst they were associated with Wolverhampton Wanderers football club:

Full International appearances:

ENGLAND
Harry Allen (5), Tom Baddeley (5), Dicky Baugh (1), Billy Beats (2), Peter Broadbent (7), Jack Brodie (3), Steve Bull (5+8 sub), Eddie Clamp (4), Chris Crowe (1), Stan Cullis (12), Norman Deeley (2), Arthur Fletcher (2), Ron Flowers (48+1 sub), Tom Galley (2), Johnny Hancocks (3), Alan Hinton (1), Emlyn Hughes (1+2 sub), Kenneth Hunt (2), George Kinsey (2), Arthur Lowder (1), Charlie Mason (3), Bill Morris (3), Jimmy Mullen (11+1 sub), Jesse Pye (1), John Richards (1), Billy Rose (1), Bill Slater (12), Tom Smalley (1), Bobby Thomson (8), Dick Topham (1), Bert Williams (24), Dennis Wilshaw (12), Harry Wood (3) and Billy Wright (105).
Goalscorers: Flowers 10, Wilshaw 10, Mullen 6, Bull 4, Wright 3, Broadbent 2, Hancocks 2, Brodie 1, Galley 1 and Wood 1.

Bert Williams, won 24 full caps for England.

SCOTLAND
Hugh Curran (4+1 sub), Andy Gray (8+5 sub), Jim McCalliog (1) and Frank Munro (6+3 sub).
Goalscorers: Gray 4, Curran 1.
IRELAND
Billy Halligan (1).
NORTHERN IRELAND
Jackie Brown (3), Robbie Dennison (12+6 sub), Derek Dougan (26), Danny Hegan (6), Bob Lutton (2), David Martin (2), Peter McParland (1), David Martin (2) and Sammy Smyth (8).
Goalscorers: Smyth 5, Dougan 4, Brown 1.
WALES
George Berry (3+1 sub), John Bowdler (2), Joseph Davies (2), Ryan Green (2), Bryn

Jones (10), Brian Law (1), Albert Lumberg (1), John Matthias (1), Teddy Peers (8), Charlie Phillips (10), David Richards (11), Dick Richards (5), Adrian Williams (6), Eric Young (1).
Goalscorers: Phillips 4, Jones 3, Bowdler 2, R. Richards 1, Williams 1.
REPUBLIC OF IRELAND
David Connolly (2+1 sub), Maurice Daly (2), David Jordan (2), Robbie Keane (5+1 sub), Mick Kearns (2), David Kelly (3+1 sub) and Jimmy Kelly (5).
Goalscorers: Keane 2, Connolly 1, Kelly 1.
DENMARK
Havaard Flo (1).
FINLAND
Mixu Paatelainen (3+1 sub).
AUSTRALIA
Steve Corica (1).
GRENADA
Jason Roberts (3) 5 goals.
NEW ZEALAND
Ricki Herbert (1).
SOUTH AFRICA
Mark Williams (3+1 sub) 3 goals.
REST OF THE UNITED KINGDOM
Billy Wright (1).
UNITED KINGDOM XI
Derek Dougan (1).

Unofficial Internationals
ENGLAND
Billy Beats (1), Alan Hinton (1) and Billy Wooldridge (1).
ENGLAND XI
Joe Blackett (1), Hill Griffiths (1) and Jack Miller (1).
ENGLAND (v Young England)
Peter Broadbent (2), Eddie Clamp (1), Ron Flowers (7), Johnny Kirkham (1), Nigel Sims (1), Bill Slater (1), Bobby Thomson (3) and Billy Wright (3).
SCOTLAND XI
Hugh Curran v Australian XI (1)

Under-23 Internationals
ENGLAND
Colin Booth (1), Peter Broadbent (1), Ted Farmer (2), Ron Flowers (2), Gerry Harris (4), Kenny Hibbitt (1), Alan Hinton (3), Ernie Hunt (2), Johnny Kirkham (2), Peter Knowles (4), Gerry Mannion (2), Jimmy Murray (2), Geoff Palmer (2), Derek Parkin (5), Barry Powell (4), John Richards (6), Alan Sunderland (1) and Bobby Thomson (15).
SCOTLAND
Frank Munro (4)

Under-21 Internationals
ENGLAND
Steve Bull (5), Paul Bradshaw (2), Bob Hazell (1), Andy Mutch (1), John Richards (2) and Alan Sunderland (1).
REPUBLIC OF IRELAND
Hugh Atkinson (1), Glenn Crowe (1+1),

Maurice Daly (1), Dominic Foley, (1), Robbie Keane (5) and John Pender (1).
WALES
Ryan Green (2), Carl Robinson (7+1).

ENGLAND WORLD CUP XI
Jimmy Mullen (1), Bert Williams (1) and Billy Wright (1).

NORTH AMERICAN/CANADIAN TOUR (FA XI) 1950
Johnny Hancocks (9), Ted Russell (6).

'B' Internationals
ENGLAND
Peter Broadbent (1), Steve Bull (5), Steve Daley (6), Mel Eves (3), Bob Hazell (1), Harry Hooper (1), Jimmy Mullen (3), Andy Mutch (3), Jesse Pye (3), John Richards (3), Roy Swinbourne (1), Bert Williams (1), Dennis Wilshaw (2) and Billy Wright (2).
REPUBLIC OF IRELAND
Noel Dwyer (1), Robbie Keane (2).
SCOTLAND
Dougie Freedman (1).
WALES
Carl Robinson (1).

Victory and Wartime Internationals
ENGLAND
Sammy Brooks (1), Stan Cullis (20), Jimmy Mullen (3), Frank Taylor (1), Dennis Westcott (4), Bert Williams (2) and Billy Wright (4).
SCOTLAND
John Harris (1)
WALES
Teddy Peers (2) and Cyril Sidlow (11).

Inter League Matches
FOOTBALL LEAGUE
George Ashall (1), Tom Baddeley (3), Mike Bailey (3), Billy Beats (5), Peter Broadbent (2), Sammy Brooks (1), Eddie Clamp (1), Stan Cullis (3), Ron Flowers (13), Tom Galley (1), Joe Gardiner (1), Hill Griffiths (1), Johnny Hancocks (2), Harry Hooper (1), Kenneth Hunt (1), Joey Jones (1), Billy Malpass (1), Jack Miller (1), Jimmy Mullen (1), Jimmy Murray (1), Derek Parkin (1), Jesse Pye (1), John Richards (1), Cecil Shaw (1), Bobby Thomson (4), Dave Wagstaffe (1), Dennis Westcott (1), Bert Williams (5), Harry Wood (4), Billy Wooldridge (1), Billy Wright (21) and David Wykes (1).

Youth Internationals (at Under-16, Under-18 and Under-20 levels)
ENGLAND
C. Beavon, J. Bray, W. Clarke, V. Cockcroft, L. Cocker, A. Corbett, C. G. Dangerfield, A. Dickson, P. R. Eastoe, A. Evans, T. Flowers, I. Hall, R. Hazell, A. Hinton, T. Jewkes, M. Jones, J. Kirkham, P. Knowles, G. Mannion, H. Middleton, C. Moss, M. Murray, L. Naylor, M. Patching, A. Proudlock, B. R. Perry, J. Skull, C. Tether.
NORTHERN IRELAND
D. Beattie, D. Clements, S.B. Devine, C. Gilmore, C. Hagan, G. Haveron, G. Simms, M. McCain, S.E. Troughton, J. Willis.
REPUBLIC OF IRELAND
K. Andrews, K. Coleman, G. Crowe, S. Crowe, M. Daly, S. Hackett, F. Hayes, R. Keane, A. Kernan, C. Larkin, J. Melligan, J. Pender, G. Quinn.
SCOTLAND
P. Buckley, D. Devlin, W. Livingstone.
WALES
J. Easter, R. Green, D. Keith, C. Robinson.

Junior International
ENGLAND
Billy Rotton (1).

Amateur Internationals
ENGLAND
Percy Corbett (7), Billy Holmes (3), Revd Kenneth Hunt (20), Dick Topham (2), Bill Slater (6).
UNITED KINGDOM (AMATEUR)
Revd Kenneth Hunt (3).

County Matches
STAFFORDSHIRE COUNTY FA
Jack Mitton (1), Harry Shaw (1).
BIRMINGHAM COUNTY FA
Len Astill (1).
BIRMINGHAM COUNTY YOUTH
P. Clark (3), P. B. Corbett (3), J. Donaghy (2), W. Gibbons (1), A. Hinton (2), W. Nicholls (2), R. Patten (1), A. Price (1), W. Weaver (1), D. Woodfield (2).
BIRMINGHAM JUNIOR FA
Dicky Rhodes (1).

Other Representative Matches
ENGLAND XI
Stan Cullis (1), Ron Flowers (1), Frank Taylor (1).
ALL BRITISH XI
Stan Cullis (1).
IRELAND XI
Lawrie Kelly (1).
ALL IRELAND XI
Billy Halligan (1).
WALES XI
Cyril Sidlow (2).
FOOTBALL LEAGUE XI
Ron Flowers (1).
FOOTBALL LEAGUE (Midlands XI)
Billy Hartill (1).
FOOTBALL LEAGUE SELECT XI
Stan Cullis (2), Dicky Dorsett (1), Tom Galley (1), Joe Gardiner (1), Billy Harrison (2), Billy Hartill (1), Alex Scott (2), Dennis Westcott (2).
RAF
Peter Broadbent (2), Ron Flowers (1).

RAF XI
Bob King (1).
BRITISH ARMY
Stan Cullis (6), Ray Goddard (3), Billy Hartill (5), Bob King (1), Dennis Westcott (1).
ARMY XI
Joe Bonson (1), Stan Cullis (21), Norman Deeley (1), Ray Goddard (7), Billy Hartill (3), Jimmy Mullen (12), Frank Taylor (10), Dennis Westcott (5).
ARMY IN ENGLAND
Stan Cullis (4), Jimmy Mullen (1), Frank Taylor (3), Dennis Westcott (1).
FA XI
Stan Cullis (4), Ron Flowers (3), FA B. King (2), Cyril Sidlow (1), Roy Swinbourne (1), Frank Taylor (1), Dennis Westcott (1), Dennis Wilshaw (2), Billy Wright (1).
FA SERVICES XI
Jimmy Mullen (1).
COMBINED SERVICES
FA B. King (1), Jimmy Mullen (1), Billy Wright (1).
WESTERN COMMAND
Jack Robinson (1), Frank Taylor (3), Billy Wright (2).
EASTERN COMMAND
Tommy Burden (1), Alex McIntosh (1), Fred Pincott (1).
NORTHERN COMMAND
Jack Dowen (4), Tom Galley (3), Jimmy Mullen (8), Cyril Sidlow (2).
ARMY PHYSICAL TRAINING CORPS
Billy Wright (1).
RHA XI
Billy Hartill (4).
RASC
Noel George (3).
BIRMINGHAM XI
Billy Blunt (1), George Garratly (1).
ENDSLEIGH LEAGUE XI (v Italy Serie 'B')
Neil Emblen (1).
SALONIKA XI
Noel George (1).

International Trials
ENGLAND
Harry Allen (1), Tom Baddeley (1), Jack Brodie (1), George Kinsey (2), Arthur Lowder (1), Harry Shaw (1), Harry Wood (2).

International facts and figures
The first Wolves player to win a full international cap was full-back Charlie Mason for England v Ireland in Sheffield on 5 February 1887.

Hugh Curran was the first Wolves player to win a full Scottish cap (v Austria in 1969); John Bowdler was the first 'Wolf' to be capped by Wales (v Scotland in 1891), Billy Halligan became the first Wolves player to represent Ireland (v England in 1912) and David Jordan was the first Wanderer to win Republic of Ireland recognition (v Switzerland in 1936).

Jack Brodie was the first Wolves player to score a goal in a full international, doing so for England against Ireland in March 1889.

Outside-right Johnny Hancocks scored twice on his debut for England v Switzerland in 1948 and Dennis Wilshaw did likewise on his first outing for his country v Wales in 1953.

Goalkeeper Tom Baddeley won the first of his five England caps on his home ground – Molineux – in February 1903 (v Ireland).

The first Wolves player to appear in an international match at Wembley was centre-half Stan Cullis v Scotland in April 1938.

When he played for England against Scotland at Wembley in 1959, Wolves' captain Billy Wright became the first player in soccer history to win a total of 100 full international caps. He skippered his country a record 90 times (in 105 starts out of a possible 108 between 1946 and 1959) and appeared in three World Cups (1950, 1954 and 1958). Wright made more appearances for England in the Home International Championship than any other player and he lined up for his country thus: 51 games at right-half, 46 in succession at centre-half and eight at left-half.

Other Wolves players who skippered their country at full international level were: Ron Flowers, Emlyn Hughes and Stan Cullis (England) and Derek Dougan (Northern Ireland). Cullis, in fact, became England's youngest skipper in 1938-39 at the age of 22.

Dennis Wilshaw scored ten goals in 12 international appearances for England. He was also the first player to score four times at Wembley – against Scotland in 1955.

Three players from Wolves – Eddie Clamp, Bill Slater and Ron Flowers – formed the England half-back line in four internationals against the USSR (twice), Brazil and Austria in May/June 1958.

Four Wolves players – Bert Williams, Flowers, Wright and Wilshaw – all lined up for England against France in May 1955.

This feat was repeated in May 1959 when Wright, Flowers, Norman Deeley and Peter Broadbent played against Brazil in Rio.

Between 1938 and 1963 England played 148 full internationals and Wolves were represented in each match by at least one player.

Ted Farmer scored four goals in his two England Under-23 appearances in 1961, including a hat-trick against Holland.

The Revd Kenneth Hunt won an Olympic gold medal for the United Kingdom in the 1908 Games in London.

On tour with the unofficial England party (the FA XI) to North America and Canada in 1950, Johnny Hancocks scored a total of 16 goals in his nine appearances. He scored four times (two penalties) in a 4-4 draw with Vancouver in British Columbia, netted the only goal against the USA in New York and grabbed hat-tricks in a 19-1 win over Saskatoon in Saskatchewan and a 9-2 victory of Essex in Ontario.

Ron Flowers and Dennis Wilshaw each scored ten representative goals for England; Jimmy Mullen netted six, Steve Bull four, Billy Wright three, Peter Broadbent and Johnny Hancocks two apiece and Jack Brodie, Tom Galley and Harry Wood one each.

Andy Gray claimed four goals for Scotland and Hugh Curran one.

Charlie Phillips (4 goals), Bryn Jones (3), John Bowlder (2) and Dick Richards (1) were on target for Wales.

Sammy Smyth (5), Derek Dougan (4) and Jackie Brown (1) netted for Northern Ireland and David Kelly was on target once for the Republic of Ireland.

Dennis Westcott hit five goals in wartime internationals for England.

Wolves players on the mark for England 'B' have been Bull (2), Steve Daley (2), Wilshaw (1), Mel Eves (1), Hooper (1), Mullen (1) and Roy Swinbourne (1).

Ted Farmer scored four times for England at Under-23 level; Alan Hinton netted three times, Jimmy Murray twice and Peter Knowles, Gerry Mannion and John Richards once apiece.

Bull (3 goals) and Bob Hazell (1) netted for England Under-21s; Dominic Foley scored once for the Republic of Ireland.

Billy Wooldridge scored four times for an England XI in the unofficial international against Germany in September 1901 and in the same year he netted a hat-trick for the Football League v the Irish League.

Other Wolves players who found the net for the Football League XI were: Billy Beats (4 goals), Mike Bailey, Peter Broadbent, Murray, Jesse Pye, Westcott, Wood, Wright and David Wykes (all one each)

Ron Flowers hit one goal for England v Young England and Alan Hinton likewise for England v the Football League.

South African striker Mark Williams notched one international goal whilst with Wolves and in 1998 he was named in South Africa's World Cup squad.

Before joining Wolves. Kevin Muscat had represented Australia in two Youth World Cup tournaments, the Olympic Games (in Atlanta) and the Victorian State side as well as the Australian senior XI.

Harry Middleton became Wolves' first England Youth international, when he was capped in 1954-55.

Gordon Simms captained the Northern Ireland Under-18 side in 1988-99.

IPSWICH TOWN

Wolves' playing record against Ipswich is:

Football League

Venue	P	W	D	L	F	A
Home	26	11	10	5	34	25
Away	26	5	3	18	25	50
Total	52	16	13	23	59	75

FA Cup

Home	4	2	1	1	4	3
Away	3	1	2	0	4	3
Total	7	3	3	1	8	6

Texaco Cup

Home	1	0	0	1	0	1
Away	1	0	0	1	1	2
Total	2	0	0	2	1	3

Wolves and Ipswich first met in the Football League in season 1961-62 and the result of the two Division One matches went in favour of the home team, Wolves winning 2-0 at Molineux but losing 3-2 at Portman Road.

Twelve goals were scored in the two matches in 1965-66: Wolves won 4-1 at Molineux but lost 5-2 at Ipswich – and all six Wolves goals were scored by different players.

Hugh Curran scored twice and Bobby Gould once in Wolves' 3-2 win at Ipswich in September 1970 and when the Suffolk side were beaten 3-1 at Molineux in March 1974 Peter Withe scored his first goal in a Wolves' shirt.

An Ipswich League double over Wolves came in season 1978-79 – both games ending 3-1 – and in the early 1990s there was a run of four draws between the clubs in three seasons.

Wolves met Ipswich five times in FA Cup football between January 1975 and February 1977. In 1993-94 after a 1-1 draw at Molineux, Wolves went to Portman Road and won the fifth-round replay 2-1 with Lee Mills and Andy Thompson on target.

Ipswich knocked Wolves out of the 1972-73 Texaco Cup after winning both legs of a second round tie.

Players with both clubs include: Len Astill, David Barnes, Ray Crawford, Danny Hegan, Derek Jefferson, Steve Sedgley, Alan Sunderland and Mark Venus.

Also associated: Bill McGarry (manager of both clubs); Sammy Chung (Assistant-manager of Town, manager of Wolves), Fred Chadwick and Fred Mitcheson (Wolves Reserves) and Jock Mulraney (Ipswich player, Wolves wartime guest).

IVERSON, Robert Thomas James

Bob Iverson was able to play as a wing-half or inside-forward, he wasn't given much of a chance at Molineux to show off his skills but after joining Aston Villa he became a firm favourite with the home fans and made over 330 appearances in the claret and blue strip (181 in wartime). Born in Folkestone on 17 October 1910, his career went as follows: Folkestone FC (August 1926), Tottenham Hotspur (August 1932), Northfleet (Spurs nursery side: 1932-33), Ramsgate, Ramsgate Press Wanderers (June 1933), Lincoln City (September 1933), Wolves (February 1935) and Aston Villa (December 1936). He retired in May 1948 to become reserve-team coach at Villa Park. Iverson guested for Birmingham, Bournemouth, Leicester City, Northampton Town, Notts County and Nottingham Forest during the war. He helped Villa win the Second Division championship in 1938 and the wartime Cup in 1944. He also found the net for Villa in just 9.3 seconds after the start of a League game against Charlton in December 1938. A keen angler and self-taught pianist, Iverson revelled in jazz. He died in Birmingham on 20 April 1953.

Wolves record: 37 apps. 7 goals.

IVILL, Edward

Ted Ivill spent only three months with Wolves (November 1932 to January 1933). Born in Little Hulton, Lancashire on 7 December 1898, he was an amateur with Bolton Wanderers and after a year with Atherton Athletic he signed professional forms for Oldham Athletic (July 1924). He had given the Latics great service, appearing in 277 games and it was thought that he was the right man to take over the left-back berth owing to an injury to Jack Smith. Alas Ivill never settled in the Midlands and after 12 weeks Wolves accepted an offer of £1,700 from Charlton Athletic and he left Molineux for the London club in January 1933 where he stayed for two years, switching to Accrington Stanley in August 1935. Ivill took over as reserve team player-coach at Peel Park and in August 1937 he left for Clitheroe where he ended his footballing career during the war. He made 331 League appearances all told. Ivill died in the Blackburn Royal Infirmary on 24 November 1979.

Wolves record: 4 apps.

JACKSON, Alan

Born in Swadlincote, Derbyshire (home town of British heavyweight boxing champion Jack Bodell) on 22 August 1938, centre-forward Alan Jackson joined Wolves as a junior in 1953 and turned professional at Molineux on his 18th birthday two years later. Initially understudy to Roy Swinbourne and Dennis Wilshaw, he was given only a handful of first-team outings by manager Stan Cullis, and owing to the form of Jimmy Murray and indeed, Barry Stobart and Bobby Mason, he subsequently left Molineux to sign for Bury in June 1959. After scoring 43 goals in 150 League outings for the Shakers he moved to Brighton and Hove Albion in November 1962 and pulled out of League action in the summer of 1964.

Wolves record: 6 apps. 2 goals.

JACKSON, Joseph G.

Born in Wolverhampton on 22 April 1966, utility forward Joe Jackson signed for Wolves as a trainee in June 1981 and became a full-time professional in August 1983. Unfortunately despite doing well at reserve and youth team level, he failed to make the grade in the senior side and was released into non-League soccer in the summer of 1984. In 1997-98 he was player-manager of Stourbridge and later took a similar position with Bilston Town.

Wolves record: 1 app.

JAMES, Ernest Josiah

Left-half Ernie James spent two seasons at Molineux where he was a diligent reserve. Born in Wolverhampton in 1885, he played for Wolverhampton Baptists and Stafford Road Juniors before joining Wolves in July 1904. On leaving Molineux he went to Langley Green (August 1906). He died in Wolverhampton c.1951.

Wolves record: 17 apps.

JEAVONS, William

Strongly built player, six feet tall and weighing 11st 5lbs, Billy Jeavons had to bide his time in the Reserves during his two years at Molineux. Born in Wolverhampton in 1886, he moved from the Hurst Hill club to Wolves in August 1907 and left Molineux for Dudley Town in October 1909, later assisting Halesowen.

Wolves record: 8 apps.

JEFFERSON, Derek

Centre or left-half Derek Jefferson was born in the North East of England in the mining village of Morpeth on 5 September 1948. He came south to East Anglia as a youngster and on leaving school joined the groundstaff at Portman Road, turning professional with Ipswich Town in January 1966. He went on to appear in 166 League and Cup games for the Portman Road club, helping them win promotion to the First Division in 1968. He left Ipswich for Wolves in October 1972 and did well during his four years at Molineux during which time he had over 50 senior outings. But soon after the team had suffered relegation (at the end of the 1975-76 campaign) he moved on, joining Hereford United in October 1976 after a month on loan to Sheffield Wednesday and a spell in the NASL. Jefferson quit League football in 1978.

Wolves record: 51+1 apps.

JOBEY, George

George Jobey's two-year reign as manager at Molineux was spent in two different Divisions. At the end of his first campaign in charge Wolves slipped into the Third Division North for the first time in the club's history, but the following year promotion was gained at the first attempt. With the former Sunderland and England international George Holley as his assistant, Jobey battled on and to his credit did an excellent job in 1923-24. Born in Heddon, near Newcastle in July 1885, he played for Morpeth Harriers, Newcastle United (1906), Woolwich Arsenal (1913), Bradford Park Avenue (1914-15), Hamilton Academical (1915-19), Leicester City (1919) and Northampton Town (as player-coach from 1920-22) prior to joining Wolves. He appeared in the 1911 FA Cup Final for Newcastle and scored the first-ever goal at Highbury – for Arsenal against Leicester Fosse in 1913. After leaving Molineux Jobey had a year out of the game before returning as manager of Derby County in 1925. He spent 16 years at the Baseball Ground. In 1941 a joint FA-Football League Commission, meeting at The Midland Hotel, Derby, found that between 1925 and 1938 Derby County Football Club had paid out illegal bonuses and inducements, balancing their books with some inventive entries. Jobey was banned from participating in football permanently and County's directors received sine die suspensions while the club itself was fined £500. Jobey's ban was lifted in 1945, yet it was not until 1952 that he re-entered football, taking over as manager of Mansfield Town, a position he held only briefly. Jobey died at Chaddesden, Derby in March 1962, aged 76.

JOHNSON, Martin

Martin Johnson was an enterprising footballer, but had far too many quality forwards to contest a place with during his short stay with Wolves. Born in Windy Nook, County Durham on 9 October 1904, Johnson played for Felling Colliery FC, Durham City (1925), Bradford Park Avenue (1925-27), Sheffield United (from June 1927) and Durham City again (July 1928) before moving to Molineux in October 1928. He left Wolves for North Shields in October 1930.

Wolves record: 8 apps. 2 goals.

JOHNSON, Thomson

Full-back Tom Johnson was a relatively unknown player from the late 1880s. Born locally c.1867, he joined Wolves July 1888 from a Wolverhampton junior club, and stayed two years with the club before moving into non-League football.

Wolves record: 1 app.

JOHNSTON, James

Outside-left Jim Johnston, despite spending three years at Molineux, made under 20 senior appearances, 15 coming in season 1892-93 when he toyed with Griffin for the left-wing position, the latter eventually playing in the FA Cup Final. Born in Edinburgh

*c.*1869, Johnston played for St Bernard's before joining Wolves in the summer of 1890. He left Molineux in May 1893 and went home to Scotland to play for East Stirlingshire.
Wolves record: 19 apps. 6 goals.

JONES, Brynmor

Inside-forward Bryn Jones was the costliest footballer in Britain when Wolverhampton Wanderers sold him to Arsenal for £14,000 in August 1938. Yet he came into League football by a most convoluted route. He was born at Penyard, Merthyr Tydfil, on 14 February 1912 and after leaving Queen's Road School, Merthyr, he worked down the pit whilst playing for Merthyr Amateurs and Plymouth United in the South Wales District League. In 1931, Southend United offered him a trial but then rejected him and instead he went to play for Glenavon in the Irish League before returning to Wales with Aberaman in August 1933. Less than eight weeks later he was a Wolves player, for a fee of £1,500, and soon made his League debut. In five years at Molineux, Jones made 177 senior appearances and scored 57 goals. He was a superb ball player who could cause havoc amongst opposing defenders. After his record transfer to Arsenal, Jones took some time to settle down and then, of course, war was on the horizon and the League shut down just after he had shown his true form, on the Gunners' 1939 summer tour to Scandinavia. During the war, Jones served in the Royal Artillery in Italy and North Africa and guested for Cardiff City. He found time to play some games for Arsenal and also added eight wartime caps for Wales to the 17 he had gained in peacetime, ten of those coming as a Wolves player. He played his last League game for Arsenal in April 1949 and altogether made 74 League and FA Cup appearances for the Gunners, scoring seven goals. He became player-coach at Norwich but retired on medical advice in 1950 and subsequently ran a newsagent's and tobacconist's shop in Stoke Newington, not far from Highbury. He died on 18 October 1985 at Wood Green, North London.
Wolves record: 177 apps. 57 goals.

JONES, Eric Norman

A Brummie, born near Villa Park on 5 February 1915, outside-right Eric Jones played his early football with Kidderminster Harriers before joining Wolves in 1936. He remained at Molineux for less than a season, quickly switching to Portsmouth and then Stoke City before teaming up with West Bromwich Albion, with whom he remained until the mid-1940s. Jones actually scored a hat-trick for the Baggies in a 3-4 home defeat against Tottenham on the eve of World War Two in September 1939. Soon afterwards the

League programme was abandoned and subsequently declared null and void. During the hostilities he guested for his former club, Portsmouth as well as Chelsea, Watford, Southend United, Tottenham Hotspur, Arsenal, Queen's Park Rangers, Nottingham Forest, Crystal Palace, Northampton Town, Fulham and Exeter City. He then signed for Brentford (1945) and in July 1946 was recruited by Crewe Alexandra, retiring out of competitive football in June 1948. He then became team manager of De Graafschap (Holland) and also acted as an FA staff coach, based at Lilleshall before becoming trainer-coach of Port Vale (June 1962). He introduced an intensive training schedule at Vale Park and kept a strict disciplinary record. Unfortunately his methods weren't to the liking of the Port Vale board and in October 1962 Jones resigned from his position for 'domestic reasons'. In his first match with Vale (a League fixture at Wrexham on 18 August 1962) Jones was hit in the face by a bottle thrown from the crowd. He was treated by first aid officials. After leaving the Potteries he went literally around ther world, coaching in some 40 different countries, including Belgium, Denmark, Egypt, Finland, Nigeria, Switzerland, Turkey, the West Indies and Zaire.
Wolves record: 3 apps.

JONES, Gwyn

Gwyn Jones was another player who found it difficult to hold down a first-team place at Molineux owing to the depth of full-back talent at the club during the time he was there. Nevertheless he stuck to his guns and always gave a good account of himself. Born in Llandwrog, mid-Wales on 20 March 1935, Jones joined Wolves from Caernarfon Town in September 1955 and left for Bristol Rovers in August 1962. He played for the Eastville club until May 1962, making 160 senior appearances.
Wolves record: 22 apps.

JONES, Harold

Outside-left Harry Jones made all his first-team appearances for Wolves in season 1910-11 when he deputised for Alf Walker. Born in Codsall in 1889, he joined the staff at Molineux in May 1909 and left the club in the summer of 1912 for Darlaston, later playing for Walsall Comrades.
Wolves record: 4 apps.

JONES, Jackery

Jack Jones was born at Wellington, Salop, on 16 March 1877, the same year that Wolverhampton Wanderers were founded, and he joined the club in 1900 from local side Lanesfield FC after first playing for Wrockwardine Wood. Jones was a fine right-back and made most of his senior appear-

Jack Jones, who made 336 appearances for Wolves.

ances for the club in that position, being an ever-present for three consecutive seasons from 1901 to 1904 and again in 1905-06 and 1906-07. He gained an FA Cup winners' medal in 1908 and teamed up first with Dick Betteley and later Ted Collins in the Wolves rearguard. Jones, who played once for the Football League (against the Irish League in 1904-05), was a Wolves regular for ten years and became trainer at Molineux after he retired from playing just after the outbreak of World War One. He was a well-known figure around the ground, always smoking his pipe and with his Cup winners' medal proudly hung from his watch chain. He was a marvellous servant to Wolverhampton Wanderers football and when he died in the town in 1945, a part of the club's history went with him.
Wolves record: 336 apps. 16 goals.

JONES, James H.

No relation to Jackery or any of the other Joneses associated with Wolves, full-back Jimmy Jones was born at Cheslyn Hay *c.*1892 and joined the Molineux staff in July 1911 from Walsall Wood junior football. He played regularly in the first team for a season, but was then, perhaps surprisingly, transferred to Shirebrook FC in September 1912 after falling out with the management at Molineux.
Wolves record: 36 apps. 1 goal.

JONES, John Joseph Alfred

Born in Wolverhampton *c.*1889, amateur full-back Jack Jones joined Wolves in August 1918 from Bristol City, having earlier been

rejected at Molineux (1913). A confident full-back, he remained with Wolves until June 1921, acting mainly as cover for George Garratly. He never wanted to turn professional and on leaving Wolves in May 1921 he became a qualified teacher, occasionally assisting Bilston Town before retiring in 1927. Jones, who attended Bristol University, died in Wolverhampton on 3 March 1940.
Wolves record: 42 apps.

JONES, Joseph William

Joe Jones (brother to Jackery above) was a Wolves player for five years: from July 1898 to May 1903. A reserve inside or outside-left, he was a very useful performer who had first Tom Worton and Billy Wooldridge and then Jack Miller ahead of him in seniority at Molineux, hence his low number of first-team outings. He did, however, make 53 Birmingham League appearances for the club, the second highest behind Tommy Green. Born in Wellington in 1880, he too played for Lanesfield.
Wolves record: 15 apps. 1 goal.

JONES, Mark

Born in Walsall on 7 September 1979, and a pupil at Idsall School, Shifnal, striker Mark Jones made his first team debut for Wolves in the Worthington League Cup first round, first leg clash against Barnet in August 1998. Capped by England at Under-17 level, he was a schoolboy footballer with Aston Villa, playing for their Under-14, 15 and 16 sides, having graduated through the Lilleshall School of Excellence. Villa claimed that Wolves 'poached' him from them and as a result the FA ordered that Wolves paid out £75,000 in compensation. Jones went into hospital in December 1998 to have a piece of floating bone removed from his left ankle but he recovered quickly only to turn down a loan move to Swindon and then rejected an extended contract offer with Wolves.
Wolves record: 0+4 apps.

JONES, Paul

Paul Jones was a tall midfielder who made over 180 appearances for Walsall before joining Wolves for £15,000 in November 1989. Born in Walsall on 9 September 1965, Jones turned professional with the Saddlers in September 1983 after two years as an apprentice. He also had a loan spell with Wrexham in March/April 1989 prior to Wolves. He was released in May 1989 and entered non-League football with Kettering Town, later assisting Stafford Rangers (from March 1992).
Wolves record: 7+8 apps.

JONES, Paul Steven

A capable goalkeeper signed as cover for Mike Stowell in July 1991 from Kidderminster Harriers for £15,000, Paul Jones was born in Chirk in mid-Wales on 18 April 1967 and played for Oswestry Boys and Shrewsbury Town as a youngster and then Bridgnorth Town prior to joining the Harriers. He made his debut for Wolves during the 1992-93 season and had a couple of spells in the team, but with Stowell in pretty good form he was transferred to Stockport County in July 1996 for £60,000, helping the Edgeley Park club win promotion from the Second Division in his first season. In the summer of 1997 Jones, after 65 games for Stockport, entered the Premiership when his former manager at Edgeley Park, Dave Jones, made him his first signing for Southampton. He won Welsh international honours whilst at The Dell and reached the milestone of 100 appearances for saints in 1998-99.
Wolves record: 44 apps.

JORDAN, David

Irishman David Jordan made his debut for Wolves against arch rivals West Bromwich Albion at The Hawthorns in October 1936 when he replaced Tom 'Pongo' Waring at centre-forward. He failed to make an impression during his brief stay at Molineux and left the club in May 1937 to join Crystal Palace. Born in Belfast c.1912, he played for Ards initially, and joined Wolves from Hull City. He returned to Ireland from Palace in October 1939, and did not play competitive football after the hostilities of World War Two.
Wolves record: 3 apps.

JORDAN, Revd William Charles

Centre-forward Billy Jordan, full of dash and vigour, was one of the many outstanding amateur footballers of his era. Born in Langley in December 1885, he won two England amateur international caps, scoring six goals against France on his debut in 1907. He played for a number of teams including Oxford University, where he was a student, Liverpool Reserves, West Bromwich Albion, for whom he starred in their 1907 FA Cup run to the semi-finals, Everton and Wolves, who acquired his services during the 1912-13 season. In 1911-12 he had been appointed curate at St Clement's Church in Nechells Green, Birmingham and thereafter devoted most of his time to the cloth, conducting several Sportsman's Services all over the country. He later worked in churches in Widnes, on the Isle of Wight, at Saltburn, Darlington and Belbroughton. In 1936 he became a director of Darlington Football Club. Jordan graduated in Natural Science at St John's College, Oxford and was ordained in 1907. He died in Belbroughton in December 1949.
Wolves record: 3 apps. 2 goals.

JUGGINS, Eleander

Wolves had Eli Juggins on their senior staff from May 1904 to June 1907. A full-back, he was reserve to Jack Jones and therefore had limited first-team football. Born in Bilston in 1879, he joined Wolves from Darlaston, having earlier starred for Willenhall Swifts, and left Molineux for Coventry City, for who he played until 1914, making over 70 appearances.
Wolves record: 22 apps.

JUVENTUS

Wolves' playing record against Juventus is:
UEFA Cup

Venue	P	W	D	L	F	A
Home	1	1	0	0	2	1
Away	1	0	1	0	1	1
Total	2	1	1	0	3	2

The great Italian club Juventus were Wolves quarter-final opponents in the 1971-72 UEFA Cup competition. The first leg in Turin on 7 March finished all square before a crowd of 35,000. This made Wolves favourites for the second leg at Molineux a fortnight later and over 40,000 turned out to see Northern Irish internationals Danny Hegan and Derek Dougan score to give the Wanderers a terrific 2-1 victory (3-2 on aggregate) and with it a place in the semi-finals.

KAY, Albert Edward

Albert Kay was a versatile defender who was born in Sheffield on 22 November 1895 and began his career with Tinsley FC and was with Birmingham from June 1919 to November 1920. He joined Wolves from Willenhall in the close season of 1921 to begin a Molineux career which lasted a decade and saw him make almost 300 senior appearances for the club. Kay was a member of the team which won the Third Division North title in 1923-24 and he also helped Wolves lift the Second Division championship in 1931-32. Kay was normally used as a defensive wing-half, but he also appeared at full-back and once in one Central League game he even kept goal in an emergency, saving a penalty in the process. Injury forced his retirement in May 1932, just after he had played his part in helping Wolves regain their First Division status. He later lived in the Tettenhall and Codsall districts of Wolverhampton and died c.1989.
Wolves record: 295 apps. 2 goals.

KEANE, Robert David

Robbie Keane made a terrific start to his Football League career – scoring twice on his Wolves debut as a 17-year-old at Norwich on 9 August 1997. A two-footed, determined, stylish and aggressive midfielder – like his namesake Roy at Manchester United – Keane was born in Dublin on 8 July 1980. He played junior football in the Republic of Ireland as a right-back with Crumlin United and Fettercairn FC (on trial) before signing YTS

forms with Wolves in June 1996. He turned professional 12 months later on his 17th birthday, agreeing a three-year contract which was later made into a five-year deal. After being capped by his country at schoolboy, Under-18, youth, Under-21 and 'B' team team levels, he then gained his first full cap and has since been a regular in the national team, setting a record by becoming Eire's youngest-ever goalscorer at the age of 18. In 1998-99 Keane, valued at £6 million by Wolves, transferred to Coventry City.
Wolves record: 74+10 apps. 27 goals.

KEARNS, Michael

Born in Banbury on 25 November 1950 goalkeeper Mick Kearns, six feet tall and 14 stones in weight, was a commanding figure between the posts. He joined Oxford United as a youngster and turned professional at the Manor Ground in July 1968. He made 67 League appearances for the 'U's; before transferring to Walsall in July 1973 after loan spells with both Plymouth Argyle and Charlton Athletic during the 1972-73 season. He performed supremely well for the Saddlers and made almost 300 appearances for the club (having one spell when he missed only five matches out of a possible 293) before signing for Wolves in July 1979 as cover for Paul Bradshaw. He made his First Division debut in the local derby with neighbours West Bromwich Albion and saved a penalty in the 0-0 draw at The Hawthorns in April 1980. Two-and-a-half years later (in August 1982) Kearns returned to Fellows Park for a second spell and later on he came back for a third spell as a non-contract player while working as a steward at a local Working Mens' Club in nearby Aldridge. In 1990 Kearns was appointed Walsall's Community officer and he did a terrific job with in the schools and youth clubs around the area. He kept himself supremely fit by playing in various charity matches and was in goal when the West Bromwich Albion All Stars won the over 35 Cup Final at Wembley in August 1992. During his Football League career Kearns, who won 18 caps for the Republic of Ireland (a record 15 with Walsall) and whose brother, Ollie, was also a professional footballer, playing with him at Walsall, amassed a total of 356 League appearances. He was also a very fine handicap golfer who won the Midland Professional Footballers' Golf Championship in 1977, while in May 1992 he established an international record for a soccer player by holing-in-one at a course in Scotland, having previously done likewise in both England and Ireland.
Wolves record: 10 apps.

KEEN, Kevin Ian

Hardworking right-sided midfield player with good pace and excellent vision, Kevin

Keen was born in Amersham on 25 February 1967 and played for West Ham United from 1982 (first as an apprentice and then as a professional, March 1984) until moving to Molineux in July 1993 for £600,000 after more than 275 appearances for the Hammers (30 goals scored). A former England schoolboy and youth international, he was sold by Wolves to Stoke City for £300,000 in October 1994 at a time when the Potters' engine-room needed stoking up. And he did a useful job before losing his place in the side in 1996. Keen's father, Mike, led Queen's Park Rangers to victory League Cup Final at Wembley and to the Third Division title in the 1966-67 season.
Wolves record: 48+6 apps. 9 goals.

KEELEY, Arthur

Outside-right Arthur Keeley had one season at Molineux. Born in Cheshire in 1915, he joined Wolves from Ellesmere Port in the summer of 1936, but never settled at Molineux and in May 1937 was transferred to Bournemouth. From Dean Court he moved to Chester (1938) and was on Portsmouth's books when he was sadly killed in action during World War Two.
Wolves record: 2 apps.

KEETLEY, Joseph Frederick S.

Joe Keetley was one of 11 brothers, the others being Bill, Albert, John, Arthur, Frank, Tom, Harold and Charlie, Lawrence and Sidney. All of them except Lawrence and Sidney played League football at various levels. Joe himself was a fine goalscoring inside-forward who was with Wolves at the same time as some other exceptionally quality marksmen and this limited his senior outings. Wanting regular first-team football, he left the club after only six months. Born in Derby on 28 June 1897, Keetley played for Victoria Ironworks, Bolton Wanderers (1920), Accrington Stanley (June 1923) and Liverpool (November 1923) before joining Wolves in May 1925. He left Molineux for Wrexham (November 1925) and later assisted Doncaster Rovers (March 1926) and Horwich RMI (1928) before retiring in 1933. He died at Allenton, Derby on 30 March 1958.
Wolves record: 10 apps. 5 goals
NB. Three of the Keetley brothers were in Doncaster's team in February 1926 – Joe joined them the following month but all four never played together.

KELLOCK, William

Billy Kellock was a powerful midfielder, born in Glasgow on 7 February 1954, who won Schoolboy caps for Scotland and represented Glasgow Boys before joining Aston Villa as an apprentice in 1970. From Villa Park he became something of a soccer nomad, serv-

ing with Cardiff City (February 1972), Norwich City (June 1973), Millwall (£25,000, July 1974), Chelmsford City (1975), Kettering Town (1977), Peterborough United (£30,000, August 1979) and Luton Town (£30,000, July 1982) before arriving at Molineux in March 1983 for £20,000. He spent just six months with Wolves, transferring to Southend United in September 19083 and later assisting Port Vale (December 1984), Halifax Town (July 1985) and Kettering Town (again). In his senior career, Kellock scored well over 80 goals in more than 350 senior appearances (78 in 298 outings in the Football League).
Wolves record: 12 apps. 3 goals.

KELLY, David Thomas

When Republic of Ireland striker David Kelly joined Wolves from Newcastle United in July 1993, for £750,000 he had just helped the Magpies gain promotion to the Premiership. Yet Kelly was really coming home to the West Midlands, for he was born in Birmingham on 25 November 1965 and played for Alvechurch and Walsall before becoming the Saddlers' record outgoing signing when West Ham United bought him for £600,000 in August 1988. It was his goalscoring prowess that had persuaded the Hammers to pay that kind of money: top scorer for Walsall in 1986-87 (26 goals) and 1987-88 (30 goals) when a superb hat-trick in the Play-off Final against Bristol City clinched promotion from the Third Division. Kelly netted 80 goals in 190 League and Cup games for Walsall and for West Ham, he scored 14 in 64 outings before being transferred to Leicester City in March 1990 for £300,000. For Leicester he netted 25 goals in 75 appearances before Newcastle bought him for £250,000 in December 1991. After helping the Magpies stave off relegation that season, his League tally of 35 goals in 70 League games proved crucial when promotion was gained from Division One in 1992-93 – and in all matches for Newcastle, Kelly claimed 39 goals in 83 appearances. At Wolves Kelly did well alongside Steve Bull, notching 14 goals in 1993-94 to be second-highest scorer next to Bull, who missed a large part of the season of course; and the top-scored in 1994-95 with a total of 22 including a second-half hat-trick in a 5-1 win at Bristol City in November. However, after over two years at Molineux, Kelly was transferred to Sunderland for a record fee of £995,000. Unfortunately he suffered injury problems at Roker Park and at the end of the 1996-97 season he left to join Tranmere Rovers. In 1998-99 Kelly reached the milestone of 600 senior appearances, having earlier passed the 200 goals barrier. He won 26 full caps, three for the Eire 'B' team, one at Under-21 level and three with the Under-23s. In November 1987 Kelly declined an invitation to play for the England Under-21 side; a week later he made his debut for the Republic of Ireland.

Wolves record: 96+7 apps. 36 goals.

KELLY, James

Born in Aldergrove, Northern Ireland on 6 February 1954, winner Jimmy Kelly played for Cliftonville before joining Wolves in December 1971. He spent seven years at Molineux, but never really established himself in the first team and actually had a loan spell with Wrexham in 1975 before moving to Walsall in August 1978. After a spell in the NASL (with team-mates Phil Parkes and Derek Jefferson). He later returned to Ireland.

One interesting point is that Kelly made his debut for Wolves against Sheffield United in February 1974 and did not play another game until March 1976, ironically against the Blades.

Wolves record: 21+ 2 apps. no goals.

KELLY, James

A Liverpudlian, born on 14 February 1973, midfielder Jimmy Kelly – no relation to the Kelly above – was signed by Wolves from Wrexham in part-exchange deal involving John Paskin in February 1992. Joining the Welsh club as an apprentice, he turned professional on his 18th birthday and played 22 League games for the Racecourse Ground club before switching to Molineux. In February 1996 Kelly, who was on loan to Walsall in March/April 1993, was sentenced to five years in jail (spending some in Sudbury Open Prison, Derbyshire) for his part in the manslaughter, in September 1994, of doorman Peter Dunphy outside the Bradford Hotel in Liverpool. In October 1997, Kelly was allowed out of prison on licence and he went straight back into football – joining the groundstaff of Vauxhall Conference side Hednesford Town, although he was not allowed to play for the non-League club being a serving prisoner. Kelly was released in October 1998 and he quickly established himself in the Pitmens' first team.

Wolves record: 5+3 apps.

KELLY, James Philip V.

During his career Jimmy Kelly won five caps for the Republic of Ireland and as well as amassing almost 150 senior appearances for Wolves and Norwich City – his two major clubs. A neat footballer with good passing ability, he was a steady rather than a quality full-back. Born in Dublin on 10 July 1939, he played for Sheldon Town (Birmingham) and Brockhill FC before joining Wolves as a professional in September 1957, signed by manager Stan Cullis as cover for Eddie Stuart, Gerry Harris and George Showell. He spent five years at Molineux before transferring to

Carrow Road in August 1962. From there he went to Lowestoft Town (May 1967) later becoming player-coach of the non-League club. He now lives in East Anglia.

Wolves record: 18 apps.

KELLY, Lawrence

Local lad Larry Kelly gave Wolves good service at left-back after making his League debut in December 1947, but made a much greater impact after he moved to Huddersfield Town. Kelly, who was born in Wolverhampton on 28 April 1925, joined Wolves as an amateur in 1940 and became a full-time professional in April 1945 – having skippered the side in season 1942-43 as a 17-year-old – possibly Wolves' youngest-ever skipper, and guested for Halifax Town. In his first season in the League side he helped Wolves finish fifth in the First Division, but the following campaign was injured in the first match of the FA Cup semi-final against Manchester United at Hillsborough and missed the Cup Final when Wolves beat Leicester. In October 1950, Huddersfield Town, looking to rebuild their side, paid £10,500 for his services and he went on to make 239 League and Cup appearances for the Town. Of course, there was not the wealth of competition that had held him back at Molineux and Kelly was first-choice at Leeds Road for six seasons, being a key figure in their 1952-53 Second Division championship side. At the end of 1955-56 Huddersfield were back in Division Two and Kelly, now 30, was thinking about his future. He became player-manager of Nuneaton in May 1957, although he spent only a few months in the job. Wolves awarded him a £750 benefit cheque when he left Molineux.

Wolves record: 70 apps.

KELLY, Robert A.

Born in Birmingham on 21 December 1964, midfielder Robert Kelly joined Leicester City as a junior at the age of 16 and became a full-time professional at Filbert Street in December 1982. A competitive performer, who loved to drive forward, he was registered with the Foxes for five years but made only 24 League appearances before transferring to Wolves in March 1987 having earlier had a loan spell with Tranmere Rovers (December 1984). He struggled with his form and fitness at Molineux and in August 1990 moved on to Burton Albion. He was forced to give the game up two years later when he returned to Molineux to join the club's backroom staff. He then moved to Watford with his coaching partner at Wolves Bobby Downes, and when Downes switched north to Blackburn Rovers in May 1997, he was quickly joined by Kelly, both men working under Rovers' new boss, Roy Hodgson.

Wolves record: 16+4 apps. 3 goal

KEMP, Frederick G.

Fred Kemp was an eager-beaver, all-action midfielder, who failed to make the grade in the top flight, but afterwards certainly did the business in the lower Divisions. Born in Salerno, Italy on 27 February 1946 (his parents stayed over there following World War Two), Kemp joined Wolves as a teenager in the summer of 1961 on leaving his school in Exeter. He turned professional at Molineux in June 1963 and two years later was transferred to Southampton. In November 1970 Kemp went north to Blackpool for £35,000 and in December 1971 he switched to Halifax Town, staying at The Shay until signing for his last League club, Hereford United, in July 1974. He dropped out of the big time in August 1976 when he joined Telford United with whom he stayed until May 1978. After that Kemp often played in local Charity matches. He accumulated more than 220 senior appearances of which 111 came in the League with Halifax Town.

Wolves record: 3 apps.

KENDALL, Mark

Goalkeeper Mark Kendall joined Wolves from Newport County in December 1986 and at the end of the season was playing in the Fourth Division Play-off Final against Aldershot, which the Shots won on aggregate. The following season, of course, Wolves went up as champions and were champions again 12 months later to complete a meteoric rise from the old Fourth to Second Divisions. Kendall shared in all these glories. He appeared in 177 senior matches for Wolves, set a club record of 28 clean sheets in 1987-88, kept 15 clean sheets in 1988-89, gained those two championship medals, and a Sherpa Van Trophy winners' medal in 1988.

Marl Kendall, 177 appearances for Wolves.

Kendall, who was born in Blackwood, Wales, on 20 September 1958, won Welsh Schoolboy caps and then signed as an apprentice for Spurs in 1974. He became a full-timer in July 1976 and made 36 senior appearances, also winning a Welsh Under-21 cap, before Newport signed him for £25,000 in September 1980 after a loan spell at Chesterfield. At Somerton Park he made 319 League and Cup appearances before Graham Turner signed him for Wolves. Kendall left Wolves for Swansea in May 1990 and in 1991-92 he had a loan spell with Barnsley, but quit football at the end of that season to join the police force (now serving in Ebbw Vale). He made more than 600 first-team appearances during his footballing career.
Wolves record: 177 apps.

KENNING, Michael John

Born in Erdington, Birmingham on 18 August 1940, Mike Kenning played on the wing for Brockhill FC before taking amateur status with Aston Villa in 1957. He signed part-time professional forms in 1958 and became full-time in October 1959. In May 1961, after failing to make an impact at Villa Park, he was transferred to Shrewsbury Town; Charlton Athletic secured his services for £10,500 in November 1982 and in December 1966 he went to Norwich City for £27,000. Wolves attained Kenning's services for £35,000 in January 1968, but he spent just over a year at Molineux before switching back to Charlton for £20,000 in March 1969. After one game for Queen's Park Rangers (May 1971) he assisted Watford from January 1972 to May 1973 before trying his luck in South Africa. He returned to England to sign for Atherstone Town in 1974, but four years later returned to South Africa to become player-manager of Germiston Callies, later taking charge of Durban United and then Wilts University. In 1986, after quitting football, Kenning was employed as a representative for a South African safety equipment company. All told he played in some 450 League and Cup games and scored almost 100 goals during his senior footballing career.
Wolves record: 40+6 apps. 6 goals.

KENT, Michael J.

Born in North Anston, near Dinnington on 12 January 1951, central defender Mick Kent played for Wolves' Yorkshire-based nursery side, Wath Wanderers, before signing professional forms at Molineux in August 1968. He hardly figured in the club's first team plans and after a couple of substitute appearances was transferred to Sheffield Wednesday in September 1973 following a loan spell with Gillingham (March/April 1971). He was not retained at Hillsborough for the 1973-74 season and moved into non-League football.
Wolves record: 0+2 apps.

KERNAN, Anthony Patrick

Tony Kernan was born in Letterkenny, Ireland on 31 August 1963 and played at youth team level for the Republic of Ireland during his early years at Molineux. He signed for Wolves as a junior, turned professional at the age of 17 (January 1981) but was not retained for the 1982-83 season.
Wolves record: 1 app.

KERR, Robert C.

Centre-forward Bobby Kerr had a fine scoring record with Wolves, averaging almost a goal every two games. Born in Leicester in 1904, he was recruited from Oadby Town in the summer of 1925 and stayed at Molineux for two years before transferring to Clapton Orient in July 1927. He later played for Kettering and Grantham.
Wolves record: 18 apps. 7 goals.

KILMARNOCK

Wolves' playing record against Killie is:

Texaco Cup

Venue	P	W	D	L	F	A
Home	1	1	0	0	5	1
Away	1	0	1	0	0	0
Total	2	1	1	0	5	1

During September 1972 Wolves played Kilmarnock twice in the Texaco Cup. At Molineux a crowd of 8,734 saw Wolves win 5-1 with two goals apiece for John Richards and Derek Dougan. The return game at Rugby Park finished goalless before 4,435 fans.

Wolves beat Kilmarnock 3-2 and 3-0 in a soccer tournament in the USA in the summer of 1969. And on their return to England the Scottish club lost 1-0 to Wolves in a friendly at Molineux (August 1969).

Player associated with both clubs: George Waddell (Wolves Reserves).

KINDON, Steven

Bustling forward Steve Kindon always let opposing defenders know he was there with his all-action display of brave attacking football, but he was also a skilful performer and when used as an orthodox outside-left, he left many a full-back in his wake. He was born in Warrington on 17 December 1950 and joined Burnley as an apprentice after leaving school in July 1965. He became a full-time professional on his 17th birthday and made his League debut for the Clarets during 1968-69. The following season he was part of a Burnley team whose average age was only 22, the youngest ever to represent the club, and whilst at Turf Moor, Kindon was also capped for England Youth. After more than 120 senior games for Burnley, he was transferred to Wolves for £100,000 in July 1972 and scored on his debut, against Newcastle United in the opening game of the 1972-73 season. But it was only in 1974-75 that

Kindon could be sure of his place. Thereafter he was in and out again, and in November 1977 returned to Burnley for £80,000. He spent two more seasons at Turf Moor and had three terms with Huddersfield Town before retiring as a player. Kindon's overall League record was a good one – 109 goals in 396 League games and in 1976 he won a 75-metre sprint race for professional footballers. After hanging up his boots he stayed in football, having a successful five-year association as promotions manager with Huddersfield Town. He then quit soccer to become a successful after dinner speaker, a role he is still enjoying today.
Wolves record: 131+36 apps. 31 goals.

KING, Andrew Edward

Midfielder Andy King had an excellent career in League football. Born in Luton on 14 August 1956, he represented Luton and Dunstable Schools, Bedfordshire Boys and Stopsley Youths and had unsuccessful trials with Tottenham Hotspur before signing apprentice forms for the Hatters as a 16-year-old, turning professional at Kenilworth Road in July 1974. He went on to appear in 33 League games for Luton before transferring to Everton for £35,000 in March 1976. During his four years at Goodison Park he amassed 151 First Division appearances and scored 38 goals, helping the Merseysiders get into the UEFA Cup for the 1978-79 season. In September 1980 King moved to Queen's Park Rangers for £425,000; 12 months later he joined West Bromwich Albion for £400,000 and was a member of the Baggies' FA Cup semi-final side (v QPR) in 1982 before returning to Goodison Park in July 1982 in an exchange deal which involved former Wolves man Peter Eastoe plus £250,000. In August 1984 King went over to Holland to sign for S.C. Cambuur, returning to England to sign for Wolves in January 1985. He spent 11 months at Molineux (finishing up as top scorer in 1985-86 under Bill McGarry) having had a loan spell with Orebo FC (Sweden) (April/May 1985). He rejoined his first love, Luton Town, in December 1985 and later assisted Aldershot (August 1986), Aylesbury 1988), Waterford (as player-manager from August 1988), Cobh Ramblers (January 1989) and Southport (August 1989). He then chose to return to Kenilworth Road as commercial manager and moved back into football management with Mansfield Town in November 1993, holding that position at Field Mill until September 1996 when he was replaced by another ex-West Brom player, Steve Parkin. In his League career King amassed exactly 350 appearances and scored almost 100 goals. He was capped twice by England at Under-21 level.
Wolves record: 30 apps. 10 goals.

KING, Frederick A. Robert

Winger Bob King was the first official transfer during World War Two, joining Wolves from Northampton Town for £2,000 in November 1939. He never played competitive League football for Wolves (owing to the war) but nevertheless he still had a useful career. Born in Northampton on 9 September 1919, he played for his home town club, Northampton Town from 1937 and returned there after the war (1947-50) having guested for Leicester City and Manchester City. He later assisted Rushden.

KINSEY, George

Wing-half George Kinsey spent the best part of his playing career with Wolves, gaining an FA Cup winners' medal and playing twice for England. Kinsey was born at Burton upon Trent on 20 June 1866 and played for Burton Crusaders, Burton Swifts and Mitchell St George's before joining Wolves in August 1891. He was a dominating figure at left-half and had a magnificent game for Wolves in the 1893 FA Cup Final against Everton before being transferred to Aston Villa in June 1894. The move to Villa Park did not work out for Kinsey and less than a year later he was on the move again, this time to Derby County. He was an ever-present in his first season with Derby, in what was their first campaign at the Baseball Ground, and at the end of 1895-96 the Rams were League championship runners-up and had reached another FA Cup semi-final, where Kinsey had a good game against Wolves. He played twice more for England and after a short spell with Notts County he helped establish Bristol Rovers (who were then Eastville Rovers) in the Southern League after joining them when they were in the Birmingham and District League. In 1900, Kinsey rejoined Burton Swifts and in 1902 was playing for Burton Early Closing FC, being reinstated as an amateur in 1904. He died on 10 January 1911.
Wolves record: 83 apps. 3 goals.

KIRKHAM, John K.

Johnny Kirkham was born at Wednesbury on 13 May 1941 and signed for Wolves as a 15-year-old (June 1956). He did so well that Wanderers took him on as a full-time professional and he made his League debut in 1959, making more of an impression in the 1961-62 season when he made 29 appearances, most at right-half in place of the injured Eddie Clamp. That season he scored in consecutive games, two goals against Forest at Molineux and then a goal at Old Trafford against Manchester United. Eventually, Freddie Goodwin was installed and in May 1965, after appearing in the last 12 League games of the relegation season, Kirkham signed for Peterborough United, and after leaving Posh he went to Exeter City

in July 1968 before dropping into non-League football with Horwich RMI in May 1969. With Wolves, Kirkham won England Youth and Under-23 caps.
Wolves record: 112 apps. 15 goals.

KIRKHAM, Reginald John

Reg Kirkham was a Wolves player during the last two League seasons leading up to World War Two. An outside-left with good pace, he was born in Ormskirk, Lancashire, on 8 May 1919, and joined the Wanderers in early August 1937 from Ellesmere Port Town. He left Molineux for Bournemouth in October 1938 and stayed at Dean Court throughout the war when he also guested for Clapton Orient and Notts County. In March 1947 he joined Burnley and retired in 1951.
Wolves record: 15 apps. 5 goals.

KNIGHT, Thomas

One of the early stars of the Wolves side, Tommy Knight could play in any forward position, but preferred the inside-right berth. Strong and powerful, he loved to dribble, head down with the ball and occasionally upset his colleagues by doing this far too much. Born in Wolverhampton 1864 Knight joined Wolves in the summer of 1886 from Pickwick. He stayed with the Wanderers until May 1890, although his career came to an abrupt end in September 1889 when he was injured playing against Stoke when occupying the right-back position (in an emergency). He had the pleasure of scoring in Wolves' first home League win – a 4-1 victory over Burnley in September 1888.
Wolves record: 33 apps. 17 goals.

KNIGHTON, Kenneth

Wing-half Ken Knighton was born in Mexborough on 20 February 1944. The tall, blond-haired Yorkshireman, who excelled in both attack and defence, joined Wolves as a junior in July 1960 and turned professional at Molineux in February 1961, having had a few games for the club's junior side, Wath Wanderers. He failed to establish himself in the Wolves' first team and was subsequently transferred to Oldham Athletic for £12,000 in November 1966, later assisting Preston North End (signed for £35,000 in November 1967), Blackburn Rovers (for a fee of £45,000 in June 1969), Hull City (for £60,000 in March 1971) and finally Sheffield Wednesday (for £50,000 from August 1973 to January 1976). He then took over as coach at Sunderland before becoming manager at Roker Park in June 1979, a position he held until April 1981. Six months later Knighton took over as boss of Leyton Orient and remained at Brisbane Road until May 1983. he later managed Dagenham (1984-85) before drifting out of football to settle in He made almost 400 appearances at senior level.

In the summer of 1969 Knighton went to New Zealand with the FA touring party. Some fans thought Knighton resembled Ron Flowers on the field.
Wolves record: 13+3 apps.

KNOWLES, Peter

A huge favourite with the girls, Peter Knowles was born at Fitzwilliam near Frickley, Yorkshire, on 30 September 1945 and came through the Wolves ranks via their nursery side Wath Wanderers before signing professional forms at Molineux, under Stan Cullis's managership, in October 1962. After accompanying the club on their USA/Canadian tour in May/June 1963, he made his League debut against Leicester City 12 months after signing as a full-time professional, and then became an established member of the first team in 1964-65. The previous Easter he had scored in England's 4-0 victory over Spain in the Final of an international youth tournament in Amsterdam. In 1965-66 he top-scored with 21 League and Cup goals in 33 games which included two hat-tricks. When Wolves won promotion back to the old First Division in 1966-67, Knowles contributed eight goals in 21 matches as they finished runners-up to Coventry City. Capped four times at Under-23 level, Knowles looked destined for even more success, but in September 1969 he dropped a bombshell on Molineux by announcing that he was turning his back on the game to become a Jehovah's Witness. He was only 24 years of age at the time and his sudden departure from football was a shock to Wolves fans young and old – and indeed to the club itself. Wolves retained Knowles' registration for several years after his departure – in anticipation that he might change his mind and return to the club. Unfortunately he never did. In 1991, a song entitled *God's Footballer* by Billy Bragg featured Knowles and ended with commentary describing one of the many goals he scored for Wolves. His brother Cyril was a full-back with Tottenham Hotspur and managed Hartlepool United before dying prematurely after suffering a brain tumour.
Wolves record: 188+3 apps. 64 goals.

KUBICKI, Daruisz

Experienced Polish international full-back Dariusz Kubicki was born in Warsaw on 6 June 1963 and made his senior debut for Wolves (with Robbie Keane) in a 2-0 Nationwide League win at Norwich City on the opening day of the 1997-98 season following his free transfer from Sunderland four days earlier. A fine player, who enjoys to get forward, he moved into English football from Legia Warsaw in August 1991 when he joined Aston Villa for £200,000. He played in 34 games for the West Midlands club before

transferring to Sunderland for £100,000 in March 1994. During his time at Roker Park, Kubicki made over 150 senior appearances and helped the Wearsiders reach the Premiership, but he was then surprisingly released after they suffered relegation in 1997. Two months after returning to Molineux from a loan spell with Tranmere Rovers (March 1998) Kubicki moved back north to sign for Carlisle United on a free transfer.
Wolves record: 16 apps.

LAKING, George Edward

Full-back George Laking was born at Harthill, near Sheffield on 17 March 1913 and played initially for Kiveton Park and Dinnington FC before joining Wolves in May 1934. His best season at Molineux was in 1935-36 when he made 20 appearances as partner to Cecil Shaw. Unable to hold down a regular place in the team, he was transferred to Middlesbrough in October 1936. During the hostilities he guested for Doncaster Rovers, Leeds United, Sheffield United and Sheffield Wednesday and played just once more for 'Boro in 1946-47 before rounding off his career with Shrewsbury Town, although he only made the odd appearance for the Shrews at non-League level. He, in fact, played more cricket than football and was a key member of the Minor Counties side, Shropshire. Laking, who had almost 100 outings for Middlesbrough, was a property repairer by trade. He died in Codsall on 5 June 1997, aged 84.
Wolves record: 29 apps.

LANGE, Anthony Stephen

Goalkeeper Tony Lange was born in West Ham on 10 December 1964, and started his League career with Charlton Athletic in December 1982. After two spells with Aldershot (one on loan) he joined Wolves for £150,000 in July 1989. In 1990 he returned to Aldershot, again on loan, and also assisted Torquay United, Portsmouth and Cheltenham Town (all on loan) before transferring to West Bromwich Albion in August 1992. A good shot-stopper, he helped the Baggies win the Second Division Play-off Final at Wembley the following year and in August 1995 switched to Fulham, who went on to gain promotion from Division Three in his second season at Craven Cottage. Lange, released by Fulham in May 1994, later played for St Leonard's (Sussex).
Wolves record: 10 apps.

LANGFORD, Thomas Sidney

Born in Wolverhampton in November 1892, Tom Langley attended Stafford Road school, but he went to Wales following his employment and became a prolific marksman with Bargoed FC, topping their scoring charts when they won the South Wales League in

1913-14. This sort of form prompted Wolves to secure his services in July 1914, but unfortunately World War One interrupted his progress at Molineux and sadly his footballing career ended abruptly after the hostilities when he failed to re-sign for Wolves. He died in April 1960.
Wolves record: 7 apps. 3 goals.

LANGLEY, Thomas William

Londoner Tommy Langley was born in Lambeth on 8 February 1958 and was first associated with Chelsea at the age of 10. He played for the colts side when he was 12 and after winning England Schoolboy honours, he joined the Stamford Bridge club as an apprentice, turning professional in April 1975. An out and out striker, he was subsequently capped by his country at Youth, Under-21 and 'B' team levels, and then went on to score 40 goals in 142 League games for the Blues before transferring to QPR in August 1980. The following March he moved to neighbouring Crystal Palace and after a brief spell in Greece with AEK Athens he teamed up with Coventry City (March 1984). It was from Highfield Road that he joined Wolves (July 1984), but his stay at Molineux was short-lived, and after a loan spell with Aldershot (March 1985) and a sojourn in Hong Kong, he signed for Aldershot in August 1986. A season with Exeter City followed (1988-89) and thereafter Langley played for Billericay Town and Slough Town. He scored 86 goals in 348 League games.
Wolves record: 26+2 apps. 4 goals.

LANGLEY, William B.

Wolves recruited reserve centre-forward Billy Langley from Tunbridge Wells Rangers in the summer of 1936. He played intermediate football during his first season at Molineux and then had a handful of senior outings in 1937-38, but was released in May 1938 when he joined Bournemouth, later assisting Poole Town. Langley was born in Wolverhampton c.1918.
Wolves record: 7 apps. 3 goals.

LAW, Brian John

Central defender, born in Merthyr on New Year's Day 1970, Brian Law signed as a trainee with QPR in June 1986 and turned professional at Loftus Road in August 1987. Capped by Wales at senior, Under-21, youth and schoolboy levels, he actually decided to quit soccer at one stage, but in December 1994 was persuaded to change his mind when, after an unsuccessful trial with Millwall, Wolves boss Graham Taylor bought him to Molineux for £134,000. After a brief loan spell with Oldham Athletic (February 1997) he was released by new boss Mark McGhee three months later and surprisingly joined Millwall in July 1997.
Wolves record: 34+6 apps. 1 goal.

LAWRENCE, Joseph

Outside-right Joe Lawrence was a reserve at Molineux for two seasons: 1891-93. Born in Willenhall c.1871, he joined Wolves from Wolverhampton Rangers, but was given little opportunity in the first team and he left the club for Darlaston in the summer of 1893.
Wolves record: 2 apps.

LAX, George

Yorkshireman George Lax was a short, stocky half-back, hard-working who spent four seasons at Molineux, from June 1929 to October 1931. A Yorkshireman, born in South Emsall, near Pontefract in 1905, he played initially for Frickley Colliery and after leaving Molineux returned to his native Yorkshire to sign for Barnsley. In 1933 he surprisingly left Oakwell and moved due south to play for Bournemouth, from where he entered non-League football with Worcester City in 1934, later going to Ireland to assist Bohemians. He retired in 1938 to continue his work as a coalminer back home.
Wolves record: 66 apps. 1 goal.

LAYTON, G. William

Outside-right Billy Layton was at Molineux for three years. He joined Wolves from Shrewsbury Town in August 1904 and left the club in the summer of 1906. Born in Newtown c.1881, he also assisted Wolverhampton Swifts and Willenhall Pickwick.
Wolves record: 34 apps. 4 goals.

LAZARUS, Mark

Mark Lazarus was a powerfully built outside-right, a former boxer (unbeaten in 10 fights). He was born in Stepney, London on 5 December 1938 and on leaving school he joined Barking and entered the Football League as a professional with Leyton Orient in November 1957. Over the next 15 years he amassed more than 400 senior appearances, playing also for Queen's Park Rangers (in three separate spells), Wolves from September 1961 to February 1962 (34 of his family came to Molineux to see him make his debut in the gold and black strip against Cardiff City), Brentford, Crystal Palace and Orient (again), finally pulling out of top-line soccer in 1972. He won a League Cup winners tankard with QPR in 1967, scoring a dramatic winner against West Bromwich Albion in that competition's first Wembley Final. Lazarus was with a promoted London club in four successions seasons – QPR in 1966-67 and again in 1967-68, Crystal Palace in 1968-69 and Leyton Orient in 1969-70. Whenever Lazarus moved from one club to another it was always during the season, never in the summer period. Lazarus's departure from Molineux followed a heated discussion with manager Stan Cullis after he had been dropped for a game at West Ham. Lazarus now runs a removal firm in Romford, Essex. His two brothers Harry and Lew were the famous Lazar boxers and his son, Nicky, is a former snooker professional. *Wolves record: 9 apps. 3 goals.*

LAZIO

Wolves played Italy's Serie 'A' side Lazio twice in the 1970 Anglo-Italian Tournament. A goal by Mike Bailey gave Wolves a 1-0 win at Molineux on 9 May when under 12,000 fans turned up and in the return fixture which was played in Italy later in the month, Lazio won 2-0 in front of a 43,073 crowd.

LEA, Thomas (Tansey)

Outside-right Tansey Lea was a member of Wolves' 1921 FA Cup Final team against Tottenham Hotspur. A willing player, he signed for the club in July 1913 from Oswestry in 1913 and spent nine years at Molineux, playing either side of World War One but getting limited opportunities until 1919. He left the club in May 1922, signing for Bristol Rovers, where he played for two seasons, making over 50 appearances. He then had a brief spell with Shrewsbury. Born in Oswestry in 1893, Lea returned to Shropshire on retiring in 1924. *Wolves record: 58 apps. 4 goals.*

LEADBEATER, Richard

Born in Gornal on 21 October 1977, Richard Leadbeater, a 6ft 1in. forward, joined the Molineux playing staff on a YTS in June 1994, turned professional in October 1996, but after a loan spell with Hereford United (December 1997 and immediately scored a hat-trick for the Bulls against Kidderminster Harriers) he failed to make an impression during his two years with Wolves and was given a free transfer in May 1998 when he signed for Hereford on a permanent basis. In February 1999 Leadbetter moved from Edgar Street to Stevenage Borough for £20,000. *Wolves record: 0+1 app.*

LECCE

Wolves met the Italian Serie 'B' side in a preliminary round of the Anglo-Italian Cup in 1994-95. The game was played in Italy and Wolves won 1-0 with a late goal by David Kelly. The attendance was a meagre 1,795.

LEE, Colin

As a player, Colin Lee was a very useful striker, who later became a confident defender. Born in Torquay, Devon on 12 June 1956, he was educated in Torbay and joined Bristol City as an apprentice in 1972, turning professional at Ashton Gate in July 1974. A loan spell with Hereford United four months later was followed by a similar spell with his native Torquay in February 1975 before he trans-

ferred to Tottenham Hotspur in October 1977, quickly scoring four goals on his debut for the London club against Bristol Rovers in a Second Division match. He went on to notch a total of 31 goals in 94 appearances for Spurs and helped them win promotion back to the top flight before switching to Chelsea for £200,000 in June 1980. In July 1987 – after winning another Second Division championship medal and a Full Members Cup medal at Wembley – he became a player and youth development officer at Brentford (linking up with his former Spurs colleague Steve Perryman). His next job saw him appointed Watford's youth team manager in July 1989 and between March and November 1990 he was team manager at Vicarage Road. Lee himself was replaced at Watford by Perryman. In July 1991 he was on the march again, this time to Reading as their youth development officer. And it was at Elm Park where he teamed up with Mark McGhee and he followed the Scot to Filbert Street and then on to Wolves, eventually taking over as boss at Molineux in November 1998 when McGhee was dismissed.

LEEDS CITY

Wolves' playing record against City is:

Football League

Venue	P	W	D	L	F	A
Home	10	7	1	2	30	14
Away	10	1	3	6	10	23
Total	20	8	4	8	40	37

Wolves registered two 5-0 home victories over City – in November 1909 when George Hedley scored twice, and in December 1911 when Irishman Billy Halligan netted two fine goals. Wolves also won 5-1 at Molineux in April 1915.

Leeds also ran up a 5-0 scoreline over Wolves at Elland Road in February 1914 and they won 5-2 again at home in December 1908. All 20 League encounters took place in the Second Division between 1906 and 1919. In fact, after they had beaten Wolves 4-2 at Molineux on 4 October 1919, City disbanded by the order of the FA and their fixtures were taken over by Port Vale, thus their last-ever League game was against the Wanderers.

Player with both clubs: Billy Halligan, Tommy Mulholland and George Swift.

Also associated: Tom Mayson (Leeds guest).

LEEDS UNITED

Wolves' playing record against United is:

Football League

Venue	P	W	D	L	F	A
Home	35	17	9	9	59	36
Away	35	6	8	21	28	59
Total	70	23	17	30	87	95

FA Cup

Venue	P	W	D	L	F	A
Home	4	0	2	2	3	6
Away	3	1	0	2	2	4
Neutral	1	0	0	1	0	1
Total	8	1	2	5	5	11

ZDSC

Venue	P	W	D	L	F	A
Home	1	0	0	1	1	2

Wolves' best ever win over Leeds United is 6-2 at Molineux in a First Division match on St Valentine's Day in February 1959. Wolves, who had netted 13 goals in their previous three homes games, were rampant again, with Jimmy Murray, Peter Broadbent and Norman Deeley each scoring twice.

On the last day of the 1971-72 season (8 May) Leeds travelled to Molineux needing to beat Wolves to win the First Division title. A crowd of 53,579 packed into the stadium, 25,000 supporting Leeds, with another

Paul Dougherty scores for Wolves against Leeds United at Elland Road in September 1984.

15,000 locked outside, but it was Wolves who spoiled the party, winning 2-1 with goals from Frank Munro and Derek Dougan. Derby County pipped Leeds to the title by a point.

Almost 37,000 fans saw Leeds record their best League win over Wolves – 4-1 in a home First Division match in September 1973.

Playing at Leeds on 12 December 1936, Wolves lost centre-half Stan Cullis with a broken collar-bone and had goalkeeper Alex Scott sent-off. The match was abandoned through fog with just seven minutes remaining and Wolves in front. The re-arranged game was played on 21 April and Wolves triumphed 1-0.

The first two encounters at League level took place in season 1920-21, Wolves winning 3-0 at Molineux, but losing by the same score at Leeds.

Elland Road was, in fact, a bogey ground for Wolves when they played United there – and it took them until April 1937 (ten League games) before they finally won (1-0).

There were some exciting contests at Molineux in the 1930s – a 3-3 draw in March 1933; a 4-1 Wolves win in February 1939 – being just two. Jimmy Mullen made his League debut for Wolves in the latter game at the age of 16 and almost 32,000 fans were present.

The last time Wolves and Leeds met in the League was in the Second Division in season 1984-85 when the Yorkshire club doubled up by winning 2-0 at Molineux and 3-2 at Elland Road.

The first FA Cup-tie between the clubs took place in January 1936, Leeds winning a third-round replay 3-1 after a 1-1 draw at Molineux.

A crowd of almost 52,500 saw Wolves succumb 1-0 to Leeds United in the semi-final of the FA Cup at Hillsborough in April 1973.

And the last attendance approaching 50,000 seen at Molineux attended the sixth-round FA Cup-tie between Wolves and Leeds United in March 1977 which the visitors won again by a single goal.

Then we had that superb sixth-round FA Cup-tie at Elland Road in March 1998 which was decided by a late goal from Don Goodman, although Leeds had only themselves to blame for going out of the competition when Dutchman Jimmy-Floyd Hasselbaink's last minute penalty was splendidly saved by Wolves' stand-in 'keeper Hans Segers.

A crowd of over 11,000 saw Leeds beat Wolves 2-1 at Molineux in the Zenith Data Systems Cup in 1990-91.

Players with both clubs include: Brian Caswell, Wilf Chadwick, Chris Crowe, Roger Eli, Ray Hankin, Bobby McDonald, Jim Melrose, Mike O'Grady, Len Smith, Ernie Stevenson and Ernie Whittam.

Also associated: Major Frank Buckley (manager of both clubs); Bill Booth (Wolves Reserves), Stan Burton, Jack Dowen, Tom Galley, George Laking, Tom Mayson and Horace Wright (all United wartime guests), Don Howe (Wolves trialist, Leeds United coach); Jim McCalliog (Leeds amateur); Bob Hazel (Leeds trialist); Les Cocker (Wolves player, Leeds trainer/coach); Jack Taylor (Wolves player, Leeds manager); Tommy Burden (Wolves Reserves).

LEES, Harold B.
Between February 1923 and September 1927 Harry Lees scored 43 goals in 129 appearances for Wolverhampton Wanderers after joining them from Ebbw Vale FC for £50. Lees was born at West Bridgford, Nottingham, on 11 May 1895 and after winning a Midland Alliance championship medal with Woodthorpe FC in 1920 he had a spell as an amateur with Notts County before moving to Welsh football. Lees helped Wolves win the Third Division North championship in 1923-24 when he scored 21 goals to become top scorer that season, which included two hat-tricks. He was a clever inside-left but his powers were waning and Wolves let him go to Darlington in October 1927. He scored five times in 26 games in the Third Division North for the Feethams club before joining non-League Shrewsbury Town in August 1929. He ended his playing days with Stourbridge and Leamington Town, retiring in 1933 to concentrate on his work as a chartered accountant in Wolverhampton. He died c.1989.
Wolves record: 129 apps. 43 goals.

LE FLEM, Richard Peter
Orthodox outside-left, born in Bradford-upon-Avon on 12 July 1942, Dick Le Flem went over to the Channel Island of Guernsey as a youngster and played his early football over there before joining Nottingham Forest as a professional in May 1960. Capped by England at Under-23 level whilst at the City Ground, he scored 18 goals in 132 League outings for Forest before transferring to Wolves in January 1964 to replace Alan Hinton in the No.11 shirt. Le Flem never really settled down in the West Midlands and spent just over a year at Molineux, switching to Middlesbrough in February 1965. He ended his senior career with Leyton Orient (March-May 1966).
Wolves record: 19 apps. 5 goals.

LEGGE, Albert E.
Albert Legge was an outside-right or centre-forward who spent six seasons at Molineux, joining the club in the summer of 1922 and departing in 1928. Born in Wolverhampton in 1902, Legge attended Prestwood Road school and played for Lewisham Athletic

before joining Wolves as a professional, manager George Robey offering him a contract after watching him score five goals in three games for his junior team. He spent the first season at Molineux in the Reserves but then broke into the first team, helping them win the Third Division North championship in 1923-24. He left Wolves for Gillingham and later assisted Charlton Athletic and Queen's Park Rangers before returning to Wolverhampton. He chose to play non-League football for Wellington Town, Hednesford and Cradley Heath before announcing his retirement in 1939-40. After the war Legge ran a pub in Heath Town and was employed as a scout for several Midlands clubs. He then worked for the Goodyear tyre company until he attained the age of 65. He was resident in Wednesfield at the time of his death, in New Cross Hospital in July 1998.
Wolves record: 56 apps. 5 goals

LEICESTER CITY (FOSSE)
Wolves' playing record against Leicester is:

Football League

Venue	P	W	D	L	F	A
Home	44	22	12	10	84	41
Away	44	11	12	21	43	74
Total	88	33	24	31	127	115

FA Cup

Home	3	2	1	0	7	2
Away	2	1	0	1	2	2
Neutral	1	1	0	0	3	1
Totals	6	4	1	1	12	6

ZDSC

Away	1	1	0	0	1	0

Wartime

Home	9	7	1	1	28	7
Away	7	2	1	4	7	15
Totals	16	9	2	5	35	22

Wolves first met Leicester when they were known as Fosse in 1906-07 and the initial two matches both ended in home wins: Wolves by 1-0 and Fosse 2-0.

Billy Blunt scored all Wolves' goals in their 4-1 home win over Leicester in December 1909 and when the Foxes were hammered 7-0 at Molineux in November 1914, centre-forward Frank Curtis scored a four-timer and inside-left Jack Needham a hat-trick.

Leicester gained sweet revenge for that heavy defeat when they also walloped Wolves 7-0 at Filbert Street in March 1923 with Albert Pynegar netting four goals, one a penalty.

Wolves' best League win of all-time in terms of goals scored, is 10-1 – against Leicester City in a First Division match at Molineux in April 1938. That afternoon a crowd of 25,540 saw two players – Dicky Dorsett and Dennis Westcott both net four-timers – the only time this has happened in Wolves' history.

When Leicester won promotion back to the First Division in 1954-55, they were

Skipper Billy Wright introduces Wolves players to the Duke of Gloucester before the 1949 FA Cup Final against Leicester City.

slammed 5-0 by Wolves at Molineux that season and after going back down and returning in double quick time they then crashed 5-1 on the same ground in February 1958.

Results were even throughout the period from 1959 to 1980, but in seasons 1982-83 and 1983-84 Leicester gave Wolves two real hidings at Filbert Street, winning 5-0 and 5-1 respectively, Steve Lynex, Alan Smith and Gary Lineker scoring in both games with Smith netting a hat-trick in the second fixture.

Wolves themselves then grabbed a 5-0 win over Leicester at Molineux in April 1990 when Steve Bull (3) and Robbie Dennison (2) scored the goals.

In the first of the six FA Cup meetings, Wolves beat Leicester 5-1 at Molineux in a fourth round tie in January 1939. Westcott and Teddy Maguire both scoring twice in front of a 43,200 plus crowd.

Two goals by Jesse Pye and a superb effort from Sammy Smyth gave Wolves a 3-1 FA Cup Final victory over Leicester City in April 1949.

And when Wolves reached Wembley again in 1960, they knocked Leicester out of the FA Cup in the quarter-final, beating them 2-1 at Filbert Street before a reported record crowd of almost 49,000.

Irish international David Kelly scored a stunning goal which clinched a 1-0 sixth-round FA Cup victory for Wolves over his former club in a fifth round tie in February 1995 in front of a record all-seater Molineux crowd of 28,544.

A Steve Bull strike at Filbert Street earned Wolves a 1-0 win over Leicester in a Zenith Data Systems Cup-tie in 1990-91 when the crowd was only 4,705.

Dennis Westcott scored a hat-trick when Wolves beat Leicester 5-0 in a Midland Regional wartime League game in December 1939 and Gerry McMahon did likewise when the Foxes were beaten 5-1 in the same competition in March 1940.

Players with both clubs include: Joe Baillie, Herbert Barlow, John Bell, Joe Blackett, Mark Blake, Steve Claridge, Wayne Clarke, Steve Corica, Dicky Davies, Derek Dougan, Peter Eastoe, John Farrington, Michael Gilkes, Jack Hamilton, Bob Hazell, David Kelly, Robert Kelly, Dave MacLaren, Lawrie Madden, Tommy McDonald, Hugh McIlmoyle, Jim Melrose, Ted Pheasant, Fred Price, Iwan

Roberts, Eddie Russell, George Swift, Mark Venus, David Walker and Maurice Woodward.

Also associated: Mark McGhee and Brian Little (managers of both clubs); Colin Lee (Wolves manager, Leicester assistant manager/coach); George Jobey (City player, Wolves manager); Gerry Summers (coach at both clubs), Emilio Aldecoa, Bill Baxter, Bob Iverson, Bob King, Jimmy Mullen, Terry Springthorpe and Billy Wright (all City wartime guests); Arthur Rowley (Wolves wartime player, Leicester's champion goalscorer in 1950s), Brian Punter, Jim Travers, Bill Tuckley and George Wills (Wolves Reserves), Chris Turner and Mike Hickman (coaches at both clubs).

LESTER, Franklyn Leslie

Secured by Wolves for just one season – as cover for Dickie Baugh and Tommy Dunn – full-back Frank Lester was a well-built defender. Born in Wolverhampton c.1871, he played for Fallings Heath Rangers before spending the 1894-95 campaign at Molineux. He returned to Fallings Heath from Wolves and later made over 70 appearances at left-back for Walsall.
Wolves record: 1 app.

LEWIS, Arthur Norman

A very safe and sound goalkeeper, Norman Lewis was born in Wolverhampton on 13 June 1908. He played for his school team and after a useful spell with the Sunbeam Works team (he was an assembler on the shop floor) joined Wolves as a professional in July 1928. After spending just one season at Molineux, Lewis went to Stoke City for £250 on 24 May 1929, signed by Potters' boss Tom Mather as cover for Dick Williams. At 5ft 10ins tall and weighing over 12 stones Lewis gained a regular place at the Victoria Ground in 1930 and was eventually replaced in the team by the former Huddersfield Town 'keeper Norman Wilkinson after 170 senior appearances for the Potters. Lewis then moved to Bradford Park Avenue (May 1936) for £300 and later served with Tranmere Rovers (November 1936 to May 1939). He helped Rovers win the Third Division North title in 1938. Lewis retired in 1942.

Wolves record: 30 apps.

LEYTON ORIENT (CLAPTON ORIENT AND ORIENT)

Wolves' playing record against Orient is:

Football League

Venue	P	W	D	L	F	A
Home	23	15	2	6	49	25
Away	23	6	6	11	26	32
Total	46	21	8	17	75	57

League Cup

	P	W	D	L	F	A
Home	1	1	0	0	2	1

Wolves registered their best League win over Orient in the second meeting between the clubs on 27 December 1906 (Division Two). Five days earlier Orient had beaten Wolves 4-0 in London, but in the return fixture, in front of 5,000 fans, Wolves raced to a convincing 6-1 victory with Arthur Hawkins and John Roberts both scoring twice. Two years later in December 1908, Wolves won 5-1 at Molineux (two goals here for Billy Blunt) and in February 1927 they ran up a 5-0 scoreline at home when Tom Phillipson netted a hat-trick.

The first time the teams played each other in the top flight was in season 1962-63. Wolves won 2-1 at Molineux and 4-0 at Brisbane Road when Barry Stobart scored twice. Bobby Mason and Norman Deeley, two ex-Wolves players, were in the Orient team at Molineux.

In a Second Division game at Orient in October 1965 two of Wolves' goals in their 3-2 win were scored by the home defender Gordon Ferry.

When winning the Second Division title in 1976-77, Wolves defeated Orient 1-0 at home and 4-2 away, John Richards weighing in with a hat-trick in the victory in London.

An eight-goal thriller at Molineux on Christmas Eve 1927 saw Wolves win 5-3, Tom Baxter scoring twice from the left-wing position.

Wolves beat Orient 2-1 in a second round League Cup-tie at Molineux in September 1972. Over 15,000 fans saw Derek Dougan and John Richards find the net.

Players with both clubs include: Scott Barrett, Gary Bellamy, Derek Clarke, Don Cock, Norman Deeley, Evan Edwards, Jack Ellis, Dick Le Flem, Roger Hansbury, Revd Kenneth Hunt, Bobby Kerr, Mark Lazarus, Albert Lumberg and Bobby Mason.

Also associated: Ken Knighton (Wolves player, Orient manager), John T. Turner (reserve), Ray King (amateur goalkeeper), Jock Mulraney (Orient trialist, Wolves guest), Andy Beattie (Orient guest, Wolves manager), James Lee (reserve), Tom Galley and Reg Kirkham (Orient wartime guests) and Joe Nicholls, who made 120 senior appearances for Orient after leaving Molineux in 1919.

LILL, Michael J.

Micky Lill was a useful goalscoring right-winger who, after winning England Youth honours, deputised for Norman Deeley at Molineux. Born in Romford, Essex on 3 August 1936, he played for Stoney Athletic prior to becoming a professional with Wolves in June 1954. He remained at the club until February 1960 when he was transferred to Everton, after failing to establish himself as a first-team regular at Molineux despite an excellent goalscoring record He moved from Goodison Park to Plymouth Argyle in June 1962 and ended his Football League career with Portsmouth (March 1963 to May 1964) and afterwards assisted Guildford, Germiston Callies in South Africa, for whom he scored 13 goals in 13 games which helped them avoid relegation. On retiring he took to coaching, having gained his FA badge whilst at Everton, and nowadays he is still based in South Africa, working as a PE teacher just outside Johannesburg. In total Lill scored 38 goals in 121 League appearances in England.

Wolves record: 34 apps. 17 goals.

LIMITED COMPANY

Wolverhampton Wanderers Football Club first became a Limited Company in 1891 when 2,000 £1 shares were issued. A new Limited Company was formed in 1923.

LINCOLN CITY

Wolves' playing record against the Imps is:

Football League

Venue	P	W	D	L	F	A
Home	11	10	1	0	29	5
Away	11	3	2	6	16	19
Total	22	13	3	6	45	24

FA Cup

	P	W	D	L	F	A
Home	1	1	0	0	2	1
Away	1	1	0	0	1	0
Total	2	2	0	0	3	1

League Cup

	P	W	D	L	F	A
Home	2	1	0	1	2	2
Away	2	2	0	0	3	0
Total	4	3	0	1	5	2

Wolves have a terrific League home record against the Imps and of their ten victories at Molineux, 4-0 is the best, achieved in January 1920 in front of 6,000 fans.

Wolves' biggest win over Lincoln is 5-1 – achieved at Sincil Bank (Division Two) in October 1910, when both the Needham brothers, Jack and Archie found the net. Wolves also won 4-0 at Lincoln in October 1906.

In the first season after World War One (1919-20) both teams won their respective home game by 4-0 – a fortnight apart.

And it was a similar story in season 1986-87 (the last time the teams met at League level) with Wolves winning 3-0 at Molineux and City likewise at Sincil Bank. Bull scored twice in the former match.

The League clash at Molineux the season before, which ended in a 1-1 draw, attracted a crowd of just 3,351.

Wolves first met Lincoln in the FA Cup in season 1911-12 when they were victorious by 2-1 in a second round tie at Molineux before a 19,700 crowd.

The second meeting in 1957-58, was an all-ticket affair and an unofficial record crowd of 25,000 packed into Sincil Bank to see Wolves win a third round clash 1-0, Jimmy Mullen the goalscorer.

Wolves lost to the Imps on the away goal rule in a first round Littlewoods League Cup-tie in 1986-87, but then won another opening round match in 1989-90, with scores of 1-0 at Molineux and 2-0 at Lincoln.

Players with both clubs include: Brian Birch, Joe Bonson, Colin Brazier, John Burridge, John Chadburn, Malcolm Clews, Mick Coady, Peter Daniel, Richard Deacon, Jackie Gallacher, Frank Higham, Bob Iverson, Jim McCalliog (player-manager of City), Steve Mardenborough, Steve Stoutt, Billy Walker, Shane Westley (also manager of Lincoln) and Tommy Yule.

Also associated: John Ward (Lincoln player, Wolves assistant manager); Jason Barnett (Wolves Reserves), Billy Ellis (Wolves junior reserve); Ian Greaves (City player, Wolves manager); Chris Turner (City goalkeeper, Wolves coach); Jason Barnett, David Felgate, Clive Ford, Ray Gaston, Dick Neal, Jim Poppitt, Brian Punter, Tommy Rudkin and Malcolm White (all Wolves Reserves), Colin Gibson (City player, Wolves wartime guest) and Arthur Rowley (Wolves reserve, City wartime guest).

Burridge holds the record for being the oldest player ever to appear in a first team game for Lincoln. He was aged 42 years, 57 days v Rochdale (Division Three) in January 1994.

LITTLE, Brian

Brian Little acted as caretaker-manager at Molineux for a period of three months, August to October 1986, having been coach at Molineux since the previous January. Born in Durham City on 25 November 1953, he played for East Durham Boys and Durham County Youths before becoming an apprentice with Aston Villa. He turned professional with the West Midlands club in June 1971, made his League debut four months later and went on to amass more than 300 senior appearances, scoring 82 goals, before injury forced him into an early retirement in 1981 at the age of 28. Capped once by England against Wales in May 1975, Little won an FA Youth Cup medal and two League Cup winners tankards with Villa and on finishing he worked briefly in the club's promotions department, occasionally assisting as a summariser on a local radio station. After leaving Wolves he served as coach to another ex-Villa star, Bruce Rioch, at Middlesbrough. In the summer of 1988 he was appointed team manager of Darlington, whom he quickly led to the Conference title – and back into the Football League – before taking over as boss of Leicester City in March 1990. He then guided the Foxes to three successive Wembley First Division Play-off Finals – first in 1992 when they lost to Blackburn Rovers; then in 1993 when they were defeated by Swindon Town; and finally in 1994 when Derby were beaten by a late Steve Walsh goal to shoot Leicester into the Premiership. Barely six months after that Wembley triumph (in the November) Little surprisingly quit Filbert Street to take over from Ron Atkinson as manager of Aston Villa, and two years later he guided Villa to victory in the Coca-Cola League Cup Final over Leeds United, taking them into the UEFA Cup competition as a result. Then shortly after the halfway stage of the 1997-98 season Little again caused big talk by leaving Villa Park. A short break outside soccer followed before he returned as manager of relegated Stoke City and then for only the second time in League soccer history, he sat in the dug-out opposite his kid brother Alan who was manager of York City when they played Stoke at the Britannia Stadium in November 1998. Little resigned in the summer of 1999 and in August was appointed WBA manager.

LIVERPOOL

Wolves' playing record against Liverpool is:

Football League

Venue	P	W	D	L	F	A
Home	43	21	8	14	65	56
Away	43	8	7	28	40	78
Total	86	29	15	42	105	134

FA Cup

Home	4	3	0	1	9	4
Away	1	0	0	1	1	2
Total	5	3	0	2	10	6

League Cup

Home	1	1	0	0	1	0

The teams first met at League level in 1894-95 (Division One) when the results were 3-1 to Wolves at Molineux and 3-3 at Liverpool.

The Merseysiders doubled up over Wolves in season 1896-97, although both games were close, Wolves having a goal disallowed in each match.

Two successive 4-1 Liverpool home victories in November 1901 and in the same month in 1902, was followed by a 4-2 triumph for Wolves at Molineux in December 1903 when Billy Wooldridge scored two superb goals.

Liverpool waltzed to a 5-1 League win at Anfield on the opening day of the 1932-33 campaign only for Wolves to win an eight-goal cracker 5-3 at Molineux in March 1935 when Bob Iverson and Billy Wrigglesworth both scored twice.

Wolves recorded their biggest League win (in terms of goals scored) in December 1946 (Division One) when they romped to a 3-1 victory at Anfield in front of 52,512 fans. Dennis Westcott scored four times that day.

Another big Wolves win was 5-3 at home in March 1935 when Bob Iverson and Bill Wrigglesworth both scored twice.

When Wolves won 5-1 at Anfield in front of 52,512 fans in December 1946 – the first League meeting between the clubs after World War Two – Dennis Westcott smashed in four terrific goals. Wolves led 4-0 at half-time.

Four years later in December 1950, two goals by Johnny Walker helped Wolves to a 4-1 win at Anfield.

Liverpool inflicted two 6-0 defeats on Wolves, both in the First Division, in the space of five years – at Anfield in September 1963 in front of 44,000 fans and at Molineux in September 1968, when almost 40,000 spectators were present. This latter result was the start of the end for Wolves manager Ronnie Allen as former Wolves star Alun Evans scored twice for the Reds.

Liverpool clinched the First Division League championship by beating Wolves 3-1 in front of 48,918 fans at Molineux on the last day of the 1975-76 season. The result also meant that the Wanderers were relegated.

In August 1983, a sweetly struck penalty by full-back Geoff Palmer after only 87 seconds play against Liverpool (after Andy Gray had been floored) gave Wolves a great start to their League programme. The game, however, ended 1-1 in front of 26,249 fans. The last time Wolves and Liverpool met in the League was in January of that season, and by winning 1-0 at Anfield with a Steve Mardenborough goal, it brought Wolves' their first victory there since 1950.

Liverpool won 17 of the 20 League encounters played between the clubs between 1951 and 1983, including 11 on the bounce from 1970, with future Wolves star Emlyn Hughes scoring in a 4-2 success in September 1972.

Hughes later scored for Wolves in a 4-1 home win over Liverpool in November 1980.

A linesman participating in the Liverpool v Wolves First Division clash at Anfield in October 1970 pulled a muscle and was replaced by John Collihole, a Watford fan, who was attending his last football match in England before emigrating to Australia.

On 11 February 1939, a record Molineux crowd of 61,315 saw Wolves keep on the Wembley road by beating Liverpool 4-1 in round five of the FA Cup.

Thirteen years later, on 2 February 1952, a record attendance at Anfield of 61,905 saw Liverpool knock Wolves out of the FA Cup by 2-1 in round four.

On their way to winning the FA Cup in 1949, Wolves beat Liverpool 3-1 at home in the fifth round in front of almost 55,000 fans.

The first FA Cup meeting between the teams took place in season 1895-96, Wolves winning 2-0 at Molineux on their way to the Final.

A crowd of 16,242 saw a fine goal by John Richards give Wolves their fifth round League Cup replay win over Liverpool on a cold Wednesday afternoon at Molineux on 19 December 1973.

Players with both clubs include: George Bowen, John Chadburn, Alun Evans, George Fleming, Dick Forshaw, Billy Hartill, Jack Hopkins, Emlyn Hughes, Fred Keetley, Jimmy Melia, Jack Sambrook, Alex Scott, Cyril Sidlow, Sammy Smyth, Paul Stewart and Mark Walters.

Also associated: Revd Billy Jordan (Liverpool reserve), George Paterson (Liverpool player, Wolves wartime guest), Stan Cullis, Dicky Dorsett and Dennis Westcott (all Liverpool wartime guests) with Dickie Dorsett also assistant trainer at Anfield, Andy Mutch (Liverpool apprentice); Stan Collymore (Wolves Reserves), Jack Hopkins (Wolves player, Liverpool reserve), Andy Beattie (Liverpool coach, Wolves manager), Ian Ross (Liverpool player, Wolves coach and caretaker-manager) and Jorgen Nielsen (on loan to Wolves).

LIVINGSTONE, William

Striker Billy Livingstone, who played for Scotland's Youth team as a teenager, had a relatively brief career as a professional footballer. Born in Coventry on 13 August 1964, he joined Wolves as an apprentice at the age of 16 (via a job opportunities scheme provided the Manpower Services Department) and was taken on the full-time staff in August 1982. He remained at Molineux for the next two seasons before transferring to Derby

County in July 1984. He quit top-class football at the end of that season.
Wolves record: 22+ 3 apps. 4 goals.

LLOWARCH, Albert

Goalkeeper Albert Llowarch took over from Isaac Griffiths between the posts for Wolves during the 1887-88 season. Born in Nechells, Birmingham in 1865, he stood six feet tall, weighed 13 stones and played his early football for Ward End Swifts and Nechells Park. He spent 12 months with Wolves (from August 1887) before joining Willenhall, later assisting Saltley Works (Birmingham).
Wolves record: 3 apps.

LLOYD, Arthur Amos

Left-half Arthur Lloyd was recruited by Wolves from Halesowen Town in May 1905, having previously been with Smethwick St Mary's and Oldbury Broadwell. He left Molineux for Hednesford Town in August 1908 after giving Wolves three years excellent service. Born in Smethwick in 1881, Lloyd retired in 1912. He died in Birmingham in 1945.
Wolves record: 80 apps. 3 goals.

LLOYD, Harold

Harry Lloyd (no relation to Arthur above) had just one season with Wolves (July 1913 to April 1914.). Born at Cannock Chase in 1888 he played his early football with Cannock Town and after spells with Walsall and Rotherham County, he moved to Molineux. On leaving Wolves he went to Hednesford Town and rounded off his career with a spell at Walsall Wood. He died c.1960.
Wolves record: 8 apps. 1 goal.

LOCALS

In season 1900-01 Wolves' 25-man strong first-team squad comprised almost all local-born players – 21 from Staffordshire and four from Cheshire.

LOCKETT, William Curfield

Bill Lockett was born in Tipton on 23 April 1893 and died in Market Harborough, Leicestershire, on 25 September 1974. A former pupil at Dudley Grammar School, he later attended Dudley Training College where he won an athletics runners-up medal in the 1912 championships as well as skippering the college cricket team and playing in a Birmingham amateur Cup Final. An inside-forward, who could also play as a wing-half, Lockett joined Wolves on amateur forms in August 1913. He became semi-professional the following month but remained at the club for just a season, leaving for Northampton Town in July 1914, later playing for Kidderminster Harriers. A schoolmaster, he served in the South Staffordshire Regiment during World War One. A fine all-round sportsman, Lockett represented Birmingham Amateurs in games against London and Lancashire and he also played for England v Wales as a 15-year-old.
Wolves record: 6 apps. 2 goals.

LOCKHART, Keith Samuel

During his nine months at Molineux (March-December 1986) the versatile Keith Lockhart appeared in a variety of positions, including those of left back and midfield. Born at Wallsend-on-Tyne on 19 July 1964, he joined Cambridge United as an apprentice in June 1980 and turned professional at The Abbey Stadium in July 1982. Two years later he moved to Wolves and from Molineux he went north to sign for Hartlepool United, later assisting Cambridge City. A fiery temper occasionally got the better of Lockhart who was sent-off three times in his career, once with Wolves.
Wolves record: 29+1 apps. 5 goals.

LOCOMOTIV LEIPZIG

Wolves' playing record against Leipzig is:
Football League

Venue	P	W	D	L	F	A
Home	1	1	0	0	4	1
Away	1	0	0	1	0	3
Total	2	1	0	1	4	4

Wolves played the East German side Locomotiv Leipzig in the second round of the 1973-74 UEFA Cup competition.

Almost 17,000 fans saw the Germans easily win the first leg 3-0 in Leipzig on 24 October and although Wolves played exceedingly well to record a famous 4-1 victory in the return fixture at Molineux a fortnight later in front of 14,530 spectators, the Germans went through on the away goal rule.

LOMAX, Geoffrey William

Geoff Lomax was a capable full-back, who was taken on loan by Wolves boss Bill McGarry from Manchester City during October/November 1985. Born in Droylsden, near Manchester on 6 July 1964, he joined the Maine Road club as a professional in July 1981 and after returning there following his sojourn at Molineux, Lomax signed for Carlisle United in December 1985 and later assisted Rochdale (from July 1987). He later became Bolton Wanderers' Football in the Community officer at the Reebok Stadium.
Wolves record: 5 apps.

LONDON CALDEONIANS

Wolves were paired with the London amateur side in the first round of the FA Cup in January 1913. A Molineux crowd of 18,189 saw the Wanderers win 3-1, two goals coming from Irish international Billy Halligan.

LONG EATON RANGERS

Wolves' record against Rangers is:
FA Cup

Venue	P	W	D	L	F	A
Home	1	1	0	0	4	1
Away	1	1	0	0	2	1
Total	2	2	0	0	6	2

Long Eaton Rangers were Wolves' first-ever FA Cup opponents, losing a first round tie at Dudley Road on 27 October 1883 by 4-1. On target for Wolves that day, in front of 2,000 fans, were Jack Brodie (who had the pleasure of securing Wolves' first-ever FA Cup goal) and John Griffiths. Both players scored twice. The other tie was played in January 1891, when two fine goals by Harry Wood gave Wolves a 2-1 first-round win after extra-time.
Player with both clubs: John Streets.

LONG SERVICE

Several people have served Wolverhampton Wanderers Football Club for 25 years or more, among them the following: Jack Addenbrooke (1877-1922 – as junior player, committee member, secretary-manager); Stan Cullis (1934-64 as player and manager); Jack Davies (trainer 1918-45); Harry Dillard (1889-1940 as reserve team manager and committee member); Jack Dowen (1935-82 as player, trainer, coach, kitman, scout and odd job man); Albert Fletcher (1886-1920 as player and trainer); Joe Gardiner (1932-64 and 1969-82 first as a player, then trainer and scout); Sir Alfred Hickman (1879-1910 as president); Albert Hoskins (1900-26 as player, office clerk, secretary and secretary-manager); Jack Howley (1923-68 as office clerk, assistant secretary, secretary and general manager); Graham Hughes (1943-99 as a supporter, odd-job man, stadium tour guide, Molineux archivist); John Ireland (1964-1988 inclusive as chairman and president); George Palmer (1946-69 inclusive as physiotherapist); George Poyser (1932-59 as player and chief scout); Albert Tye (1919-50 as groundsman); Dot Wooldridge (1959-97 as office worker, lottery clerk and assistant secretary); Billy Wright (1938-59 as player and then 1990-95 inclusive as a director).

Jack Howley arrived at Molineux as an office junior in 1923 and stayed with Wolves for the rest of his working life, retiring in 1968 after 45 years service. He was club secretary for 20 years, the last five being combined with the duties of general manager. He died on 23 March 1971. Jack's daughter, Christine, has followed in her father's footsteps as an ardent Wolves supporter, being a season ticket holder at Molineux since Jack's death.

LOS ANGELES WOLVES

In the summer of 1967, under Ronnie Allen's managership, Wolves – masquerading under the name of Los Angeles Wolves – won the North American Summer Soccer League, a competition sponsored by a Canadian millionaire.

This was Wolves' programme of matches:

27	May	v	Bangu	1-1
31	May	v	Cerro	2-0
3	Jun	v	Stoke City	0-0
7	Jun	v	Hibernian	2-1
11	Jun	v	Sunderland	5-1
14	Jun	v	Glentoran	4-1
20	Jun	v	Aberdeen	1-1
25	Jun	v	Shamrock Rovers	1-1
28	Jun	v	ADO The Hague	0-1
1	Jul	v	ADO The Hague	2-1
4	Jul	v	Cagliari (Italy)	2-2
8	Jul	v	Dundee United	2-2
10	Jul	v	Aberdeen	0-3
14	Jul	v	Aberdeen	6-5*

*The final victory came after extra-time and Davey Burnside scored a hat-trick for Wolves. Frank Munro played at centre-half for the Dons and was later signed by Wolves.

The match against Aberdeen on 10 July was a replay of the fixture staged on 20 June following the Scottish club's protest over the illegal use of a substitute by Wolves.

LOVELLS ATHLETIC

Wolves' playing record against Lovells:

FA Cup

Venue	P	W	D	L	F	A
Home	1	1	0	0	8	1
Away	1	1	0	0	4	2
Totals	2	2	0	0	12	3

Wolves played Lovells Athletic in the transitional season after World War Two, beating them 12-3 over two legs in the third round.

Two goals by Ken Davies helped Wolves to a 4-2 win before 10,000 fans at Lovells and there were 14,885 present at Molineux to see the return leg which Wolves eased through with goals by Tom Galley (3), Billy Wright (2), Jimmy Mullen, Bob King and Jimmy Dunn.

Associated with both clubs: George Brewster, Billy Lucas (Wolves Reserves).

LOWDER, Arthur

Born in Wolverhampton on 11 February 1863, and a former pupil at St Luke's school, Blakenhall, Arthur Lowder joined Wolves in September 1882 and retired through injury in October 1891. In later years he went over to Europe where he coached in France, Germany and Norway, before returning to England in 1924 to become chairman of the Brewood Parish Council, a position he held for 12 years. He prefered the left-half berth although he did occasionally figure in the forward-line. He appeared in Wolves' first-ever FA Cup-tie in 1883 and then followed up by playing in the club's first Football League game v Aston Villa five years later. He wasn't a tall man, standing 5ft 5ins. yet he loved a challenge and never gave an inch. A grand competitor he was capped by England against Wales a month after playing for Wolves v Preston in the 1889 FA Cup Final. Lowder died in Taunton, Somerset, on 4 January 1936.
Wolves record: 71 apps. 3 goals.

LOWTON, Wilfred George

Right-back Wilf Lowton was already an experienced defender in the Third Division when he joined Wolves from Exeter City, his hometown club, in 1929. Born in the Devon city on 3 October 1899, he joined the Grecians from local amateur club Heavitree United in 1924 and eventually won his place over the great Exeter full-back Bob Pollard in 1928. Lowton made 75 League appearances for the St James' Park club before joining Wolves for £1,400 and he proved a great success in the 1930s, being a key figure in the 1931-32 Second Division promotion side when he was successful with 11 out of 12 penalties and skippered the side, a job he did for four seasons. In May 1935, after Wolves had again struggled in their efforts to raise themselves into the upper reaches of the First Division, he returned to Exeter. Lowton made a further 18 League appearances for the Grecians before spending three months as their assistant trainer and then retiring in 1939. Lowton – who was a keen model railway enthusiast – died in Exeter on 12 January 1963.
Wolves record: 209 apps. 27 goals (20 penalties)

LUMBERG, Arthur Albert

One-time furniture remover Albert Lumberg was an efficient right-back, who was good enough to win four caps for Wales at full international level (one with Wolves). Born in Connah's Quay, Flintshire on 20 May 1901, he played for Connah's Quay and Shotton United, Mold Town (early 1924) and Wrexham (November 1924) before joining Wolves in May 1930. Acting as reserve to Wilf Lowton, he spent most of his three year-stay at Molineux in the second team. On leaving Wolves in June 1933, he signed for Brighton and Hove Albion for £650. In May 1934 he switched to Stockport County and the following January moved south to London to sign for Clapton Orient, diverting north again to Lytham FC in July 1935. Four months later he was recruited by New Brighton (November 1935) and after a two-year spell with Winsford United (from July 1936) he became player-manager of Newry Town (June 1938). After the war Lumberg remained in Ireland for a while, but returned to England to become Wrexham's 'A' team trainer in 1950. Thereafter he acted as coach at the Racecourse Ground and also assisted Wrexham Old Boys FC. He played in 169 League games for Wrexham with whom he won a Welsh Cup winners medal in 1925. He died in Wrexham on 16 February 1986.
Wolves record: 22 apps.

LUNN, Thomas Henry

Goalkeeper Tommy Lunn was signed by Wolves from Brownhills Albion in August 1904 having moved down to the area after being educated in County Durham. Born in Bishop Auckland on 9 July 1883, he helped Wolves win the FA Cup in 1908 and went on to play for the club until the end of the 1909-10 season when he was transferred to Tottenham Hotspur (April 1901). For the Londoners he made 106 first-team appearances before joining Stockport County in June 1913. Unfortunately after playing only twice for the Edgeley Park club he suffered a serious leg injury which forced him into an early retirement which saw him return to London. He died in the capital, in an Edmonton hospital on 29 March 1960.

Tommy Lunn, 142 appearances in Wolves' goal.

One interesting point is that Lunn appeared for Spurs against Wolves in the first-ever Football League game staged at White Hart Lane – on 1 September 1908.
Wolves record: 142 apps.

LUTON TOWN

Wolves' record against the Hatters is:

Football League

Venue	P	W	D	L	F	A
Home	12	5	2	5	26	20
Away	12	4	2	6	19	25
Total	24	9	4	11	45	45

FA Cup

Away	2	2	0	0	6	2

League Cup

Home	1	0	0	1	1	3

Wartime

Home	3	3	0	0	13	2
Away	3	0	1	2	2	6
Total	6	3	1	2	15	8

The first time Wolves and Luton met in the Football League was in season 1955-56 (Division One) and the Hatters certainly called the tune in both games, winning 5-1 at Kenilworth Road and 2-1 at Molineux. Roy Swinbourne was badly injured in that encounter at Luton and as a result he was forced to quit the game.

Wolves' first League victory arrived in style and it turned out to be one of the greatest post-war League matches ever seen at Molineux in terms of football. It was in August 1956 when Wolves won a nine-goal thriller 5-4 in front of 46,781 fans. Full-back Gerry Harris made his debut for Wolves, but star of the show was Jimmy Murray who netted twice for the Wanderers who led 5-3 at half-time. This game kicked-off at 7pm and was partly played under floodlights.

In April 1959 – just before Luton played Nottingham Forest in the FA Cup Final – they crashed 5-0 to Wolves at Molineux in a First Division League game. Peter Broadbent scored twice and made two more goals for the rampant Wanderers.

Wolves followed this up with another goal-rush at Kenilworth Road five months later when they beat Luton 5-1 with Norman Deeley netting twice.

When Wolves won 5-2 at home in March 1975, star of the show was Kenny Hibbitt with a brilliant hat-trick.

Luton beat Wolves 4-0 at home and 2-1 at Molineux in Wanderers' relegation season of 1983-84. And in April 1995, Wolves were 2-0 down at Kenilworth Road in a First Division game, but bounced back to earn a point from a 3-3 draw.

En route to FA Cup glory at Wembley in 1959-60, Wolves ousted Luton in the fifth round, beating them 4-1 at Kenilworth Road before a crowd of 25,714. Bobby Mason scored twice

The Hatters knocked Wolves out of the League Cup at Molineux in a second round tie in August 1977 when the attendance was 10,101.

Dennis Westcott scored a hat-trick in Wolves' 6-1 Midland Regional League win over Luton in April 1940.

Players with both clubs include:Joe Blackett, Gordon Brice, Bill Bryant, Mark Burke, Steve Claridge, Mark Crook, Bob Hatton, Bob Hazell, Billy Kellock, Andy King (also commercial manager of Luton), Bertie Lutterloch, Jack Nelson, Jesse Pye, Mike Small, Stacey North, Graham Rodger, Mike Small, John Smith, Alan Steen, John E. Taylor and Bobby R. A. Thomson.

Also associated: Richie Barker (coach at both clubs), Jimmy Jinks, Jimmy Mulvaney and Bernard Streten (Luton players, Wolves wartime guests), Harry Keeling, Joe McBride, John Read and John Sanderson (all Wolves Reserves), Dave Richards (Wolves Reserves, Luton player – 150 games) and Cameron Buchanan (Wolves wartime player).

LUTTERLOCH, Bert Richard

Inside-forward Bertie Lutterloch was a Cockney, born in Poplar, East London on 16 May 1910. A one-time marketer, he started his career at the age of 21 with Tufnell Park and after spending two years playing and working in France, with Nice (1932) and FC Lille (1933), he joined Wolves in readiness of the start of the 1934-35 season, having done well in a friendly match against the Wanderers in a tour match in 1933. Unfortunately he failed to gain a regular place in the side at Molineux and in 1935 was sold to Aldershot, later assisting Luton Town (from June 1936). He played for Vauxhall Motors after leaving Kenilworth Road and retired during World War Two.
Wolves record: 2 apps.

LUTTON, Robert John

Winger 'Bertie' Lutton was born in Banbridge, Northern Ireland on 13 July 1950. He joined Wolves as a 15-year-old and turned professional at Molineux in September 1967. Basically a reserve, his first-team outings were rather limited and after four years at the club he was transferred to Brighton and Hove Albion in September 1971, later assisting West Ham United (January-May 1973). He won six caps for Ireland, two of them whilst at Molineux (v England and Scotland in season 1969-70).
Wolves record: 19+6 apps. 1 goal.

LYDEN, Joseph

Slimly built inside-forward, born in Walsall in February 1870, Joe Lyden played for Bloxwich St Luke's and Walsall Pilgrims before having a shade over a season with Wolves (April 1896 to September 1897). He then returned to non-League football with Darlaston and died c.1940 in Wolverhampton.
Wolves record: 8 apps. 3 goals.

McALLE, John Edward

John McAlle had a magnificent career with Wolverhampton Wanderers, making his debut for them as a teenager and going on to make 406 League appearances and over 500 in all matches. He was born in Liverpool on 31 January 1950 and signed for Wolves as an apprentice in July 1965, turning professional in February 1967, although he did not become a first-team regular until 1970. He made his debut in the defence against Chelsea in April 1968, helped Wolves win the Texaco Cup in 1971 and was ever-present in 1971-72, the season they met Tottenham Hotspur in the UEFA Cup Final. Club commitments denied him an England Under-23 cap, but he won a League Cup winners' trophy in 1974, when Wolves beat Manchester City at Wembley and was in the side that won the Second Division championship in 1976-77. He was awarded a richly deserved testimonial in 1978-79. In February 1980 McAlle was introduced from the subs' bench during a FA Cup-tie against Watford at Molineux, but before he had touched the ball he fractured his leg in a tackle. He was never the same player again and in August 1981 was transferred to Sheffield United for £10,000, moving to Derby County in April 1983. Alas, he was one of several players who fell out with the Rams management when Peter Taylor returned to the Baseball Ground and in 1984 he left Derby, who had just been relegated to the Third Division. McAlle went into non-League football, playing for a team called Harrisons. In 1988 he was appointed head groundsman at the Merryhill shopping centre at Brierley Hill, and afterwards soon started his own landscape gardening business.
Wolves record: 495+13 apps. 3 goals.

McALOON, Gerald Padva

Scotsman Gerry McAloon was born in the Gorbals district of Glasgow on 13 September 1916. He played junior football with St Francis Juniors and joined Wolves from Brentford in March 1939. But World War Two severely disrupted his progress at Molineux and after the hostilities were over he returned to Griffin Park, later assisting Celtic (Glasgow) and Belfast Celtic. A well-built inside-forward, McAloon died in Bridgeton on 13 April 1987.
Wolves record: 2 apps. 1 goal.

McCALL, William

Outside-left Billy McCall joined Wolves in June 1922 from Blackburn Rovers. A sprightly footballer with good skills, he was born in Wallacetown, Scotland on 5 May 1898 and played initially for Queen of the South Wanderers and Dumfries before being engaged at Ewood Park in December 1920. He lined up in the first 12 League games of the 1922-23 season for Wolves before being replaced by Len Rhodes. The two men then contested the left-wing berth over the next few months. But McCall, unable to hold down a regular place in the side, then became disillusioned and was transferred to Southampton in January 1923. After a bright start he never quite fitted the bill at The Dell and after scoring twice in eight outings for

the Saints (over a period of 18 months) he was sold to Queen of the South in September 1925 for a reduced fee of £250.
Wolves record: 16 apps. 1 goal.

McCALLIOG, James

Midfielder Jim McCalliog was born in Glasgow on 23 September 1946 and began his career as an amateur with Leeds United in 1962-63 before they released him and he joined Chelsea as a professional on his 17th birthday. McCalliog could not establish himself in Chelsea's first team, making only 12 appearances (five in the League Cup) before they let him go to Sheffield Wednesday for £37,500 in July 1965, which made him Britain's costliest teenage footballer at the time. His mother and father, three brothers and a sister moved to Yorkshire with him, all living in the same house near Hillsborough. For the Owls, McCalliog made 150 League appearances, playing in the 1966 FA Cup Final against Everton, before Wolves signed him for £70,000 in October 1969. The fee was well spent and McCalliog remained at Molineux for almost five years, making 210 appearances and scoring 48 goals. He left in March 1974, when a £60,000 deal took him to Manchester United. He helped them regain their First Division place but was soon on the move again, this time to Southampton for £40,000. McCalliog won an FA Cup winners' medal in 1976 (when Southampton beat his former club, Manchester United at Wembley) and made 72 League appearances for the Saints before becoming player-manager of Lincoln City in September 1978. He had also appeared for Chicago Sting in the North American Soccer League and in March 1979 was appointed player-manager of non-League Runcorn. McCalliog eventually drifted out of football but in April 1990 he came back as manager of Fourth Division strugglers Halifax Town. It was a thankless task and in October 1991 he went the way of all the men who have tried their luck as boss at The Shay. His personal honours from the game included five full Scottish caps (one with Wolves) as well as Under-23 and Schoolboy caps. McCalliog, a publican since 1982, was the licensee of the George and Dragon at Wetherby in 1997.
Wolves record: 204+6 apps. 48 goals.

McDONALD, John Christopher

John McDonald was a useful utility forward, who played for Wolves during the last two seasons before World War Two. A Yorkshireman, born in Maltby on 27 August 1921, he moved to Molineux from non-League football in August 1937, as cover for the main attackers. Unfortunately his chances were restricted and in March 1939

he was one of the many ex-Wanderers' who went south to join Bournemouth. The war disrupted McDonald's career but in 1946 he re-entered League soccer with Bournemouth and later played for Fulham (1948-52, making 75 League appearances), Southampton (for season 1952-53) and Southend United before dropping into non-League football with first Weymouth and then Poole Town. McDonald made over 200 League appearances during his career (64 goals scored).
Wolves record: 2 apps.

McDONALD, Robert

Left-back Bobby McDonald had a fine career in League football, amassing well over 500 appearances for five different clubs. Born in Aberdeen on 13 April 1965, he was educated north of the border and won Scottish Schoolboy caps as a 15-year-old. After playing for King Street Sports Club (Aberdeen) he joined Aston Villa as an apprentice in June 1971, turning professional in September 1972. During the next four years he played for his country's Youth team, gained Junior Floodlit League Cup and FA Youth Cup winners medals in 1972, collected a League Cup winners tankard in 1975 and helped Villa win promotion from the Second Division. In August 1976 he was transferred to Coventry City for £40,000. Four years later he moved to Manchester City, being one of John Bond's first signings in October 1980, and in February 1987 was recruited by Leeds United for £25,000. McDonald was then on loan to Wolves in February/March 1988 (signed to fill in for the injured Andy Thompson) but soon after returning to Elland Road he quit the big time to sign for VS Rugby (July 1988), later assisting Burton Albion (1990), Redditch United (1991), Armitage (1991-92) and Burton Albion again (1993-93).
Wolves record: 7 apps.

McDONALD, Thomas

Right-winger Tommy McDonald was born in Glasgow on 24 May 1930 and after service with the Edinburgh club, Hibernian, he moved to Wolves in April 1954 as cover for England international Johnny Hancocks. McDonald found it difficult to get first-team football at Molineux and in July 1956 was transferred to Leicester City for £6,000. He scored 27 goals in 113 League games for the Foxes before moving back to Scotland to sign for Dunfermline Athletic in July 1960. He later assisted Raith Rovers (December 1962 to June 1963), Queen of the South (from August 1963) and finally Stirling Albion (December 1963-May 1964). He won a Scottish 'B' cap during his time at Easter Road.
Wolves record: 6 apps. 2 goals.

McDOUGALL, Alexander Lindsay

Born in Flemington near Motherwell in 1900, Alex McDougall was signed by Wolves boss Fred Scotchbrook from Wishaw Juniors in February 1925 as cover for Jack Mitton. He had earlier had trials with Motherwell and had assisted Wishaw White Star and Carluke. After leaving Molineux in August 1928 he had a spell with Derby County before returning to Scotland to sign for Barrhead (September 1929). He died in Scotland in 1975.
Wolves record: 22 apps. 1 goal.

McGARRY, William Harry

Bill McGarry had two separate spells as team manager of Wolves – the first one lasted seven-and-a-half years from 25 November 1968 to 5 May 1976, the second just 61 days from 4 September to 4 November 1985. Born in Stoke-on-Trent on 10 June 1927, McGarry played at first as an inside-right for Northwood Mission before becoming a professional with Port Vale in June 1945. At both of these clubs he played behind Ronnie Allen whom he succeeded as manager at Molineux in 1968. After switching to right-half he spent six good years with the Valiants, up to March 1951 when he was transferred for £10,000 to Huddersfield Town where he remained until March 1961 when, for a fee of £2,000, he became player-manager of Bournemouth.

McGarry made over 500 senior appearances for the Town, helping them into the First Division. He also gained four full England caps and represented his country at 'B' team level (1954-56). From Dean Court he took charge of Watford (July 1963 to October 1964) and after serving in the same capacity at Ipswich Town, he arrived at Molineux, after being wanted by the club's directorate for quite some time.

During his first spell with Wolves McGarry saw Wolves reach the 1972 UEFA Cup Final and win the League Cup two years later. He rebuilt the whole team and signed some excellent players as well as baptising plenty more who went on to become superb footballers. Unfortunately things started to go wrong for McGarry – and the Wolves team – in season 1975-76 and after relegation had been suffered he departed company, handing over the reins to Sammy Chung, who had previously been trainer-coach and assistant-boss at the club. At this juncture McGarry went abroad to coach in Saudi Arabia and the United Arab Emirates (June 1976 to October 1977). Between November 1977 and August 1980 he was manager of Newcastle United, and after scouting briefly for Brighton and Hove Albion during the first half of the 1980-81 season, he went off to coach in Zambia, at club level with Power

Dynamo and the Zambian national team. He then turned down a lucrative job in South Africa, before returning to Molineux for a second term of office in September 1985 following Wolves' disastrous start to the season. Sadly he stayed for just two months after seeing Wolves win twice in 12 games. McGarry was then out of football for quite a while before taking a coaching job in Bophuthatswana in 1993.

McGARVEY, Scott Thomas

Scott McGarvey was a useful inside-forward who spent more than 12 years in the Football League (1979-91). Born in Glasgow on 22 April 1963, he joined the groundstaff of Manchester United as a teenager and turned professional at Old Trafford in April 1980. He assisted Wolves on loan from March to May 1984 and finally left United for Portsmouth in a £100,000 deal in July 1984. He later assisted Carlisle United (from January 1986), Grimsby Town (signed for £30,000 in March 1987), Bristol City (September 1989), Oldham Athletic (April 1990) and Wigan Athletic before entering non-League football with Redbridge Forest. Capped four times by Scotland at Under-21 level, McGarvey made over 200 appearances at senior level.

Wolves record: 13 apps. 2 goals.

McGHEE, Mark Edward

Born in Glasgow on 25 May 1957, Mark McGhee was an excellent goalscorer, who played, in turn, for Bristol City (initially as an amateur); Greenock Morton (37 goals in 64 League games); Newcastle United (signed for £150,000 in December 1977 – five goals in 28 League outings); Aberdeen (bought for £80,000 in 1979 – scored 100 goals in 263 matches in all competitions for the Dons); SV Hamburg (for £285,000 in 1984 – seven goals in 30 appearances); Celtic (£200,000 in 1985); Newcastle United (for a second time in 1989) and then Reading (initially as player-manager in 1991).

All told he netted over 200 goals in more than 500 senior appearances at club and international level. He gained four full caps for Scotland and one with the Under-21 side. With Aberdeen and Celtic he won four Scottish League championships, five Scottish Cups (1982-89) and in 1983 helped the Dons lift the European Cup-winners' Cup. After holding office at Elm Park for three years, during which time the Royals won the Second Division title (1994), he took over as manager of Leicester City, replacing ex-Wolves caretaker-boss Brian Little, who switched to Aston Villa. But then, just like Little had done before him, McGhee walked out of Filbert Street to take over the reins at Molineux, moving to Wolves in December 1995.

Forty-eight hours after taking office McGhee admitted that the squad he had inherited was short on both physical and mental strength, certain players are under-coached and have practically no desire to try and appreciate tactics. It took an awful lot of hard work to change that, and at the end of his first season in charge Wolves finished a poor 20th in the First Division. The following term they reached the Play-offs, only to miss out on a trip to Wembley after losing to Crystal Palace over two legs. Unfortunately he saw Wolves struggle in 1997-98, despite an appearance in the FA Cup semi-final – beaten by Arsenal – and after some more disappointing results during the first third of the following campaign, when Wolves were dumped out of the Worthington League Cup by lowly Bournemouth, McGhee left the club by mutual consent (in November 1998). This was his record as Wolves' boss. games played 159, won 65, lost 55, drawn 39.

McILMOYLE, Hugh

Few players have moved around the Football League as much as all-action striker Hughie McIlmoyle. Born at Cambuslang, Scotland, on 29 January 1940, McIlmoyle was involved in ten separate transfer deals during a career which saw him play for Carlisle United in three different spells as well as Leicester City, Rotherham United, Wolves, Bristol City, Middlesbrough and Preston North End. This after starting his career with Port Glasgow and also playing for Morton in the Scottish League. A good old-fashioned centre-forward, he scored well over 170 goals in 450 senior games for eight clubs. He began his English career as an apprentice with Leicester in August 1959, then, after playing in the 1961 FA Cup Final against Tottenham with just seven first-team outings under his belt, he moved to Rotherham. Joining Wolves for £30,000 in October 1964 after his first spell with Carlisle, McIlmoyle scored 45 goals in 105 games in his spell at Molineux before being transferred to Bristol City in March 1967. He rejoined Carlisle in September 1967, then went to 'Boro (September 1969), Preston (July 1971) and Morton (August 1973) before ending his career with yet another spell at Brunton Park, from July 1974 to May 1975. In his two and a half years at Molineux he developed a good understanding in attack with players like Ray Crawford, Jimmy Melia, Ernie Hunt, Terry Wharton, David Burnside and Dave Wagstaffe. He scored his first goal for Wolves at home to Blackburn Rovers in January 1965 and netted one hat-trick, against Aston Villa in an FA Cup fifth round second replay at The Hawthorns in March the same year. Nine days later he scored twice against Manchester United in the quarter-final, but Wolves went down 5-3. That season Wolves

were relegated, but before leaving for Ashton Gate, McIlmoyle helped set them on the road back to the old First Division with 13 goals in 24 League games.

Wolves record: 104+ 1 apps. 45 goals.

McINTOSH, Alexander

Inside-right Alex McIntosh played competitive football before, during and after World War Two. Born in Dunfermline on 14 April 1916, and a junior with St Mirren (amateur), Hearts of Bleith FC, he was playing for Folkestone Town when Wolves spotted his undoubted talent and recruited him to Molineux in October 1937. He became a regular in the Wolves League side in 1938-39 and was in their line-up against Portsmouth in that season's FA Cup Final. He played for the Wanderers when he could during the hostilities and he also guested for Newport County and Watford. He made almost 40 appearances for Wolves in the war and gained a League Cup winners medal in 1942 (v Sunderland) despite spending some time inside a prisoner-of-war camp in Holland having served with the Hearts Regiment. But afterwards McIntosh found if difficult to get into the first team under manager Ted Vizard. In January 1947 he was transferred to Birmingham City and after helping Blues on their way to winning the Second Division championship, he left St Andrew's for Coventry City in February 1948. He ended his League career in 1950 when he moved to Kidderminster Harriers, later assisting Bilston Town and Hednesford Town before retiring in 1953.

Wolves record: 50 apps. 9 goals.

McLEAN, Angus

Gus McLean was unusual in that he was born a Welshman of Scottish parents. He was born at Queensferry on 20 September 1925 and after appearing for Aberystwyth Town was playing for Hilton Main when Wolves signed him during the early days of wartime football. At first he appeared as a wing-half, but later played in both full-back positions, centre-half and even at centre-forward. McLean signed as a professional in November 1942 and after 125 appearances during the war, he quickly made his mark in the Football League and FA Cup competitions. Although he played in a Wolves side that was always challenging for First Division honours, McLean was denied an FA Cup winners' medal in 1949 when a cartilage injury kept him out of the Final against Leicester City. The nearest he came to an international honour was when he was selected as reserve for Wales against Scotland in 1947-48. In May 1951, he left Wolves to become player-manager of Aberystwyth Town and then took over as first-team trainer at Bury in May 1953. He

later worked for Crewe Alexandra and was manager of Hartlepools United from May 1967, when he took over from Brian Clough, to April 1970. With Clough's team he won Hartlepools their first-ever promotion, from the Fourth Division, but they were relegated the following season and after having to seek re-election at the end of the next campaign, he was sacked. A brief spell in charge of Bromsgrove Rovers followed before he announced his retirement from full-time involvement in football in May 1975, though he did continue to work as a scout for a number of Midlands-based clubs. McLean died in 1979.
Wolves record: 158 apps.

McLOUGHLIN, Paul Brendan

Midfielder Paul McLoughlin was born in Bristol on 23 December 1963 and played his early football in the South West having trials with Bristol City in 1979 and serving with Yeovil Town (1980). Soon afterwards he went to New Zealand, collecting several medals in domestic competitions while playing for Gisborne FC before returning to Britain to sign full-time professional forms with Cardiff City in December 1984. He won Welsh international honours at Ninian Park where he played until 1986. He then returned to Ashton Gate as a non-contract player, transferring to Hereford United in June 1987. From Edgar Street, McLoughlin moved to Wolves for £45,000 in July 1989. He never really settled in at Molineux and after a loan spells with Walsall (September 1991, when former Wolves favourite Kenny Hibbitt was in charge of the Saddlers) and York City, he joined Mansfield Town in a £35,000 deal in January 1992, staying at Field Mill until May 1994.
Wolves record: 12+17 apps. 4 goals.

McMAHON, Douglas David Alexander

Inside-right Doug McMahon made his League debut for Wolves against Blackpool (away) in December 1938, having joined the club the previous month from Caledonian Juniors in his homeland in Winnepeg, Canada, where he was born in 1915. He returned to Winnepeg in March 1939 joining the Union Weston Sencor club.
Wolves record: 1 app.

McMAIN, Joseph

Following Charlie Henderson's departure from Molineux at the end of the 1895-96 season, Wolves quickly recruited Joe McMain from Kettering Town as his replacement. Born in Wolverhampton c.1872, McMain, a previously with Stafford Rangers, did a splendid job for the club and scored some cracking goals including six in five matches in December 1898. In the summer of 1899,

after suffering a couple of niggling injuries, he left Molineux for Notts County and returned to Kettering Town.
Wolves record: 51 apps. 19 goals.

McMILLAN, Stuart Thomas

Outside-right Stuart McMillan had one good season with Wolves, making 23 senior appearances in 1922-23 under manager George Robey. But when Robey left Molineux in May 1924, so did McMillan, who immediately joined Bradford City. He spent three years at Valley Parade, making 73 appearances, before transferring to Nottingham Forest in June 1927. He left Forest in August 1928 after only 10 outings to sign for Clapton Orient, retiring in 1930. In 1942 he become football advisor with Derby County and managed the Rams from January 1946 to November 1953. He then turned his hand to scouting. Born in Leicester on 17 August 1896, McMillan was educated in Rutland, yet played his early League football with Derby County (December 1914 to June 1919). He then had two years with Chelsea before moving to Gillingham in March 1921, from where he joined Wolves in June 1922. McMillan died in Ashbourne, Derbyshire on 27 September 1963.
Wolves record: 39 apps. 5 goals.

McNAB, Robert

In his prime Bob McNab was a fine full-back with good ball control and excellent vision. A Yorkshireman, born in Huddersfield on 20 July 1943, he played local junior football in his home town and for Rawthorpe CSM and Mold Green Civic Youth Club before joining Huddersfield Town as an amateur in June 1961, turning professional at Leeds Road in April 1962. After more than 70 games for the Town he was transferred to Arsenal for £40,000 in October 1966 and over the next nine years became a star performer with the Gunners, helping them win the Fairs Cup in 1970, complete the League Championship and FA Cup double 12 months later, finish runners up in the FA Cup in 1972, as well as collecting two League Cup runners-up medals in 1968 and 1969. He made 365 appearances for Arsenal and was also capped four times by England and represented the Football League. He signed for Wolves in July 1975, but stayed only a season at Molineux before going over to America to play for San Antonio in Texas. Returning to this country in September 1977, McNab signed for non-League Barnet, but he remained at Underhill for only a short time prior to becoming a publican in Tottenham. He later went abroad to coach in Vancouver where he now resides with his wife and family.
Wolves record: 16 apps.

McPARLAND, Peter James

Peter McParland was a brilliant goalscoring outside-left, fast, direct, with a grand shot in either foot, who came to Wolves far too late in his career. Born in Newry, County Down, Northern Ireland on 25 April 1934, 'Packy' McParland joined Dundalk on leaving senior school in Newry. In August 1952, while serving his apprenticeship as a coppersmith and having been watched over a period of time, George Martin, the Aston Villa manager, paid £3,880 for his services and in the next ten years he gave the Birmingham club supreme service, scoring 120 goals in 341 appearances. He netted both goals when Villa beat double-chasing Manchester United 2-1 to win the 1957 FA Cup Final, he helped Villa take the Second Division championship in 1960 and then captured a League Cup winners tankard in 1961. In between times he represented the Football League XI and gained 33 caps for Northern Ireland (he added another to his collection when a Wolves player). He moved from Villa Park to Molineux in January 1962 but a year later switched due south to sign for Plymouth Argyle for £30,000. A spell in America with Atlanta Chiefs preceded a brief association with Peterborough United and after serving with Worcester City from 1966, he returned to Ireland where he became player-manager and then manager of Glentoran from 1968 to 1971. Thereafter McParland coached in Kuwait, Libya and Hong Kong and was also briefly in charge of No.1 Club of Kuwait before returning to England to take up residence in Bournemouth, where he ran a successful property business with his son.
Wolves record: 21 apps. 10 goals.

McVEIGH, James

Jimmy McVeigh was a reserve defender at Molineux during a four-year period to 1970. Born in Hathersage on 2 July 1949, he joined the Wolves apprentice staff in 1966, turned professional in May 1968, but just over two seasons later was released to join Gillingham in October 1970. He remained at the Priestfield Stadium until May 1972, making 51 League appearances.
Wolves record: 2 apps.

MACLAREN, David

Goalkeeper Dave MacLaren was born in Auchterarder on 12 June 1934. He played for St Johnstone juniors before entering the RAF for his National Service. In February 1956 he became a professional with Dundee, before joining Leicester City in January 1957. He made almost 100 senior appearances during his three and a half years at Filbert Street before transferring to Plymouth Argyle in June 1960. At Home Park he became a firm favourite with the fans and had 131 League outings for the Pilgrims prior to his transfer to Wolves in January 1965. He did well at Molineux where he contested the No.1 position with Fred Davies. In September 1966, however, MacLaren was sold to Southampton after playing in the opening game of that season under Wolves boss Ronnie Allen. From The Dell MacLaren switched back to the Midlands to play for Worcester City (July 1967), retiring two years later.

In 1954, when serving in the RAF, he won both the Sportsman of the Year award and unofficial representative honours for Malaysia and in 1970 he returned to that country as a coach, assuming the management of the Malaysian national team in 1972. He also coached the Australian club, Hakoah in 1973-74.

His two brothers, Jimmy and Roy, both kept goal in League football.
Wolves record: 47 apps.

MACCLESFIELD TOWN

Wolves have yet to meet Macclesfield at any level of senior football.
Player with both clubs: Jim Melrose.

MADDEN, Lawrence David

Lawrie Madden was already a studious, experienced defender when he joined Wolves on a free transfer from Sheffield Wednesday in August 1991. Born in London on 28 September 1955, he commenced his career with Arsenal, but failed to make the breakthrough at Highbury and subsequently made his League debut for Mansfield Town as a non-contract player in March 1975.

He moved from Field Mill to Charlton Athletic and made over 120 appearances for the Addicks before drifting out of competitive football to assist Boston United. He returned to the fray with Millwall in March 1982 and in August 1983 teamed up with Sheffield Wednesday. After playing in more than 250 games for the Owls he became surplus to requirements at Hillsborough and a loan spell with Leicester City (January 1991) preceded his move to Wolves. Madden, who helped Wednesday win the League Cup in 1991 (v Manchester United) was given a free transfer from Molineux in May 1993 and four months later he signed for Darlington, later assisting Chesterfield (from October 1993). Madden was 37 years, 222 days old when he last played for Wolves against Derby County on 8 May 1993. (See *Age*)
Wolves record: 71+5 apps. 1 goal.

MAGUIRE, James Edward

During the late 1930s Teddy Maguire was part of two excellent wing pairings – first on the right with big Tom Galley and then on the left with hard-shooting Dicky Dorsett. Maguire, in fact, could occupy either wing position and he was also a very useful inside-forward. Keen and aggressive, he was born in Meadowfield on 23 July 1917 and joined Wolves from Willington FC early in the 1936-37 season, claiming a regular first-team place by the November. During the war he guested for Hartlepools and remained at Molineux until May 1947 when he transferred to Swindon Town, later assisting Halifax Town (from October 1948-May 1950) and retiring out of League football a year later after a brief spell with Spennymoor United. Maguire played outside-left for Wolves in the 1939 FA Cup Final defeat by Portsmouth. In his League career he netted 19 times in 162 games.
Wolves record: 85 apps. 9 goals.

MALPASS, William

Half-back Billy Malpass had a 'storming' game when Wolves won the 1893 FA Cup Final against Everton at the Crystal Palace. And three years later, as skipper, he was again outstanding in the Final, although on this occasion Wolves went down 2-1 to Sheffield Wednesday. Yet in that same 1895-96 season, Malpass, together with team-mates Tommy Dunn and Alf Griffin, had been suspended by the club for allegedly not trying on the pitch. It was a remarkable indictment, especially when made against Malpass, who had given Wolves such yeoman service since joining them from Wednesbury Old Athletic in August 1891. Born in Wednesbury on 5 March 1867, Malpass's Wolves career lasted almost eight years, until May 1899, when he was forced to retire because of a knee injury. Most of his games were at centre-half, although he also appeared at wing-half, doing so in the 1893 Final, when he skippered the side. In November 1896 he played for the Football League against the Irish League in Belfast, in a team which included nine Midlands-based players, three of them from Wolves, the others being Beats and Wood. Billy Malpass died at Darlaston just before World War Two.
Wolves record: 155 apps. 9 goals.

MANAGERS

Here is a list of Wolves' managers down the years:

August 1877-July 1885	George Worrall
August 1885-June 1922	John Addenbrooke
June 1922-May 1924	George Robey
June 1924-March 1926	George Hoskins
March 1926-June 1927	Fred Scotchbrook
June 1927-March 1944	Major Frank Buckley
April 1944-May 1948	Ted Vizard
June 1948-September 1964	Stan Cullis
September 1964-September 1965	Andy Beattie
September 1965-November 1968	Ronnie Allen
November 1968-May 1976	Bill McGarry
June 1976-November 1978	Sammy Chung
November 1978-November 1981	John Barnwell
February-August 1982	Ian Greaves
August 1982-April 1984	Graham Hawkins
June 1984-July 1985	Tommy Docherty
August-September 1985	Sammy Chapman
September-November 1985	Bill McGarry
November 1985-August 1986	Sammy Chapman
October 1986-March 1994	Graham Turner
March 1994-December 1995	Graham Taylor
December 1995-November 1998	Mark McGhee
November 1998 to date	Colin Lee

See under individual personal entries for details of all Wolves' managers.

Club Record
John (Jack) Addenbrook held the position of secretary-manager for a club record 37 years (1885 to 1922).

Caretaker Managers
For seven games (from 19 September 1964 to 31 October 1964 inclusive) senior players Ron Flowers and Gerry Harris, along with physiotherapist George Palmer, looked after team affairs until Andy Beattie officially took over as manager on 1 November 1964.

Former player Jack Dowen (trainer) and coach Gerry Summers were put in charge of the team against Newcastle United on 23 November 1968 prior to the arrival of Bill McGarry.

Senior coach Brian Garvey took control of the side for two League matches (11 November 1978 and 18 November 1978) before John Barnwell moved into office.

Ian Ross held the team together for four games (16 January 1982 to 2 February 1982 inclusive) prior to the arrival at Molineux of Ian Greaves.

And Jim Barron assumed the role of caretaker-boss for five League games in the mid-1980s (28 April 1984 to 12 March 1984) until Tommy Docherty took over. Brian Little was in charge from August-October 1986. Peter Shirtliff was in charge in March 1994 between Graham Turner and Graham Taylor.

Bobby Downes acted as caretaker-boss at Molineux from mid November 1995 to mid December 1995 during which time Wolves played six League games, winning two and losing three. And when Mark McGhee left the club in November 1998, Colin Lee took charge of team affairs on a caretaker-basis until being given the job full-time, albeit on a short term contract.

Player to Manager
Here is a list of some of the many ex-Wolves players (at all levels) who later became managers of senior football clubs:
John Addenbrooke (Wolves 1885-1922)
Mike Bailey (Brighton and Hove Albion 1981-82, Charlton Athletic 1980-81, Hereford United 1978-79)
Jock Basford (Exeter City 1966-67, Mansfield Town 1970-71).
Phil Chard (Northampton Town 1992-93)

Stan Cullis (Wolves 1948-64, Birmingham City 1965-70)

Peter Daniel (Lincoln City 1987)

Ron Flowers (Northampton Town 1968-69)

Bobby Gould (Bristol Rovers 1981-83 and 1985-87), Coventry City 1983-84 and 1992-93, West Bromwich Albion 1991-92, Wimbledon 1987-90, Wales national team 1996-1999).

Jack Hamilton (Bristol City 1915-19)

Ray Hankin (Darlington 1991-92)

John Harris (Chester 1956-59, Sheffield United 1959-68)

Joe Harvey (Barrow 1955-57, Workington 1957-62, Newcastle United 1962-75)

Graham Hawkins (Wolves 1982-84)

George Hedley (Bristol City 1913-15)

Kenny Hibbitt (Walsall 1990-94, Cardiff City 1995-97)

Albert Hoskins (Wolves 1924-26)

Emlyn Hughes, OBE (Rotherham United 1981-82)

Eric Jones (De Graafschap, Holland 1950s)

Andy King (Waterford 1988-89, Mansfield Town 1993-96)

Ken Knighton (Sunderland 1979-81, Leyton Orient 1981-83)

Jim McCalliog (Halifax Town 1990-91)

Angus McLean (Hartlepool United 1967-70)

Stuart McMillan (Derby County 1946-53)

Jimmy Melia (Aldershot 1969-72, Crewe Alexandra 1972-74, Southport 1975, Brighton and Hove Albion 1983, Beleneses of Portugal 1983-85, Stockport County 1986).

Ian Ross (FC Valur, Iceland 1984-88, Huddersfield Town 1992)

Arthur Rowley (Shrewsbury Town 1958-68, Sheffield United 1968-69, Southend United 1970-76)

Jack Rowley (Plymouth Argyle 1955-60, Oldham Athletic 1960-63 and 1968-69, Wrexham 1966-67, Bradford Park Avenue 1967-68).

John Rudge (Port Vale 1984-99)

Jack Smith (West Bromwich Albion 1948-52, Reading 1952-55)

Cyril Spiers (Cardiff City 1948-54, Crystal Palace 1954-58, Exeter City 1962-63, Norwich City 1946-47)

George Swift (Southampton 1911-12)

Frank Taylor (Stoke City 1952-60)

Jack Taylor (QPR 1952-59, Leeds United 1959-61)

Harry Thompson (Headington United – now Oxford United – 1949-56)

Les Wilson (Vancouver Whitecaps (1974-83)

Peter Withe (Wimbledon 1991-92, Thailand national team 1998-99)

George Worrall (Wolves 1877-85)

Billy Wright (Arsenal 1962-66)

NB. wartime guests have not been included.

Managerial Odds and Ends

Brothers Arthur and Jack Rowley, and Jock Basford were all registered as amateurs with Wolves during the 1938-45 wartime period.

Addenbrooke and Hoskins both played in various Wolves teams before becoming the club's manager.

Don Howe was an amateur with Wolves, who, in later years managed several Football League clubs including Arsenal, West Bromwich Albion, QPR and Coventry City.

John Rudge was a junior player at Molineux in 1959. He later became Port Vale's longest-serving manager (15 years).

After his association with Vancouver Whitecaps, Les Wilson was appointed manager/administrator of the Canadian national team.

Former Wolves reserve and coach George Poyser had trials with Mansfield Town as a youngster and later returned to become assistant manager of the Stags. He was also assistant manager of Manchester City.

Stan Cullis was the youngest manager of an FA Cup winning team when he guided Wolves to success in 1949 at the age of 33 years, 187 days.

Reserve-Team Manager

In July 1892, Wolves appointed their first-ever reserve-team manager. He was Harry Dillard (christened Henry James) who had done so much to help develop the club during its early years in the Football League. Dillard was to hold the position until 1918.

Born in Tewkesbury, in April 1862, he was taken to Sheffield by his parents at the age of three but later returned to the Midlands and attended Wesley School in Pelsall. A founder-member of Walsall Swifts in 1874 he played for that club until a serious knee injury forced him into an early retirement at the age of 24, upon which he became an official club umpire, a key position in the 1870s and 1880s, prior to the innovation of linesmen. From 1918 to 1940 Dillard was Wolves' representative on the Birmingham County FA and was duly rewarded with a long service medal before World War Two. Indeed, during his lifetime in association football Dillard received over 30 medals for various deeds performed within the game. A much respected figure and avid Wolves supporter until the day he died in 1961.

MANCHESTER CITY

Wolves' playing record against City is:

Football League

Venue	P	W	D	L	F	A
Home	48	27	12	9	122	68
Away	48	11	10	27	71	119
Total	96	38	22	36	193	187

FA Cup

Home	2	2	0	0	5	1
Away	1	0	1	0	2	2
Total	3	2	1	0	7	3

League Cup

Home	1	0	0	1	0	2
Away	2	1	0	1	5	5
Neutral	1	1	0	0	2	1
Total	4	2	0	2	7	8

Wartime

Home	2	1	0	1	3	3
Away	2	0	0	2	1	5
Total	4	1	0	3	4	8

Wolves and City first met in the Football League 100 years ago in season 1899-1900 (Division Two) when both games ended in 1-1 draws.

In 1903-04 City whipped Wolves twice – winning 4-1 at Molineux and 6-1. The legendary Welsh wizard, Billy Meredith, scored for City in both games.

Indeed, around this time City held the upper hand in tussles with Wolves. They won both games in 1904-05 (5-1 at home, 3-0 away) and doubled up again in 1905-06 (4-0 at home, 3-2 at Molineux).

And in December 1909, a hat-trick by Irving Thornley helped City to another emphatic 6-0 home win over the Wanderers.

An excellent 4-1 home victory for Wolves in April 1927 (Wilf Chadwick scored twice) was followed six years later by a thumping 8-0 triumph, again at Molineux, when Charlie Phillips (3), Jack Beattie (2) and Ivor Jones (2) led the goal rush in front of 21,640 fans.

By coincidence, both First Division League games in 1934-35 ended in 5-0 home wins – Wolves racing to success three days before Christmas at Molineux and City collecting the points on the last day of the campaign at Maine Road.

A seven-goal epic went Wolves' way by 4-3 at Molineux in December 1935 and in season 1937-38 City were beaten twice for the first time, Wolves winning 3-1 at home and 4-2 away, Gordon Clayton scoring a hat-trick in the victory at Molineux.

Nearly 40,000 fans saw Wolves triumph at Maine Road on New Year's Day, 1938. Tom Galley opened the scoring for Wolves early on from the penalty spot and later added a second goal, while Welshman Bryn Jones, soon to move to Arsenal, scored a cracker past Frank Swift. Peter Doherty scored for City.

It was all square (one win apiece) over Easter 1949, but three years later, in November 1952, Roy Swinbourne scored a 20-minute hat-trick as Wolves – playing their 1,000th League game at home – whipped luckless City 7-3 at Molineux. And it was hot-shot Swinbourne again who haunted City when he helped himself to another four goals in Wolves' brilliant 7-2 home win in August 1955.

Swinbourne netted total of 11 League goals for Wolves against City in the early 1950s.

Jimmy Murray (who had replaced

John Richards (No. 9) hits the winning goal against Manchester City in the 1974 League Cup Final.

Swinbourne) grabbed four goals in Wolves' 5-1 home win on the first day of the 1956-57 season and in November 1957, Wolves found themselves 3-1 down at Maine Road in a First Division game, but they stormed back to beat Manchester City 4-3 in front of 45,121 fans. The return fixture at Molineux ended 3-3, when City centre-half Dave Ewing conceded a spectacular own-goal.

Wolves scored five goals in a 15-minute spell either side of half-time when they hammered City 8-1 at Molineux in a First Division game August 1962. Ted Farmer was a four-goal hero on this occasion.

When Wolves lost 2-1 at Maine Road in August 1965, both City's goals were scored by Wolves players: George Miller and Bobby Thomson.

In the return fixture at Maine Road five days later, David Woodfield became the first Wolves player to be sent-off for 30 years after a clumsy challenge on Mike Summerbee. City made the extra man count and eventually won 4-2.

Francis Lee hit a hat-trick in City's 5-2 home win over Wolves in January 1972, and another four goals were scored in a 17-minute spell against City in the League match at Molineux ten years later, in April 1982, when Wolves won 4-1.

When Manchester City beat Wolves 4-0 at Maine Road in a one-sided encounter in December 1984, former Wanderers' star Jim

Melrose set up all his side's goals.

Robbie Dennison scored his last goal for Wolves in a 3-0 home win over Manchester City in November 1996 – and what a cracker it was too.

The first FA Cup-tie between the teams took place in 1910-11 when Wolves won a second round tie 1-0 at Molineux in front of a 25,032 crowd.

The next two encounters were staged in 1951-52 and again it was Wolves who took the honours, winning a third round clash 4-1 after a replay. Defender Jack Short, playing at centre-forward, scored twice for Wolves, as did Jimmy Mullen. The Molineux attendance was almost 44,000.

Wolves lost a seven goal thriller by 4-3 to Manchester City in a second round League Cup-tie at Maine Road in September 1971. Wolves were, in fact, 3-1 ahead with only ten minutes remaining but City stormed back to score three times late on to win.

But two-and-a-half years later, in March 1974, and in front of 97,886 fans at Wembley (receipts £161,500 – with terrace tickets only 80p) revenge was sweet as Wolves won the League Cup trophy for the first time by beating City 2-1 in the Final, John Richards hitting the winning goal.

Wolves sold Steve Daley to Manchester City in September 1979 for a then British record transfer fee of £1,150,000.

Wolves' centenary game in August 1977

was a friendly against Manchester City when almost 15,000 fans witnessed a 2-1 win for the visitors.

Players with both clubs include: Chic Brodie, John Burridge, Wayne Clarke, Keith Curle, Steve Daley, Geoff Lomax, Bobby McDonald, Jim Melrose, Jimmy Murray, Eric Nixon, Paul Simpson, Paul Stewart, Barry Stobart, Mike Stowell, Dave Wagstaffe, Dennis Westcott and Ken Whitfield.

Also associated: Major Frank Buckley (City player, Wolves manager), Mick Docherty (City player, Wolves coach), Terry Park, Bob Robinson and Davey Robson (Wolves Reserves), Andy Beattie (City wartime guest, Wolves manager), Bob King (City wartime guest), Harry Iddon and Jock Mulraney (Wolves guests), George Poyser (Wolves reserve, scout and coach, City assistant manager); Dicky Davies (City reserve); Fred Ramscar (City amateur); Mel Eves (City trialist), Ronnie Ekelund (Wolves trialist).

MANCHESTER UNITED

Wolves' playing record against United is:

Football League

Venue	P	W	D	L	F	A
Home	40	21	9	10	81	55
Away	40	9	5	26	44	80
Total	80	30	14	36	125	135

FA Cup

	P	W	D	L	F	A
Home	4	1	0	3	8	12
Away	1	0	1	0	1	1

Neutral	2	1	1	0	2	1
Total	7	2	2	3	11	14
Wartime						
Home	1	1	0	0	2	0
Away	1	0	0	1	0	2
Total	2	1	0	1	2	2

Wolves first met United (then known as Newton Heath) at senior level in October 1892 – and against all the odds, the Heathens went goal-crazy, winning 10-1 in heavy rain at their Monsall Road ground in a Second Division match. And at the time they were bottom of the table. This defeat (in terms of goals conceded) is the heaviest suffered by Wolves in a major competition.

Amazingly, the return fixture, played at Molineux in mid-December, resulted in a 2-0 win for Wolves, who fielded the same defence except for their goalkeeper.

As a consequence of being based in different Divisions, there were no League encounters between the clubs between 1894-95 and 1921-22, and from then to 1930-31 there were only four.

But over the festive season of 1931, 12 goals were scored in the two second Division matches. United won 3-2 at Old Trafford on Christmas Day, only for Wolves to romp to an impressive, all-action 7-0 victory at Molineux 24 hours later.

United made two changes from the first game, Wolves none, and 37,207 fans saw Walter Bottrill and Billy Hartill both score twice in Wolves' runaway win.

Wolves boss Major Buckley fielded two 16-year-old wingers in his side which beat Manchester United 3-1 in a First Division match at Molineux in March 1939.

Wolves and Manchester United were two of the top teams in the country immediately after the war and when the sides met at Molineux in November 1947, a crowd of 44,309 saw United win comfortably by 6-2, Johnny Morris and Stan Pearson scoring two apiece.

United, the FA Cup holders, came to Molineux in September 1948, and almost 43,000 fans saw Wolves win 3-2 with Johnny Hancocks scoring twice. The return clash at Old Trafford took place a week later and United gained revenge with a 2-0 victory, Pearson again on target.

On 4 October 1952, close on 40,000 spectators saw Roy Swinbourne score a hat-trick in a 6-2 triumph, Wolves' best-ever home win over United – and five weeks later Swinbourne netted another treble against United's arch rivals Manchester City.

As reigning League champions, Wolves doubled up over United in 1954-55, winning both matches 4-2, Johnny Hancocks scoring in each one.

Another Wolves double arrived in 1957-58 when they triumphed 3-1 at home and 4-0 at Old Trafford. The latter game was the re-arranged fixture after the scheduled one in February had to be postponed because of the Munich Air Disaster.

The Wolves 'M' squad got into action at Molineux in November 1958 when Jimmy Murray (2), Bobby Mason and Jimmy Mullen scored in a thumping 5-0 win.

Wolves completed the League double over united in seasons 1959-60 and 1960-61 before United returned the gesture with two victories over Wolves in 1962-63, 1964-65 and 1967-68.

Those two League matches between Wolves and United over the Christmas period in 1967 attracted more than 117,000 spectators. There were 63,450 at Old Trafford and 53,940 at Molineux.

League honours were even during the 1970s, although United did storm to an impressive 4-2 win at Molineux in October 1978 when the Greenhoff brothers found the net in front of a near 30,000 crowd.

Jimmy McIlroy scored a hat-trick in United's resounding 5-0 home win over Wolves in October 1981 in front of 46,837 fans. And in February 1984, just over 20,000 fans saw Wolves hold United to a 1-1 draw at Molineux in the last League meeting between the two clubs to date.

Two of Wolves' three away FA Cup-ties with United were in the semi-final of 1948-49. After a nail-biting 1-1 draw at Hillsborough, a single goal by Sammy Smyth in the Goodison Park replay was enough to take Stan Cullis' men through to Wembley.

A total of 14 goals were scored in two FA Cup games between Wolves and United in successive seasons in the mid-1960s and both times it was those at Molineux who saw the action. In March 1965, a crowd of 53,581 witnessed United's 5-3 triumph and 12 months later 53,428 fans were present to see United win again, this time by 4-2 after Wolves had been 2-0 ahead inside 10 minutes thanks to two Terry Wharton penalties. Denis Law scored twice in each tie for United.

A crowd of 28,145 saw United beat Wolves 2-1 in a pre-season friendly at Molineux in August 1994.

Players with both clubs include: Brian Birch, George Bisset, Bill Bryant, Joe Davies, Darren Ferguson, Billy Harrison, Jim McCalliog, Scott McGarvey, Sid Tyler and Billy Wrigglesworth.

Also associated: Major Frank Buckley (United player, Wolves manager); Ian Greaves (United player, Wolves manager); Arthur Rowley (Wolves reserve, United guest – making his debut for the Reds aged 15 years, six months in November 1941 v Liverpool alongside his brother Jack), Jack Rowley (United player, Wolves reserve and wartime guest), Gregg Fellows (United reserve, Wolves coach); Mark Todd (United junior), John Griffiths and Charlie Mitten (Wolves wartime guests); Arthur Allman, Ben Morton, Bill Prendergast, Jim Travers and Jeff Wealands (Wolves Reserves); Arthur Potts (United amateur); Paul Bradshaw (United trialist); Hugh Curran (United amateur), Mick Martin (Wolves trialist), Billy Halligan (United guest); Chris Turner (United goalkeeper, Wolves coach).

Action from the sixth-round replay against Manchester United at Molineux in March 1976.

MANNION, Gerry Patrick

Right-winger Gerry Mannion had pace, good skills, an appetite for the game and he could score goals as well as make them. Unfortunately from Wolves' point of view he did far better after leaving Molineux than he did while he was there, although to be fair he did have some competition for the No.7 shirt during his time with the Wanderers. Born in Rugby League territory at Burtonwood near Warrington on 21 December 1939, Mannion joined Wolves as a youngster and turned professional in November 1957. After winning England youth honours and two Under-23 caps, he was transferred to Norwich City in September 1961 for £13,000 and during the next six-and-a-half years he appeared in 119 senior games for the Canaries, scoring 21 goals. From Carrow Road he switched to Chester (January 1968) and pulled out of League football five months later.

Wolves record: 21 apps. 7 goals.

MANSFIELD TOWN

Wolves' playing record against the Stags is:

Football League

Venue	P	W	D	L	F	A
Home	1	1	0	0	6	2
Away	1	0	0	1	1	3
Total	2	1	0	1	7	5

FA Cup

Home	1	0	0	1	0	1
Away	1	1	0	0	3	2
Total	2	1	0	1	3	3

League Cup

Home	1	1	0	0	2	1
Away	1	0	0	1	0	1
Total	2	1	0	1	2	2

The first League game between Wolves and Mansfield took place at Molineux on 17 December 1988 and it produced eight goals, Wolves winning a Third Division contest 6-2 in front of 12,134 fans. Steve Bull scored a hat-trick. The Stags won the return fixture 3-1 at Field Mill when over 9,000 fans attended.

Wolves of the Second Division were humbled by Mansfield Town from the Midland League in the third round of the FA Cup in January 1929. The Stags came to Molineux and won 1-0 in front of 21,837 fans.

On a mud bath of a pitch at Field Mill, Wolves came back from 2-0 down to beat plucky Mansfield 3-2 in the third round of the FA Cup-tie in January 1995, Lee Mills notching the winner on 71 minutes.

Wolves' first League Cup win was 2-1 at home against Mansfield in September 1966. Bob Hatton and Terry Wharton scored the Wanderers' goals that evening in front of a 12,098 crowd. The Stags gained revenge nine years later, winning a fourth round tie at Field Mill 1-0 in November 1975.

Players with both clubs include: Tommy Baxter, John Chadburn, Nicky Clarke, Simon Coleman, Mel Eves, Walter Featherby, Henry Hargreaves, Reg Hollingworth, Henry Howell, Emlyn Hughes (Town non-contract), Paul McLoughlin, Lawrie Madden, Harry Middleton, Jack Needham, Jack Streets, David Thompson, Harry Thompson, Albert Thorpe, Stuart Watkiss, Ernie Whittam, Frank Wignall.

Also associated: Andy King (Wolves player, Town manager); Jock Basford (Wolves reserve, Mansfield manager), Sammy Chapman (Town player, Wolves manager); Ian Greaves and George Jobey (managers of both clubs); George Poyser (Wolves reserve, scout and coach, Mansfield junior); Rod Arnold, Peter Clarke, Ivan Flowers, Gerry Darville, Ian Hall, Neville Hamilton, Colin Harrington, Harry Keeling, Jonathan Laws, Frank Perfect, Cyril Poole, Richard Smith, Alf Somerfield, Alwyn Statham, David Synett, John Thomas, Mark Todd and Fred Wilson (all Wolves Reserves), Andy Poole (Wolves reserve, Mansfield apprentice); John Jarman (Wolves junior and coach, Mansfield coach); Charlie Mitten (Wolves wartime guest), Bill Baxter and Roy Pritchard (Mansfield wartime guests), Tom Pritchard (Wolves player, Town trainer).

MARDENBOROUGH, Steven Alexander

Utility forward Steve Mardenborough had the pleasure of silencing the Anfield kop when he scored a dramatic winning goal (his only one for Wolves) against Liverpool in a First Division match there in January 1984. A native of Birmingham (born on 11 September 1964), he joined Coventry City as a professional in 1962 and after a brief spell with Birmingham City, he switched to Molineux, making his League debut in September 1983. After a loan spell with Cambridge United (February 1984) Mardenborough signed for Swansea City (July 1984) and a year later went to neighbouring Newport County, transferring to his third Welsh club, Cardiff City, in March 1987. He switched from Ninian Park to Hereford United and after assisting IFK Osterlund (Sweden) and Cheltenham Town he re-entered League football with Darlington (June 1990). In July 1993 he moved to Lincoln City for £10,000, switched to Scarborough in February 1995 and after a brief spell with Stafford Rangers he was recruited by Colchester United in August 1995. Four months later he teamed up with Swansea City and in 1996 signed for Merthyr Tydfil, later assisting Inter Cardiff (League of Wales). Fast and direct, Mardenborough made well over 300 appearances during his professional career, including more than 80 as a substitute.

Wolves record: 9+2 apps. 1 goal.

MARR, Andrew

A Wolves player during the last season prior to the suspension of the competition in 1915, outside-right Andy Marr found it difficult to get first-team football at Molineux and after the hostilities he did not re-sign for Wolves. Born in Gateshead c.1893, he played for Coventry City before moving to Molineux.

Wolves record: 3 apps.

MARSDEN, Christopher

Yorkshireman Chris Marsden, an astute and highly competitive midfielder, was born in Sheffield on 3 January 1969. He joined his home town club Sheffield United as an apprentice in June 1985 and turned professional at Bramall Lane in January 1987. In July 1988 after 18 first-team games for the Blades he was transferred to neighbouring Huddersfield Town and in the next six years amassed 155 League and Cup appearances for the Terriers before moving to Wolves for £250,000 in January 1994 after a loan spell with Coventry City (November 1993). Unfortunately he failed to make an impact at Molineux although injuries (including a broken leg) didn't help matters and in November 1994 he went to Notts County, also for £250,000, switching to Stockport County for £70,000 in January 1996. He helped the Edgeley Park club gain promotion from the Second Division in 1997. In October 1997, after 86 games, Marsden left Stockport to sign for Birmingham City for a fee of £500,000 in October 1997 and on his debut for Blues he scored the winner in a 1-0 Nationwide League win over Wolves. In January 1999, Marsden left St Andrew's and signed for Southampton in a £850,000 deal.

Wolves record: 11 apps.

MARSDEN, Frederick

Fred Marsden was a steady, reliable half-back, standing well over six feet tall, who was reserve to George Laking during his time at Molineux. A Lancastrian, born in Blackburn on 6 September 1911 he attended Blackburn Council School and played for Clitheroe, Manchester Central and Accrington Stanley before joining Wolves in January 1935 with Jack Aspin in a combined deal worth £750. He left Molineux in May 1936 for Bournemouth and later assisted Weymouth (from June 1949) prior to retiring in 1952. Marsden died in Bournemouth in November 1989.

Wolves record: 1 app.

MARSHALL, George Harold

Left-back George Marshall made his League debut for Wolves on the opening day of the 1920-21 season, and what an unemorable occasion it was – a 2-0 defeat at Craven Cottage in the Second Division. But by the end of the same season, Marshall was turning out in a FA Cup Final at Stamford Bridge where Wolves lost to Tottenham Hotspur. He missed only four games that season, all through injury, and in all made well over 100 senior appearances for Wolves before being

transferred to Walsall in February 1924 after the emergence of Harry Shaw saw him unable to regain his place after another injury. Marshall was born at Walker-on-Tyne on 3 March 1896 and after beginning his career with the Newcastle club Shankhouse FC, he had trials for Portsmouth in 1913-14 before being signed by Southend United in July 1914. War was declared before his career could get going but in August 1919, Wolves signed him and after a season in their reserve side he made his League debut in August 1920. He was with Walsall for only a short time before being transferred to Reading, moving to Bournemouth in 1924-25 and then ending his career with Darlaston in 1925-26. Marshall died c.1978.
Wolves record: 111 apps. 1 goal.

MARSHALL, John

Outside-right Johnny Marshall appeared in Wolves' first team during the last pre-war season of 1938-39. Born in Cambridgeshire c.1917, he was recruited to the Molineux staff from Norwich City in June 1938, but owing to the hostilities his career was cut short and he never appeared in the League again.
Wolves record: 1 app

MARSHALL, William Harry

Wing-half or inside-forward Harry Marshall (no relation to George or John) was born in Hucknall, Notts on 16 February 1905. He started out with his local club, Hucknall Primitives and after brief spells with Bromley Athletic and Bromley United he joined Nottingham Forest (February 1924), later playing for Southport (July 1926) before signing for Wolves in March 1928. He was transferred from Molineux to Port Vale for a substantial fee in March 1930 and played over 50 games for the Valiants before switching to Tottenham Hotspur in March 1932. Over the next few years he assisted Kidderminster Harriers (July 1933), Brierley Hill Alliance (1934), Rochdale (August 1935) and Linfield (June 1938), retiring during the 1939-40 campaign. Marshall died in Linby, Notts on 9 March 1959. Brother Bob played for Sunderland and Manchester City.
Wolves record: 54 apps. 13 goals.

MARSON, Frederick

Inside-left Fred Marson had a fair amount of ability, but failed to settle at Molineux following his transfer from Darlaston in July 1923. Born in Darlaston on 18 January 1900, he played for a number of local clubs early in his career and after leaving Wolves in 1925 he joined Sheffield Wednesday, later assisting Swansea Town (1928-29) before returning to play in the Black Country, first with Darlaston, then Wellington Town and back to Darlaston, retiring in 1938.
Wolves record: 8 apps. 4 goals.

MARTIN, David Kirker

Irish centre-forward David 'Boy' Martin was born in Belfast on 1 February 1914 and played and scored for his home town club, Belfast Celtic, before joining Wolves in December 1934. Formerly an orphanage lad, Martin came to the fore when leading the Royal Ulster Rifles and Army attacks while serving in the forces as a drummer (hence his nickname.).He was engaged by Celtic in 1932 at a cost of just £5 and quickly set the footballing fraternity in Ireland alight with some superb displays. He went on to win nine full caps for his country (four against Scotland, three against England and two against Wales). Unfortunately he never really settled down at Molineux despite scoring plenty of goals especially for the Reserves, and he left Wolves in August 1936, transferring to Nottingham Forest for whom he accumulated a fine record – 48 goals in only 86 appearances. He then had a season in the Third Division (South) with Notts County, hitting 26 goals in 26 League games in 1938-39, before returning to Ireland to play for Glentoran. 'Boy' Martin, who was a prize boxer in his youth, died on 9 January 1991.
Wolves record: 27 apps. 18 goals.

MARTIN, James Colin

Inside-forward Jimmy Martin spent one season at Molineux (from September 1923 to July 1924), acting as reserve to strikers Stan Fazackerly and Tom Phillipson. Born at Basford, North Staffs on 2 December 1898, he played for Stoke St Peter's before joining Stoke for £750 in July 1916, and on leaving the Victoria Ground in June 1921 (after 16 games) Martin switched to Aberdare Athletic. During a lengthy career (1914-38) he also assisted Reading (from July 1924), Aberdare again (June 1925), Bristol City (May 1926), Blackpool (February 1928), Southend United (February 1929), Halifax Town (July 1929) and Congleton Town (August 1930 to May 1931). He died in Stoke on 27 June 1969.
Wolves record: 11 apps. 6 goals.

MARTIN, Tudor James

Tudor Martin was a prolific goalscorer. Born in Caerau, near Bridgend on 20 April 1904, he played for Careau Corinthians and Bridgend Town before joining West Bromwich Albion in October 1926 at a time when the Baggies were well blessed with forwards, all of them exceptional goalscorers. Consequently Martin never got a first team outing at The Hawthorns and he duly left for Newport County in July 1929, switching to Wolves in May 1930. He scored in over half his first-team games during his stay at Molineux – and 74 for the Reserves in League and Cup games – but in July 1932 became surplus to requirements and boss Major

Frank Buckley sold him to Swansea Town. At the Vetch Field Martin did extremely well, netting 45 goals in 116 League games for the Swans, up to July 1936, when he moved to London to sign for West Ham United, later assisting Southend United (February 1937 to May 1939). He retired at the age of 35 and returned to south Wales where for many years he worked for a tube manufacturing company and regularly attended Newport County's home matches at Somerton Park. A Welsh international, capped against Northern Ireland in 1930, Martin scored a club record 49 second team goals (in League and Cup) for Wolves in season 1931-32. He died in Newport on 6 September 1979.
Wolves record: 15 apps. 9 goals.

MASCOT

The wolf has always been regarded as the Wolves' mascot – but in early the 1990s – in unison with a lot of other clubs – Wolves introduced their mascot, named Wolfie, to their supporters, and immediately he became a hit especially with the younger element. However, Wolfie – an ardent Wanderers fan suitably dressed up in a Wolves strip and donning the appropriate headgear – began to hit the headlines for all the wrong reasons in the late 1990s when he got involved in a couple of pitch scuffles with certain rival, namely Baggie Bird (the West Bromwich Albion mascot) and the Bristol City Piglets – all three of them.

"All good fun" said one spokesman but occasionally the antics between the respective mascots out on the pitch did get a little out of hand. And following an incident in the local derby (Wolves against Albion) at Molineux in April 1999, the FA launched an inquiry after a 'brawl' between Wolfie and Baggie Bird.

MASON, Charles

Robust full-back Charlie Mason was born in Wolverhampton on 13 April 1863. Founder member of Wolverhampton Wanderers after leaving St Luke's School in 1877, he went on to enjoy 15 splendid years with the club, making almost 300 appearances, including over 100 in the League and FA Cup competitions before announcing his retirement during the summer of 1892. When he was capped for England against Ireland in 1887, he was the first current Wolves player to appear in an international match and he won further caps in 1888, against Wales, and in 1890, against Ireland again. He was at left-back when Wolves played in their first FA Cup Final against double winners Preston in 1889, and he played all but four games in their first season in the Football League (1888-89). Indeed, he seems to have been in at the start of every facet of Wolves' history, appearing in the club's first-ever FA Cup-tie and their first Football League game. In May 1888, Mason guested for West Bromwich Albion, the FA Cup holders, when they met Renton, winners of the Scottish Cup, in the so-called 'Championship of the World'. Mason died in Wolverhampton on 3 February 1941.

Wolves record: 108 apps. 2 goals.

MASON, James

Well built footballer of some merit, Jimmy Mason played as an inside-forward for Wednesfield Rangers prior to joining Wolves in August 1907. He was given limited opportunities in the first team during his two years at Molineux and left Wolves for Bristol Rovers in July 1909. He later served with Wrexham (August 1910), Llandudno Town (1913) and Rhyl Athletic (1914-15). Mason was born in Wolverhampton in 1885 and died in Llandudno in 1952.

Wolves record: 8 apps. 1 goal.

MASON, Jeremiah

Hardy left-back, no relation to Charles (above) Jerry Mason was born in Wolverhampton in 1865 and played for Blakenhall St Luke's before joining Wolves in July 1889. He spent two years at Molineux, as a reserve to Charlie, before leaving for Willenhall Swifts in May 1891. He died in 1941.

Wolves record: 7 apps.

MASON, Robert Henry

Inside-right Bobby Mason won League championship medals with Wolverhampton Wanderers in consecutive seasons, 1957-58 and 1958-59, but missed the 1960 FA Cup Final after losing his place to the young Barry Stobart. Mason, who was born in Tipton on 22

Bobby Mason, won consecutive League championship medals but missed the 1960 FA Cup Final.

March 1936, spent two seasons as an amateur on the Molineux staff before becoming a full-time professional in May 1953. His League debut was hardly an auspicious occasion when in November 1955, Wolves were hammered 5-1 at Kenilworth Road, but he went on to play in two championship-winning sides. He opened Wolves' second championship season with a hat-trick in a 5-1 home win over Nottingham Forest and in his time at Molineux he was never out of place in a front-line which included such stars as Norman Deeley, Mickey Lill, Jimmy Mullen, Jimmy Murray, Peter Broadbent, Dennis Wilshaw and Colin Booth. In May 1962, after a short period with Chelmsford City in the Southern League, Mason joined Leyton Orient for £10,000. He made 23 League appearances for the O's before retiring from first-class football in 1965 after a spell with Poole Town. He returned to the Midlands to work, although in later years he moved to Christchurch in Dorset where he resides today.

Wolves record: 173 apps. 54 goals.

MASTERS, Neil Bradley

An Irishman, born in Ballymena on 25 May 1972, full-back Neil Masters played over 50 games for AFC Bournemouth before joining Wolves for £300,000 three days before Christmas, 1993. He started his career in his homeland and came over to England to sign for the Cherries in August 1990 after representing his country at youth team level. Unfortunately niggling injuries disrupted his performances at Molineux and in March 1997 he joined Gillingham for £150,000.

Wolves record: 10 apps. 2 goals.

MATCHES

Longest

A wartime League Cup (North) game between Wolves and Birmingham City played at Molineux on 14 April 1945, lasted 133 minutes before Bill Morris scored a dramatic winner for Wolves (1-0) in the 63rd minute of added time. The game started at 3pm and finished close to 6.45pm.

The Wolves-Derby County second-round FA Cup-tie, played in February 1904 went to a second replay before the Rams won 1-0.

Likewise, Sunderland beat Wolves at third attempt in a sixth-round FA Cup clash in March 1937, the Wearsiders eventually winning 4-0 after 1-1 and 2-2 draws at Molineux and Roker Park respectively.

The fifth-round FA Cup encounter between Aston Villa and Wolves in February/March 1965 also went to a third game before Wolves went through 3-1 at The Hawthorns.

The Coventry-Wolves third-round FA Cup-tie in January 1984 took three games to decide, the Sky Blues finally going through 3-0 after two 1-1 draws.

Non-League Chorley ousted Wolves from the FA Cup competition in the first round in November 1986, winning 3-0 at Bolton after two 1-1 scorelines at Molineux and Burnden Park.

Wolves' fifth-round League Cup match against Grimsby Town in December 1979 went to a third meeting before Wolves won 2-0 to progress into the semi-finals where they met (and beat) Swindon Town.

The Staffordshire Cup-tie between Wolves and Tamworth in 1967 lasted 240 minutes. The tie was played over two legs and Wolves' winning goal from Riley came in the 148th minute of the second encounter which went into extra-added time.

Most in a Season

The most competitive games played by Wolves in a season is 61 – in 1987-88 (46 League, three FA Cup, four League Cup and eight in the Sherpa van Trophy). They played 59 in season 1972-73.

MATLOCK

On 30 October 1886, Wolves defeated non-League Matlock 6-0 in a first-round FA Cup-tie at Dudley Road. A crowd of 2,500 saw Jack Brodie (2), Ben Griffiths (2), Harry Allen and Tom Hunter score the goals.

MATTHEWS, Michael

Born in Hull on 25 September 1960, Mick Matthews represented Yorkshire Boys as a teenager before joining Wolves as an apprentice in August 1976, turning professional at Molineux in October 1978. A midfielder, he did well with the Wanderers before transferring to Scunthorpe United for £5,000 in February 1984. After a brief spell with Peterborough United (no first-team outings), he assisted the Humberside club North Ferriby (August 1985) before joining Halifax Town in September 1986. A little over two years later, in December 1988, a fee of £25,000 took Matthews to Scarborough; he switched to Stockport County for £15,000 in February 1989; went back for a second spell with Scarborough for £15,000 in December 1989 and after serving Peterborough United (again) from June 1990, he played briefly for North Ferriby United (again) before being recruited for a second time by Hull City in August 1991, staying at Boothferry Park until May 1992, when he went back to play for Halifax Town, quitting the League scene in May 1993 with 434 appearances under his belt, having dome extremely well in the lower Divisions. He was later a member of the over '35s Wolves team.

Wolves record: 79+4 apps. 7 goals.

MATTHIAS, John Samuel

Before he was forced to retire through injury in May 1902 at the age of 23, Jack Matthias had performed superbly well as a full-back

and central defender with Shrewsbury Town (August 1896), Wolves (May 1897) and Wrexham (from August 1901 to May 1902). Born in Broughton near Wrexham in June 1878, he came through his early footballing career with Brymbo Institute (from 1891) before joining Shrewsbury. A Welsh international, capped five times between 1896 and 1900 (capped as a Wolves player) Matthias was as keen as mustard, always totally committed, his career was ended after receiving a bad knee injury playing for Wales against Scotland when he collided with John Bell. Thereafter he struggled to regain full fitness. When he joined Shrewsbury he became one of the Shropshire club's first paid players. A fine cricketer with Broughton CC, Matthias worked at Brymbo Steel Works for many years and played in the work's band. He was also a caretaker and Sunday School teacher at a local church, positions he held until his death in the village of Moss, near Wrexham, on 16 November 1938.
Wolves record: 45 apps.

MAY, George James

Wing-half George 'Kosher' May did far better in non-League circles than he did with Wolves. Born in Aston, Birmingham in May 1891, he was educated in Bromsgrove and played for Redditch and Verity Athletic (Birmingham Works Association with Ted Collins) before signing professional forms at Molineux in July 1908. He stayed with Wolves for two seasons before transferring to Nuneaton Town in May 1910, later assisting Atherstone (1912-14). He died in Warwick c.1947.
Wolves record: 16 apps.

MAYSON, Thomas F.

Adroit in footwork, Tom Mayson was a classy forward, a star on his own in some games, who was well into his thirties when he joined Wolves. His age was certainly against him and he never really adapted to the system used at Molineux. Born in Whitehaven on 8 December 1886, he spent quite some time playing in the Northern Alliance with Walker Celtic before entering the Football League with Burnley in December 1907. From Turf Moor he moved to Grimsby Town (£350,000, October 1911) and after spells with Everton (July 1919) and Pontypridd (£350,000, July 1920) he was recruited by Wolves in August 1921. Ten months later (in June 1922) he moved to Aberdare Athletic where he stayed until May 1926 and on retiring he became trainer at Queen's Park Rangers (to 1933). During World War One Mayson guested for Leeds City and gained a Welsh Cup winners medal with Pontypridd in 1921. He broke a leg during the 1912-13 season. He died in Cleveland in 1972.
Wolves record: 2 apps.

MEEK, Harold Leonard

Harry Leek spent only five months at Molineux – November 1925 to March 1926. An inside-left, born in Belfast in 1903, he played initially for Belfast Rangers and then Cliftonville and Glentoran before joining Wolves. On leaving Molineux he returned to Ireland to sign for Shelbourne, later assisting Burradon.
Wolves record: 8 apps. 1 goal.

MELIA, James John

Inside-forward Jimmy Melia was born in Liverpool on 1 November 1937, being the fifth of 11 children. He played for Liverpool Boys and was on the groundstaff at Anfield in 1953, turning professional with Liverpool in November 1954. A clever schemer, with good vision and passing technique, he spent the next ten years on Merseyside before transferring to Wolves for £55,000 in March 1964 after helping the Reds win promotion to the First Division in 1962. He stayed with Wolves for seven months, failing to settle in the Midlands and consequently, in the November was sold to Southampton for £30,000. Four years later he went to Aldershot for £9,000 and was player-manager at the Recreation Ground from April 1969 to January 1972. Melia took up a similar position with Crewe Alexandra (May 1972 to December 1974) and was in charge of Southport for three months, from July-September 1975. After that he coached in the Middle East before joining California Lasers as their head coach. Brighton and Hove Albion took on Melia as their team manager in March 1983 and two months later he strolled out at Wembley for the FA Cup Final against Manchester United, a game Brighton should have won, but eventually lost 4-0 in a replay. In October 1983 Melia took over as boss of Belenenses (of Portugal), remaining there for two years. From July to November 1986 he managed Stockport County and in 1992 he went to coach in Texas. He remained in football for a short time after that, taking a variety of jobs before going over to coach in the Far East in 1993-94 and also in Texas. In his League career Melia, easily recognisable by his receding hairline, scored 105 goals in 571 League games (76 in 269 for Liverpool). He was capped twice by England at senior level, having earlier represented his country as a schoolboy and youth team player. He also turned out for the Football League XI.

It is interesting to know that Melia helped Liverpool win the First Division title in 1963-64, was relegated with Wolves the following season and then gained promotion back to the top flight with Southampton in 1966-67.
Wolves record: 24 apps. 4 goals.

MELROSE, James Millsopp

Ginger-haired Jim Melrose was a useful strik-

er, born in Glasgow on 7 October 1958, who played for Eastercraigs FC before joining Partick Thistle in 1975. After that he became a soccer nomad, serving, in turn, with Leicester City (signed for £25,000 in July 1980), Coventry City (player-exchange deal involving Tommy English, September 1982), Celtic (£100,000, August 1987), Wolves (on loan, September-October 1984), Manchester City (£40,000, November 1984), Charlton Athletic (£45,000, March 1986), Leeds United (£50,000, September 1987), Shrewsbury Town (on loan, February 1988, joining the Shrews for £50,000 the following month), Macclesfield Town (July 1989) and Curzon Athletic (October 1990).

He won eight Scottish Under-21 caps and twice represented for the Scottish League XI. With Celtic Melrose gained runners-up medals in both the FA Cup and League Cup competitions in 1984 and then played for Charlton in the Full Members Cup Final at Wembley in 1987. A year later Melrose received a fractured cheek-bone during an incident involving Swindon's Chris Kamara. At Shrewsbury Magistrates Court Kamara was found guilty of assault, and fined £1,200 (plus costs). In his professional career north and south of the border, Melrose scored 131 goals in 486 appearances.
Wolves record: 8+1 apps. 4 goals.

MERCANTILE CREDIT LEAGUE CENTENARY COMPETITION

Wolves entered this Wembley celebratory competition in April 1988. Playing in the Second Phase, they were knocked out by Everton 3-2 on penalties after a 1-1 draw in normal time. Robbie Dennison was the goalscorer. The crowd was 21,446.

MERTHYR TOWN

Wolves defeated the Welsh team 1-0 in the opening round of the 1922-23 FA Cup competition at Merthyr. The attendance was officially given as 13,000 and centre-forward Stan Fazackerley scored the all-important goal.

Players with both clubs include: Charlie Cross, Evan Edwards, Walter Featherby, Joe Hodnett and Steve Mardenborough.

Also associated: Alf Bishop (Town guest), Sid Protheroe, Billy Richards, Alun Smith, and Joe Smith (Wolves Reserves).

METCALF, Thomas Clark

Wolves recruited half-back Tommy Metcalf from Salisbury City in July 1906 as cover for Ken Hunt, Alf Bishop. He got few opportunities to show what he was made of and left Molineux in March 1909 for Bristol Rovers. Born in Burton upon Trent in 1879, Metcalf went abroad before World War One.
Wolves record: 9 apps.

MICKLEWRIGHT, William

Billy Micklewright was a stocky right-winger, reserve to Billy Harrison, who spent three years at Molineux: June 1909 to May 1912. Born in Reading *c*.1890, he moved to Molineux from Wellington Town and on leaving Wolves went into non-League football in Berkshire.
Wolves record: 5 apps.

MIDDLESBROUGH

Wolves' playing record against 'Boro is:
Football League

Venue	P	W	D	L	F	A
Home	39	17	7	15	73	54
Away	39	4	12	23	37	74
Total	78	21	19	38	110	128

FA Cup

Home	3	3	0	0	11	3
Away	1	0	1	0	1	1
Total	4	3	1	0	12	4

The initial League games between Wolves and 'Boro took place in 1902-03 and ended level, each team winning its home fixture by 2-0.

In season 1904-05 the two League encounters produced 12 goals – Wolves winning 5-3 at Molineux with a hat-trick from Fred Bevin.

In 1928-29 the two Second Division matches produced 17 goals. It was 3-3 at Molineux but at Ayresome Park, Middlesbrough took the honours with an emphatic 8-3 victory, their best over Wolves.

On target for 'Boro that day in front of 14,636 fans were Billy Pease (4, including two penalties) and George Camsell (3), who in 1926-27 had scored a staggering 63 goals for the Ayresome Park club.

Charlie Phillips scored twice for Wolves in their 5-3 home League win over 'Boro in March 1935 and Billy Wrigglesworth netted twice in a 4-0 Wolves win in May 1936.

And Dennis Westcott and Dicky Dorsett grabbed two goals apiece when Wolves raced to a 6-1 home win in March 1939.

A thrilling 4-4 draw took place at Middlesbrough in March 1949 (Jesse Pye scoring twice for Wolves) and a seven-goal thriller at Molineux in October 1950 went Boro's way by 4-3.

The 1951-52 season's results saw both teams win their home game by 4-0, Pye again netting twice for Wolves, and when Wolves won the First Division title in 1953-54 they only bagged one point off relegated 'Boro – a 3-3 away draw as they lost 4-2 at Molineux.

A break of 11 years ensued before the teams met again in 1965-66, Wolves winning 3-0 at home but losing 3-1 on Teesside. And after some close exchanges during the 1970s, which 'Boro got the better of, Wolves won 4-0 at Molineux in December 1982 with Mel Eves scoring twice.

On the opening day of the 1989-90 League programme, 'Boro beat Wolves 4-2 at Ayresome Park.

The first of the four FA Cup matches between the clubs was played in 1892-93 when Wolves beat Middlesbrough, then an amateur side, 2-1 at Molineux on their way to the Final.

In season 1936-37 Wolves trounced 'Boro 6-1 at home in a third round tie which attracted a 38,459 crowd to Molineux. All five Wolves forwards scored that afternoon with outside-left George Ashall netting twice.

The last two Cup encounters took place in season 1980-81 when Wolves won a sixth-round replay 3-1 at Molineux.

Players with both clubs include: David Black, Joe Blackett, Walter Bottrill, Mark Burke, Simon Coleman, Dick Le Flem, Vic Fox, George Laking, David Miller, Ray Hankin, Hugh McIlmoyle, Eddie Russell, Dave Thomas and Bob Young.

Also associated: Dick Forshaw and George Heppell (Wolves Reserves, 'Boro wartime guests), Mick Fenton ('Boro player, Wolves wartime guest), Mick Hollifield ('Boro trialist), Arthur Rowley and Guy Wharton ('Boro wartime guests) and Brian Little ('Boro coach, Wolves manager).

MIDDLETON, Harold

Centre-forward Harry Middleton was the first Wolves player to be capped by England at youth international level. Unfortunately he became the odd man out at Molineux simply because there were so many other strikers registered with the club at the same time. Consequently he missed out and was transferred to Scunthorpe United in September 1959. Born in Birmingham on 18 March 1937, Middleton started off as an amateur at Molineux, turning professional in August 1954. Then, over the next five years, he made only one senior appearance – in a 2-1 defeat at Everton in April 1956 when he deputised on the right-wing for Johnny Hancocks. From Scunthorpe, he switched to Portsmouth in June 1961 and eight months later he joined Shrewsbury Town. After netting 37 goals in 85 League games for the Shrews he was transferred to Mansfield Town in November 1964 and continued to score regularly for the Stags (24 goals in 46 League outings). In March 1966 he returned to the West Midlands to sign for Walsall and at Fellows Park he again did well, scoring 30 goals in 65 senior appearances for the Saddlers. He left Walsall in May 1968 for Worcester City, retiring in 1970. In his League career Middleton scored 103 goals in 236 games – and his claim to fame with Wolves was his five goals in a 10-0 FA Youth Cup win over his future club Walsall in 1954-55.
Wolves record: 1 app.

MIDLAND INTERMEDIATE LEAGUE

Wolves Reserves (and youth team players) won the championship of this competition in successive seasons of 1987-88 and 1988-89.

They played a total of three seasons in the competition their full record being:

P	W	D	L	F	A	Pts
71	39	6	26	164	103	123

Wolves' best win of the 39 recorded is a 9-0 hiding of Peterborough United (h) in October 1988.

Their two heaviest defeats are those of 7-4 at Walsall in October 1986 and 5-2 at Nottingham Forest in February 1988.

Goalkeeper Vince Bartram made a record 52 Intermediate League appearances for Wolves (1986-89). Defender Nicky Clarke made 45 during the same period.

Jackie Gallagher and Colin Taylor scored most 'Intermediate' goals – 12 each; Jon Purdie netted 11.

MIDLAND YOUTH CUP

Wolves beat Walsall 6-4 on aggregate in the Final of the 1998-99 Midland Youth Cup Final. The Wanderers won 4-2 at The Bescot Stadium and were held at 2-2 by the Saddlers at Molineux. A crowd of 1,325 saw the second leg.

Wolves defeated Notts County in the Final in 1997-98 in front of 5,000 fans at Molineux.

MILLER, David

David Miller was able to occupy a number of positions, including those of left-half, inside-forward or winger. Born in Middlesbrough on 21 January 1921, he played for South Bank FC before becoming a professional with Middlesbrough in 1938. Near the end of the war (when he served in the RAF) he moved from Ayresome Park to Molineux (August 1945) and spent two seasons with Wolves before transferring to Derby County in April 1947. From the Baseball Ground he moved to Doncaster Rovers (January 1948) and after a short spell with Aldershot (March to May 1954) rounded off his career by assisting Boston United, retiring through injury in 1957. In fact, during his time with Boston he returned to his old stamping ground at Derby and helped inflict upon the Rams a hefty 6-1 FA Cup hammering in 1955-56. Miller appeared in more than 150 games during his six years with Doncaster whom he helped win the Third Division North championship in 1950.
Wolves record: 2 apps.

MILLER, George

George Miller was a long-striding wing-half, who played in an international trial for Scotland, represented the Scottish League XI

and played in the 1962 Scottish Cup Final while with Dunfermline Athletic, the club he assisted for four years prior to joining Wolves for £26,000 in October 1964. Born in Larkhall, Lanarkshire on 20 May 1939, his performances at Molineux were mixed and he left the club to sign to return to Scotland in May 1966, retiring in 1970.
Wolves record: 45 apps. 3 goals.

MILLER, Thomas John

Outside-left Jack Miller was born in Hednesford early in 1875 and joined Wolves from Hednesford Town in September 1895, initially as cover for David Black and Alf Griffin. After establishing himself in the side, he was virtually an ever-present from September 1896 to November 1904. Miller, who represented the Football League in 1899-1900, left Molineux for Stoke for £400 in the summer of 1905 and after scoring five goals in 63 games for the Potters he moved, in April 1907, to Willenhall. He retired in 1910 to become a publican. He died in 1935.
Wolves record: 249 apps. 49 goals.

MILLS, Rowan Lee

Tall, hardworking and very efficient goalscorer, born in Mexborough on 10 July 1970, Lee Mills played his early football with Stocksbridge Park Steels, joining Wolves as a full-time professional in December 1992. He failed to establish himself in the side at Molineux and in February 1995 was transferred to Derby County for £400,000, moving on to Port Vale in August 1995 in a £475,000 deal involving Robin Van Der Laan (Mills being rated at £200,000). He did very well at Vale Park (under manager John Rudge) but was perhaps surprisingly sold (certainly as far as the ardent Vale supporters were concerned) to Bradford City for £1 million in August 1998. In season 1998-99 he top-scored for the Yorkshire club, helping them reach the Premiership as runners-up to Sunderland.
Wolves record: 19+14 apps. 4 goals.

MILLWALL (ATHLETIC)

Wolves' playing record against the Lions is:

Football League

Venue	P	W	D	L	F	A
Home	12	7	4	1	26	9
Away	12	3	3	6	13	16
Total	24	10	7	7	39	25

FA Cup

Home	1	1	0	0	1	0
Away	1	1	0	0	2	1
Total	2	2	0	0	3	1

League Cup

Home	1	1	0	0	5	1

Wartime

Home	1	0	0	1	1	2
Away	1	0	0	1	0	2
Total	2	0	0	2	1	4

Wolves and Millwall first met each other in the Football League in season 1928-29 (Division Two), and after losing 1-0 at Molineux very early on in the campaign, Wolves gained sweet revenge with an excellent 5-0 victory in London a week later when centre-forward Reg Weaver scored a fine hat-trick.

Eighteen months later (in March 1930) Wolves returned to Millwall and this time were hammered 4-0.

When the Second Division championship was won in 1931-32 Wolves defeated Millwall twice – 5-0 at home and 1-0 away – Billy Hartill netting a hat-trick at Molineux.

There was then a gap of 35 years before the teams met again – Wolves winning 2-0 at home and drawing 1-1 at The Den in 1966-67.

It was then a further ten years before the Wolves and the Lions did battle again at League level – and once more Wolves collected three points from a 3-1 home win and a 1-1 away draw.

In December 1990, Wolves beat Millwall 4-1 at Molineux – Gary Bellamy (with a rare goal), Steve Bull and Colin Taylor (2) the scorers and when the Lions were beaten 3-1 on the same ground in May 1993, debutant Shaun Bradbury was Wolves' hero with two smart goals.

The first of the two FA Cup-ties with Millwall was played in London in January 1897 before an 18,000 crowd, Billy Beats and Jack Tonks scoring in Wolves' narrow 2-1 win in front of 18,000 fans.

The second encounter took place at Molineux in February 1973 when Wolves won a fifth round tie 1-0 with a goal by John Richards.

Wolves' 5-1 home League Cup win over Millwall was achieved in September 1968 in front of a 17,000 plus crowd. John Farrington netted twice that night with Frank Munro also figuring on the scoresheet.

Players with both clubs include: John Bell, Willie Carr, Hugh Curran, Neil Emblen, Walter Featherby, Malcolm Finlayson, Hillary Griffiths, Billy Kellock, Brian Law, Lawrie Madden, Fred Ramscar, Tony Towner, Sid Tyler and Jermaine Wright.

Also associated: Arthur Allman, Maurice Doyle, Davey Robson and Jim Travers (all Wolves Reserves) Jimmy Jinks (Wolves guest) and Frank Taylor and Horace Wright (Athletic wartime guests).

MITTON, John

Solid defender Jack Mitton was born at Todmorden on 7 November 1895 and played his early football for Brierfield FC and as an amateur for Burnley before guesting for Bury from 1916. By the time World War One had ended, Mitton was on Exeter City's books, but in October 1920, Sunderland, then a

force in the First Division, thought enough of him to pay the Grecians £250 for his signature after he had made 11 League appearances in Exeter's first season in the new Third Division. In the Southern League he had been ever-present in 1919-20 and his brother James had also played in the same Exeter team. For the Wearsiders, Mitton made 82 senior appearances, scoring seven goals before Wolves signed him for £500 in May 1924, just after they had won the Third Division North championship. As they re-established themselves in the Second, finishing sixth, Mitton made 36 League appearances and the Molineux fans loved his powerful performances in defence. He also skippered the side occasionally. In May 1927, Wolves sold him to Southampton for £150, after he had made over 100 senior appearances. But he played only eight times for the Saints before being released in the 1928 close season. After a spell in the Hampshire County League he retired in 1930. Mitton died in Kings Lynn on 5 August 1983.
Wolves record: 107 apps. 6 goals.

MOLINEUX

Wolves have been playing at Molineux since 1889, the ground being named after the Molineux family, which first came to England with Isabella of France, wife of Edward II, almost 700 years ago, in 1307. At the time when the Flemish wool-workers were frequenting this country teaching the British their trade.

The Molineuxs chose to reside in a large mansion on the outskirts of Wolverhampton town centre which they named, appropriately, Molineux House.

At the time Wolverhampton was a very important wool town and as time progressed, so did Wolverhampton itself and it quickly became famous throughout Europe.

The house was made one of the town's principal buildings, and on local maps it was referred to as Mr Molineux's Close, being situated between Wadham's Hill and Dunstall Lane.

Come 1792 it was the residence for a family of French refugees and the grounds were later developed into a pleasure park by Mr. A. J. Brewster, with several galas and fetes being held there at regular intervals during the summer months in favourable weather conditions.

In 1869, a South Staffordshire Industrial Firm and Fine Arts Exhibition was held in the grounds of Molineux House with the old English game of croquet taking place on the lush lawns where it was dominated by the ladies.

Two years later further developments were carried out, making the Molineux complex into a much more accomplished, sporting venue which incorporated some quite superb gardens, a spacious boating lake, a rather elegant band stand and most important of all, an excellent cycle and athletics track which went round the spacious sports field. Indeed, so good was the playing surface that Wolves themselves played there in a Walsall Cup semi-final against Walsall Town on 20 March 1886, three years before they actually made Molineux their home.

Wolves played out their first season in the Football League (1888-89) at their Dudley Road ground, but facilities there were now rather poor and the club desperately wanted new head-quarters.

The Northampton Brewery had by now purchased the Molineux sports complex as well as the old house, which had been converted into a smart hotel. The brewery, therefore, came to the assistance of Wolves, and within a matter of months a good quality football ground was forthcoming, with dressing rooms, an office, a respectable grandstand (able to seat 300 spectators), and a shelter on the perimeter embankment where some 4,000 fans could escape from the inclement weather, all for a yearly rent of £50. At the same time Aston Villa were renting their Perry Barr ground for £200 per annum.

Opening of ground
Molineux was officially opened on Monday 2 September 1889 when Aston Villa were invited to play a friendly match which resulted in a 1-0 win for Wolves in front of almost 4,000 fans.

The old and the new – Molineux, always a famous stadium.

The match kicked-off at 5.30pm and David Wykes scored the only goal halfway through the first-half, Warner in the Villa goal allowing his feeble shot (from Harry Wood's centre) to pass through his hands.

The Wolves team for this historic encounter, was: Rose; Baugh, Mason; Fletcher, Allen, Knight; Worrall, Perry, Wykes, Wood and Booth.

Villa lined up with: Warner; Aldridge, Coulton; Burton, Jas. Cowan, Devey; Brown, Allen, Hunter, Garvey and Dickson.

The first League game at Molineux followed five days later when Notts County were the visitors. The result was a 2-0 victory for Wolves, Arthur Worrall and Wykes the scorers before 4,000 spectators.

During the 1890s Molineux was the venue for several Football League Committee meetings and in March 1891 England played Ireland there in a full international. England won 6-1 before a crowd of 15,231. Two Wolves players – goalkeeper Billy Rose and Jack Brodie, lining up at left-half, were in the England team.

In February of the following year, the first of ten FA Cup semi-finals took place at Molineux when West Bromwich Albion played Nottingham Forest.

In February 1903 a second international on Wolves' ground saw England defeat Ireland 4-0, goalkeeper Tom Baddeley being Wolves' only representative in the England side.

Two further full internationals took place at Molineux – in February 1936 when England lost 2-1 to Wales, and in December 1956 when England beat Denmark 5-2 in a World Cup qualifier.

There have also been Under-21 and Under-23 internationals staged at the ground, the last of these in October 1996 when England Under-21s drew 0-0 with their counterparts from Poland.

Molineux has also been the venue for one wartime international between England and Wales in October 1942 when over 25,000 fans saw the Welsh win 2-1. There have also been three Inter League games (one in 1952 when Bolton's Nat Lofthouse scored netted five goals for the Football League side against the Irish League). There were four other wartime matches staged on Wolves' territory, including a Football League XI against an All British XI in December 1939 and the Western Command v RAF (North West) in February 1944, when almost 23,000 spectators were present. Youth internationals have been held there, including a goalless draw between England and Ireland in 1951-52 which attracted a 10,000 crowd, along with various Cup semi-finals and, indeed, Cup Finals.

The most recent Schoolboy international to be played at Molineux was between England and Wales on 4 March 1999, England won 2-1.

Rugby Union matches were played at Molineux in 1926-27 when the Wolverhampton Rugby Club celebrated its 75th anniversary by playing a season on Wolves' soccer pitch.

A special centenary match between Commander W. J. A. Davies' XV and the Wolves Rugby Club was arranged and attracted a 6,000 crowd.

And during the early 1950s the first boxing tournaments took place at the ground, the ring being erected in the centre-circle.

In June 1967 around 8,000 fans saw the British heavyweight title fight between Henry Cooper and Jack Bodell.

At the outset (in 1889) it is believed that Molineux could house around 20,000 spectators – and the first time a five-figure attendance was recorded was when 19,000 fans saw Blackburn Rovers defeat Wolves 4-2 on Boxing Day 1889 in a Football League game.

Developments

Developments and improvements to Molineux were carried out when funds permitted, and although it was rated one of the best grounds in the country early in the 20th century, it still required an awful lot of attention, especially along one side which backed on to a busy main road.

Immediately after World War One when Wolves were based in the Second Division, Molineux was said to be below standard and when an extra large attendance was present, scores of supporters were unable to see the action out on the pitch.

Those who chose to stand on the Molineux Street side of the ground complained that the sloping bank made their feet ache, while others who were privileged to get a seat in the Waterloo Road stand moaned about toilet facilities, the exits, gangways, and even the type and style of their seat.

The Wolves directors did look into all this but it was quite some time before money was found to carry out improvements.

In 1919, the loyal Wolves supporters misbehaved at Molineux during a game against Bury and as a result, Wolves were forced to play two 'home' matches on a neutral ground, choosing The Hawthorns to entertain Barnsley and Stockport County halfway through that first post-war campaign. They failed to win either.

In 1923, disaster hit Wolves when relegation was suffered to the Third Division North. But this demotion was, in fact, a hidden bonus, for a new limited company was formed and immediately the freehold of Molineux was purchased from the Northampton Brewery Company for what was described as a 'very reasonable price' for such a massive site – just £5,607.

Twelve months later Wolves regained their Second Division status and in mid September 1925, the first major stand, approximately 200 feet long with dressing rooms, was erected on the Waterloo Road side of the ground at a cost of £15,000. The old roof, covering that side of Molineux had been earlier transferred to the opposite side of the ground – but unfortunately it didn't last long and following a fierce gale it was ruthlessly blown away on 4 January 1925.

The Molineux Street side of the ground was gradually made to look compact and in 1932 it was completed in time to celebrate Wolves' return to the top flight.

This stand was capable of holding 8,000 spectators: 3,450 seated, 4,550 standing. It had a multi-span roof and there was a clock mounted in the centre overlooking the halfway line. There were only a few other stands in the country at the time which were of similar design including those at Highbury, The Valley and Old Trafford.

During Major Frank Buckley's reign as manager (late 1930s) the crowds flocked to Molineux in their thousands and thankfully, the terracing at each end of the ground, the South Bank and North Bank (Cow Shed) were both covered, aiding the supporters in wet weather.

In February 1939, a record crowd of 61,315 packed Molineux to see Wolves taken on Liverpool, in the FA Cup. It is still the best Molineux attendance.

In 1953 floodlighting (costing £10,000) was installed for the first time and four years later a new set went up at a cost of £25,000.

During the ten year period up to 1963, Wolves played host to many of Europe's big clubs in friendly and European matches and attendances often topped the 50,000 mark with 30,000 packed onto the South Bank, which at the time was one of the biggest kops in the country, on par with The Penistone Road End at Hillsborough, The Holte End at Villa Park, Anfield's Kop and Birmingham City's Tilton Road.

During the next 15 years, up to 1978, few changes were made to Molineux, a splash of paint here and there, a few sets replaced, but nothing major. The ground capacity however was cut – to 41,900 – for safety reasons and the South Bank could now house 23,000 instead of 30,000.

The 'new' Molineux

Then, following the introduction of the Government's new legislation – The Safety of Sports Grounds Act – it was unanimously agreed by the club's directors and by senior police officers and heads of the Fire Service, that the Molineux Street side of the ground would not pass the required standards. An immediate plan was put into operation and it was agreed that this side of the ground should be redeveloped.

In 1979 Wolves purchased 71 terraced houses in Molineux Street, knocked them all down and started to build a £2 million luxury stand, now called the John Ireland Stand, which can seat 9,500 fans.

This excellent structure also contains 42 executive boxes, and has eye-catching red plastic seats, which contrast splendidly with the gold fascia. It was designed by the architects Atherden and Rutter, who were also responsible for the magnificent stands at Old

Trafford and who were later the brains behind the superb two-tiered cantilever stand at White Hart Lane.

While this stand was being built Wolves were doing fairly well out on the pitch and they also got themselves involved in two massive transfers when Andy Gray was signed and Steve Daley sold with well around £3 million involved in the two deals.

Home crowds were not all that good and the club struggled to meet the costs of building that new stand.

However, as time passed by, Wolves almost went into liquidation, but were bailed out by former player Derek Dougan, who came along and led a consortium of businessmen (mainly from Allied Properties) to rescue the club from extinction.

It happened at the start of the 1982-83 season and in fact Wolves were just three minutes away from execution when Dougan and Property Developer Doug Hope saved the club by fronting a successful bid of £2.3 million.

It seemed cut and dry at first that consortiums led by Walsall's chairman Ken Wheldon and Doug Ellis were favourites to takeover at Molineux but the mystery bankers on 30 July were Allied Properties for whom the Bhatti brothers pulled the strings.

Manager Ian Greaves was dismissed, replaced by ex-player Graham Hawkins. Out also went secretary Phil Shaw and commercial manager Jack Taylor, who was replaced by former *Evening Mail* and *Sports Argus* reporter Eric Woodward.

Wolves battled on with very little money in the bank to carry out with ground redevelopment – but they survived, just.

Three years later, after promotion and relegation and another change of manager, the club found itself in all sorts of trouble once again, almost £2 million in debt, with soaring interest rates on the John Ireland Stand their biggest headache.

On 29 July 1985 Allied Properties were taken to court and the judge ordered Wolverhampton Wanderers Football Club to be wound up – it was 1982 all over again.

But a ten-day stay of execution was granted and Mick Channon (ex Southampton, Manchester City and England) was reported to be in line to become the first player-manager of Wolves. But this never materialised and Sammy Chapman was given the manager's job, but he was replaced by Bill McGarry and things progressed.

Attendances had dropped alarmingly – only 1,618 spectators turned up to watch Wolves play Torquay United in a Freight Rover Trophy game in January 1986 – and after the Bhatti brothers moved on, so Wolves' fate grew grimmer by the hour.

On 2 July 1986, for the third summer in five years, and with the club now in the old Fourth Division, the Official Receiver was called in and news bulletins were posted all over the world indicating that the once mighty Wolverhampton Wanderers Football Club was about to fold – again.

Thankfully the club was saved at the 11th hour when the local council purchased Molineux for £1.12 million, also buying the surrounding land, while Gallagher Estates Limited, in conjunction with the ASDA Superstore chain, agreed to pay off all the outstanding debts, subject to them gaining building and planning permission to erect a giant supermarket next to the ground itself. The football club was to be run by a consortium containing chairman Dick Homden and director Jack Harris, the president being Sir Jack Hayward, OBE. The former Aston Villa forward Brian Little, who was coach at Molineux, was put in charge of the team and secretary Keith Pearson showed the spirit of the club by volunteering to work without pay for a said period of time.

In the summer of 1985, after the fire service had carried out more stringent safety tests on the ground, following the Bradford City fire and the trouble at the Heysel Stadium in Brussels, Wolves were forced to shut down the Waterloo Road Stand to fans on matchdays, although the television gantry, dressing rooms, press area, scoreboard, players' lounge and the odd offices remained in use.

Even the North Bank (the Cow Shed End) was declared out of bounds to all supporters. Fortunately the South Bank was allowed to stay open and with the room allocated in the John Ireland Stand, Molineux's capacity in 1985 was dramatically cut from 41,000 to 25,000.

The buzz slowly returned to Molineux, and after the arrival of Steve Bull and manager Graham Turner, plus the celebration a Wembley victory and two successive promotion campaigns, things were looking much brighter for all concerned.

Step forward multi-millionaire businessman Sir Jack Haywood.

An avid supporter since he was a young lad, Sir Jack bought Wolverhampton Wanderers Football Club in May 1990 and immediately placed his son, Jonathan, and Wolves legend Billy Wright, on the board of of directors. Immediately he set about redeveloping the Molineux Stadium and in the next seven years he put £19.7 million into the club as Wolves strove to get into the Premiership. The ground was completed in 1993 and officially opened by HM the Queen in June 1994.

Wolves spent over £200,000 on their Molineux pitch and a new under-soil heating system in 1997.

Molineux is now a luxury 28,550 all-seater stadium with some of the best facilities anywhere in the country, not only for football.

Molineux Fact File

The record crowd to date at the 'all-seater' Molineux stadium is 28,544 for the sixth-round FA Cup-tie with Leicester City (won 1-0) in February 1995.

Prior to that 28,369 fans had witnessed a Coca-Cola League Cup-tie with Nottingham Forest in October 1994, while the best League attendance so far has been that of 28,298 against Stoke City in January 1995.

Molineux can accommodate 76 wheelchairs and there are 46 disabled parking spaces along with 16 disabled toilets, one wheelchair lift and six ramps. And 15 stewards are trained to look after these people on matchdays.

There are 50 seats allocated for blind supporters with radio commentary supplied via the club's own Radio Wolves network. There are 300 reserved seats for non-wheelchair disabled supporters and there is also one disabled rest room.

There are another 50 seats for the hard of hearing with a loop for PA announcements.

In 1994 Molineux won the Sports Council's UK Sports Stadia Award for the most effective provision for disabled spectators.

Molineux is equipped with 42 executive boxes in the John Ireland Stand and a further 18 (on a larger scale) in the Billy Wright Stand.

The club offices and changing rooms are situated in the Billy Wright Stand, along with a Health and Fitness Centre, press and photography rooms, a radio studio, a Conference and Banqueting Centre, private lounges (for the Executive Club members), the Captain's Club and President's Club and Sir Jack Hayward's 'special room' – a top-class restaurant from where diners can look over the Molineux pitch.

The Stan Cullis Stand houses the Terrace Bar and Johnny Hancocks Community Room as well as the club's Ticket Office, Consumer sales Office, Travel and Members office, Cyber bar and promotions department.

The Molineux Superstore is situated on the corner between the Billy Wright and Stan Cullis Stands. The interior of the Jack Harris Stand contains the nerve centre of all security and safety operations at Molineux and sections of the John Ireland Stand is leased out to the Wolverhampton University for office facilities.

There are two giant video-walls, which are positioned in the corner areas between the Billy Wright and Stan Cullis and Jack Harris and John Ireland Stands.

There is a police station inside Molineux with cells in the Jack Harris stand.

There will be 25 police officers and some 250 stewards on duty when a first team game takes place at Molineux.

The pitch at Molineux has under-soil heating and is fitted with a hi-tech computerised watering system.

A family of foxes live under the John Ireland stand.

A hawk is allowed to fly over and around the stadium one a week to keep the pigeons away.

Wolverhampton Wanderers has its very own radio station, named Radio Wolves.

There is a time capsule underneath the floor of the main reception at Molineux. This was buried there in December 1992 when the foundations of the Billy Wright stand were initially laid. The capsule contains a copy of the *Express and Star* newspaper, a Wolves matchday programme, copies of contracts for both Steve Bull and Billy Wright, plus a pair of their boots.

The first supporters' open day at Molineux took place in the summer of 1977 when around 10,000 fans turned up to look behind the scenes.

When the Wolves v Crewe Alexandra Nationwide League game was called off because of a waterlogged and snow covered pitch in March 1999, it was the first fixture lost to the weather at Molineux for nine years.

MORRIS, William Walker

Bill Morris was born a goalkick away from West Bromwich Albion's ground at The Hawthorns, on 26 March 1913, and was educated at Handsworth New Road and Niniveh Road schools. He played his early football for Handsworth Old Boys and the Baggies' colts side and was also with Halesowen Town before Albion let him slip through their net and he signed for Wolves as a professional in May 1933. Morris was the regular centre-half until the emergence of Stan Cullis, after which he switched to right-back and it was in that position that he won three full England caps in 1938-39, the same season he played in the FA Cup Final against Portsmouth at Wembley. Morris, who was famed for running backwards at speed, was only 24 when the Football League was suspended on the outbreak of war (in September 1939) and when competitive soccer resumed in August 1946 he was past his 30th birthday, having guested for Wrexham during the hostilities. The following year (June 1947) he retired. Morrism made only ten appearances in that first post-war season when Wolves finished third in Division One, and altogether he totalled close on 200 senior appearances as well as starring in 68 wartime games. In fact, during one League Cup North game against Birmingham in 1944-45 he scored a dramatic winning goal in the 153rd minute of a prolonged encounter. After leaving Wolves he enjoyed two seasons with Dudley Town in the Birmingham Combination, playing at

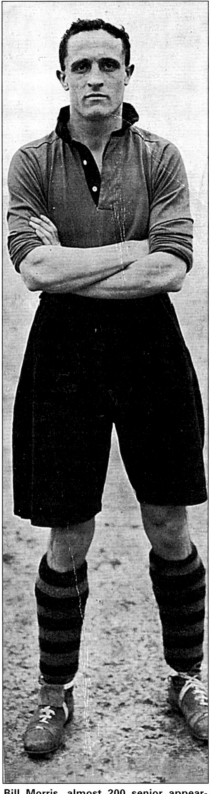

Bill Morris, almost 200 senior appearances for Wolves.

centre-forward. Indeed, it was as a forward that he joined Wolves in the first place.
Wolves record: 197 apps. 3 goals.

MORRISSEY, John Joseph

Left-winger Johnny Morrissey followed his dad into League football, Morrissey senior having played for Liverpool, Everton and Oldham between 1957 and 1973. Morrissey

junior was born in Liverpool on 8 March 1965 and signed as a junior for Everton in 1981, turning professional at Goodison Park in March 1983. After representing England at youth team level and making only two appearances for the Merseysiders he was transferred to Wolves in August 1985. Playing in a struggling team, he never really settled at Molineux and in October 1985 was sold to Tranmere Rovers for £8,000. Over the next decade and more he did very well at Prenton Park, scoring more than 60 goals in over 550 senior appearances. Morrissey was awarded a testimonial for his service to Tranmere (a game against his former club Everton in July 1999).
Wolves record: 6+5 apps. 1 goal.

MOSCOW DYNAMO AND MOSCOW SPARTAK

These two famous Russian club sides visited Molineux to play Wolves in friendly matches under floodlights in the 1950s.

Spartak were the first to come to town, losing 4-0 to Wolves in November 1954 in front of 55,184 enthralled supporters. Johnny Hancocks scored twice.

Dynamo followed their arch rivals to the Black Country 12 months later in November 1955 and again a bumper crowd, this time numbering 55,480, saw Wolves rise to the occasion and win 2-1 with goals from Bill Slater and Jimmy Mullen. The great 'black cat' Lev Yashin kept goal for Dynamo.

In August 1955 Wolves made a short tour of Russia where they played both Spartak Moscow and Moscow Dynamo, losing 3-0 and 3-2 respectively.

In March 1982 Moscow Dynamo returned to Molineux to play Wolves in John Richards' testimonial match and they won a good contest by 4-2.

MOSS, Craig A.

Born in Birmingham on 11 March 1961, left-winger Craig Moss, whose brother Paul was also on Wolves' books in the mid-1970s, had a relatively short career in League football. He joined the apprentice ranks at Molineux in June 1977 and turned professional in March 1979. Unfortunately he became surplus to requirements and left the club in 1982, moving into non-League soccer, first with Worcester City, then Trowbridge Town and Worcester again.
Wolves record: 4 apps.

MOUNTFIELD, Derek Neal

Wolves signed experienced defender Derek Mountfield from Aston Villa for £150,000 in November 1991 and by the time new manager Graham Taylor released him in May 1994 Mountfield had made over 90 senior appearances for the club. He was born at Liverpool on 2 November 1962 and began

his professional career with Tranmere Rovers in November 1980 after two years as an apprentice at Prenton Park. He had made only 29 appearances for Tranmere when Everton paid £30,000 for his signature in June 1982. It was a good move for him and he went on to make 154 appearances for the Goodison club, scoring 25 goals and helping them to the Football League championship in 1985 and 1987, the FA Cup in 1984 and the European Cup-winners' Cup in 1985. Villa paid £450,000 for Mountfield in June 1988 and he made 120 appearances for them before moving to Wolves. From Molineux Mountfield went to Carlisle United on a free transfer in August 1994 and after a loan spell with Northampton Town (October 1995) he switched back to the Midlands to sign for Walsall (November 1995). In July 1997 he was appointed player-coach at The Bescot Stadium and whilst with the Saddlers took his senior appearance tally to past the 600 mark. In September 1998 Mountfield joined Bromsgrove Rovers and in January 1999 became caretaker-assistant manager of soon-to-be-demoted Scarborough under Colin Addison. He represented England once at both Under-21 and 'B' team levels.
Wolves record: 87+4 apps. 5 goals.

MULHOLLAND, Thomas
Reserve inside-forward at Molineux, Tommy Mulholland (5ft 6ins tall, 10st 4lbs in weight) was born in Ireland in 1890 and played for Distillery and Leeds City (May 1909) and Distillery again before joining Wolves in November 1912. He spent less than a season at Molineux, moving to Brewood and then on to Scunthorpe and Lindsey United. In 1913 he went back 'home to sign for Belfast Celtic and played briefly for Hartlepools United before ending his career in Ireland with Cliftonville. Mulholland died in Belfast *c.*1950.
Wolves record: 6 apps. 1 goal.

MULLEN, James
Speedy left winger Jimmy Mullen was another of the great names in a magnificent Wolves side of the post-war era, a player who always seemed to destined to be a star from his schooldays and who gave Wolves 23 years' splendid service. He gained three League championship medals with the club, an FA Cup winners' medal, 12 full England caps as well as 'B' caps and games for the Football League and helped Wolves win the wartime League (North) Cup in 1942. Guesting for Leicester City and Darlington during the war, he also played for Northern Command against Western Command, scoring a hat-trick in the last ten minutes of this game to earn his side a 3-3 draw. One of his full caps came as a substitute for Stan Mortensen against Belgium in Brussels in 1950. It was the first time that England had used a sub

and 15 minutes after coming on, Mullen scored. In all he appeared in more than 480 senior games for Wolves and scored well over 100 goals, and that was in addition to his 91 wartime appearances (27 goals), when he was also an Army Corporal. Mullen, who was born at Newcastle-upon-Tyne on 6 January 1923, had a terrific shot and he was already an England Schoolboys star when he joined the Molineux staff in July 1937, when he was still only 14. He made a somewhat sensational League debut, when he played against Leeds in February 1939, when he was barely 16, and Major Frank Buckley signed him on professional forms as soon as he could, in January 1940. With Mullen on the left flank and Hancocks on the right, the Wolves forward line of the 1940s and early 1950s played some of the most attractive attacking football the game has ever seen. Indeed, the pair were rated the best club wingers in the country. Jimmy Mullen was only 64 when he died in October 1987.
Wolves record: 486 apps. 112 goals.

MUNRO, Francis Michael
Sturdy centre-half Frank Munro made almost 300 League appearances for Wolves after Chelsea had released him after he had been on amateur forms at Stamford Bridge. Munro was born at Broughty Ferry, near Dundee, on 25 October 1947 and after leaving Chelsea signed for Dundee United with whom he won four Scottish Youth caps and two Amateur caps before becoming a professional in July 1963. In October 1966 he was transferred to Aberdeen and the following year played on the losing side in the Scottish Cup Final. Wolves came to take an interest after he had scored a hat-trick (including two penalties) against them in a summer tournament in the USA in 1967 and he joined them for £55,000 in January 1968. A tough-tackling defender he was banned for a month during the 1969-70 season, but came back with great tenacity. For Wolves he played in the 1972 UEFA Cup Final and gained a League Cup winners' trophy in 1974. He was also capped four times for Scotland Under-23s and won nine full caps whilst with Wolves. Munro helped Wolves win the Second Division title in 1976-77, but in December 1977 they allowed him to move for Celtic for £20,000 after he had been on loan to the Parkhead club for two months. He appeared for Celtic in the 1978 Scottish League Cup Final and then went into Australian football, playing for Hellas and later coaching Albion Rovers, Hamlyn Rangers and Keilor Austria. He returned to England but, alas, in 1993 he suffered the first of two strokes. Wolves fans loved him and he scored some vital goals as well as being a magnificent defender.
Wolves record: 365+6 apps. 19 goals.

MURRAY, James R.
Jimmy Murray had a magnificent scoring record for Wolves, and all told in his professional career (he also served with Manchester City and Walsall) he struck 211 goals in 404 League games. With Wolves he gained two League championship winners' medals and an FA Cup winners' medal and also won two England Under-23 caps and represented the Football League. Born in Dover on 11 October 1935, Murray joined Wolves as a full-time professional in November 1953 after George Poyser, the man who also spotted Peter Broadbent, recommended him to championship-chasing Wanderers. In 1955, he was brought in to the side to replace the injured Roy Swinbourne and soon settled down, stayed there for the rest of the season, scoring 11 goals in 25 games as Wolves finished third. In the first of two successive championship seasons, 1957-58, he was leading scorer with 29 goals, and he top scored with 21 when the title was retained the following season. In 1960 he played in the side which beat Blackburn Rovers in the FA Cup Final and the following year he set a Wolves record by scoring a double hat-trick (six goals) for the Reserves against Chesterfield in a Central League match. Although he stood only 5ft 9in, Murray gave opposing defenders plenty to think about and after he moved to Manchester City for £27,000 in November 1963 he continued his rich vein of form in a sensational start at Maine Road. In his first six games for City he scored 12 goals including two hat-tricks as he formed a great striking partnership with former West Brom and England centre-forward Derek Kevan. After 43 goals in 70 games for City, Murray was transferred to Walsall and netted 15 goals in 64 League and Cup games for the Saddlers before dropping into non-League football with Telford United in August 1969 and helping the Shropshire club to consecutive FA Trophy Finals at Wembley. He retired in 1971 and ran a very successful greengrocery business in Tamworth for 24 years until 1995. Murray now lives in Lichfield and works for a contract car hire firm.
Wolves record: 299 apps. 166 goals.

MUSCAT, Kevin Vincent
Despite being born in Crawley, Sussex on 7 August 1973, left-back Kevin Muscat was brought up in Australia. Now an established Antipodean, he represented the Victoria State side, played in two Youth World Cup tournaments (1991 and 1993) and in the Olympic Games in Atlanta, and South Melbourne before entering English League football by signing for Crystal Palace for £35,000 in August 1996. An Aussie international (nine caps gained) he made over 60 appearances for the London club, helping them gain Premiership status, before trans-

ferring to Wolves in October 1997. The £1 million deal of which £200,000 was placed on Muscat's had, also saw striker Dougie Freedman move to Molineux from Selhurst Park, while Jamie Smith went in the opposite direction. Muscat, who made his debut for Wolves in the Nationwide home League game against Tranmere Rovers 24 hours after joining the club, had his disciplinary problems at Molineux, picking up 10 yellow cards in 27 games in 1997-98 and another handful the following season. In December 1998 he appeared before the FA after an alleged over-the-top-tackle on Norwich City Welsh international Craig Bellamy. He had also been involved in an incident with Charlton's Matty Holmes the previous season which resulted in the London-based player suffering a broken left leg which required lengthy surgery whereby a metal rod was inserted into his limb.
Wolves record: 70+2 apps. 7 goals.

MUTCH, Andrew Todd

Striker Andy Mutch, a former Liverpool and Everton apprentice who was born on Merseyside on 28 December 1963, was playing in non-League football with Southport when Wolves boss Sammy Chapman gave him another chance to make the grade. Wanderers signed him in February 1986 and after making his League debut the following month he ended the season with seven goals in 15 games. Alas, he came too late to prevent Wolves dropping into the Fourth Division, but the following season they lost out in the Play-off Final and then in consecutive seasons jumped from the Fourth Division to the Second with Mutch enjoying a lucrative goals partnership with Steve Bull. In addition, Wolves won the Sherpa Van Trophy in 1988 and Mutch scored in the Final against Burnley. In that spectacularly successful season he and goalkeeper Mark Kendall were the only ever-presents in the Wolves team. In the summer of 1989 his marksmanship was rewarded by England 'B' honours, when he played against Switzerland, Norway and Iceland. As Wolves consolidated themselves in the Second Division (which, of course, eventually became the First when the Premier League was formed), Mutch continued to find the net, although the goals were fewer in the higher sphere and he also missed much of the 1990-91 season. In August 1993, Swindon Town, newly promoted to the Premiership, paid £250,000 for his signature, but the Robins found life desperately difficult in the top flight and it did not prove a happy move for Mutch who, after a loan spell with Wigan Athletic (August-September 1995) moved to Stockport County in April 1996. He helped the Edgeley Park club win promotion to the First Division the following year. In July 1998 Mutch left Stockport to

Andy Mutch – England 'B' caps and over 300 games and 100 goals for Wolves.

sign for the Conference side Barrow, later rejoining his old club Southport (January 1999) before linking up with Telford United early in 1999 as player/assistant manager.
Wolves record: 325+13 apps. 105 goals.

MYERS, James Henry

Outside-left Jim Myers played for Wolves in season 1938-39, acting as reserve to Teddy Maguire and Dicky Dorsett. A Yorkshireman, born in Barnsley on 5 March 1920, he was signed from Barnsley (where he hadn't made a first-team appearance) in June 1938 and left Molineux for Cardiff City during the first part of the war. He did appear in League football when it recommenced in 1946.
Wolves record: 3 apps.

MYNARD, Leslie Daniel

Left-winger Les Mynard was born in Bewdley on 19 December 1925. He played for his home town club, Bewdley FC, before joining Wolves for season 1945-46. Basically a reserve at Molineux, his first-team appearances were limited and in July 1949 he was transferred to Derby County, later assisting Scunthorpe United (August 1952 to May 1953) before reverting back to non-League soccer.
Wolves record: 3 apps.

NAYLOR, Lee Martyn

Defender Lee Naylor made his Football League debut for Wolves in the televised local derby against Birmingham City at St Andrew's in October 1997, which Wolves lost 1-0. Born in Walsall on 19 March 1980 and educated at Sneyd Community School, Walsall, he joined Wolves in the summer of 1996, turning professional on his 18th birthday. He represented Wolverhampton Boys

before embarking on his career at Molineux and has since played for England at youth team level, representing his country in the 15th European Under 18 championships in Spain in April 1999. He prefers the left wingback position.
Wolves record: 39+8 apps. 2 goals.

NEEDHAM, Archibald

Forceful inside-forward Archie Needham spent one season at Molineux when he played alongside his brother Jack (below). Born in Sheffield in August 1881, he represented Sheffield Schools before joining Sheffield United for the 1901-02 season. Four years later (1905) he was transferred to Crystal Palace for whom he scored 27 goals in 104 outings. After a spell with Glossop North End (from June 1909) he signed for Wolves in August 1910 and left Molineux for Brighton and Hove Albion in July 1911. He did not play football after World War One and died in Sussex in 1961.
Wolves record: 35 apps. 7 goals.

NEEDHAM, John

Jack Needham (Archie's younger brother) was a goalscoring utility forward, who starred for Wolves between April 1910 and January 1920. Needham was born at Newstead, Notts on 4 March 1887 and played for Mansfield Wesleyans and Mansfield Invicta before joining junior side Mansfield Town in July 1907 (the present day Mansfield Town did not come into being until the summer of 1910). From here Needham – known as 'Mr Consistency' switched to Birmingham and scored five goals in 20 games for the Blues between June 1909 and April 1910, when he was transferred to Wolves. He made his debut in the last game of that season, scoring in a 3-2 win over Manchester City at Molineux. The following season Needham was Wolves' top scorer with 13 goals. Before the war he formed an excellent left-wing partnership, first with Archie Walker, then Sammy Brooks and occasionally Tommy Yule. Needham, who guested for Port Vale in 1916-17, was still in the Wanderers side when the Football League resumed in 1919-20, but towards the end of that season was transferred to Hull City who probably remembered the hat-trick he had scored against them in an 8-0 drubbing at Molineux back in November 1911. By now, though, Needham's powers were waning and he managed only one goal in 18 games for the Tigers before drifting out of League football in 1922. He died c.1956.
Wolves record: 206 apps. 61 goals.

NEIL, Patrick Thomas

Born in Portsmouth on 24 October 1937, left winger Pat Neil won an amateur cap for England as a teenager with

Wolves in 1933-34

Portsmouth, whom he joined on leaving school in 1953. He never turned professional and after scoring three goals in nine League games for Pompey he was transferred to Wolves in August 1956. Recruited by Stan Cullis, he was basically a reserve at Molineux and never really threatened the club's regular wingers, Jimmy Mullen and Norman Deeley. He left Wolves for Pegasus in the summer of 1957 and later returned for a second spell at Fratton Park (1962) before quitting League soccer the following year.

Wolves record: 4 apps. 1 goal.

NELSON, John Henry

Jack Nelson was born in Chorley on 15 March 1906 and worked in a bleach factory in the Lancashire town whilst playing for the local club, Chorley All Saints and then Town. He became a full-time professional with Preston North End in March 1926 and was transferred to Wolverhampton Wanderers in November 1932, after making 72 League appearances for Preston. Initially, he came as cover for the centre-half position in a Wolves team which had just returned to the First Division and was struggling in their first season back in the top flight, eventually finishing 20th. Nelson, a 'policeman' type of defender standing 6ft 2ins. tall, played an important part in their fight against instant relegation. He stayed with Wolves for another two seasons, in which they battled to improve on lowly positions before moving to Luton Town in May 1935. Nelson spent two seasons at Kenilworth Road, making 134 appearances and helping the Hatters win the Third Division (South) title in 1936-37. He later returned to Molineux as Wolves' trainer and prior to, during and immediately after World War Two Nelson acted as trainer/coach at Walsall. Also a very fine cricketer and tennis player, Jack Nelson eventually returned to Wolverhampton where he died in May 1986.

Wolves record: 75 apps. 4 goals.

NEW BRIGHTON

Wolves' playing record against New Brighton is:

Football League

Venue	P	W	D	L	F	A
Home	1	1	0	0	5	1
Away	1	1	0	0	1	0
Total	2	2	0	0	6	1

FA Cup

	P	W	D	L	F	A
Home	1	1	0	0	5	1

The two League games between Wolves and New Brighton took place in season 1923-24 and were a week apart. After winning 5-1 at Molineux on 24 November, when Harry Lees scored a hat-trick. Wolves travelled to Merseyside the following Saturday and edged home with a Stan Fazackerley goal.

Billy Wooldridge scored a hat-trick in Wolves emphatic 5-1 FA Cup win over New Brighton in February 1901, this being the only senior meeting between the two clubs in the competition. Players with both clubs include: Jack Hopkins, Albert Lumberg, Billy Walker, George Walker and Dennis Westcott.

Also associated: Edward Anderson, Alan Steen and Tom 'Pongo' Waring (wartime guests for New Brighton), Tom Grimley (Wolves trialist), George Wallace Bruce, Sid Clewlow, Bill Prendergast, George Waddell and Wilfred Walker (all Wolves Reserves).

NEWCASTLE UNITED

Wolves' playing record against the Magpies is:

Football League

Venue	P	W	D	L	F	A
Home	38	25	8	5	78	36
Away	38	8	8	22	48	89
Total	76	33	16	27	126	125

FA Cup

Venue	P	W	D	L	F	A
Home	3	3	0	0	6	2
Away	2	0	2	0	3	3
Neutral	3	1	1	1	4	3
Total	8	4	3	1	13	8

It was back in season 1898-99 when Wolves first met Newcastle in the Football League and it was the former who had the better of those initial exchanges, winning 4-2 on Tyneside after a 0-0 draw at Molineux. Billy Beats scored two of the four Wolves goals in that victory at St James' Park.

Centre-half Ted Pheasant became the first Wolves defender to score a hat-trick when he obliged with treble in a 3-0 victory over Newcastle in March 1902. It was 93 years before another defender equalled Pheasant's feat, John De Wolf scoring three times at Port Vale in 1995.

Wolves' first League double over United came in 1902-03 when they triumphed 3-0 at home and 4-0 away, Adam Haywood scoring twice in the game at Molineux.

United, the reigning League champions, went to town and hammered Wolves 8-0 at St James' Park in November 1905, Bill Appleyard scoring a hat-trick.

There were no more League meetings until the 1930s and it was United who had the better of the exchanges with successive home wins of 3-2 and 5-1 in October 1932 and April 1934, Bill Imrie claiming a hat-trick in the latter game.

The results were fairly even through to the late 1950s, although there were some exciting affairs. Two of the best ended in Wolves wins – the first in March 1949 when Dennis Wilshaw, on his Wolves' League debut, hit a second-half treble in a 3-0 win at St James' Park and ten years later, in February 1959, Micky Lill scored twice in a 4-3 victory for Wolves, also on Newcastle's ground.

An eight-goal bonanza finished level at 4-4 at St James' Park in October 1960, when Peter Broadbent was in sparkling form for Wolves with two goals. And in 1968-69, the two encounters produced ten goals, Wolves winning 5-0 at Molineux, with two goals for Peter Knowles, one being a superb overhead kick, and United gaining revenge with a 4-1 victory on the last day of the season.

In season 1975-76, thanks mainly to a John Richards hat-trick, Wolves won 5-0 at Molineux, but crashed 5-1 at St James' Park, and two years later (in December 1977) United again ran up a big score, winning 4-0 on home soil.

Steve Bull scored all Wolves goals in their 4-1 demolition of Newcastle United at St James' Park in a Second Division game on 1 January 1990, when a specially chartered plane flew ardent Wolves' supporters north to St James' Park after they had celebrated the New Year's Eve in the Midlands.

Wolves first encountered United in the FA Cup in the Final of 1908 at Crystal Palace and they triumphed 3-1 with all the game's goals being scored by four players whose surname began with the letter 'H' – Harrison, Hedley and Hunt for Wolves and Howie for United.

Wolves beat United 1-0 at home in a third round tie in January 1934, but lost to the Magpies 2-1 after a replay in the 1951 FA Cup semi-final, United scoring twice in a

Steve Bull and Andy Mutch battle it out against Newcastle United in March 1992.

minute after Johnny Walker had fired the Wanderers in front.

Wolves knocked the St James' Park side out of the Cup by 4-2 at Molineux in a third-round replay in January 1960 after 62,443 spectators had attended the initial 2-2 draw in the North East.

The last FA Cup meeting was a fourth replay in February 1979 when a Norman Bell goal gave Wolves a 1-0 home win.

Steve Watson became the youngest player ever to don a Newcastle jersey when he made his debut against Wolves as a substitute in a Second Division match on 10 November 1990 at the age of 16 years 223 days.

Players with both clubs include: Dave Beasant, Joe Blackett, John Burridge, David Kelly, Tom Phillipson, Billy Rafferty and Peter Withe.

Also associated: Bill McGarry (manager of both Wolves and Newcastle United); Pavel Srnicek (Wolves trialist from Newcastle); Harry Bowden and Colin Gibson (United players, Wolves wartime guests), Alex McIntosh and Jimmy Mullen (United guests), George Jobey (United player, Wolves manag-

er); Mick Martin (Wolves trial), Mark McGhee (United player, Wolves manager), Joe Harvey (Wolves reserve, later Newcastle player and manager, who made 247 appearances for the Geordies between 1945-53, leading them to a FA Cup Final triumph) and Ray King (amateur goalkeeper with both clubs).

NEWELL, Percy John

Full-back Percy Newell deputised for Dickie Baugh in Wolves' defence during his three seasons at Molineux. Born in Wolverhampton in 1901, he played for Stourbridge before joining Wolves in May 1920. He returned to Stourbridge on leaving the club in August 1923 and later assisted Bloxwich Strollers.

Wolves record: 10 apps.

NEWPORT COUNTY

Wolves' playing record against County is:

Football League

Venue	P	W	D	L	F	A
Home	2	1	1	0	3	3
Away	2	1	0	1	4	4
Total	4	2	1	1	7	7

Wartime

Home	1	1	0	0	5	2
Away	1	1	0	0	3	1
Total	2	2	0	0	8	3

The teams first met in the League in 1985-86, County winning both matches: 2-1 at Molineux and 3-1 at Somerton Park.

Two years later – in April 1988 – Wolves clinched promotion from Division with a 3-1 win at Newport, Steve Bull scoring twice, including his fiftieth goal of the season. Ex-Wolves 'keeper Paul Bradshaw played for Newport.

Players with both clubs include: Joe Bonson, Paul Bradshaw, Arthur Brooks, Don Cock, Ted Collins, Vic Fox, Mark Kendall, Steve Mardenborough, Fred Pincott, Fred Price, Tom Pritchard, Jack Smith, Nigel Vaughan, Reg Weaver, Joe Wilson, Bobby Woodruff and Harry Wright.

Also associated: Alex McIntosh (County wartime guest). Tom Wood (Wolves wartime guest), Len Weare junior (Wolves trialist) and Walter Akers, Fred Chadwick, Ernie Hackett, Billy Lucas, Matthew O'Mahoney, Cyril Pearce and George Smith (all Wolves

Reserves). Lucas, who left Molineux in 1937 for Swindon Town, was player-manager of County from 1953-61 and manager from 1962-67 and again from 1970-74. He made over 100 appearances for the Welsh club.

NICHOLAS, Alfred

Smart, determined outside-right, Alf Nicholls was born in Birmingham c.1875 and after attending Abbey Road School, he played, in turn, for Hockley Brook, Hockley Belmont, Walsall Primitives, Wednesbury Royal and Wednesbury Old Athletic before joining Wolves in August 1896. He spent just a season at Molineux, moving to Walsall Alma in April 1897. He later assisted Alma Swifts and Bushbury Park, and scored six goals for the latter club against Featherstone in 1900. He died in Rugby in 1932.
Wolves record: 3 apps. 2 goals.

NIESTROJ, Robert

Tall, hard-working midfielder, Robert Niestroj was signed from Fortuna Dusseldorf for £350,000 in October 1998. He had been associated with the Dusseldorf club since he was a 14-year-old and had been a professional in the Bundesliga since 1993. He agreed a three-and-a-half year contract at Molineux. Born in Germany on 2 December 1974, he made his Wolves debut, as a second-half substitute, in the local derby with neighbours West Bromwich Albion at the Hawthorns in November 1998.
Wolves record: 3+3 apps.

NIGHTINGALE, John Gladstone

Wolves recruited left-winger Jack Nightingale from Kidderminster Harriers in December 1919. Born in Oldbury in June 1899, and a player with Brandhall Rovers, he unfortunately failed to make the grade at Molineux and left for Shrewsbury Town in July 1920. He switched to Brighton and Hove Albion in 1921 for whom he made almost 200 senior appearances up to 1927, when he returned to Shrewsbury. On retiring Nightingale moved down to Sussex, living in Hove until his death in December 1967.
Wolves record: 3 apps.

NIXON, Eric Walter

Goalkeeper Eric Nixon has had a fine career in the Football League. Born in Manchester on 4 October 1962, he began his soccer life with Curzon Ashton and entered League action with Manchester City in 1983. He remained registered at Maine Road until March 1988 when he was transferred to Tranmere Rovers for £60,000. During his five years with City, Nixon played on loan with Wolves (August-November 1986 – during which time he saved two penalties), Bradford City (November 1986) and Carlisle United

(January-March 1987). He went on to amass 431 senior appearances for Tranmere, up to May 1997 when he joined Stockport County for £100,000, having in between times served on loan with Reading (January 1996) and Blackpool (February 1996). In September 1998, Nixon joined Wigan Athletic (on loan from Edgeley Park). He helped Tranmere win the Leyland DAF Trophy at Wembley in 1990 and during the course of the 1996-97 season passed the milestone of 600 League and Cup appearances. One interesting point is that Nixon played in every Division of the Football League over a period of six months from August 1986 to January 1987, lining up for Wolves (Division Four), Bradford City (2), Southampton (1) and Carlisle United (3) – the quickest in League history.
Wolves record: 16 apps.

NORTH, Stacey Stewart

Blond central defender Stacey North had an exceptionally long throw, once catapulting the ball almost 75 yards from the right-hand touchline when playing for Luton Town. Born in Luton on 25 November 1964, North was on loan at Molineux from The Hatters during November and December 1985, having initially joined the staff at Kenilworth Road as a junior in 1980, turning professional in August 1982. Capped by England at youth team level, he went on to play in 25 League games for the Hatters before moving to The Hawthorns in December 1987. He left Albion for Fulham in October 1990 for £135,000 after making more than 100 senior appearances for the Baggies. Unfortunately North was forced to quit football with serious knee and back injuries in January 1993.
Wolves record: 3 apps.

NORTHAMPTON TOWN

Wolves' playing record against the Cobblers is:

Football League

Venue	P	W	D	L	F	A
Home	3	2	1	0	5	3
Away	3	1	0	2	6	5
Total	6	3	1	2	11	8

Sherpa Van Trophy

	P	W	D	L	F	A
Home	1	1	0	0	3	1

Wartime

	P	W	D	L	F	A
Home	5	3	1	1	13	9
Away	5	1	3	1	9	8
Total	10	4	4	2	22	17

Wolves first met the Cobblers in the Football League in season 1966-67 (Division Two) and both games went in favour of the Molineux men, who won 1-0 at home and 4-0 at the County Ground, Ernie Hunt scoring a hat-trick in the latter contest.

Wolves clinched the Third Division championship with a 3-2 home win over Northampton in May 1989.

Goals by Mick Gooding, Robbie Dennison and Nigel Vaughan gave Wolves a 3-1 victory over the Cobblers in a Sherpa Van Trophy game at Molineux in February 1989 and took them into the Area semi-final.

Dennis Westcott scored four times when Wolves defeated the Cobblers 7-2 at Molineux in a Midland Regional League game in October 1939.

Wolves crashed 7-2 at Northampton in a Football League North match in March 1944.

The first official transfer in wartime football saw forward Bob King sold by Northampton to Wolves for £2,000 on 22 November 1939.

Players with both clubs include: Andy Blair,

Ally Robertson keeps an eye on Northampton Town's Paul Cooper in May 1989 as Wolves moved towards the Third Division championship.

Chic Brodie, John Burridge, Phil Chard (also assistant manager and manager of Northampton), Bill Coley, Bob Coy, Richard Deacon, Dean Edwards, Evan Edwards, John Farrington, Ron Flowers, Bob Hatton, George Henson, Micky Holmes, Bill Lockett, Derek Mountfield, Martin Patching, Fred Ramscar, Phil Robinson, Tom Smalley, Harry Thompson, Mark Turner, Alf Walker and Kim Wassall.

Also associated: John Barnwell (managed both clubs), George Jobey (Town player-coach, Wolves manager); Ian Ross (Town player, Wolves coach, caretaker-manager); Frank Upton (Town player and coach at both clubs); George Ashall, Andy Beattie – later Wolves manager – Bob Iverson, Eric Jones, Fred Pincott and Horace Wright (all Cobblers wartime guests), Tom Allen, Bill Barron, Vic Cockcroft, Arthur Ford, Stuart Garnham, Arthur Hartshorne, Andy Poole, Darren Shaw, Dave Syrett and Gareth Williams (all Wolves Reserves). Poole made 141 League appearances for the Cobblers, 1978-82.

NORWICH CITY

Wolves' playing record against the Canaries is:

Football League

Venue	P	W	D	L	F	A
Home	14	11	2	1	33	12
Away	14	5	6	3	19	13
Total	28	16	8	4	52	25

FA Cup

Home	2	1	1	0	6	2
Away	1	1	0	0	3	2
Total	3	2	1	9	9	4

League Cup

Home	1	1	0	0	1	0
Away	1	0	1	0	1	1
Total	2	1	1	0	2	1

Wolves and Norwich first met at competitive level at Carrow Road in October 1965 (Division Two). And it was the visitors who took the honours with an easy 3-0 victory.

The return game at Molineux that season saw Wolves double up with a 2-1 win.

Wolves did the double over the Canaries the following season, taking all four points with a 4-1 win at Molineux and a 2-1 triumph at Carrow Road. Derek Dougan scored twice in the 4-1 victory.

Six goals were shared at 3-3 in the League game at Molineux in March 1978 (Steve Daley netted twice for Wolves) and hot-shot from the spot Kenny Hibbitt netted two penalties in Wolves' 4-0 win over Norwich in the First Division game at Carrow Road in February 1980.

When Wolves beat the Canaries 5-0 in a First Division game at Molineux in January 1998, they were 4-0 up at half-time and Dougie Freedman scored a hat-trick, two of his goals coming in 90 seconds just before the interval.

A crowd of more than 29,000 saw Wolves beat the Canaries 5-1 at Molineux in a third-round FA Cup-tie in January 1971. Bobby Gould and Jim McCalliog both scored twice. It was a much closer affair when the teams met in the same competition in 1979-80 and this time Wolves went through to round five after a replay (1-1 and 3-2).

A 2-1 semi-final aggregate victory over Norwich City in 1973-74 took Wolves to Wembley for their Final showpiece with Manchester City. After a 1-1 draw at Carrow Road, John Richards became the Molineux hero with the winning goal in the second leg before a 32,605 crowd. He had also scored at Norwich.

Players with both clubs include: Paul Blades, Lewis Botto, Bill Brown, Paul Cook, Hugh Curran, Walter Featherby, Roger Hansbury, Bryn Jones (Town player-coach), Billy Kellock, James Kelly, Mike Kenning, Gerry Mannion, Iwan Roberts, Robert Rosario, Tom Smalley, John Smith, Jack Taylor, Albert Thorpe, Shane Westley and Les Wilson.

Also associated: Major Frank Buckley (manager of both clubs); Ron Bradley (Norwich player, Wolves coach), Jack Acquaroff (Wolves wartime guest), Cameron Buchanan (Wolves wartime player), Cyril Spiers (Wolves player, Norwich manager); Guy Wharton (City wartime guest), Tommy Hunt, Harry Keeling, John Marshall, Frank Perfect, Sid Plunkett and Jim Travers (all Wolves Reserves), Sid Taylor (Wolves trialist), Justin Bray (Wolves reserve, City schoolboy).

NOTTINGHAM FOREST

Wolves' playing record against Forest is:

Football League

Venue	P	W	D	L	F	A
Home	51	35	9	7	120	57
Away	51	11	11	29	57	101
Total	102	46	20	36	177	158

FA Cup

Home	1	1	0	0	2	0
Away	2	0	0	2	3	5
Total	3	1	0	2	5	5

League Cup

Home	1	0	0	1	2	3
Neutral	1	1	0	0	1	0
Total	2	1	0	1	3	3

FA Charity Shield

Home	1	1	0	0	3	1

Wartime

Home	2	2	0	0	11	0
Away	2	0	2	0	0	0
Total	4	2	2	0	11	0

There were plenty of goals in the first ten League games between Wolves and Forest which took place between 1892 and 1897.

There were 44 in fact with Wolves winning 3-1, 6-1 and 4-1 at home and Forest doing likewise by 7-1 and 3-1. Wolves' six-goal romp came in March 1896 when both Billy Beats and Harry Wood scored twice.

Forest's seven-goal haul was achieved on the opening day of that 1893-94 season (2 September) when Jimmy Collins scored a hat-trick.

Future West Brom winger Ben Shearman scored twice in Forest's 5-0 home in over Wolves in January 1904 and when Wolves completed the seasonal double over Forest in 1913-14 (winning 4-1 at home and 3-1 away) outside-left Sammy Brooks was on the score sheet in both matches.

Forest were beaten 5-1 at Molineux the following season and shortly after World War One (November 1919) they lost 4-0 on Wolves' soil with Albert Groves netting a hat-trick.

Wolves again doubled-up over Forest in 1925-26, winning 4-0 at home and 4-1 away, and in 1930-31 it was again Wolves who took the honours with victories of 4-2 at Molineux and 4-3 at the City Ground. Billy Hartill scored twice in game for Wolves.

There was no action between the clubs between 1932 and the mid-1950s but then Wolves ran up five successive wins over Forest, the best being a 5-1 victory at Molineux in August 1958 when Bobby Mason rattled in a hat-trick in front of a bumper opening day crowd of 52,656.

There were fireworks galore on 5 November 1960 when Wolves beat Forest 5-3 at Molineux and there were plenty more when Forest were felled 6-1 by a rampant Wolves in April 1968, Derek Dougan scoring a treble on this occasion.

Wolves drew 0-0 with Forest in a First Division League game at Meadow Lane (home of Notts County) in November 1968. This was due to the City Ground being out of bounds because of fire damage. And the following season 12 goals were scored in the two encounters (3-3 at Molineux and a 4-2 Forest win by the River Trent).

Another flurry of goals greeted the Wolves-Forest League clashes of the 1970s, with 19 coming in the four games in 1970-71 and 1971-72. Wolves won 4-0 and 4-2 at home and 3-1 away while Forest took the points with a 4-1 home success in between times.

As reigning European Champions, Forest came to Molineux and beat Wolves 4-1 in a First Division game on Boxing Day 1980 and on Guy Fawkes Day 1983 they again fired a few rockets when thumping Wolves 5-0 at the City Ground, Steve Hodge scoring twice.

Wolves first met Forest in the FA Cup in season 1926-27 when they won a home fourth round tie 2-0 in front of 41,112 fans.

Forest won a thrilling long-delayed third round tie at the City Ground by 4-3 in January 1963. The bitterly cold arctic weather disrupted football all over the country around this time, yet almost 39,000 fans witnessed this seven-goal thriller in which Barry Stobart netted twice for Wolves.

An easy tap-in goal from two yards by Andy Gray – following a mix-up involving Peter Shilton and Dave Needham – was enough to give Wolves a 1-0 victory over Forest in the 1980 League Cup Final at Wembley Stadium in front of 96,527 spectators (receipts £625,000).

A stunning last minute goal by England full-back Stuart Pearce earned Forest a 3-2 third round League Cup win over Wolves in October 1994 when the crowd of 28,369 set a new record for the rebuilt Molineux. (This was beaten in February 1995 for the visit of Leicester City in the FA Cup).

Goals by Micky Lill, Jimmy Murray and Peter Broadbent gave Wolves a 3-1 win over Nottingham Forest in the FA Charity Shield match at Molineux in August 1959.

Dennis Westcott scored a double hat-trick (six goals) when Wolves whipped Forest 7-0 at home in a Football League South game in December 1941.

Players with both clubs include: Jim Barron, Dave Beasant, Colin Booth, George Bowen, Chris Crowe, Dick Le Flem, Dougie Freedman, John Galley, Hillary Griffiths, Alan Hinton, Dick Le Flem, Stuart McMillan, Billy Marshall, David 'Boy' Martin, Robert Rosario, Hans Segers, Geoff Thomas, Frank Wignall, Joe Wilson and Peter Withe.

Also associated: Andy Beattie (manager of both clubs); John Barnwell (Forest player, Wolves manager); Stan Collymore (Wolves Reserves), Albert 'Sailor' Brown and Frank O'Donnell (Forest players, Wolves wartime guests), Dick Forshaw, George Heppell, Bob Iverson, Eric Jones, Cecil Shaw and Tom Waring (all Forest wartime guests); Phil Chard (Forest amateur); Ian Miller (Forest player, Wolves coach).

When Alan Hinton and Frank Wignall were selected to play against Wales in November 1965 it was the first time two Nottingham Forest players had received full England recognition since 1902. Both players were also associated with Wolves.

NOTTS COUNTY

Wolves' playing record against County is:

Football League

Venue	P	W	D	L	F	A
Home	33	20	8	5	67	32
Away	33	7	11	15	40	71
Total	66	27	19	20	107	103

FA Cup

Home	2	1	1	0	6	2
Away	4	4	0	0	11	6
Total	6	5	1	0	17	8

Sherpa Van Trophy

Home	1	1	0	0	3	0
Away	1	0	1	0	1	1
Total	2	1	1	0	4	1

As founder members of the Football League, Wolves first met County in season 1888-89 and honours were shared with Wolves winning 2-1 at Dudley Road, while County took the points with a 3-0 victory at Meadow Lane.

Wolves had the better of the meetings during the first decade of League competition but in October 1900 County won 4-1 at home in a game which could have seen them reach double figures.

The following season (1901-02) 12 goals came from the two encounters with Wolves triumphant by 3-1 at Molineux and County 5-3 victors in Nottingham.

Twenty-five goals were scored in the four League games between the clubs in 1904-05 and 1905-06. Wolves doubled up with 3-1 and 4-3 wins in the former campaign and they won again by 6-1 a year later, while County gained some joy with a 5-2 home win as well. Wolves' outside-left Jack Pedley was a hat-trick hero in that six-goal feast.

County won five home League games on the trot before Wolves ended that run in 1927 with a 2-2 draw, and in October 1929, Billy Hartill slammed in all five goals as County crashed 5-1 to Wolves at Molineux in a Second Division fixture.

Surprisingly Wolves and County did not meet each other at League level for 44 years (from 1932) but then it was stalemate as both games ended in draws in 1976-77.

During the early 1980s County ran up four successive home League wins over Wolves with scores of 4-0, 4-0, 4-1 and 4-0 and they also won twice at Molineux.

Wolves have a 100 per cent away record against County in the FA Cup. They commenced with a 4-3 replay win in February 1896 and since then their best victories at Meadow Road have been those of 4-0 in January 1935 and 3-1 in January 1980, each time in the third round.

By beating County 4-1 on aggregate in the Area semi-final of the Sherpa Van Trophy in 1987-88, Wolves went through to play Burnley in the Final at Wembley.

Players with both clubs include: John Burridge, John Chadburn, Ray Chatham, Don Cock, Ted Collins, Will Devey, Keith Downing, Walter Featherby, Dominic Foley, Tom Galley, Andy Gray, George Kinsey, Harry Lees, Joe McMain, Chris Marsden, David 'Boy' Martin, Dennis Pearce, Frank Pope, Roy Pritchard, Jesse Pye, Paddy Ratcliffe, Phil Robinson, Eddie Russell, Peter Russell, Alex Simpson, John Streets, George Swift (also County manager), John E. Taylor and Albert Thorpe.

Also associated: John Barnwell and Major Frank Buckley (managers both clubs); Andy Beattie (Wolves manager, County coach and professional advisor with Peter Doherty); Richie Barker (County player and manager,

Wolves coach); Ian Ross (coach and caretaker-manager of Wolves, County player); Frank Upton (County player, Wolves coach); Jack Abthorpe, Terry Harkin, Terry Thompson and Gordon Wills (Wolves Reserves), George Poyser (Wolves reserve and scout, County assistant manager); Andy Beattie (Wolves manager), Bill Baxter, Roy Bicknell, John Griffiths, Bob Iverson, Reg Kirkham, Roy Pritchard, Cyril Sidlow and Billy Wright (all County wartime guests), Tommy Asher and Frank Broome (County players, Wolves wartime guests) and Harry Keeling, Jim Poppitt and Sid Protheroe (Wolves Reserves; Eric Lister (amateur), Vic Povey (Wolves junior) and Bernard Streten (guest).

Wolves played Nottingham Forest in a First Division League game at County's Meadow Lane ground in November 1968 owing to fire damage at the City Ground.

NUMBERING OF PLAYERS

Shirt-numbering for Football League games was first made compulsory for the 1938-39 season – and it is believed that the first time Wolves players wore shirts numbered 2-11 was against Stoke City in the League Jubilee Fund game in August 1938.

NURSE, Daniel G.

Right-half Dan Nurse was born in Princes End, Tipton in June 1873. He attended Princes End School, played for Princes End FC and then Coseley before joining Wolves in June 1894. He spent seven excellent years at Molineux although he was only a regular in the first team in 1895-96. In May 1901 he was transferred to West Bromwich Albion and at the end of his first season at The Hawthorns collected a Second Division championship medal as skipper of the Baggies. In 1903 he represented the Football League and went on to play in 88 games for Albion before injury forced him into an early retirement in April 1905. Five years later he became a director at The Hawthorns, a position he held until May 1927. He was also elected a Life Member of Albion in 1920 (in recognition of his sterling efforts in saving the club from going into liquidation in 1910). Nurse's grandson, David, is now an Albion shareholder. Dan Nurse died in West Bromwich in April 1959.
Wolves record: 39 apps. 1 goal.

O'CONNOR, John Patrick

Small, frail-looking outside-right or inside-forward, Jack O'Connor was born in Wolverhampton *c*.1901. He played for Lea Hall Ramblers and Quarry Bank Rangers before joining Wolves in May 1923. He spent two years as a reserve at Molineux before transferring to Gillingham in August 1926. He later assisted Tranmere Rovers, Darlington and Crewe Alexandra (all in season 1927-28), Flint Town (1928), Stafford Rangers (October 1929), Darlaston, Halesowen Town, Dudley Town, Netherton and Cradley Town, retiring in 1939-40 on the outbreak of World War Two.

Wolves record: 11 apps. 2 goals.

O'GRADY, Michael

Despite his Irish-sounding name, Mike O'Grady was a Yorkshireman, born in Leeds on 11 October 1942. A smart utility forward, able to occupy both flanks as well as an inside berth, he joined Huddersfield Town on leaving school and turned professional with the Town in October 1959. He did well at Huddersfield, scoring 26 goals in 160 League games, winning the first of his two full England caps and also lining up for his country in three Under-23 internationals. In October 1965 he was transferred to Leeds United for £30,000 and over the next four years became part of that fine Don Revie footballing-machine at Elland Road. He netted 12 goals in 91 First Division appearances and helped United reach successive Fairs Cup Finals in 1967 and 1968 (gaining a winners medal in the latter) and carry off the League championship in 1969. He also added his second England cap to his collection, and represented the Football League on three occasions. In September 1969, O'Grady joined Wolves for £80,000, remaining at Molineux for three years, although during this time he was plagued by injury and, indeed, he hardly got a first team outing after his initial campaign with the club. After a loan spell with Birmingham City (February 1972 – being Blues' first loan player to make a League appearance) he was transferred to Rotherham United where he stayed until retiring through injury in May 1974.

Wolves record: 35+6 apps. 6 goals.

O'HARA, Gerald John

Midfielder Gerry O'Hara was born in Wolverhampton on 3 December 1956. He joined Wolves on leaving school in the summer of 1972 and turned professional at Molineux in December 1974. He spent the next four years or so in the Reserves, making only fleeting first-team appearances before being released in May 1978. Three months later (August 1978) he signed for Hereford United as a non-contract player, dropping out of League soccer in 1979 after only one game for the Bulls. O'Hara played for Bilston Town (two spells), Worcester City, Redditch (two spells), Willenhall, Dudley Town and Bridgnorth Town before retiring in 1995.

Wolves record: 9+2 apps.

OLD CARTHUSIANS

Wolves' playing record against Carthusians is:

FA Cup

Venue	P	W	D	L	F	A
Home	2	2	0	0	6	3

The amateur club, Old Carthusians, who themselves had won the coveted 'English Cup' in 1881, were ousted from the competition by Wolves in the opening round of the 1888-89 tournament, losing 4-3 at Molineux in front of 6,000 spectators. Tommy Knight scored twice for Wolves. A year later, at the same stage, around 13,000 fans saw England international Harry Wood score both goals in a 2-0 Wolves triumph.

OLDERSHAW, Walter

Full-back Wally Oldershaw was reserve to Charlie Mason during his one season with Wolves (1889-90). His only outing for the club was against Accrington on New Year's Day when Wolves were beaten 6-3. Oldershaw was born in Walsall in 1867. He joined the club from Walsall Alma and left Molineux for Wednesbury Town. He died c.1938.

Wolves record: 1 app.

OLDFIELD, John Stephen

Goalkeeper John Oldfield was born in Lindrick on 19 August 1943. He joined Huddersfield Town on leaving school and turned professional at Leeds Road in August 1961. He made over 150 League appearances for the Town before transferring to Wolves in December 1969. A competent 'keeper, with good reflexes, he remained at Molineux for two years, acting in the main as reserve to Phil Parkes. A month before leaving Wolves he had a loan spell with Crewe Alexandra (November) and signed for Bradford City in December 1971, remaining at Valley Parade until May 1973, making 34 appearances for the Bantams.

Wolves record: 19 apps.

OLDHAM ATHLETIC

Wolves' playing record against the Latics is:

Football League

Venue	P	W	D	L	F	A
Home	19	9	6	4	34	19
Away	19	4	2	13	19	42
Total	38	13	8	17	53	61

FA Cup

Venue	P	W	D	L	F	A
Home	1	1	0	0	4	1
Away	2	0	1	1	2	3
Total	3	1	1	1	6	4

The first time Wolves met the Latics at League level was in 1907-08 (Division Two) when each club won its home game.

The results were fairly even up to October 1928 when Wolves won 4-0 at Boundary Park with Wilf Chadwick scoring twice.

The Latics quickly gained revenge, hammering Wolves 6-0 on the same ground in November 1929 when Fred Worrall and Stewart Littlewood both netted twice.

Over 20,000 fans saw Wolves' handsome 7-1 home victory (their best to date over Oldham) in April 1932 (on their way to clinching the Second Division championship). Billy Hartill scored three times that day and Wilf Lowton tore a hole in the net with a penalty kick.

There was a break of some 45 years before the teams met at League level again and then (in 1976-77) Wolves won 5-0 at Molineux and 2-0 at Boundary Park, on their way to taking the Second Division title.

Oldham had by far the better of the League exchanges during the 1990s, twice winning 4-1 at home. Andy Ritchie scored a hat-trick in one of those triumphs on Boxing Day 1994.

Almost 25,000 fans saw a third-round FA Cup-tie between the Latics and Wolves at Boundary Park in January 1967. The game ended 2-2 and over 39,000 saw Wolves win the replay in style by 4-1.

Players with both clubs include: Brian

Tony Evans scores against Oldham Athletic at Boundary Park in October 1984.

Birch, Bill Boswell, Billy Halligan, Ted Ivill, Ken Knighton, Scott McGarvey and Nicky Sinclair.

Also associated: Ian Greaves (Oldham player, Wolves manager), Jack Rowley (Wolves reserve and guest, Oldham manager: two spells), Arthur Bailey (Latics player, Wolves wartime guest) and George Waddell and Jeff Wealands (Wolves Reserves).

OLDROYD, Darren Robert

It was anticipated that Darren Oldroyd would take over the right-back berth from Geoff Palmer at Molineux, but unfortunately he was dogged by injury and a promising career ended abruptly in 1988. Born in Ormskirk on 1 November 1966, Oldroyd joined Everton as an apprentice in 1982 and turned professional at Goodison Park in November 1984. He came to Molineux in August 1986, but was released in May 1987 when he joined Southport. He later played occasional local non-League soccer until 1996.
Wolves record: 13 apps.

ORDISH, Cyril Stanley

The versatile, red-faced Cyril Ordish was a neat and tidy footballer, who played as a full-back, Wing-half or outside-right who found it difficult to break into Wolves' first team. Born in Chesterfield, Derbyshire in 1910, he served with Blackwell FC before joining his hometown club, Chesterfield in 1933, moving to Molineux in May 1936. He spent two seasons with Wolves and in May 1938 when he was transferred to Reading. He retired during the war.
Wolves record: 2 apps.

OSBORN, Simon Edward

Midfielder Simon Osborn was born in Croydon on 19 January 1972 and was taken on as a trainee by Crystal Palace in June 1988, turning professional with the Eagles in January 1990. Over the next four years he did reasonably well at Selhurst Park, appearing in over 70 first-team games before transferring to Reading for £90,000 in August 1994. After just a season at Elm Park he switched back to London to sign for Queen's Park Rangers for £1.1 million, but failed to settle down at Loftus Road and after only 11 outings was snapped up by his former manager at Reading, Mark McGhee, who bought him to Wolves for £1 million in December 1995. A player with great stamina, he's always seeking the ball and loves to have a shot at goal, especially from long distances.
Wolves record: 126+4 apps. 13 goals.

OVERSEAS OPPOSITION AND PLAYERS
Opposition

Wolves have played the following overseas clubs at competitive level: Academica Del Coimbra, Ascoli, Atalanta, FK Austria, Barcelona, Belenenses, Carl Zeiss Jena, FC Den Haag, PSV Eindhoven, Ferencvaros, Fiorentina, Juventus, Lazio, Lecce, Lokomotiv Leipzig, FC Porto, Red Star Belgrade, FC Schalke '04, Venezia, and ASK Vorwaerts. (See also *Friendlies*)

Wolves made their first official foreign tour in 1931 to France where they were beaten 3-1 by the Spanish club Santander and 4-2 by First Vienna of Austria in Paris.

They re-visited France in 1933; visited Ireland in 1937 and again in 1938 when they also went on their first full and lengthy European tour which took them to Poland, Czechoslovakia, Hungary, France and Belgium. The following year – before World War Two – they travelled to play games in Denmark and Holland.

Since 1945 tours/trips/visits have taken them all over the world.

The longest journey (in terms of duration) undertaken by a Wolves party was to America in 1967 (where they played 14 games in just 49 days). It was here that they assumed the title Los Angeles Wolves and won the prearranged tournament, beating Aberdeen in the Final.

The furthest Wolves have travelled to play football was to New Zealand in 1972.

Players

Here are some of the overseas-born players who have served Wolves at first team level over the years: Emilio Aldecoa (Spain – wartime player), Steve Corica (Australia), Isidro Diaz (Spain), Jens Dowe (Germany), Cliff Durandt (South Africa), Haavard Flo (Norway), Don Gardner (Jamaica), Fernando Gomez (Spain), Ricki Herbert (New Zealand), Des Horne (Johannesburg), Dariusz Kubicki (Poland), Doug McMahon (Canada), Robert Niestroj (Germany), Mixu Paatelainen (Finland), Serge Romano (France), Jesus Garcia Sanjuan (Spain), Hans Segers (Holland), Eddie Stuart (South Africa), Robin Van der Laan (Holland), Raphael Villazan (Uruguay), Mark Williams (South Africa), Les Wilson (Canada), John de Wolf (Holland) and Eric Young (Singapore).

OWEN, Brian Ernest

Brian Owen had a fine career as a energetic wing-half. Born in Harefield on 2 November 1944, he joined Watford as an apprentice in June 1960, turned professional in July 1962 and went on to appear in 153 League games for the Hornets, lining up for them in the 1970 FA Cup semi-final against Chelsea. Two months after that game he went to Colchester United and switched to Wolves in January 1972, staying at Molineux until May 1973. He later returned to the club as trainer-coach and in 1997-98 became physiotherapist at Layer Road.
Wolves record: 7 apps.

OWEN, L. Trevor

When Trevor Owen joined Wolves in September 1899, he was already the holder of two full Welsh caps won whilst serving with Crewe Alexandra earlier that year. Owen was born at Llangollen in May 1873, the son of a local flannel factory owner, and played for Llangollen Rovers before joining Wrexham in 1892. The Welsh club was in the Combination League and in 1892-93 Owen was their top scorer with nine goals in 19 League and Cup matches. A knee injury then interrupted his career, but he stayed with Wrexham until 1896, by which time he had helped them to consecutive Welsh League championships and two Welsh Cup Finals. He was described as 'the best forward in Wales' and 'a scientific forward who always gives a good account of himself'. There followed a spell with rivals Druids, with whom he won a Welsh Cup winners' medal, and then with Crewe Alexandra in the Birmingham League. He played against Scotland and England in 1899 and Wolves gave him a chance of League football when he was 26. Owen soon acquitted himself well at Wolves, but just when it looked as though he would thrive at a higher level, he suffered ill health and after returning to Crewe, was forced to retire in 1901. Owen died in Acrefair on 1 June 1930.
Wolves record: 12 apps. 3 goals.

OWEN, William

Bill Owen was a key member of the Wolves first team during the middle to late 1890s when he had two separate spells with the club. A full-back or wing-half, he was born in Brierley Hill in 1869 and played for Dudley Road Excelsior and Loughborough before making his senior debut for Wolves against Bolton Wanderers at Molineux in a First Division match in September 1893, replacing George Swift at left-back. But after 19 outings that term he returned to his former club Loughborough, only to switch back to Wolves in the summer of 1895. He quickly became a permanent fixture in the left-half position and lined up against Sheffield Wednesday in the 1896 FA Cup Final. He was an ever-present in the Wanderers' side for two successive seasons before transferring to Everton in July 1898, being replaced in the team by George Fleming, who he had played alongside the previous year when occupying the centre-half berth. Owen died c.1930.
Wolves record: 117 apps. 8 goals.

OXFORD UNITED

Wolves' playing record against United is:
Football League

Venue	P	W	D	L	F	A
Home	9	5	2	2	16	10
Away	9	1	4	4	7	15
Total	18	6	6	6	23	25

League Cup

Away   1   0   0   1   0   1

The first recorded meeting at first team level between Wolves and Oxford was in the form of a friendly at the Manor Ground in July 1969, when Wolves won 5-1 with Hugh Curran, later to play for Oxford, scoring twice.

The first League encounters took place as recently as 1984-85 when Wolves lost both Second Division matches to united: 2-1 at Molineux and 3-1 at the Manor Ground.

Wolves' best League win over the Us is 3-1, achieved on two occasions, both at home – in September 1992 when Robbie Dennison, Steve Bull and Tim Steele found the net all in the first half and on Boxing Day 1996 when Simon Osborn scored twice in front of 26,512 fans.

Oxford crushed Wolves 4-0 at home in April 1994, Mark Venus conceding an own-goal and in September 1997 Wolves were beaten 3-0 at the Manor Ground, producing one of the worst displays of the season.

Wolves suffered their League Cup defeat at Oxford in September 1970, this being the first senior meeting between the clubs.

Players with both clubs include: Jim Barron, Steve Biggins, Colin Booth, Derek Clarke, Hugh Curran, Mick Kearns, Bobby McDonald, Jon Purdie, Paul Simpson, Harry Thompson (player-manager of United) and Colin Tether.

Also associated: Ian Greaves (manager of both clubs); Sammy Chung (Oxford player, Wolves manager); Ron Atkinson (Wolves junior, Oxford player); Gerry Summers (Wolves coach/assistant manager, Oxford manager), Colin Beavon, Ray Gaston, Colin Harrington, Maurice Kyle and John Love (Wolves Reserves/juniors/amateurs).

PSV EINDHOVEN

Wolves' playing record against PSV is:

UEFA Cup

Venue	P	W	D	L	F	A
Home	1	1	0	0	1	0
Away	1	0	0	1	1	3
Total	1	1	0	1	2	3

Following their victory in the 1980 League Cup Final, Wolves therefore gained entry into the following season's UEFA Cup competition, but unfortunately they failed to get past the first round, losing 3-2 on aggregate to the Dutch side. Almost 29,000 fans saw PSV win their home leg and there were 19,939 spectators at Molineux to see Wolves battle it out for a well-earned victory in the return leg.

PAATELAINEN, Mika Matti

Born in Helsinki, Finland on 3 February 1967, blond stocky striker Mixu Paatelainen joined Wolves from Bolton Wanderers for a £200,000 in August 1997 – having helped the Trotters win the First Division championship the previous season. Nicknamed the 'Moose' he came over to Britain in October 1987 to sign for the Scottish club Dundee United from the Finnish side Valkeakosken and he became an instant hit north of the border, scoring 47 goals in more than 170 appearances. Capped over 50 times by his country, Paatelainen moved from Dundee to Aberdeen in March 1992 and again he did the business in Scotland, netting 28 goals in less than 100 outings for the Dons. In July 1994, a fee of £300,000 took him from Pittodrie to Bolton Wanderers and in his first season at Burnden Park he linked up extremely well with John McGinlay to claim 15 goals, in 56 games as the Trotters climbed into the Premiership. Unfortunately in 1995-96 and again in 1996-97 he was plagued by injury and loss of form and after amassing a record of 18 goals in 83 outings for Bolton, he switched to Molineux. He scored a stunning goal on his debut in the Coca-Cola League Cup clash with QPR in August 1997. Paatelainen left Molineux for the Scottish club Hibernian in September 1998, helping the Easter Road club win promotion (as First Division champions) back to the Scottish Premier League.

Wolves record: 18+15 apps. 5 goals.

PALMER, Geoffrey

Uncompromising full-back Geoff Palmer spent two separate spells with Wolves, totalling 16 years in all, helping them win the Football League Cup in 1974 and 1980 and twice gain promotion from the old Second Division as his tally of appearances passed the 500 mark to make him one of the finest servants the club has ever known. Palmer was born in Cannock on 11 July 1954 and became a Wolves apprentice in July 1970 before signing full-time professional forms on his 17th birthday. The majority of his appearances came in his first period at Molineux during which time Wolves twice played at Wembley with Palmer in the team on both occasions, and they were twice promoted from the Second Division, in 1977 as champions and in 1983 as runners-up. In that championship-winning season he was ever present and in the second promotion campaign missed only two League games. An England Under-23 international, Palmer had made 388 League appearances and been awarded a testimonial game against Leicester City in 1983 when he was transferred to Burnley, who were then in the Third Division, in November 1984 for £5,000. The Clarets were relegated at the end of that season, although Palmer missed the closing weeks of the campaign, and in December 1985 he returned to Wolves. He added a further 22 League appearances to his total before quitting professional football to join the West Midlands Police Force. He continued to play soccer for the Cannock Police team and also for the senior Birmingham Police side in the Midland Combination as well as acting as part-time coach under ex-Wolves man Steve Daley at Bromsgrove Rovers (1998-99).

Wolves record: 489+7 apps. 15 goals.

PARFITT, George

Full-back George Parfitt was an efficient reserve at Molineux, acting as cover for Ted Collins and George Garratly. Born in Longton, Staffs, *c.*1890, he played for Newcastle St George's before joining Wolves in May 1913. He left Molineux for Cocknage in September 1920.

Wolves record: 4 apps.

PARKER, William David

Bill Parker spent just a season at Molineux (1938-39) when he deputised for full-back Bill Morris. He made his debut at Old Trafford in November 1938 in front of a near 33,000 crowd. Born in Liverpool on 27 May 1915, Parker played for Marine and Hull City (making 30 League appearances for the Tigers in 1937-38) before linking up with Wolves in August 1938. Parker was killed whilst on active service during the war. He had guested for Crewe Alexandra. He was aged 28.

Wolves record: 3 apps.

PARKES, Philip Arthur

Goalkeeper Phil Parkes was born in West Bromwich on 14 July 1947, but it was Wolverhampton Wanderers who snapped him up when he left West Bromwich Grammar School in the summer of 1962. Parkes, 6ft 2ins. tall, became a full-time professional at Molineux in September 1964 but did not break into Wolves' first team until November 1966. Standing in for Fred Davies, he marked his first appearance by saving a penalty against Preston at Molineux as Wolves won 3-2. He managed 14 games that season, returning for the last 13 games of the campaign as Wolves won promotion to the First Division. Although he had a reputation for inconsistency, being brilliant one week and then making mistakes the next, Parkes battled hard to retain his place and eventually became a regular first choice, altogether making over 380 senior appearances for the Molineux club. Only the great Bert Williams (420) had kept goal more times for Wolves, and Parkes also established some records of his own: between September 1970 and September 1973 he made 127 consecutive League appearances to beat the old club record set by fellow 'keeper Noel George; and in all made 171 appearances on the trot. Parkes helped Wolves finish fourth in Division One 1970-71, the year they won the

Texaco Cup, and he gained a UEFA Cup runners-up medal in 1972, but missed the 1974 League Cup Final win over Manchester City and did not play at all when Wolves won the Second Division title in 1976-77. The following season he was awarded a testimonial and at the end of that campaign retired from League football. Parkes assisted Vancouver Whitecaps in the North American Soccer League in 1976 and he returned there in 1979 to help them win the Soccer Bowl. He also played for Chicago Sting, Toronto Blizzard and San Jose Earthquakes in the NASL. After leaving League football Parkes starred in goal for Marstons FC and Wolves Old Stars in charity matches, and managed several local clubs in the Wolverhampton area before taking over as coach at Telford United in 1997 (under ex-Wolves man Steve Daley). Then when Daley became boss of Bromsgrove Rovers (1998-99) Parkes and another former Wolves star, Geoff Palmer went with him as part-time coaches. A keen cricketer, he turned out regularly for Fordhouses CC in the 1990s.
Wolves record: 382 apps.

PARKIN, Derek
Derek 'Squeak' Parkin was born in Newcastle upon Tyne on 2 January 1948, and made a record number of senior appearances for Wolves during his 14 years at Molineux. He helped the club twice win the League Cup (1974 and 1980) and also the Second Division championship in 1977, as well as

Derek Parkin, Wolves record appearance holder.

gaining five caps for England at Under-23 level and representing the Football League. Parkin started his career with Huddersfield Town as a junior, turning professional at Leeds Road in May 1965. He moved to Molineux on St Valentine's Day 1968 for

£80,000. In March 1982 Stoke manager Richie Barker secured his services on a free transfer and Parkin spent a season at the Victoria Ground, making 45 appearances for the Potters. He then retired to concentrate on his landscape gardening business near Bridgnorth. A fine handicap golfer, Parkin now resides in the same locality as Bert Williams and Willie Carr.
Wolves record: 607+2 apps. (501 in the League), 10 goals.

PARSONAGE, Harold
A tall inside-forward, quick at times, Harry Parsonage was signed from Walsall by Wolves manager Jack Addenbrooke in July 1911. Born in Aston, Birmingham in October 1889, he had been with the Saddlers since 1909 and spent two seasons with Wolves before leaving Molineux for Dudley Town in June 1913, later assisting Shrewsbury Town (1913-14). He died in Birmingham in 1979.
Wolves' record 20 apps. 6 goals.

PARSONS, Dennis Ronald
Goalkeeper Dennis Parsons was reserve to England's Bert Williams at Molineux and then understudy to Welsh international Keith Jones at Aston Villa. Born in Birmingham on 29 May 1925, he was playing for BSA Cycles FC when Wolves spotted his talent and brought him to Molineux in February 1944. Unfortunately the war was still on and the luckless Parsons had to wait three years before making his League debut, ironically against the team he was to join later in his career, Aston Villa. In the summer of 1951 Parsons left Molineux to assist Hereford United (of the Southern League) and he rejoined the big time to sign for Aston Villa in September 1952. Four years and 41 games later he moved to Kidderminster Harriers (September 1956) and was forced to retire through injury in May 1960.
Wolves record: 27 apps.

PASKIN, John William
Centre-forward John Paskin was born in Capetown, South Africa on 1 February 1962. Tall, raven-haired, direct in his approach, he played for his school team in Capetown and then for Hellenic (from 1979-80) before joining Toronto Blizzard (Canada) in May 1983. The following year he assisted South China, then played for FC Seiko in Hong Kong (1985), KV Kortrijk of Belgium (1986) and Dundee United (on trial, August 1987) before signing for West Bromwich Albion in March 1988. After almost 30 games for the Baggies Paskin moved to Wolves for £75,000 in June 1989 and in February 1992 was transferred to Wrexham, with Jimmy Kelly moving to Molineux in a player-exchange deal. During his stint with Wolves, Paskin, who failed to hold down a regular first-team

place, was loaned out to three clubs in 1991-92, namely Stockport County (September), Birmingham City (November) and Shrewsbury Town (February). In July 1994 he signed for Bury on a free transfer and at the end of that season was in the Shakers' line-up which lost to Chesterfield in the Play-off Final. Paskin left Gigg Lane in the summer of 1996 after taking his League and Cup record in England to 183 appearances and 35 goals.
Wolves record: 25+15 apps. 3 goals.

PATCHING, Martin
Utility forward Martin Patching won England Schoolboy honours and followed up by representing his country at youth team level. Rated a great prospect as a teenager, he did reasonably well with Wolves, but failed to build on his early success and after five years' at Molineux, he joined Watford. Born in Rotherham on 1 November 1958, Patching arrived at Wolves as an apprentice in June 1974 and turned professional in March 1976 and played in that year's FA Youth Cup Final defeat by West Bromwich Albion. He went to Vicarage Road in December 1979 and after a loan spell with Northampton Town (January-February 1983) he was forced to quit top-class football in the summer of 1984. He later became a publican in Berkhamstead near Watford.
Wolves record: 86+15 apps. 11 goals.

PAYNE, Charles Edgar
Reserve outside right Charlie Payne played for Wolves between 1907 and 1910. Understudying Billy Harrison he was given very little opportunity in the first team and he left Molineux in June 1910 to sign for Blakenhall. His only goal for Wolves, was the winner in a 3-2 away win at Bradford in his last but one outing for the club. Payne was born in Wednesfield c.1888 and died in Wolverhampton in 1957.
Wolves record: 12 apps. 1 goal.

PEARCE, Dennis Anthony
Full-back or defensive midfielder Dennis Pearce spent four years with Aston Villa before joining Wolves on a free transfer in July 1995. Having signed for Villa as a junior, he turned professional in June 1993 but failed to make the first team at Villa Park. He arrived at Molineux to bolster the club's reserve strength, but was released from his contract at the end of the 1996-97 season. He immediately joined Notts County and had the pleasure of helping the Magpies win the Third Division championship in his first season at Meadow Lane. Pearce, who had trials with Wycombe Wanderers in 1997-98, was born in Wolverhampton on 10 September 1974.
Wolves record: 9+2 apps.

PEARSON, Alfred

Hard-working wing-half Alf Pearson was one of Wolves' most consistent players in the mid 1880s. Born in Wolverhampton *c.*1861, Pearson played for St Luke's before joining Wolves in August 1884. He left the club for Stafford Road in September 1887. He died *c.*1933 in Wolverhampton.

Wolves record: 12 apps.

PEDLEY, John

Jack Pedley, a former steel-worker, was playing for Wednesbury Old Athletic when Wolves signed him in November 1905. The Wanderers had been looking for a good outside-left ever since Jack Miller's departure and Pedley, who was born in West Bromwich in February 1881, fitted the bill. Wolves had been particularly attracted by his ability to beat an opponent by sheer speed over 20 yards, but he also had overall class and was a clever 'one-touch' player. In his first season at Molineux Pedley scored ten goals in 21 League games to finish second highest scorer and his goals included a hat-trick in a 6-1 win over Notts County in the penultimate game of the campaign. Wolves won their last game 7-0 over Derby County but it was not enough to prevent them from being relegated and consequently the following season Pedley found himself in Division Two. In 1907-08 he helped Wolves, still a Second Division side, beat Newcastle United in the FA Cup Final and was a regular in the team until the end of the 1909-10 season. In May 1919 Pedley joined Wrexham but was forced to quit football through injury at the age of 30. He returned to the steel industry and later ran the Plumber's Arms in Tyndal Street, West Bromwich for a number of years. Pedley died *c.*1946.

Wolves record: 168 apps. 28 goals.

PEERS, Edward John

Goalkeeper Teddy Peers started his football life as an outside-right and then switched to full-back before finding lasting success as a goalkeeper. Born at Connah's Quay on 31 December 1886 he played as an amateur with Oswestry St Clare's and Chirk, then after a trial with Shrewsbury Town played for three local clubs in Connah's Quay, gaining a Welsh Cup winners' medal with Connah's Quay FC in 1911 and a Welsh Amateur Cup winners' medal with Connah's Quay Juniors before that. He first appeared for a Wolves team in April 1911 before being signed as a professional eight months later. After taking over from Frank Boxley during the last few weeks of the 1911-12 season, he was a regular in the team until Noel George replaced him in 1921. Peers thus missed that season's FA Cup Final, although he had returned to first-team duties in the weeks leading up to the Final. Peers won eight full caps for Wales whilst with Wolves and also played in two Victory internationals in 1919, but after he had joined Port Vale in August 1921, he made only four more international appearances because Vale were reluctant to release him all that often. Peers, who guested for Stoke and Walsall during World War One, left Vale in May 1923 and ended his playing career with Hednesford Town. He took over the New Inn public house in Bilston Road, Wolverhampton, then another in Bilston, and died in Wolverhampton on 20 September 1935.

Wolves record: 198 apps.

PEMBLE, Arthur

Arthur Pemble played in goal for Wolves in season 1908-09, deputising for Tommy Lunn in two away games when he conceded a total of six goals. Born in Bridgnorth *c.*1885, he played for Beacon Rangers prior to joining Wolves and Willenhall Pickwick after leaving Molineux (July 1909). He later assisted Lowton Manor and Fordhouses FC. Pemble died *c.*1954.

Wolves record: 2 apps.

PENALTIES

Inside-forward Joseph Heath scored the first-ever penalty in a Football League game – doing so for Wolves against Accrington at Molineux on 14 September 1891, helping Wolves to a 5-0 win.

The *Birmingham Gazette* describing the penalty (Wolves' second goal) reported the historic moment with none of the hysterical outburst today's press uses on penalties: "One of the Accrington half-backs acted as goalkeeper and the new rule, which gives a free kick to the attacking side with no one but the defending goalkeeper in front, was enforced. Heath took the kick and shot the ball through with a clean, hard shot."

Harry Allen is thought to be responsible for missing the first spot-kick for Wolves, doing so during a League game against West Bromwich Albion at Stoney Lane five days later when the Throstles won 4-3.

In the first floodlit League game at Molineux in April 1956, Bill Slater stroked home two penalties as Wolves beat Tottenham Hotspur 5-1.

Wolves led Manchester United 2-0 after 10 minutes of their FA Cup-tie at Molineux in 1965-66 thanks to two Terry Wharton penalties. But United came back to win 4-2.

Goalkeeper John Oldfield saved two penalties in quick succession over Easter 1970 in games against Arsenal and Liverpool.

There were four penalties awarded during the Bristol City v Wolves League game at Ashton Gate in August 1977. City scored from their two spot-kicks while Willie Carr missed one and scored one as Wolves won 3-2.

Jim McCalliog missed two penalties against his future club Southampton at The Dell in March 1972, but Wolves still won 1-0.

Kenny Hibbitt scored a record nine penalties for Wolves in season 1974-75. And 20 years later in season 1994-95, his tally was equalled by left-back Andy Thompson.

Goalkeeper Phil Parkes was Wolves' hero when he stopped two penalties in the UEFA Cup-tie against Ferencvaros in 1971-72. Parkes had earlier saved a penalty on his League debut for Wolves against Preston in November 1966.

Goalkeeper Eric Nixon saved two penalties during his short period on loan at Molineux – v Swansea City and Leyton Orient in 1986.

Paul Bradshaw was Wolves' hero at Tottenham in November 1978 when he saved two penalties before getting injured. He was replaced in goal by Kenny Hibbitt, but Wolves still lost the game 1-0.

In a League game of three penalties, Wolves' 'keeper John Burridge saved two as the ten men of Sheffield Wednesday were beaten 1-0 at Molineux in March 1983.

Wolves 'keeper Paul Jones saved a penalty in normal time against Sheffield Wednesday in a fourth-round FA Cup-tie at Hillsborough in January 1995 to earn his side a 1-1 draw. Then in the replay he was again a hero as Wolves won the resulting penalty-shoot out 4-3 after Wednesday had once led 3-0 on spot kicks.

PENDER, John Patrick

John Pender was a permanent feature of Wolves' defence for three during the mid-1980s. He was born in Luton on 19 November 1963 but came to live in the West Midlands as a youngster and it was his performances as a goalscoring centre-forward with Lichfield Social in the Lichfield Sunday League that alerted Football League scouts. Pender had trials with several clubs, including Wolves, whilst he was still at school and then joined the Molineux staff as an apprentice in June 1979 before becoming a full-time professional in 1981. He was now playing in defence as a healthy six-footer and developing well, winning Republic of Ireland caps at both youth and Under-21 levels, having qualified for the Republic through his parentage. In March 1982, with Wolves fighting a losing battle against relegation, he was given his League debut at centre-half, replacing Joe Gallagher at home to Swansea. The following season he missed only three games as Wolves went back into Division One as runners-up. Twelve months later, alas, they were down again, Pender playing 34 times in the relegation team. This time there was no quick way back – just the opposite in fact – and in July 1985, with Wolves facing Third Division football, Pender was transferred to Charlton Athletic for £35,000. He made 41 appear-

ances for the Addicks before moving to Bristol City in October 1987 and helped the Ashton Gate club to promotion to the old Second Division. In October 1990, after a month's loan at Turf Moor, he signed for Burnley for £70,000 and was in the Clarets side that won the old Fourth Division championship in 1992. He skippered Burnley and in 1994 was in their line-up that beat Stockport County in a stormy Second Division Play-off Final at Wembley. In August 1995 Pender switched to Wigan Athletic and two years later he joined Third Division Rochdale. In 1998-99 he passed the career milestone of 600 League and Cup games at club level.
Wolves record: 127+2 apps. 4 goals.

PERRETT, William Walter

Bill Perrett served Wolves for three years, from 1909 to 1912, during which time he was initially first reserve to centre-half Bill Wooldridge. Well built, with a fair kick, he was born in Willenhall in 1888 and played for Wood Cross Links, Fazeley and Bilston United before moving to Molineux. On leaving Wolves Perrett went briefly to Dudley and later assisted Halesowen before a broken leg ended his playing career in 1913.
Wolves record: 4 apps.

PERRY, Walter

A naturally gifted footballer, able to play as a forward or wing-half, Walter Perry came from a sporting family, two of his brothers, Tom and Charlie, both represented England. Born in West Bromwich in October 1868, he attended and played for Christ Church School and after a spell with West Bromwich Excelsior, joined West Bromwich Albion in August 1886. He spent three years with the Throstles, moving to Molineux in December 1889. The following year he switched to Warwick County and thereafter served with Burton Swifts, Albion again (from October 1894 when he played with his two brothers) and Burton Swifts for a second time, retiring in June 1900. He was later appointed manager of Albion's reserve team (1906-07) and also qualified as a Football League linesman (1909). Perry died in West Bromwich in September 1928.
Wolves record: 8 apps. 3 goals.

PETERBOROUGH UNITED

Wolves' playing record against Posh is:

Football League

Venue	P	W	D	L	F	A
Home	4	1	1	2	5	8
Away	4	3	1	0	6	3
Total	8	4	2	2	11	11

Sherpa Van Trophy

Home	1	1	0	0	4	0

Anglo-Italian Cup

Home	1	1	0	0	2	0

Wolves first met Posh in League football on New Year's Day 1987 when a Molineux crowd of 4,399 saw the visitors win a Fourth Division game by 3-0. Wolves gained revenge later in the season with a 1-0 victory at London Road.

Wolves doubled up over Peterborough in 1992-93, winning 4-3 at home and 3-2 away, Mark Burke scoring in both games.

Two goals from Steve Bull helped set Wolves up for a convincing 4-0 home victory over Posh in the Sherpa Van Trophy clash at Molineux in February 1988.

And just over 3,000 fans saw Wolves beat Peterborough 2-0 in an Anglo-Italian Cup-tie at Molineux in September 1992.

Steve Bull – regaining match fitness after suspension – scored five goals in Wolves' 8-1 Midland Intermediate League win over Peterborough United in 1997-98.

Players with both clubs include: Kevin Ashley, Jim Barron, George Berry, Paul Bradshaw, Campbell Chapman, Phil Chard, Eddie Clamp, Derek Dougan, Walter Featherby, Jackie Gallagher, John Galley, Mick Gooding, Francis Green, Ray Hankin, Billy Kellock, John Kirkham, Fred Ramscar, Darren Roberts, Nigel Sims, Mike Small and Paul Walker.

Also associated: John Barnwell (manager of both clubs); Richie Barker (Posh player, Wolves coach); Ian Ross (Posh player, Wolves coach and caretaker-manager); Bobby Downes (Posh player, Wolves coach), Mick Matthews (Posh reserve); Stuart Garnham, Tony Read, Tommy Rudkin and Dave Syrett (Wolves amateurs/Reserves); Mick Martin (Wolves trialist).

PHEASANT, Edward

Ted 'Cock' Pheasant packed a great deal into his 33 years. Born in the back streets of Wednesbury on 15 February 1877, he was a bustling forward with his Joseph Edward Cox School team and with Wednesbury Excelsior and Wednesbury Old Athletic. Wolves signed him as an 18-year-old in the summer of 1895 and he made his debut in the forward line in September 1896, in a 4-3 defeat at Derby. He missed the following season because of injury, but returned at centre-half in 1898-99 and it was in that position where he settled down, going on to make well over 160 appearances for Wolves. He was, by all accounts, a fearsome character who would shave his head and roll his sleeves up and his socks down to appear as fearsome as possible to opposing forwards. He was physically dominating anyway, standing 6ft 2in tall and weighing 15st, and he skippered the Wolves side for a time. He was a fierce hitter of a dead ball, took free-kicks and penalties, and in March 1902 scored a hat-trick against Newcastle United at Molineux, one of the goals coming from a 35-yard free-kick. To

mark the feat, Wolves chairman M. T. H. Stanley presented Pheasant with a specially inscribed gold watch. He was reportedly the highest paid Wolves player of his day earning £3 10s (£3.50) per week during the season and £3 in the summer. On one occasion he was selected to represented the Football League, but preferred to play for Wolves instead – such was his dedication. In November 1904 Pheasant moved to West Bromwich Albion and made over 150 appearances for the Baggies, scoring 22 goals, before Leicester Fosse signed him in July 1910. Alas, he was never able to play for Leicester; because two weeks after leaving The Hawthorns he was admitted to a Birmingham hospital with peritonitis and died on 17 July that year.
Wolves record: 168 apps. 19 goals.

PHILLIPS, Cuthbert

Cuthbert Phillips, who was always known as Charlie, was born in Victoria, Monmouthshire, on 23 June 1910 and won Welsh Schoolboy honours while working as a boilerman and playing Welsh League football for Ebbw Vale in 1925. Several clubs wanted to sign him and he had offers from Plymouth Argyle, Torquay United and Cardiff City before signing professional forms for Wolves in August 1929. He was a speedy forward, mostly at home on the right wing, and that is where he played the majority of his 200 plus senior games for Wolves. He was capped ten times for Wales while at Molineux, and he helped Wolves win the Second Division championship in 1931-32, scoring 18 goals. Phillips netted on his international debut against Northern Ireland at Wrexham in 1931 and captained his country on six occasions. At Christmas 1935 he was sent off whilst skippering Wolves against Bolton and a month later, in January 1936, he was transferred to Aston Villa for £9,000. He was capped three more times as a Villa player, but made only 25 appearances for the Birmingham club and although he scored on his debut (in a 3-1 win at Derby) he could not save them from relegation. When they returned as Second Division champions in 1937-38 he managed only a handful of games before moving across the city to play for Birmingham in March 1938. In 1939 Phillips went into non-League football with Chelmsford City, then guested for several clubs until retiring at the end of the war. Phillips was a fine all-round sportsman who also excelled at cricket, golf, tennis, rugby union and various athletics events. He was later a licensee in Bushbury and Lichfield, dying in the latter city on 21 October 1969.
Wolves record: 202 apps. 65 goals.

PHILLIPSON, William Thomas

Tom Phillipson is one of the best strikers ever

to play for Wolves. Born at Ryton-on-Tyne on 31 October 1898, he once scored 14 out of his school side's 15 goals in one Saturday morning match and then netted ten in the next game. He joined Newcastle United from Scotswood in December 1919, but made only 15 League and FA Cup appearances for the Magpies, scoring five goals, before they let him go to Swindon Town in May 1921. Wolves, then in the Third Division North, paid £1,000 for his signature in December 1923 and he made a great start to his Molineux career with a hat-trick in only his fourth game, against Ashington. At the end of the season he had 14 goals to his credit and Wolves were Northern Section champions. In the next four seasons, Phillipson scored another 97 goals, including a club record 37 in League and Cup games in 1925-26 and 33 goals the following season. In April 1926 he scored four goals past Barnsley and on Christmas Day the same year netted five in a game against Bradford City. Having captained the side, he surprisingly moved to Sheffield United in February 1928, but spent only a short time at Bramall Lane before returning to the West Midlands to play for Bilston United and then had a season with Walsall (1931-32). On retiring he concentrated on his business interests in Wolverhampton and went into local politics. In 1938 he was elected Lord Mayor of Wolverhampton and in 1947 watched Dennis Westcott surpass his scoring record for the club. Tom Phillipson died in Wolverhampton on 19 November 1965, aged 77.
Wolves record: 159 apps. 111 goals.

PICKEN, Albert Henry
Albert Picken played for Wolves between 1921 and 1925. A reserve outside-left, he was given very little scope at senior level and left the club for Bolton Wanderers, later playing for Derby County Reserves, Gillingham (1928-29), Wellington Town and Crewe Alexandra before retiring in 1934. Born in Wellington in 1900, Picken, who joined Wolves from Audley FC, later became a bricklayer.
Wolves record: 12 apps.

PICKERELL, Jack
Inside-forward Jack Pickerell was born in Bilston c.1875, and was given a month's trial by Wolves in March 1890 after having starred for Dudley Road Swifts. He failed to catch the eye and left Molineux for Dudley Town, later assisting Netherton St Luke's (1900-02). Pickerell died in Wednesbury c.1919.
Wolves record: 1 app.

PIERCE, Gary
Goalkeeper Gary Pierce was born in Bury on 2 March 1951. After playing local park's football he signed for Mossley in 1969 before Huddersfield Town took him on as a full-time professional in February 1971. He appeared in 23 games for the Town before Wolves signed him in June 1973, as cover for Phil Parkes. He went on to play in more than 100 senior games for Wanderers, having initially got into the first team in September 1973, going on to have 19 outings that term, the highlight coming in March when he made his first League Cup appearance for Wolves in the 2-1 Wembley Final win over Manchester City. It was a memorable way to celebrate his 23rd birthday. For two seasons he and Parkes shared the goalkeeping position, but in 1976-77, with Wolves back in Division Two, Pierce was ever-present as Wanderers won the title. His joy was short-lived, however, and after Paul Bradshaw had been signed from Blackburn, he did not play at all in 1977-78 and managed only three games in 1978-79. In July 1979, his future at Molineux bleak, Pierce was allowed to join Barnsley. He made 81 appearances in four years at Oakwell and then had 27 games for Blackpool before his contract was cancelled in May 1984. He later managed Accrington Stanley, Netherfield, Radcliffe Borough (1991-92) and Ainsworth FC (Bolton Combination).
Wolves record: 111 apps.

PILSBURY, Charles
Charlie Pilsbury was a reserve centre-forward at Molineux in season 1903-04 – but he certainly made his mark, scoring in his only senior outing for the club in a 6-1 home defeat by Manchester City when he came in for the injured Billy Wooldridge. Born in Bilston in 1881, Pilsbury played his early football with Queen Street Methodists and Dudley Central. On leaving Molineux he signed for Bilston Swifts and later served with Tipton Victoria. He died in June 1964.
Wolves record: 1 app. 1 goal.

PINCOTT, Frederick Charles
Fred Pincott played for Wolves' first team in season 1932-33 when he deputised for George Bellis at centre-half in two games – against Arsenal and Manchester City – when Wolves were defeated 7-1 at home and 4-1 away respectively. Born in Bristol on 19 March 1913, Pincott represented Bristol Royal Victoria before moving to Molineux in the summer of 1931. A six-footer, weighing almost 11st 5lbs, he did far better at reserve-team level and on leaving Wolves in 1934 he joined forces with a number of former Wanderers' players at Bournemouth before drifting into non-League soccer just before the war, first with Dartford and then with Gravesend. During the hostilities he guested for Bristol City, Chester and Northampton Town. In season 1947-48 Pincott had 14

League outings with Newport County before rounding off his career with Bideford Town, retiring in 1951.
Wolves record: 2 apps.

PLATT, Frederick Douglas
Reserve outside-right Fred Platt spent three seasons with Wolves from 1897 to 1900, during which time he was reserve to Jack Tonks. Born in Wolverhampton in 1869 he played for Lanesford Boys before joining Wolves and after leaving Molineux he played in turn for Oxley, Castle Hill Rovers and St Augustine's. Platt died c.1940.
Wolves record: 6 apps.

PLAYING RECORD
This is Wolves' complete playing record at first team level: 1883 to 1997

Competition	Seasons	P	W	D	L	F	A
Football League	100	4,012	1,630	920	1,462	6,596	6,042
League Play-Offs	3	8	3	1	4	7	10
FA (English) Cup	106	335	157	76	102	613	430
League Cup	33	100	43	19	38	147	129
European Cup	2	8	2	2	4	12	16
Cup-winners' Cup	1	4	1	1	2	6	5
UEFA Cup	4	20	13	3	4	41	23
FA Charity Shield	5	5	1	3	1	11	12
Texaco Cup	2	12	6	2	4	20	9
Watney Cup	1	1	0	0	1	0	2
Anglo-Italian Cup	4	12	5	3	4	17	15
FRT/SVT	4	20	13	5	2	43	16
ZDS Cup	2	4	1	0	3	2	4
Totals		4,544	1,875	1,037	1,632	7,518	6,717

For Wolves' record in wartime football – see **War Football**.

PLYMOUTH ARGYLE
Wolves' playing record against the Pilgrims is:
Football League

Venue	P	W	D	L	F	A
Home	9	7	1	1	17	8
Away	9	2	3	4	10	13
Total	18	9	4	5	27	21
FA Cup						
Home	1	1	0	0	3	0
Away	2	1	1	0	3	2
Total	3	2	1	0	6	2
Wartime						
Home	1	0	1	0	1	1
Away	1	0	0	1	2	3
Total	2	0	1	1	3	4

Wolves and Argyle first met in season 1930-31 when 12 goals were scored in the two Second Division encounters. Wolves won 4-3 at Molineux while Argyle were 3-2 victors at Home Park. Charlie Phillips scored in both games for Wolves.

In 1966-67 Wolves doubled up over Argyle as they surged on towards the First Division and in 1976-77, after beating Plymouth 4-0 at home, Wolves gained a point from a 0-0 draw at Home Park late on in the campaign to clinch promotion to the First Division.

Sammy Smyth's goal against Plymouth Argyle in the 1950 FA Cup third-round replay.

Steve Bull scored twice in Wolves' 3-1 home win over the Devon club in September 1990 – the last time the Pilgrims have played at Molineux.

The three FA Cup games between the clubs took place in successive seasons. In 1949-50, after drawing 1-1 at Home Park, Wolves brought Argyle back to Molineux and beat them 3-0 to reach the fourth round. And a year later, Wolves again travelled to South Devon, but this time they won at the first attempt by 2-1, Jimmy Dunn and Johnny Walker on target before a 39,262 crowd.

Players with both clubs include: Davey Burnside, John Chadburn, Glenn Crowe, Noel Dwyer, Walter Featherby, Ray Goddard, Archie Goodall, Mick Kearns, Micky Lill, Dave MacLaren, Peter McParland, Billy Rafferty, Paddy Ratcliffe.

Also associated: Andy Beattie (manager of both clubs), Ernie Carless, Geoff Crudgington, Richard Flash, Fred Mitcheson, John Timmins, George Willis (Wolves juniors/Reserves), Jack Rowley (Argyle player and manager, Wolves reserve and guest), Harry Bowden (Wolves wartime guest), Joe Gardiner and John Kirkham (Argyle guests), George Poyser (Wolves reserve and scout); Charlie Phillips (Argyle trialist).

POPE, Frank W.

Frank Pope was a strapping 12 stone inside-right, who found it hard to get first-team football at Molineux. Born in Brierley Hill c.1880, he played initially for Pensnett Albion and then Cradley Heath before linking up with Wolves for the first time in August 1903. He left Molineux for Stourbridge in July 1904, only to return to the Wanderers' camp in May 1905. After another year, spent mainly in the Reserves, he was sold to Notts County (August 1906) and followed up by assisting Walsall (June 1907) and Netherton (1909-11). Pope died in Dudley c.1947.
Wolves record: 8 apps.

POPE, Harvey Frank

Frank Pope was a reserve centre-forward, no relation to Frank (above) who spent two years with Wolves: 1900-02. Well built, he was signed as cover for Billy Beats and George Harper, but got very little opportunity, although he did score a cracking goal in in a 3-1 home win over Notts County in October 1901. Born in Wolverhampton in 1879, Pope had played for Compton Rovers immediately before joining Wolves and on leaving Molineux he signed for Darlaston, but was injured after two games. He died c.1955.
Wolves record: 5 apps. 1 goal.

POPPITT, James

Right-winger Jim Poppitt spent two seasons at Molineux at the turn of the century, appearing in over 20 first-team games. Fast and clever, and perhaps a shade too eager and over-elaborate at times, he was born in Shropshire c.1879 and joined Wolves in 1900 from Wellington. Poppitt left Molineux for Swindon Town (in May 1902), and then played in turn for Reading (1903-04), Swindon again, Notts County (1905-07) and Lincoln City. In 1908 he moved back to the Midlands and signed for Walsall Wood, later assisting Gnosall Olympic. Poppitt died in 1940.
Wolves record: 21 apps. 3 goals.

PORTO (FC)

Wolves' playing record against Porto is:
UEFA Cup

Venue	P	W	D	L	F	A
Home	1	1	0	0	3	1
Away	1	0	0	1	1	4
Total	2	1	0	1	4	5

The Portuguese side Porto knocked Wolves out of the UEFA Cup at the first hurdle in season 1974-75. They won their home leg comfortably in front of 39,529 fans and then held on for an aggregate 5-4 victory following a two-goal defeat at Molineux where the attendance was almost 16,000. Wing-half Mike Bailey scored in both games for Wolves.

PORTSMOUTH

Wolves' playing record against Pompey is:

Football League

Venue	P	W	D	L	F	A
Home	36	22	9	5	91	36
Away	36	10	9	17	39	53
Total	72	32	18	22	130	89

FA Cup

	P	W	D	L	F	A
Home	3	2	0	1	9	5
Away	1	0	1	0	0	0
Neutral	1	0	0	1	1	4
Total	5	2	1	2	10	9

FA Charity Shield

	P	W	D	L	F	A
Neutral	1	0	1	0	1	1

Wartime

	P	W	D	L	F	A
Home	1	1	0	0	4	0
Away	1	1	0	0	2	0
Total	2	2	0	0	6	0

The first League meeting between Wolves and Pompey ended in a 2-2 draw at Fratton Park in October 1924, but the return fixture at Molineux was a disaster for the Wanderers who crashed 5-0 – their heaviest defeat to date against Portsmouth.

Revenge though was soon gained as Pompey were whipped 4-1 on Wolves' soil in September 1925 when Bobby Kerr scored on his home debut.

There were seven different scorers when Wolves beat Pompey 5-2 at home in January 1933 and when Wolves raced to an emphatic 5-0 win at Molineux in November 1937 there were two goals apiece for Bryn Jones and Dennis Westcott.

In 1948-49 and 1949-50, Portsmouth were First Division champions but they managed only one win over Wolves during that time – 5-0 at home in April 1949 when they were in sight of their first championship crown.

There were some excellent Wolves wins during the fifties including those of 4-1, 4-3, 3-1 ad 6-0 in the space of five years at Molineux and 4-1 and 3-2 at Fratton Park.

Dennis Wilshaw scored twice in that six-goal romp in October 1956.

And when Wolves beat Portsmouth 4-3 in September 1953, they led 2-0 inside three minutes with Wilshaw scoring both goals. He later completed his hat-trick.

Wolves put 12 goals past luckless Pompey in the space of 24 hours in December 1958. They won 5-3 on Fratton Park on Boxing Day (a hat-trick here for Peter Broadbent) and the following afternoon Colin Booth and Norman Deeley both claimed trebles in Wolves' 7-0 victory.

In November 1965 Wolves were 7-0 up in their home Second Division match against Pompey after an hour's play on a snow-covered pitch. They eventually won 8-2, John Holsgrove, Hugh McIlmoyle and Bobby Woodruff all scoring twice.

After scoring in Wolves' 3-2 win at Portsmouth in February 1967, Peter Knowles belted the ball clean out of Fratton Park. He

was made to pay for it afterwards (cost £25).

In September 1989 Steve Bull found the net twice in another 5-0 Wolves home win and some ten years later in April 1999, Wolves enhanced their Play-off chances with a 2-0 home win over Pompey, who had Frenchman Jeff Peron sent-off when the game was goalless.

One of the most disappointing results Wolves have suffered against Pompey was to lose the 1939 FA Cup Final. Major Buckley's team were red-hot favourites to lift the coveted trophy, but on the big day the players froze and the prize went to the underdogs who won in style by 4-1 with Herbert Barlow and Guy Wharton (both ex Wolves players) starring for the winners. In front of a 99,370 crowd, Barlow scored first for Pompey on 30 minutes and before the break Johnny Anderson lobbed in number two. Soon after half-time Cliff Parker made it 3-0 and although Dicky Dorsett reduced the arrears, Parker scored his second goal of the game to clinch matters for the Fratton Park club.

In January 1958 Wolves knocked Pompey out of the competition by hammering them 5-1 in the fourth round at Molineux. Peter Broadbent scored twice that afternoon in front of 43,522 fans.

Portsmouth dented Wolves' FA Cup hopes in January 1997 at the first hurdle, beating them 2-1 at Molineux with a last gasp goal.

Wolves (the FA Cup holders) met Pompey (the reigning League champions) in the annual FA Charity Shield game at neutral Highbury in October 1949 and in front of a 35,140 crowd shared the honours in a 1-1 draw. Johnny Hancocks scored for Wolves.

Players with both clubs include: Herbert Barlow, Mark Blake, Steve Claridge, Ray Crawford (also Pompey coach), Derek Dougan, George Harris, Jackie Henderson, Rob Hindmarch, Ron Howells, Eric Jones, Tony Lange, Micky Lill, Scott McGarvey, Harry Middleton, Pat Neil, Billy Rafferty, Billy Smith, Kenny Todd (later Pompey youth team manager), Dave Thomas, Andy Turner, Ted Watson, Guy Wharton, Bob White, Clive Whitehead and Guy Whittingham.

Also associated: Mike Bailey (Wolves player, Pompey coach), Sammy Chapman (Portsmouth player, Wolves manager); Harry Wood (Wolves player, Portsmouth trainer); George Marshall (Pompey trialist) and Ron Bennett, Charles Brawn, Arthur Keeley, Michael Read and Eden Taylor (Wolves Reserves).

PORT VALE (BURSLEM)

Wolves' playing record against the Valiants is:

Football League

Venue	P	W	D	L	F	A
Home	20	13	3	4	43	19
Away	20	10	6	4	38	24
Total	40	23	9	8	81	43

FA Cup

	P	W	D	L	F	A
Away	1	1	0	0	2	0

League Cup

	P	W	D	L	F	A
Home	1	0	1	0	0	0
Away	1	1	0	0	2	1
Total	2	1	1	0	2	1

Sherpa Van Trophy

	P	W	D	L	F	A
Home	1	1	0	0	5	1

Wartime

	P	W	D	L	F	A
Home	2	1	0	1	3	2
Away	2	1	0	1	3	2
Total	4	2	0	2	6	4

The first time Wolves met the vale in the Football League was in November 1906 and they beat 6-2 at Molineux, George Hedley scoring a hat-trick.

Wolves doubled up over the Vale in seasons 1921-22, 1925-26, 1928-29, 1930-31 and 1931-32, winning 4-0 at home and 4-1 away in 1928-29.

When Wolves slammed Vale 7-1 in the Potteries in December 1931, Wilf Lowton netted with two block-busting penalties and all five Wolves forwards found the net.

Wolves and Vale didn't meet each other at League level for some 56 years from April 1932, and when they recommenced operations, a crowd of over 14,000 witnessed a six-goal thriller at Molineux which ended all square at 3-3 in October 1988.

Wolves were unbeaten on Vale soil in 12 visits between 1927-28 and 1997-98. The registered a fine 4-2 win in February 1995 when Dutchman John De Wolf scored a hat-trick, thus becoming the first Wolves defender to perform such a feat for 92 years, since Ted Pheasant's treble against Newcastle United in March 1902.

Two penalties by Andy Thompson – on his way to equalling Kenny Hibbitt's club record of nine spot-kick conversations in a season – gave Wolves a 2-1 home League win over the Vale in October 1994.

Wolves' FA Cup win over Vale was achieved in the fourth round in season 1993-94 when almost 22,000 fans packed into Vale Park to see their triumph 2-0.

Wolves beat Vale on aggregate by 2-1 in the second round of the League Cup in season 1984-85.

A Steve Bull four-timer helped Wolves whip Vale 5-1 in their Sherpa Van Trophy game at Molineux in December 1988.

Players with both clubs include: Harry Aston, Tom Baddeley, Tom Baxter, Billy Beats, Steve Biggins, Alan Boswell, Mark Burke, Alan Dodd, George Eccles, Fred Goodwin, Billy Harrison, Graham Hawkins (also Wolves manager), Bob Hazell, Joe Holyhead, Harry Jones, Billy Kellock, Harry Marshall, Lee Mills, Teddy Peers, Roy Pritchard, Valentine Rouse, Jack Shelton, Mick Stowell, Bobby A. Thomson, Kenny Todd, Robin Van der Laan and Alf Walker (later coach at Vale).

Former Wolves player Lee Mills is challenged by Keith Curle at Vale Park in 1996-97.

Also associated: Ronnie Allen (Vale player, Wolves coach and manager), Arthur Allman (reserve), Jimmy Baker (Wolves junior and reserve), Bill Booth, George Bowen, Roy Burns, Matthew Carrick, Chris Dangerfield, Richard Danks (Vale guest), Albert Flatley (Wolves trialist), Arthur Ford (amateur), Sammy Brooks, Ted Collins, Albert Groves, Henry Howell, Eric Jones – later trainer-coach at Vale Park, 1962, Jack Needham, Fred Price and Dennis Wilshaw (all Vale wartime guests), Terry Harkin, Arthur Hartshorne, George Heppell, and Dennis Isherwood; Arthur Bailey, John Griffiths, Lionel Hayward and Mick Fenton (Wolves wartime guests), Billy Holmes, Cliff Johnson, Bill McGarry (Vale player, Wolves manager); Fred Mitcheson (Vale guest), Chris Pearce, Andrew Poole (Wolves Reserves), George Poyser, (Wolves reserve and scout), Harold Prince (Wolves amateur), Bob Pursell (Vale trialist), Len Smart, Albert R. Spencer, Richard Twiss, Frank Whitehouse, George Willis, Dave Richards (Wolves Reserves) and Tommy Yule, Bill Asprey (Vale defender, Wolves coach); Ray King and Sid Blunt and Graham Newton (Wolves amateurs); Bobby Downes (coach at both clubs); John Rudge Wolves junior, Vale's manager); Peter Withe (Wolves player, Vale community officer); Ian Miller (coach at both clubs and youth development officer at Vale); Tony Lacey (player, coach at Vale, youth recruitment officer at Wolves).

Phil Shaw was secretary of Wolves and later on administration the staff at Vale Park.

POTTS, Arthur Arnold

Inside-left Arthur Potts was born in Cannock on 26 May 1888 and was on Wolves' books for two full seasons: 1920-22. He attended Cannock Council School and played for Willenhall Swifts before turning professional with Manchester City. He failed to make the grade at Maine Road and moved across the city to join arch rivals Manchester United for whom he made 27 League appearances either side of World War One. Having guested for Birmingham during the hostilities, he switched to Molineux in May 1920 and left Wolves for Walsall, playing one game for the Saddlers prior to serving Bloxwich Strollers. After quitting football in 1925 Potts became licensee of the Blue Ball pub in Pipers Row, Wolverhampton. He died in Walsall in 1981.

Wolves record: 42 apps. 10 goals.

POWELL, Barry Ivor

Barry Powell has been in football since June 1970 when he joined Wolves as an apprentice. He was born at Kenilworth on 29 January 1954 and played for Warwickshire Schools before signing for the Wanderers. Powell became a full-time professional in January 1972 and made his League debut in midfield in season 1972-73, appearing ten times as Wolves finished fifth in Division One. He came on as substitute in Wolves' 1974 League Cup Final win over Manchester City at Wembley. He began his footballing travels in September 1975 moving from Molineux to Coventry City. Thereafter he served with Derby County, Portland Timbers (he had two spells in the NASL), Bulova, Burnley, Swansea City and the South China club before returning to Wolves as player-coach in November 1986. He was basically a reserve second time round but managed to get into the side which lost the Fourth Division Play-off Final second leg (and consequently the tie on aggregate) against Aldershot in May 1987, and although he made one FA Cup appearance in 1987-88, as a substitute in the first round against Cheltenham Town, he did not play in the side at all when the the Fourth Division championship trophy was lifted that season. That Cup game turned out to be his last in senior football and he worked as reserve-team and youth-team manager at Molineux before becoming Coventry City's assistant youth development officer in 1991. He also played, ironically, for Cheltenham Town, under Ally Robertson's management, and for Moor Green, and returned to Highfield Road as football in the community officer in 1993. Powell made 392 senior appearances for his five League clubs and scored 45 goals. He also won four England Under-23 caps with Wolves. Powell became manager of Aberystwyth Town in 1999.

Wolves record: 83+13 apps. 8 goals.

PREECE, John Causer

Full-back John Preece was signed by Wolves from Sunbeam Motors FC in March 1934. He played twice in the Wanderers' League side (in place of the injured Wilf Lowton) but didn't quite fit the bill. Born in Wolverhampton on 30 April 1914, he earned a living in a local car factory and played for its football team before going to Molineux. Preece joined Bristol Rovers in 1935 and made 79 League appearances for the Pirates before joining Bradford City in 1938. After the war he assisted Southport and Swindon Town (both in the Football League) and ended his career by having two seasons with Chippenham United.

Wolves record: 2 apps.

PRESIDENTS OF WOLVES

1879-1910	Sir Alfred Hickman
1910-1923	Brigadier General Hickman
1923-1931	No official club president
1931-1946	Sir Charles Mander
1946-1976	No official club president
1976-1988	John R.Ireland
1988-to date	Sir Jack Hayward

PRESTON, Henry

Useful inside or centre-forward Harry Preston was on Wolves' books for four seasons: from August 1901 to May 1905. Born in Shropshire *c*.1880, he joined Wolves from Ironbridge and acted as reserve to Billy Beats, Adam Haywood and Billy Wooldridge. He made his Wolves debut in a 2-0 home win over Grimsby in November 1901 and his only goal was in the 3-1 home defeat of Liverpool in March 1902. On leaving Molineux, Preston joined Kidderminster Harriers

Wolves record: 26 apps. 1 goal.

PRESTON NORTH END

Wolves' playing record against North End is:

Football League

Venue	P	W	D	L	F	A
Home	46	27	9	10	95	52
Away	46	10	11	25	70	107
Total	92	37	20	35	165	159

FA Cup

Away	3	0	0	3	2	10
Neutral	1	0	0	1	0	3
Total	4	0	0	4	2	13

League Cup

Home	1	0	0	1	2	3
Away	1	0	0	1	0	1
Total	2	0	0	2	2	4

As founder members of the Football League, Wolves and Preston first met in this competition on 15 September 1888 – and in front of 5,000 spectators at Dudley Road, the visitors won in style by four goals to nil. The following month Preston doubled up by winning 5-1 at Deepdale.

Wolves' initial League win over the Lillywhites came in October 1889 and, in fact, they were the first team to beat Preston at Deepdale in a League match, taking the points with a 2-0 victory.

However, Wolves' next trip to Preston's ground ended in a 5-1 hammering in October 1890 and they lost 4-0 there in April 1893.

The League results between the two clubs evened themselves out between the mid 1890s until just before World War One when Preston won 5-3 at Deepdale in March 1915. After that Wolves classed Deepdale as one of their bogey grounds, failing to win any of their next 11 League and Cup games on

Preston soil, although they were more successful at Molineux.

There were two nine-goal thrillers at Preston, Wolves losing out both times by 5-4. The first clash took place in January 1928 and the second in September 1930, both in Division Two.

In contrast Preston simply couldn't win at Molineux and they too went 11 games without success between 1929 and 1951, finally ending the run with a 4-1 victory in November 1951 in front of more than 37,000 fans.

Gordon Clayton scored twice in Wolves' 5-0 home win over Preston in January 1937 and both Jesse Pye and Johnny Hancocks were on target in Wolves' 4-1 and 4-2 home wins in March 1947 and April 1948 respectively.

Preston were 3-0 up in a First Division game at Molineux in November 1956, but Wolves stormed back and helped by a fine Harry Hooper hat-trick, took the points with a superb 4-3 victory after scoring three times in the last 14 minutes. And season 1959-60 Wolves netted three goals in both League games against North End but failed to win either, losing by the odd goal in seven at Deepdale and drawing at Molineux.

The last League meeting between the team was in May 1989 when 14,126 fans witnessed

Bert Williams and Terry Springthorpe guard the Wolves goal against Preston North End in April 1948.

another 3-3 draw at Deepdale (Division Three). Earlier in the season (November 1988) Steve Bull netted four times in Wolves' emphatic 6-0 victory at Molineux – their best-ever win over the Lillywhites.

Wolves' 2,000th Football League game was against Preston North End at Molineux in November 1952, when they lost 2-0.

Preston became the first team to win the League and FA Cup double, doing so in 1888-89. They clinched this feat when beating Wolves 3-0 in the Cup Final at The Kennington Oval on 30 March in front of a record 22,250 crowd.

Wolves have not had the best of luck in FA Cup clashes with North End and the last time they met in the competition – in January 1953 – they crashed to a 5-2 defeat at Deepdale.

Wolves were knocked out in the second round of the 1983-84 League Cup by Preston, who won both legs (3-2 at Molineux, 1-0 at Deepdale) to go through 4-2 on aggregate.

Players with both clubs include: Micky Bennett, George Berry, Paul Birch, George Eccles, Willie Forbes, Archie Goodall, Billy Halligan, Jack Hampton, Graham Hawkins (also Wolves manager), Jack Hetherington, Ken Knighton, Hugh McIlmoyle, Jack Nelson, Tom Pritchard, Fred Ramscar, Mark Rankine, Dale Rudge, Mike Stowell, Sammy Thomson and Peter Zelem.

Also associated: Andy Beattie (Preston player, Wolves manager); Tommy Docherty (Preston player and manager, Wolves manager); Matt Carrick and George Waddell (Wolves Reserves); Harry Iddon and Frank O'Donnell (Wolves wartime guests), Billy Crispin Rose; Stan Fazackerley (Preston trailist);

PRICE, Arthur Bertrand R.

Arthur Price was a tall inside-right, born in Birmingham c.1883, who was given a trial by Wolves in April-May 1907, but failed to make an impact. He played his early football with Sheldon Heath and Moor Green and after his brief association with Wolves, joined Acocks Green. He died in Birmingham c.1941.
Wolves record: 1 app.

PRICE, Frederick

Right-half or right-winger Fred Price was born at Brierley Hill in 1888 and played for Aston FC, Wellington Street Citadels and Dudley Town, winning Junior international honours for England, before signing for Wolves in June 1912. He got his chance in the first team in February 1913, playing in the last 15 games of the season after Albert Groves had been moved into the forward line. In fact he missed only three out of the 91 games Wolves played up to World War One. During the hostilities Price served in the Army, guest-

ed for Port Vale and Sunbeam Motors FC and then made two appearances for Wolves in the Midland Victory League prior to the resumption of the Football League. In that first post-war season of 1919-20 he played 28 times before losing his battle against a knee injury. Val Gregory took over his position. Price was then transferred to Port Vale in May 1920 and he served Newport County from July 1921 to May 1922 before retiring at the age of 34. He later became licensee of the King's Head, Mill Street, Brierley Hill. He died at Dudley c.1960.
Wolves record: 124 apps.

PRICE, Frederick Thomas

Outside-left Fred Price spent two seasons with Wolves: July 1925 to May 1927. Born in Ibstock on 24 October 1901, he played for Whitwick Imperial before becoming a professional with Leicester City in 1922. From Filbert Street he moved to Southampton (1925) and from The Dell he joined Wolves. On leaving Molineux, after failing to establish himself in the senior side, he signed for Chesterfield (season 1927-28) and later assisted Burton Town, Nuneaton Borough and Midland Red Sports before retiring c.1938. Price died in Leicester in November 1985.
Wolves record: 41 apps. 8 goals.

PRICE, John A.

Centre-forward or outside-right Jack Price was a reserve at Molineux during the early 1920s. Born in Blackburn c.1900, he joined the staff at Molineux in July 1920 (from Barnoldswick Town) and left Wolves for Heanor Town in May 1922, later playing for Buxton and Clitheroe. His only goal for Wolves proved to be the winner in a 2-1 success at South Shields in December 1920.
Wolves record: 13 apps. 1 goal.

PRITCHARD, Roy Thomas

Former Bevin Boy Roy Pritchard joined Wolves as a full-time professional in August 1945 after being associated with the club since 1941 when he left Dawley Council School. Born in Dawley on 9 May 1925, he was a full-back who guested for Mansfield Town, Notts County, Swindon Town and Walsall during the war, made his League debut in the first post-war season, playing four times in the Wolves team that eventually finished third in Division One. He established himself in the team the following season when he played 20 times and in 1948-49 he appeared in 30 League games and played his first games in the FA Cup. By the end of that season he had collected a winners' medal after Wolves had beaten Leicester City 3-1 in the Final at Wembley. When Wolves won the League championship in 1953-54, Pritchard played in 27 matches and by the time he was transferred to Aston Villa in February 1956,

he had made over 200 senior appearances for Wolves. He had the misfortune to mark his first League outing in a claret and blue shirt by breaking his jaw against Arsenal. That proved to be his only appearance of the season and he played only once in 1956-57 and once the following term before joining Notts County in November 1957. Eighteen League games for County were followed by a move to Port Vale in September 1958, where he made 24 appearances before ending his career with Wellington Town (August 1960 – June 1964). Pritchard continued to appear in charity games right up until 1990. He died at Willenhall in January 1993. In the 1990s Wolves introduced the Roy Pritchard trophy for their Young Player of the Year.
Wolves record: 223 apps.

PRITCHARD, Thomas Francis

Wolves signed centre-half Tom Pritchard from Newport County for £1,000 in September 1927 following injuries to Sammy Charnley and Jack Williams and spent two seasons at Molineux. Pritchard was born at Wellington, Shropshire, on 18 June 1904 and began his career with the Great Western Railway works side whilst working as a boiler maker. He had trials with Wolves as a youngster but was working in a cycle factory and playing for Sunbeam FC before signing amateur forms for Stockport County in June 1925. Newport signed him in the summer of 1926 and he was a Wolves player just over a year later. Pritchard, a tall, commanding centre-half, made 35 League appearances in 1927-28 and 21 in 1928-29 as Wolves hovered around the lower half of Division Two. In May 1929, he was transferred to Charlton Athletic and made 43 appearances for them, his run being interrupted after he broke a leg when Charlton visited Molineux on Boxing Day 1929. In November 1931, he signed for Thames FC, the club with a fleeting League presence, and played 27 times in the Third Division South before spending a year in the French League with Olympique Marseilles. He returned to England to play for Preston North End, then spent a season with Lancaster Town before becoming Mansfield Town's trainer in June 1935, playing in one League game for the Stags in August of that year. Pritchard, who made over 150 League appearances in his career, died c.1980.
Wolves record: 58 apps. 3 goals.

PROFESSIONALISM

Wolverhampton Wanderers officially became a professional football club on 20 August 1885 and among their first paid footballers were Jack Baynton, Jack Brodie, Jimmy Hill, Arthur Lowder and Charlie Mason. Jack Addenbrooke immediately became the club's secretary-manager.

Professionalism in football was strongly

opposed by a number of senior clubs and indeed, by many responsible people in the game, including Charles Crump, representing the Birmingham FA.

At a specially arranged meeting of the Football Association, on 19 January 1885, the voting was 112-108 against allowing professionalism into the sport. And two months later another meeting went almost the same way. However, on 20 July 1885, the progressives finally won the day, professional was introduced and as they say, the rest is history.

PROGRAMMES

Wolves, like all the other clubs in League football, has seen many and varied styles of programmes over the years although up until the mid-sixties the formats tended to last for many years rather than one or two seasons.

Very little is known about issues that date from before World War One. It is doubted if programmes were released, except for odd games such is the rarity of information or copies of them.

Certainly there are are only two known instances of programmes from that era – a single card for the England v Ireland international at Molineux in 1903 and a 12-page issue for the FA Cup replay with Bradford City five years later.

The latter contained a list of all the club's officials and there was, of course, the team line-ups and fixtures for both the Wolves' first and reserve teams as well as details of all the other cup games played the previous weekend. The remainder of the programme was made up of advertisements.

In 1920, Paulton Brothers of Berry Street, Wolverhampton, took over the printing and publishing of the club programme and they

Programme for the World Cup qualifier held at Molineux in 1956.

continued to do so until the summer of 1968.

Programmes issued between the wars were large sized ones that were heavily advertised. Consisting of 16 pages they contained club notes, a small section on the visitors, fixtures and League tables. The odd picture was used occasionally but easily three-quarters of the programme was taken up by advertisements.

During World War Two all programmes were small, golden coloured single sheets with the team details on the front and fixtures on the back. Even the publication for the wartime Cup Final between Wolves and Sunderland in 1942 comprised of just a single sheet.

In 1945-46, and the following season, the size of the programme increased to four pages before normality began to return in 1947 when a 12 page issue was produced. This included two pages of topical soccer talk from journalist Ivan Sharpe who contributed until his death in 1967.

The cover of the Wolves programme, with a coloured drawing of Molineux and the silhouettes of players, was to remain basically unaltered until 1957 when a different image of the ground was used and gold rather than white was the predominant colour on the rest of the programme. The silhouettes remained.

The pagination was reduced in 1952 to eight pages with most issues containing a single back and white action photograph from a recent game. In 1949-50 each programme carried a picture of the FA Cup on the cover – Wolves being the holders of the trophy.

In the 1965-66 season, and the two ensuing campaigns, the covers changed – for two years with a black wolf against a golden background, then a white cover with gold text and a black and white action shot remained unaltered through the season. It was the last of the Paulton Brothers issues.

From the mid sixties through to the 1970s the programmes contained a copy of the *Football League Review* complete with colour photographs.

Then came the innovative 'Molinews'. Larger in size, and comprising 24 pages, it was the first of the magazine style programme with many more pictures than in any previous Wolves programmes. They style remained for five seasons during which time colour photographs were used for the first time in the programme for the UEFA Cup Final against Tottenham Hotspur in 1972.

Then, for two seasons, the size of the programme was reduced though it still contained 24 pages before, in 1975, it went back to a larger style with the number of pages reduced to 16.

An oblong shaped programme with 16 pages, with a colour cover, was released over the next three years until 1979 when the

largest issue ever, at A4 size and 16 pages, was used for a season.

The two campaigns that followed saw the programme reduced in size twice. It remained at 16 pages in 1980-81, but incorporated a 20-page insert called Programme Plus which included anything from general football articles to pop music and car news.

The insert disappeared after 12 months and although the size shrank once more the pagination increased to 32 pages. Then came three seasons of almost square design before the club's fall from grace resulted in a 16-page programme that was in keeping with the football at Molineux at the time.

As fortunes improved the page content went up by four pages in each of the following two seasons. Then came the outsized A5 issue that was to remain for 12 years to date.

Initially 32 pages with colour and black and white, it has now grown to a 48 page, all colour issue that scooped the Programme of the Year award for the Nationwide League Division One and finished second overall in the *Football Directory* honours list in 1997-98. The Wolves programme has been produced in house since 1994.

PUBLIC PRACTICE MATCHES

These matches were generally played pre-season between the Wolves first and second teams or the Reserves against the trailists. There were sometimes three matches of this nature played in the fortnight or so leading up to the start of a League season.

The first recorded Public Practice match was played on 26 August 1893 when the Wolves first team beat the Reserves 3-2 with Harry Wood (2) and David Black scoring the senior goals.

The last such game took place at Molineux on 12 August 1967 when the Whites beat the colours 4-2 thanks to a Terry Wharton hat-trick.

Other hat-tricks in Public Practice Matches were scored by Harper (4) in 1900; Pope (4) in 1901; J. Smith (3) in 1903; Hayward (3) in 1903; Roberts (3) in 1906; Hedley (4) in 1908; Groves (3) in 1909 and (3) in 1913; Radford (3) in 1909; Halligan (4) in 1912; Sambrooke (3) in 1920; Weaver (3) in 1928; Hartill (3) in 1932; Thompson (3) in 1936; Westcott (4) in 1937; Dorsett (3) in 1939 and Mullen (3) in 1946.

Some of the biggest scorelines in these games were 6-4 in 1894, 7-4 in 1906, 8-0 and 6-0 in 1908, 7-2 in 1913, 6-4 in 1930, 5-5 in 1937, 9-2 in 1939, 8-2 in 1944, 6-5 in 1958 and 5-5 in 1965.

In 1942 and 1943 with many of the Wolves players serving in the armed forces, the club invited Wath Wanderers to take part and Wolves beat them twice, 3-0 and 2-1 respectively.

In 1959, Billy Wright made his last appearances as a Wolves player in that pre-season's public practice match.

PURDIE, Jonathan

Jon Purdie will be remembered for scoring a spectacular winning goal for non-League Kidderminster Harriers against Birmingham City in the FA Cup in January 1994, but earlier in his career he had given Wolves excellent service on the left wing. Purdie, who was born in Corby on 22 February 1967, started his career with Arsenal, joining the Gunners as an apprentice in 1983 and signing full-time professional forms in January 1985. An England Schoolboy international, he failed to break into the first team at Highbury and joined Wolves in July 1985. Wolves were relegated to Division Four in his first season, when he missed only five games, but he helped them to the Play-off Final the following year. By the time they were Fourth Division champions a year later, however, Purdie managed only nine appearances (two as substitute) and was loaned to Cambridge United in October that season. In July 1988, Purdie moved to Oxford United and later played for Brentford and Shrewsbury Town before entering non-League soccer with Worcester City. He played for Cheltenham Town before joining Kidderminster Harriers in January 1993 and after helping the Harriers win the Conference in 1994 he was transferred to Telford United, having earlier been on tour with the famous Middlesex Wanderers club. In August 1997 Purdie was

appointed assistant manager to Steve Daley (ex-Wolves) at Bucks Head. But in 1998 he moved to Bromsgrove Rovers, only to return to his former club Kidderminster Harriers in January 1999, soon after Graham Allner had quit as manager. Then in February 1999, Purdie switched to Worcester City.
Wolves record: 94+9 apps. 13 goals.

PYE, Jesse

Jesse Pye, who was born in the village of Treeton near Rotherham on 22 December 1919, had plenty of experience of life by the time he became a professional footballer. An apprentice joiner, he played for his village team and for Catliffe FC in the Rotherham Intermediate League and was an amateur trialist with Sheffield United before World War Two broke out. He served with the Royal Engineers in several theatres of the conflict as well as playing alongside some fine players in services football and listed his most memorable performance as scoring seven goals (three penalties) for 556 Coy RE in the Tripoli Army League. In August 1945, Pye signed for Notts County, but after less than 12 months at Meadow Lane, during which time he played in a Victory international for England, the goalscoring inside-forward was transferred to Wolves, who paid out a club record fee of £12,000 in May 1946. Pye, who had been the target of several leading clubs, immediately won over the Molineux fans with a hat-trick on his debut, in a 6-1 win over Arsenal. He scored 20 League goals in

that first season with Wolves, then netted 16 the following campaign and was leading scorer in 1948-49 with 21 in League and FA Cup, when Wolves won the Cup by beating Leicester City 3-1 at Wembley, Pye scoring twice. He continued to score regularly for Wolves until leaving for Luton Town in July 1952. He had also appeared for the Football League, won three England 'B' caps and played once for the full international team, against the Republic of Ireland in September 1949. From Luton, where he scored 31 goals in 60 League games, Pye joined struggling Derby County in October 1954 but was unable to halt their slide into the Third Division North. He was on the fringes of the team when the Rams won the Northern Section title in 1956-57, and in July 1957 he signed for Wisbech Town, taking over as player-manager from March 1960 to 1966. Pye died in Blackpool on 20 February 1984.
Wolves record: 209 apps. 95 goals.

QUEEN ELIZABETH II

Her Majesty Queen Elizabeth II has visited Molineux twice. The first occasion was in the summer of 1962, to inspect soldiers of the North and South Staffordshire Regiments and present them with their colours. Over 30,000 people turned up to watch. Her second visit was in the summer of 1988 when she officially opened the newly-designed stadium. On this occasion there were 2,000 onlookers outside but thousands more round the streets of Wolverhampton.

Queen Elizabeth II visits Molineux in 1962.

QUEEN'S PARK RANGERS

Wolves' playing record against QPR is:

Football League

Venue	P	W	D	L	F	A
Home	9	4	2	3	15	14
Away	9	2	3	4	13	16
Total	18	6	5	7	28	30

FA Cup

Venue	P	W	D	L	F	A
Home	1	0	0	1	0	1
Away	1	0	1	0	1	1
Total	2	0	1	1	1	2

League Cup

Venue	P	W	D	L	F	A
Home	2	1	0	1	2	2
Away	3	1	1	1	4	4
Total	5	2	1	2	6	6

Wolves first did battle against Rangers in the League soccer in 1968-69 (Division One). And it was the Wanderers who came out on top, winning both games, 3-1 at Molineux and 1-0 at Loftus Road.

In October 1973 Rangers won 4-2 at Molineux and they repeated that scoreline on home soil in February 1976 despite two goals by Bobby Gould.

Wolves ran up three successive 1-0 home wins over Rangers between 1977 and 1980 and then whipped the Londoners 4-0 at Molineux in December 1982 when three defenders, John Humphrey, Alan Dodd and Geoff Palmer all got on the scoresheet.

The following season, in September 1983, Rangers turned things round and whipped Wolves 4-0 on the same pitch.

The two FA Cup meetings between the clubs were in season 1899-1900 when non-League Rangers won 1-0 in a first-round replay at Molineux after the sides had fought out a 1-1 draw in front of 7,000 spectators in London.

Wolves' first League Cup win over Rangers was achieved at Molineux when they defeated the Londoners 1-0 in a fourth-round replay in November 1979, the goalscorer being Willie Carr in front of 26,014 fans. And their second victory came at Loftus Road in August 1997 when they beat Rangers 2-0 in a first round, first leg clash only to lose the return fixture at Molineux by 2-1 to go through 3-2 on aggregate.

Players with both clubs include: John Burridge, Peter Eastoe, George Goddard, Adam Haywood, Bob Hazell, Mike Kenning, Andy King, Tommy Langley, Mark Lazarus, Simon Osborn, Fred Ramscar, Dave Thomas, Ken Whitfield.

Also associated: Dougie Freedman (QPR reserve), Jack Taylor (Wolves player, QPR manager); Tommy Docherty and Ted Vizard (managers of both clubs); Tom Mayson (Wolves player, QPR trainer); Dave Richards (Wolves reserve, rangers trainer: 1930s); Don Howe (Wolves trialist, QPR assistant manager and manager); Dickie Dorsett, Eric Jones and Bill Wrigglesworth (Wolves players, QPR wartime guests), George Paterson (QPR player, Wolves wartime guest), Jim Travers and Ernie Whatmore (Wolves Reserves).

RADFORD, Walter Ivor Robert

Goalscoring inside-forward Wally Radford had two spells with Wolves but his second was much more productive for goals and, indeed, ended with an FA Cup winners' medal. Radford was born in Wolverhampton in July 1886 and first joined the Molineux staff in August 1905. That season he played only twice for Wolves and in 1906-07 was on the books of Southampton, for whom he scored twice in nine Southern League matches, both goals coming at Northampton Town in April 1907. Radford then rejoined Wolves, having failed to make an impression at The Dell, but in 1907-08 he hit nine goals in 26 Second Division games and was at inside-left in the team that beat Newcastle in the FA Cup Final. In 1908-09 he top-scored with 24 goals and then hit 11 the following season before joining Southport Central in the summer of 1910. When Radford retired in 1913 he took up refereeing and later officiated in the Football League. He died in 1940.
Wolves record: 94 apps. 48 goals.

RAFFERTY, William Harry

Glaswegian centre-forward Billy Rafferty (born on 30 December 1950) had a fine career which spanned almost 20 years. After starting his goalscoring exploits with Port Glasgow in Scotland he entered League soccer with Coventry City in 1968-69 and thereafter travelled round the country playing, in turn, for Blackpool (from October 1972), Plymouth Argyle (March 1974), Carlisle United (May 1976), Wolves (March 1978), Newcastle United (October 1979), Portsmouth (December 1980) and AFC Bournemouth (February 1984). He retired from competitive action in 1985 after appearing in more than 500 senior games and scoring in excess of 150 goals, including 40 in 102 League outings for Pompey and 35 in 90 matches for Plymouth. Rafferty now runs two health, fitness and beauty salons with his wife in Carlisle and nearby Cockermouth.
Wolves record: 47+3 apps. 8 goals.

RAMSCAR, Frederick Thomas

As a 20-year-old, Fred Ramscar was called up to fight in World War Two and served in France and Germany. Born in Salford on 24 January 1919, he had represented Salford Boys and played as an amateur for both Manchester City and Stockport County prior to entering the Army and serving in France and Germany. In August 1945 he was recruited by Wolves and remained at Molineux until October 1947 when he switched to Queen's Park Rangers. A ball-playing inside-forward with a good right-foot shot, Ramscar then switched to Preston North End in November 1949 where he teamed up with Tom Finney. From Deepdale he moved to Northampton Town (July 1951) and after spells with Millwall (from September 1954) and Peterborough United, he returned to Northampton to coach the club's youngsters. He later served with Wellingborough and retired out of football in 1960. Ramscar scored 56 goals in 159 games for Northampton and on the day he joined Stockport he was offered a contract by Manchester United, but decided to stay with the Edgeley Park club. It is believed he is now living in Northampton.
Wolves record: 17 apps. 1 goal.

RANGERS (GLASGOW)

Wolves' playing record against Rangers is:

European Cup-winners' Cup

Venue	P	W	D	L	F	A
Home	1	0	1	0	1	1
Away	1	0	0	1	0	2
Total	2	0	1	1	1	3

The famous Ibrox Park club defeated Wolves in the semi-final of the European Cup-winners' Cup competition in season 1960-61.

The first leg in Scotland on 29 March was attended by over 79,000 fans who saw Rangers take a two-goal lead. After a brave fight Wolves could only draw at Molineux in front of 45,163 spectators and bowed out of the competition on aggregate.

In August 1972 Wolves defeated Rangers 2-0 in a friendly at Molineux.

Players with both clubs: Andy Gray, Walter Featherby, Sammy Thomson, George Waddell, Mark Walters and Steve Wright.

RANKINE, Simon Mark

The versatile Mark Rankine was born in Doncaster on 30 September 1969 and after representing the school team and Doncaster Boys, he went on to play in almost 200 games for his home town club Doncaster Rovers before joining Wolves for £70,000 in January 1992. Rankine, who prefers the right-back or right-half berths, did well at Molineux before losing his place to Jamie Smith, hence his transfer to Preston North End in September 1996 for £100,000. He was in North End's Second Division Play-off team in 1998-99.
Wolves record: 142+25 apps. 1 goal.

RATCLIFFE, Patrick Christopher

Irishman Paddy Ratcliffe was born in Dublin on 31 December 1919. He played Gaelic football at school and in 1935 joined Bohemians. As an Air Gunner during the war, his plane was shot down in Essen, Germany. Fortunately he parachuted to safety, but was captured and forced to spend two years in a PoW camp with shrapnel still embedded in

his left leg, a legacy from that horrific incident. After being liberated Ratcliffe returned to Ireland and continued his association with Bohemians. In 1945 he was transferred to Notts County, but failed to impress at Meadow Lane and in June 1946 was signed by Wolves boss Ted Vizard. A useful full-back, he found it difficult to get first-team football at Molineux and in June 1947 moved to Plymouth Argyle. He gave the Pilgrims sterling service, appearing in almost 250 games up to May 1956 when he pulled out of League football. He and his family later emigrated to America where he died c.1973.
Wolves record: 2 apps.

RAYBOULD, Thomas

Tom Raybould spent two seasons at Molineux (1905 to 1907) during which time he acted, in the main, as a versatile reserve half-back who deputised for the likes of Bishop, Corfield, Lloyd, Ward Whitehouse and Williams. Born in Wilden in July 1884, he joined the Molineux staff from Kidderminster Harriers and left in the summer of 1907 for Grimsby Town. He failed to make the first team at Blundell Park and in 1908 switched to Worksop, later returning to the Midlands to play for Brierley Hill (1909) and Stourbridge (1910). Raybould died in Birmingham in 1944.
Wolves record: 15 apps. 1 goal.

RAYNES, William

Yorkshireman Billy Raynes was a steady, unspectacular but hard-working midfielder. A Yorkshireman born in Sheffield on 30 October 1964, he represented Sheffield and District Schools and played for Heanor Town from 1981 before joining Rotherham United as a professional in September 1983. A loan spell with Stockport County (January 1985) preceded his transfer to Wolves in December 1985. Unfortunately he failed to fit in at Molineux and quit English football for the NASL in May 1986.
Wolves record: 7+1 apps.

READING

Wolves' playing record against the Royals is:
Football League

Venue	P	W	D	L	F	A
Home	11	7	2	2	19	11
Away	11	2	2	7	11	23
Total	22	9	4	9	30	34

FA Cup

Home	1	1	0	0	5	0
Away	1	1	0	0	1	0
Total	2	2	0	0	6	0

League Cup

Away	2	0	0	2	2	5

Wolves and Reading first met at League level in season 1926-27 (Division Two) and as you can see from the statistics the results over the years have been fairly equal.

Both teams amazingly ran up four successive homes wins between 1927 and 1931 and there were no League meetings for 54 years (1931 to 1985). And then it was Wolves who hit the headlines, ending Reading's run of 14 successive League wins from the start of the season when they forced a 2-2 draw at Elm Park in October 1985.

In December 1994 Wolves lost 4-2 at Reading – their heaviest League defeat at the hands of the Royals.

The best of Wolves' two FA Cup wins over Reading was that of 5-0 at Molineux in January 1910 in the first round. A crowd of 6,000 saw centre-forward Billy Blunt score four times for in-form Wolves. This tie was initially scheduled to take place at Elm Park but Wolves offered Reading £400 (rising to £450) to switch the game to Molineux and they did. (It was officially registered as a Reading home game but for the record books it has been marked up as a Wolves' home tie).

Reading's first League Cup win over Wolves was by a goal to nil at Elm Park in a second round tie in August 1978 when the crowd was 13,107. They recorded their second victory in October 1997 with an excellent 4-2 triumph as manager mark McGhee returned to his former club.

Players with both clubs: Billy Beats (also Reading trainer), Gordon Brice, John Chadburn, Keith Curle, Roy Davies, Walter Featherby, George Getgood, Michael Gilkes, Mick Gooding (also joint manager of Reading), Val Gregory, Hillary Griffiths, Bob Hazell, John Humphrey, Harry Marshall, Eric Nixon, Cyril Ordish, Simon Osborn, Jim Poppitt, Floyd Streete, Nigel Vaughan, Johnny Walker, Percy Whittaker, Ernie Whittam, Frank Wildman, Adrian Williams and Billy Wrigglesworth.

Also associated: Mark McGhee (manager of both clubs), Colin Lee (coach and assistant manager at both clubs, manager of Wolves); Chris Westwood (Wolves player, Reading trialist), Joe Blackett (Wolves player, Reading trainer); Sammy Chung (Reading player, Wolves manager); Jack Smith (Wolves player, Reading manager), George Coyle, John Curtis, Gerry Dareville, Martin Jones, Arthur Kelsey, Trevor Long, David Meeson (all Wolves Reserves), George Paterson (Reading player, Wolves wartime guest), Graham Newton (Wolves junior, Reading player) and Andy Gurney (Reading player, Wolves trialist).

RED STAR (BELGRADE)

Wolves' playing record against Red Star is:
European Cup

Venue	P	W	D	L	F	A
Home	1	1	0	0	3	0
Away	1	0	1	0	1	1
Total	2	1	1	0	4	1

The Yugoslavian giants met Wolves over two legs in the first round of the 1959-60 European Cup competition. There were 62,000 fans present for the first clash in Belgrade on 11 November that ended in a draw. Then, for the return encounter at Molineux, almost a fortnight later, a crowd of 55,519 saw Wolves win comfortably with Bobby Mason netting twice.

REDFEARN, Leslie F.

This player's name has been seen spelt two ways – Redfern and Redfearn. An inside-forward, born in Burton upon Trent on 6 December 1911, he played for Stafford Rangers (with whom he won a Staffordshire Senior Cup medal) before joining Wolves in April 1931. After two full seasons at Molineux he moved to Southend United and later played for Crewe Alexandra and Folkestone. He was reserve to Walter Bottrill and Jimmy Deacon at Molineux. In March 1933 he rejoined Stafford Rangers and during the war guested for several non-League clubs.
Wolves record: 6 apps. 1 goal.

REED, Johnson

Well-built inside-right, born in Bruselton in 1908, John Reed played for Bruselton FC and Spennymoor United before spending six weeks at Molineux (February-April 1931). He never really fitted the bill and after his release from Wolves he went on to have an excellent spell with Walsall, making over 120 appearances for the Saddlers before retiring through injury in the summer of 1938 at the age of 30.
Wolves record: 1 app.

REFEREES

Former Wolves player Walter Perry became a local referee and a Football League linesman after retiring as a player. And 1930s full-back Cecil Shaw took up refereeing in the Oldbury and District League in season 1959-60. Jack Taylor refereed a World Cup Final and was later commercial manager at Molineux.

REGIS, Cyrille

One of the great goalscorers of the late 1970s and 1980s, Cyrille Regis made a rapid rise from non-League football with Hayes to reach the FA Cup semi-final with West Bromwich Albion in the space of eight months. Born in Maripiasoula, French Guyana on 9 February 1958, he cost Albion a mere £5,000 in May 1977 having been spotted by former Wolves boss and Baggies centre-forward Ronnie Allen. He scored on his Central League, Football League, FA Cup and League Cup debuts for Albion and went on to claim a total of 140 goals in 370 outings for the Baggies' first team including a record of 112 goals in 302 competitive appearances, playing in three major Cup semi-finals and

in the UEFA Cup. Capped four times by England at senior level whilst at The Hawthorns, he also appeared in three 'B' internationals and lined up for the Under-21s on six occasions. In October 1984, he left Albion for Coventry City in a £250,000 deal and three years later helped the Sky Blues win the FA Cup – and he added another full cap to his collection. After 282 outings for Coventry (62 goals scored) the 'big fella' moved to Aston Villa in July 1991. He then switched to Wolves on a free transfer in August 1993 (joining mainly as a squad player) and left Molineux for Wycombe Wanderers, also on a free transfer in August 1994, ending his senior career with a brief spell at Chester City. Regis, who in May 1996 became the oldest player ever to appear for Wycombe in a senior game (aged 37 years, 86 days against Leyton Orient) retired through injury in the summer of 1996, having netted over 200 goals in more than 700 League and Cup games for his six major clubs. In fact, Regis became the first player to be registered as a professional, and to play at senior level, for the following four West Midlands clubs – Albion, Coventry, Villa and Wolves. He returned to his first club, West Brom, as reserve-team coach in the summer of 1997 under Ray Harford's management. A very popular player and true gentleman.
Wolves record: 10+13 apps. 2 goals.

RESERVES

Wolves have had a reserve team since 1884 and the first recorded match was against Astbury (Handsworth) in the Birmingham Junior Cup on 15 November of that year.

Wolves won 10-1 with goals by Brazier 4, Cliff 2, Jenks 2, Mason and Price. They reached the semi-final that season before losing 2-1 to Bilston at Perry Barr.

Since then the reserve side has played in various competitions, namely the Shropshire League, the Birmingham and District League and Cup, the Central/Pontins League and Cup, the Midland Intermediate League and Cup, the Birmingham Senior Cup, the Staffordshire Cup, the Walsall Senior Cup, the Tittotson Cup, the Keys Cup and the Birmingham Charity Cup.

Wolves' Reserves have played their home matches at Molineux, Aldersley Stadium, Berwick Rangers (Worcester), Castlecroft, Dudley Road, Oldbury Town FC and Telford United.

In all competitions Wolves Reserves have played almost 4,000 matches of which over 1,900 have been won, 750 drawn and more than 1,250 lost. The players have scored well over 7,900 goals and conceded more than 5,900, amassing some 4,500 points.
(See under separate categories: i.e *Central League*).

REYNOLDS, Charles J.

Outside-right Charlie Reynolds played for Wolves' first team during season 1894-95. He was born locally in Wolverhampton c.1873 and played for the Church Taverners before joining the staff at Molineux in the summer of 1893. He was introduced to League action following an injury to David Wykes in September 1894 and made a reasonable contribution before losing his form and his place before the turn of the year. He left Molineux in June 1895 and signed for Berwick Rangers (Worcester), quickly switching to Banbury before retiring through injury in 1902.
Wolves record: 14 apps. 5 goals.

RHODES, Leonard

No relation to Dicky (below) Len Rhodes was an outside-left, who played for Wolves during the early 1920s, having one good season with the club (1922-23). Born in Darlaston c.1900, he played initially for Willenhall and moved to Wolves in May 1920. On leaving Molineux in May 1922 he signed for Shrewsbury Town.
Wolves record: 19 apps. 1 goal.

RHODES, Richard Alma

Dicky Rhodes was one of the most skilful half-backs in the Football League in the early 1930s and a big influence when Wolves returned to the First Division in 1931-32. Born in Wolverhampton on 22 June 1908, Rhodes joined Wolves from Redditch United in July 1926. In those days he was a centre-forward, a position he had occupied as a schoolboy when playing for Wolverhampton Town Boys in 1922-23 and winning England Junior honours against Scotland in the 1924-25 season. Major Frank Buckley switched him to right-half and Rhodes went on to make over 150 appearances, winning a Second Division championship medal in 1931-32 when he missed only two games. He was transferred to Sheffield United in October 1935 and later played for Swansea Town and Rochdale before hanging up his boots in 1939. After the war Rhodes returned to Wolverhampton and became landlord of the Old Still pub in the town and later of the Posada in Lichfield Street. He was also a champion canary breeder and won the national title in 1973 when he beat off the challenges of 1,500 competitors. He had his aviary at Wednesbury and was also a keen pigeon fancier as a member of the Lower Gornal Homing Society. He died in Wolverhampton in January 1993.
Wolves record: 159 apps. 7 goals.

RICHARDS, David Thomas

'Dai' Richards was born in Abercanaid near Merthyr on 31 October 1906 and his early clubs were River Field, Bedlingog and Merthyr Town, who were then a Third Division South side, before he signed for Wolverhampton Wanderers in August 1927, for £300. Originally a full-back, Richards was converted to a scheming left-half and occasionally inside-forward by Major Frank Buckley. He remained at Molineux for nine seasons, helping Wolves to the Second Division championship in 1931-32. He forged a good understanding with fellow countryman Charlie Phillips and won 11 of his 21 full Welsh caps as a Wolves player. In November 1935 he was transferred to Brentford for £3,500. The Bees were in their first-ever season in Division One but although Richards earned some excellent reports, he did not settle in London and in March 1937, he moved to Birmingham in the most extraordinary circumstances. Richards woke up one Saturday morning expecting to play for Brentford against Birmingham but was transferred before the start and when kick-off time came around he was opposing his former colleagues. In July 1939,

Wolves Reserves, 1946-47. Back row (left to right): Kirkham, Pritchard, Parsons, A. Crook, Sanderson. Front: Davies, Dunn, Chatham, Ramscar, Darby, Bicknell.

Birmingham allowed him to join Walsall on a free transfer, but the coming season was only three games old when war was declared. He played a few times in the early wartime seasons, but by 1945 had left for Sedgley, at the age of 39. His trade was a builder and contractor and he was also a good cricketer and keen motorist. His brother Billy made 31 senior appearances for Wolves from 1927 to 1929. Richards died at Yardley, Birmingham on 1 October 1969.
Wolves record: 229 apps. 5 goals.

RICHARDS, Dean Ivor

Described as a 'classy central defender' when he joined Wolves on loan from Bradford City in March 1995, Dean Richards made such an impact at Molineux that he was signed on a full contract for an agreed club record fee of £1.8 million during the close season which followed (Wolves initially paying £1,300,000 and adding the final payment of £500,000 in November 1998). Born in Bradford on 9 June 1974, Richards was a trainee at Valley Parade before turning professional with City in July 1992. He played over 100 times for the Yorkshire club before transferring to Wolves. Capped four times by England at Under-21 level, he had an excellent first full season at Molineux, but in 1996-97 and again the following term he was dogged by injury, one after being involved in a car crash on an icy road, which badly damaged his knee. Nevertheless, when fit and chosen, Richards was named Wolves skipper in 1996, but two years later, after some injury and contractual problems he was placed on the transfer list by Wolves in December 1998. In July 1999 he moved to Southampton under the Bosman ruling.
Wolves record: 128+6 apps. 6 goals.

RICHARDS, John Peter

Centre-forward John Richards was the most prolific scorer in Wolves' history until his record was beaten by Steve Bull. Richards, who was born in Warrington on 9 November 1950, joined Wolves after leaving school in July 1967 and turned full-time professional two years later. He made his debut at The Hawthorns in February 1970 and claimed his first senior goal away to Fiorentina in May of that year, in the Anglo-Italian Cup. Thereafter Richards scored in every season for Wolves up to and including the 1981-82 campaign. He netted almost 200 goals, a record at the time, which included 144 in the Football League and 24 in the FA Cup, three of which were netted against Charlton in 1976 after coming on as a substitute, as well as 18 in the Football League Cup and four in European competitions. And he has the distinction of scoring one of the fastest-ever goals for Wolves, netting after only 12 seconds against Burnley at Turf Moor in November 1975 in a First Division game. Richards appeared in the 1974

and 1980 League Cup Finals, scoring the winner against Manchester City in the first game, and he won a Second Division championship medal in 1976-77 and a UEFA Cup runners-up medal in 1971-72. The following season Richards was the country's leading scorer with 33 goals, but he won only one full England cap for his efforts, in 1973 against Northern Ireland at Wembley. He had been capped at Schoolboy, Under-21 and Under-23 level prior to that and his scant reward at full level was certainly a surprise considering his goalscoring record with Wolves. Richards is the only Wolves player to receive two benefits: in 1982 and 1986. But he left the club in unhappy circumstances, moving to the Portuguese side Maritimo Funchal of Madeira in August 1983, after a short loan spell with Second Division strugglers Derby County. He was in Wolves Reserves when he offered his experience to the Rams in what turned out to be a successful battle against relegation that season. He scored twice in ten games for Derby. Whilst working for Wolverhampton Leisure Services Department he was made a director of the club, in 1995, and in October 1997 Wolves' owner Sir Jack Hayward appointed Richards as the club's managing director on a salary of £150,000 a year.
Wolves record: 461+25 apps. 194 goals.

RICHARDS, Richard William

Dick Richards played for Wolves from 1913 to 1922, World War One excepted of course. He was born at Chirk, a one-time hotbed of Welsh football, on 14 February 1890, and first played serious soccer for Bronygarth FC in 1907. He then served Chirk and Oswestry United before joining Wolves in July 1913, after trials with both Wrexham and Everton. He managed only 13 games in the last two pre-war seasons but in 1919-20 was top scorer with ten goals. He played in only half the games in 1920-21, missing the FA Cup Final against Spurs, and managed 27 League outings the following season before transferring to West Ham United in June 1922. He scored six goals in 53 games for the Hammers and played in the first-ever Wembley FA Cup Final in 1923 against Bolton Wanderers. His career then took in Fulham (1924-25), Mold Town (1925-27) and Colwyn Bay United (1927-28) before he was forced to retire because of a serious back injury sustained when unloading electric light pylons. He had returned to North Wales for domestic reasons and had taken a job with an electricity company. The injury eventually led to his death in a Salford hospital on 27 January 1934, aged 43. Richards won five Welsh caps as a Wolves player and added three more to his total with West Ham and another with Mold, the only time a player from this small club has ever achieved full international hon-

ours, although at the time they were pioneers of big spending in the Welsh National League. In his early international career Richards played with Wolves goalkeeper Teddy Peers and Ted Vizard, who was to be his boss at Upton Park and who later managed Wolves.
Wolves record: 94 apps. 26 goals.

RICHARDS, William Edward

Brother of David Thomas Richards, Billy Richards was born in Abercanaid in August 1905 and worked in the pits, while also playing junior football with Troedyrhiw Carlton and then Mid-Rhondda (July 1923). More than useful at outside-right, fast raiding, he joined Wolves in July 1927 was a member of Wolves' first-team squad for two seasons before moving to Coventry City in March 1929. Richards scored 12 goals in 80 appearances during a two-and-a-half-year spell at Highfield Road and then, in the summer of 1931, he moved south to Fulham, helping the Cottagers win the Third Division (South) championship in 1931-32. He later assisted Brighton and Hove Albion, Bristol Rovers and Folkestone Town. Winner of one Welsh cap against Northern Ireland in 1933 (whilst with Fulham – being the first from that club to win full international honours), Richards, who was a competent cricketer and good golfer, died in Wolverhampton on 30 September 1956.
Wolves record: 31 apps. 2 goals.

RICHARDSON, Jonathon T.

Defender Jon Richardson was born in Durham *c*.1905. He joined Wolves from Spennymoor Black and Whites in June 1928 and stayed two years at Molineux before transferring to Southend United in June 1930. He later played for Waterford Celtic in Ireland (August 1931-32).
Wolves record: 3 apps.

RILEY, Alfred

Half-back Alf Riley played for Wolves before and after World War One. He began as a centre-half and was relatively small for that position – he stood only 5ft 7in – but in those days that mattered little because the position was not purely a defensive one. He was born at Stafford on 7 December 1889 and played his early football for Stafford Excelsior (1905), Bostocks FC (in two spells), Stafford Rangers Reserves, Siemens Institute and Wellington Town, whom he joined in 1910. In August 1911 he went back to Stafford Rangers and two years later he signed for Wolves. It was the start of useful association with the club and Riley made his League debut against Huddersfield Town in April 1914. He appeared ten times in 1914-15 and during the hostilities guested for Wellington for three years from 1915 to 1918. When

League football resumed after World War One, he became a regular in the left-half position at Molineux, gaining a FA Cup runners-up medal in 1921. Riley made his last appearance in November 1922, at Meadow Lane, and at the end of that season he was forced to retire through injury. His only goal for Wolves came in a 3-0 home win over Leicester City in April 1921. Alf Riley died c.1958.

Wolves record: 130 apps. 1 goal.

ROBERTS, Brian Leslie Ford

'Harry' Roberts could play in either full-back position or as a central defender and made well over 500 appearances during a useful career. Born in Manchester on 6 November 1955, he joined Coventry City as an apprentice in June 1972 and turned professional in May 1974. The following February he gained experience as a loan player with Hereford United and afterwards went on to star in almost 250 games for the Sky Blues before transferring to Birmingham City for £10,000 in March 1984. After overcoming the boo-boys at St Andrew's, Roberts amassed 213 outings for the Blues up to June 1990 when he was recruited by Wolves on a free transfer. Ever-reliable and a sound competitor, he was released in May 1992 and immediately rejoined his former club Coventry as a scout and was later appointed reserve-team coach. Now a sports teacher he also wrote a witty column in a local sportspaper.

Wolves record: 20+4 apps.

ROBERTS, Darren

Striker Darren Roberts made a terrific start to his Football League career – scoring a hat-trick on his debut for Wolves against Birmingham City in the televised Sunday game on 27 September 1992 in front of 14,391 fans at St Andrew's. Born in Birmingham on 12 October 1969, the six-foot Roberts joined Wolves in March 1992 from Burton Albion for £20,000 and he quickly helped the Reserves win promotion from the Pontins League Division Two before making a name for himself in League action. Unfortunately he failed to carry on the good work and after a loan spell with Hereford United in March 1994 he left Molineux four months later for Doncaster Rovers but quickly switched to Chesterfield within 12 days. After two loan spells with Telford United, he moved to Darlington in July 1996. Another loan period followed, this time with Peterborough United in February 1998, before Roberts joined Scarborough in January 1999.

Wolves record: 13+11 apps. 5 goals.

ROBERTS, Iwan Wyn

Welsh international striker at four levels (Full, 'B', Youth and Schoolboy) Iwan Roberts (6ft 3ins. tall and weighing more than 14 stones) joined Wolves for £1 million from Leicester City in July 1996. Born in Bangor on 26 June 1968, he initially signed apprentice forms for Watford in 1985 and turned professional at Vicarage Road in July 1988. He scored 12 goals in 83 games for the Hornets before transferring to Huddersfield Town for £275,000 in August 1990. After almost three-and-a-half seasons at Leeds Road, during which time he netted 68 times in 182 appearances, he switched to Leicester City, signing for the Foxes in November 1993 for £100,000. He continued to hit the target during his time at Filbert Street and when he moved to Wolves had claimed 45 goals in 111 outings for the East Midland club. Roberts did well at Molineux, teaming up with co-strikers Steve Bull and Don Goodman and there is no doubt that the highlight of his stay with Wolves was his hat-trick in a 4-2 win at neighbours West Brom early in the 1996-97 season, when he became the first Wanderers player ever to score a treble against the Baggies at The Hawthorns. He was perhaps surprisingly sold by manager Mark McGhee to Norwich City for £1 million in June 1997, being replaced at Molineux by the Finnish international Mixu Paatelainen, signed from Bolton.

Wolves record: 28+10 apps. 12 goals.

ROBERTS, Jack

Left-winger Jack Roberts was a member of Wolves' first-team squad during the 1894-95 season when he challenged for a place in the side along with Messrs Fleming, Griffin and Brockstopp. Born in Wednesbury c.1873 he had played for Swan Athletic (West Bromwich) and Tipton Excelsior before teaming up with Wolves. After leaving Molineux he returned to non-League soccer with Ewells.

Wolves record: 1 app.

ROBERTS, John

Utility forward Jack Roberts had one excellent season with Wolves (1906-07) when he formed a fine left-wing partnership with winger Jack Pedley. Born in Walsall c.1885, he was signed from Darlaston and left the club for Bristol Rovers for whom he appeared in 85 League games, scoring 28 goals. He returned to the Midlands in 1911 to play for Stourbridge and then Walsall Phoenix and in 1914-15 went off to War. It seems that he quit playing football after the hostilities.

Wolves record: 25 apps. 14 goals.

ROBERTSON, Alistair Peter

Ally Robertson had already enjoyed a remarkable career with another certain Black Country club before he joined Wolves in September 1986. The tough-tackling, resilient Scottish defender, who was born at Philipstoun, Lothian, on 9 September 1952, first played for Linlithgow Academy and Uphill Saints before spending 18 years with West Bromwich Albion. Joining them as an apprentice in July 1968, Robertson made his League debut as a 17-year-old against Manchester United, facing Charlton, Best and Co, in October 1969. He then overcame a broken leg, suffered in a League Cup-tie against Charlton in 1970 and went on to total over 620 first-team appearances, although he never won a major honour with Albion and even his international appearances were limited to Schoolboy and Youth caps. He was in the Albion sides that lost three major semi-finals, one in 1978 and two in 1982, and also featured in the 1969 FA Youth Cup Final defeat v Sunderland. Considering the number of games he played for West Brom, his lack of personal silverware was remarkable enough. Yet after moving to Wolves and playing in more than 100 League games, he managed championship medals in the old Fourth and Third Divisions and also gained a Sherpa Van Trophy winners' medal at Wembley. He also helped Wolves to the Fourth Division Play-off Final against Aldershot at the end of his first season at Molineux. Robertson was released in June 1990 and became player-manager of Worcester City and then manager of Cheltenham Town, before leaving football altogether in 1992 to become a car salesman in Dudley.

Wolves record: 136 apps

ROBINSON, Carl Phillip

Midfielder Carl Robinson was born in Llandrindod Wells on 13 October 1976 and went to Shrewsbury Town as a 16-year-old trialist, but was released and ended up at Molineux as a trainee, turning professional with Wolves in July 1995. Capped by Wales at 'B' and Under-21 levels, he was a frequent member of the Wolves' first-team squad during seasons 1996-99 and actually went back to Gay Meadow on loan in March 1996 and won Welsh Cup runners-up medal with the Shrews.

Wolves record: 71+11 apps. 11 goals.

ROBINSON, Philip John

Equally adept in defence or midfield, the red-headed Phil Robinson always gave a good account of himself out on the park. Born in Stafford on 6 January 1967, and educated at the town's Rising Brook High School where he gained eight 'O' levels, he represented Stafford and District Schools before joining the groundstaff of Aston Villa at the age of 14. He then became an apprentice (June 1983) and signed professional forms at Villa Park in January 1985. Wolves paid £5,000 for his services in June 1987 and he went on to help the Wanderers win both the Fourth and

Third Division championships as well as the Sherpa Van Trophy before transferring to Notts County for £67,500 in August 1989. He was a key member of County's Third Division promotion-winning side in 1990 and whilst on loan from Meadow Lane, he helped Birmingham City lift the Leyland DAF Cup at Wembley in 1991. In September 1992 he was sold by County to Huddersfield Town and after a two month loan period with Northampton Town (September-October 1994) he joined Chesterfield in December 1994. Robinson had a second loan spell with Notts County (August 1996) and during the 1997-98 season he passed the personal milestone of 300 senior appearances at club level. In July 1998 he became one of Brian Little's first signings for Stoke City.
Wolves record: 80+10 apps. 9 goals.

ROBSON, David

Dave Robson was a well built, stocky defender who spent two seasons with Wolves, making his debut on the last day of the 1893-94 campaign at Burnley when he replaced George Swift at left-back. Born in Scotland c.1869, he played for Ayr United and Ardwick before joining Wolves in August 1893. He left Molineux for in May 1895, returning to Ardwick (who by now had become Manchester City). He played 57 League games for City before moving to London to play for Millwall (1896-98). He then returned to Scotland, retiring in 1900.
Wolves record: 5 apps.

ROCHDALE

Wolves' playing record against the Dale is:
Football League

Venue	P	W	D	L	F	A
Home	3	1	2	0	2	0
Away	3	2	1	0	4	0
Total	6	3	3	0	6	0

Wolves and Rochdale battled it out for the Third Division North championship in season 1923-24 and in the end it was the Wanderers who took the prize, pipping their Lancashire rivals by a single point. Both games between the clubs that term ended goalless. The third encounter, in November 1986, also finished 0-0 at Molineux, in Division Four, before Wolves finally registered their first win, 3-0 at Spotland in April 1987. The following season, when Wolves took the Fourth Division title, they achieved the double over Rochdale, winning 2-0 at home and 1-0 away, Micky Holmes hitting the winner in the latter contest which attracted just over 2,800 fans.

Players with both clubs: Alan Ainscow, Brian Birch, Joe Blackett (player-manager of Rochdale), Micky Holmes, Geoff Lomax, Billy Marshall, John Pender, Dicky Rhodes, Jimmy Seal, Alan Steen, Geoff Thomas, Tony Towner,

Also associated: Neville Hamilton was signed by Wolves on a free transfer from Rochdale in 1984. He was ready to make his debut but suffered a heart attack in training that ended his career. Billy Halligan and Tom Wildsmith (Wolves players, Rochdale wartime guests); Laurie Calloway, Matt Carrick, Vic Cockcroft, David Felgate, Dennis Isherwood, Bert Latham, Ron Morgan, Chris Pearce and Sid Protheroe (all Wolves Reserves); Tony Lacey (Rochdale player, Wolves youth recruitment officer) and Bobby Downes (Rochdale player, Wolves coach).

RODGER, Graham

Graham Rodger was a competent Scottish centre-half, who became one of a fine plethora of excellent defenders at Grimsby Town during the 1990s. Born in Glasgow on 1 April 1967, Rodger joined Wolves as an apprentice in 1983, but before he had the chance to turn professional at Molineux, he was whisked away by Coventry City (February 1985). A little over two years later, after signing full-time for the Sky Blues, he stepped out at Wembley and helped City win the FA Cup Final against Spurs. He made over 40 appearances during his stay at Highfield Road that ended in August 1989 when he was transferred to Luton Town for £150,000. From Kenilworth Road he switched to Blundell Park for a then record fee for the Mariners of £135,000 (January 1992) and over the next five years was a regular member of Grimsby's senior squad, amassing more than 165 appearances, In the summer of 1997 he joined the coaching staff at Blundell Park while still a player and in the July 1998 Rodger left the Cleethorpes-based club to sign as a player-coach for Hull City.
Wolves record: 1 app.

ROMANO, Serge

French full-back Serge Romano, who was born in Metz on 25 May 1964, joined Wolves on a free transfer from FC Martigues in August 1996, having previously played for his home town club Metz and Toulouse. Unfortunately he never adapted to the pace of the English game, looking far too fragile. He was released in May 1997 when his contract expired and returned home to France.
Wolves record: 2+3 apps.

ROONEY, John

John Rooney was born in Newcastle in 1919. A useful centre-half, signed from Romsley, he broke into the first team at Molineux in season 1938-39, but the following year, like so many other footballers, he went into the forces to serve his country. He was sadly killed in Italy in 1943, aged just 24.
Wolves record: 2 apps.

ROPER, Francis L.

Frank Roper stepped out for his one and only appearance for Wolves in a 3-0 home defeat by Blackpool in a Second Division match in March 1920 when he replaced Jack Sambrook in the attack. Born in Walsall in 1899, he joined Wolves from Pleck in July 1919 – when the club was engaging several relatively unknown players after the war – and left Molineux for Wolverhampton Rangers in May 1920.
Wolves record: 1 app.

ROSARIO, Robert

Tall, raven-haired striker, Robert Rosario won England youth honours as a teenager. Born in Hammersmith, London, on 4 March 1966, he joined Norwich City from non-League Hillingdon Borough in December 1983 and during his time at Carrow Road he added four England Under-21 caps to his collection. He made only 20 League appearances for the Canaries in his first three years with the club and in January 1986 was loaned to Wolves. After returning to Norwich the following month, he quickly established himself in the first team and went from strength to strength, netting 29 goals in 158 games up to March 1991 when he moved to Coventry City for £600,000.

In March 1993 – after netting ten goals in 67 games for the Sky Blues – he went to Nottingham Forest for £400,000, staying at The City Ground until May 1996.
Wolves record: 4 apps. 1 goal.

ROSE, William Crispin

Goalkeeper Billy Rose, was born in St Pancras, London on 3 April 1861 and was one of the leading 'keepers of the 1890s. He began his career with Small Heath (later Birmingham City) before making his name with the Swifts club of London. He played for Wiltshire, Staffordshire and London in county matches and also appeared for Preston North End (in 1885-86) and Stoke (who he joined in August 1886) before signing for Wolves in January 1889. Rose enjoyed a fine career with the club, appearing in more than 150 senior games overall and gaining an FA Cup winners' medal in 1893, although he missed another Final three years later because of injury. He was capped four times for England before joining Wolves and won another cap as a Wolves player. In his five internationals he conceded only four goals. In July 1894 his Wolverhampton career was interrupted when he was sacked and he had a brief spell with Loughborough Town. The Loughborough club was elected to the Second Division in the summer of 1895, but by then Rose was back with Wolves, who he finally left 12 months later. In 1893 he had circulated a letter in which he stated that he was 'instrumental' in forming a Players'

Union. It was that which apparently upset Wolves. After he finished playing, Rose ran a pub in Birmingham, then another in Wolverhampton, and also had a shop in Bordesley Green, near St Andrew's. He died in Bordesley Green on 4 February 1937.

Wolves record: 155 apps.

ROSS, Ian

Early in 1982 player-coach Ian Ross, ex-Aston Villa and Liverpool and former manager of FC Valur, took over as caretaker-manager of Wolves. He held the team together for four games from the 16 January 1982 to 2 February 1982 inclusive prior to the arrival at Molineux of Ian Greaves.

ROSS, Stewart

Stewart Ross was a full-back or midfielder, who made his League debut for Wolves in front of almost 54,000 fans at Old Trafford in December 1967. Born in Woking on 11 September 1945, and a former Wolverhampton Grammar School pupil, Ross joined Wolves on schoolboy forms, became an amateur in June 1965 and signed as a part-time professional at Molineux five months later, staying there until May 1971, basically as a reserve. He then qualified as a Chartered Accountant (the profession he's in today) and between 1977 and 1980 he assisted Old Wulfrunians.

Wolves record: 1+2 apps.

ROSTANCE, James Colin

Jim Rostance was one of a number goalkeepers registered with Wolves for the first season after World War One (1919-20). Born the son of a local foundry worker in Penkridge, Staffs. in May 1898, he joined the Molineux staff in April 1913 from Siemen's FC, having earlier played for Cannock Town and Featherstone Boys Club. He was unlucky to be between the posts when Wolves crashed to a 10-3 defeat at Hull City in December 1919 and seven months later was transferred to Hednesford Town, later assisting Rugeley Swifts and Cannock Welfarers.

Wolves record: 9 apps.

ROTHERHAM UNITED (COUNTY)

Wolves' playing record against the Millers is:

Football League

Venue	P	W	D	L	F	A
Home	9	7	1	1	20	5
Away	9	1	3	5	11	16
Total	18	8	4	6	31	21

FA Cup

Home	3	2	1	0	8	4
Away	3	1	0	2	3	7
Total	6	3	1	2	11	11

Wolves lost their first two League games against Rotherham in season 1919-20 but then won four in succession at home during the 1920s including two by three goals to nil, the second en route to taking the Third Division North championship in 1923-24.

Having been relegated the previous season, Wolves beat Rotherham 4-1 at Molineux but lost 4-3 at Millmoor in their Second Division campaign of 1965-66 and on their way to regaining their top-flight status next term they beat the Yorkshire club 2-0 at home and drew 2-2 away.

Wolves suffered their heaviest FA Cup defeat of all-time when they crashed 6-0 to Rotherham in a first round tie at Millmoor in November 1985. Defender Nicky Clarke was sent-off and, in fact, this was Wolves heaviest reverse at senior level since 1968.

Prior to that Wolves had run up two 3-0 Cup wins over the Millermen – in the third round in 1946-47 and in the fourth round in 1964-65, the latter coming in a replay.

In January 1977 Rotherham were beaten 3-2 at Molineux in the third round before 23,605 fans, John Richards scoring twice.

Players with both clubs: Alan Birch, Paul Blades, Walter Bottrill, Albert Brookes, Arthur Brooks, Pat Buckley, John Galley, Mick Gooding, Henry Hargreaves, Leslie Heelbeck, Francis Hemingway, Arthur Hetherington, Micky Holmes, Emlyn Hughes (Rotherham player-manager); Harry Lloyd, Hugh McIlmoyle, Mike O'Grady, Willie Raynes, Paul Stancliffe, Mark Todd, Tony Towner, Jack Turner and Ernie Whittam.

Also associated: Tommy Docherty (manager of both clubs); Herbert Barlow, Billy Gold and Frank Wildman (all Rotherham wartime guests); Mick Martin (trialist) and John Fantham, David Felgate, Fred Hanson, Joe Miller, Roy Poole and Fred Robinson (all Wolves juniors/Reserves).

ROTTON, William Harry

Amateur inside-forward Billy Rotton was born in Wednesbury c.1909. He played local intermediate football in the West Bromwich and Walsall areas before joining Wolves as a reserve in August 1927. After only one season at Molineux he began his tour of the Midlands, playing in turn, for Shrewsbury Town (August 1928), West Bromwich Albion (May 1929), Brierley Hill Alliance (May 1930), Cradley Heath (March 1931), Walsall (August 1931), Hereford United (1933), Worcester City (1934) and Dudley Town (October 1935-May 1936). He won a Junior International cap for England whilst with Wolves (1928).

Wolves record: 4 apps. 1 goal.

ROUSE, Valentine Alfred

Although born at Hoddesden, near Harlow, on 14 February 1898 (St Valentine's Day – hence his Christian name) left-half Val Rouse started his playing career in South Wales with Pontypridd, where, in 1921, he was discovered by an eagle-eyed Wolves scout. He made only a handful of senior appearances during his brief stay a Molineux before transferring to Stoke for £1,000 in 1922. A gentleman both on and off the field, Rouse scored twice in 94 outings for the Potters, up to May 1925, when he returned to South Wales to sign for Swansea Town. He returned to the Potteries in June 1926 and joined Port Vale for whom he made 103 appearances in three seasons. He next assisted Crewe Alexandra and later played for Connah's Quay and Shotton FC before retiring in 1933. Rouse died in Hereford in 1961.

Wolves record: 5 apps.

ROWBOTHAM, Harold

Wolves signed Harry Rowbotham as a reserve half-back in June 1900. He remained at Molineux for three seasons, making only seven first-team appearances, occupying all three middle-line positions as well as that of inside-right. Born in Bilston c.1879, he played for Bilston Town prior to joining Wolves and on his departure from Molineux Rowbotham signed for Stourbridge, later assisting Netherton and Oldbury St Michael's. He died in Birmingham in 1969.

Wolves record: 7 apps. 1 goal.

ROWLEY, Kenneth F.

Utility forward Ken Rowley joined Wolves as a professional in October 1947, a few weeks before entering the Army. Born in Pelsall on 29 August 1926, he originally came to the club from Elkington's FC in June 1946 as an amateur and after his national service he returned to play for Wolves until January 1951 when he moved to Birmingham City, later assisting Coventry City (November 1954 to May 1955) when he quit League football.

Wolves record: 3 apps.

RUDGE, Dale Anthony

Dale Rudge did a reasonable job in the midfield engine-room for Wolves during his short time at Molineux. Born in Wolverhampton on 9 September 1963, he represented Staffordshire Boys before joining Wolves as an apprentice in July 1979, turning professional in August 1981. In July 1984 he moved to Preston North End and after a three-year spell in Norway with FC Djvre 1919 (January 1987 to June 1990) he rounded off his career with Hednesford Town (to 1992). He then became a market trader in Kingswinford, and later worked for Dudley Council Adult Education (catering for special needs) while also running a junior football team, Ashwood Boys in Wordsley, Stourbridge.

Wolves record: 25+4 apps.

RUSSELL, Edward Thomas

Wing-half Eddie Russell was signed by Wolves from St Chad's College during the 1945-46 season. He turned professional immediately and went on to play 30 League games during his time at Molineux which lasted until December 1951 when he switched north to join Middlesbrough. From Ayresome Park he moved to Leicester City (October 1953) and after 101 appearances for the Foxes, he rounded off his senior career with Notts County (August 1958 to May 1959). Russell was born in Cranwell on 15 July 1928.

Wolves record: 33 apps.

RUSSELL, Peter W.

Born in Gornal, near Dudley on 16 January 1935, half-back Peter Russell joined Wolves as a junior in 1950 and turned professional at Molineux in October 1952. With so many excellent footballers occupying the same position around that time, Russell's first-team outings were limited and in March 1956 he was transferred to Notts County for whom he played more than 100 League games before quitting the big time in May 1959.

Wolves record: 4 apps.

RUTTER, Hubert

Full-back Hubert Rutter acted as cover for Dickie Baugh during his short spell at Molineux. Born in Walsall *c.*1869, he played initially for Bradley Swifts and was recruited by Wolves in March 1891. He stayed with the club for barely three months before moving to Ashwood Villa, later assisting Tutbury Town and Dresden Celtic.

Wolves record: 2 apps.

RYAN, Derek A.

A reserve inside-forward or winger at Molineux, Derek Ryan joined Wolves as an apprentice in June 1982. He signed professional forms in October 1984 and had three fairly good years at the club before being released in May 1987 by manger Graham Turner. Born in Dublin on 2 January 1967, he returned to Ireland after leaving the Midlands.

Wolves record: 29+11 apps. 5 goals.

SAMBROOK, John Henry

Good class centre-forward who joined Wolves towards the end of World War One and was a valuable member of the first-team squad for two seasons: 1919-21. Born in Wednesfield on 10 March 1899, he played initially for Willenhall Town and after leaving Molineux he signed for Liverpool in 1922, appearing in two League games, and thereafter assisted Stockport County, Willenhall Swifts and C & L Hills FC, retiring in 1937. Sambrook died in Heathtown, Wolverhampton on 30 December 1973.

Wolves record: 21 apps. 7 goals.

SAMWAYS, Vincent

Midfielder Vinny Samways was on loan to Wolves from Everton in December 1995. Born in Bethnal Green, London on 27 October 1968, he joined Tottenham Hotspur on leaving school and turned professional at White Hart Lane in November 1985. A determined player, he went on to score 17 goals in almost 250 appearances for Spurs, helping them win the FA Cup in 1991. He was transferred to Everton for £2.2 million in August 1994 but never really settled on Merseyside and, indeed, after his loan spell at Molineux he had a similar one at Birmingham City (February 1996). Samways, who won five England Under-21 caps while with Spurs and also represented his country at youth team level, joined the Spanish club Las Palmas in September 1996.

Wolves record: 3 apps.

SANJUAN, Jesus Garcia

Spanish midfielder Jesus Sanjuan – known as the 'Bulldozer' – was signed on loan for three months from Real Zaragoza by Wolves boss Mark McGhee in September 1997. He scored on his debut in a 1-0 Coca-Cola Cup win at Fulham but never really fitted the bill and returned home before his 12 weeks were up. He was born in Zaragoza on 22 August 1971 and represented his country at Under-21 and Under-23 honours and gained a European Cup-winners' Cup winners' medal in 1995 as substitute against Arsenal.

Wolves record: 6+1 apps. 1 goal.

SCARBOROUGH

Wolves' playing record against Scarborough is:

Football League

Venue	P	W	D	L	F	A
Home	1	0	1	0	0	0
Away	1	0	1	0	2	2
Total	2	0	2	0	2	2

The two games played between Wolves and Scarborough were in the old Fourth Division in season 1987-88. A crowd of 7,314 packed into Boro's McCain Stadium on the opening day of the campaign to see the two Steves – Stoutt and Bull – score for Wolves, while at Molineux in mid-February 11,391 spectators witnessed a disappointing 0-0 scoreline. During the clash at Scarborough, a Wolves supporter fell through the roof of one of the stands and was seriously injured. As a result of those mindless fans being held responsible for causing damage and unsatisfactory behaviour, Wolves were fined £5,000, and supporters were banned from travelling away for six matches and then they had to purchase tickets in advance for the remainder of the season.

Players with both clubs include: John Burridge, Leslie Heelbeck, Steve Mardenborough, Mick Matthews, Darren Roberts and Billy Wrigglesworth.

Burridge, in fact, is the oldest player ever to appear for 'Boro in a League game – he was 41 years, 338 days old when he lined-up against Doncaster in November 1993, and he was 45 when he played his last game for 'Boro in 1996.

Also associated: Kevin Charlton (Wolves apprentice), Mark Todd (reserve) and Derek Mountfield (Scarborough's assistant manager).

SCHALKE '04

Wolves' playing record against Schalke is:

European Cup

Venue	P	W	D	L	F	A
Home	1	0	1	0	2	2
Away	1	0	0	1	1	2
Total	2	0	1	1	3	4

The Germans were Wolves' first-ever opponents in a major European competition. They came to Molineux for a European Cup first round first leg encounter on 12

Norman Deeley (left) in action against Schalke '04 in the European Cup.

November 1958 and earned a crucial draw before a 45,767 crowd. Peter Broadbent scored both Wolves goals. The return game in Germany, which was played six days later, resulted in a narrow defeat for Wolves in front of 25,000 fans, allowing Schalke going through 4-3 on aggregate.

SCOTCHBROOK, Frederick

Fred Scotchbrook was Wolves' manager from March 1926 to June 1927. Born in Horwich, near Bolton in 1886 and on leaving school, played for two local clubs, Gymnasium FC and Horwich. In 1914 he joined Bolton Wanderers as a professional, but failed to make the grade at Burnden Park and retired during the war to become Wanderers' coach, later taking over as assistant-secretary at the Lancashire club. He left Bolton in 1924 to become manager of Stockport County, moving to Molineux two years later to succeed Hoskins. Wolves had finished Fourth in the Second Division at the end of the 1925-26 season, but the following year they slipped to 15th. Then, shortly after the club's annual meeting in June 1927, Scotchbrook had a heated argument with two directors and was subsequently relieved of his duties, allowing Major Frank Buckley to take over the reins. He quit football at this juncture.

SCOTT, Henry T.

Inside-right Harry Scott was a tall, well built six-footer, weighing over 12 stones, who made opponents realise his presence in no uncertain terms. Born in Newburn, Northumberland on 4 August 1897, Scott played for Newburn Grange before teaming up with Sunderland in 1922. After three years at Roker Park he was transferred to Wolves (July 1925). He stayed at Molineux until November 1926 when he signed for Hull City, later assisting Bradford Park Avenue (from June 1928), Swansea Town (July 1932), Watford (1933-34) and Nuneaton Borough (July 1934). On his retirement in 1936, Scott chose to live in Warwickshire and he died in that county c.1970.
Wolves record: 37 apps. 6 goals.

SCOTT, Robert Alexander

Alex Scott, an eminently safe goalkeeper, cost Wolves just £1,250 when signed from Burnley in February 1936. Bringing a secure style of goalkeeping to Molineux which was to be of inestimable value over the next ten years, Scott went on to play in almost 130 League and FA Cup games for the Wanderers, plus 68 in wartime, collecting two League Division One runners-up medals in his first two seasons at Molineux, when he missed only four matches out of 84. Scott, who also finished on the losing side in the 1939 FA Cup Final, was originally a centre-half. Born in Liverpool on 29 October 1913,

he won England schoolboy honours and was also a fine baseball pitcher for Oakmere in the Zingari League while playing soccer for Forest Dynamos. Standing 6ft 4ins. tall, he joined Liverpool in 1930, but at that time there was another goalkeeper called Scott in charge at Anfield – Elisha (no relation) – along with a big South African, Arthur Riley, and consequently after failing to break through into the first team, Scott was transferred to Burnley in May 1933. He made 60 appearances for the Turf Moor club, helping them to a FA Cup semi-final in 1935, before switching to Wolves. Scott, a big man with the ability to kick the ball huge distances downfield, was sent off twice playing for Wolves in December 1936 against Huddersfield and Leeds, although the latter game was abandoned late on. The FA suspended Scott for seven days and fined him £8 (a week's wages) and manager Major Buckley no doubt had something to say as Wolves lost 4-0 at Huddersfield. Scott, who had played for England at baseball, represented the Football League and played for an All British XI in the first wartime season of 1939-40 and he also guested for Aston Villa and Southport during the hostilities. With Bert Williams installed at Molineux after the war, Scott left for Crewe Alexandra in August 1947 and made 44 League appearances for the Railwaymen before quitting the big time in 1949. He later ran a general stores in Dunstall Road, Whitmore Reans, Wolverhampton and became a detective in the Wolverhampton Borough Police Force. He died in 1962.
Wolves record: 129 apps.

SCUNTHORPE UNITED

Wolves' playing record against the Iron is:
Football League

Venue	P	W	D	L	F	A
Home	2	2	0	0	5	1
Away	2	2	0	0	3	0
Total	4	4	0	0	8	1

All four League games were played in Division Four during the 1980s. In 1986-87 Wolves won 1-0 at home and 2-0 at Scunthorpe and the following season they were 4-1 victors at Molineux and 1-0 winners at The Old Show Ground. Steve Bull and Andy Mutch both scored twice in that four-goal win in August 1987.

Players with both clubs include: Ian Arkwright, Mark Atkins, Alan Birch, Joe Bonson, Roger Eli, Ron Howells, Mick Matthews, Harry Middleton, Tom Mulholland, Les Mynard, Geoff Sidebottom and Albert Thorpe.

Also associated: Ron Bradley (Scunthorpe manager, Wolves coach); Ian Miller (Scunthorpe player, Wolves coach) and Les Andrews, Jack Angus, Gordon Brown, Jimmy Conde, Paul Moss and Barrie Wood (all Wolves Reserves).

SEAL, James

Striker Jimmy Seal was born in Pontefract on 9 December 1950 and joined Wolves on leaving school in 1966, turning professional at Molineux in March 1968. Unfortunately he had far too many established forwards to battle against for a place in the first team at Molineux and consequently, in May 1971, he was transferred to Barnsley having had a lengthy loan spell with Walsall the previous year. From Oakwell he switched to York City (July 1972) and at Bootham Crescent he did extremely well, scoring 43 goals in 161 League outings before joining Darlington in November 1976. Again he did the business at Feethams, claiming 19 goals in his 122 League outings up to November 1979 when he left the Quakers for Rochdale. After a fine career Seal eventually pulled out of big time football in 1981 with a record of 92 goals in 420 League matches.
Wolves record: 1 app.

SECRETARIES

Wolves first appointed a club secretary in 1888 (when the entered the Football League), and ever since then they have had a man in that position.
Here is a full list of Wolves' secretaries, 1888 to date:

August 1888 to June 1922	Jack Addenbrooke
June 1922 to March 1926	Albert Hoskins
March 1926 to June 1927	Alfred Scotchbrook
June 1927 to March 1944	Major Frank Buckley
April 1944 to June 1948	Ted Vizard
June 1948 to June 1968	Jack Howley
July 1968 to August 1982	Philip Shaw
August 1982 to February 1985	Peter Redfearn
February 1985 to November 1994	Keith Pearson, ACIS
February 1995 to October 1996	Thomas Finn
December 1996 to date	Richard Skirrow

Jack Howley joined the Molineux staff as an office junior in 1923 and stayed with Wolves for the rest of his working life, retiring in 1968 after 45 years service with the club. He was Wolves' secretary for 20 years, the last five being combined with the duties of general manager. He died on 23 March 1971 (See Long service).

During his 14 years as secretary Phil Shaw contributed greatly to the Wolves' match day programme. A member of the Wombourne cricket club, he was a junior footballer with Wolves and was also in line for an England youth cap. He worked in the offices at Molineux before assuming the role of secretary.

Peter Redfearn joined Wolves initially as an office clerk; he then became assistant to Phil Shaw and took over as secretary in 1982. He left the club for a position with Marks and Spencer.

Keith Pearson, a West Brom supporter as a lad, joined Wolves as an accountant in October 1977 and held that position as well as being club secretary and a member of the board of of of directors until 1995, when he left to join Derby County as secretary. Born and bred in Stafford, he played soccer at schoolboy and amateur levels, and at the age of 16 took up football refereeing, qualifying as a Class 1 official. Also a keen cricketer, he is a member of the Milford Hall Cricket Club.

SEDGLEY, Stephen Philip

Born in Enfield, Middlesex on 26 May 1968, Steve Sedgley joined Wolves in June 1997 from Ipswich Town in a £650,000 deal which took fellow defender Mark Venus (rated at £150,000) from Molineux to Portman Road. He made his debut against Norwich City on the opening day of that 1997-98 season, starring in a 2-0 win. Sedgley began his career as an apprentice with Coventry City, signing professional forms at Highfield Road in June 1986. He remained with the Sky Blues until July 1989, when a fee of £750,000 took him to Tottenham Hotspur. Two years later Sedgley helped Spurs win the FA Cup. Capped 11 times by England at Under-21 level, he made over 220 appearances during his five-year spell at White Hart Lane, before leaving the London club for Ipswich in a £1 million deal in June 1994. During the 1997-98 season Sedgley passed the milestone of 450 senior appearances in his career.
Wolves record: 70+5 apps. 3 goals.

SEGERS, Johannes

Six weeks after being found not guilty in the footballers' bribe case (with Bruce Grobbelaar, John Fashanu and a Malaysian businessman) Dutch goalkeeper Hans Segers signed a one year contract with Wolves in September 1997 after being at Molineux as a non-contract player the previous season. Born in Eindhoven, Holland on 30 October 1961, Segers came over to England from his hometown club, PSV Eindhoven (whom he joined as a 16-year-old in 1977) to sign for Nottingham Forest for £50,000 in August 1984. He made almost 70 appearances under Brian Clough and during his time at the City Ground he was loaned out to Stoke City. He also assisted both Sheffield United (November/December 1987) and Dunfermline Athletic (March 1988) before transferring to Wimbledon for £180,000 in September 1988, replacing Dave Beasant. Segers remained with the Dons until the summer of 1996 when he moved to Wolverhampton Wanderers as cover for Mike Stowell, having made more than 320 appearances for the London club. In March 1998, his late penalty save helped Wolves to an FA Cup quarter-final victory over Leeds. In July that year, Segers left Wolves to become goalkeeping coach at Tottenham, who still retained his players'

registration, making him one of Ian Walker's deputies.
Wolves record: 13 apps.

SEQUENCES
(see also *Unbeaten Runs*)

Wolves' record unbeaten run in League football is 20 matches – in season 1923-24.

Their best spell at home was to remain unbeaten in 27 matches, also in 1923-24.

Wolves' best sequence of successive League wins is eight, achieved on four separate occasions in 1915, 1967, 1987 and 1988.

Wolves suffered a record eight successive League defeats in season 1981-82.

Wolves went 17 League games without a win between May 1983 and November 1983.

The team went a club record 19 League matches without a win between December 1984 and April 1985.

A record run of 11 away League games was set up in season 1953-54, and in this same campaign Wolves went a record 14 home games without defeat.

Wolves failed to record a single away League win between March 1922 and October 1923 – a total of 32 matches.

Wolves went eight matches without conceding a goal in 1982-83.

SHAW, Bernard

Full-back Bernard Shaw was born in Sheffield on 14 March 1945. He joined Sheffield United as a junior and made 134 League appearances for the Blades between October 1962 and his transfer to Wolves in July 1969. Shaw was a steady defender who won England Youth and Under-23 caps and he played for Wolves in the 1972 UEFA Cup Final against Tottenham Hotspur. He partnered Derek Parkin in a number of games before being transferred back to Sheffield – this time to play for Wednesday in May 1976. He had served in a period of relative success under Bill McGarry and afterwards made 113 senior appearances for the Owls before being released in May 1976 after Wednesday had dropped to the lower reaches of the Third Division. His brother Graham was also a Sheffield United full-back, who later played for Bristol Rovers.
Wolves record: 152+4 apps. 2 goals.

SHAW, Bertram

Born in Lower Gornal in 1863, Shaw was a utility forward who played for Gornal Wood before joining Wolves in July 1887. He remained with the club for two seasons, leaving for Willenhall in September 1889.
Wolves record: 3 apps. 1 goal.

SHAW, Cecil Ernest

Full-back Cecil Shaw was born at Mansfield on 22 June 1911 and played for Mansfield Boys, Mansfield Invicta, Blidworth Juniors,

Rainworth Church and Rufford Colliery before Wolves signed him in February 1930. He signed the appropriate forms outside a cinema. Shaw had spent some of his early career as a centre-forward but at Wolves he was used exclusively as a full-back after making his League debut in a 2-0 defeat against Hull City at Anlaby Road on the last day of the 1929-30 season. He did not come back into the side until the final nine games of the following season and managed only ten games the following season, when Wolves won the Second Division championship. He was more regular in 1932-33 and then, as Wolves began to settle down in the First Division, he became virtually a permanent fixture in the side until his departure for West Brom in December 1936. A left-back with a fiercesome challenge, Shaw made over 180 appearances altogether, all but those first 20 in the First Division. From 4 November 1933 (at Ewood Park) to 19 September 1936 (at home to Arsenal) he made 121 consecutive League appearances. Shaw had been a penalty expert with Wolves and had never missed from the spot, but he fluffed the first one he took for West Brom, in an FA Cup-tie against Coventry City. With Albion he made 127 senior appearances and after guesting for Blackpool and Nottingham Forest during World War Two, he joined Southern League Hereford United in June 1947. He retired three years later and took up refereeing in the Oldbury and District League, where he remained for ten years. He then spent three years scouting for his former club West Brom. Shaw, who was a very capable cricketer, died in Handsworth on 20 January 1977.
Wolves record: 183 apps. 8 goals.

SHAW, Harold

Harry Shaw was another splendid left-back, who served Wolves exceedingly well between the two World Wars. Born at Hednesford on 5 February 1906, he was only 15 when he made Hednesford Town's first team while working as an engineer's fitter. Wolves' boss George Jobey signed him at the end of the 1922-23 season and, still in his early 20s, Shaw was the baby of the side which won the Third Division North championship in 1923-24. He missed only five League games that season and was a regular for the rest of that decade, making almost 250 senior appearances altogether. He formed a good partnership with Ted Watson and later with Len Williams followed by Wilf Lowton, and Wolves fans were surprised when Major Frank Buckley sold Shaw to Sunderland for just over £7,000 in February 1930. He was with the Roker Park club when they won the League championship in 1935-36, but played only once that season in what turned out to be the last League game of his career. Shaw

retired in May 1938, after making 217 appearances for Sunderland. He had been an ever-present for them in 1931-32 and claimed the first goal of his career that season against Everton at Goodison Park in January 1932. Always a keen golfer, he was a member of the South Staffs and Penn club. He also worked as an engineer's fitter at Cannock Colliery. Shaw died in 1960.
Wolves record: 249 apps.

SHEARGOLD, Arthur L.

Born in Princes End, Tipton in April 1888, Arthur Sheargold was a competent goalkeeper, who played three seasons with Great Bridge Unity before joining Connah's Quay, moving to Wolves in the summer of 1910. He remained at Molineux for two years, acting as reserve to Frank Boxley and Teddy Peers. In May 1912 he signed for Dudley Town and later played for Netherton and Gornal Town.
Wolves record: 4 apps.

SHEFFIELD UNITED

Wolves' playing record against the Blades is:
Football League

Venue	P	W	D	L	F	A
Home	40	18	13	9	82	51
Away	40	7	13	20	56	81
Total	80	25	26	29	138	132

FA Cup

Home	6	2	3	1	8	7
Away	5	3	0	2	10	9
Total	11	5	3	3	18	16

ZDSC

Away	1	0	0	1	0	1

On 30 September 1893 the first crowd disturbances of any real threat were seen at Molineux when Sheffield United beat Wolves 4-3 in the first League game between the two clubs. The match referee was attacked by a group of irate home supporters in the 7,000 crowd.

After losing their first four League encounters with the Blades, Wolves finally registered a victory in September 1895 when they triumphed 4-1 at Molineux, David Black scoring twice. Three years later, in November 1898, they repeated that scoreline thanks mainly to a Joe Blackett hat-trick.

United's Billy Beer netted a treble and Peter Boyle scored from 50 yards as Wolves crashed 5-2 at Bramall Lane in October 1899 and 18,000 spectators saw Wolves hammered 7-2 on United soil in October 1903, this being the Blades' best-ever win over the Wanderers.

Each side won its home game by 4-2 in season 1904-05 with Adam Haywood and Jack Smith for Wolves and Johnny Lang for United scoring in both matches.

After a break of more than 25 years Wolves commenced League duties against United with a 5-1 home win in October 1932, Jimmy Deacon scoring two splendid goals, and soon after World War Two, Jimmy Dunn, Dennis Wilshaw and Jimmy Mullen all netted braces as Wolves – Wembley bound – whipped United 6-0 at Molineux – their biggest victory over the Yorkshire club.

When Wolves won the League championship in 1953-54 they beat United 6-1 at home and drew 3-3 at Bramall Lane, Johnny Hancocks, Roy Swinbourne and Wilshaw scoring in both fixtures.

When Wolves' 'keeper Fred Davies was injured at Bramall Lane in March 1964, centre-forward Ray Crawford took over between the posts. But despite his heroics the Blades went on to record a 4-3 victory, Crawford netting twice for Wolves.

In 1975-76 Wolves ran up two impressive wins over United – 5-1 at home and 4-1 away. John Richards and Kenny Hibbitt both scored twice in the home game.

In April 1995 Wolves drew 3-3 at Bramall Lane. After Don Goodman, Steve Bull and David Kelly had scored second half goals, Wolves were robbed of victory by a 92nd minute equaliser from Jostein Flo.

United dumped Wolves out of the FA Cup in the third round in March 1901, beating them 4-0 at Molineux. Future Wolves player George Hedley scored one of his side's goals and United's 'keeper 'Fatty' Foulke saved Ted Pheasant's penalty when the score was 1-0. The Blades went on to reach the Final where the lost to Spurs in a replay.

In a fourth round tie at Molineux Wolves beat United 3-0 in front of a near 50,000 crowd and then as holders of the trophy they again knocked the Blades out of the competition in the fourth round in February 1950, beating them 4-3 at Bramall Lane after a goalless draw at Molineux.

The last of the 11 FA Cup meetings took place at Molineux in February 1966 when Wolves won a fourth round tie 3-0 when a youthful Peter Knowles hit the target twice.

United beat Wolves by the only goal of a Zenith Data Systems Cup-tie at Bramall Lane in 1989-90 when the attendance was under 5,000.

Players with both clubs include: David Barnes, Pat Buckley, John Burridge, Gordon Cowans, Mel Eves, George Farrow, Stan Fazackerley, Roger Hansbury, Bob Hatton, George Hedley, Charlie Henderson, George Henson, Martin Johnson, John McAlle, Chris Marsden, Archie Needham, Tom Phillipson, Dicky Rhodes, Hans Segers, Bernard Shaw, Paul Simpson, Paul Stancliffe, Mark Todd, Tony Towner, Peter Withe.

Also associated: John Barnwell (United player, Wolves manager); Andy Beattie (Wolves manager, United assistant manager); John Harris (Wolves reserve and wartime player, United manager, also General manager and scout); Arthur Rowley (Wolves wartime player, later United manager), Willie Morgan and Roy Poole (Wolves Reserves), George Laking (United wartime guest), Jesse Pye (amateur with United); Gerry Summers (United player, Wolves coach/assistant—manager).

SHEFFIELD WEDNESDAY

Wolves' playing record against the Owls is:
Football League

Venue	P	W	D	L	F	A
Home	40	27	8	5	92	45
Away	40	6	12	22	40	82
Total	80	33	20	27	132	127

FA Cup

Home	5	1	2	2	7	6
Away	4	0	1	3	2	6
Neutral	1	0	0	1	1	2
Total	10	1	3	6	10	14

League Cup

Home	2	1	0	1	4	3

Wolves and Wednesday first met at League level in 1892-93 when both encounters went Wolves' way – 2-0 at home, 1-0 in Sheffield. It was the same story the following season, Wolves again doubling up with a 3-1 home victory and a 4-1 success at Owlerton. Wolves, in fact, won six of the first seven meetings – and in their 4-0 victory at Molineux in September 1895, David Wykes scored a brilliant goal after beating four men in a mazy dribble. And they made it eight wins out of 12 with a 5-0 romp at home on the last day of the 1897-98 campaign.

Wednesday strung together a run of 14 successive home wins over Wolves between January 1904 and October 1934, 11 coming in the Football League, including those of 4-0 (twice), 5-1 and 6-0, the latter in April 1921 which is still Owls' best over the Wanderers.

In October 1932 Wednesday, with a four-timer from Jack Ball, won 5-3 at Molineux but Wolves quickly gained revenge with a crushing 6-2 victory on the same ground 12 months later when Charlie Phillips netted twice and Wilf Lowton burst the ball with his penalty kick. This is Wolves' best League win of the 33 to date over the Owls.

Wolves remained unbeaten in 16 successive home League games against Wednesday between October 1933 and February 1965. During that sequence 13 games were won, 12 in succession, including victories of 4-0, 4-1, 4-2 and 4-3 either side of World War Two.

There were three penalties awarded during the Wolves v Wednesday Football League game at Molineux in March 1983. Wolves' 'keeper John Burridge saved two as 10-men Wednesday were beaten 1-0.

Eight years later, in March 1991, Wolves scored twice in the first 12 minutes at home to Wednesday, Andy Mutch netting the first goal after only 29 seconds. The Owls came back to 2-2 before Steve Bull notched the winner at 3-2.

After meeting, and beating, Wednesday for

Action in the Burnley goalmouth during the 1988 Sherpa Van Trophy Final at Wembley.

the first time in the FA Cup by 3-0 in the third round in March 1889, the next encounter between the teams in this competition was in the 1896 Final which Wednesday won 2-1 at Crystal Palace, Scotsman David Black scoring a fine goal for Wolves in front of 48,836 spectators.

After two drawn games and 210 minutes of hard fought football, Wolves finally beat Wednesday 4-3 on penalties in a fourth-round FA Cup replay at Molineux in January 1995. Don Goodman netted the winning spot-kick after Wolves' 'keeper Paul Jones had performed heroics both at Hillsborough in the initial game, which ended 1-1, and during the tense Molineux penalty shoot-out.

In October 1973 Wolves beat the Owls 3-2 in a home fourth round League Cup-tie, but in a second round clash three years later on the same ground Wednesday won 2-1.

Players with both clubs include: Andy Blair, Simon Coleman, Tom Davison, Ernie Hatfield, John Holsgrove, Derek Jefferson, Mick Kent, Ken Knighton, Jim McCalliog, Lawrie Madden, Fred Marson, Dicky Rhodes, Bernard Shaw, Peter Shirtliff, Guy Whittingham and Len Williams.

Also associated: Arthur Hetherington (Wednesday trailist); Richie Barker (Wednesday coach and assistant manager, Wolves coach); Ron Atkinson (Wolves junior, Wednesday manager), Meynell Burgin, Stan Burton and George Laking (Wednesday wartime guests), Dave Clements and Frank Moss (Wolves Reserves),Chris Turner (coach with both clubs and player with Wednesday), John Harris (Wolves wartime player, Wednesday coach).

SHELTON, John

Right-half or inside-forward Jack Shelton was born at Wolverhampton in June 1884 and played for Willenhall Pickwick and Compton Rovers before signing for Wolves in March 1907. He had to wait until the following season to make his League debut, at right-half against Derby County at Molineux in October, but soon moved into the forward line with great effect – he scored a hat-trick against Grimsby in only his fifth game up front – and by the end of the season had collected an FA Cup winners' medal. Shelton's overall career at Molineux saw him as a provider for others rather than as an out-an-out scorer. Shelton

joined Port Vale in 1911 and helped them win the Staffordshire Cup, Birmingham Cup and North Staffordshire Infirmary Cup. He also played briefly for Stourbridge and Dudley Town and his son, also Jack, played for Walsall either side of World War Two. Jack Shelton senior was killed in action in September 1918 and his widow married Jack Needham, the former Wolves player of the 1910-20 era. Shelton's brother George Henry also played football for Port Vale and Wellington Town.
Wolves record: 94 apps. 17 goals.

SHERPA VAN TROPHY

The Sherpa Van Trophy replaced the Freight Rover Trophy for season 1987-88 and what an entry Wolves made. They went all the way to the Final and won the competition at the first attempt, beating Burnley 2-0 in front of 80,841 fans at Wembley. On their way to the Final, Wolves played Swansea, Bristol City, Peterborough, Brentford, Torquay and Notts County. They scored a total of 19 goals with Steve Bull netting 12.

The following season Wolves were knocked out in the area Final by Torquay, losing 2-0 at home after winning the first leg 2-1 at

Plainmoor. In an earlier round Bull scored four times in a 5-1 win over Port Vale – Wolves' best victory in the Sherpa Van Trophy.
Summary

P	W	D	L	F	A
20	13	5	2	43	16

SHINTON, Bertram

Bert Shinton was a reserve inside-forward, born in Wednesbury in November 1885 who joined Wolves from Ettingshall Church in July 1909. He spent only one season at Molineux, scoring the winning goal on his only appearance against Stockport |County in a 2-1 win. On leaving Wolves he moved to Halesowen and he died in Wolverhampton c.1959. Shinton's brother Fred played for West Bromwich Albion, Bolton Wanderers and Leicester Fosse.
Wolves record: 1 app. 1 goal.

SHIRTLIFF, Peter Andrew

Sturdy central defender Peter Shirtliff was born in Hoyland on 6 April 1961. He played over 200 games for Sheffield Wednesday between October 1978 and August 1986 before transferring to Charlton Athletic for £125,000. He added a further 125 appearances to his tally with the Addicks and then returned to Hillsborough for a second spell in July 1989 for £500,000. Again he served the Owls well, having another 135 outings for the Yorkshire club before signing for Wolves for £250,000 in August 1993. He stayed at Molineux for two seasons, leaving the club to sign for Barnsley for £125,000 in August 1995. Two years later he celebrated as the Tykes gained a place in the Premiership. In 1997 Shirtliff reached the personal milestone of 600 senior appearances at club level.
Wolves record: 83+2 apps.

SHOP

Wolves' first souvenir shop was opened in 1968 at the North Bank End of Molineux. It was initially managed by the folk singer, Harvey Andrews.

SHORT, John

Yorkshireman Jack Short was born in Barnsley on 18 February 1928. He moved to the Midlands as a youngster and played for Wath Wanderers (the Molineux nursery side) during the latter stages of the war before joining Wolverhampton Wanderers as a professional in May 1948. A competent fullback, he waited patiently in the wings behind a posse of good defenders before breaking into Wolves' first team in 1950. Short made well over 100 appearances for the club, helping them win their first League title, but with so much talent at Molineux, he was allowed to leave for Stoke City in June 1954, Potters manager Frank Taylor (a former Wolves fullback) acquiring him to 'bolster up his

defence'. Short played 55 times for the Potters before returning home to sign for Barnsley in a £3,000 deal in October 1956. He made 109 League appearances for the Tykes, up to 1960 when he announced his retirement. Short died after a brief illness in 1976.
Wolves record: 107 apps. 2 goals.

SHORTHOUSE, William Henry

Defender Bill Shorthouse, nicknamed 'The Baron' by his Wolves teammates, was born at Bilston on 27 May 1922 and joined the Molineux club as an amateur in June 1941. By the time he turned professional in April 1945, Shorthouse had guested for Burnley, served in the Army and been wounded on a Normandy beach on D-Day. He had learned his football at St Martin's School, Bilston, and with St

Bill Shorthouse – wounded in the D-Day landings he recovered to give Wolves tremendous service.

Mirren Old Boys in the Wolverhampton and District League, and his early days with Wolves were spent at the Wath Wanderers nursery club. From 1947-48, Shorthouse was a regular member of the Wolves first team, winning an FA Cup winners' medal in 1949 and a League championship medal in 1954. He played in all the Cup rounds in 1948-49 and when the League title went to Molineux for the first time, in 1953-54, he missed only two games all season. He was only ever out of the side through injury, never dropped, and altogether played in almost 380 senior matches. The majority of his career was spent a centre-half but in 1954 he switched to full-back

when Billy Wright took over the number five shirt. After retiring during the 1956-57 season – some 44,000 saw his last game, against Birmingham City at Molineux in September that season – Shorthouse worked as a coach. He gained a fine reputation working with young players and was coach briefly to the England Youth team in 1970-71 and also served Birmingham City and Aston Villa, guiding Villa to an FA Youth Cup Final victory in 1980. At the height of his playing career, one writer described him as 'resolute, determined, strong-tackling and a dedicated club man…one of the game's most conscientious players'. He now lives at Penn, Wolverhampton.
Wolves record: 376 apps. 1 goal.

SHOWELL, George

George Showell was another Bilston-born defender who served Wolves well, although it took him some considerable time to become established. Born on 9 February 1934, Showell played for South-East Staffordshire Boys before joining Wolves straight from school in July 1949. He became a full-time professional two years later, but the club had such a strong squad that he had to wait until March 1955 before making his first-team debut, at home to Preston North End. By the end of the 1958-59 season he had managed less than 40 League appearances, despite having been with the club for almost a decade. However, during the next six campaigns Showell's fortunes improved and by the time he moved to Bristol City in May 1965, his total number of senior appearances had risen past the 200 mark (he also had 196 outings for Wolves' second team in League and Cup competitions). Showell missed out on League championship medals when Wolves won the title two seasons running, simply because he never made enough appearances to qualify, but he did gain an FA Cup winners' medal in 1960 and always proved a versatile performer, playing at full-back, centre-half and even as a centre-forward for Wolves. He spent only a short time at Ashton Gate before being transferred to Wrexham in November 1966, and in May 1968 he quit playing to concentrate on coaching. In a long association with Wrexham, Showell saw the club rise from the Fourth Division to the Second and back again and qualify many times for European competition as winners of the Welsh Cup.
Wolves record: 218 apps. 3 goals.

SHREWSBURY TOWN

Wolves' playing record against the Shrews is:
Football League

Venue	P	W	D	L	F	A
Home	2	0	1	1	2	3
Away	2	1	0	1	3	2
Total	4	1	1	2	5	5

FA Cup

Home	1	0	1	0	1	1
Away	1	1	0	0	3	1
Total	2	1	1	0	4	2

League Cup

Home	1	1	0	0	6	1
Away	1	0	0	1	1	3
Total	2	1	0	1	7	4

The four League matches between the two clubs spanned three years.

The first clash on 27 December 1982 at Gay Meadow ended in a 2-0 win for Wolves and the last meeting at Molineux on 6 April 1985 saw the Shrews take the honours with a 1-0 victory.

Wolves met Shrewsbury in the quarter-finals of the FA Cup in 1978-79 and after a hard fought 1-1 draw at Molineux, the replay went in favour of Wolves by 3-1 with Peter Daniel, Willie Carr and Billy Rafferty on target in front of a 15,000 plus crowd.

The two League Cup encounters were in the second round of the 1991-92 competition and after winning hands down in the first leg at Molineux, Wolves eased up at Gay Meadow where Shrewsbury gained a creditable victory only to bow out on aggregate.

Players with both clubs include: Pat Bartley, Steve Biggins, Alan Boswell, Jack Bowlder (founder member of Shrewsbury Town), Frank Boxley, Peter Broadbent, Alf Canavan, Wayne Clarke, Arthur Coley, Fred Davies (also assistant manager and manager of Shrewsbury), Harry Davies, Richard Davies, Dean Edwards, George Getgood, Paul Jones, Mick Kenning, Bill Layton, Tancy Lea, John Matthias, Jim Melrose, Harry Middleton, Jack Nightingale, John Paskin, Jon Purdie, Len Rhodes, Carl Robinson, Billy Rotton, Darren Simkin, Alex Simpson, Tim Steele, Barry Stobart and Ernie Whatmore.

Also associated: Arthur Rowley (Wolves reserve, later record scorer for Shrewsbury with 167 League and Cup goals); Richie Barker (Shrewsbury manager, Wolves coach); Graham Turner (player and manager at Gay Meadow, manager of Wolves); Graham Hawkins (assistant manager of Shrewsbury, player and manager of Wolves); Sid Blunt, Terry Harkin (Wolves Reserves); Arthur Allman and Tom Trevellyan Jones (Wolves Reserves); Jock Mulraney, Bernard Streten and Tom Wood (Wolves wartime guests, Town players), Teddy Peers (Town guest).

Shrewsbury's 25-year-old former Danish Under-21 international goalkeeper Benny Gall was a given a one-match trial by Wolves in 1997, playing against Sunderland in a Pontins League match. He was not taken on the staff.

SHROPSHIRE COUNTY LEAGUE

Wolves' second team played in the Shropshire County League in 1891-92,

attaining this record to carry off the championship:

P	W	D	L	F	A	Pts
16	15	1	0	84	9	31

Their biggest wins were those of 14-0 against Newport and 12-0 over Ironbridge. John Heath scored five goals in the latter victory.

They registered 15 consecutive victories during the course of the season.

Wolves' first League game in this competition was against Wellington St George at home on 5 September 1891 which they won 5-0.

SIDEBOTTOM, Geoffrey

Goalkeeper Geoff Sidebottom was born in Mapplewell, Yorkshire on 29 December 1936. He played his early football with the local village side and then Wath Wanderers before joining Wolves in January 1954, turning professional at Molineux the following September. Despite being told by his doctor not to play football because of a chest complaint, Sidebottom developed quickly as understudy to the great Bert Williams. His debut at West Bromwich in November 1958 saw Wolves lose 2-1 but he came through that experience and did well before leaving Wolves to join Aston Villa in February 1961, where he was reserve to another ex-Molineux man, Nigel Sims. He went on to make 88 appearances for Villa, up to January 1965 when he transferred to Scunthorpe United, later assisting New York Royal Generals (1968-69) when he also coached the Columbia University side in the States and Brighton and Hove Albion (from January 1969). He retired through injury in May 1971 after recovering from serious head injuries suffered in a reserve game in October 1970. He gained a League Cup winners prize with Villa in 1961 and was awarded a testimonial by Brighton ten years later.
Wolves record: 35 apps.

SIDLOW, Cyril

Although goalkeeper Cyril Sidlow played in only a handful of peacetime League games for Wolves he helped the club win the wartime League (North) Cup in 1942, enjoyed a successful career elsewhere in the First Division, was capped for Wales and might have done much more with Wolves, the club he rejoined in later years, but for the intervention of World War Two. Sidlow, who guested for Wrexham during the hostilities, was born at Colwyn Bay on 26 November 1915. He played for Colwyn Bay United (in two spells), Abergele, Flint Town and Llandudno Town before signing for Wolves in July 1937. He made his League debut in a 3-2 home win over Birmingham in April 1938 and played in the next two matches, the last a 10-1 home win against Leicester, and made one appearance the fol-

lowing year. War ended League football for seven years and by the time peace was restored, Bert Williams was the first-choice and in February 1946, Wolves felt able to let Sidlow go to Liverpool for £4,000. Ironically, he had a fine game in the last match of the 1946-47 season when Liverpool clinched the League championship at Molineux. During the war Sidlow had guested for Notts County, Wrexham, Darlington and Hartlepools United as well as helping Wolves win a wartime Cup competition and representing the Army Northern Command, and he also appeared in 11 wartime internationals for Wales before making his full international debut in 1947. In all he won seven full caps. After 146 League appearances for Liverpool and an appearance in the 1950 FA Cup Final, he moved to New Brighton in August 1952 and returned to Molineux as emergency cover for Williams in 1953. Sidlow did not appear in the first team again, though, and after coaching the youngsters he retired in 1955 and returned to his former trade as a carpenter. He lives at Codsall, near Wolverhampton.
Wolves record: 4 apps (plus 92 apps in wartime).

SIMKIN, Darren

Left-back or central defender Darren Simkin was born in Walsall on 24 March 1970. He joined Wolves from non-League Blakenhall Town for £10,000 in November 1991 and made his debut in a 1-1 draw at Luton in April 1993. He failed to establish himself in the first team at Molineux, despite some excellent performances in the Reserves, and subsequently left Wolves for Shrewsbury Town in a £35,000 deal in December 1994. He spent three years at Gay Meadow during which time he also had a loan spell with Telford United.
Wolves record: 15+1 apps.

SIMPSON, Alexander

Wing-half Alex Simpson was born in Glasgow on 24 November 1924 and played for the local Scottish junior team, Benburb before moving south to sign professional forms for Wolves in January 1947. He stayed at Molineux until October 1949 during which time he found it difficult to get first-team football due the abundance of talent at the club and moved on to Notts County. After 80 appearances for the Magpies he was transferred to Southampton (November 1952) and after three years and 68 League outings for the Saints, he signed for Shrewsbury Town in June 1955, eventually pulling out of competitive football in May 1959 after more than 100 games for the Gay Meadow club.
Wolves record: 2 apps.

SIMPSON, Paul David

A left-winger with pace and a free-kick specialist, Paul Simpson joined Wolves initially on a month's loan from Derby County in October 1997, making his debut in a 1-0 League defeat away to Birmingham City. Born in Carlisle on 26 July 1966, Simpson joined Manchester City as a junior in 1982 and turned professional at Maine Road in August 1983. He went on to score 24 goals in 155 outings for City, gaining England youth and Under-21 honours in the process before transferring to Oxford United for a record fee for the 'Us' of £200,000 in October 1988. At the Manor Ground he improved his scoring record considerably, netting exactly 50 times for the Us in 168 appearances, up to February 1992 when he moved to Derby County for £500,000. Again he did well at the Baseball Ground and in the next four years was a regular in the Rams' first team. He went on loan to Sheffield United in December 1996 and by the time he arrived at Molineux, his record for County was a useful one: 57 goals in a little over 225 senior outings. He struggled to establish himself in the first team at Wolves and during the 1998-99 season he had two separate loan spells with neighbours Walsall (he appeared in ten League games and helped the Saddlers win promotion to the First Division) and one with Sheffield United. Nevertheless, he finished the season in Wolves' first team.
Wolves record: 34+6 apps. 6 goals.

SIMS, Nigel David

For his size and build Nigel Sims was a tremendously agile goalkeeper. Born in Coton-in-the-Elms near Burton upon Trent on 9 August 1931, he played for Coton Swifts and Stapenhill FC before joining Wolves in August 1948, turning professional the following month. With Bert Williams bedded in as first-choice 'keeper at Molineux, Sims bided his time in the Reserves, having only a few senior outings, although he did gain an England 'B' cap in 1954 before being transferred to nearby Aston Villa in March 1956. He performed superbly well over the next eight years at Villa Park, amassing 309 senior appearances, collecting an FA Cup winners medal (1957), a Second Division championship medal (1960) and a League Cup winners' tankard (1961). He was also voted Villa's 'Terrace Trophy' winner in 1958, represented Young England against the Football League and in May 1959 he even guested for Arsenal. Sims left Villa for Peterborough United in September 1964 and the following year went over to play for Toronto City in Canada and then Toronto Italia (1966). On his return to England he worked for an Insurance Company in Wolverhampton.
Wolves record: 39 apps.

SINCLAIR, Nicholas J.T.

Defender, born in Manchester on 3 January 1960, Nicky Sinclair preferred the full-back position and did well with Oldham Athletic, making 75 League appearances for the Latics between June 1978 and September 1984. He then had a month on loan with Wolves (September 1984) and on leaving Molineux was transferred from Boundary Park to Tranmere Rovers where he ended his senior career in 1986.
Wolves record: 1 app.

SINGLE MEN

In season 1937-38 Wolves had 40 players registered with the club and not one of them was a married man.

SLATER, Robert David

Wolves manager Mark McGhee, desperate to bolster up his midfield, signed Australian international Robbie Slater from Southampton for £75,000 in March 1998. But the 33-year-old never really settled in at Molineux and cited family reasons for wanting to leave Wolves. He returned to his home in Lens, France, with only seven first-team outings to his name after his contract was not renewed at the end of the 1997-98 season. Capped 39 times by Australia, Slater had unsuccessful trials with Nottingham Forest (1981) prior to going to Australia to play for St George's (1982). He then served with RSC Anderlecht (Belgium) and the French club Lens before helping Blackburn Rovers win the Premiership title in 1994-95. In August 1995 he was transferred to West Ham United for £600,000 and switched from Upton Park to The Dell for £250,000 in September 1996 with less than 50 League appearances under his belt in English soccer. In September 1998, Slater returned to Australia to sign for Northern Spirit in Sydney. He was born in Ormskirk, Lancashire, on 22 November 1964 and qualified to play for Australia by virtue of his grandparents. He played for Australia in the 1988 Olympic Games.
Wolves record: 4+3 apps.

SLATER, William J, OBE, CBE, BSC

Bill Slater was an amateur when he appeared in the 1951 FA Cup Final for Blackpool against Newcastle United at Wembley. He finished on the losing side that day, but nine years later, now a professional with Wolverhampton Wanderers, he at last collected a winners' medal as captain of the side that defeated Blackburn Rovers at Wembley. Born at Clitheroe, Lancashire, on 29 April 1927, Slater played in the Lancashire and District Youth League before joining Blackpool in 1944. At the same time he was also turning out for Yorkshire Amateurs and Leeds University. After scoring nine goals in

Bill Slater – the last amateur to appear in an FA Cup Final, with Blackpool, he won England honours as a professional with Wolves.

30 League games for the Seasiders he was transferred to Brentford in December 1951. He played only seven times in the Bees' League team before Wolves signed him in August 1952, still as an amateur. Slater made his League debut for the club as an inside-forward that season, but was at wing-half when Wolves won the League championship the following campaign, when he missed only three games. In February 1954 he became a part-time professional and went on to win two more League championship medals and that FA Cup winners' medal. He had been capped 21 times at Amateur level and played 12 times for the full England team. In 1960 he gained a B.Sc. degree and was voted Footballer of the Year, although he had started the Cup winning season out of the first team. In the summer of 1963 he returned to Brentford, having played for Wolves in all three half-back positions. After a season at Griffin Park he played for Northern Nomads before retiring late in 1964. Slater became deputy director of the Crystal Palace Sports Centre and later worked as director of P.E. at both Liverpool and Birmingham Universities. In 1982 he was awarded the OBE for his services to sport and in 1998 received the CBE. From 1984 to 1989, Slater was director of National Services and in July 1989 was elected president of the British Gymnastics Association. Slater is now a member of the National Olympic Committee and also sits on the Panel of the National lottery. His daughter, Barbara, a for-

mer national champion gymnast, represented Britain in the 1976 Olympic Games and later worked for Central TV.

On 2 May 1956, an aeroplane was chartered to fly Slater, who was at the time working at Birmingham University, for an evening League game at Sheffield United. The Auster pilot was unable to locate the landing strip and when the aircraft finally came down, unheralded, at the RAF aerodrome at Worksop, it was surrounded by fire-tenders, ambulances and angry security officers. When Wolves kicked-off against the Blades, Slater was still hitch-hiking a lift to Bramall Lane, having been replaced in the team by George Showell.

Wolves record: 339 apps. 25 goals.

SMALL, Michael

Born in Birmingham on 2 March 1963, six-foot striker Mike Small played for Bromsgrove Rovers, Luton Town (October 1979), Peterborough United (on loan October 1982), Twente Enschede (Netherlands), Standard Liege (Belgium), Go Ahead Eagles (Netherlands), PAOK Salonika and Brighton and Hove Albion (August 1990) before joining West Ham United in the summer of 1991 for £400,000. He top-scored with 13 goals in 40 League games in his first season at Upton Park, but then lost his place in the side that led to him getting unsettled at Upton Park. In September 1993 he was loaned out to Wolves for a month and then assisted Charlton Athletic in the same capacity in March 1994 before being released by the Hammers at the end of that 1993-94 season.

Wolves record: 3+1 apps. 1 goal.

SMALLEY, Thomas

Wing-half Tom Smalley joined Wolves from South Kirkby Colliery, Yorkshire in May 1931. Born at Kingsley, near Barnsley, on 13 January 1912, he remained at Molineux until August 1938, when he was transferred to Norwich City. Capped once for England, against Wales at Molineux in October 1936, all but two of his League outings for Wolves came in the First Division. After appearing in 43 League games for the Canaries Smalley joined Northampton Town in October 1941 and by the time he left League football ten years later he had amassed over 400 senior appearances for the Cobblers, half of them in wartime football when he also guested for West Bromwich Albion. Smalley later spent two years as player-coach with Lower Gornal (1952-53). A good club cricketer, he resided in Wolverhampton until his death on 1 April 1984.

Wolves record: 196 apps. 12 goals.

SMART, Frederick Laurence

Fred Smart was the cousin of the Aston Villa and England full-back Tommy Smart and brother of Herbert Smart, a Wolves reserve who was with Fred at Molineux. Born in Birmingham in 1899 inside-forward Fred Smart was given little opportunity with Wolves, whom he joined in September 1919 from Redditch having earlier assisted Cotteridge FC. He left Molineux for Aston Villa in November 1921 and later served with Kings Norton (January 1922 to May 1924). He died in Birmingham in 1972.

Wolves record: 7 apps. 2 goals.

SMART, Herbert Horace

Bert Smart was a well built reserve full-back, who served Wolves for two seasons from August 1912 to May 1914. Born in Smethwick in April 1892 and a junior with Bilston United, he joined the playing staff at Molineux from Aston Villa for whom he made one League appearance. He left Molineux for Willenhall and later played for Dudley Town and Bloxwich Strollers.

Wolves record: 3 apps.

SMITH, Alun Arnold

Amateur left-half who was recommended to Wolves by his Welsh colleague and friend, Dai Richards, Alun Smith was born in Aberaman in 1906 and played initially for Merthyr Town, joining Wolves in August 1930. He spent just the one season at Molineux, deputising for Richards in the side before leaving for Caerphilly in May 1931 and later assisting Pontypridd.

Wolves record: 4 apps.

SMITH, Arthur John

Jack Smith was a good quality full-back, not the flashy type, but a player who enjoyed a bold confrontation. Born in Merthyr on 27 October 1911, he had trials with West Bromwich Albion in 1928 when playing for Aberaman, and before joining Wolves as a professional in September 1929 he assisted Aberdare Athletic. After five years at Molineux he moved to Bristol Rovers, and then served with Swindon Town before assisting Chelsea (from 1937). During the war he guested for Cardiff, WBA and Wolves. Smith's playing career came to an end in late 1943 when he slipped on a Wolverhampton kerbstone whilst out walking and a bus, driven by a Wolves supporter, ran over his foot. He returned to Molineux as coach in 1946 after guesting for both Wolves and West Bromwich Albion during World War Two and starring for a Welsh International XI against Birmingham in November 1941. In June 1948 Smith was appointed manager at The Hawthorns, holding office for four years (until April 1952) and steering the Baggies to promotion to the First Division in 1949. From 1952 to 1954 Smith was in charge of Reading and later became a hotelier in Dorset. He died in hospital in Weymouth on 7 June 1975.

Wolves record: 27 apps.

SMITH, Edwin Eric

An all-purpose defender who could play as a full-back or left-half, Eric Smith was born in Wednesbury c.1880 and served with Key Hill FC, Wednesbury Old Athletic (1899), Walsall Unity (1900) and Bilston United before joining Wolves in August 1903. He remained at Molineux until May 1906 when he transferred to Darlaston, later assisting Dudley Town. He died c.1955.

Wolves record: 15 apps.

SMITH, Gordon Melville

Winner of ten youth and four Under-23 caps for Scotland, full-back Gordon Smith played in well over 150 League games in England following his transfer from St Johnstone to Aston Villa for £80,000 in August 1976. Born in Glasgow on 3 July 1954 he was educated in Perth and was watched by a number of leading clubs before he chose to join Villa. He replaced Charlie Aitken at Villa Park and won a League Cup winners medal in 1977. Smith moved to Tottenham Hotspur in February 1979 for £150,000, but sadly missed out on two FA Cup Final appearances with Spurs before switching to Molineux in August 1982. With Wolves he took over the no.4 shirt and played only occasionally at full-back before leaving Molineux for South Africa in May 1984. In 1996 Smith moved across the world to begin working for an advertising agency in Spain.

Wolves record: 39+3 apps. 3 goals.

SMITH, James Jade Anthony

Right-back Jamie Smith was born in Birmingham on 17 September 1974. He joined Wolves as a trainee at the age of 16 and turned professional at Molineux in June 1993. He made rapid progress and after establishing himself in the first team at Molineux he gained representative honours when coming on as substitute for the Football League Under-21 side against Italy's Serie 'B' XI. Excellent on the over-lap, Smith was able to release some fine crosses and his speed in recovery helped him out of many difficult situations. He was transferred from Molineux to Crystal Palace in October 1997 in a £1 million deal that saw two Palace players – Kevin Muscat and Dougie Freedman – move to Molineux. Later that season – March 1999 – Smith moved from Selhurst Park to neighbours Fulham and duly helped the Cottagers clinch the Second Division championship.

Wolves record: 97+7 apps. 1 goal.

SMITH, John

Jack Smith joined Wolves in July 1902. Born at Wednesfield in April 1882, he first played for Cannock and then Stafford Road FC before signing moving to Molineux. A short, stocky forward, he soon established himself

in the team, scoring nine goals in 25 games in his first season. Standing only 5ft 3ins. tall, he formed a very useful left-wing partnership with Jack Miller, but following Wolves' relegation to Division Two in 1906, he surprisingly left the club for Birmingham. He made only six appearances for the Blues before switching to Bristol Rovers. For the Pirates he hit ten goals in 31 games and then netted 24 in 41 outings for Norwich City between 1908 and 1910. He then assisted Luton Town before retiring in 1912. Smith died c.1961.
Wolves record: 114 apps. 43 goals.

SMITH, John James

Born in Penn in 1875, inside-right Jack Smith played for Springfield Royal Star before joining Wolves in December 1897. He failed to impress at Molineux and was released in August 1898 when he signed for Dudley Town. He died in Wolverhampton in 1929. For his only outing for Wolves, he replaced England international Harry Wood in a 2-0 win over Bolton at Molineux in April 1898.
Wolves record: 1 app.

SMITH, Leslie Joseph

Les Smith was a fast, clever and direct winger, who was seen by Wolves as an eventual successor to either Johnny Hancocks or Jimmy Mullen having joined the club as an amateur in June 1945. Born at Halesowen on Christmas Eve 1927, Smith became a full-time professional in April 1946 and made his League debut the following season, at Stoke in the April. He played only four times in the 1953-54 League championship season and it was not until 1954-55 that he really broke through, playing in 34 games as Wolves finished runners-up in the table behind Chelsea. In February 1956, with Hancocks and Mullen still the regular wingers, Smith, who scored 78 goals in 214 reserve team appearances for Wolves (League and Cup) moved to Aston Villa for £25,000. At Villa Park he found less competition and went on to make 130 appearances, scoring 25 goals and collecting an FA Cup winners' medal against Manchester United at the end of his first season in the claret and blue strip. An Achilles tendon injury forced Smith into an early retirement in 1960.
Wolves record: 94 apps. 24 goals.

SMITH, Reginald George Charles W.

Born in Westbury in 1916, Reg Smith replaced Bryn Jones at inside-left in two League games for Wolves in December 1937. A compact footballer he spent just a season as a reserve at Molineux before leaving to join Tranmere Rovers, failing to re-appear after the war. Prior to moving to Wolves, Smith played for Westbury Town, Trowbridge Town and Bristol City (from 1935).
Wolves record: 2 apps.

SMITH, William Courtney

Billy Smith was a useful centre-half, who was born in Hednesford in September 1912. He learnt his football with Denaby United, moving to Molineux in the summer of 1932 as cover for Bellis and Nelson. He was called upon only infrequently and left Wolves to join Southend United in late 1933. He remained with the Shrimpers until 1936, helping them win the prestigious Hospital Cup.
Wolves record: 5 apps.

SMITH, William R.

Billy Smith was an excellent goalscorer for Wolves whom he served from July 1896 until November 1898 when he joined Portsmouth. He remained at Fratton Park until May 1908, amassing an excellent record of 74 goals in 231 League appearances. He then had a brief spell with Gosport United before retiring in 1911. Born in Bilston c.1872 he played for Willenhall prior to his move to Molineux.
Wolves record: 62 apps. 19 goals.

SMYTH, Samuel

For five years, from 1942, inside-forward Sammy Smyth had played only amateur football in his native Northern Ireland, serving with Distillery and Linfield, and a handful of junior clubs. In the summer of 1947, after agreeing to sign professional forms for Dundella, which allowed him to be transferred for a fee, he moved to England to join Wolves for £1,100. A schoolboy international trialist, he had gained several amateur caps for Ireland (with Distillery) and also represented the Irish League, and once at Molineux he quickly made an impact, netting eight goals in 30 games in his first season there. He was immediately upgraded to senior international football (he won a total of nine full caps) and at the same time continued to impress at Wolves, collecting an FA Cup winners medal in 1949 when he scored twice in the 3-1 Final win over Leicester City. He left Wolves for Stoke City for £25,000 in September 1951 and netted 19 times in 44 games for the Potters before switching to Liverpool for £12,000 in January 1954. He spent only five months at Anfield, quitting competitive League football at the age of 29 to return home to Belfast where he got married and took a full-time job, later working for a bookmaker prior to running his own sports shop. He is now an agent for the sportswear company of Halbro and Falcon. Smyth is also an enthusiastic golfer and became both captain and president of the Clandeboye 36-hole complex in Ireland. Born in Belfast on 25 February 1925, Smyth hit 72 goals in 187 League games in English football.
Wolves record: 116 apps. 43 goals.

SOUTHAMPTON

Wolves' playing record against the Saints is:

Football League

Venue	P	W	D	L	F	A
Home	23	11	8	4	38	23
Away	23	5	3	15	31	53
Total	46	16	11	19	69	76

FA Cup

	P	W	D	L	F	A
Home	2	1	0	1	5	3
Neutral	1	1	0	0	2	0
Total	3	2	0	1	7	3

League Cup

	P	W	D	L	F	A
Home	1	0	0	1	0	2
Away	1	0	1	0	2	2
Away	2	0	1	1	2	4

Wartime

	P	W	D	L	F	A
Home	1	1	0	0	3	2
Away	1	1	0	0	4	2
Total	2	2	0	0	7	4

Wolves first met Southampton in the Football League in season 1922-23 (Division Two), and after a 0-0 draw at Molineux Saints won the return fixture at the Dell by 3-0.

It took Saints 13 attempts before they finally won a League game on Wolves' soil, breaking their duck in April 1971 with a 1-0 scoreline.

In between times Wolves had won on nine occasions including a 4-1 triumph in October 1925 (Tom Phillipson scored twice) and a 5-1 victory in February 1932 when Billy Hartill netted a hat-trick.

On the south coast Saints beat Wolves 4-2 in February 1926 and 4-1 in October 1927.

Southampton's best League win over Wolves is 9-3, achieved at The Dell in a Second Division game in September 1965. And it was Wolves, in fact, who took the lead in this game, scoring after only 35 seconds.

Wolves doubled up over Southampton in 1969-70 and 1971-72 but in season 1976-77 Saints, the reigning FA Cup holders, took revenge with a thumping 6-2 win at Molineux and a 1-0 victory at The Dell. Nick Holmes and Mick Channon both scored twice in that big win in the Black Country.

Jim McCalliog missed two penalties against his future club Southampton at The Dell in March 1972, but Wolves still won 2-1 thanks to Gerry Taylor's floated winner.

Saints had by far the better of the 12 League encounters, winning six and drawing four, three of them in succession at Molineux: 1979-81.

Wolves beat Saints 2-0 in the semi-final of the FA Cup at Stamford Bridge in 1907-08. Their goals came from Wally Radford in the first half and George Hedley halfway through the second. The attendance was 44,696.

After a battling performance at The Dell in a third round League Cup-tie in October 1984, Wolves lost the Molineux replay by 2-0.

Young teenager Cameron Buchanan scored a hat-trick when Wolves beat Southampton 4-2 at The Dell in a Football

League South game in October 1945.

Players with both clubs include: Dave Beasant, Davey Burnside, John Burridge, Cuthbert Counden, Tim Flowers, George Getgood, Michael Gilkes, Harry Haynes, George Hedley, Henry Howell, Fred Kemp, Dave MacLaren, Jim McCalliog, John McDonald, Chris Marsden, Jimmy Melia, Jack Mitton, Eric Nixon, Fred Price, Walter Radford, Alex Simpson, Robbie Slater, Ernie Stevenson, David Thompson, Johnny Walker, Harry Wood and Billy Wrigglesworth.

Also associated: Tom Allen, Arthur Hartshorne, Billy McCall, Billy Moore, Frank Perfect, Tommy Rudkin and Arthur Wilson (all Wolves Reserves), Dave Emanuel (wartime guest), Dickie Dorsett and John Harris (Saints wartime guests); Gerry Summers (Wolves coach, Saints scout), Ronnie Ekelund (Wolves trialist).

SOUTHEND UNITED

Wolves' playing record against Southend is:

Football League

Venue	P	W	D	L	F	A
Home	8	5	1	2	19	6
Away	8	2	3	3	8	9
Total	16	7	4	5	27	15

League Cup

	P	W	D	L	F	A
Home	1	1	0	0	1	0

The first two League meetings between the Wolves and Southend in 1986-87 (Division Four) both ended in victories for the Shrimpers: 2-1 at Molineux and 1-0 at Roots Hall.

Since then Wolves have held the upper hand, winning their last four home matches by scores of 3-0, 5-0 (September 1994), 2-0 and 4-1 (April 1997).

Steve Bull scored the 200th goal of his career for Wolves against Southend in April 1995 and then made his 500th senior appearance for the Wanderers in the 4-1 First Division League victory over the Shrimpers at Molineux in April 1997, scoring to celebrate the occasion.

In a first round League Cup-tie in September 1968, a goal by John Farrington gave Wolves a hard-earned 1-0 victory over the Shrimpers in front of 18,667 fans at Molineux.

Players with both clubs include: Sammy Brooks, Francis Burrill, John Burridge, Simon Coleman, Cuthbert Counden, Bill Crew, Jimmy Deacon, George Goddard, Ernie Hatfield, Bryn Jones, Martin Jones, Billy Kellock, George Marshall, Tudor Martin, Billy C. Smith, Andy Turner, Shane Westley, Maurice Woodward.

Also associated: Les Redfearn (trialist); Stan Collymore and Jon Richardson (Wolves Reserves), Eric Jones (Wolves player, Southend wartime guest) and Arthur Rowley (Wolves reserve and wartime player, Southend manager).

Steve Bull in action against Southend United in December 1986.

SOUTHERN JUNIOR FLOODLIT CUP

Wolves reached the Final of this competition in 1998-99. They beat Portsmouth on penalties after the aggregate scores over the two-legs had finished 3-3 with each team winning at home by 3-1. A crowd of just under 1,000 attended Fratton Park and 1,091 saw Wolves win the shoot-out 8-7 to lift the trophy in their first season of entering.

SOUTHPORT

Wolves' playing record against Southport is:

Football League

Venue	P	W	D	L	F	A
Home	1	1	0	0	2	1
Away	1	0	1	0	0	0
Total	2	1	1	0	2	1

These two League games were played in 1923-24 when Wolves took three valuable points off Southport on their way to winning the Third Division North championship. Just over 4,500 fans saw the game at Haig Avenue, while at Molineux a week later, the turnout was 14,665, outside-left Evan Edwards scoring both goals for Wolves.

Players with both clubs include: George Bellis, Fred Goodwin, Chris Greene, Andy King, Billy Marshall, Andy Mutch, John Preece and Peter Withe.

Also associated: Jimmy Melia (Wolves player, Southport manager); Nicky Boland, Tom Bond, Terry Harkin and John Preece (all Wolves Reserves) and Alex Scott and Tom Wildsmith (Southport wartime guests).

SOUTH AFRICA

Wolves toured South Africa in May and June 1951, playing a total of 12 matches and winning them all, scoring 50 goals in the process. Their best victories were those of 13-0 against Eastern Transvaal and 7-0 against Northern Transvaal.

Six years later Wolves made a return trip there and this time won all their eight matches, scoring 49 goals on this occasion. Their best wins came in the space of 72 hours – a 10-1 drubbing of Southern Rhodesia followed by an 11-1 triumph over Northern Rhodesia.

Three South Africans who made the grade with Wolves were Eddie Stuart, Des Horne and Cliff Durandt. Later on strikers John Paskin and Mark Williams both played at Molineux in the 1990). Two players associated with Wolves – Danny Hegan and Peter Withe – both did well in South Africa. Two Wolves full-backs, Terry Springthorpe and Gordon Smith also went over to South Africa.

On 30 September 1953 the South African national team officially 'switch on' the Molineux floodlights, losing 3-1 to Wolves in a friendly.

SOUTH SHIELDS (GATESHEAD)

Wolves' playing record against South Shields is:

Football League

Venue	P	W	D	L	F	A
Home	8	7	1	0	15	4
Away	8	3	4	1	13	11
Total	16	10	5	1	28	15

All 16 games were played in the Second Division between 1919 and 1928. South Shields collected their first point off Wolves when they drew 0-0 at Molineux in a Second Division match on Boxing Day 1919. Wolves' best win of the ten they recorded is 3-0, at home, in December 1920, when under 7,500 fans turned up on a freezing cold afternoon. The teams fought out a cracking 3-3 draw at South Shields in September 1924 when right-half Jack Mitton scored twice for Wolves, one a superb 25 yard drive into the roof of the net. South Shields became Gateshead in 1930.

Player with both clubs: Joe Blackett and John Burridge.

Also associated: Jimmy Utterson (Gateshead juniors).

SPIERS, Cyril Henry

Goalkeeper Cyril Spiers was born in Witton, Birmingham on 4 April 1902 and played his early football with Witton Star, Birchfield Boys Brigade, The Swifts (Perry Barr), Brookvale United, Soho Rovers and Handsworth Central, and after a useful spell with Halesowen he was signed by Aston Villa in December 1920. Standing bolt upright at 6ft 1in. tall and weighing over 12 stones, Spiers had all the necessary attributes for a 'keeper. He was both agile and alert and during his first two years at Villa Park he understudied Tom Jackson, finally establishing himself in the League side in 1922, only to

lose it back to Jackson and then reclaim it again in 1924. He stayed with Villa until August 1927, amassing 112 appearances before transferring to Tottenham Hotspur where he spent another six years, accumulating a further 186 senior appearances. In September 1933 he was recruited by Wolves boss, Major Frank Buckley, as reserve to Alex Scott and proceeded to have just eight games between the posts before quitting the club in 1935. He later became a successful manager with Cardiff City (1939-46), Norwich City (1947), Crystal Palace (1954-58) and Exeter City (1962-63). Spiers died on 21 May 1967. *Wolves record: 8 apps.*

SPRINGTHORPE, Terence

If World War Two hadn't intervened full-back Terry Springthorpe may well have developed into an England international...that was the firm belief of Wolves' manager Major Frank Buckley. Born in Draycott, Shropshire on 4 December 1923, Springthorpe joined Wolves as a 15-year-old in the summer of 1939 and virtually throughout the war was a part-time professional, guesting for Leicester City and Wrexham before finally signing as a full-time professional in 1947. With so many quality defenders on the books at Molineux, he found it hard to hold down a first team position but there is no doubt he was certainly a fine player, and in 1949 he helped Wolves win the FA Cup, replacing the injured Lawrie Kelly against Leicester City in the Final. In December 1950, after more than 11 years' service with Wolves, Springthorpe was transferred to Coventry City, where he stayed for a year, making just 12 League appearances for the Highfield Road club. He went over to South Africa soon afterwards and then moved to America where he played for New York Americans, who, in 1956, became known as the Amerts after amalgamating with Hakoah. Springthorpe lived 200 miles from the New York ground and chose to fly to home games. *Wolves record: 38 apps.*

STAFFORD RANGERS

Wolves met Rangers in the Final of the Staffordshire Senior Cup in season 1935-36 and beat them 2-1 in a very entertaining game at Molineux in front of 6,000 fans.

Players with both clubs (various levels): George Berry (also commercial manager at Stafford); Billy Blunt, Billy Caddick, Dean Edwards, Tony Evans, Joe Hassall, David Heywood, Joe Hodnett, Tommy Horton Revd Kenneth Hunt, Paul Jones, John O'Connor, Les Redfearn, Alf Riley, Jack Rostance, Les Snape, Bobby R. A. Thomson and Dennis Westcott.

Also associated: Dennis Isherwood (Rangers guest); Ian Miller (Rangers player,

Wolves coach); Stan Collymore, Harry Hughes, Harry Prince and Francis Wragge (all Wolves Reserves); Tony Lacey (Rangers player, Wolves youth recruitment officer).

STAFFORD ROAD

Wolves record against Stafford Road:

FA Cup

Venue	P	W	D	L	F	A
Home	1	1	0	0	4	2

Wolves' first official game was against Stafford Road on 13 January 1877. A crowd of 600 at Windmill Field on Goldthorn Hill saw Wolves beaten 8-0, fielding these players in a 12-a-side contest: Harry Barcroft in goal; Frank Hampson, David Hedges, James Adams, Oscar Rowbotham, George Worrall and Walter Kendrick in defence and John Baynton, Ernest Newman Richard Myatt, Billy Jacks and Jack Foster as forwards. John Ward was Wolves' official umpire for this prestigious match.

Eight years later, Wolves played and beat local rivals Stafford Road 4-2 at Dudley Road in a second-round FA Cup-tie in November 1885 – the first major competitive match between the clubs, Jack Aston (2), Harry Aston and Harry Wood scored for the Wanderers in front of 3,000 fans.

Players with both clubs include: Ted Anderson, Walter Annis, Jack Aston, Dickie Baugh junior, Dickie Baugh senior, Richard Danks, Edmund Hadley, Ernie James, Joe McMain, Alf Pearson, John Smith and Tom Tomkyes.

STAFFORDSHIRE SENIOR CUP

The Staffordshire Senior Cup competition has been in existence since 1877. Wolves, however did not enter until 1884-85, reaching the Final at the first attempt.

Wolves put out their strongest side on a regular basis right up until 1905 when the Reserves took over before the club quit the competition in 1954, returning in the mid-1960s.

Here are details of Wolves' appearances in the Final of the Staffordshire Cup:

1884-85	v Walsall Town (at Stoke)	lost 1-2
1887-88	v WBA (at Stoke)	drew 0-0
Replay	v WBA (at Stoke)	drew 0-0(aet)
2nd replay	v WBA (at Stoney Lane)	won 2-1
1893-94	v Aston Villa (at Stoney Lane)	lost 1-2
1894-95	v Burton Wanderers (at Stoke)	drew 1-1
Replay	v Burton Wanderers (at Stoke)	lost 0-2
1896-97	v Stoke (at Stoke)	lost 0-0
Replay	v Stoke (at Molineux)	won 2-0
1900-01	v Stoke (at Molineux)	won 3-1
1903-04	v Stoke (at Stoke)	drew 2-2
Replay	v Stoke (at Molineux)	drew 2-2(aet)
		(Trophy shared)
1904-05	v Small Heath (at Coventry Road)	lost 0-4
1921-22	v Walsall (at Molineux)	won 2-1
1922-23	v Walsall (at Fellows Park)	lost 2-3

1931-32	v WBA (at The Hawthorns)	lost 2-3
1934-35	v Stoke City (at Molineux)	won 6-2
1935-36	v Stafford Rangers (at Molineux)	won 2-1
1936-37	v Birmingham (at Molineux)	won 4-1
1937-38	v WBA (at Molineux)	won 5-3
1949-50	v Walsall (at Molineux)	won 3-1
1950-51	v WBA (at The Hawthorns)	lost 0-1
1951-52	v Stoke City (at Molineux)	won 9-0
1966-67	v Tamworth (on aggregate)	won 3-2

Wolves' biggest Staffordshire Senior Cup win is 12-1 against Stafford Road on 1 October 1887.

Aston Villa beat Wolves 9-1 at home in a Staffs. Cup-tie in November 1908

Wolves were thrown out of the competition in 1891 when they refused to contest the Final against Stoke at Burslem. They re-entered in 1893.

In the first round of 1893-94 Billy Beats netted a hat-trick for Burslem Port Vale but Wolves won the tie 6-4.

Wolves beat Birmingham 8 0 in 1899 1900 (Beats scoring another hat-trick). In 1928-29 Dicky Rhodes claimed four goals for Wolves against Burton Albion and Tom Galley netted two hat-tricks in 1934-35 – against Port Vale in the semi-final and Stoke in the Final.

Dennis Westcott notched five goals against Stafford Rangers in 1937-38 when Wolves went all the way to the Final against West Bromwich Albion which they won thanks to a four-timer from Billy Langley.

In season 1951-52 Wolves beat Burton Albion 7-0 and then trounced Stoke City 9-0 in the Final when Ken Whitfield scored four times.

STAFFORDSHIRE JUBILEE

On 15 November 1926, a landmark in regional football history was commemorated at Molineux when the Jubilee of the Staffordshire FA brought together two star-studded sides – a Staffs FA XI and an FA XI. A crowd of 5,848 saw the FA XI win 6-4 with two goals for Dixie Dean. Harry Shaw of Wolves played at left-back for the Staffs FA, where he was partnered by Dicky Baugh (WBA) who had left Molineux for The Hawthorns in 1924.

STANCLIFFE, Paul Ian

Born in Sheffield on 5 May 1958, central defender Paul Stancliffe had almost 20 years in League football. He signed for his first club, Rotherham United, as a junior in June 1974 and turned professional at Millmoor in March 1976. During the next seven years he appeared in well over 300 games for the Millermen before transferring to Sheffield United in August 1983. At Bramall Lane he continued to do well at senior level and added a further 337 League and Cup appearances to his tally before joining Rotherham United and Wolves (both on loan) in

September and November 1990 respectively. He then transferred to York City from Bramall Lane in July 1991 and skippered the Minstermen to promotion from Division Three in 1993. He became assistant manager/coach at Bootham Crescent on his retirement as a player in 1996 and later (in 1998) was appointed the Minstermen's youth team manager.
Wolves record: 20 apps.

STANFORD, Sidney

Wolves signed inside-forward Sid Stanford from Mossley White Star in August 1884. He spent two seasons with the club, playing in several friendly matches as well as two FA Cup matches against Derby St Luke's in November 1884. Born in Wolverhampton *c.*1860, he was not retained for the following season.
Wolves record: 2 apps.

STANLEY, John

Durable full-back Jack Stanley had Dick Betteley barring his way to the first team at Molineux, but he still managed to play in half of the games during his only season with the club. Born in Cheshire *c.*1880, he served with Crewe Alexandra before joining Wolves in August 1905 and from April 1906 to October 1909 he was with Bolton Wanderers for whom he made over 70 senior appearances. Thereafter he played for Burton United, retiring in 1912.
Wolves record: 22 apps.

STEELE, Timothy Wesley

Tim Steele was born in Coventry on 1 December 1967 and played over 60 games as a wide midfielder for Shrewsbury Town (from December 1985) before transferring to Wolves in February 1989 for a fee of £80,000. He had a couple of good seasons at Molineux, but after a loan spell with Stoke City in February/March 1992, he was allowed to leave Molineux for Bradford City on a free transfer in July 1993. Steele later assisted Hereford United from January 1994, although injuries which required surgery disrupted his performances at Edgar Street.
Wolves record: 85 apps. 10 goals.

STEEN, Alan William

On 2 October 1943, Alan Steen who had made his senior debut as a 16-year-old for Wolves during the 1938-39 season, was reported missing after a bombing raid over Germany. He was captured by the enemy and spent the remainder of the war as a PoW in Stalag IV 3. On returning to England, he went on to play on the wing for Luton Town (May 1946), Aldershot (June 1949), Rochdale (June 1950) and Carlisle United (December 1951), moving into non-League soccer in May 1952 after more than 80

League appearances in total. Born in Crewe on 26 June 1922, Steen joined Wolves from local junior football and turned professional at Molineux in the summer of 1939. He guested for New Brighton during the first part of the war.
Wolves record: 1 app. one goal.

STEVENSON, Ernest

Utility forward Ernie Stevenson was a Yorkshireman, born in Rotherham on 28 December 1923. He played for Wolves' junior team, Wath Wanderers during the early part of World War Two, signing on a full-time basis at Molineux in 1943. He made over 30 appearances during the hostilities – when he also guested for Blackpool and Tranmere Rovers – but only a handful afterwards before transferring to Cardiff City in November 1948. In March 1950 he surprisingly left Ninian Park for Southampton but failed to settle down as he had hoped at The Dell and after only 23 games for Saints (8 goals scored) he went to Leeds United in February 1951. He later switched to Wisbech Town (July 1952) where he ended his career. Stevenson died in St Helens on 15 October 1970.
Wolves record: 9 apps.

STEWART, Paul Andrew

Utility forward Paul Stewart spent a month on loan at Molineux soon after the start of the 1994-95 season (September/October). Born in Manchester on 7 October 1964, he signed for Blackpool as a junior in June 1980 and turned professional at Bloomfield Road in October 1981. Capped by England at youth team level he went on to score 62 goals in 225 games for the Seasiders before transferring to Manchester City for £200,000 in March 1987. He did well at Maine Road, adding 30 goals in 63 starts to his record up to June 1988 when he moved to London to sign for Tottenham Hotspur for £1.7 million. He stayed at White Hart Lane for four seasons during which time he netted 37 more goals in 172 outings for Spurs, helping them win both the F.A Cup and Charity Shield in 1991. In July 1992 Stewart went north to Liverpool, who paid £2.3 million for his services, hoping he would fit in alongside Ian Rush. Unfortunately he never really settled down at Anfield and during the next four years managed only 42 outings (three goals scored) for the Reds, while also having loan spells with Crystal Palace (January 1994), Wolves, Burnley (February 1995) and Sunderland (August 1995). In March 1996 Stewart signed permanently for the Roker Park club on a free transfer and quickly helped them clinch the First Division championship, having achieved a similar feat with Palace two years earlier. He moved from Sunderland to Stoke City, again on a free transfer in July 1997. Capped three times by his country at senior level, on five occasions by the 'B' team and once by the Under-21s, Stewart is perhaps only one of a handful of footballers who has played in four major local derbies – the North-East, Black Country, Merseyside and North London. In season 1998-99 he left League football to sign for Workington.

Wolves record: 7+3 apps. 2 goals.

STOBART, Barry

After making only five first-team appearances, inside-forward Barry Stobart was called into Wolves' 1960 FA Cup Final team against Blackburn Rovers as a late replacement for Bobby Mason, manager Stan Cullis having no second thoughts about playing the 21-year-old in front of 100,000 fans at Wembley. Stobart did a good job and celebrated with a winners' medal after helping his teammates beat Rovers 3-0. Born in the village of Dodsworth, near Doncaster on 6 June 1938, Stobart attended the local school and played for Wath Wanderers before joining Wolves as an amateur in 1953, turning professional in December 1955. He found it hard to get a game in the first team at Molineux with so many talented goalscorers in the squad, but he stuck in there and went on to create a record of scoring 110 goals in the Central League for Wolves in 197 appearances. He remained at Molineux until August 1964 when a £20,000 fee took him to Manchester City. Unfortunately Stobart failed to settle at Maine Road and he quickly switched to Aston Villa (for £22,000) in the November. He hit 20 goals in 53 games for the Villa who then released him to Shrewsbury Town for £10,000 in October 1967. Three years later Stobart left the League scene to join Willenhall Town. He later ran a successful grocer's shop and was team manager of Willenhall for two seasons (1979-81) and then held a similar position with Dudley Town (from 1984 to 1990).

Wolves record: 54 apps. 22 goals.

STOCKIN, Ronald

Inside-forward Ronnie Stockin was born in Birmingham on 27 June 1931. He played junior football before World War Two and local services soccer during the hostilities. In 1950 he became an amateur with West Bromwich Albion and the following year teamed up at the same level with Walsall, turning professional at Fellows Park in January 1952. The following month Wolves manager Stan Cullis recruited Stockin for £10,000 (as cover for his main goalscorers). He remained at Molineux for two and a half years before switching to Cardiff City for £12,000 in June 1954, having had six League games during Wolves' First Division championship winning campaign. He stayed at

Ninian Park for three years before moving to Grimsby Town in June 1957 for £5,000. He dropped out of big time football in July 1960 when he signed for Nuneaton Borough. It was Stockin who scored Cardiff's goal when they lost 9-1 to Wolves in a League game in 1955. Stockin now lives in West Bromwich.

Wolves record: 21 apps. 7 goals.

STOCKPORT COUNTY

Wolves' playing record against County is:

Football League

Venue	P	W	D	L	F	A
Home	16	12	3	1	32	11
Away	16	5	6	5	18	20
Total	32	16	10	6	54	31

After first meeting each other at League level in season 1906-07, the opening ten encounters were evenly balanced before Wolves won 2-1 at Stockport and 4-0 at Molineux in 1911-12. The following season County whipped Wolves 5-1 at Edgeley Park but lost the next two fixtures at Molineux.

Stockport drew 2-2 away with Wolves in a Second Division game in December 1919 at The Hawthorns following a League ban that closed Molineux for two matches. Eight days later County won 4-1 at home.

Wolves won four home games running during the 1920s including a 5-1 romp in April 1926 when Tom Phillipson netted a hat-trick.

There was a break of 60 years before the teams met again and when they did, in September 1986, Wolves won 2-0 on Stockport soil, following up with a 3-1 victory at Molineux later in the season.

Wolves were beaten 4-3 at Molineux by Stockport in a First Division game in April 1998, after being 2-1 ahead at half-time.

Players with both clubs include: Scott Barrett, Pat Bartley, Tom Bennett, Alan Birch, John Blunt, Peter Broadbent, Paul Cook, Gordon Cowans, George Farrer, Freddie Goodwin, John Griffiths, John Holsgrove, Paul Jones, Albert Lumberg, Tommy Lunn, Chris Marsden, Mick Matthews, Andy Mutch, John Paskin, Tom Pritchard, Billy Raynes, Jack Sambrook, Eddie Stuart, Bobby R.G. Thomson, Jack Turner and Len Williams.

Also associated: Andy Beattie (manager of both clubs); Fred Scotchbrook (manager of both clubs); Jimmy Melia (Wolves player, County manager); Edward Anderson (County training staff); Fred Ramscar (County amateur) and Alf Lythgoe (Wolves Reserves).

STOCKTON

Wolves record against Stockton is:

FA Cup

Venue	P	W	D	L	F	A
Away	1	1	0	0	4	1

Wolves beat the Northern-based non-League

club comfortably by 4-1 on a mud-heap in the first round of the 1903-04 FA Cup competition in front of 7,000 spectators. Jack Smith scored twice for Wolves. At the time Stockton were the Amateur Cup holders.

Players with both clubs include: John Farley and Jack Taylor.

STOKE CITY

Wolves playing record against the Potters:

Football League

Venue	P	W	D	L	F	A
Home	61	35	14	12	124	67
Away	61	19	11	31	75	105
Total	122	54	25	43	199	172

FA Cup

Venue	P	W	D	L	F	A
Home	6	6	0	0	22	3
Away	2	1	1	0	3	2
Total	8	7	1	0	25	5

Anglo-Italian Cup

Venue	P	W	D	L	F	A
Away	1	0	1	0	3	3

Wartime

Venue	P	W	D	L	F	A
Home	7	3	2	2	16	14
Away	8	1	2	5	11	24
Total	15	4	4	7	27	38

Wolves and Stoke were founder members of the Football League and they first met at this level on 17 November 1888 in the Potteries. Wolves won the contest 1-0 and then completed the double with a 4-1 home victory the following month.

There were several high-scoring games between the clubs during the late 1800s; Wolves twice winning 4-2 and registering another 4-1 success while Stoke also registered a 4-1 victory.

Arthur Capes netted a hat-trick in Stoke's 5-1 win over Wolves at the Victoria Ground in December 1903 and after spending 11 years out of the League, Stoke returned in 1919-20 only to lose 4-0 at Molineux before winning the return fixture 3-0 five days later.

Wolves' best home win over Stoke in the 1920s was a 5-1 home success in February 1926 and they started the 1930s off in a similar vein, winning by the same score at Molineux in September 1930 when Billy Hartill scored a hat-trick.

Just before World War Two Stoke defeated Wolves 4-1 and 5-3 at the Victoria Ground and immediately after the hostilities Wolves won both First Division matches in 1946-47 with 3-0 scorelines.

Wolves won 3-0 in successive home matches in 1952 and 1953 and had to wait until 1963 before winning again owing to Stoke dropping into the Second Division.

Then unknown to perhaps everyone inside the ground, Wolves kicked off at the start of each half of their home First Division game with the Potters in August 1963 before eventually taking the points with a 2-1 victory Two former Wolves players, Eddie Stuart and Eddie Clamp, returned to Molineux for this game.

Stoke's Denis Smith (5) and Wolves goalkeeper Paul Bradshaw have a few things to say to each other at the Victoria Ground in November 1979.

Wolves were 3-0 down at home to Stoke in a First Division game in November 1967. They fought back to get level, but eventually lost 4-3 in the dying seconds after a gallant fight.

An eight-goal thriller went Wolves' way by 5-3 at Molineux in September 1972 (John Richards scoring a hat-trick) and in 1979-80 Wolves completed their 13th League double over the Potters with wins of 3-0 at home and 1-0 away.

Victory at Stoke towards the end of the 1981-82 season would have preserved Wolves' First Division status. As it was they went down 2-1 and the Potters stayed up.

A crowd of just 8,679 witnessed the 0-0 draw with Stoke at Molineux in December 1983. This was the first time the crowd had dropped below 10,000 for a Wolves home League game since March 1937.

Paul Maguire scored all Stoke's goals (two of them penalties) in their crushing 4-0 home win over relegated Wolves in May 1984 – this being their best win (in terms of goal-difference) over their Staffordshire rivals for 79 years.

In October 1995, Wolves were rocked at Molineux when Stoke pulled out all the stops to win 4-1.

Wolves first met Stoke in the FA Cup in 1889-90, but after winning their third round tie 4-0 at Molineux, the Potters complained about the poor state of the pitch and a replay was ordered. This time Wolves doubled their score and raced to an emphatic

8-0 victory, Jack Brodie registering five of their goals (he had also scored once in the first game).

Wolves beat Stoke 3-0 at home on their way to reaching the 1895-96 FA Cup Final and they did likewise (1-0) en route to winning the trophy in 1908. And when they went all the way to the Final again in 1921, they defeated Stoke 3-2 at Molineux in the first round with George Edmonds scoring twice.

The last time the clubs met in the FA Cup was in 1980-81 when Wolves went through to the fourth round after a 2-1 replay win.

A healthy crowd of 9,092 witnessed Stoke's 3-3 draw with Wolves in an Anglo-Italian Cup-tie at Molineux in 1993-94.

Wolves lost 9-3 at Stoke in a wartime Football League North game in January 1944.

Players with both clubs include: Arthur Arrowsmith, Tom Baddeley, Charlie Baker, Scott Barrett, Pat Bartley, George Berry, Wilf Chadwick, Eddie Clamp, Wayne Clarke, Harry Davies, Alan Dodd, Keith Downing, James Gorman, Kevin Keen, Norman Lewis, Jim Martin, Jack Miller, Derek Parkin, Phil Robinson, Valentine Rouse, Ken Scattergood, Hans Segers, Jack Short, Brian Siddall, Sammy Smyth, Tim Steele, Paul Stewart, Bill (Ed) Stevenson, Eddie Stuart, Billy Tompkinson, Mark Walters, Bob White, Jack Whitehouse and Dennis Wilshaw.

Also associated: Brian Little (manager of both clubs); Frank Taylor (Wolves full-back, Stoke manager); Richie Barker (assistant-boss/coach at Molineux, manager of Stoke); Sammy Chung (Wolves manager, assistant-boss at Stoke); Brian Caswell (Wolves player, reserve-team coach with Stoke); Arthur Hartshorne and Frank Whitehouse (Wolves Reserves); Henry Howell (Stoke reserve and guest); Harry Watson (Wolves junior); George Swift (Stoke trialist); Eric Jones (Stoke reserve and wartime guest); John Griffiths, Jack Shelton and William Crispin Rose (all Stoke wartime guests), Griffiths and Neil Franklin (Wolves wartime guests), Billy Burns (Stoke trialist), Chris Evans (Stoke reserve, Wolves coach); Tony Lacey (Stoke player and coach, Wolves' youth recruitment officer).

STOKES, David

When he turned out in his last League game for Wolves against Sheffield Wednesday at Hillsborough in April 1921, Stokes was over 40 years of age – the oldest player ever to line-up for the club at senior level. A utility forward, born in Ketley, Staffordshire in March 1880, he played for Kingswinford Albion, Wordsley Olympic, Halesowen, Brierley Hill Alliance, and Aston Villa Reserves in the Birmingham and District League before joining Bolton Wanderers in December 1901, the Lancashire club having to pay Villa 10 guineas for his signature. A right-winger, he scored 46 goals in 420 senior games for Bolton, helping them win promotion three times (in 1905, 1909 and 1911) collecting a Second Division championship medal in 1909. He also appeared in the 1904 FA Cup Final and represented the Football League against the Irish League in Belfast. Having worked in a munitions factory during World War One, he left Burnden Park inn the summer of 1920, rejoining his old club Brierley Hill. But in an injury crisis he was signed by Wolves during their Second Division campaign of 1920-21 and deputised for both Tancy Lea and Harry Lees in the first team. He was released from Molineux in May 1921. Stokes died c.1958.

Wolves record: 7 apps.

STOUTT, Stephen P.

Steve Stoutt was a good, solid performer able to occupy a number of defensive berths and a player who was always confident in his own ability. Born in Halifax on 5 April 1964, he was one of manager Tommy Docherty's last signings for Wolves when the team was heading towards the Second Division. He had done very well in Yorkshire junior football before joining Huddersfield Town on non-contract terms in January 1984. He switched to Molineux in April 1985 and spent three years with Wolves before moving to Grimsby Town in August 1988. He later assisted Lincoln City from December 1989.

Wolves record: 114+3 apps. 5 goals.

STOWELL, Michael

Born in Preston on 19 April 1965, goalkeeper Mike Stowell played initially for Leyland Motors FC before joining Preston North End as a professional in February 1985. Over the next five years, before signing for Wolves on a permanent basis, he made only 55 senior appearances while assisting Everton – whom he joined as cover for Neville Southall in December 1985 – Chester City, York City, Manchester City, Port Vale, Wolves and Preston North End, the latter six clubs all on loan. He first appeared for Wolves in March and April 1989, making seven appearances, and was then signed on a full contract for £250,000 from Goodison Park in August 1990 and over the last nine years has given the Molineux club excellent service. Standing 6ft 2in, he has fine reflexes, good positional sense and is a fine shot-stopper. In November 1998 Stowell kept his 100th clean sheet for Wolves at Norwich and soon afterwards he set a club record for most senior appearances for Wolves by a goalkeeper – beating Bert Williams' tally of 420 when he turned out against neighbours West Bromwich Albion in a Nationwide League Division One game on 29 April 1999.

In November 1990 Stowell hired a tractor to beat severe snow drifts in the West Midlands in order to report for international duty in Algeria with the England 'B' team.

Wolves record: 424 apps.

STREETE, Floyd Anthony

Tough-tackling central defender Floyd Streete was born in Jamaica in the West Indies on 5 May 1959 and after plying his trade in the sun with Rivet Sports he entered English football with Cambridge United in July 1976. He played in 125 League games for

Floyd Streete twice helped Wolves win promotion also the Sherpa Van Trophy.

United over the next seven years before signing for the Dutch club, Utrecht, later assisting SC Cambuur. He returned to the Football League with Derby County for the 1984-85 season and was transferred to Wolves in October 1985 at a time when Molineux was a rather depressing place to be (attendances were down to around the 4,000 mark). He came through well with Wolves and went on to give the club excellent service, helping them twice win promotion (from the Fourth and Third Divisions) and also carry off the Sherpa Van Trophy at Wembley. In May 1990 after being released by Wolves Streete joined Reading, staying with the Royals for two seasons. He is now a PE teacher at a senior boys' school in Berkshire.

Wolves record: 192+2 apps. 6 goals.

STREETS, John William

Born in Nottingham in November 1893, inside-forward Jack Streets played for Long Eaton Rangers before joining Wolves in August 1913. He stayed at Molineux for just one season, transferring to Notts County in the summer of 1914 and later assisting Mansfield Town. He did not re-appear in the Football League after World War One. Streets died in Mansfield in 1949.

Wolves record: 2 apps.

STRINGER, James

Jimmy Stringer was a sound, vigilant goalkeeper whose height (6ft 1in.) and weight (13 stones) enabled him to dominate his area when high crosses came over. Born at Netherton, Dudley, in May 1878, he represented Netherton and Dudley Schools and played for Netherton Rovers before joining Wolves as a professional in August 1900. He did well in the Reserves at Molineux, but found it hard to gain a regular place in the first team. Consequently in April 1905 he was transferred to near neighbours West Bromwich Albion whom he served until October 1910, making a total of 172 senior appearances. Stringer wound down a useful career with Dudley Town (1910-12) before becoming trainer of Port Talbot. He retired out of football in 1915 and died back home in Dudley in December 1933.

Wolves record: 16 apps.

STUART, Edward Albert

South African full-back Eddie Stuart was born in Middleburg, Cape on 12 May 1931. He played intermediate football in his homeland for Rangers FC before joining Wolves as a professional in January 1951. He went on to appear in over 300 games for Wolves after surprisingly making his League debut as a centre-forward against West Bromwich Albion in April 1952, scoring a goal to celebrate the occasion. Stuart helped Wolves win the First Division championship in 1954, 1958 and 1959 and then he added an FA Cup winners' medal to his tally in 1960. In July 1962 after 11 years' excellent service, he was transferred to Stoke City for £8,000, and in his first season at the Victoria Ground skippered the Potters to the Second Division title. He netted twice in 71 games for Stoke up to August 1964 when he moved to Tranmere Rovers for £4,000. In July 1966 he signed for Stockport County and helped them win the Fourth Division crown in 1967. Retiring from competitive football in 1968 with 510 League appearances under his belt, Stuart then had an excellent two-year spell with Worcester City, making 110 appearances. Thereafter he managed the non-League club and in the late 1970s/early 1980s, while living in Tettenhall, he played in several charity matches in the Midlands as well as running a successful hairdressing business with shops in Wolverhampton, Codsall and Newcastle (Staffs).

NB – In 1952, Stuart had to return to South Africa after being infected by a 'mystery illness'. Thankfully he responded to treatment and came back to England to continue his career.

Wolves record: 322 apps. 1 goal.

SUBSTITUTES

Substitutes were first introduced into the Football League programme in England at the start of the 1965-66 season.

The first League substitute for Wolves was wing-half Freddie Goodwin, who replaced inside-forward Ernie Hunt during the home game with Middlesbrough in October 1965.

The following season Les Wilson became the club's first Cup substitute when he came on during Wolves' third-round FA Cup replay win at home to Oldham Athletic.

Wilson also had the pleasure of becoming the first Wolves' sub to score – achieving the feat after replacing Dave Wagstaffe during the away First Division game at Everton in September 1967.

Paul Walker had the honour of becoming Wolves' first sub in the League Cup, taking over from Wagstaffe in the tie at QPR in October 1969.

Les Wilson and Kenny Hibbitt were the first subs used by Wolves in European competition. They replaced Gerry Taylor and Jim McCalliog respectively in the UEFA Cup clash with Den Haag in Holland in October 1971.

John Richards had the pleasure of scoring a hat-trick for Wolves in their 3-0 FA Cup win over Charlton Athletic at Molineux in February 1976 – this after coming off the subs' bench to replace the injured Dave Wagstaffe.

Norman Bell netted twice as sub for Wolves in their 3-1 FA Cup victory over Wrexham at Molineux in February 1981.

During his entire career Steve Mardenborough was used as a substitute in more than 80 League games.

The player who made most substitute appearances for Wolves has been Robbie Dennison with 37. Steve Kindon made 36.

The versatile Jackie Gallagher had 17 appearances as a sub for Wolves in season 1987-88 (13 in the League, three in the Sherpa Van Trophy and once in the League Cup).

Steve Kindon was used as a sub. on 15 occasions by Wolves in 1972-73 (11 in Football League matches).

'Pee-wee' Paul Dougherty was a Wolves' playing sub in 11 Division Two games in 1984-85.

Norman 'Super Sub' Bell was utilised as a sub in 12 matches in 1980-81 while fellow striker John Richards came off the bench in 12 League and Cup games for Wolves in 1970-71.

The two substitute ruling was introduced in 1987-88 and three players were allowed to come off the bench in season 1995-96.

SUNDERLAND

Wolves' playing record against Sunderland is:

Football League

Venue	P	W	D	L	F	A
Home	46	23	9	14	77	64
Away	46	10	11	25	56	102
Total	92	35	21	40	133	166

FA Cup

	P	W	D	L	F	A
Home	3	2	1	0	5	2
Away	4	0	3	1	4	6
Neutral	1	0	0	1	0	4
Total	8	2	4	2	9	12

League Cup

	P	W	D	L	F	A
Home	1	0	1	0	1	1
Away	1	0	0	1	0	5
Total	2	0	1	1	1	6

Wartime

	P	W	D	L	F	A
Home	1	1	0	0	4	1
Away	1	0	1	0	2	2
Total	2	1	1	0	6	3

Wolves were the first team to win a League game at Sunderland – doing so in September 1890 by four goals to three. In fact, this was Wolves' first League encounter against the Wearsiders and 5,000 fans were present.

In contrast, Wolves' next three trips to the north east all ended in big defeats: 5-2 in September 1891 (when Jimmy Millar scored a hat-trick), 5-2 again in January 1893 (a treble here for Jimmy Hannah) and 6-0 in November 1893 (when Millar again registered three goals).

Another impressive win for Sunderland was achieved in January 1901 when Wolves crashed 7-2 – that man Millar once more weighing in with a hat-trick.

Wolves bounced back with a 4-2 home win in September 1901, but four-and-a-half years later (in March 1906) they were hammered again 7-2 at Roker Park, having beaten Sunderland 5-2 at Molineux four months earlier.

After a break of more than 25 years Wolves and Sunderland commenced their League battles in 1932-33 and the following season 13 goals were scored in the two games, Sunderland winning 6-1 at Molineux and being held 3-3 at Roker Park.

Sunderland won 6-2 at home in March 1937 (Patsy Gallacher netting a hat-trick) but Wolves gained revenge with a 4-0 victory at Molineux six months later, Dennis Westcott scoring twice for the Wanderers.

There wasn't much to choose between the teams during the late 1940s and early fifties, with each team claiming one impressive victory – Sunderland by 5-2 at Roker Park in December 1952 and Wolves by 5-0 at Molineux in August 1957.

Surprisingly there has very little to choose between the clubs over the last 40 years, although they met only once in the 1970s, in March 1970 when Sunderland won 2-1 at Roker Park.

Sunderland won the FA Cup in 1937 and in the quarter-finals they met Wolves three times, eventually going through 4-0 in a second replay at Hillsborough after draws of 1-1 at Molineux and 2-2 at Roker Park. More than 168,500 fans witnessed those three encounters with 61,796 packing Roker Park for the first replay.

After being held to a 1-1 draw by

Johnny Hancocks gets in a shot during the 2-1 win over Sunderland in September 1950.

Sunderland in a second round League Cup-tie in October 1982, the Wearsiders romped to an impressive 5-0 win at Roker Park to inflict upon Wolves their joint heaviest defeat in the competition.

Wolves won the 1942 wartime Football League North Cup by defeating Sunderland in the Final which was played over two legs in May. A crowd of 34,776 saw the teams fight out a 2-2 draw at Roker Park and there were 43,038 present at Molineux to see Wolves win the return leg 4-1 to take the trophy 6-3 on aggregate. Dennis Westcott, Frank Broome and Jack Rowley (2) scored for Wolves in the second game.

Players with both clubs include: Joe Blackett, Mike Coady, Peter Daniel, George Goddard, Don Goodman, George Harper, Danny Hegan, Rob Hindmarch, Harry Hooper, David Kelly, Dariuz Kubicki, Jack Mitton, Harry Scott, Harry Shaw, Paul Stewart and Harry Thompson.

Also associated: Billy Ellis (Wolves junior reserve, then over 200 appearances for Sunderland: 1919-27); Ken Knighton (Wolves player, Sunderland manager); George Holley (Sunderland player and coach, Wolves trainer/coach); Mick Docherty (Sunderland player and manager, Wolves coach); Chris Turner (Sunderland goalkeeper, Wolves coach), Guy Wharton (Sunderland wartime guest) and Tom Allen (Wolves Reserves).

SUNDERLAND, Alan

During his time at Molineux, the versatile Alan Sunderland donned nine different shirts for Wolves – nos. 2, 3, 4, 7, 8, 9, 10, 11 and 12. Originally billed as an out-and-out striker, he did play in a variety of positions including those of right-back, defender, midfielder (all under manager Bill McGarry), winger and target man – and he did a good job wherever he appeared. Born in Mexborough on 1 July 1953, he signed as an apprentice for Wolves in July 1969 and turned professional in June 1971. He made intermittent first-team appearances during seasons 1971-72 and 1972-73 before establishing himself in the side in 1973-74 which culminated with League Cup glory at Wembley. Six months after helping Wolves regain their First Division status – and recovering from a double fracture of the leg suffered in a training session – Sunderland was transferred to Arsenal for £240,000 in November 1977 and with the Gunners he did even better than at Molineux. He appeared in 321 senior games for the Londoners and scored 101 goals, including a last-ditch winner against Manchester United in the 1979 FA Cup Final. Sunderland left Highbury for Ipswich Town in February 1984 where he added a further 12 goals in 50 outings to his tally before going over to Ireland to serve with Derry City

(1986-87). Capped by England at senior and Under-21 levels, he accumulated a fine set of statistics in an excellent League career: 422 appearances and 96 goals.
Wolves record: 176+22 apps. 34 goals.

SWALLOW, John E.

Jack Swallow played as a reserve with Wolves in season 1895-96. A useful goalkeeper in his own right, he understudied Joe Hassall and then Billy Rose and had very few first team opportunities. Born in Wednesbury in February 1873, he was six feet tall and weighed 12 stones, and his two appearances were four weeks apart. In June 1896 following the arrival of Billy Tennant, Swallow was transferred to Darlaston. He later served with Walsall Town, Dudley Phoenix and Hill Top Victoria, retiring in 1912. He died in 1944, aged 71.
Wolves record: 2 apps.

SWANSEA CITY (TOWN)

Wolves' playing record against the Swans is:

Football League

Venue	P	W	D	L	F	A
Home	12	5	4	3	22	15
Away	12	4	4	4	18	22
Total	24	9	8	7	40	37

FA Cup

Home	1	1	0	0	5	3
Away	1	1	0	0	4	0
Total	2	2	0	0	9	3

Sherpa Van Trophy

Away	1	0	1	0	1	1

Wartime

Home	1	1	0	0	1	0
Away	1	1	0	0	5	2
Total	2	2	0	0	6	2

Wolves and Swansea first met each other at League level in 1925-26. The Welsh side won 3-2 at Molineux, Wolves having earlier took the points with a 4-3 victory at The Vetch Field.

On their next two visits to Swansea, Wolves conceded ten goals, losing 4-1 in January 1927 and 6-0 eight months later.

Wolves came back and recorded three successive home wins – 4-1, 3-1 and 2-0.

With Swansea spending most of their time in the lower divisions there were no League meetings for 49 years from 1932, but Swansea quickly made up for lost time by winning 1-0 on Wolves' soil in March 1982, following up soon afterwards with an impressive 5-1 victory at Molineux in September 1985, having gone 5-0 up after 55 minutes.

Dennis Westcott scored a hat-trick when Wolves beat Swansea 4-0 at The Vetch Field in a third-round FA Cup-tie in January 1938 and when the Welsh club were beaten 5-3 at the same stage of the competition in January 1957, Joe Bonson found the net twice in front of a near 38,400 crowd.

Just 2,886 fans saw Steve Bull score Wolves'

goal in their 1-1 draw at Swansea in the Sherpa Van Trophy game in October 1988.

Players with both clubs include: Robbie Dennison, Noel Dwyer, Evan Edwards, Chris Greene, George Henson, Emlyn Hughes, Mark Kendall, Steve Mardenborough, Frank Marson, Barry Powell, Dicky Rhodes, Val Rouse, Harry Scott, Kim Wassall and Len Williams.

Also associated: Billy Lucas (Wolves junior and reserve, later Swansea player – 208 League appearances – and Swans' manager: 1967-69), Arthur Allman, Tom Gracie Paton and Cyril Pearce (Wolves Reserves), Dave Emanuel (wartime guest), Arthur Buttery (Swansea trialist), John Harris (Wolves wartime player, Swansea defender).

SWIFT, George Harold

Full-back George Swift was born in St George's, Wellington on 3 February 1870, was educated at St George's Church of England School (Oakengates) and played for Wellington St Swifts, Wellington Town (1885), Stoke (trialist 1886), Wellington St George's and Crewe Alexandra (from 1888) before joining Wolves in August 1891. Two years later he gained an FA Cup winners medal, but in August 1894, after three excellent seasons at Molineux, he was transferred to Loughborough. In August 1896 he switched to Leicester Fosse, later assisting Notts County (from June 1902) before retiring in June 1904 to become trainer of Leeds City. (He was called out of retirement to play in one League game in March 1906). In August 1907 Swift was appointed secretary-manager of Chesterfield; between April 1911 and April 1912 he worked in the same position with Southampton (Saints' first ever manager incidentally) and thereafter lived on the Isle of Wight until his death during World War Two. Swift won Football League representative honours.
Wolves record: 66 apps. 1 goal.

SWIFT, Walter George

Born in Coseley in 1874, inside-forward Walter Swift made a scoring debut for Wolves against Grimsby Town in November 1901 – his only outing for the first team. Recruited as cover for the main three central strikers, he arrived at Molineux in the summer of 1894 and was released in May 1902 when he joined Bilston United. He made a record 84 consecutive Birmingham and District League appearances for Wolves' second team between January 1895 and December 1899. Prior to his arrival at Wolves he had played for Tipton St Phillip's and Coseley Town. Swift died in Nottingham c.1938.
Wolves record: 1 app. 1 goal.

SWINBOURNE, Royston Harry

Roy Swinbourne was a fine goalscoring centre-forward whose career came to an prema-

ture end in 1957 after a serious knee injury. A Yorkshireman, born in Denaby Main on 25 August 1929, the son of a former Aston Villa reserve defender, he joined Wolves' nursery side, Wath Wanderers as a 15-year-old in 1944 and turned professional on his 17th birthday in 1948. He made his League debut in December 1949 and scored the first of his 114 goals for Wolves in the local derby against Aston Villa that same month. He established himself in the first team in 1950-51 (netting 22 goals in 48 first-team games) and although injuries disrupted his progress the following season, he bounced back with 21 more goals in 1952-53 and then, playing in a terrific forward-line, he helped bring the League championship to Molineux in 1953-54 by netting 24 goals in 40 First Division outings. He weighed in with another 18 goals in 1954-55 and in the opening 12 League games of the 1955-56 campaign he found the net 17 times before badly injuring himself when he tried to avoid a group of cameramen who were crouched near the by-line during Wolves' away game at Luton. He came back to play in two just more matches, but never looked right and despite going through a sometimes painful and certainly strenuous fitness programme, Swinbourne was forced to quit the game in the summer of 1957, shortly before his 28th birthday. Capped by England 'B' against Germany he would surely have gained full international honours had not fate intervened when it did. Swinbourne is now living in the village of Kinver, near Kidderminster.
Wolves record: 230 apps. 114 goals.

SWINDON TOWN

Wolves' playing record against Swindon is:
Football League

Venue	P	W	D	L	F	A
Home	6	3	2	1	9	7
Away	6	1	0	5	5	10
Total	12	4	2	6	14	17

FA Cup

Home	1	1	0	0	2	0

League Cup

Home	4	4	0	0	9	4
Away	4	0	1	3	3	8
Total	6	4	1	3	12	12

It wasn't until season 1989-90 that Wolves first met Swindon in the Football League and then it was the Robins who drew first blood, winning 3-1 at the County Ground, only for Wolves to gain revenge with a 2-1 victory in the return fixture at Molineux.

Since then Swindon have had slightly the better of the exchanges, certainly at home.

The only FA Cup meeting between the clubs was in 1907-08 when Wolves won a third round tie 2-0 in front of almost 27,000 fans at Molineux.

Wolves reached the 1980 League Cup by defeating Swindon 4-3 on aggregate in the two-legged semi-final. They trailed 2-1 after the first leg at Swindon, but bounced back to take the return leg 3-1 in front of an excited Molineux crowd of 41,031. Wolves narrowly went out of the League Cup to the Robins in 1993-94 and 1996-97, losing on aggregate each time – 3-2 and 2-1 respectively.

Players with both clubs include: Jim Barron, John Chadburn, Mark Crook, Peter Eastoe, Tony Evans, Tim Flowers, Jack Hetherington, Joe Hoyhead, Ernie Hunt, Teddy Maguire, Andy Mutch, Tom Phillipson, Jim Poppitt, John Preece, Jack Smith, George Taylor, Paul Walker, Mark Walters, Frank Wildman and Bobby Woodruff.

Also associated: John Harris (Wolves wartime player, Swindon amateur), Ian Miller (Swindon player, Wolves coach); John Musgrave (Wolves trialist), Roy Bicknell, Roy Pritchard and Frank Wildman (all Swindon wartime guests), George Paterson (Wolves wartime guest), Harry Keeling, Billy Lucas, Ben Morton, John Preece and Jim Travers (all Wolves Reserves). Lucas made 74 League appearances for Swindon (1937-39).

TAGG, Ernest

Reserve outside-right Ernie Tagg made his debut for Wolves in April 1939, in front of 51,000 fans at Molineux when Aston Villa were beaten 2-1. That was his only game for the club. Born in Crewe on 15 September 1917, he had scored seven goals in 19 games for Crewe Alexandra before moving to Wolves in the summer of 1938. In May 1939 he transferred to Bournemouth and after guesting for his former club Crewe during the hostilities, after the war he went on to make 80 League appearances for the Cherries before moving to Carlisle United in November 1948. Tagg retired from first class soccer the following May and was appointed trainer of Crewe Alexandra, later taking over as manager at Gresty Road (November 1964-1971). He then held the post of club secretary (1972) before becoming caretaker-boss of the Railwaymen (December 1974-January 1975). Tagg later served on the board of directors at Gresty Road for seven years (1976-83).
Wolves record: 1 app.

TATEM, Frank Arthur

Born in West Bromwich in 1888, goalkeeper Arthur Tatem was a loser in each of his first-team outings for Wolves against Chesterfield and Leeds City in 1907-08. He joined Wolves in July 1907 from Willenhall Pickwick and left Molineux for Brierley Hill in June 1909. He later played for Stourbridge and Netherton.
Wolves record: 2 apps.

TAYLOR, Colin

Colin Taylor was a useful goalscoring inside or centre-forward, who did very well at youth and reserve team level for Wolves, but failed to establish himself in the first team, owing mainly to the fact that he had Messrs Bull and Mutch to content with.

Born in Liverpool on Christmas Day 1971, he came to Molineux on the YTS in the summer of 1987 and turned professional with Wolves in March 1990. Capped by England at Under-18 level, he went on loan to Wigan Athletic in January 1992 and was released by Wolves in June 1993, joining non-League Telford United, later assisting Runcorn.
Wolves record: 10+14 apps. 3 goals.

TAYLOR, Douglas

Centre-forward Doug Taylor was an amateur with West Bromwich Albion before turning professional with Wolves in October 1949. Born in West Bromwich on 20 April 1931, he was understudy to the likes of Jesse Pye, Roy Swinbourne, Dennis Wilshaw and Ken Whitfield (among others) during the next six years, getting very few first team opportunities. Then, in November 1955, he was transferred to Walsall for whom he scored eight goals in 38 Third Division (South) games before entering non-League football in 1957.
Wolves record: 3 apps.

TAYLOR, Frank

Full-back Frank Taylor was born in Hemsworth, Yorkshire on 30 April 1916. Educated at Barnsley Grammar School, he joined Wolves in July 1936 and spent eight years at Molineux before being forced to retire through injury in August 1944. He made over 100 appearances for Wolves (all games including wartime fixtures), his best moment coming in the 1939 FA. Cup Final when he partnered England international Bill Morris. During the hostilities Taylor also won an England cap, playing against Scotland at Hampden Park in April 1944 in front of 133,000 fans, and he guested for Aldershot, Darlington, Millwall and St Mirren. On his retirement he was taken on the coaching staff at Molineux before taking over as manager of Scarborough in June 1948. From there he became Major Frank Buckley's managerial-assistant at Hull City, briefly in mid-1950, and did a similar job at Leeds United, for two years, prior to becoming team manager of Stoke City in June 1952, a position he held for eight years until June 1960. Taylor was a track-suit manager who loved to be out on the field training with the players and he was so keen that he placed a sign in the dressing room at Stoke which read 'Are you 90 minutes fit? It's the last 20 minutes that count – train for it.' Taylor's brother, Jack, played with him at Molineux. Frank Taylor died at Chapeltown, Sheffield on 10 January 1970.
Wolves record: 57 apps.

TAYLOR, Gerald W.

Gerry Taylor was a neat and tidy defender, able to play at full-back (his best position) or as a centre-half. He had a good career at Molineux where, for the first eight years of his professional career, he acted, in the main, as reserve to first Joe Wilson and Bobby Thomson and then Derek Parkin and Bernard Shaw before finally gaining a regular place in the League side in 1972. A dedicated club man, Taylor, who made 210 reserve team appearances for Wolves, helped the senior side gain promotion to the First Division in 1967, win the Texaco Cup in 1971 and reach the UEFA Cup Final 12 months later. Following a loan spell with Swindon Town (October 1975) he retired from the professional game in 1976 and joined the Staffordshire Constabulary, playing for the Cannock Police team. He progressed to the rank of sergeant and was later based at Wombourne and Kinver.
Wolves record: 187+5 apps. 1 goal.

TAYLOR, Graham

Graham Taylor was team manager at Molineux from 29 March 1994 until 12 November 1995, during which time he took Wolves into the First Division promotion Play-offs where they lost to Bolton Wanderers. As a defender, full-back Taylor served as a professional with Grimsby Town from July 1962 until July 1968 when he moved to Lincoln City, staying at Sincil Bank until the summer of 1972 when he retired to become Imps' team manager a position he held for five years, leading the team to the Fourth Division championship in 1976. He appeared in 189 League games for the Mariners and 152 for Lincoln. From Sincil Bank he switched to Vicarage Road to become team boss of Watford under the club's owner Elton John (having rejected an offer from West Bromwich Albion) and whilst at Vicarage Road he did a superb job, guiding the Hornets into Europe and the 1984 FA Cup Final, having earlier seen the team rise from the Fourth to the First Division in double-quick time, taking Fourth Division title in 1979 and finishing runners-up in the Football League in 1983. After leaving Watford in 1987 Taylor took charge of Aston Villa, and after winning promotion to the top flight he took them to League runners-up in 1989-90. That year he was appointed England manager but after subsequent World Cup failure in the finals – and much personal abuse from sections of the media – he lost the job. After a short spell out of the game he was brought back into League football by Wolves, who appointed him manager in late March 1994. Taylor failed to bring eagerly awaited Premiership football to Molineux and was subsequently dismissed after less than 18 months in office. Soon

Graham Taylor can count Wolves and England among his managerial jobs. He took Wolves to the First Division Play-offs, and then guided Watford into the Premiership.

afterwards he returned to his former club Watford, as general manager and guided them to promotion from Division Two. In November 1998 Taylor was rushed to hospital with a throat infection. He made a full recovery as the Hornets' bid for promotion to the Premiership fizzled out after Easter. A year later, however, he led unfancied Watford into the Premiership via the Play-offs.
Wolves won 38 and drew 28 of the 92 competitive games played during Taylor's reign at Molineux.

TAYLOR, Jack, OBE

Wolverhampton-born Taylor refereed the 1974 World Cup Final between West Germany and Holland in the Olympic Stadium, Munich – and awarded the Dutch a first minute penalty from which Johan Neeskins scored. After retiring as a League official he became the first officially appointed commercial manager at Molineux, a position he held from 1978 to 1982.

In February 1999, Taylor had bestowed upon him at a ceremony in Barcelona, a place in the FIFA Hall of Champions.

Jack Taylor was granted a testimonial match in season 1977-78. It was staged at Villa Park between a Midlands XI and an England XI. John Richards (Wolves) scored twice for the Midlanders, who won 2-1.

TAYLOR, John

Born in Barnsley on 15 February 1914 and brother of Frank, defender Jack Taylor left Barnsley Grammar School and played briefly for Wordsborough Bridge FC (Barnsley) and joined the groundstaff at Molineux in June 1931, turning professional in January 1934. In five League games during the 1936-37

campaign he played alongside his brother and the following season he was a key member of the team before being sold to Norwich City for £4,500 in June 1938. During the war Taylor guested for Barnsley and Watford and after the hostilities went to Hull City (1947), leading the Tigers to the Third Division North title in 1949. In May 1950 he was appointed player-manager of the Southern League side Weymouth, later taking over as team boss of Queen's Park Rangers (from June 1952) before moving in as team boss of Leeds United (from May 1959 to March 1961). Taylor, who was fine tennis player, died in Barnsley on 22 February 1978.
Wolves record: 89 apps.

TAYLOR, John E.

Centre-forward Jack Taylor started his career with Stockton before entering League football as a professional with Luton Town in February 1949. He netted 29 goals in 85 League games for the Hatters, gained an England 'B' cap and left Kenilworth Road for Wolves in May 1952. He remained at Molineux until February 1954, deputising in the main for Dennis Wilshaw. Taylor wanted regular first-team football though, and he subsequently left for Notts County, for whom he struck 19 goals in 53 League outings before rounding off his senior career with Bradford Park Avenue (July 1957 to May 1958).
Wolves record: 10 apps. 1 goal.

TEASDALE, John S.

A Scotsman, born in Glasgow on 15 October 1962, left-winger John Teasdale joined Wolves from Nairn County in December 1980, as understudy to Mel Eves. He didn't

get too many opportunities in the first team at Molineux and in March 1982 was transferred to Walsall, where he stayed for ten months before joining Hereford United as a non-contract player in January 1983. He later assisted Blackpool in the same capacity during November/December 1984.
Wolves record: 6+2 apps.

TENNANT, William
Goalkeeper Billy Tennant was a hefty fellow, weighing over 14 stones, who cost Wolves a mere £30 when signed from Hartshill Unity in January 1896. With a heavy moustache and often seen wearing a neck-tie, he replaced Billy Rose between the posts at Molineux and did an excellent job before surprisingly leaving the club for Walsall for £75 in the summer of 1897, a year after playing in the FA Cup Final against Sheffield Wednesday. Born in Wolverhampton in July 1865, Tennant played initially for Willenhall Pickwick (1881-85) having earlier tried his luck at rugby with Moseley where it is reported that he was on the verge of representative honours. After his days with Walsall he switched to Grimsby Town (May 1901), but made only 13 appearances for the Mariners before retiring to become second team manager at Blundell Park (September 1903, occasionally taking over the first team). He quit football soon after the war and went into the fish business in Hull. He did in that city on 6 December 1927, aged 62.
Wolves record: 45 apps.

TETHER, Colin
Full-back Colin Tether never got a real chance at Molineux owing to depth of talent at the club during his brief spell there. Born in Halesowen on 11 August 1938, he joined the Wolves groundstaff in 1954 and turned professional in August 1955. Five years later, after having represented England at youth team level, and seemingly confined to reserve team football at Molineux, he was transferred to Oxford United where he stayed until May 1962, making 32 appearances in the Southern League.
Wolves record: 1 app.

TEXACO CUP
Wolves entered this short-lived competition (also known as the British Isles Cup) on two occasions – in 1970-71 and again in 1972-73. They won the trophy in that initial season, defeating Heart of Midlothian 3-2 in the two-legged Final, having earlier ousted Dundee (2-1 over two legs), Greencock Morton (3-2) and the Irish club Derry City (5-0, including a home leg triumph of 4-0 which saw a rare goal from Derek Parkin).

After a 3-1 success at Tynecastle in the first game when the crowd topped 26,000, Wolves relaxed at Molineux and were lucky to hold on for a 3-2 aggregate victory.

Missing out in 1971-72, Wolves took part in the tournament again the following season, but this time fell at the second hurdle, losing 3-1 over two legs to Ipswich Town having earlier accounted for Kilmarnock (0-0 away, 5-1 at home). John Richards and Derek Dougan both scored twice in that big win at Molineux.

Wolves' full Texaco Cup record:

P	W	D	L	F	A
12	6	2	4	20	9

Bobby Gould top-scored with five of the 20 Texaco Cup goals netted by Wolves. Hugh Curran claimed four and John Richards three.

THOMAS, Archibald Albert
An early 1920s player with Wolves, Archie Thomas was born in Birmingham *c.*1900. He was a reserve at Molineux from July 1920 to May 1922, making almost a dozen senior appearances. He played for Hall Green before joining Wolves and on leaving the club he assisted Stourbridge and later Cradley St Luke's.
Wolves record: 11 apps.

THOMAS, David W.
An England international left-winger, who won eight full and 11 Under-23 caps, as well as representing his country at youth team level, Dave Thomas had a fine career, which spanned 15 years. Born in Kirkby-in-Ashfield on 5 October 1950, he joined Burnley as a junior in 1966 and turned professional at Turf Moor in October 1967. He went on to score 19 goals in 157 League games for the Clarets before transferring to Queen's Park Rangers in October 1972 for a record fee of £165,000. After notching a further 29 goals in 182 First and Second Division games for the London club, he switched to Everton in August 1977 and was given over 75 first-team outings by the Merseysiders before moving to Wolves in October 1979. He never settled down at Molineux and after less than eight month he went over to play for Vancouver Whitecaps in the NASL. In March 1982 he returned to England to sign for Middlesbrough and eventually rounded off his senior career with a spell at Portsmouth (July 1982 to May 1985).
Wolves record: 16 apps.

THOMAS, Geoffrey Robert
Geoff Thomas was born in Manchester on 5 August 1964, and played his early football with Littleborough FC before entering the League scene with Rochdale in August 1982. A powerful midfielder, over six feet tall and weighing more than 13 stones, and a player who loves to drive forward, Thomas moved from Spotland to Crewe Alexandra in March 1984, and it was here, at Gresty Road, under the shrewd guidance of manager Dario Gradi, where his career took off. He played in almost 140 games for the Alex who then sold him to Crystal Palace for a bargain fee of £50,000 in June 1987. Over the next eight years Thomas developed into an international footballer, winning nine full and three 'B' caps for England, as well as appearing in some 250 matches for the Eagles, helping them win the Full Members Cup in 1991 and reach the 1990 FA Cup Final (v Manchester United). Wolves, requiring a grafter in the centre of the park, secured his services for £800,000 in June 1993. In first season at Molineux he scored four goals in his first eight games but then missed the rest of the campaign through injury. He struggled desperately to get fit again and made only two substitute appearances in 1995-96 before undergoing surgery on his right knee which eventually resulted in him having his cruciate ligament removed. He came back briefly in 1996-97 but at the end of that campaign went on a free transferred to Nottingham Forest. Sadly, after one reasonable campaign at the City Ground when Forest won promotion, injuries again ruined Thomas's game as Forest battled to stay in the Premiership.
Wolves record: 44+9 apps. 8 goals.

THOMPSON, Andrew Richard
Andy Thompson was born at Featherstone, near Cannock, on 9 November 1967. And after playing junior football for Featherstone Primary School, Wednesfield Social U/16s, Featherstone Boys (under mentor George Hewitt) and Cresswell Wanderers, he became an apprentice with West Bromwich Albion (after being recommended to the club by scout Sid Day), turning professional at The Hawthorns in November 1985. A midfielder, with grim determination despite being on the small side at 5ft 4ins.'Thommo' was given limited first-team football by Albion and in November 1986, along with Steve Bull, was transferred to Wolves, his fee going down as £35,000. Over the next 11 years, Thompson became Wolves' penalty expert (he equalled the club record of nine successes from the spot in 1994-95) and was one of the most versatile players at Molineux, playing in five different positions for the Wanderers. He produced some outstanding performances when helping Wolves climb up from the Fourth to the Second Division in rapid time and he also gained a Sherpa Van Trophy winners medal at Wembley in 1988. After a well deserved testimonial (v Chelsea in July 1996) he was released by manager Mark McGhee 12 months later and joined forces with Tranmere Rovers where he played as an orthodox left-back.

During his time with Wolves 'Thommo' wore every outfield jersey at first team level and he even went in goal during a friendly match against Worcestershire CCC soccer XI at Molineux.

Wolves record: 431+20 apps. 43 goals.

THOMPSON, David S.

Born near the racecourse at Catterick Camp on 12 March 1945, Dave Thompson was a useful outside-right, fast and alert, who signed for Wolves as a junior before turning professional at Molineux in April 1962. His first-team outings were restricted and in August 1966 he was transferred to Southampton where he remained for more than four years prior to joining Mansfield Town in October 1970. He did exceedingly well with the Stags and scored 24 goals in 131 League games whilst at Field Mill, moving to Chesterfield in December 1973. He dropped out of League soccer in the summer of 1974.

Wolves record: 10 apps. 1 goal.

THOMPSON, Harold

Inside-left Harry Thompson was a player with Wolves from May 1935 to November 1938 when he moved to Sunderland. Born in Mansfield on 29 April 1915, he played for Mansfield Invicta and Mansfield Town Reserves before coming to Molineux. A brief spell with York City (1939) followed his time at Roker Park and between 1946 and 1949 he made 38 League appearances for Northampton Town before joining Headington United (now Oxford United) as their player-manager, some 13 years before the Us entered the Football League.

Wolves record: 73 apps. 17 goals.

THOMSON, Robert Anthony

Born in Smethwick on 5 December 1943, Bobby Thomson emerged as a classy right-back, who went on to play for his country at both Under-23 and senior levels, winning eight full caps. He joined Wolves as a youngster in June 1959 on leaving Lyndon High School and turned professional at Molineux in July 1961. He made his first team debut in an FA. Cup-tie against West Bromwich Albion the following January and thereafter gave the Wanderers excellent service, right up until March 1969 when he moved to Birmingham City for £40,000. In July 1972, he switched to Luton Town, played next for Hartford U.S. Bi-Centennials in the NASL (April 1976); assisted Port Vale (from October 1976 to April 1977) and then, after another spell in America as player-coach of the Connecticut Bi-Centennials (formerly Hartford), he returned to England to play for Worcester City, soon becoming player-manager of Stafford Rangers (August 1979-1981). After that he served with Memphis Rogues (NASL), Brewood, Solihull Borough, Tipton

Town, and for some years ran a sports shop in Sedgley, near Wolverhampton. During the 1980s Thomson played in several Charity matches around the Midlands area.

Wolves record: 299+1 sub. 3 goals.

THOMSON, Robert George

Scottish inside-forward Bobby Thomson had a splendid career after leaving Molineux in June 1959. Born in Dundee on 21 May 1937, he represented Dundee and Dunblane Schools and was an amateur with Albion Rovers and Airdrieonians (August 1952) before joining Wolves as a junior in 1953, turning professional in August 1954. Although he scored in his only senior game – a 2-0 home win over Newcastle in April 1957 – he was unable to gain regular first-team football and left Wanderers for Aston Villa five years later in an £8,000 deal. At last his career took off. He went on to score 70 goals in 171 appearances in four seasons with Villa, helping them win the Second Division championship (1960) and the League Cup (1961) as well as gaining a runners-up medal in the latter competition against his future club in 1963. Thomson left Villa to sign for their arch rivals Birmingham City in September 1963. He stayed at St Andrew's for a further four years, hitting 25 goals in 129 games before rounding off his League duties by having six months with Stockport County (December 1967 to May 1968). He then had a spell with Bromsgrove Rovers (to 1970) and thereafter kept himself supremely fit by playing squash and tennis on a regular basis.

Wolves record: 1 app. 1 goal.

THOMSON, Samuel

Wolves recruited Scotsman Sammy Thomson from Preston North End in the summer of 1890 after he had scored 124 goals in 34 League games for the Deepdale club, whom he helped complete the double in 1888-89, playing against Wolves in that season's FA Cup Final. A dashing, all-purpose forward, able to adapt, he was born in Lugar on 14 February 1862, he joined Preston from Glasgow Rangers in the summer of 1888. From Wolves he moved to Everton and from Goodison Park he went to Accrington, retiring to live and work in Preston, the town where he died on 23 December 1943, aged 81.

Wolves record: 24 apps. 9 goals.

THORPE, Albert Edward

Albert Thorpe played for Wolves in season 1928-29, replacing Bill Brown in the away game at Nottingham Forest in December – his only first team outing for the club. Born in Pilsley on 14 July 1910, Thorpe played for Shirebrook FC and represented East Derbyshire schools in 1924 before joining the Molineux camp in May 1928. On leaving

Wolves in the summer of 1929 he signed for Mansfield Town, later serving with Notts County, Norwich City (61 League appearances between 1932-35,helping them canaries win promotion from Division Three South in 1933-34), Crystal Palace, Scunthorpe United and Hereford United, retiring in 1939. Thorpe died in Langwith on 3 January 1971.

Wolves record: 1 app.

TIMMINS, Beniah

Ben Timmins was an early 1920s star with Walsall for whom he played over 100 League games before being transferred to Wolves (with Bowen) in March 1924 for a combined fee of £130. Timmins could occupy either full-back spot and was always willing to occupy a more central position if required. Born in Great Barr, Birmingham in August 1898, he attended Christ Church School and played for Beeches Road Methodists and Dartmouth Victoria before signing for Walsall in 1920. He was unfortunately badly injured in 1926 and as a result decided to retire to go and work in a factory. Timmins died in Birmingham, on 13 August 1965.

Wolves record: 11 apps.

TODD, Kenneth

Born in Butterknowle on 24 August 1957, busy midfielder Todd joined Wolves as a junior in 1974 and turned professional in August 1975. Given very little opportunity at Molineux, he was eventually bought by Port Vale in August 1978 for a record fee of £37,000. After 45 League and Cup games (9 goals) for the Valiants, he rounded off his League career with a spell at Portsmouth, moving south for £20,000 in October 1979, staying at Fratton Park until to May 1980, when he switched to Fareham Town. He later assisted Waterlooville prior to making a return to Pompey as youth team manager in 1985.

Wolves record: 4+1 sub. app. 1 goal

TOMKYES, Thomas

Tommy Tomkyes was with Wolves for two seasons, from August 1887 to May 1889. He made only one League appearance, at Notts County in January 1889, replacing Jack Brodie at centre-forward. Born in Heath Town Wolverhampton c.1867, he joined Wolves from Stafford Road, returning there after leaving the Wanderers.

Wolves record: 1 app.

TONKS, John

Dashing outside-right Jack Tonks (sometimes referred to as Joe) was a useful goalscorer in his time. As keen as mustard, tricky with a good shot, he played for Walsall Unity before joining Wolves in July 1894 and left Molineux for Walsall in June 1900. Born in Wednesfield in 1872, Tonks went into the building trade after retiring in 1904. He was given a benefit match by Wolves in 1899. He died in 1948.

Wolves' record 119 apps. 23 goals.

TOOTILL, Alfred

Towards the end of the 1928-29 season Wolves introduced a promising new goalkeeper by the name of Alf Tootill, who made his senior debut against Notts County at Molineux on 2 April, helping his side win 3-1. That was the start of a fine career for Tootill, who was born in Ramsbottom, Yorkshire on 12 November 1908. Nicknamed the 'Birdcatcher', he was small, acrobatic with great ability and a safe pair of hands, who in later years was described as 'brainy with a fine eye.' He starred for Ramsbottom United in the Bury and District Amateur League for two years before signing as a full-time professional for Accrington Stanley in September 1927. After playing in the Third Division North for 18 months he was transferred to Wolves for £400 in March 1929 and quickly made an impression at Molineux. He was first choice 'keeper from 1929 to November 1932, helping Wolves win the Second Division title in 1932. Then, after conceding seven goals against Arsenal, he was sold to Fulham by Major Frank Buckley for £1,000, Tootill actually signing the appropriate forms after being called out of a cinema. He did as well at Craven Cottage as he'd done at Molineux, and after 214 appearances for Fulham he moved to Crystal Palace in May 1938, staying at Selhurst Park until after the war. In his professional career Tootill appeared in well over 400 senior games, 372 in the Football League and during the war he turned out for Palace more than 150 times in regional competitions. Outside football Tootill enjoyed a game of cricket, turning out regularly for Ramsbottom in the Lancashire League. He died in London on 31 August 1975, aged 66.

Wolves record: 143 apps.

TOPHAM, Robert

Utility forward 'Dick' Topham was born in Ellesmere Port on 3 November 1867 and remained an amateur throughout his career. A speedy player, difficult to contain, he played his early football at Oswestry school and whilst attending Keble College Oxford, he assisted Oxford University and Oswestry FC, being selected by Wales against Scotland in 1885, but declined his first cap. Afterwards he starred for the Casuals (London), Chiswick Park FC and the Corinthians (1894-98), being registered to play for Wolves between 1891 and 1896. A schoolmaster at Brighton College from 1892 to 1905, Topham gained an FA Cup winners medal in 1893, having earlier collected a Welsh Cup runners-up prize with Oswestry in 1885. He

later received a second runners-up medal with Casuals in the FA. Amateur Cup of 1894. Topham appeared in several amateur internationals for England and won two full caps against Ireland in February 1893 and Wales in March 1894. His best season at Molineux was in 1891-92 when he netted 12 goals in 13 games. After retiring from football and in his spare time, Topham became a highly respected hop grower in Kent. He died on 31 August 1951.

Wolves record: 32 apps. 19 goals.

TORQUAY UNITED

Wolves' playing record against United is:

Football League

Venue	P	W	D	L	F	A
Home	2	1	0	1	2	2
Away	2	1	1	0	2	1
Total	4	2	1	1	4	3

Freight Rover Trophy

	P	W	D	L	F	A
Home	1	0	1	0	1	1

Sherpa Van Trophy

	P	W	D	L	F	A
Home	2	1	0	1	1	2
Away	1	1	0	0	2	1
Total	3	2	0	1	3	3

The four League games between Wolves and the Gulls were all in Division Four in the late 1980s. Wolves completed the double in season 1986-87, winning 1-0 at home and 2-1 at Plainmoor – their first ever visit to the seaside club's ground.

When Wolves were held to a 1-1 draw by United at Molineux in the 1985-86 Freight Rover Trophy the attendance of just 1,618 was one of the lowest on record for any Wolves home game at competitive level.

It was Steve Bull's goal which gave Wolves a 1-0 win over United in the Sherpa Van Trophy game at Molineux in March 1988 – a result which took the Wanderers into the

Area Final before they embarked on the trip to Wembley to play (and beat) Burnley.

As holders of the SVT. In fact, Wolves were close to going to Wembley again in 1988-89, but Torquay denied them a place in the Final after beating them 3-2 on aggregate in the Area semi-final, winning 2-0 at Molineux after losing their home game 2-1.

Players with both clubs include: Ted Anderson, Bill Coley, Keith Curle, Paul Dougherty, Dean Edwards, Jackie Gallagher, Francis Hemingway, Micky Holmes, Sammy Holt, Tony Lange and Jason Roberts.

Also associated: Colin Lee (United player, later Wolves manager), Garry Pendrey (United player, Wolves coach); Tom Bond, Cliff Johnson, Harry Keeling, Ron Morton, Sid Protheroe, Arthur Wilson and Francis Wragge (all Wolves Reserves); Andy Gurney (United player, Wolves trialist).

TOTTENHAM HOTSPUR

Wolves' playing record against Spurs is:

Football League

Venue	P	W	D	L	F	A
Home	37	20	7	10	76	52
Away	37	4	7	26	49	94
Total	74	24	14	36	125	146

FA Cup

	P	W	D	L	F	A
Home	1	0	0	1	0	2
Away	2	0	1	1	1	3
Neutral	3	0	1	2	3	6
Total	6	0	2	4	4	11

League Cup

	P	W	D	L	F	A
Home	2	1	0	1	2	2
Away	1	0	1	0	2	2
Total	3	1	1	1	4	4

UEFA Cup

	P	W	D	L	F	A
Home	1	0	0	1	1	2
Away	1	0	1	0	1	1
Total	2	0	1	1	2	3

Jesse Pye heads a goal against Spurs at White Hart Lane in November 1951.

Wartime

Home	1	1	0	0	4	2
Away	1	1	0	0	4	1
Total	2	2	0	0	8	3

Wolves were the first team ever to play a Football League game at White Hart Lane, losing 3-0 there on the opening day (1 September) of the 1908-09 season – the London club's first in the competition. The return game at Molineux that term ended in a 1-0 win for Wolves.

In season 1919-20 Spurs completed their first of eight doubles over Wolves, winning 3-1 at Molineux and 4-2 in London.

The 12 League games between the clubs over the seven-year period: 1928-35, produced 52 goals, Wolves winning all their six home games and losing five out of six on Spurs' soil.

Wolves' best win in that sequence was by 6-2 in January 1935 when Billy Hartill scored a hat-trick in front of 28,189 spectators.

In the 1950s/early 1960s Wolves and Spurs were two of the finest teams in the country and between them they lifted the Football League championship no fewer than five times and the FA Cup on three occasions. There were some cracking matches both at Molineux and White Hart Lane, with both teams being practically unbeaten in front of their own supporters.

In fact, Spurs won only three times in 15 visits to Wolves' territory between 1950 and 1964 while Wolves hated White Hart Lane, just two successes in their 15 attempts.

Wolves secured their first and so far only double over Spurs in 1953-54.

Bobby Smith scored four times in Spurs' 5-1 home win over Wolves in October 1959 and 12 months later the Londoners whipped the Wanderers 4-0 at Molineux, on their way to the League and Cup double.

The first League game to be played under the Molineux floodlights was that between Wolves and Spurs in April 1956. A crowd of 29,890 saw Wolves win 5-1 with Bill Slater scoring with two penalties.

Bill Slater had to retake two penalties in Wolves' game at Tottenham in September 1958. He failed to score from the spot, but Eddie Clamp did as Spurs won 2-1.

An 11-goal thriller at White Hart Lane in March 1965 was watched by a crowd of less than 26,000. Those present saw Spurs lead 3-1, 4-2, 5-3 and 5-4 before two late penalties ended Wolves' gallant challenge to give the London club a splendid 7-4 victory.

Paul Bradshaw saved two penalties to no avail when Wolves lost a League game 1-0 at Tottenham in November 1978.

When Spurs overwhelmed Wolves to the tune of 6-1 at White Hart Lane in February 1982, their Argentinian World Cup star Ricky Villa scored a hat-trick in front of a near 30,000 crowd.

The last time Wolves and Spurs met at League level was in March 1984 when Micky Hazard's goal gave the Londoners a 1-0 home win before a disappointing crowd of 19,296.

Wolves first met Spurs in the FA. Cup Final in April 1921, when the Londoners won 1-0 at a rain-swept Stamford Bridge, Jimmy Dimmock scoring the all-important goal in front of 72,805 spectators.

Exactly 60 years later, in April 1981, Wolves and Spurs were again paired together in the FA. Cup semi-final and it was the London side who once more took the honours, winning 3-0 in the Highbury replay after a 2-2 draw at Hillsborough, where Kenny Hibbitt netted a late penalty for Wolves in front of a 50,174 crowd.

In season 1994-95 Wolves were knocked out of the FA. Cup by Spurs in the fourth round. After a 1-1 draw at White Hart Lane, Wolves went down 2-0 at Molineux in the replay before a 27,846 crowd, which paid record attendance receipts at the time.

A goal by Jim McCalliog gave Wolves a 1-0 League Cup win over Spurs at Molineux in September 1969.

Three seasons later a place at Wembley was the reward when the two teams met in the League Cup semi-final of 1973. After a 2-1 win at Molineux, Spurs, always the favourites, duly won through to Wembley with a 4-3 on aggregate victory after holding out for a 2-2 draw against a plucky Wolves side in the return leg.

In between times, despite a fine away performance, Wolves were beaten 3-2 on aggregate by Tottenham Hotspur in the 1972 UEFA Cup Final. This was, in fact, the first major European club Final to feature two British clubs and it was also Wolves' first European Final.

Players with both clubs include: David Black, Sammy Brooks, Henry Hargreaves, Bob Iverson, Mark Kendall, Tommy Lunn, Billy Marshall, Vinny Samways, Steve Sedgley, Gordon Smith, Cyril Spiers, Paul Stewart and Andy Turner.

Also associated: Colin Lee (Spurs player, Wolves assistant manager, then manager); Jack Rowley (Wolves reserve and wartime guest, Spurs guest), Shane Westley (Spurs apprentice), Andy King (Spurs trailist), Eric Jones (Wolves player, Spurs wartime guest), John Harris (Wolves wartime player, Spurs defender).

TOWNER, Anthony J.

Wide-midfielder Tony Towner was born in Brighton on 2 May 1955. Between January 1973 and October 1978, he played 162 League games for his home town club, Brighton and Hove Albion before transferring to Millwall. In August 1980 (after 68 outings for the Lions) he moved to Rotherham United for whom he starred in more than 100 senior matches. A loan spell with Sheffield United (March 1983) preceded his departure from Millmoor to Molineux in August 1983. With Wolves he did reasonably well but with a struggling side he never really enjoyed his football and in September 1984 was sold to Charlton Athletic, later assisting both Rochdale (November 1985) and Cambridge United (March/May 1986) as a non-contract player. Towner then quit League football that summer, having amassed a useful record in the competition of 419 appearances and 54 goals.

Wolves record: 29+6 apps. 2 goals.

TRANMERE ROVERS

Wolves' playing record against Rovers is:

Football League

Venue	P	W	D	L	F	A
Home	9	7	1	1	18	8
Away	9	2	4	3	10	14
Total	18	9	5	4	28	22

FA Cup

	P	W	D	L	F	A
Away	1	1	0	0	1	0

League Cup

	P	W	D	L	F	A
Home	1	1	0	0	2	1
Away	1	0	1	0	1	1
Total	2	1	1	0	3	2

Anglo-Italian Cup

	P	W	D	L	F	A
Away	1	0	0	1	1	2

Wartime

	P	W	D	L	F	A
Away	1	0	0	1	1	3

Wolves won the Third Division North championship in 1923-24 thanks to three precious points they took off Rovers whom they met twice during the eight days of the season. Wolves won 3-0 at Molineux on 26 April and then drew 0-0 in Birkenhead on 3 May to take the title by just a single point (63-62) from Rochdale.

It was then more than 60 years before the teams met again in the League, Wolves doubling up in 1986-87 with a 2-1 home win and a 1-0 victory at Prenton Park.

It was a 3-0 home win for each club the following season and a seven-goal thriller at Tranmere in February 1992 went in favour of Rovers by 4-3, former Molineux winger John Morrissey scoring twice, including the winner in the 90th minute.

Steve Bull netted his 250th goal of his career against Tranmere Rovers (away) in May 1995 and it earned Wolves a point to ensure them a place in the Play-offs.

And Bully's 300th senior goal also came against Tranmere, in a League game in March 1997 when Wolves won 3-2.

Under 11,000 fans saw Wolves beat Tranmere 1-0 thanks to a Kenny Hibbitt goal in a third-round FA Cup-tie at Prenton Park in January 1983.

During the time of the electricity strike and three-day working week, Wolves and Tranmere met in a third round League Cup-tie in October/November 1973 and after a 1-1 draw at Prenton Park, the midweek afternoon replay went Wolves' way by 2-1 with goals by Derek Dougan and Barry Powell.

Only 3,361 spectators saw Tranmere's 2-1 Anglo-Italian Cup win over Wolves in season 1992-93.

Players with both clubs include: Ted Anderson, Paul Cook, Billy Crew, Jack Curnow, Mick Hollifield, David Kelly, Rob Kelly, Norman Lewis, Johnny Morrissey, Derek Mountfield, Eric Nixon, John O'Connor, Nicky Sinclair, Reg Smith, Eddie Stuart, Andy Thompson, Tom 'Pongo' Waring and Bob White.

Also associated: George Bellis, Bill,Coley and Ernie Stevenson (all Rovers wartime guests) and Ted Buckley and Frank Perfect (both Wolves Reserves).

TRANSFERS

Record transfers received:

Steve Froggatt – Wolves to Coventry City for £1.9 million – September 1998

Steve Daley – Wolves to Manchester City for £1,437,500 – September 1979

Alan Sunderland – Wolves to Arsenal for £240,000 – November 1977

Alun Evans – Wolves to Liverpool for £100,000 – June 1968

Record transfers paid:

Dean Richards – Bradford City to Wolves for £1,800,000 – May 1994

Tony Daley – Aston Villa to Wolves for £1,250,000 – June 1994

Andy Gray – Aston Villa to Wolves for £1,150,000 – September 1979

Peter Daniel – Hull City to Wolves for £185,000 – March 1978

Transfer Talk

The first official transfer during World War Two saw Bob King sold to Wolves from Northampton Town for £2,000 in November 1939.

Dean Richards' initial final transfer fee was £1,300,000 – rising to £1,800,000, with the last payment being made by Wolves in November 1998.

TRIP

The longest journey a Wolves team has made to play a game of football was when they travelled to New Zealand in June 1972. They had two games Down Under, beating a Wellington Invitation XI 6-0 and a South Island XI 2-0.

TROUGHTON, Samuel E.

Inside-forward Sammy Troughton was born in Lisburn, Northern Ireland on 27 March 1964 and joined Wolves from Glentoran in December 1983. Capped by his country at both Schoolboy and Youth team levels, he stayed at Molineux until May 1984 when he returned to his homeland because Wolves refused to pay £5,000 to his former club

Glentoran after Troughton had made a certain number of appearances (20).
Wolves record: 20 apps. 2 goals.

TUFT, Walter ELI

Wally Tuft was a sold player, a reserve to full-back George Eccles. Born in Wolverhampton in 1875, he played for Tettenhall St Peter's before having half a season at Molineux (September 1897 to January 1898). He then joined Darlaston and later assisted Castle Hill Rovers (Dudley).
Wolves record: 8 apps.

TURNER, Graham J.

Graham Turner was Wolves' manager from October 1986 to mid November 1995, having collected his last Manager of the Month award in September 1994. During that nine-year spell in the Molineux job, Turner, without doubt, did a terrific job in guiding the club up from the depths of the Fourth Division and taking them to Wembley, as well as making some excellent signings, among them a certain Steve Bull.

Born in Ellesmere Port, Cheshire on 5 October 1947, Turner was a defender, who played as a professional for Wrexham from July 1965 to January 1968, winning an England youth cap during his time at the Racecourse Ground. He went on to appear in more than 250 games for Chester before transferring to Shrewsbury Town in January 1973. He then remained at Gay Meadow for 13 years, until July 1984, when he became manager of Aston Villa. During his last season with the Shrews he acted as player-manager and all told chalked up in excess of 400 first-team appearances for the Shropshire club (355 in the Football League). He struggled to come to terms with the situation at Villa Park and left to take charge of Wolves just three months into the 1986-87 season. He quickly snapped up Messrs Bull and Andy Thompson from neighbouring West Bromwich Albion and slowly built a squad which proved good

enough to win promotion from the Fourth and then Third Divisions in successive seasons, as well as capturing the Sherpa Van Trophy at Wembley.

But once into the reconstructed First Division, Turner began to feel the frustration creeping in (from the fans especially) as Wolves struggled to put in a strong enough challenge to win a place in the top flight and eventually this sort of form inevitably led to him being axed in November 1995 (after a 0-0 home draw with Charlton Athletic). Into his place stepped another Graham – Taylor – the former England, Watford and Aston Villa boss. Turner was out of football for quite awhile, but returned in the summer of 1996 when he took over the reins at Hereford United, who, sadly under his control, lost their Football League status in May 1997, after failing to win their last game of the season at home to Brighton and Hove Albion. In 1999 Turner was chairman and director of football at Edgar Street.

TURNER, Graham Mark

Manager Graham Turner's son, Mark Turner was with Wolves for three seasons during which time he made only one senior appearance. Born in Bebbington on 4 October 1972, he was signed as a wide midfielder by his father from Paget Rangers in July 1991 and was released in June 1994 when he signed for Northampton Town. He failed to make an impact with the Cobblers, who allowed him to leave for Telford United in December 1995. His father then re-signed him again in March 1997, this time for Hereford United.
Wolves record: 1 app.

TURNER, John Alan

Wolves signed goalkeeper Jack Turner from Stockport County in August 1928 as cover for Lewis Botto and Alf Canavon. Born in Swallownest, Sheffield in 1906, he had previously had a trial at Molineux (in 1924 from Silverwood Colliery FC.) but was rejected and went to Edgeley Park, appearing in 38 games for County before switching to Molineux. He conceded 14 in his seven outings for the club, including four against Hull and five at Preston, before leaving in November 1927 to sign for Watford, later playing for Rotherham United.
Wolves record: 7 apps.

TYLER, Sidney

Described as a 'polished full-back' Sid Tyler spent three years at Molineux where he acted as reserve to Ted Watson. Born in Wolverhampton on 7 December 1904, he played for Stourbridge from May 1921 before joining Manchester United in May 1922 (making one senior appearance). In May 1924 he was recruited by Wolves and left Molineux for Gillingham in August 1927. He later assisted Norwich City (on trial) and Millwall (from April 1929), before rounding off his career with Colwyn Bay United (June 1931 to May 1933) and then Chamberlain and Hickham FC (Birmingham) as an amateur from September 1933 to his retirement in 1935. Tyler died in Walsall on 25 January 1971.

Wolves record: 18 apps.

UNBEATEN RUNS

The longest unbeaten League run in Wolves' history was achieved in season 1923-24 when they went 20 Third Division North games without defeat on their way to winning the championship and ultimate promotion back to the top flight.

That terrific spell started with a 5-1 home victory over New Brighton on 24 November 1923 (when Harry Lees netted a hat-trick) and ended on 7 April 1924 with a 2-1 defeat at Walsall. Out of those 20 matches, 13 were won and seven drawn.

Wolves' went a club record 27 home games without defeat between March 1923 and September 1924 (Derby County ended that sequence with a 4-0 win).

Wolves' best unbeaten away spell in the League is 11 matches – from September 1953 to January 1954.

The most successive League wins Wolves have achieved is eight – registered four times in 1915, 1967, 1987 and 1988. Their best run of successive home victories is 14 between March and November 1953 and their best sequence of wins is five – recorded three times in 1938, 1962 and 1980.

Wolves went 12 FA Cup games without defeat between January 1949 and February 1950.

Their best run in the League Cup is eight unbeaten matches (on two occasions) and in the Sherpa Van Trophy Wolves played 14 games without defeat between October 1987 and April 1989.

UNITED STATES OF AMERICA

Wolves have visited the USA five times.

They first crossed the Atlantic to play in there in May and June of 1963 and besides taking on teams from America, they also met sides from Canada and Brazil (Bangu), a Mexican Select XI, the Ukranian Nationals and FC Schalke '04 (from Germany). In all they played ten matches, remained unbeaten, scored a total of 38 goals (Ted Farmer was top man with 11) and 6-0 against CYO All Stars, was their best victory of the nine. Around 22,000 fans saw them win their opening game of this tour, 5-0 against Montreal Cantalla.

Wolves' second trip to the States came in May, June, July 1967. They had just regained their First Division status and under manager Ronnie Allen, they celebrated promotion by entering – and winning – the prestigious Los Angeles tournament, playing under the name of the local team, Los Angeles Wolves.

They played 14 matches on the tour – winning six. Bangu were there again as well as seven from nearer home, namely Hibernian, Stoke City, Sunderland, Dundee United, Glentoran, Shamrock Rovers and Aberdeen, the latter adopting the name Washington Whips, ADO (The Hague) and FC Cerro (from Uruguay) were also over there.

The Final of the heavily sponsored and extremely well supported tournament was attended by 17,824 fans in the Los Angeles Coliseum, and they saw Wolves defeat Aberdeen 6-5 in a thrilling contest, Davey Burnside scoring a hat-trick and Dougan conceding a rare own-goal. Frank Munro had a superb game for the Dons, scoring a hat-trick including two penalties, and his display led to Allen signing him for Wolves.

The third trip made by Wolves to America was two years later – in May 1969. On this occasion they again played in a well planned tournament which comprised four other teams with a total of eight matches on the agenda, two against each participating club.

Wolves won six of their eight fixtures: 2-1 and 5-0 over Midland neighbours Aston Villa, 4-2 against West Ham United and 3-2 and 3-0 against Kilmarnock to end up as champions.

In May 1972, Wolves went on their fourth venture to Canada and the USA and this time they played four exhibition games with Aberdeen, losing 3-1 in San Francisco, and 3-0 in Seattle, while winning 3-0 in Vancouver and 4-0 in Los Angeles.

Wolves' last visit to the States was in May 1981, when they were beaten 4-1 by the Jacksonville Teamen in a one-off friendly.

UTTERSON, James

Giant goalkeeper, upright, smart, Jimmy Utterson was at Molineux during the mid-1930s. Born in Gateshead on 26 November 1914, he played as a junior with South Shields and for Glenavon (Ireland) before moving to Molineux for £300 in the summer of 1934 as cover for Alex Scott. He represented the Irish League against he Football League whilst with Glenavon. Sadly Utterson died shortly before Christmas in December 1935, when only 21 years of age. He had suffered a serious head injury in a 4-2 defeat at Ayresome Park in September 1935 and died in hospital of brain damage.

Wolves record: 14 apps.

VAN DER LAAN, Robertus Petrus

Robbie Van der Laan was a hardworking Dutch midfielder who played a handful of games for Wolves whilst on loan from Derby County in 1996-97. Born in Schiedam in the Netherlands on 5 September 1968, Van der Laan played for SVV Schiedam and FC Wageningen in his homeland before joining Port Vale for £80,000 in February 1991. He went on to appear in well over 200 first-class games for the Valiants, helping them win promotion to the First Division in 1994, a year after lifting the Autoglass Trophy at Wembley. He left Vale Park for Derby County in a £475,000 deal (involving Lee Mills) in July 1995, a month after being hit in the face by a Stoke City supporter who was later fined £100 for assault. He was a key figure in the Rams midfield when they stormed into the Premiership in 1996, but in July 1998 Van der Laan moved again, this time to Barnsley for £500,000.

Wolves record: 7 apps.

VAUGHAN, Nigel Mark

Welsh international midfielder Nigel Vaughan was a hardworking player, a waif like figure who had a will o' the wisp tendency to ghost in and make the most of the half chances. He gave Wolves excellent service for three years, putting in some sterling performances. Born in Caerleon, near Newport, Wales on 20 May 1959, Vaughan joined Newport County straight from school (June 1975) having played for The Lodge and the Cwmbran representative side. He turned professional at Somerton Park in May 1977. After 224 League games for County (34 goals scored) he was transferred to Cardiff City in September 1983 and in his four years at Ninian Park Vaughan netted a further 42 goals in 149 League outings. After a loan spell with Reading (February-March 1987) he moved to Molineux for £12,000 in August 1987 and remained with Wolves until May 1990 when he switched to Hereford United, staying at Edgar Street for two seasons. During his time with Wolves Vaughan gained Fourth and then Third Division championship medals and a Sherpa Van Trophy winners medal at Wembley. And he scored in six successive League matches between 17 October and 24 November 1987 – quite a feat for a midfield player. He represented Wales at youth and Under-21 levels before gaining 10 full caps (1983-85). Unfortunately he broke his leg while playing with Hereford and was out of the game for quite a while. In 1996-97 Vaughan became caretaker-manager of Newport AFC (Wales) after spells with Worcester City, Stourbridge and Pershore. A fully qualified FA coach, he was appointed manager of Bridgnorth Bandon (Banks Premier League) in 1999.

Wolves record: 110+10 apps. 13 goals.

VENEZIA

Italy's Serie 'B' side Venezia defeated Wolves 2-1 at home in an Anglo-Italian Cup game in October 1994. The attendance of just 750 was the lowest Wolves have ever played in front of at competitive level. Defender Mark Venus netted for Wolves.

VENUS, Mark

Born in Hartlepool on 6 April 1967, Venus occupied a number of positions during his time at Molineux, lining up as a full-back, central defender, sweeper, left-sided midfielder and an occasionally as an emergency attacker. And he always gave a good account of himself, especially in defence where he was confident, using his excellent left foot to good effect. Venus started his career with his home town club, Hartlepool United whom he joined initially as a junior, turning professional in March 1985. In September of that same year he was transferred to Leicester City and went on to make almost 70 appearances for the Foxes before moving to Wolves for £40,000 in March 1988. He was placed in the League side immediately and at the end of his first season at Molineux collected a Third Division championship medal. During his nine-year stay he became a valuable member of the senior squad and passed the milestone of 300 competitive appearances for Wolves before his transfer to Ipswich Town (in a deal involving Steve Sedgley) in June 1997. Venus then gave great service to the Portman Road club, twice helping them into the Play-offs where they were denied each time.
Wolves record: 319+18 apps. 10 goals.

VEYSEY, Arthur John

Reserve outside-right Arthur Veysey had a fine record, albeit relatively small, during the 1904-05 – scoring on each of his two League outings for Wolves against Middlesbrough at home (won 5-3) and Stoke away (lost 2-1). Born in Willenhall c.1884, he played initially for Featherstone Boys and on leaving Molineux in May 1905 he joined Oxley, later playing for Brewood. Veysey died c.1955.
Wolves record: 2 apps. 2 goals.

VILLAZAN, Raphael

Born in Uruguay on 19 September 1957, Raphael Villazan was hard-tackling midfielder who was recruited to Molineux from Huelva Sporting club in May 1980 by manager John Barnwell. Unfortunately he never really fitted the bill although injuries didn't help his cause and after less than 30 first-team outings he was released in May 1982, returning to Uruguay.
Wolves record: 24+3 apps.

VIZARD, Edward

Ted Vizard was Wolves' manager for four years – April 1944 to May 1948. Born in Cogan, Wales, 7 June 1889, he attended St David's County school and played soccer for Cogan Old Boys and rugby for Penarth

before establishing himself as an outside-left with Barry Town in 1909. He joined Bolton Wanderers in December 1910 and remained as a player at Burnden Park until May 1931, having guested for Chelsea during World War One. After hanging up his boots Vizard was appointed Bolton's scout and he also coached the 'A' team to April 1933. In that same month he became manager of Swindon Town, a position he held for five years before taking over at Queen's Park Rangers (May 1939 to April 1944). From Loftus Road he switched to Wolves (April 1944) and nine months after leaving Molineux he was given the manager's job at non-League Cradley Heath (February 1949). He quit football in May 1950 and was later licensee of the Tettenhall Hotel, Wolverhampton (1950-53). A very accomplished footballer, Vizard was capped 22 times by Wales; he gained two FA Cup winners' medals with Bolton (1923 and 1926) and also made 467 League appearances for the Lancashire club (64 goals). He scored 70 times in 512 outings in all competitions for Bolton and was the oldest player ever to appear for the Lancashire club, aged 41 years, 287 days against Sunderland in March 1931. He died in Wolverhampton on Christmas Day 1973.
Wolves' playing record (League and Cup) under Vizard was a good one – played 94, won 48, drawn 18 and lost 28.

VORWAERTS (ASK)

Wolves' playing record against Vorwaerts is: European Cup-winners' Cup

Venue	P	W	D	L	F	A
Home	1	1	0	0	2	0
Away	1	0	0	1	1	2
Total	2	1	0	1	3	2

Wolves were paired with the Austrian club, A.S.K. Vorwaerts, in the preliminary round of the 1959-60 European Cup competition.

The first leg was played in Austria on 30 September and Wolves battled hard before losing narrowly in front of 65,000 fans. The return leg, a week later, attracted an audience of 55,747 to Molineux and this time Wolves played exceedingly well to win the game and so go forward into the next round 3-2 on aggregate. Peter Broadbent scored in both games.

WAGSTAFFE, David

Outside-left Dave Wagstaffe, an all-time great of Wolverhampton Wanderers, was a terrific crosser of the ball. He had both pace and skill and was a big favourite with the supporters. There was no finer sight in the eyes of the Molineux faithful than to see the flying 'Waggy' racing down the touchline and swinging over a pin-point cross aimed for his goal-seeking strikers. 'Waggy' did this frequently during his 11 years with Wolves and there is no doubt whatsoever that he was one

of the most accurate crossers of a ball in the game during the late 1960s and early 1970s. Born in Manchester on 5 April 1943, Wagstaffe joined Manchester City as a junior on leaving school, turning professional at Maine Road in May 1960. He went on to make 161 appearances for City (eight goals scored) before transferring to Wolves for what was to prove a bargain fee of £30,000 on Boxing Day 1964. He soon started to produce the goods at Molineux, but sadly Wolves were relegated at the end of his first season with the club. However, his form never waned and he was instrumental in helping the team regain their First Division status in 1967 when he was an ever-present in the side. He played in two major Cup Finals for Wolves, collecting a winners medal when his former club Manchester City were defeated 2-1 in the 1974 League Cup Final at Wembley and a loser's prize after Spurs had beaten Wolves on aggregate in the UEFA Cup Final two years earlier. In January 1976, after more than 400 appearances for the club, 'Waggy' was sold to Blackburn Rovers. He later switched to neighbouring Blackpool (March 1979) and decided to retire from competitive football in May of that same year with a League record of 564 appearances and 42 goals scored. Not for the want of trying, 'Waggy' received very few representative honours, playing for England at both schoolboy and youth team levels and getting one outing with the Football League XI. In later years he returned to Molineux to run Waggy's bar and later acted as steward of the Old Wulfrunians Club, Castlecroft, a position he filled until January 1993. One record 'Waggy' isn't proud of is that he was the first League footballer to be shown the red card when playing for Blackburn Rovers at Bolton in a Second Division match on 2 October 1976.
Wolves records: 404 apps. 32 goals.

WAKE, Bertram B.

Born locally in Wolverhampton c.1888, inside or centre-forward Bert Wake was registered with Wolves for two seasons, initially signing for the club in July 1907 from St Augustine's. Deputising for Jack Shelton and George Hedley during the second-half of that 1907-08 season, he left Molineux in the summer of 1909, when he joined Bloxwich, later assisting Bilston. On retiring he worked on the railway.
Wolves record: 4 apps. 1 goal.

WALDRON, Joseph John

Outside-right Jack Waldron played for Wolves in season 1883-84, making one senior appearance in the FA Cup-tie against Wednesbury Old Athletic. Born in Wolverhampton c.1861, he also served with St Paul's, Springfield Rovers (before joining

Wolves) and Whitmore Reans, Wednesfield and Wolverhampton Nomads before retiring in 1896. Waldron died c.1935.
Wolves record: 1 app.

WALKER, Alfred J. Samuel
A Londoner, born c.1887, left-winger Alf Walker played for Northampton Town and Brentford before joining Wolves for the 1909-10 season. He spent two years at Molineux, the first in the Reserves, but then he had some useful outings as partner to Jack Needham, having replaced Jack Pedley. In July 1911 Walker was sold to Port Vale and he went on to play in almost 100 first-team games for the Potteries' club before moving to Scotland to sign for Dunfermline Athletic in the summer of 1914. He later returned to Stoke-on-Trent where he became an ardent Port Vale supporter, while also coaching the younger footballers in the area. Walker died in Newcastle-under-Lyme on 14 September 1961.
Wolves record: 35 apps. 2 goals.

WALKER, David
Walker made only two League appearances for Wolves, but after leaving Molineux he became a highly effective inside-forward with Bristol Rovers, West Bromwich Albion and Leicester Fosse. Born in Oakdene, Walsall in July 1884, he attended Pleck Road school and played for Walsall White Star and Birchfield Villa before joining Wolves in March 1905. He spent only five months with the Wanderers before transferring to Bristol Rovers in August of that same year, switching back to the Black Country to join Albion in April 1907. From The Hawthorns he transferred to Leicester in May 1908 for £700 (plus Arthur Randle), and then returned for a second spell with Bristol Rovers in August 1911. He rounded off his career with Willenhall Swifts (1912-13) and Walsall (from 1914), retiring in May 1920. Walker possessed a powerful right-foot shot and scored on his debut for Albion against Wolves. He died in October 1935, aged 51.
Wolves record: 2 apps.

WALKER, George William
Defender George Walker who appeared at full-back and centre-half and initially was an able deputy for Ted 'Cock' Pheasant. Born in West Bromwich in December 1877, he played for several local teams including West Bromwich Sandwell signing for Wolves in July 1899 from Willenhall Pickwick. After four years at Molineux, he became a founder-member of Crystal Palace in August 1905, but remained with the London club for only a short time before switching to Gillingham only to return to Palace for as second spell in 1907. Walker had three footballing brothers, one of whom served with Aston Villa and was the father of Billy

Walker, the famous England international of the 1920s who later managed Sheffield Wednesday and Nottingham Forest. George Walker died in 1945, aged 67.
Wolves record: 132 apps. 2 goals.

WALKER, John
Jack Walker, a tall, blond, red-faced left-half, played in two League games for Wolves in season 1903-04, replacing Billy Annis on both occasions (at Villa Park and at Stoke). Basically a reserve he spent three seasons at Molineux, initially joining the Wanderers from Coseley in the summer of 1902, and leaving in May 1905. Born in Gornal c.1882, Walker played his early football with several local teams including Tipton Excelsior and Toll End, from where he moved to Molineux.
Wolves record: 2 apps.

WALKER, John Young Hilley
A Glaswegian, born in Anderston on 17 December 1928, wing-half or inside-forward Johnny Walker played for three major League clubs over a period of 17 years: 1947-64. And during that time he amassed a fine record of more than 100 goals in well over 500 competitive matches (93 coming in 496 League appearances). Starting his career north of the border with Campsie Black Watch FC at the tail end of the war, he joined Wolves as a professional in July 1947. But with so many talented forwards already established at Molineux, Walker did not break into the first team until February 1950, making his debut against Portsmouth. However, he quickly made an impact and scored eight goals in his 12 outings that term, doing well once more the following season with 16 goals in 27 League and Cup games. Then perhaps surprisingly, in October 1952, he was transferred to Southampton for £12,000. At The Dell he impressed all and sundry and in his 186 outings for the Saints he registered another 52 goals before asking and getting a transfer, and duly moving to Reading in December 1957 for just £2,500. He continued to do well at Elm Park and added a further 26 goals in more than 300 senior appearances for the Biscuitmen, up to 1965 when he retired. After ten years out of the game, Walker returned to Elm Park where he became Reading's youth and reserve-team coach, a position he held until 1979. Walker, who was employed by the Royal Mail, Reading, is now living in the Berkshire village of Theale and still follows the fortunes of all his clubs very closely.
Wolves record: 44 apps. 26 goals.

WALKER, Paul G.
Although he never really hit the heights with Wolves, Yorkshireman Paul Walker had a useful career as a utility forward. Born in Bradford on 3 April 1949, he was an amateur with his home town club, Park Avenue before

becoming a professional at Molineux in October 1966. He stayed with Wolves for five years and then in December 1971 moved to Watford, later serving with Swindon Town (March 1973), Peterborough United (July 1973), Barnsley (July 1975), Ottawa Tigers (Canada), Huddersfield Town (November 1976 to April 1977) and then in non-League football in Yorkshire. Walker made more than 125 appearances in the Football League (over 80 with Posh).
Wolves record: 21+ 11 apps.

WALKER, William Stanley
Goalkeeper Billy Walker made only one appearance for Wolves – in the 7-3 defeat at West Bromwich Albion in December 1929 – and that only lasted 38 seconds before he fractured his right ankle in a goalmouth mêlée. Unfortunately he never played for Wolves again, yet he recovered and went on to star in 40 League games for New Brighton in 1931-32 and in a further 20 for Doncaster Rovers the following season. Born in Waddington, Lincolnshire in 1907, he had been with Wolves a year and a half before his making debut, having acted as understudy to the likes of George, Botto, Canavan, Turner, Lewis and Tootill. Before arriving at Molineux he played briefly for Waddington FC, Lincoln City, Gainsborough Trinity and Grantham. Walker retired in 1937.
Wolves record: 1 app.

WALLACE, Ian R.
Wallace was a professional at Molineux for just one season (1966-67). Born in Hedley, Northumberland on 12 September 1948, he came to Wolves as an apprentice in July 1964, but after failing to make an impact after turning professional in September 1966, he was released by the club and went into non-League soccer in the north of England. His only appearance for Wolves was as a substitute in the 4-0 win over Blackburn in September 1966.
Wolves record: 0+1 app.

WALSALL
Wolves' playing record against the Saddlers is:

Football League

Venue	P	W	D	L	F	A
Home	2	0	2	0	0	0
Away	2	0	1	1	2	3
Total	4	0	3	1	2	3

FA Cup

	P	W	D	L	F	A
Home	3	3	0	0	10	3

League Cup

	P	W	D	L	F	A
Home	1	0	0	1	0	1
Away	1	0	1	0	1	1
Total	2	0	1	1	1	2

Wartime

	P	W	D	L	F	A
Home	9	4	4	1	17	15
Away	8	5	1	2	17	16
Total	17	9	5	3	34	31

The first of the four League meetings between the clubs took place in December 1922 when a crowd of over 16,400 witnessed a 0-0 draw in a Third Division North encounter at Molineux. Later in the season, with Wolves going for the championship, the Saddlers beat them 2-1 at Fellows Park in front of a 10,000 crowd.

The other two clashes were in the Third Division in 1985-86, and both ended in draws: 0-0 at Molineux and 1-1 at Walsall.

Wolves' three FA Cup wins all came during the period from 1885 to 1889, the best being an emphatic 6-1 victory in February 1889 in front of 5,000 fans, who saw Tommy Knight score a fine hat-trick.

The two League Cup encounters took place in season 1985-86. On 20 August a crowd of 11,330 saw Walsall held 1-1 at Fellows Park, but in the return leg, at the start of the following month, a similar crowd of 11,310 saw Nicky Cross net the all important goal to give the Saddlers a 2-1 aggregate victory.

Dicky Dorsett netted a four-timer as Wolves beat Walsall 5-3 in a wartime Midland Regional League game in December 1939.

Players with both clubs include: Harry Allen, Pat Bartley, Alan Birch, Alan Boswell, Bill Boswell, Tommy Bowen, Colin Brazier, Francis Burrill, Arthur Buttery, Brian Caswell, Derek Clarke, Wayne Clarke, Billy Crook, Chris Crowe, Steve Daley, Ken Davies, Will Devey, Peter Eastoe, Alun Evans, Tony Evans, Jack Gardiner, George Garrattly, Alf Griffin, Sid Grosvenor, Albert Groves (also player-manager of Walsall), Bill Guttridge (also Walsall coach), Johnny Hancocks, Ian Handysides, Gerry Harris, John Harris, Irvine Harwood, Harry Haynes, John Heath, Frank Higham, Ron Howells, Paul Jones, Mick Kearns (also Walsall Community officer), David Kelly, James Kelly, Jimmy Kelly, Franklyn Lester, Harry Lloyd, Paul McLoughlin, George Marshall, Harry Middleton, Derek Mountfield, Harry Parsonage, Tom Phillipson, Frank Pope, Arthur Potts, David Richards, Jack Richards, Billy Rotton, Jimmy Seal, Bernard Shaw, Paul Simpson, Darren Simkin, Ronnie Stockin, Doug Taylor, John Teasdale, Billy Tennant, Ben Timmins, Joe Tonks, David Walker, Stuart Watkiss, Terry Wharton, Bert Williams, Dennis Wilshaw, Harry Wood and David Wykes.

Also associated with both clubs: Ronnie Allen (manager of both clubs); John Barnwell (manager of both clubs); Andy Beattie (Wolves manager, Walsall coach); Major Frank Buckley (manager of both clubs); Kenny Hibbitt (Wolves player, Walsall manager); Tom Hunter (Walsall reserve); Garry Pendrey (Walsall player, Wolves coach); Gerry Summers (Walsall player, Wolves trainer/coach); Davey Burnside (Wolves player, Walsall asssistant manager); John Jarman (Walsall player, Wolves junior and coach); Mark Crook (Wolves player and scout, Walsall scout); Henry J. Dillard (Walsall player and club umpire, Wolves reserve-team trainer); Harry Bird (Walsall reserve), Jack Nelson (Wolves player, Walsall trainer/coach), Stan Collymore (Wolves reserve, Walsall junior), Sid Gibbons, Ron Hewitt, Billy Long, Jack Pitt, Johnson Reed, Lol Woodward and Francis Wragge (all Wolves Reserves); Irvin Methley (Wolves junior/reserve and wartime guest, Walsall player), Norman Deeley (Walsall steward); Graham Newton (Wolves junior); Jack Beattie, Arthur Buttery, Teddy Peers, Roy Pritchard, Jack Rowley and Billy Wrigglesworth (all Walsall wartime guests) and Ron Jukes (scout for both clubs).

WALSALL SENIOR CUP

This competition was first introduced in 1883-84. Wolves entered regularly until the turn of the century, appearing in the Final six times, winning the trophy in 1895-96 (2-0 against Wellington St George at the Oval, Wood Green), 1897-98 (4-1 against Aston Villa at Walsall) and 1899-1900 (1-0 against Aston Villa at Molineux). They were beaten Finalists in 1886-87 (beaten 3-0 by Walsall Town in a replay at The Oval), in 1898-99 (lost 4-1 to Aston Villa at Villa Park) and in 1904-05 (humbled 5-0 by Stoke at the Victoria Ground).

Tom Worton scored five goals and Jack Miller three when Wolves beat Wellington Town 8-0 at home in March 1896.

WALTERS, Mark Everton

Wing-forward Mark Walters occupies either flank. A tricky player with pace and telling shot, he crosses a ball with great precision and has one marvellous feature whereby he drags his foot over the ball before gliding past a defender. Born in Birmingham on 2 June 1964, he joined Aston Villa as a teenager from the Holte Grammar School in Lozells and remained with the Midlands club until moving to Scotland to sign for Glasgow Rangers for £500,000 in December 1987. From Ibrox Park he moved to Liverpool for £1.25 million in August 1981 and after loan spells with Stoke City (March/April 1994 and Wolves (September/October 1994) he moved to Southampton (January 1996) on a free transfer, later switching to Swindon Town, also on a free transfer in July 1996. Winner of one full, one 'B', nine Under-21 and both schoolboy and youth caps for England, Walters gained a European Super Cup winners medal with Villa (1982) and three Scottish Premier Division and two League Cup winners medals while at Ibrox, plus an FA Cup winners medal with Liverpool in 1992. Walters passed the personal milestone of 600 senior appearances at club level during the 1998-99 season. He had also hit the 125 goal mark in the process.
Wolves record: 11 apps. 3 goals.

WARD, Samuel

Rather on the small side for a defender, Ward was nevertheless a useful performer who did well in the Wolves side before losing out to Ted Collins. Born in Wolverhampton c.1880, he joined the Molineux staff from Springfield FC in April 1906 and spent over four years with Wolves before transferring to Dudley Town in July 1910, later assisting Brierley Hill Alliance (1912-13). His only League goal for Wolves was a real gem, scored against Burton United (away) in March 1907 – sadly to no avail as his side lost 4-1.
Wolves record: 47 apps. 1 goal.

WARING, Thomas

Tall, long striding, six feet two inches of sinew, muscle and bone, Tom 'Pongo' Waring was a free-scoring centre-forward, supremely confident in his own ability. A colourful character, with plenty of dash, the stories about him apocryphal or otherwise are legion. Over 23,000 fans witnessed his debut for Aston Villa in a reserve team fixture against Birmingham in February 1928, shortly after he had scored six goals for Tranmere Rovers in an 11-0 win over Durham City in a Third Division North game. Born in Birkenhead in October 1906, Waring attended school in his native town and was a chocolate seller outside Prenton Park besides playing at weekends for Tranmere Celtic. He then joined Tranmere Rovers as a professional in February 1926, succeeding the great Dixie Dean in their attack, and two years later moved to Aston Villa for £4,700. In his ten years at Villa Park, he netted 167 goals in 226 first-team appearances. An England international (five caps won in 1931 and 1932). Waring claimed a record 49 League goals for Villa in 1930-31 when he was dubbed the 'Gay Cavalier' as he streaked past defenders time and again to smash the ball into the net. Indeed, every kid around Villa Park wanted to be 'Pongo' Waring – for he was more popular than the Prime Minister. He was sensationally sent off while playing against Spurs in January 1934, and as he walked, head bowed, from the field he received a bigger cheer than the whole team would have got if they'd won the FA Cup. In July 1936, Waring moved to Molineux but he failed to settle down to Wolves' style of play and after barely three months with the club he returned to Tranmere (October 1936), later playing for Accrington Stanley (November 1939 to July 1939). He served with Bath City up to the outbreak of the war and after guesting for

Crewe Alexandra, New Brighton, Northampton Town, Nottingham Forest and Wrexham during the hostilities, he then went on to assist Ellesmere Port, Graysons FC, Birkenhead Dockers and Harrowby whilst working in the Merseyside docklands. In a sparkling career, Waring, who was also referred to as the 'Birkenhead Bombadier' and the 'Claret and Blue Torpedo', scored 245 goals in 362 League games. He won one medal at club level – helping Tranmere take the Third Division North championship in 1937-38. He died in December 1980, aged 74. *Wolves record: 10 apps. 3 goals.*

WARTIME FOOTBALL

Wolves' record in wartime football (Regional League/Cup and other organised competitions) was:

Seasons	P	W	D	L	F	A
1918-19	6	2	3	1	9	9
1939-46	229	96	47	86	442	412
Totals	235	98	50	87	451	421

NB – The three void First Division League matches which were played at the start of the ill-fated 1939-40 season, are included in these figures, but the four FA Cup-ties, played in August/September 1946, are not included (see under **FA Cup**).

Wartime Dispatches

Wolves' six competitive matches in 1918-19 were in the Midland Victory League and 5-2 over Aston Villa was their best win. Prior to that they had played several friendly games and in April 1916 a hat-trick by Edwin Dunn gave them a 5-2 win over Birmingham. In November of that same year a strong Wolves side beat an Aston Villa/West Bromwich Albion select XI 9-2 at Molineux and on Boxing Day 1917 Wolves' first team defeated an Army XI 3-2.

Dennis Westcott scored four goals in Wolves' 7-2 Midland Regional League home win over Northampton Town in October 1939.

Dicky Dorsett netted a four-timer when Wolves beat Walsall 5-3 away in the same competition in December 1939.

Taylor claimed four goals when Wolves defeated rivals West Bromwich Albion 5-4 at Molineux in May 1939.

Wolves won the Midland Regional League Championship in season 1939-40 with a record of 19 wins and three draws from their 28 fixtures. They scored 76 goals and conceded 44, amassing 41 points. Dennis Westcott was leading scorer with 27 goals (including four hat-tricks); Dicky Dorsett netted 15. Wolves' average home 'League' attendance this season was 4,344. Their best attendance was 9,412 against WBA and their lowest just 2,016 against Northampton Town.

Their best win was 7-2 against North-ampton and their heaviest defeat 5-0 at West Brom.

Wolves lost 7-2 to Coventry City over two legs in the wartime League Cup in May 1940.

On 22 May 1940, Westcott was paid £4 to play for Cheltenham Town against Worcester City. The maximum wage at the time was 30 shillings (£1.50).

West Bromwich Albion beat Wolves 8-2 at Molineux in a League (South) fixture in November 1941.

A double hat-trick (6 goals) by Westcott earned Wolves an emphatic 7-0 League South home victory over Nottingham Forest on 13 December 1941.

In January 1942, Wolves crashed 6-1 at Blackpool in a League Cup game.

Guests Jack Rowley (5 goals) and Frank Broome (3) were the stars in Wolves' 11-1 home win over Everton in a League Cup-tie in March 1942.

Wolves won the wartime League Cup in season 1941-42, beating Sunderland 6-3 in the two-legged Final. They drew 2-2 at Roker Park on 23 May in front of 34,776 fans and then defeated the Wearsiders 4-1 at Molineux seven days later when the attendance was 43,038. Hot-shot Westcott scored in both matches.

Wolves had defeated Manchester United 6-5 on aggregate to reach that Final.

Wolves drew 1-1 with the London Cup winners Brentford at Stamford Bridge in June 1942.

In 1942-43 Larry Kelly skippered Wolves at the age of 17 – possibly the club's youngest-ever skipper.

Billy Wright netted two hat-tricks for Wolves in season 1942-43 – against Stoke City and Crewe Alexandra in League North games.

Wolves beat Derby County 8-1 in November 1942 and guest striker Jack Rowley scored all eight goals (a club record). A week later County won 3-1 at the Baseball Ground. Crewe Alexandra beat Wolves 8-1 at Gresty Road in a League Cup (Second Competition) game in April 1943.

In season 1943-44, Wolves lost 9-3 at Stoke, 7-2 at Northampton, 5-0 at West Brom and 4-0 at home to Chester, all in League North (Second Competition) matches.

Guests Jimmy Jinks and Jack Acquaroff both netted hat-tricks when Wolves beat Chester 6-1 and Wrexham 4-1 respectively in League North (Second Competition) matches in January/February 1945.

Bolton Wanderers ousted Wolves from the League Cup (North) competition in season 1944-45, beating them 4-3 on aggregate in the two-legged semi-final.

In the last wartime season of 1945-46, Wolves defeated Lovells Athletic 12-3 on aggregate in the first round of the FA Cup

(they won 4-2 away and 8-1 at Molineux). Tom Galley scored a hat-trick in the latter game.

In the Football League South, Wolves ran up two successive 5-2 wins over Welsh opposition, beating Newport County (home) and Swansea Town (away) in March 1946. Westcott scored a hat-trick against Newport.

The first season of wartime football in 1939-40, cost Wolves £17,717, a liability which seemed injudicious to increase, thus they didn't play at all in 1940-41. And due to this the club still lost £4,846. During the first four World War Two seasons period (1939-43) Wolves lost a total of £24,763

Jimmy Mullen celebrated his 17th birthday by making his first appearance as a full-time professional when Wolves beat Coventry 3-0 on 6 January 1940.

On 27 September 1941 against Leicester City (away) Wolves created a record by fielding a team whose average age was just 17 years, one month. Derek Ashton, at 18 years six months was the veteran of the side.

Eighteen months earlier, the average age of the Wolves side which beat Birmingham 3-1 on 16 March 1940 was 19 years, seven months. Included in the line-up were two 16-year-olds – Billy Wright and Terry Springthorpe.

In September 1942, Scotsman Cameron Buchanan (born in Airdrie on 31 July 1928) became the youngest-footballer ever to play in a competitive game in the UK when, at the age of 14 years 57 days, he made his debut for Wolves in a League North (First Competition) game against West Bromwich Albion at Molineux.

On 23 April 1945, pre-war Wolves player Alex McIntosh was reported missing on active service. He survived and became a PoW

The first official transfer to take place during World War Two was that of Bob King, who moved from Northampton Town to Wolves for £2,000 in November 1939.

Eric 'Ned' Robinson (Wolves) lost his life on military service during World War Two (drowned on exercises).

A crowd of 105,145 saw England beat Scotland 4-0 in a wartime international at Hampden Park and during the course of the game the Wolves centre-half Stan Cullis, skippering England, was injured in an off the ball incident involving the Clyde striker Wallace. Wallace never represented his country again.

On 2 October 1943 Alan Steen, who had made his debut as a 16-year-old for Wolves during the last peacetime season, was reported missing after a bombing raid over Germany. He was captured by the enemy and spent the remainder of the war as a PoW in Stalag IV 3. On returning to England, Steen went on to play for Luton Town, Aldershot,

Rochdale and Carlisle United, moving into non-League soccer in 1952.

On 24 March 1945 when Wolves beat Aston Villa 2-1 at Villa Park, the deciding goal was scored by 20-year-old Jimmy Anderton with his first-ever penalty kick.

On 14 April 1945, Wolves defeated Birmingham 1-0 at Molineux in a second round, second leg Regional League Cup-tie. The winning goal, scored by Bill Morris, came in the 63rd minute of extra-time. After the scheduled 90 minutes of normal playing time, plus 30 minutes of extra-time, the referee told the players that the game would end when a goal was scored. Morris netted at approximately 5.45pm, the game having kick-off at 3pm.

Westcott top-scored for Wolves in 1939-40 with 27 goals; in 1941-42 with 28 and again in 1942-43 with 18 (in all competitions). During World War Two, Westcott scored 89 goals; Dicky Dorsett netted 40 and Billy Wright 33.

Derek Ashton appeared in most competitive games for Wolves during World War Two – 147 in total. Angus McLean had 125 outings, Billy Crook 122, Billy Wright 111, Jack Alderton 110, Jimmy Dunn 100, Cyril Sidlow 93, Jimmy Mullen 84, Dennis Westcott 71 and Tom Galley 62.

A total of 91 players registered with Wolves were on active service during World War Two. Crystal Palace topped the poll with a total of 98.

Wolves utilised a total of 182 players in their competitive war games between 1939 and 1946 and 21 were called up during the 1915-19 period.

At the end of the 1945-46 transitional season, Wolves went on tour to Sweden where they fulfilled five matches. They lost 3-0 in Gothenburg and 3-1 in Stockholm, drew 2-2 with Gavle and defeated Sundsvall 7-1 and FF Malmo 3-2.

During World War Two Wolves' Reserves played 40 competitive games in total, taking part in both the Birmingham and District League and Cup competitions, the Birmingham Combination, the Tittotson Cup, the Keys Cup and the Worcestershire Senior Cup. They won only six, drew two and lost 32. Their goal-average was 63-174.

Their biggest win was that of 10-0 against RAF Hednesford (a) in March 1942 when Billy Crook scored a hat-trick, while their heaviest defeat was a 15-1 thrashing at Darlaston in April 1940. Both matches were in the Birmingham Combination.

Wolves Reserves hammered Bloxwich Strollers 17-0 in a friendly match in November 1944. Larry Kelly scored five times.

Guest Players

During World War Two, Wolves recruited 42 guest players (see under **Guest Players**).

Jimmy Mullen guested for both Darlington and Leicester City during World War Two..

Several Wolves players also guested for other clubs, among them: Emilio Aldecoa (Leicester City), Jim Alderton (Chester), Ted Anderson (Everton, Wrexham), Bill Baxter (Leicester City, Mansfield Town, Notts County), Roy Bicknell (Notts County, Swindon Town), Billy Crook (Aldershot, Chelsea), Stan Cullis (Aldershot, Fulham, Liverpool), Dicky Dorsett (Grimsby Town, Liverpool, Southampton), Tommy Galley (Aldershot, Clapton Orient, Leeds United, Watford), Johnny Hancocks (Chester, Crewe Alexandra, Wrexham), John Harris (Grimsby Town, Southampton), Larry Kelly (Halifax Town), Bob King (Leicester City, Manchester City), Alex McIntosh (Newcastle United, Watford), Teddy Maguire (Hartlepools United), Bill Morris (Wrexham), Jimmy Mullen (Darlington, Leicester City), Bill Parker (Crewe Alexandra), Roy Pritchard (Mansfield Town, Notts County, Swindon Town, Walsall), Jimmy Rooney (Cardiff City), Arthur Rowley (Crystal Palace, Brighton and Hove Albion, Lincoln City, Manchester United, Middlesbrough), Alec R. Scott (Aston Villa, Southport), Bill Shorthouse (Burnley), Cyril Sidlow (Wrexham), Terry Springthorpe (Leicester City, Wrexham), Frank Taylor (Aldershot, Darlington, Fulham), Dennis Westcott (Brentford, Cheltenham, Liverpool, Watford), Bert Williams (Chelsea, Derby County), Dennis Wilshaw (Port Vale, Walsall), Horace Wright (Aldershot, Bolton Wanderers, Leeds United, Millwall, Northampton Town, Wrexham) and Billy Wright (Leicester City, Notts County).

WASSALL, Kim D.

Strong-running forward, who preferred the left-wing position, Kim Wassall was on West Bromwich Albion's books, initially as a junior before turning professional in June 1975, but he failed to make the grade at The Hawthorns. Born in Wolverhampton on 9 June 1957, he left the Baggies for Northampton Town in September 1977 and later served, as a non-contract player, with Hull City (August 1983), Swansea City and finally Wolves (from October to December

1983). Then, over the next decade or so, he played non-League soccer for various clubs. *Wolves record: 2 apps.*

WATFORD

Wolves' playing record against the Hornets is:

Football League

Venue	P	W	D	L	F	A
Home	8	3	4	1	12	9
Away	8	1	2	5	7	13
Total	16	4	6	6	19	22

FA Cup

	P	W	D	L	F	A
Home	3	2	0	1	12	4
Away	3	1	2	0	5	2
Total	6	3	2	1	17	6

Mo Johnston scored a hat-trick for Watford in their emphatic 5-0 Division One victory over Wolves at Molineux in December 1983 – the first League meeting between the two clubs. The return fixture that season ended goalless.

Wolves' first win over the Hornets arrived in August 1991 when goals by Andy Mutch and Steve Bull gave them a 2-1 victory at Molineux in front of 13,547 fans.

A tenth minute own-goal by Mark Venus gave Watford a 1-0 win at Vicarage Road in September 1993 and nearly 26,000 spectators saw Wolves beat the Hornets 3-0 at home in March 1996, Steve Froggatt and Simon Osborn (2) their scorers.

Wolves recorded their best ever FA Cup win at Molineux when they thrashed luckless Watford 10-0 in a first-round replay in January 1912. After playing out a goalless draw at Watford, Wolves went to town in the midweek replay and score at will through Irishman Willie Halligan (3), Jack Needham (2), Sammy Brooks (2), George Hedley and Billy Harrison and Dick Young. The attendance was 8,751.

Watford caused a shock by beating Wolves 3-0 at Molineux in a fifth-round FA Cup-tie in February 1980 but the following year Wolves gained revenge by ousting the Hornets from the competition in a fourth-round replay (1-1, then 2-1).

The last FA Cup-tie between the clubs was staged at Vicarage Road in the third round in January 1993 when Wolves raced to a convincing 4-1 victory.

Players with both clubs include: David Barnes, David Connolly, Tony Daley, George Edmonds, John Farley, Jack Ferguson, Dominic Foley, Val Gregory, Jack Hamilton, Jack Harris, Jack Hetherington, Mick Kenning, Brian Owen, Martin Patching, Iwan Roberts, Harry Scott, Jack Turner, Paul Walker, Bob White, Guy Whittingham and David Woodfield.

Also associated: Graham Taylor (manager of both clubs); Bill McGarry (manager of both clubs); Sammy Chung player and manager of Watford, manager of Wolves); John Ward (player and assistant manager/coach of

Watford, assistant manager of Wolves), Bobby Downes (Watford player and later director of Youth football and Wolves coach), Rob Kelly (coach at both clubs); Colin Lee (coach at Watford, assistant manager and manager of Wolves); Tom Gracie Paton (Wolves Reserves), Jackie Brown, Tom Galley, Eric Jones, Alex McIntosh, John Taylor and Dennis Westcott (all Watford wartime guests), Brian Garvey (Watford player, Wolves coach) and Dave Richards (Wolves reserve, Watford player).

WATH WANDERERS

Wath Wanderers were Wolves' nursery club from the town of Wath in Yorkshire. They were formed by the ex-Wolves player of the 1930s, Mark Crook, who took over the facilities of Brampton Welfare FC and most of their better players who eventually found their way to Molineux.

WATKISS, Stuart Paul

Stuart Watkiss was a tall, brave defender, who enjoyed a challenge. Born in Wolverhampton on 8 May 1966, and a pupil at Ward's Bridge School, he was taken on at Molineux as an apprentice in 1982 and signed professional forms for Wolves in July 1984. Unfortunately he failed to make an impression in the gold and black strip and in February 1986 was transferred to Crewe Alexandra. He then dropped out of League football for a while and played for Rushall Olympic before re-entering the big time with Walsall in August 1993. He went on to play in more than 75 games for the Saddlers, who then released him on a free transfer to Hereford United in February 1996.
Wolves record: 2 apps.

WATNEY CUP

Wolves took part in this short-lived sponsored Cup competition just once – losing their only game 2-0 to Bristol Rovers on 29 July 1972 before a crowd of almost 12,500 at Rovers' old Eastville Stadium.

WATSON, Edward George

Defender Ted Watson was born in Felling-on-Tyne on 28 April 1895. He played for Felling Colliery FC, Portsmouth and Pontypridd before joining Wolves in May 1921. He spent eight years at Molineux, establishing himself in the first team in 1924-24 when he replaced Val Gregory in the Third Division North Championship winning side. On leaving Wolves in March 1929 he signed for Coventry City and made over 100 appearances for the Highfield Road club prior to rounding off his career with Oakengates Town (1933-35).
Wolves record: 206 apps. 4 goals.

WEARE, Arthur John

Goalkeeper Jack Weare, like his predecessor Frank Wildman, conceded five goals on his League debut for Wolves – against Newcastle United (away) in a First Division game in April 1934. As it happened he was given ample time to get over that debacle because his second outing for the club was not until the following February and then, by coincidence, Weare conceded another five goals, this time away at West Bromwich Albion. Born in Newport, South Wales on 21 September 1912, Weare stood 6ft tall and weighed a fraction over 12 stones. He joined Wolves from Lovells Athletic in March 1934 and in total made 42 appearances during his time at Molineux, which ended in August 1936 when he agreed to sign for St Mirren. Unfortunately he never confirmed the move to Paisley and quickly went south to join West Ham United. During the war, having made 60 first-class appearances for the Hammers, he guested for Bristol Rovers, and after the hostilities went on to appear in more than 150 League and Cup games for the Eastville Stadium club before announcing his retirement in 1952 after a brief spell with Barry Town. Weare's son, Len (born in 1934) played in 526 League games for Newport County between 1955 and 1969.
Wolves record: 42 apps.

WEATHER

On the opening day of the 1906-07 season – 1 September – Wolves played Hull City at Molineux in temperatures topping 90 degrees – this being perhaps the hottest weather a Wanderers team has ever had to handle in Britain.

Wolves have played in higher temperatures when on tour, especially when they visited South Africa in 1951 and 1957, America and Canada in 1963, the Caribbean in 1964 and Malta in 1985, and, indeed, the temperatures touched the high eighties when they visited Russia in 1955.

One of the coldest places a Wolves team has ever played in was when they met Carl Zeiss Jena in East Germany in the UEFA Cup in November 1971.

WEAVER, Reginald William

Reg Weaver and his brother Walter (below) were playing colleagues with Wolves in season 1927-28. And it was Reg who became the more prominent player of the two and in all he served with five different clubs in an excellent career. Born in Clutton on 14 September 1905, he first played for Llanhilleth United and then Newport County, joining the Welsh club in the 1925-26 season. He transferred to Wolves in November 1927 and did very well in the gold and black strip, top-scoring for the Wanderers in 1928-29 with 18 goals before switching to Chelsea in March 1929. After leaving Stamford Bridge he spent a season with Bradford City (June 1932 to March 1933) and after a brief spell with Chesterfield, he returned to Newport County in 1934. A fast-raiding winger, who preferred the left flank, Weaver won the Welsh Powderhall Sprint title at Caerphilly in July 1931. Weaver died in Gloucester on 16 July 1970.
Wolves record: 51 apps. 29 goals.

WEAVER, Walter

Walter Weaver, brother of Reg (above) was born in Birkenhead on 9 November 1898, He played initially for Royal Ivanhoe FC and then South Liverpool before joining Burnley as a professional in 1921. He then had a spell with Everton before returning to Turf Moor in 1924, transferring to Wolves in October 1926. He remained with Wolves until December 1927 when he left to sign for Accrington Stanley. He retired through injury in 1930, and then chose to live and work in the Lancashire town. Basically an outside-left, Weaver could also occupy the inside-left position and that of left-half. Strong and determined, he did well during his 15-month stay at Molineux. Weaver died in Accrington on 8 June 1965.
Wolves record: 47 apps. 13 goals.

WEDNESBURY OLD ATHLETIC

A crowd of just 1,000 saw Old Athletic beat Wolves 4-2 at home in the second round of the English (FA) Cup in December 1883 – this being Wolves first-ever defeat in the competition.

Players with both clubs include: George Harris, George Hawkins, Joe Holyhead, Billy Malpass, Alf Nicholls, Jack Pedley, Ted Pheasant and Edward Smith.

WEIGHT

In the 1940s defender Angus McLean was one of the heaviest footballers to don a Wolves shirt, once weighing over 14 stones.

Full-back Cecil Shaw also weighed around the 14 stone mark when he was at Molineux during the 1930s. Early 20th century goalkeeper Jim Stringer was another player who tipped the scales at 14 stones as was Bill Shorthouse (at times) during the 1950s.

Of the many lightweights who have represented Wolves at senior level, Paul 'pee-wee' Dougherty and Norman Deeley (earlier in his career) are two who weighed under eight stone at one time.

WELLINGTON TOWN (TELFORD UNITED)

Wolves have never played Wellington Town (Telford United) in a major competitive first team match, but there have been links between the two with several players serving with both clubs (various levels) including: Kevin Ashley, Derek Ashton, George Bellis,

Steve Biggins, Frank Boxley, Chris Brindley, Billy Caddick, Wayne Clarke, Steve Daley (Telford player-manager), Dean Edwards, Mel Eves, Ron Flowers (Telford player-manager), Paul Grainger, Jack Hampton, Johnny Hancocks, Arnold Henshall, Joe Holyhead, Richard Howells, Dennis Isherwood, Jack Jones, Fred Kemp, John Kirkham, Reg Kirkham, Fred Marsden, Andy Mutch, Albert Picken, Jim Poppitt, Roy Pritchard, Alf Riley, Stewart Ross, Darren Simkin, Colin Taylor, brothers Edward and Joe White and Len Williams.

WEMBLEY STADIUM
Wolves have played at Wembley Stadium on seven occasions – in the 1939, 1949 and 1960 FA Cup Finals; in the 1974 and 1980 League Cup Finals; in the 1988 Sherpa Van Trophy Final and in the Football Festival, also in 1988, which was organised to celebrate the Football League's Centenary. Robbie Dennison is the only Wolves player to score in two club games at Wembley (both goals coming in 1988 – in the Sherpa Van Trophy Final against Burnley and the Festival encounter with Everton) and Jesse Pye (1949) and Norman Deeley (in 1960) are the only three Wanderers' stars to score twice for the club at the Empire Stadium.

Billy Wright (as an England player) starred many times at Wembley for his country at international level and he skippered Wolves to the victory in the 1949 FA Cup Final. He also gained his 100th England cap (against Scotland in 1959) at the Empire Stadium.

WEST BROMWICH ALBION
Wolves' playing record against Albion:

Football League

Venue	P	W	D	L	F	A
Home	65	32	16	17	125	88
Away	65	17	19	29	90	118
Totals	130	49	35	46	215	206

FA Cup

Home	5	1	0	4	4	8
Away	5	0	2	3	3	8
Totals	10	1	2	7	7	16

FA Charity Shield

Home	1	0	1	0	4	4

United Counties League

Home	1	1	0	0	4	2
Away	1	0	0	1	1	3
Totals	2	1	0	1	5	5

Wartime

Home	12	7	3	2	26	22
Away	12	2	3	7	15	33
Totals	24	9	6	9	41	55

Wolves and Albion have now met each other almost 250 times at first team level (including friendly matches).

The rivalry between the two Black Country clubs commenced on 20 January 1883 when they met in the third round of the Birmingham Cup at Dudley Road (Wolverhampton). Albion took the honours, winning 4-2.

Wolves gained their first victory over Albion on 25 May 1885 when they won 2-0 in a friendly in Wolverhampton.

At League level, the first encounters took place in the inaugural season of 1888-89, and Wolves won them both, 2-1 at home (Molineux) and 3-1 on Albion territory (Stoney Lane).

The first time the clubs were paired together in the FA Cup was in season 1885-86 when Albion won a fourth-round tie 3-1 at Stoney Lane on 2 January before a crowd of 5,196.

In 1886-87 Wolves met Albion seven times – the most important fixtures being the semi-final of the Staffordshire Cup (which Albion won) and the semi-final of the Birmingham Charity Cup (which Wolves won at Stoney Lane after two replays).

The clubs opposed each other a further seven times in 1887-88. Albion beat Wolves

2-0 in a third-round FA Cup-tie and by the same score in the semi-final of the Birmingham Cup, but Wolves ousted Albion from the Staffordshire Cup in the semi-final at Stoney Lane.

The first penalty kick ever awarded at Albion's Stoney Lane ground was missed by the Wolves defender Harry Allen in a League game on 19 September 1891. Albion won the match 4-3.

Wolves' record win (League or Cup) over Albion is 7-0, achieved at Molineux in a re-arranged First Division game on 16 March 1963. Almost three months earlier, on Boxing Day, snow caused the scheduled game to be abandoned at half-time with Wolves 2-0 ahead. Terry Wharton netted a hat-trick in that 7-0 victory as Wolves rattled in five goals in the last quarter of the game. Albion's goalkeeper Tony Millington had played in a Central League game on the same ground earlier in the season and let in eight goals – he conceded seven this time and so saw 15 fired past him by some eager Wolves players.

On 29 December 1929, Albion crushed Wolves 7-3 in a home Second Division match, but the victory was marred when the Wanderers goalkeeper, Billy Walker, making his debut, broke his ankle just before half-time.

Wolves also trounced Albion 6-1 in a home League game over Christmas 1896 and in mid-January 1899 they again thrashed the Throstles, this time by 7-0 in an away second round Birmingham Cup-tie.

Wolves' heaviest defeat at the hands of Albion (in League and Cup) is 8-0 – in a First Division game at Molineux on 27 December 1893. At the time Wolves were FA Cup holders and this remains as Albion's best ever away League win while it is also Wolves' heaviest ever home defeat.

The first clash between the two clubs in the Second Division took place on 29

A Wolves goal for Bobby Gould in the centenary match at The Hawthorns in March 1971.

September 1906 at Molineux – and it turned out to be a great day for four ex-Wanderers players – Jim Stringer, Dick Betteley, Ted Pheasant and Adam Haywood – who helped Albion to a 3-0 victory.

A rare own-goal by Wolves defender Keith Curle gave Albion a 1-0 Nationwide League win at The Hawthorns in September 1997.

On 2 March 1895, a FA Cup-tie was played at Stoney Lane, which Albion won 1-0 before a then record crowd of 20,977.

There was a tremendous confrontation between the clubs in the third round of the FA Cup in February 1924. In the initial game at The Hawthorns, Albion of the First Division, were held to a 1-1 draw by Wolves of the Third Division North before 53,649 fans. But it was the Throstles who came out tops in the replay, winning 2-0 in front of a midweek Molineux crowd of 40,283.

During Albion's double-winning season of 1930-31 they defeated Wolves twice in the League (2-1 at The Hawthorns and 4-1 at Molineux) and also knocked the Wanderers out of the FA Cup, winning a sixth-round replay 2-1 at Molineux after a 1-1 draw. These four matches were watched by a combined total of 175,264 spectators with over 99,000 witnessing the two cup clashes.

During the 1930s Wolves remained unbeaten in home League games against Albion while similarly the Baggies never lost to Wolves at The Hawthorns.

In May 1940, Wolves beat Albion 5-4 to clinch the wartime Midland Regional League championship.

Eighteen months later – in November 1941 – Albion ran out 8-2 winners over Wolves in a League (South) game. But Wolves quickly gained revenge by knocking Albion out of the wartime League Cup 7-0 on aggregate in the two-legged semi-final in May 1942 (winning 4-0 at The Hawthorns, 3-0 at Molineux).

Albion's biggest wartime crowd at The Hawthorns – 38,077 – witnessed the 1-1 draw against Wolves in a Football League (South) game on 23 April 1946.

Wolves and Albion met for the first time after the restoration of League football in 1946 at Molineux on 26 February 1949 in the sixth-round of the FA Cup. Wolves scraped through 1-0 with a goal by Jimmy Mullen. This is Wolves' only FA Cup victory over Albion and they went on to win the trophy at Wembley that year.

A record League crowd at The Hawthorns – 60,945 – saw Albion held to a 1-1 draw by Wolves on 4 March 1950.

Wolves and Albion were involved in a titanic battle for the League championship in 1953-54 – and it was Wolves who finally took the star prize. They beat Albion twice (1-0 on both occasions) the vital victory coming at The Hawthorns on 3 April courtesy of Roy

Swinbourne's 58th minute goal, which virtually ended Albion's chances of taking the title.

Wolves (the League champions) and Albion (the FA Cup holders) played out a tremendous 4-4 draw at Molineux in the FA Charity Shield in September 1954. Over 45,000 fans saw Ronnie Allen score a hat-trick for the Baggies, who trailed by two goals with 14 minutes remaining.

Over a period of ten years – 1953 to 1963 – Albion lost eight times in ten League visits to Molineux, winning only once – 5-1 under floodlights in March 1962.

Earlier that season Albion knocked Wolves out of the FA Cup, winning 2-1 at Molineux in the fourth round, when full-back Bobby Thomson made his senior debut for the Wanderers.

Phil Parkes saved a sixth-minute penalty from Tony Brown but was later sent off in the 3-3 draw at Molineux soon after Wolves had returned to the First Division in August 1967. Over 52,400 fans had seen Wolves hold a 3-1 lead in this game, but Albion came back and their late equaliser was contentious.

The return game at The Hawthorns a week later ended: Albion 4 Wolves 1.

Wolves' 1,000th post-war Football League game was at The Hawthorns in March 1970 when they drew 3-3 with Albion in front 37,819 fans.

The 100th League meeting between the clubs took place at The Hawthorns on 20 March 1971. Wolves came out on top, winning a First Division game 4-2 with Bobby Gould (soon to join Albion) among the scorers. Albion were 1-0 up at half-time in this game.

When holding Wolves to a 0-0 draw at home on 13 January 1996, Albion ended a sequence of 11 successive League defeats – the worst run in the club's history.

Welsh international Iwan Roberts became the first Wolves player to score a hat-trick on Albion territory when he obliged with a treble in a 4-2 win at The Hawthorns in a First Division match in September 1996.

When Albion beat Wolves 2-0 in November 1998 it was the first time they had achieved three victories on the bounce over their arch rivals since 1952 – and the gate receipts from that game at The Hawthorns created a new record for a League game between the two clubs on that ground – and indeed a local derby – of £243,949.

Mike Stowell beat Bert Williams' record for most senior appearances by a Wolves' goalkeeper when he played in his 421st game for the club in the local derby against Albion at Molineux in April 1999. A best-of-season League crowd of over 27,000 witnessed the 1-1 draw.

Away from first team action, in May 1963 Wolves' Reserves beat Albion's second string

8-3 in a Central League game at Molineux, Ted Farmer scoring four times. This is Wolves' best win over the Baggies at this level – and in 1998 the Wanderers went to The Hawthorns and won 5-0. Albion's reserve team beat Wolves' second team 6-0 at home in September 1924; five years later they won 5-1 at Molineux and in April 1936 a nine-goal thriller at this level ended Wolves 4 Albion 5 at Molineux. In season 1947-48, Wolves Reserves won both games against Albion by the same scoreline of 5-2.

Players with both clubs include: Harry Aston, Dicky Baugh, Dick Betteley, Paul Bradshaw, Steve Bull, Davey Burnside, John Chadburn, Sid Corfield, Ray Crawford, Robbie Dennison, Peter Eastoe, Paul Edwards, Don Goodman, Bobby Gould, Andy Gray, Adam Haywood, Danny Hegan, Eric Jones, Billy Jordan, Andy King, Tony Lange, Stacey North, Dan Nurse, John Paskin, Walter Perry, Ted Pheasant, Cyrille Regis, Alistair Robertson, Cecil Shaw, Jimmy Stringer, Andy Thompson, David Walker, Clive Whitehead, George Woodhall, Tom Worton and Harry Wright.

Bull went on to become Wolves' record marksman of all-time, netting over 300 goals for the Molineux club (up to 1999).

Also associated with Wolves and Albion: Ronnie Allen (Albion player, manager and coach, also coach and manager of Wolves; Billy Elliott (Wolves junior); Fred Hartland (amateur at Albion before Wolves; Meynell Burgin (Wolves reserve before Albion); Bill Morris (Albion junior before Wolves: 1933-47): Arthur Rowley (amateur with Wolves before Albion); Don Howe (Wolves trialist before Albion); Joe Butcher (FA Cup winner with Wolves but before he could make his debut for Albion a knee injury forced him to quit the game at the age of 21); Jack Ellis (amateur with Albion before Wolves); Josiah Davies (Albion reserve before Wolves); Harry Wilkes (Albion amateur before Wolves); Arthur G. Kelsey (Albion player, Wolves reserve), Tudor Martin (Albion reserve, later with Wolves); David Felgate and John T. Turner (Reserves), Ronnie Stockin (Albion amateur, later with Wolves); Mick Martin (on loan to Wolves having earlier played for Albion). Mark Jones (apprentice at Albion, brief spell with Wolves); Vince Bartram, (Wolves goalkeeper, on loan to Albion); Mel Eves (Wolves player, later Albion non-contract); ex-Wolves stars Alan Birch, Cavan Chapman, his brother Campbell and Paul Dougherty all wore Albion colours; Jimmy Dunn (Wolves player, Albion trainer); Doug Taylor (Albion amateur, Wolves player); Ron Bradley (Albion player, Wolves coach); Garry Pendrey (Albion player, Wolves coach); Jack Screen (Albion full-back, Wolves trainer);. Jack Smith (Wolves player, Albion manager); John Jarman (trainer/coach at both clubs);

Gordon Dimbleby (commercial manager at both clubs, also Albion secretary); Kim Wassall (Albion reserve, later Wolves); Bobby Downes (Albion reserve, later assistant manager to Graham Taylor at Wolves); Lee Hughes (Wolves junior, later Albion striker); Jesse Pennington, (Albion defender, later Wolves scout); Bobby Hope (Albion player later Wolves coach); Ron Atkinson and Keith Burkinshaw (both amateurs at Wolves, later Albion managers); Fred Pedley (physiotherapist at Albion and Wolves); Bob Burton (groundsman at both clubs). Thirteen players guested for both Wolves and Albion in World War Two: Jack Acquaroff, George Billingsley, Lester Finch, John Griffiths, Jimmy Jinks, Jim McCormick, Jock McDonald, Laurie Scott, Jack Shelton, Tom Smalley, Jack Smith, Les Smith and Tom Wood. Wolves' Jack Brodie guested for Albion in 1886 as did Charlie Mason against Renton in 'Championship of the World' game in 1888. Ex-Wolves star Derek Dougan scored for Albion in Johnny Giles' testimonial match against Leeds in 1975 and Manchester United's George Best netted for Wolves in Mike Bailey's testimonial against Albion in 1976. Tom Wildsmith, a Wolves player in the 1930s, later became Albion's scout in the Sheffield area.

Striker Ally Brown, who spent 11 years at The Hawthorns, was all set to join Wolves from Albion in March 1983 – and was actually photographed in a Wolves shirt. But the deal fell through and he moved to Crystal Palace instead, quickly transferring to Walsall and then to Port Vale for whom he scored against Wolves in a Milk Cup-tie in 1984.

WEST HAM UNITED

Wolves' playing record against the Hammers is:

Football League

Venue	P	W	D	L	F	A
Home	26	13	6	7	40	29
Away	26	3	7	16	25	60
Total	52	16	13	23	65	89

FA Cup

Home	1	0	0	1	1	5

Wartime

Home	1	0	1	0	3	3
Away	1	0	0	1	1	2
Total	2	0	1	1	4	5

Wolves first met the Hammers at League level in season 1919-20. After a 1-1 draw at Molineux, a crowd of 16,000 saw the Londoners win the return fixture 4-0 at Upton Park.

The following season the Hammers completed the first of three successive League doubles over Wolves, and included in that run of six straight wins was a 4-1 victory at Molineux in December 1922.

With the Hammers in the Second Division, Wolves' first League success did not

arrive until April 1960 when goals by Jimmy Murray (2), Eddie Clamp, Des Horne and Gerry Mannion gave them a convincing 5-0 scoreline at Molineux in front of more than 48,000 fans.

West Ham, though, quickly avenged that defeat by beating Wolves by exactly the same score at Upton Park eight months later when Bobby Moore scored one of the goals.

Wolves recorded their best win on Hammers' soil in August 1962, Ted Farmer netting twice in a 4-1 victory.

The two League matches in 1964-65 produced 12 goals. Wolves won 4-3 at Molineux just a week after crashing 5-0 a Upton Park, Geoff Hurst scoring twice in the latter game.

A total of 11 goals were scored in the two encounters in 1974-75. Wolves won 3-1 at home but lost 5-2 in London when ex-Wolf Bobby Gould scored for the Hammers.

Wolves crashed 4-0 at Upton Park on the final day of the 1989-90 season and the last time the teams met in the League saw Wolves win 2-1 at Molineux in February 1991, Steve Bull and Paul Birch the scorers.

A crowd of 17,000 saw the Hammers of the Southern League crush Wolves 5-1 in a second-round FA Cup-tie at Molineux in February 1910.

Wolves played the Hammers twice in a tournament in the USA in 1969, winning one game 4-2 and losing the other 3-2.

Players with both clubs include: Ted Anderson, Francis Burrill, Stan Burton, Richard Deacon, Jack Dowen, George Eccles, Joe Gallagher, Bobby Gould, Noel Dwyer, Harry Hooper, Kevin Keen, David Kelly, Tudor Martin, Dick Richards, Robbie Slater, Mike Small, Jack Weare and Bob Young.

Also associated: Dennis Westcott (West Ham trial), Joe Musgrave (Wolves trial), Arthur Wilson (reserve).

WESTCOTT, Dennis

Dennis Westcott was a prolific goalscorer. Born in Wallasey on 2 July 1917, he played for England at schoolboy level and after unsuccessful trials with West Ham United, he joined New Brighton as a junior for the 1932-33 season. After turning professional he moved to Molineux in February 1937 while still a teenager and over the next ten years became one of the finest marksmen in the game. He played his first game for the Wanderers on the right-wing in an FA Cup replay against Grimsby Town, starring in a 6-2 win. His first League goal came soon afterwards against Stoke City – the first of 128 for Wolves at this level. Thereafter he established himself in the centre-forward shirt in 1938, remaining there for ten years, until his transfer to Blackburn Rovers in April 1948. He was Wolves' leading scorer in seasons 1937-38 and 1938-39 and despite the war (when he was a sergeant in the Royal Artillery and

guested for Brentford, Cheltenham Town, Liverpool and Watford) again in 1939-40, 1941-42, 1942-43 and 1946-47. His tally of 43 goals in the 1938-39 season, which included a four-timer against Grimsby Town in the FA Cup semi-final at Old Trafford, remained a club record until beaten by Steve Bull in 1987-88 with 52. Westcott played for Wolves in their 1939 FA Cup Final defeat by Portsmouth and was a winner when Sunderland were beaten over two legs in the 1942 wartime League Cup Final. He was desperately unlucky not to have won a full England cap, but he did represent his country in four Victory internationals (1945-46) and starred for the Football League XI against the Scottish League in 1947. For Blackburn, he scored 37 goals in only 63

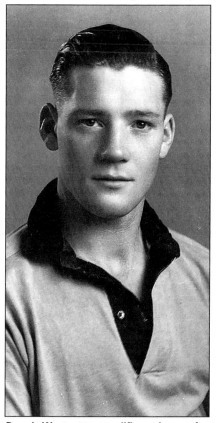

Dennis Westcott – a prolific goalscorer for Wolves either side of World War Two.

League outings and after leaving Ewood Park he added 37 more goals to his tally in 72 starts for Manchester City whom he served from February 1950 to June 1952. He wound down his senior career by netting 21 goals in 40 League matches for Chesterfield before retiring from first-class soccer in 1953. He then spent a short time with Stafford Rangers, ending his playing days in May 1959. Westcott netted a total of 19 hat-tricks for Wolves (seven League, two FA Cup and ten wartime) – a record which still stands to day with Steve Bull having claimed 18. In May 1940, (as a guest) Westcott was paid £4 to play for Cheltenham against Worcester City – the maximum wage at the time was just £1.50. Dennis Westcott died on 13 July 1960 in Stafford, still a relatively young man. *Wolves record: 144 apps. 124 goals (also 72 wartime apps. 91 goals).*

WESTLEY, Shane Lee Mark

Shane Westley was a sound defender, able to play in a variety of positions, but it was as a centre-back where he produced his best displays. Born in Canterbury on 16 June 1965, he attended Windcheap Primary and Frank Hooker Secondary schools in London, and was a junior with Tottenham Hotspur before signing for Charlton Athletic as an apprentice in 1981, turning professional with the Addicks in June 1983. Two years later, after a loan spell at Roots Hall, he was transferred to Southend United for £15,000, and made over 150 appearances for the Shrimpers before switching to Wolves for £150,000 in June 1989. He had two good seasons at Molineux, but loss of form and injury problems led to him moving to Brentford for £100,000 in October 1992. After a loan spell with his former club Southend (February/March 1995) he went to Cambridge United on a free transfer in August 1995 and a little over two years later he switched to Lincoln City for £7,500. After deciding to retire in 1997 Westley – who by now had become a qualified FA coach – was appointed assistant manager at Sincil Bank to John Beck, and when Beck was dismissed in March 1998, Westley took over as caretaker-boss of the Imps. He then became full-time manager at Sincil Bank in June 1998, but was dismissed after poor results in November 1998. In January 1999 Westley became assistant manager at Barrow under his former boss at Lincoln John Beck. *Wolves record: 55+2 apps. 3 goals.*

WESTWOOD, Christopher

Born in Dudley on 13 February 1977, utility defender Chris Westwood made his first full appearance for Wolves at the age of 20 in a 1-0 Coca-Cola Cup win at Fulham in September 1997, along with the Spaniard, Jesus Sanjuan. He did well for the remainder of that season, receiving high praise at times from his manager and coaches. Unfortunately he didn't develop as anticipated and in May 1998 Westwood was given a free transfer by Wolves. After trials with Reading he later linked up with Hartlepool United, managed by the former Wolves coach Chris Turner. *Wolves record: 4+2 apps. 1 goal.*

WHARTON, Guy

Wing-half Guy Wharton was an FA Cup winner at Wembley with Portsmouth in April 1939 (against Wolves) having left Molineux for Fratton Park a few weeks before the last pre-war Final. Born in Broomfield, Kent, on 5 December 1916, he played initially for Broomfield Rangers and started his League career with Chester in 1935, joining Wolves in readiness for the 1936-37 season. He stayed with the club until his departure to Fratton Park in March 1939. During the war Wharton guested for Chester, Darlington, Middlesbrough, Norwich City and Sunderland and went on to play for Pompey until July 1948, when he transferred to Darlington. *Wolves record: 35 apps. 2 goals.*

WHARTON, Terence J.

Terry Wharton was a fine goalscoring outside-right, who was first choice at Molineux for six years: 1962-67 inclusive. He and his fellow winger Dave Wagstaffe were, in fact, two of the finest wing-forwards in League football during the mid-sixties with Wharton adding goalscoring prowess to his ability. A wartime baby, born in Bolton on 1 July 1942, he joined Wolves on his 15th birthday in 1957 and became a full-time professional at Molineux in October 1959, making his Football League debut against Ipswich Town the following month, scoring in a 2-0 win. Wharton went on to keep that No.7 short for the next five and a half seasons, during which time he appeared in more than 240 first-class games, helping the club regain their First Division status in 1966-67. In November 1967 he was transferred to his home town club, Bolton Wanderers for £60,000 and after more than 100 games for the Trotters he went south to sign for Crystal Palace (January 1971). From Selhurst Park he switched to South Africa, having a brief spell with Durban City before returning to England in November 1973 to assist Walsall. He retired from competitive football in 1974 with almost 100 goals to his credit in close on 350 League appearances. Wharton then tripped round the non-League scene – as player-manager of Dudley Town and Tividale, and manager of Stourbridge and Brewood. He later acted as part-time coach with Wombourne Rovers and also coached at Ounsdale School. A keen cricketer, Wharton spent 13 years with Brewood CC. Son of Johnny Wharton, the former Preston North End, Manchester City, Blackburn Rovers and Newport County outside-right, Terry was a fine penalty-taker, netting over 20 times from the spot during his career. *Wolves record: 241+1 apps. 79 goals.*

WHATMORE, Ernest

Ernie Whatmore was a reserve centre-forward at Molineux during the early 1920s. Born in Kidderminster on 25 April 1900, he joined the Wolves playing staff from Stourbridge in July 1922 and was released in January 1923 when he moved to Shrewsbury Town. Returning to League football with Bristol Rovers at the start of the 1923-24 campaign, he went on to play over 140 senior games for the Pirates and then added another 80 to his tally with Queen's Park Rangers (1928-32) before rounding off his career with Shepherds Bush. Whatmore died in his native Kidderminster on 31 July 1991, aged 91. *Wolves record: 2 apps.*

WHITE, Edward

Capable inside-left Ted White was born in Wolverhampton in 1900 and died in Shrewsbury in 1970. Brother of Joe (below) he played one season with Wolves (May 1922-July 1923) having been signed from Wellington Town. He returned to his former club on leaving Molineux and later played for Welshpool. *Wolves record: 11 apps. 3 goals.*

WIIITE, Joseph

Born in Wolverhampton in 1903, inside-right Joe White's only senior outing for Wolves was against South Shields (away) in January 1923. Like his brother Ted (above) he, too, played for Wellington before and after leaving Wolves. He died in Shropshire *c.*1974. *Wolves record: 1 app.*

WHITE, Robert Nelson

Right-winger Bob White had a useful career in the game, serving with a number of clubs, starting off with Prudhoe Colliery, he then played for Prudhoe Castle FC in 1919 before joining Huddersfield Town, from where he switched to Stoke in May 1924. He transferred to Tranmere Rovers in March 1925; had a brief spell with Yeovil and Petters *c.*1928 and was then associated with Wolves in season 1929-30. He later assisted Watford, Portsmouth, Carlisle United and North Shields, retiring in 1939. White was born in the village of Walbottle near Newburn-on-Tyne on 11 August 1902 and died on 10 July 1977. *Wolves record: 3 apps. 2 goals.*

WHITE, Walter

Walter White scored twice for Wolves in their first-ever Football League victory, a 4-1 home triumph over Burnley in September 1888. Born in Halesowen in 1864, he played for Coombs Wood before joining Wolves in readiness for that initial League campaign of 1888-89. Unfortunately he failed to establish himself in the first team and was released by the club in April 1890, when he teamed up with Cradley St Luke's. White died in Walsall *c.*1930. *Wolves record: 4 apps. 2 goals.*

WHITEHEAD, Clive R.

Clive Whitehead had a fine career, serving with Bristol City, West Bromwich Albion and

Wolves at League level. Able to play as a full-back, in midfield or left-winger, he was born on 24 November 1955 in Birmingham and played for Northfield Juniors before turning professional with Bristol City in August 1973. After winning England Youth international honours he went on to play in more than 250 games for the Ashton Gate club before transferring to West Brom in November 1981. During his six years at The Hawthorns, the versatile Whitehead skippered the Baggies and made almost 200 League and Cup appearances for the club prior to his transfer to Portsmouth in June 1987, having been on loan to Wolves in January 1986. After leaving Fratton Park he assisted Exeter City, first as a player then as player-manager before being sacked in April 1991 after only six months in charge. He then served with Yeovil Town and in 1996 returned to his first club, Bristol City, as youth team coach in 1997, a position he held for 15 months. Whitehead's wife gave birth to twins whilst he was at The Hawthorns.

Wolves record: 4 apps.

WHITEHOUSE, John

A very stylish, yet competitive half-back, the fair-haired Jack Whitehouse was a regular in Wolves' League side for five years from 1901 (he was sent-off at least once during his time with Wolves). Born in Swan Village, West Bromwich in August 1878, Whitehouse, who had four brothers, two of them footballers, played for Great Bridge School and Wednesbury Town before moving to Molineux in July 1900. Acting initially as reserve to Ted Pheasant, he finally claimed his place in the first team the following year, but after a misdemeanour within the club (he was involved in a flare-up with two colleagues) Whitehouse was banished to Stourbridge for two months to 'cool down.' He came back and gave Wolves more sterling service before leaving to sign for Stoke in October 1906. He played in two League games for the Potters the following month and was released early in 1907. He then went on to play for a number of Black Country sides, including Bloxwich Strollers, Darlaston, Dudley and Gornal Wood. He retired in 1915.

Wolves record: 155 apps. 1 goal

WHITFIELD, Kenneth

Ken Whitfield had a difficult time at Molineux – not in terms of playing football, simply because there were so many other quality forwards at the club around the same time. He began his career as an amateur with Shildon Colliery in County Durham, arriving at Molineux in December 1947. He spent the next six years with Wolves playing mainly in the Reserves and youth teams, although he did hit the headlines with a cracking hat-trick in a 3-0 home win over Blackpool in

December 1951. Thus, with the likes of Peter Broadbent, Dennis Wilshaw, Jesse Pye, Roy Swinbourne and Johnny Walker occupying the three inside-forward berths between them, Whitfield was allowed to leave for Manchester City in March 1953. He spent a shade over a season at Maine Road before moving south to play for Brighton and Hove Albion for whom he made almost 200 senior appearances. He rounded off his major career by having a season with Queen's Park Rangers (1959-60).

Wolves record: 10 apps. 4 goals.

WHITTAKER, Percy

Goalkeeper Percy Whittaker was born in Swinton on 19 November 1905. He played his early football with Grantham and joined Wath Wanderers in 1929 before becoming a full-time professionalism at Molineux in August 1930. Acting as reserve to Alf Tootill and Jack Ellis but with injuries interrupting his progress he found it difficult to get regular first-team football and with less than a dozen senior appearances under his belt plus a Central League Championship medal won in 1931, he left Wolves for Reading in June 1933. He did very well at Elm Park and amassed over 160 outings for the Biscuitmen prior to the outbreak of World War Two. He played occasionally during the hostilities, but retired from the League scene in 1945-46 to concentrate on his business while keeping goal for Redditch United on a part-time basis.

Wolves record: 11 apps.

WHITTAM, Ernest Alfred

Inside-forward Ernie Whittam was blind in one eye, but still managed to have a useful footballing career. Born in Wealdstone on 7 January 1911, he played, in turn, for Deighton Council School, Huddersfield Town (as an amateur from December 1926, turning professional in November 1928), Chester (signed for £500 in May 1933), Mansfield Town (May 1935), Wolves (from February 1936), Bournemouth (September 1936), Reading (1937) and Rotherham United (1945-46) and Leeds United, retiring in 1947. His outings were restricted at Molineux due to the presence of so many utility forwards, but all told he scored 57 goals in a total of 202 League appearances in a very useful career.

Wolves record: 1 app.

WHITTINGHAM, Guy

Guy Whittingham was a goalscoring centre-forward in the Army when he decided to buy himself out of the forces and become a professional footballer with Portsmouth in June 1989, having assisted Yeovil Town for a season prior to that. Born in Evesham on 10 November 1964, Whittingham did supremely

well at Fratton Park, scoring 104 goals in 188 first-class matches (including a club record 47 in 1992-93) before transferring to Aston Villa for £1.2 million in August 1993. Unfortunately he failed to match those goalscoring exploits with Villa and after a loan spell with Wolves (February/March 1994) he was sold to Sheffield Wednesday for £700,000 four days before Christmas, 1994. At Hillsborough Whittingham was eventually asked to play in midfield where he succeeded, contributing much to the Owls' excellent 1996-97 season, laying on five goals in a 7-1 Coca-Cola Cup win over Grimsby Town. He reached the milestone of 100 senior appearances for Wednesday early in the 1997-98 campaign but then, during the first half of 1998-99, under new boss Danny Wilson, he found himself out of the side and consequently returned to Wolves for a second loan spell in November 1998. After that was over he returned to Hillsborough, but in January 1999 Whittingham chose to go back to his former club Portsmouth for another loan spell. And on the transfer deadline in March 1999 he moved to Watford, again on loan.

Wolves record: 23+1 apps. 9 goals.

WIGAN ATHLETIC

Wolves' playing record against Athletic is:

Football League

Venue	P	W	D	L	F	A
Home	2	1	1	0	4	3
Away	2	0	1	1	4	6
Total	4	1	2	1	8	9

FA Cup

Away	1	1	0	0	3	1

Wolves and Wigan drew 2-2 at Molineux in the first League meeting between the two clubs in December 1985. In the return fixture at Springfield Park that season Wigan won a thrilling encounter 5-3 in front of 4,029 fans. Warren Aspinall scored a hat-trick for the Latics who led 3-1 after 26 minutes and after Wolves had drew level on the hour, scored twice more to sew up the points.

Wolves recorded their only League win in October 1988 – just over 10,000 fans seeing Steve Bull and Jackie Gallagher hit the net in a 2-1 victory at Molineux.

Wolves' FA Cup success over Wigan came in season 1987-88, Robbie Dennison, Gallagher and Phil Robinson scoring in a 3-1 win.

Players with both clubs include: Paul Cook, Isidro Diaz, Scott McGarvey, Andy Mutch, John Pender and Colin Taylor.

WIGAN BOROUGH

Wolves' playing record against Borough is:

Football League

Venue	P	W	D	L	F	A
Home	1	0	1	0	3	3
Away	1	0	1	0	1	1
Total	2	0	2	0	4	4

The two League encounters took place in Wolves' 1923-24 Third Division North championship-winning season. Evan Edwards scored in both games for the Wanderers, including a great 25-yard drive in the six-goal thriller at Molineux which attracted 21,425 fans.

Player with both clubs: Billy Crew.

WIGNALL, Frank

Goalscorer Frank Wignall had a fine career in League football that began in 1959 and ended in 1973. Born in Blackrod near Chorley, Lancashire on 21 August 1939, he played for Horwich R.M.I. before becoming a professional with Everton in May 1958. He made his League debut for the Merseysiders the following year and in June 1963, after scoring 15 goals in 33 First Division games, was transferred to Nottingham Forest. At the City Ground he did extremely well and netted 47 times in 156 League outings before moving to Molineux in March 1968. He remained with Wolves for just under a year, leaving for Derby County in February 1969. After claiming another 15 League goals for the Rams (in 45 matches) he switched to his last senior club Mansfield Town in November 1971. He stayed at Field Mill until the end of the 1972-73 season, by which time he had taken his record in League football to 107 goals in 322 appearances. After leaving Mansfield Wignall went on to play for a number of non-League clubs including King's Lynn and Burton Albion. Capped twice by England against Belgium and Holland in 1964, Wignall also represented the Football League.
Wolves record: 35+1 apps. 16 goals.

WILDMAN, Frank Reginald

Goalkeeper Frank Wildman was a Yorkshireman, born in Pontefract in August 1910. He joined Wolves from South Kirkby Colliery FC in November 1932, shortly after Alf Tootill had left Molineux for Fulham. Unfortunately he made a disastrous entry into League football, conceding five goals on his debut at Craven Cottage on Christmas Eve, 1932. Poor old Wildman, in fact, let in 22 goals in his first eight outings for the club before losing his place in the side to Jack Ellis. In 1933-34 he bounced back and played in 34 games that season before being replaced between the posts early in the 1934-35 campaign by Cyril Spiers. With Arthur Weare also pushing for a first-team place, Wildman was then sold to Reading in February 1935. He later assisted Swindon Town (94 League games) and thereafter played for a number of non-League clubs including Frickley Colliery until retiring in 1945 having guested for Grimsby Town, Rotherham United and Swansea Town during the hostilities. Wildman was also a very useful all-round

cricketer and once scored a century in a Bank Holiday fixture as well as taking 5-35 with his slow left-arm all-sorts. He was a competent tennis player as well.
Wolves record: 56 apps.

WILDSMITH, Thomas B.

Acting as a reserve to Jack Nelson, right-half Tom Wildsmith played once in Wolves' League side – away at Sheffield United in February 1933. He was signed from Hadfield Sports FC in November 1932 and left Molineux for Bristol Rovers in August 1933, later assisting Doncaster Rovers (1935-37) and Rochdale, and then guested for Southport during war. He retired in 1945 and returned home to live in his native Sheffield. In the 1940s and 1950s Wildsmith was appointed West Bromwich Albion's scout in the Sheffield area. Born on 8 January 1913, Wildsmith was an efficient, reliable and steady player who did very well after leaving Molineux.
Wolves record: 1 app.

WILKES, Gilbert Harry

Born in West Bromwich in 1882, Harry Wilkes was related to the famous Wilkes family of photographers. He was a reserve inside-left and played his only League game for Wolves against Derby County (away) in December 1905. He was a pupil at Beeches Road school, played for St Phillip's Church team, West Bromwich Standard and West Bromwich Albion (as an amateur) before being recruited by Wolves in September 1905. He left Molineux for Dudley Town in May 1906. Wilkes died in Walsall in 1942.
Wolves record: 1 app.

WILLIAMS, Adrian

Born in Reading on 16 August 1971, defender Adrian Williams joined his home town club as a 16-year-old and turned professional at Elm Park in March 1989. He went on to play in more than 240 games for Reading before joining Wolves for £750,000 in July 1996, teaming up again with his former boss Mark McGhee. After suffering a knee injury on Wolves' summer tour to Austria he played in only eight senior team games in his first season at Molineux, six of them resulting in victories. Even during the 1997-98 campaign he struggled with injuries but the resilient Williams battled on and was rewarded with a recall to the Welsh international squad for the European Championship qualifiers by team manager Bobby Gould in 1998-99. Williams has ** full caps to his credit – with more to come one feels. He helped Reading win the Second Division title in 1993-94.
Wolves record: 33+2 apps. 1 goal.

WILLIAMS, Bertram Frederick

There is no doubt that Bert Williams was a great goalkeeper. He was Wolves' number

one for a total of 12 seasons, from September 1945 until April 1957, and during that time starred in well over 400 senior matches, including 381 in the First Division of the Football League. Quite brilliant at times, he was agile, alert, fearless and utterly reliable. Known as 'The Cat' he won 24 England caps between 1949 and 1955 and played in the 1954 World Cup Finals in Switzerland.

Born in Bilston on 31 January 1920, Bert played for Thompson's FC on leaving school and after a brief spell on the Fellows Park groundstaff, turned professional with Walsall in April 1937. During World War Two, Williams served in the RAF (reaching the rank of sergeant) and guested for Chelsea and Derby County, and when the hostilities were over he left the Saddlers to join Wolves for a bargain fee of £3,500 in September 1945, playing in 30 League games in that transitional season. In 1949 he helped Wolves win the FA Cup and five years later gained a League Division One championship medal. He retired from first-class football at the end of the 1956-57 season, handing over his goalkeeping duties at Molineux to Malcolm Finlayson. For a number of years afterwards Bert ran a highly successful sports-outfitters shop in Bilston, as well as organising a goalkeeping school for youngsters in the area. Today he lives in Shifnal.
Wolves record: 420 apps. (606 goals conceded).

WILLIAMS, Evan

Despite his Welsh-sounding surname, goalkeeper Evan Williams was born in Dumbarton, Scotland on 15 July 1943, having an English father and a Scottish mother. He was a capable goalkeeper with good technique who acted as first reserve to both Phil Parkes and Fred Davies at Molineux. He began his playing career with Third Lanark who signed him straight from school in 1958, making him a professional on his 17th birthday. He had 26 games for the now-defunct Scottish League club before joining Wolves for £5,000 in March 1966. Williams was loaned out to Aston Villa in August/September 1969 and after returning to Molineux he finally quit Wolves in March 1970, going back to his homeland to sign for Celtic. He retired from first-class football in 1972.
Wolves record: 15 apps.

WILLIAMS, George Harvey

Wing-half George (sometimes referred to as Charlie) Williams spent three seasons at Molineux (August 1903 to October 1906), playing reserve team football in his initial campaign before going on to establish himself in the first team. Born in Shirebrook in 1882, he was signed from Blakenhall and joined Tettenhall Rangers on leaving the club. He died in Bilston in 1939.
Wolves record: 51 apps.

WILLIAMS, Leonard Horace

An efficient footballer, good on the ball and always totally committed, full-back Len Williams took over from Ted Watson in the Wolves team and did a good job until the arrival of Wilf Lowton. Born in Rotherham in 1902, he graduated with Wath Athletic in 1922 before signing as a professional with Sheffield Wednesday in July 1923. From Hillsborough he switched to Stockport County (May 1926) and arrived at Molineux in June 1927. On leaving Wolves, he was recruited by Swansea Town (September 1930) and after spells with Oswestry Town and Wellington. Williams retired four years later.

Wolves record: 50 apps.

WILLIAMS, Mark Frank

South African striker (born in Johannesburg on 11 August 1966), Mark Williams was a £300,000 signing by Wolves from RWD Molenbeek in September 1995. Capped several times by his country prior to his arrival at Molineux, he scored two early goals for Wolves, but failed to earn a work permit by not appearing in 75 per cent of the games he was available for, and consequently he was released at the end of that season.

Wolves record: 8+8 apps. 2 goals.

WILLIAMS, Nigel J.

Steady defender, relaxed in his style whose first-team outings were limited owing to the form of full-backs Geoff Palmer, Derek Parkin, Bernard Shaw and Gerry Taylor. Born in Canterbury on 29 July 1954, he joined Wolves as an apprentice in July 1970 and turned professional in August 1972. Four years later he was transferred to Gillingham (July 1976) and stayed with the Kent club for two years before dropping into non-League football.

Wolves record: 11 apps.

WILLIAMS, Walter

Wally Williams could play on either wing. He was recruited by Wolves from Ettinghsall in the summer of 1905, initially as cover for Jack Hopkins, but then Jack Pedley arrived to challenge him for the outside-left berth. Fast and tricky, he made four League appearances in the 1905-06 season before switching to the opposite flank, and then he had 22 games on the right in 1906-07 prior to Billy Harrison arriving on the scene. Williams found it hard to get into the first team after that and he left Molineux in June 1908, joining Darlaston, later assisting Willenhall Swifts. He was born in Stafford in 1883 and died in Wolverhampton c.1950.

Wolves record: 34 apps. 4 goals.

WILLIAMS, Walter John

After establishing themselves in the Second Division in 1924-25, Wolves added several players to their first-team squad, one being sturdy defender Jack Williams, a centre-half, who was recruited from Wednesfield Rovers. Unfortunately he failed to make his mark in the League side despite spending four seasons with the club, and left Molineux for Gillingham in June 1928, quickly switching to Brighton and Hove Albion for whom he made over 40 senior appearances prior to pulling out of League soccer in 1931. Born on 18 July 1906 in Wolverhampton, Williams was 76 when he died in a Brighton hospital on 26 July 1982.

Wolves record: 3 apps.

WILSHAW, Dennis James

Wilshaw was a natural goalscorer – a player who, in today's game, would have fitted into any forward-line superbly. Born in Packmoor, Stoke-on-Trent on 11 March 1926, Wilshaw was a pupil at Hanley High School and played junior football for the Packmoor Boys Club (for whom he once scored ten goals in a 16-0 win over Michelin Tyres). From here he signed for Wolves in September 1943 and within seven days he made his debut in a wartime game against neighbours West Bromwich Albion. In 1945 Wilshaw was loaned out to nearby Walsall and he also guested for Port Vale against Stoke in May 1946, when the Vale were beaten 6-0. He returned to Molineux in 1949 and scored a hat-trick on his League debut against Newcastle United, lining up in the No.11 shirt. Indeed, during his long association with Wolves he played in four front-line positions, outside-right being the odd one out. Wilshaw established himself in the Wolves' first team in 1952 and two years later was a key member of the team which landed the First Division championship. He also won two 'B' and 12 full caps for England, becoming the first player to net four goals against Scotland at Wembley in that emphatic 7-2 victory in April 1955. He moved from Molineux to Stoke in December 1957, and was a vital cog in the Potters' forward-line for four years before breaking a leg against Newcastle United in a FA Cup-tie in 1961. It was ironic that he should play his first and last senior games of his career against the Geordies as he was forced to retire after that second injury. Wilshaw scored exactly 50 goals in over 100 games for the Potters, and on leaving the Victoria Ground, concentrated on his profession as a schoolmaster, rising to the Head of Service and Community Studies at Crewe and Alsager College. He also scouted for Stoke for a short while and, being a keen golfer, he was made chairman of his golf club at Newcastle-under-Lyme. Wilshaw had a heart attack in 1993, from which he thankfully recovered.

Wolves record: 232 apps. 117 goals.

WILSON, Joseph

Joe Wilson was a right-back who made over 500 appearances during his professional career which spanned 17 years. Born in Workington on 6 July 1937, Wilson played as a junior for Workington (from May 1955) before turning professional in January 1956. In March 1962 he was transferred to Nottingham Forest, switching to Wolves in March 1965. Two years later, in May 1967, he was sold to Newport County and then returned to his former club, Workington as player-coach in September 1968. He retired from football in 1973.

Wolves record: 63 apps.

WILSON, Joseph Frank

Outside-left Frank Wilson played in two League games for Wolves in 1892-93, replacing Will Devey each time. Born in Hockley, Birmingham in 1871 and the younger brother of the Albion player Joe Wilson, he spent just the one season at Molineux before leaving for Castles Blues FC (Shrewsbury), returning to the Black Country to play for Walsall Wood and then Dudley Town. Earlier in his career he assisted Smethwick Swifts and Elwells. Wilson died in Handsworth, Birmingham 1949.

Wolves record: 2 apps.

WILSON, Leslie John

Nicknamed 'The Revd', Les Wilson had the honour of being the first substitute used by Wolves when he was called off the bench during a League game with Everton at Goodison Park in September 1967. A player who could occupy a full-back or midfield position, he was born in Manchester on 10 July 1947. Moving to Canada with his parents at an early age, he attended school in Vancouver but returned to England to sign apprentice forms with Wolves on his 16th birthday, turning professional in September 1964. He established himself in the first team at Molineux in the late 1960s, but was then sold to Bristol City in March 1971. In September 1973 he moved to Norwich City but at the end of that season (May 1974) he decided to try his luck in his adopted country, entering the NASL with Vancouver Whitecaps as player-coach. He held a coaching position with the Whitecaps until 1983 when he was appointed manager/administrator of the Canadian national team becoming a very important figure in Canadian soccer. He holds a Canadian passport.

Wolves record: 103+13 apps. 8 goals.

WIMBLEDON

Wolves' playing record against the Dons is:

Football League

Venue	P	W	D	L	F	A
Home	1	0	1	0	3	3
Away	1	0	1	0	1	1
Total	2	0	2	0	4	4

FA Cup

Home	1	1	0	0	2	1
Away	1	0	1	0	1	1
Total	2	1	1	0	3	2

The two League matches between the clubs took place in 1984-85 in Division Two. Just over 7,000 fans witnessed the 3-3 draw at Molineux when full-back David Barnes scored a rare goal for Wolves and there were a mere 3,277 spectators present to see the draw at Plough Lane.

The two FA Cup matches were played in season 1997-98. The first game was at Selhurst Park and after Wolves' had earned a 1-1 draw they came back to beat the Dons 2-1 at Molineux with a late goals from Dougie Freedman and Carl Robinson. The attendance was 25112.

Players with both club: Dave Beasant, Keith Curle, David Galvin, Hans Segers and Dave Wintersgill and Eric Young.

Also associated: Bobby Gould and Peter Withe (both Wolves players and Wimbledon managers); Don Howe (Wolves trialist, Wimbledon coach, assistant manager and chief scout).

WINTERSGILL, David

Dave Wintersgill was a reserve defender with Wolves, making only a handful of first-team appearances. A Yorkshireman, born in Northallerton on 19 September 1985, he was a junior at Molineux from June 1981 before turning professional in June 1983. After a loan spell with Chester City (March/April 1984) he had a brief spell with Wimbledon and played in Finland for two years before returning to this country to sign for Darlington in November 1986. He dropped out of League football the following year.
Wolves record: 3+1 apps.

WITHE, Peter

Peter Withe was a goalscoring nomad, who had a splendid playing career in the game which spanned almost 20 years. He netted well over 200 goals in more than 600 appearances while serving Southport (1970), Skelmersdale, Preston North End (1971), Barrow (also in 1971), Wolves (November 1973 to August 1975), Birmingham City, Nottingham Forest (1976), Newcastle United (August 1978), Aston Villa (signed for £500,000 in 1980), Sheffield United (1985), Birmingham City (again, on loan) and Huddersfield Town (player-coach in season 1988-89). He also went abroad to play in South Africa with Port Elizabeth and Arcadia Shepherds in 1972-73 and in 1987 he assisted Portland Timbers in the NASL. He won League and Cup medals with Nottingham Forest and Villa, scoring the winning goal in the 1981 European Cup Final for the latter club. He was also capped 11 times by England and was a big favourite with the fans

standing at the Holte End of Villa Park. After leaving Huddersfield he returned to Villa Park as assistant to manager Josef Venglos and later had a spell as team manager of Wimbledon before embarking on a position as football in the community officer with Port Vale. He then became a football summariser on local radio and in 1996 was appointed chief scout at his old club, Aston Villa. Two years later Withe took over as coach of the Thailand national team – amidst a lot of publicity.
Wolves record: 12+5 apps. 3 goals.

WOOD, George

Outside-left George Wood spent two seasons with Wolves: 1885-87, during which time he partnered his namesake, Harry Wood, in the forward-line. Born locally in Wolverhampton c.1862, he played for Goldthorn Villa and Wolverhampton Druids before joining Wolves and after leaving the club he served with Wednesbury Town and Willenhall Pickwick, retiring in 1891 after breaking his right leg.
Wolves record: 5 apps.

WOOD, Harry

England international utility forward Harry Wood was born in Walsall on 2 August 1868 and died in Portsmouth on 5 July 1951. A real gentleman, he was a model professional who played the game with great skill and enthusiasm. A pen-picture printed in 1889 described him as 'clever in ball manipulation and staidly exact in distribution. He certainly gave the fans something to cheer about during his two spells with the Wanderers.

On leaving school Wood played briefly for Walsall Town Swifts, joining Wolves in the summer of 1885 and making his senior debut for the Wanderers in an FA Cup-tie against Derby St Luke's on 31 October of that year. His first spell with Wolves lasted six years, until July 1891 when he re-signed for Walsall. But he was persuaded to return to Molineux five months later and remained at the club for a further six years before transferring to Southampton in June 1898. In his first spell Wood scored 46 goals in 87 League and Cup matches for the Wanderers while in his second he netted another 80 goals in 202 appearances. He finished up with an impressive record of more than 125 goals in just under 300 first-team games, and became the first Wolves player to claim 100 competitive goals. He won three full England caps between 1890 and 1896 and also represented the Football League. He starred in three FA Cup Finals with Wolves, those of 1889, 1893 and 1895, collecting a winners medal in his second against Everton when he had an exceptionally fine match. He went on to skipper Southampton for seven years (up to 1905) when he retired at the age of 37. He scored 62

goals in 158 games for Saints; played for them in two losing FA Cup Finals (1900 and 1902) and also gained four Southern League championship medals (1899, 1901, 1903 and 1904). After hanging up his boots Wood – nicknamed 'Wolf' – was appointed trainer of Portsmouth, a position he held until 1912 when he became landlord of the Milton Arms public house, situated 200 yards from Fratton Park. Wood spent the rest of his life in Portsmouth, passing away at the age of 83. His son, Arthur, also played for Southampton and Clapton Orient.
Wolves record: 289 apps. 126 goals.

WOODFIELD, David

Dark, curly-haired Dave Woodfield was a dogged centre-half, honest and competitive, who could also play as a full-back or wing-half and even centre-forward if required. He gave Wolves excellent service during the 1960s, amassing well over 270 senior appearances. Born in Leamington Spa on 11 October 1943, he joined Wolves as an amateur in January 1959 and turned professional on his 17th birthday. He broke into the first team towards the end of the 1961-62 campaign and made the No.5 shirt his own early in the following season. A fine stalwart, Woodfield helped Wolves gain promotion from Division Two before leaving Molineux for Watford in a £30,000 deal in September 1971. The following month he made his debut for the Hornets against Wolves and was carried off injured and never played again that season. He retired out of first-class soccer in 1974 after returning to Molineux to celebrate a deserved testimonial.
Wolves record: 273+3 apps. 15 goals.

WOODHALL, George

George 'Spry' Woodhall made his name as a goalscoring inside-forward with West Bromwich Albion, helping the Throstles win the FA Cup in 1888 when he hit one of the goals which beat Preston North End 2-1 at Kennington Oval. Born in West Bromwich on September 1863, he attended Hateley Heath school and played for West Bromwich All Saints and Churchfield Foresters before signing for Albion in May 1883, turning professional two years later. He went on to score 20 goals in 74 senior games for Albion, winning two England caps against Wales and Scotland in 1888 and also lining up in two more FA Cup Finals (1886 and 1887). He was almost 30 when he joined Wolves in July 1892 and did well during his brief spell at Molineux. He left the club in April 1894, signing for Berwick Rangers (a Birmingham League side). He later played for Oldbury Town (October 1894 to May 1898) before announcing his retirement. Woodhall died in West Bromwich on 16 September 1924.
Wolves record: 18 apps. 1 goal.

WOODRUFF, Robert

Bobby Woodruff had a tremendous throw in, sometimes hurling the ball a distance of 60 yards from the touchline to the far post and beyond. A wing-half or inside-forward, he made more than 570 League appearances during his career which spanned 19 years. Born in Highworth, Wiltshire on 9 November 1940, he was a junior with Swindon Town (September 1956) before turning professional at the County Ground in May 1958. He cost Wolves £40,000 when he transferred to Molineux in March 1964 and spent just over two years with the Wanderers before switching to Crystal Palace in a £35,000 deal in June 1966. In November 1969, Cardiff City recruited his services for a fee of £25,000 and in August 1974 he moved to Newport County for £5,000. Woodruff remained at Somerton Park until May 1976 when he quit major competitive soccer, winding down his career by playing at non-League level in South Wales. He helped Swindon gain promotion from Division Three in 1963 and then helped Palace win a place in the First Division in 1969. Woodruff's son, Bobby junior, played for Swindon Town and Newport County.
Wolves record: 72 apps. 21 goals.

WOODWARD, Maurice

Centre-half or right-back Maurice Woodward was a professional footballer for 12 years during which time he appeared for Leicester City (from August 1912), Southend United (June 1914), Wolves (from May 1919) and Bristol Rovers (June 1922 to May 1924). Born at Enderby, Leicestershire on 23 February 1892, Woodward started out with Enderby Town and played for Wolves in the 1921 FA Cup Final against Tottenham Hotspur. In the mid 1920s he was licensee of the Royal Oak, Compton Road, Wolverhampton. He died in 1968, aged 76.
Wolves record: 37 apps. 1 goal.

WOOLDRIDGE, William T.

Billy Wooldridge appeared in more than 350 games for Wolves. He was born in Netherton, Dudley on 19 August 1878 and played his early football with Netherton St Mary's, Dudley Road and Cradley St Luke's before joining Wolves in July 1899. Over the next 12 years, he gave the Molineux club excellent service, first as an attacker (he scored two hat-tricks, one against New Brighton in an FA Cup-tie in 1901 and another against Derby County in a League match in April 1906) and then as a centre-half. He scored four goals in England's 10-0 unofficial international match victory over Germany in September 1901 and he also starred for the Football League against the Irish League in that same season when he netted another treble. Wooldridge retired as a player in 1911.

He worked and lived in the area for a number of years before his death in Dudley in April 1945, at the age of 66.
Wolves record: 356 apps. 90 goals.

WORLD CUP FINALS

Jimmy Mullen, Bert Williams and Billy Wright (in 1950) and Williams, Dennis Wilshaw and Wright (in 1954), Peter Broadbent, Eddie Clamp, Bill Slater and Wright again (in 1958), Ron Flowers (1962 and in the initial 1966 squad) and Steve Bull (1990) – all England players – are the only Wolves stars to represent their country in the World Cup finals.

WORRALL, Arthur G.

Arthur Worrall was a utility forward who spent two seasons with Wolves: 1889 to 1891, his best campaign being his first (1889-90) when he made 25 first-team appearances on the right wing or as an inside-forward. Born in Wolverhampton *c*.1869, he joined the club from Fallings Heath Rangers and left Molineux for Goldthorn Villa, later playing for St Paul's and Whitmore Reans. Worrall died in 1935.
Wolves record: 37 apps. 13 goals.

WORRALL, George

George Worrall (no relation to Arthur) was one of the club's early players, who acted as team manager/secretary/committee member during an eight-year period from August 1877 to the summer of 1885. In fact, his position at the club was secretary rather than manager. Born locally, Worrall was a Wolves man through and through, and after giving up his job at the club, he remained a true supporter, cheering the team on from the terraces, first at the old Dudley Road ground and then at Molineux. He died *c*.1930.

WORTON, Thomas

Tom Worton was a sharp-shooting, all-purpose inside-left – a creator, driver and instigator from centre-field. Born in Heath Town, Wolverhampton on 5 February 1878, he played for Heath Town FC and Cannock Road schools before joining Wolves as a junior in 1895, turning professional in March 1896. After more than 50 League appearances and a record 158 outings in the Birmingham and District League for the Wanderers, he was transferred to West Bromwich Albion in May 1901. He helped the Throstles win the Second Division title in his first season at The Hawthorns before retiring through injury in June 1905. Worton died on 20 July 1940.
Wolves record: 59 apps. 12 goals.

WREKIN CUP

Wolves entered this short-lived competition just once in season 1883-84. And they won

the trophy without conceding a goal. They beat Hadley (a Shropshire club) 11-0 in the Final.

Earlier Wolves eliminated St Paul's (Lozells) 7-0 (a hat-trick here for Jack Brodie), Stafford Road 5-0 and Shrewsbury Castle Blues 5-0 (in a replay after Shrewsbury had made a successful protest following their first game defeat by 2-0).

Brodie scored six goals in the Final, Arthur Lowder (3), Jack Griffiths and Dicky Baugh got the others.

WREXHAM

Wolves' playing record against Wrexham is:

Football League

Venue	P	W	D	L	F	A
Home	3	1	0	2	3	5
Away	3	0	2	1	4	6
Total	6	1	2	3	7	11

FA Cup

Home	2	2	0	0	12	2

Wartime

Home	5	4	0	1	15	3
Away	5	1	3	1	9	8
Total	10	5	3	2	24	11

The first of the six League games between the clubs took place at the Racecourse Ground on 19 January 1924, Wolves taking a point from a 1-1 draw. A hat-trick by Harry Lees gave Wolves a 3-0 win in the return fixture at Molineux a week later.

The last four encounters were in the Fourth Division during the mid-eighties, Wrexham winning three of them, including a 3-0 victory on Wolves' soil in November 1986 and a 4-2 romp at home in April 1988, the last time the teams met.

Wolves beat Wrexham 9-1 at Molineux in a third-round FA Cup-tie in January 1931 before a 28,000 plus crowd. Billy Hartill (4) and Charlie Phillips (3) led the goal-race. Fifty years later, in February 1981, Wolves won a fifth round match at Molineux 3-1 and this time almost 33,800 fans were present to see substitute Norman Bell score twice.

Players with both clubs include: Ian Arkwright, George Bellis, Alf Bishop, Bill Bryant, Sid Corfield, Billy Harrison, Albert Hill, Harry Jones, Paul Jones, Fred Keetley, James Kelly, Jimmy Kelly, Albert Lumberg (later Wrexham trainer and coach), James Mason, John Matthews, Trevor Owen, John Paskin, George Showell (also trainer, coach etc. at Wrexham), Darren Wright.

Also associated: Graham Turner (Wrexham player, Wolves manager); Jack Rowley (Wolves reserve and guest, Wrexham manager), Jack Screen (Wrexham player, Wolves trainer); Freddie Haycock (Wrexham player, Wolves wartime guest), Ted Anderson, Bill Morris, Cyril Sidlow, Terry Springthorpe, Tom Waring and Horace Wright (all Wrexham wartime guests); Dick Richards (Wrexham trialist); Matt Carrick, Ron

Hewitt, Dennis Isherwood, Arthur Nelson, Chris Pearce, Bill Prendergast, Alf Somerfield and Lee Williams (all Wolves Reserves).

WRIGGLESWORTH, William Herbert

Born in South Elmsall on 12 November 1912, Billy Wrigglesworth was a small, lightweight left-winger, a veritable box of tricks who had a very deceptive body swerve. He played his early football with Frickley Colliery, joining Chesterfield as a professional in May 1932. From there he was transferred to Wolves in December 1934. He did very well at Molineux, pairing up initially with Welsh international Bryn Jones. He then lost his place to George Ashall and after a few games on the opposite flank he was sold to Manchester United in January 1937. During the war he guested for Arsenal, Brentford, Chelsea, Cardiff City, QPR, Walsall and York City and after scoring ten goals in 37 outings for United he moved on to Bolton Wanderers in January 1947, later playing for Southampton and Reading before becoming player-manager of Burton Albion in 1949. He joined Scarborough as a player in December of that year and remained with the seaside club until May 1950. He later coached at a Hampshire school and in July 1952 was appointed trainer of Accrington Stanley. He pulled out of football in 1955 and died on 11 August 1980.

Wrigglesworth's brother Walter also played for Chesterfield

Wolves record: 58 apps. 22 goals.

WRIGHT, Darren James

Darren Wright looked a good prospect as a youngster, but sadly he never reached the heights his coaches had anticipated. Born in West Bromwich on 14 March 1968, he joined the Molineux staff on the YTS in June 1983 and turned professional in July 1985. He was released in May 1986 and two months later after a trial at The Racecourse Ground he signed for Wrexham, where he stayed until May 1991 before drifting into non-League soccer with Worcester City (after suffering a knee injury). He later assisted Bilston Town, Willenhall, Atherstone United and Cheltenham Town (from July 1997). Wright made almost 150 appearances for Wrexham, gaining a Welsh Cup runners-up medal in 1988 and helping his side win promotion via the Play-offs in 1989.

Wolves record: 1 app.

WRIGHT, Harry Fereday

Harry Wright was an energetic forward who could occupy any position in the front-line, usually preferring the inside-right berth. A gritty performer, he was born in West Bromwich on 12 October 1888 and represented both Beeches Road and St Phillip's

Schools (West Bromwich) before playing for West Bromwich St Mark's and Wednesbury Athletic. In November 1906 he was taken on as a full-time professional by West Bromwich Albion, but after three years at The Hawthorns he was transferred to Stourbridge, returning to the Baggies for a second spell in June 1910. He helped Albion win the Second Division title and reach the FA Cup Final in successive years – 1911 and 1912 – before moving to Molineux for £500 in November 1919. In September 1920, he switched to Newport County, moved north to Chesterfield in August 1921 and announced his retirement in May 1922. Wright, who guested for Oldbury Town and Bilston during World War One, died in West Bromwich on 17 September 1950.

Wolves record: 21 apps. 4 goals.

WRIGHT, Horace Raymond

Yorkshireman Horace Wright was born in Pontefract on 6 September 1918 and played his early football with Woodbourne Athletic before joining Wolves in September 1937. A useful inside-forward, he remained at Molineux until July 1946 when he transferred to Exeter City, later playing for Yeovil and Petters United (1948-49). He scored 11 goals in his 55 League games for Exeter and during the war when playing in Regional games for Wolves, he was sometimes mistaken on the team-sheet for Billy Wright and occasionally had the same problem while guesting for Aldershot, Bolton, Leeds United, Millwall, Northampton Town and Wrexham.

Wolves record: 8 apps. 1 goal.

WRIGHT, Jermaine Malaki

Born in Greenwich, London, on 21 October 1975, Jermaine Wright had an unsuccessful trial with Bolton Wanderers before joining Millwall as a trainee in July 1991, turning professional at The Den in November 1992. He failed to make the Lions' first team despite gaining an England youth cap and in December 1994 was transferred to Wolves for £60,000. An exciting winger, with good pace and skills, he found it hard to settle into a rhythm at Molineux and, indeed, get a regular run out in the first team. Consequently after a loan spell with Doncaster Rovers (March/April 1996) Wolves boss Mark McGhee sold him to Crewe Alexandra for £25,000 in February 1998.

Wolves record: 5+20 apps. 1 goal.

WRIGHT, Stephen

Scotsman Steve Wright was taken on loan by Wolves from Rangers in March 1998 and made his debut in a 3-0 defeat at Ipswich. A right-back, born in Belshill near Glasgow on 27 August 1971, he played his early football with Eastercraigs FC before joining Aberdeen in November 1987. He played 176 games for

the Dons prior to moving to Ibrox Park in July 1995. Capped by his country twice at senior level, he also played in two 'B' and 14 Under-21 internationals, but made only 19 appearances for Rangers, mainly due to injuries. At the end of the 1997-98 season Wright signed for Bradford City on a free transfer.

Wolves record: 3 apps. no goals.

WRIGHT, William Ambrose, CBE

Born in Ironbridge, Shropshire on 6 February 1924, former Madeley schoolboy Billy Wright was actually turned away from Molineux in 1938 by the then manager Major Frank Buckley when he went along as a frail-looking 14-year-old asking for a trial. "You're too small – come back when you've put on some weight," said the Major. Wright did just that – and became one of the greatest players ever to serve the club and, indeed, ever to play for England, gaining a then record 105 caps and captaining his country a record 90 times. He also played for the United Kingdom side against Wales in 1951. After that initial meeting with Buckley at Molineux, Wright went off to build himself up and develop his game with Cradley Heath and he duly returned to sign for Wolves (in exchange for three bars of chocolate) on 2 June 1938, earning £2-a-week as a playing-member of the groundstaff. He was an outside-left in those days and made his first team debut at the age of 15 years, seven months and 17 days in that position against West Bromwich Albion in September 1939, in a Midland Regional League game but after the war (during which he guested for Leicester City and Notts County) Wright was converted into a cool, footballing centre-half by new manager Ted Vizard. He had served with the King's Shropshire Light Infantry, attaining the rank of sergeant/PE instructor during the hostilities and made 113 appearances for Wolves (35 goals scored) before peacetime football resumed in earnest in 1946-47. By this time Wright had become a fully-fledged professional at Molineux and in 1949 – under Stan Cullis's leadership – he skippered Wolves to victory in the FA Cup Final at Wembley. Three years later he was voted Footballer of the Year and two years after that, in 1954, he lifted the League championship trophy, following up with two more League titles in 1958 and 1959. He announced his retirement as a player at the end of the latter campaign, having accumulated 490 League appearances for Wolves and over 650 first-team outings all told. In June 1959, Wright was awarded the CBE for services to football and then in a blaze of publicity in October 1960, he was appointed manager of the England youth team, later taking charge of the Under-23 side. In May

The most famous player in Wolves history, Billy Wright was the first man to reach the milestone of 100 international appearances.

1962, with the press and media again taking full advantage of the story, Wright became manager of Arsenal, a position he held until June 1966. Thereafter he was associated with sports coverage on ATV, being in control of the station's sports output until his retirement in 1989. He was made an honorary member of the FA and also became a member of the Pilkington Commission on Television Broadcasting, before joining the board of directors at Molineux in May 1990 – a position he held until his death on 3 September 1994. Wright, who was married to Joy, one of the Beverly sisters, was living in Whetstone, North London, at the time of his death. A stand at Molineux is named after him and there is a sculpture standing proudly outside the main entrance to the Wolves stadium in recognition of the service Wright gave to the club over many years as a player and director. In July 1998, Wright was named in the list of 100 Football League legends.

A true sportsman in every sense of the word, Wright never refused to give someone his autograph, and would occasionally sign two at the same time because he was ambidextrous.
Wolves record: 541 apps. 16 goals

WYKES, David

David Wykes was a thrustful, goal-hungry inside-forward who sadly died in a Wolverhampton hospital of typhoid fever and pneumonia at the age of 28, just 24 hours after playing his last game for Wolves against Stoke in a First Division fixture on 5 October 1895. Born in Walsall on 15 September 1867, he played initially for Bloxwich Strollers, Wednesbury Town and his home club Walsall before signing for Wolves in August 1888. Lithe and subtle in play, his mobility and enthusiasm was sorely missed by Wolves.
Wolves record: 179 apps. 69 goals.

YORK CITY

Wolves' playing record against York is:

Football League

Venue	P	W	D	L	F	A
Home	1	1	0	0	3	2
Away	1	0	0	1	1	2
Total	2	1	0	1	4	4

Players with both clubs: Hugh Atkinson, Walter Bottrill, Sam Charnley, Paul McLoughlin, Jimmy Seal, Paul Stancliffe, Mike Stowell and Harry Thompson.

Also associated: Billy Ellis (Wolves junior reserve); Cliff Johnson and Bert Latham (Wolves Reserves); John Ward (York City manager, Wolves assistant manager), Albert Flatley (Wolves trialist) and Billy Wrigglesworth (City wartime guest).

York City were managed by Alan Little, the brother of the former Wolves boss Brian Little.

YOUNG, Eric

Welsh international centre-back Eric Young, easily recognisable by a cavalier headband, worn just above his eyes to prevent scars re-opening, was born in Singapore on 25 March 1960. He played his early football in this country with Slough Town before becoming a full-time professional with Brighton and Hove Albion in November 1982. He went on to appear in almost 150 games for the Seagulls before transferring to Wimbledon for £70,000 in July 1987. Twelve months later he starred in the Dons; defence as they lifted the FA. Cup at Wembley. Young played 125 times for Wimbledon, up to August 1990, when he moved to Crystal Palace for £850,000. He served the Eagles exceedingly well over the next five years, amassing a further 204 first-class appearances, helping the London club win the Full Members Cup in 1991 and gain promotion to the First Division in 1994. He also took his total number of international caps won at senior level with Wales to 21 – Palace's most capped player. Wolves acquired Young's services in September 1995, signing him on a free transfer from Selhurst Park and he did a good job initially at Molineux before his release in the summer of 1997. He later joined Egham Town of the Ryman League.
Wolves record: 40 apps. 2 goals.

YOUNG, Robert T.

Craggy Scot Bob Young was born in Stonehouse, Lanarkshire in September 1886. He had a useful career as a solid, uncompromising defender, playing in his home country, London, the Midlands, the North of England and on Merseyside. He signed for Paisley St Mirren at the age of 15 and in July 1907 switched south to join West Ham United. He stayed with the Hammers for one season, switching to Middlesbrough in October 1908. In January 1910 he was on the move again, this time across country to Everton. Wolves signed him in August 1911 and he stayed at Molineux until May 1914 when, aged only 27, he announced his retirement owing to injury and ill-health. Young later returned home to Scotland where he died in 1955

Wolves record: 73 apps. 11 goals.

YOUTH FOOTBALL

Wolves first formed a youth team in the early 1920s. The club entered a side initially in the Staffs County League and then transferred to the Birmingham Combination in 1932. In January 1939 Wolves' youngsters beat Atherstone 16-0 to create a record of the highest score ever made by a team representing the club. This was in a Birmingham Combination game.

In August 1952 the FA Youth Cup was introduced and Wolves have entered this competition every year since, winning the trophy in 1958 when they defeated Chelsea 7-6 over two legs in a memorable Final. They also appeared in the Finals of 1953 against Manchester United (lost 9-3 on aggregate); in 1954, again against Manchester United (lost 5-4 on aggregate); in 1962 against Newcastle United (lost 2-1 on aggregate) and in 1976 against neighbours West Bromwich Albion (lost 5-0 on aggregate). (See FA. Youth Cup).

Two Wolves players, who graduated through the youth ranks at Molineux, were both later transferred for seven-figure fees – midfielder Steve Daley went to Manchester City for £1.15 million in 1979 and full-back Jamie Smith moved to Crystal Palace in 1997 in a £1 million deal which involved Kevin Muscat and Dougie Freedman who came to Molineux.

Wolves' Youth team won the double in season 1997-98 – taking the Midland Melville League Championship and capturing the Midland Youth Cup. A crowd of 5,000 at Molineux saw them beat Notts County 2-0 in the Final of the Cup competition.

YULE, Thomas

Wolves signed Tommy Yule from Lincoln City in the summer of 1911 to replace Alf Walker (sold to Port Vale). A sprightly winger with good pace, he scored six goals in 25 League games in his first season at Molineux, but was injured at Bury in October 1912 and thereafter struggled to get back into the first team. He, like Walker, moved to Port Vale in 1913, staying with the Potteries club until January 1915 when he went to war. There is no record of Yule playing football after the hostilities. Born in Douglas Water on 4 February 1888 he played for Portbello FC before joining Lincoln in 1909 and scored seven League goals in 63 games for the Imps.

Wolves record: 33 apps. 7 goals.

ZELEM, Peter R.

Born in Manchester on 13 February 1962, steady defender Peter Zelem played well over 130 senior games for Chester before joining Wolves – then under manager Tommy Docherty – in January 1985. Just over two years later, on the transfer deadline of March 1987, Zelem was transferred to Preston North End; five months after that he switched to nearby Burnley and in May 1968, he quit the big time after amassing a total of 209 League appearances and scoring 19 goals.

Wolves record: 54 apps. 1 goal.

ZENITH DATA SYSTEMS CUP

Wolves entered this short-lived competition three times between 1989 and 1992. They played four matches as follows:

1989-90 v Sheffield United (a) 0-1
1990-91 v Leicester City (a) 1-0
       v Leeds United (h) 1-2
1991-92 v Grimsby Town (a) 0-1
Summary:

P	W	D	L	F	A
4	1	0	3	2	4

Subscribers

Albert Nick Abbotts
John Abela
Frank A'Court
Derek Adams
Geoffrey Adams
Jackie Adams
Stephen Adams
Glenys Adkinson
Anwar Ahmed
Colin Allen
Les Allen
Thomas Allen
Geoff Allman
B S Andrews
Rod Anning
Cecil James Anslow
Kevin Arlott
D W J Arnold
Alan James Arthur
Simon D Asbury
Michael Ashmore
P Nell Ashton
David T Asprey
Martin Astley
Paul Aston
E Atkin
Ben Atkins
Douglas J Aulton
Anthony Austin
Phil Austin
Mr J R Bache
Simon Bagley
Mike 'Jat' Bailey
Ronald James Bailey
David Baker
Kevin Baker
Christopher Ball
Andrew Banham
Chris Barber
David R Barnett
S A Barnett
S J Barnett
Lloyd Baron
Ryan Barrows
Stephan Bartlett
Hannah Bassett
Jeremy Bassett
M K Bate
Don Bates
John Bates
Nigel Bates
S J Bayley
Kalvin Bayliss
R J Bedward
Colin Bennett
David Samuel Bennett
Paul Bennett
Reg Benton
Neil C Berry
Simon Betteridge
Dr A S Bill

Edward Bill
Phil Bilton
Francis Bird
Ashley David Bloor
Mark Blore
David Bloxham
Kelvin James Boddy
Mark Anthony Bodin
Bones
Anthony Bourke
Keith Bourne
Liam Bowden
Alan Bowen
Terence W Bown
Mr C A Bowyer
Christopher John Boys
David Bracher
Steven Bradford
Andrew Bradley
T E Bradley
Barry L Brant
Lewis Brazier
Dominic Brett
J D Brewe
Mark Bridgewater
E J Bridgewood
Adam Brinsdon
Maurice J Briscoe
Des Brittain
Colin K Britton
Mick Broadhurst
Keith Brooks
Mick Brooks
Paul Brookes
Mrs Hilary Broster
Paul Buckerfield
Rachel Bulkeley-Jones
Ivan Bull
Paul Bullimore
William Derek Burgwin
Mark A Burke
Mr David Paul Burrows
Harry Burt
Roy Burton
Tom Butler
Graham Caddick
Mr Roy Harvey Caddick
Glynn Cadman
Sean Cairney
Arthur Campbell
Michael and Linda Capewell
Adrian Carrington
Roger W Carter
Dennis Cartwright
Fran Cartwright
G Carvey, New Zealand
Lloyd Catton
Pete Cecil
Campbell Chalmers
Jeremy Chamberlain
Terry Chell

John Chorzempa
Richard Churchill
Christopher Clark
Gary Clark
David Cleveland
William Cockbill
Nick Cole
Steve Cole
David Collett
Ian A Collett
Paul Collins
Barry Compton
David Cook
Peter J Cook
Robert Cooke
Craig Cooper
Geoff Cooper
John W Cooper
Joshua James Cooper
Tony Cowley
Ben Cox
Frederick Cox
Matt Cox
Richard Cox
Steven Cox
V Ernest Cox
Wayne Craddock
John A Cross
Rosemary Crump
Colin J Cutts
Curt Daly
Gordon L Dangerfield
John Daniel
Brian Daniels
Dennis Danks
John E Dannatt
Harry Davenhill
Rob Davies
Roy S Davies
S J Davies
Wallace Davies
Glyn Davis
Warwick B Davis
Miss B Dawson
Christopher J Day
Peter J Deans
Ian Dempsey-Robbins
Rhys and Bethany Denner
R J Dimmock
Edna Dix
Sheryl Dowen
Mr and Mrs B L Drew (Canada)
Chris Driver
Keith Duberley
J E Dudley
Teresa B Dudley
Michael Duffield
David R Dungar
Paul Dyson
Daniel Eade
Colin Eagle

Frank Eardley
Elke Edwards
John Edwards
Neil Egerton
Nick Egerton
Betty Ellis
Glyn Ellis
Michael D Ellis
Mike Ellis
Adrian Elmore
Dave Embrey
David Mark Emery
Steve English
Alex Evans
Eric Evans
Glyn David Evans
Peggy Evans
John A Everitt
Mark E Everitt
G W Evers
Derek J Fairfield
Keith Farley
David John Farmer
Garry Fellows
Ian Felton
S J Fennell
Susan Fennell
Andrew Fereday
Paul Ferguson
Phillip Ferguson
Bill Fern
William H Fern
Paul H Fieldhouse
Ray Finch
Roger Finch
Mr A Firm
William H Firmstone
Mrs J A Fish
Joseph Fish
Don Fisher
Stephen Flavell
John H Fletcher
Foal
Norman Follows
Karl Foster
Laurence Foster
Oliver Foster
Mr William C Francis
Roger Freeman
Christine Frost
Leslie W Fullelove
Ron Fullwood
G E Galleymore
Mr Stan Garner
James Garner-Woodberry
Andre Gauden
Kate Gelsthorpe
Alan George
Raymond Gibbons
Don Giles
Frank Giles
Scott Paul Giles
Calum Gill
Owen Gill
Wendy Gill
Lee Gillett
F D Gilson, South London Harriers
P E Godson

Stephen Goodey
Fred Goodman
James Gough
Steve Gower
Mr A W Grainger
M J Grainger
David James Green
Jace Green
Michael Benedict Green
Peter L Green
R J Green
Robert H Green
Vincent James Green
Stephen Greenway
Peter Greybanks
John Griffin
Alan Griffiths
Peter R Griffiths
Alan Grove
Eileen Guest
Malcolm Guest
Peter Guest
N T Gwilliam
T J Hadlington
Hadlo Ltd
Gareth Hale
Rob Hale
Graham Hammersley
Bob Hammonds
David Hammonds
John Hammonds
Peter Hand
Peter Hands
Mrs B G Harley
Fred Harley
Mr R Harley
Mr Carl Harper
David Harper
Melvyn Harper
Graham Harridence
Steve Harriman
Adam Harris
Mrs B Harris
Reg and Greg Harris
William H Harrison
Brian Hart
James Hart
Edward Hartill
John Hartshorn
Stephen Hateley
Les Hatton
Richard M Hawkins
Darren Lee Haycock
David Haytree
Brian William Hayward
Glen Robert Hayward
W W Hazlehurst
Peter Henton
Mathew Henworth
Matthew Hepwood
Norman Heritage
Paul David Hickman
William John Hickman
Thomas Higgs
A D Hill
Alwyn H Hill
Martin A Hill
Michael H Hill

Rod Hill
Scott Hilton
Albert F Hingley
Mark Hipkiss
Matthew Hobbs
J V Hodgens
Barry Hodgkiss
David Ronald Hodgkiss
Mr Brian Holden
Derek Norman Holding
Horace John Holding
Ken Holland
Roy Holloway
Ernie Holmes
Jason Paul Homer
Nick Hone
Alan Hooper
Stephen John Hopkins
Ian Hopson
Martin Horne
Mark Horton
Mr P A Horton
Robert Horton
Stephen Horton
D Hough
Shaun Houghton
Mr Alan Roy Howe
Robert A Howe
Christopher Howell
Derek Hubbard
Rex Hudson
David Noel Hughes
Keith 'Yug' Hughes
Leniva Hughes
Lawson Hunt
Melvyn Hunt, Windsor NSW
Michael Huntbatch
Clive Ibbison-Steele
Alexander Neil Ives
Malcolm Ives
Charlie Jacks
The Jackson Family
Phil Jackson
R E James
Mr P Jasper
John Jeavons
Keith Jeavons
Peter J Jeavons
Nicky Jetimik
A Jenkins
Geoffrey Jenkins
Adam Jewkes
Paul Jewkes
Phillip John
Lee Johnson
Robert Johnson
Olive Johnston
Christopher Jones
Colin Jones
D L Jones
F W Jones
Graham Jones
Horace Jones
Mr K T Jones
Kenneth Jones
Kevin I Jones
Kevin Paul Jones
Michael Jones

Mike Jones
Peter Jones
Philip Jones
Ray Jones
Steven Jones
Thomas Jones
Alan Jordan
Les Jordan
John Jowicz
Eric Joyce
David Judson
Dave Keeling
Martin Kendrick
Mike Kendrick
Tony Kendrick
David Key
Lawrence Kilkenny
Reginald John Trafford Knipe
Steve Knowles
Alec Kokinis
Robert Lacey
John R Laidlow
Paul Robert Lancett
Michael W Lane
Henry Larard
Paul Latham
Steven Lawlor
Miss Gaynor Leary
Jamie Lee
James Lee
C M Levett
Edward Lewis
W Lewis
Ian Lickis
David Liggins
Jerry Lloyd
Malcolm Lloyd
Mr M Lockett
C Lockley
Paul Lockley
Ian M Lones
Mr Sandy Love
David John Lowe
Peter Christopher Lowe
Grenville Lucas
Ian MacDonald
Robert J McEwan
Sean McGahey
John D McKenna
Joe Mackett
Hannah McLeod
Robert McLeod
Paddy McShane
Philip Magness
Jason Maiden
Kevin Maiden
Clive Male
Ken Male
Stephen Male
Tony Mallam
Anthea Mander
Leslie Marratt
Barry Marsden
Lee Martin
Ian Nicholas Mason
Jack Mason
Lynton Mason
Jonathan Matthews

Martin Melhuish
E J Mellor
John Mellor
Barry J Millar
Eric 'Barrs' Millington
Edward Mills
Paul Millward
Eileen Mincher
David Mohammed
Alan Moore
Andrew Moore
Dave Moore
Owen Moore
John Noel Moorhouse
S Moreton
Jim Morgan
John Morgan
Gary Morris
George Morris
John Leslie Morris
Paul Morris
Phil Morris
Thomas Mortimer
Mr S Morton
Larry Muir
Matthew Mullin
Matthew Mycock
A D Narraway
G Narraway
P G Narraway
Warwick Nash
G H Newman
Antony D J Nicholls
Debbie A Nicholls
Kent Nicholls
Chris Nock
Les Nock
John Nuttall
Andy Onions
Martin Orme
Roy Orr
John O'Shea
Alex Overton
Gerald Owen
Keith Alexander Owen
Paul William Owen
Phil Owen
Robert Stephen Owen
Christopher Paint
Malcolm F Palmer
Robert Palmer
Keith Parkes
John Parkes
Philip Parkes
Stuart Parry
David A Pauling
Mr N J R Payton
Paul Peacock
Andrew Pearce
Mick Pearce
Mr R G Pearce
Douglas John Pearl
Brian John Pearson
John Brian Pearson
David Pedley
Rosamund Pedley
R C Pendrell
David Pepper

Billy John Perkins
Matthew Perry
Ian Peters
Robert Piper
Roger Pitt
Gerry Plant
Matthew Plested
Mr Kevin Ponder
John Pope
Matthew Potter
Phil Porter
Rob Poulton
Graham Powell
E S Preston
Bill Price
Edward Price
Peter C Price
Tony Price
Neil Priest
Edward Pritchard
Martyn Andrew Pritchard
Paul Pritchard
Mrs D M Prosser
Robert Purnell
I H Purves
Dale Randle
Jack Randle
Bob Ratcliffe
Graham Alexander Rath
H H Raybould
Clyde Redfern
Mike Redfern
Ian Redmond
Gordon Terence Reed
David Rees
Warren Reid
Brian Restall
M D Rhodes
Mark Rhodes
Alan Richards
Dave Richards
Kevin Richards
Paul Richards
T A Robbins
Colin Roberts
Patrick Roberts
Richard Roberts
Stephen Roberts
Arthur Robertson
Don Robinson
Ronald Robinson
RAJ Rogers
Gregory Rollason
Mark Rollason
Andrew Rotherham
Mrs A J Rowland
Mr P A Rowland
Alwyn Royans
Arthur and Jane Rudge
A A Rudkin
Peter W Russell
Larry Ryder
Mr J C Salmon
John Salmons
A E Salusbury
M R Sambrooks
Christopher N Sargent
Mark J Savage

THE A-Z OF WOLVES

Frank E Scott
Patrick Scriven
Geoffrey Scrivens
J Geoffrey Shakespeare
Adam Shamma
David Shamma
Ian Shamma
Diane Sharp
Nigel Sharp
Jim Sharples
Nick Sharples
Raymond Noah Sheldon
Fred Shenton
Charlie Shepherd
A J and E A Sherwood
Peter Shore
Phil Shuker
Arthur Simmonds
Chris Simmonds
Ivor R Simpkins
Ranjit Singh
Dave Slape
Stan Slater
Gordon Small
Clive Smith
Ian Smith
John T Smith
Matthew Smith
Michael Smith
Patrick J Smith
Peter J Smith
Reg Smith
Ron Smith
W Smith
Keith Southall
David J Spooner
David Sproson
Tony Stafford
Kerry Stanhope
J P Starkey
Darren Statham
James Steed
Mark Stevens
Bill Steventon
Matthew Steward
Adam Stott
David Summers
Gurvinder Sunger
George Susilovic
Sveinung Svanberg
Chris Swatman
Steven Sweet
Colin Talbot
Lynzi Tanner
Owen and Hayley Tanner
Oskar Targosz
Phil Tart
Andrew Peter Taylor
Brian Taylor
Mr C B Taylor
David Taylor
Glynn Taylor
Mr J Taylor
Mr R E Taylor
Roy Thomas Taylor
Scott Allan Taylor
Steve Taylor
Christopher A Teed

Tom Terry
John Thompson
Dave Tilley
W Timmington
Ken Timmis
David Tomlinson
Mr T Toner
Christine Tonks
Graham Tonks
Allen Townsend
Lee Tredwell
Jim Trinder
Richard Trumper
Stephen Trumper
Dean Turner
Leslie Turner
Philip F Turner
A J Turpin
Adam Turpin
Peter Turton
Peter C Vaughan
Roger and Marlene Venney
Paul Joseph Vernon
Craig John Vickers
Samuel David Vickery
Dr P A Vingoe
Richard Vodrey love The Vodreys
Daniel Wain
Geoffrey P Wakelam
C D Walker
Dave Walker
G A Walker
Steve Walker
Mark Waller
Daniel Wallis
Kevin Wallsgrove
Tyrone Sean Walsh
Miss J Walters
Bill Ward
Greg Ward
James E Ward
Steven J Warner
I P Warren
Phil Washburn
David Waterfield
Alfred Watkins
Michael Watkiss
William C Watterson
Mark Webb
Steven Wells
D M Westley
G Westwood
Joan Westwood
Christopher Wheatley
Mark Stanley White
Tessa Dawn White
Adrian Whitehurst
Brian Whitfield
Kenneth Thomas Whitfield
James Whitter
Elizabeth Wilde
Robin J Wilding
Chris A Wilkes
Ken Wilkinson
Albert Williams
Bryan Williams
Jean Williams
Judith A Williams

Mark Williams
Nigel Williams
Phil Williams
David Willis
Gavin Wills
Luke Wilson
Terry Wilson
Ian Windsor
Alan Winmill
David Winterbottom
Darren Winwood
Southport Wolf
Thomas Wolverson
Carl Wood
Stuart Wood
Kevin J Woodall
Les Woodberry
Peter Woodifield
Russell Woodland
Richard Woodward
Paul Wooldridge
T Woolford
David Woolley
Spencer Wootton
W D Worrall
Alex Wright
Ken Wright
Michael J Wright
Mick Wright
Nicola Wright
Peter Harry Wright
Tony Wright
Brian Wynn
John R Wythes
Mr C R Yates
Thomas Yates